First Canadian Edition

The FUTURE of BUSINESS

First Canadian Edition

The FUTURE of BUSINESS

Norm R. Althouse
University of Calgary

Shirley A. Rose
Mount Royal College

Laura A. Allan
Wilfrid Laurier University

Lawrence J. Gitman
San Diego State University

Carl McDaniel
University of Texas, Arlington

THOMSON

NELSON

Australia   Canada   Mexico   Singapore   Spain   United Kingdom   United States

THOMSON

NELSON

The Future of Business
First Canadian Edition

by Norm R. Althouse, Shirley A. Rose, Laura A. Allan,
Lawrence J. Gitman, and Carl McDaniel

Editorial Director and Publisher:
Evelyn Veitch

Acquisitions Editor:
Anthony Rezek

Marketing Manager:
Don Thompson

Senior Developmental Editor:
Karina Hope

Photo Researcher:
Indu Ghuman

Permissions Coordinator:
Indu Ghuman

Production Editor:
Carrie McGregor

Copy Editor:
Valerie Adams

Proofreader:
Valerie Adams

Indexer:
Belle Wong

Production Manager:
Renate McCloy

Creative Director:
Angela Cluer

Interior Design:
Michael H. Stratton

Interior Design Modifications:
Katherine Strain

Cover Design:
Katherine Strain

Cover Images:
©2002 Stockbyte

Compositor:
Gerry Dunn

Printer:
Transcontinental Printing Inc.

**National Library of Canada
Cataloguing in Publication Data**

The future of business /
Lawrence J. Gitman ... [et al.]. —
1st Canadian ed.

Includes bibliographical references
and index.

ISBN 0-17-622438-6

1. Management—Canada.
2. Marketing—Canada.
3. Business enterprises—Canada.
I. Gitman, Lawrence J.

HD70.C3F87 2004   658
C2003-905890-5

BRIEF CONTENTS

CONTENTS

PREFACE

THE BOOK THAT BUILDS THE FOUNDATION

Today's employees must manage multiple tasks that require new skills, new perspectives, and new resources. In this new century, the primary competitive tool in the work force is knowledge. This knowledge must extend beyond the scope of an employee's own job to encompass other areas of the business as well.

Organization

The **Introduction** to *The Future of Business,* **First Canadian Edition**, discusses the importance of this textbook to students, whether they are presently working or hope to work in business in the future. It explains that it is not only important to be introduced to the different elements of business, but also to be able to see the different elements working together to create a business entity as a whole. *The Integrative Model of a Successful Business* is explained as the "framework" for the book.

To either introduce or refresh the students' awareness of certain elementary, but critical components, ***The Future of Business*** begins with *Business Trends and the Business Environment* (Part One). In Part One, students consider the fundamental Economic Systems and Competition (Chapter 1); The Global Marketplace and Governments' Roles (Chapter 2); Social Trends, Social Responsibility, and Ethics (Chapter 3); and Technology, the Internet, and Business Success (Chapter 4). With this basic fundamental knowledge, students can begin to see how the integrative model works.

Part Two introduces the concepts of *Canadian Business.* Students learn about Forms of Business Ownership (Chapter 5); Entrepreneurship: Starting and Managing Your Own Business (Chapter 6); and Corporate Governance, the Legal Environment, and Taxes (Chapter 7).

Part Three encompasses the *Functional Areas of Business,* starting with Marketing—The Customer Focus (Chapter 8) and followed by Marketing—Product, Price, and Promotion (Chapter 9). Next there is a discussion of Achieving World-Class Operations and Distribution (Chapter 10). Students then study accounting and financial basics—Understanding and Using Accounting Information (Chapter 11) and Financial Management and the Securities Markets (Chapter 12). Part Three concludes with Human Resource Management (Chapter 13).

In Part Four, the *Management Process* is discussed. This includes Management and Planning in Today's Organization (Chapter 14), Designing Organizational Structures (Chapter 15), Leadership and Motivation (Chapter 16), and Information Systems and Effective Control (Chapter 17).

Some schools may cover the *Management Process* in specific courses. If this is the case, the instructor may use Part Four as an introduction to the materials presented in another management course or choose to eliminate Chapters 14, 15, and 16, and only cover Chapter 17 (Information Systems and Effective Control).

Bringing It All Together is the conclusion to the textbook and shows how all the functional areas of business are integrated through the use of a real-world example. A manager from the Hudson's Bay Company, one of Canada's most recognizable companies, provides insights into his successful, 34-year career with the company. The conclusion gives the students a real-life integration of the material presented in the book.

The Future of Business also includes a short appendix that discusses Business Research, Reports, Executive Summaries, and Presentations. These helpful hints are included to enhance the students' understanding of the unique features of business reports and the presentation of their contents or findings. The appendix is especially useful in courses that require students to prepare or present either primary or secondary business research, and it can be modified for particular business environments. Organizations (including secondary education) use different formats for reports, so this section is only intended as a guide, and any particular institution may choose not to include it in the curriculum.

New Angles on Business

The new shape, pace, and spirit of the global economy require new ways of looking at business. We've organized every chapter of *The Future of Business* with a unique chapter structure to support three essential themes.

1. Business in the 21st Century

Students begin their study of each chapter with a glimpse into the strategies of popular business organizations and business practices. This lively section draws the students into the chapter and stimulates classroom discussion by providing a "living" example of current business principles and practices. Students learn what is happening in today's business with examples from the largest global corporate giants, such as McCain Foods Ltd., to the smallest entrepreneurships.

2. Capitalizing on Trends in Business

The second part of each chapter explores new business trends and how they are reshaping today's business and altering tomorrow's competitive environment. Technology and the global economy are covered extensively in every trends section. We expose students to the fundamental factors that are reshaping the business world in which they will soon, if they have not already done so, begin professional careers. With this preview of the future, students will gain a keen advantage when entering the workplace.

3. Applying This Chapter's Topics

This unique feature, found only in *The Future of Business,* brings the chapter topics to life for students with relevant and interesting tips for making the most of the professional career, making intelligent investment decisions, or becoming a smart consumer. Students can utilize these suggestions throughout their careers, and many are applicable in everyday life.

Topics Up Close

Today's most fundamental business trends and topics are thoroughly covered—this means more value added for students. Some examples of the topics shaping the future of business covered in this edition are:

- Customer value
- Knowledge management
- Relationship management
- The Euro and the European Union
- The new Internet economy
- Launching an e-business
- Global mergers
- Entrepreneurs/intrapreneurs
- Database marketing
- Mass customization
- Web advertising
- Global management skills
- Motivational job design
- Virtual corporations
- Online trading
- Online banking
- Risk management
- Agile manufacturing
- Intranets and extranets

Technology and E-Commerce

Technology not only touches all areas of business, it often revolutionizes it. Chapter 4 (Technology, the Internet, and Business Success) looks at the impact of the Internet on business operations and describes the growth of e-commerce in both consumer and business-to-business markets. Chapter 4 also clarifies what many have difficulty in distinguishing: e-commerce and e-business. Also discussed are the concepts of business-to-business, business-to-consumer, consumer-to-consumer, consumer-to-business, and business-to-enterprise.

Chapter 4 also explores the process for launching an e-business and looks ahead to the future of the Internet in business ("click versus brick"). No other introductory business textbook offers such comprehensive coverage of the profound impact of technology and the Internet on business. In addition, each chapter addresses how businesses are applying technology to improve processes and maximize value to the customer.

Keeping Pace with Business

The Future of Business uses an integrated learning system as its framework to introduce students to the new business environment.

Integrated Learning System

To anchor key concepts and provide a framework for study, an integrated learning system links all major concepts with the chapters, end-of-chapter material, and supplements package. Learning goals at the beginning of each chapter out- line the goals for study. Major headings within the chapter are identified by icons and supported with concept checks and a chapter summary. In addition, the Instructor's Manual, the Test Bank, and PowerPoint slides are all framed around the integrated learning system. Each piece of the integrated learning system reinforces the other components to help students learn quickly and to ease lecture preparation.

Hundreds of Actual Business Applications

We focused this book on the needs, abilities, and experience of the typical student. We drew on our experiences inside and outside the classroom to create the most readable and enjoyable textbook in business. We believe that the actual business applications interspersed throughout the chapters set the standard for readability and lucid explanation of key concepts.

Chapter Features

Making the Connection introduces each chapter. This section shows how the chapter concepts relate to "The Integrative Model" to help students connect the chapter concepts to business as a whole.

Learning Goals (lg) are provided at the beginning of each chapter to highlight the learning expectations for students as they read the chapter. These help to guide students' learning by providing key concepts that are presented in the chapter.

Many texts use short stories to open the chapters but fail to make connections to these stories elsewhere in the chapters. We take a different approach. We begin each chapter with an **opening vignette** about a prominent, student-friendly company or a business professional that actually previews that chapter's content. We then provide several questions to prompt critical thinking. The chapter discussion materials are concluded with **Looking Ahead**, where the opening vignette is revisited with a short discussion of what the future may hold for the company or the business professional.

Unlike most traditional textbooks that have review or study questions at the end of each chapter, *The Future of Business* has **Concept Checks** throughout the chapter. These concept checks are meant to challenge the students' learning as they progress through the chapter. By eliminating the end-of-chapter questions and using concept checks, students can follow the learning goals more easily. If they are unable to respond to the concept checks, they can simply review the previous few pages instead of trying to search through the entire chapter to locate the information.

Hot Links give the student an opportunity to connect to various Web sites to expand on the information presented in the chapter. Instructors may also choose to send students to the Web site links to fulfill assignments.

Key Terms help students to master the business vocabulary. Every key business term is carefully defined within the text. Each term appears in bold type and is defined in the margin where the term is first introduced. A complete glossary of all key terms is also included at the end of the book.

The **Try It Now!** boxes, found near the end of every chapter, encourage students to actively use the material learned in the chapter. These activities include Web-based exercises and other hands-on approaches to using the information.

End of Chapter Resources

A **Summary of Learning Goals** at the end of each chapter helps students to focus on the relevant material in a concise manner. As a supplement to this summary, the Key Terms that were used in the chapter are listed along with their page numbers.

Students often require more of a challenge to learn more about concepts that are of interest to them. The **Working the Net** section suggests Web sites that the instructor can choose to assign for discussion purposes, assignments, etc. Or they can be used as general interest to the students. The Web sites provided encourage further learning of some of the topics presented in the chapter.

A **Creative Thinking Case** concludes each chapter. The cases can be used as learning tools whereby students analyze the situation and apply the chapter material. The **Critical Thinking Questions** at the end of each case allow for a discussion or can be used for assignments or other testing.

At the end of each of the four parts of the textbook, there are two **Video Cases** that relate to concepts discussed in the part. The videos focus on issues that are important to Canadian business and are presented by CBC's *Venture*. These can be useful for discussion and testing.

Supplements

The Future of Business is supported by the following supplements:

Instructor's Manual

At the core of the integrated learning system for the text is the *Instructor's Manual* prepared by the authors of the textbook. Developed in response to numerous suggestions from instructors teaching this course, each chapter is designed to provide maximum guidance for delivering the content in an interesting and dynamic manner. Each chapter begins with learning goals that anchor the integrated learning system. A lecture outline guides professors through key terminology and concepts. Lecture enhancers provide additional information and examples from actual businesses to illustrate key chapter concepts. Each chapter includes lecture support for integrating PowerPoint™ slides and other visuals that illustrate and reinforce the lecture. A comprehensive Video Guide includes the running time of each video segment, concepts illustrated in the video segments, teaching objectives for the case, and solutions for video case study questions. A complete set of transparency masters is available to create overhead acetates. The transparency masters include exhibits from the text and additional teaching notes designed to add fresh examples to your lectures.

PowerPoint™ Slides

Over 300 slides of key chapter concepts and actual business examples not included in the text are available in PowerPoint presentation software to improve lecture organization and reduce preparation time. The PowerPoint slides were prepared by Vic de Witt of Red River College.

Test Bank

The comprehensive Test Bank is organized by learning goals to support the integrated learning system. With over 1700 true/false, multiple-choice, fill-in-the-blank, and short-answer questions, tests can be customized to support a variety of course objectives.

The Test Bank is available in print and software format with the ExamView™ Testing System. ExamView offers both a Quick Test Wizard and an Online Test Wizard that guides instructors step by step through the process of creating tests, while its unique WYSIWYG capability allows you to see the test on screen exactly as it will appear in print or online. With ExamView's complete word processing capabilities, you can enter an unlimited number of new questions or edit existing questions. The Test Bank was prepared by Kristi Harrison of Centennial College.

Instructor's Resource CD

For maximum convenience, the Instructor's Manual, the PowerPoint™ slides, the ExamView Testing System, and Test Bank are all available on a CD.

Videos

Designed to enrich and support key concepts, each of the video segments present real business issues faced by a variety of service and manufacturing organizations. The videos focus on Canadian issues that are important to Canadian business and are presented by the CBC program *Venture*. The instructor's video guide is included in the Instructor's Manual and outlines the key teaching objectives for each video case, and suggests answers to the critical thinking questions.

Web Site (www.futureofbusiness.nelson.com)

The Web site for *The Future of Business* provides rich content to maximize student learning and build online skills. Each text chapter is supported by an online Test Yourself quiz (written by Angela Davis of the University of Winnipeg) that tests student understanding and offers clear, customized feedback for incorrect answers. Also included on the Web site are Web Links, Crossword Puzzles, News Room, Stock Market Game, downloadable supplements, and much more.

InfoTrac™

Now you can give your students an entire library for the price of one book. With InfoTrac™, students gain complete, 24-hour-a-day access to full-text articles from hundreds of scholarly journals and popular periodicals such as *Canadian*

Business, Business Week, Canadian Business Review, and *HR Professional.* Thousands of full-length, substantive articles spanning the past four years are updated daily, indexed, and linked. And because they're online, the articles are accessible from any computer with Internet access. InfoTrac™ is perfect for all students, from dorm-dwellers to commuters and distance learners.

ACKNOWLEDGEMENTS

This book could not have been written and published without the generous, expert assistance of many people. We have benefited from the detailed and constructive contributions of many individuals. Specifically, we would like to thank the following people for their insight and contributions to *The Future of Business*.

Carolyn Anderson
Janice Bodnarchuk
Diane Bond
Victoria Calvert
Bob Channing
Linda Craig
Gordie Cruikshank
Doug Dokis
Randall Gossen
Christopher Halpin
Donna Harlamow
Marc Jerry
Robin Lynas
Robert Malach
Sandra E. Malach
Arden Matheson
Jim McCutcheon
Doug McDonnell
Fred (Scoop) McKay
Tim Morgan
Ron Murch
Albert Nasaar
Margaret Nemeth
Gino Panucci
Blair Phillips
Shabira Pradhan
Bruce Ramsay
Barry Sadrehashemi
Steve Smith
Frank Thirkettle
Maureen Warmington
Elizabeth Watson
Justine Wheeler
Claire Wright

We would also like to recognize the contribution of Lawrence Gitman and Carl McDaniel, authors of the U.S. edition of *The Future of Business*. Their original work served as the foundation for our writing and set a standard of excellence we conscientiously followed.

And, of course, we would also like to thank our talented and patient editorial and production staff at Nelson Thomson.

We have benefited from the detailed and constructive reviews provided by many individuals. In particular, we wish to thank the following educators who have served as reviewers:

Barry Boothman, University of New Brunswick
F. Alex Boultbee, Seneca College
Elisabeth Carter, Douglas College
Angela Davis, University of Winnipeg
Vic de Witt, Red River College
Jane Forbes, Seneca College
Robert Fournier, Red Deer College
Walter Isenor, Acadia University
Ed Leach, Dalhousie University
Alan McGee, Acadia University
Erica Morrill, Fanshawe College
William Thurber, Brock University
Leslie Wilder, Red River College

ABOUT THE AUTHORS

Norm R. Althouse

Norm Althouse received his Bachelor of Business Administration (Accounting) and worked in the public sector for ten years before returning to continue studies in the Master of Business Program. He has studied in Canada, Australia, Ireland, and Hungary. Currently, Norm teaches at the Haskayne School of Business at the University of Calgary. He has also taught at the University of Lethbridge and Mount Royal College.

After several years of teaching in the Human Resource area at the University of Calgary, Norm transferred to the Strategy and Global Management Area and currently teaches in the Business and Environment Area. Initially, Norm's primary responsibility was to develop a required core-course in business for first- and second-year business students. His commitment to "continuous improvement" has resulted in many new developments, including the integration of materials and changes in the pedagogy of the course.

Norm's research activities include: team building, the changing nature of management and managers, and most currently, studying values and diversity in the workplace. Additionally, Norm has presented at such conferences as the Administrative Sciences Association of Canada ("*The Gendering Component of Diversity: How is it Faring?*") and has been published in a book of readings from the Global Business and Technology Association—Budapest, Hungary ("*Hierarchies in Transition: Hungary and Canada*").

Shirley A. Rose

Shirley Rose received her Bachelor of Business Administration from the University of New Brunswick in 1980. She then moved to Alberta to assume a position with the Alberta Provincial Government in the Department of Advanced Education. After some time in industry, Shirley returned to university and completed an MBA at the University of Calgary in 1989. Upon completion of the MBA, Shirley taught in a variety of full- and part-time positions at the University of New Brunswick, Athabasca University, Simon Fraser University, University of Calgary, University of Lethbridge, and the University College of the Cariboo. She was accepted into a PhD program at the University of Bath in the UK and completed two years of study. Shirley's research and consulting activities are in the fields of health care, oil and gas, union-government relations, and unemployment.

Shirley Rose has been with the Bissett School of Business at Mount Royal College since 1998. During that time she has taught in the areas of management, organizational behaviour, and general business. She served as Program Chair from 2000–2003 and was responsible for programs in marketing, human resources, general business, and aviation. Shirley is on the Board of Directors for Aviation Alberta and is Vice President of the Canadian Association of Aviation Colleges. She has authored test banks and study guides, as well as serving as a contributing author for textbooks in management and introduction to business.

Laura A. Allan

Laura Allan received her Honours Bachelor of Business Administration from Wilfrid Laurier University, and after a brief stint in the private sector working for an advertising agency, she went on to get her Masters of Business Administration in Marketing at York University. Laura went back to her alma mater to teach in 1984, and apart from taking brief time off to have her two children, she has been there ever since. Laura teaches primarily first-year undergraduate classes, but has also taught a second-year decision-making course. She also teaches executive development seminars for the Laurier Institute. Laura has been academic editor on another introductory text, written a study guide, and contributed chapters for two introductory textbooks. She has also co-authored the lab manual for the two first-year courses each semester since 1998, and has developed an on-line version of both courses for the university's distance education department.

Laura's commitment to the integrative approach to teaching business led to a complete redesign of the first-year courses. Most recently she helped design the first annual Nordia New Venture Competition for first year students. Currently, Laura serves as co-coordinator for the first year program at Wilfrid Laurier University, and has been recognized as one of the "most popular profs" in *MacLean's* magazine since 2000.

Lawrence J. Gitman

Lawrence J. Gitman is a professor of finance at San Diego State University. He received his Bachelor's Degree from Purdue University, his M.B.A. from the University of Dayton, and his Ph.D. from the University of Cincinnati. Professor Gitman is a prolific textbook author and has over 45 articles appearing in *Financial Management, Financial Review, Journal of Financial Planning, Journal of Risk and Insurance, Journal of Financial Research, Financial Practice and Education, Journal of Financial Education,* and other publications. He currently serves as an associate editor of *Journal of Financial Planning* and *Financial Practice and Education.*

His singly authored major textbooks include *Principles of Managerial Finance: Brief,* Second Edition, *Principles of Managerial Finance,* Ninth Edition, and *Foundations of Managerial Finance,* Fourth Edition. Other major textbooks include *Personal Financial Planning,* Eighth Edition, and *Fundamentals of Investing,* Seventh Edition, both co-authored with Michael D. Joehnk. Gitman and Joehnk also wrote *Investment Fundamentals: A Guide to Becoming a Knowledgeable Investor,* which was selected as one of 1988's ten best personal finance books by *Money* magazine.

An active member of numerous professional organizations, Professor Gitman is past president of the Academy of Financial Services, the San Diego Chapter of the Financial Executives Institute, the Midwest Finance Association, and the FMA National Honor Society. In addition he is a Certified Financial Planner (CFP) and a Certified Cash Manager (CCM). Gitman recently served as Vice-President,

Financial Education, for the Financial Management Association and as a Director of the San Diego MIT Enterprise Forum. He currently serves on the CFP Board of Standards. He lives with his wife and two children in La Jolla, California, where he is an avid bicyclist.

Carl McDaniel

Carl McDaniel is a professor of marketing at the University of Texas—Arlington, where he is Chairman of the Marketing Department. He has been an instructor for more than 20 years and is the recipient of several awards for outstanding teaching. McDaniel has also been a District Sales Manager for Southwestern Bell Telephone Company. Currently, he serves as a board member of the North Texas Higher Education Authority, a US$300 million financial institution.

In addition to this text, McDaniel also has co-authored a number of textbooks in marketing. McDaniel's research has appeared in such publications as *Journal of Marketing Research, Journal of Marketing, Journal of Business Research, Journal of the Academy of Marketing Science,* and *California Management Review.*

McDaniel is a member of the American Marketing Association, Academy of Marketing Science, Southern Marketing Association, Southwestern Marketing Association, and Western Marketing Association.

Besides his academic experience, McDaniel has business experience as the co-owner of a marketing research firm. Recently, McDaniel served as senior consultant to the International Trade Centre (ITC), Geneva, Switzerland. The ITC's mission is to help developing nations increase their exports. McDaniel also teaches international business each year in France. He has a Bachelor's Degree from the University of Arkansas and his Master's Degree and Doctorate from Arizona State University.

INTRODUCTION

This text on business is important whether you are working in a business today or hope to work in a business in the future. Even if your major is in the arts or sciences, you will likely work in an organization that is considered to be a business. Profit or nonprofit, the same principles apply.

If you want to be as successful as you can be, and make your business as successful as it can be, then it is critically important that you understand how a successful business works. Most introductory textbooks and courses do a good job of introducing you to the different elements of a business, but often fail to show you how these elements fit together. This objective is achieved mostly in senior business courses. The problem is that by that point you are so used to studying each piece separately that it's very difficult to see them working together to create the business entity as a whole. And what's important to see is that *"the whole" really is greater than the sum of its parts*. To truly understand what makes a business successful, you must accept it as a fully integrated entity, and as you study each of its parts, study them with the whole in mind.

To this end, we have used an integrative model (shown below) of a successful business as our framework or base for this book. Each chapter will focus on a specific part of this model, and you will be reminded of where and how each piece fits with the other aspects of the model at the beginning of each chapter.

Before we get into the model in detail, take a look at the title—*The Integrated Model of a Successful Business*:

- It is *integrative*. All the elements of the model work together to create a unified whole. Each piece depends on the others, and they all affect each other. One of the most important lessons to learn about business is that you can't make a decision in one area of a business without considering the impact that it will have on other areas of the business.

For example, according to *Report on Business Magazine*'s annual "Top 1000" issue published in July 2002, General Motors is the number-one ranked private company in Canada (wholly owned by General Motors Corp. U.S.) on the basis of revenue. This company has clearly shown that it knows what it takes to be successful. If the *operations* department of GM was to find a new, less expensive source for a material that it uses in the making of its cars, could it use this material

The Integrated Model of a Successful Business

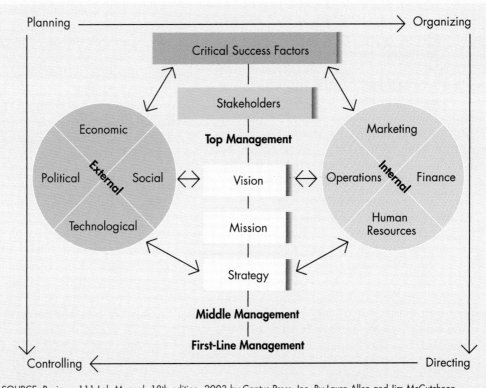

SOURCE: Business 111 Lab Manual, 18th edition, 2003 by Captus Press, Inc. By Laura Allen and Jim McCutcheon.

without any impact on other areas of the business? If the material was also of lesser quality, or was perceived to be of lesser quality, this would affect the image of the product in the mind of the consumer, making it difficult for the *marketing* department to sell the cars. Therefore the marketing department would be affected in terms of the sales of the product, which in turn means that the *finance* department would be affected, as it would affect the expected income for the year, and this might mean that the labour contracts negotiated by the *human resources* department would be lower, and so on. All the elements of the business or areas of its *internal environment* (shown by the green circle on the model) affect one another.

By the same token, what if a new *technology* was developed that would allow GM to produce its cars by way of machine only, with no human input? Then layoffs would likely result and affect the *economy* of the towns where the plants were located. This, in turn, would have an impact on the *social* environment of the business with respect to the relationship it has with the residents of the community, and may lead to the government stepping in to enact a *political* solution for the community.

All the areas of the *external environment* (shown by the pink circle on the model) impact on each other as well as on the business as a whole. These four areas of the external environment together can be remembered as the acronym PEST—for political, economic, social, and technological. The external environment can indeed be a pest to business! But it can also create enormous opportunities, as you will see.

To make our model more fully integrated, changes in this external environment set off another chain reaction inside the internal environment of the business. For example, what if GM's supplier can sell materials to GM for less *because* it uses this new technology? The interactions are endless. It's not necessary that you see all these connections. But what is necessary is that you understand as we go through the material section by section, that these sections of material cannot be treated as if they are separate areas of a business that can act on their own. They all work together.

- It is a *model*. This means several things. A model represents reality—this *is* how a *real* business works! A model simplifies reality—you are learning how a successful business works, and that's very complicated. A model summarizes the essential elements in a simple form to give you a base on which to build your knowledge. A model integrates ideas into a whole, as we discussed above. And lastly, a model provides a framework so that you can see how the pieces fit together and how you can build on it in later business courses.

- It is a model of a *successful* business. We're not discussing what all businesses do. We are discussing what successful businesses do that makes them successful over time—not just one year, but consistently outperforming year after year. That's how we learn about business—by studying those successful businesses that are leaders in their fields.

What does it mean to be truly successful? Is it simply making money? What does it take to make money? The *critical success factors* for any business, or the factors that indicate success are:

- Achieving financial performance.
- Meeting and exceeding customer needs.
- Providing value—quality products at a reasonable price.
- Encouraging creativity and innovation.
- Gaining employee commitment.[1]

Most businesses exist to make money, but what is often left out of the discussion is how a business becomes successful in the first place. Can a business be truly successful at generating income if it ignores the other four factors? For example, can it make money by selling products that do not satisfy customers' needs, with inferior quality at an unreasonable price, using yesterday's ideas (when the competition is ten steps ahead), while displaying a negative attitude toward the customer as demonstrated by its employees? Even one of these points would result in lower income, and a less successful business.

It's important to remember as well that these factors are also integrative—they all affect each other. It is virtually impossible to find a successful business in which all of these factors have not been achieved. They work together to make the company truly successful. For example, consider Chrysler. To *meet customer needs*, Chrysler was the first to design a mini-van with a second passenger sliding door, but it took *creativity and innovation* to come up with the design, a *committed work force* to follow through, and a commitment to *providing value through quality at a reasonable price* to achieve success. Because of these factors, the company is able to achieve *financial performance*.

Achieving financial performance is measured in three ways: profit, cash flow, and net worth. A company needs to have a healthy profit or "bottom line," but it also needs to earn a good profit relative to the money it has invested—the equity of the owners or shareholders. But this means nothing, of course, if it can't pay its bills. It's important to understand that a company that is profitable can still go bankrupt. For instance, while it is waiting for its customers to pay for the products they have purchased, it still has to pay its bills. The timing of the cash flows can put an otherwise profitable business into a very precarious position. And lastly, the net worth of the company is important, measured either by its stock price multiplied by the number of shares outstanding, or in terms of its assets (what it owns) relative to its liabilities (what it owes).

Meeting and exceeding customer needs means that companies must be sensitive to the needs of customers, anticipate changes in their needs, and of course work to meet these needs in a proactive fashion—before a customer complains. However, today companies cannot just provide what the customer wants. They need to satisfy customers beyond their expectations.

Providing value means that a business must constantly strive to improve the quality of its products and services, and do so at a reasonable cost. Customers demand quality and will stand for nothing less, but they will not pay for quality just because it's quality. They will pay a price that gives them value for their money—the quality that they demand at a price that makes it worthwhile or valuable to them.

Encouraging creativity and innovation involves the process of being creative (or "thinking outside the box") as well as harnessing that creativity in order to create the innovations that keep the company one step ahead of the competition. Danger exists when the company becomes comfortable with its level of success, as it may resist change. But remember, there are only two kinds of businesses—those that constantly innovate and those that go out of business. In today's business world, one of the only constants is change. The status quo doesn't work any more. Companies need to become "learning organizations," proactively seeking to learn and move ahead every day in everything they do.

And lastly, probably the most important success factor is *gaining employee commitment.* Employees need to be empowered to act and motivated to meet the company's objectives in each of the first four factors, or those objectives won't be met. Therefore, every company needs to understand the needs of its employees. It is only then that it can gain the commitment of its employees, for they will only be committed to meeting the goals of the company if their own goals are met at the same time. It is, again, an integrative relationship.

Underneath the critical success factors are the *stakeholders* of the business. These are individuals and groups that have a "stake" in what the business does. They are affected by the decisions that the business makes and therefore the business has a responsibility to consider them in those decisions.

The three most critical and obvious stakeholder groups are the owners of the business (or shareholders in the case of a corporation), the employees of the business (and their union if represented by one), and the customers. But there is a much wider world out there that must be considered—the government, special interest groups, the community surrounding the business, its suppliers, and so on. All of these groups interact with the business and keep it operating.

The business cannot operate in a vacuum as if these groups did not exist. They must be considered in every decision the business makes. If we change this material, how will our customers react? Will they keep buying our product? If we move the business, how will it affect the community? How many employees will we lose? If we cut down these trees to build the new plant, how will the environmentalist groups respond? How will the community and the local government respond? If earnings drop in the fourth quarter as expected, will our shareholders sell their shares, making the share price fall even lower? Achieving the critical success factors clearly depends on an intimate knowledge of and relationship with the stakeholders of the business.

It is primarily *top management*'s external focus that keeps the business looking at the stakeholders. It is the responsibility of the top management of the company to look outward and chart a course for the company. They examine the external environment of the business and match the threats and opportunities in the external environment with both the expectations of the stakeholders and the strengths and weaknesses of the company, in order to determine the direction the company should take in the future—their *vision* for the future of the company. This is further refined into a *mission* statement for the company. Next they determine the *strategy* for the company to pursue to achieve this mission—how to go about achieving the company's goals in the future.

For example, perhaps opportunities exist in the external environment to take the company global. Perhaps needs exist within foreign countries for the type of product the company sells and little competition exists from other firms at the present time. If the company has the internal marketing, operations, human, and financial strength to achieve this objective, then top management may determine that the vision for the future of the company is to make it a strong global competitor. The strategy would then need to take into account such decisions as what countries to enter first, whether to search out foreign firms with which to form a joint venture, to pursue a licensing arrangement with a foreign firm, or build its own plants.

It is then *middle management*'s job within each of the functional areas of the business to determine and plan out what each area needs to do to help achieve this overall corporate strategy. For example: What type of marketing campaigns will be most successful in these new foreign markets? Do we build new plants or lease/purchase and renovate existing plants? What new skills and attributes are needed to staff our operations in these new foreign markets? Where will the money come from and how will the budgets be realigned?

First-line management manages the workers that do the actual work in each of the functional areas. It is their job to make sure the plans at the higher levels are implemented, and—most importantly—by committed workers who are motivated to achieve the goals of the company.

Top managers, middle managers, and first-line managers are responsible for managing the company and its employees to ensure that all five of the critical success factors are achieved. They do this by:

- *planning* what the goals are (to achieve the critical success factors) and how to achieve them,
- *organizing* the resources of the company—human, physical, and financial—to achieve the goals,
- *motivating* the workers to gain their commitment to the goals,
- and then measuring results and making any changes necessary to continue to steer the company in the direction of the goals, thus maintaining *control* over the achievement of these five critical success factors.

This is the model we will use in this text to help you to integrate the different topics covered into an understanding of how a successful business works as a whole. By studying the topics presented in this textbook, you will have a solid foundation on which to build your further understanding of successful business practices.

Evolving Economic Systems and Competition

In this chapter you'll learn about different economic systems, basic economic concepts you need to understand how the economy works, and the role of competition in the economic environment. But where does all this fit into our understanding of a successful business?

Take a look at the model below.

The most obvious relationship between this chapter and the model of a successful business is in the external environment. Remember that the PEST model of the external environment is an acronym for the political, economic, social, and technological environments that interact with business.

The *economic* environment is part of our PEST model of the external environment. The chapter describes the economic system of a country as a "combination of policies, laws, and choices made by its government." Remember, our model is an integrative model. Here we see a direct link between the *political* and economic environments. But as you'll

see throughout the chapter, the economy has an impact on all the other aspects of the external environment, as well as on the internal environment of a business and how it operates.

Take, for example, DaimlerChrysler AG's "Smart" car discussed in this chapter. It is as a result of pressure from governments and *society* to reduce fuel emissions that cause pollution that the company worked to create the *technology* for the Smart car. This affects the economic environment because it is a competitive action. The internal environment of the business interacts by creating the product to *meet the needs of the customer*—a critical success factor. This involves *marketing* working with *operations* to design and build the product through the *human resources* of the company and with the *financial* resources of the company. This is a very innovative move on the part of the company, which will take several years to create a return. But it is this commitment to *innovation* in response to an environmental threat that allows DaimlerChrysler AG to remain a competitive company and turn what would have been a threat into an opportunity for the business. That is what competition and success is all about.

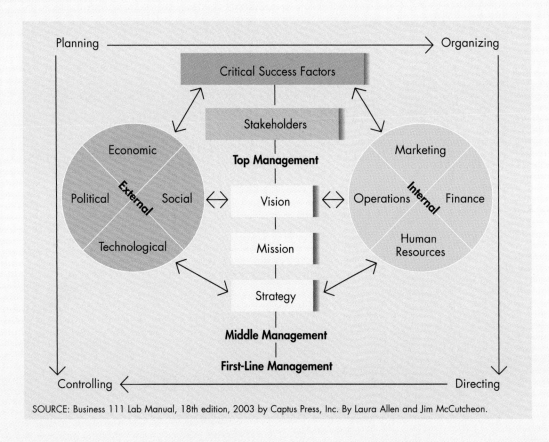

SOURCE: Business 111 Lab Manual, 18th edition, 2003 by Captus Press, Inc. By Laura Allen and Jim McCutcheon.

Economic systems are described in this chapter as differing on the basis of how they manage the factors of production. Factors of production involve the resources needed to produce a company's products. These factors are provided by the *stakeholders* of the business—employees provide human resources and owners provide financial resources, for example. Therefore the economic system that exists in a society depends partly on the relationship between the stakeholders, business, and the government. This stakeholder relationship to the economic environment can also be seen in the discussion of economics as a "circular flow"—resources are provided by the stakeholders, who then receive something in return from the business. This circular flow also clearly demonstrates the integrative nature of a business, as changes in one flow affect the others.

The chapter provides numerous examples of the integrative nature of business. Examples of news stories that deal with economic matters are given to show that you're exposed to economics more than you may realize. Looking at that from a different perspective, how does this news affect a business? Consider the following:

- *"The Bank of Canada lowers interest rates."* This would affect the financial decisions of the company, perhaps making it more financially feasible to expand—affecting the company's overall strategy, as well as affecting the ability of the company to meet the needs of the customer by offering better financing packages.
- *"The Minister of Finance proposes a cut in income taxes."* Lower personal income taxes result in customers having more disposable income to spend on the company's products, and lower corporate taxes make the economic environ-

ment more favourable to business investment domestically and make it easier to compete with companies from countries with lower taxes.

There are numerous examples throughout the chapter of how factors in the economy affect business decisions—what to produce (marketing and operations), how to price these products (marketing and finance), and how many people to employ and how much to pay them (human resources and finance). The impact of inflation, business cycles, and fiscal and monetary policy all provide examples of how economics affects business. If you look at the factors that cause demand and supply curves to shift, you can also see many other aspects of the environment at play; for example, technology shifts the supply curve, and buyer's preferences (social environment) shift the demand curve.

The critical success factors of the business are also affected by the economy. Many trends in the economic environment relate to these success factors. The chapter states that the "key to building and sustaining a long-range advantage is a commitment to delivering *superior customer value.*" This is a result of better-educated and more demanding customers from the social environment, new technology, and the globalization of markets in the economic environment creating more competition. It also states that "creating customer value and building long-term relationships require a world-class work force." Better training and better technology to improve worker productivity help to build a *work force committed* to meeting the *quality* needs of the customer. Trends in technological development come about as a result of a commitment to innovation. All these factors result in better meeting the needs of customers and therefore achieving better *financial performance.*

Evolving Economic Systems and Competition

CHAPTER 1

Learning Goals

→ **lg 1** What is an economic system and what economic systems are prevalent in the world today?

→ **lg 2** What is economics, and how are the three sectors of the economy linked?

→ **lg 3** How do economic growth, full employment, and price stability indicate a nation's economic health?

→ **lg 4** What is inflation, how is it measured, and what causes it?

→ **lg 5** How does the Bank of Canada and the government use monetary policy and fiscal policy to achieve their macroeconomic goals?

→ **lg 6** What are the basic microeconomic concepts of demand and supply, and how do they establish prices?

→ **lg 7** What are the four types of market structure?

→ **lg 8** Which trends are reshaping micro- and macroeconomic environments?

The Smart Car—Today Europe, Tomorrow the World

It's as big as an oversized go-cart with a plastic exterior that never rusts or dents. It can be swapped for another colour for about the price of a good-quality business suit. Designed for city commuting, it can turn on a dime, goes easy on fuel, and barely pollutes.

Alexis Mannes, a Brussels car dealer, says, "This may be the car that will change the car business." That's just what DaimlerChrysler AG has in mind for its "Smart" car, an ultra-light, ultra-fuel-efficient two-seater car being marketed as the ideal European city car, with a lead-in price of the equivalent of about $10 000.

DaimlerChrysler AG has no current plans to market the Smart car in Canada, but views the project as a laboratory experiment. The company sees the Smart car as an idea factory for the automotive technology and industrial cooperation of the future. "Daimler sees the Smart as a playground to test things," says Peter Soliman, a consultant with Booz-Allen Hamilton in Düsseldorf. "Even if it never makes any money, it has already taught the operation a lot about manufacturing, research and development, and distribution that they can carry over to their main business."

Some rival automakers scoff at the idea of plastic doors, hoods, and trunks. But the lightweight materials are critical in increasing fuel efficiency, which is important in Europe, where automakers have agreed to reduce their fleets' carbon dioxide emissions by some 25 percent by the year 2008. The Smart car is one of Europe's most fuel-efficient autos; the three-cylinder engine averages about 4.8 litres of gasoline per 100 kilometres, compared to 6.8 litres for Ford Motor Company's Ka and 6.6 litres for a Volkswagen Polo.

To make the car dramatically smaller than existing subcompacts, DaimlerChrysler AG was forced to redesign the basic "three-box" concept of the traditional car, which has a hood, a cockpit, and a trunk. Designers put the engine in the back, as in the original Volkswagen Beetle. Then they shoved the rest of the car's mechanics below the passenger cabin, something that had previously been done only with minivans. As a result, the Smart factory in France is capable of building 575 cars a day with virtually no parts inventory of its own (e.g., Magna, a Canadian auto parts manufacturer, supplies the body of the vehicles). Because only 25 percent of the Smart's value is added in final assembly, it takes just 4.5 hours to assemble one car, compared with 20 hours for a Volkswagen Polo.[1]

Auto history is littered with cars of tomorrow that landed on the scrap heap, including the Edsel, the Tucker, and the DeLorean sports car. And for every Smart enthusiast there seems to be a Smart skeptic. "Too expensive," says Shuhei Toyoda, chief engineer for Toyota Motor Corp.'s new Yaris, another small city car. Ferdinand Piech, chairman of rival Volkswagen AG, suggests that the Smart car isn't even new: "We already have a city car," he scoffs, referring to the VW Polo. "And it has four seats."[2]

CRITICAL THINKING QUESTIONS

As you read this chapter, consider the following questions as they relate to the Smart car:

- What factors determine the price of the Smart?
- In what type of environment does DaimlerChrysler AG compete?
- How can the changing economic environment affect the demand for the Smart?

→ lg 1

economic system
The combination of policies, laws, and choices made by a nation's government to establish the systems that determine what goods and services are produced and how they are allocated.

factors of production
The resources that are necessary to produce goods and services: labour, capital, entrepreneurs, physical resources, and information.

market economy
An economic system based on competition in the marketplace and private ownership of the factors of production (resources); also known as the *private enterprise system* or *capitalism*.

BUSINESS IN THE 21ST CENTURY

Whether the Smart car will be a success will depend in part on the economic systems of the countries where it is marketed. A nation's **economic system** is the combination of policies, laws, and choices made by its government to establish the systems that determine what goods and services are produced and how they are allocated. Economic systems found in the world today include market economies (capitalism), command (planned) economies, socialism, and mixed economies, all of which are discussed below.

This chapter will help you understand how economies provide jobs for workers and also create and deliver products to consumers and businesses. You will also learn how governments attempt to influence economic activity through policies such as lowering or raising taxes. Next, we discuss how supply and demand determine prices for goods and services. We conclude by examining trends in evolving economic systems and competition.

Evolving Economic Systems

As noted above, there are four primary types of economic systems in the world today: market economies, command economies, socialism, and mixed economies. The primary difference between the types of economic systems is how they manage the **factors of production**. Factors of production include all the resources needed to produce goods and services. These resources include human resources (labour), funds (capital), people who start and operate the business (entrepreneurs), physical resources (natural and manufactured), and knowledge (information). Managers must understand and adapt to the factors of production and the economic system or systems in which they operate to be successful.

The Market Economy (Capitalism)

A remarkable trend in global economies today is the move toward **market economies** (also known as capitalism or as the private enterprise system). Sometimes, as in the case of the former East Germany, the transition to a market economy has been painful, but fairly quick. In other countries, such as Russia, the movement has been characterized by false starts and backsliding. Market economies are based on competition in the marketplace and private ownership of the factors of production. In a competitive economic system, a large number of people and businesses buy and sell products and services freely in the marketplace. In pure capitalism all the factors of production are owned privately, and the government does not try to set prices or coordinate economic activity.

A market economy guarantees certain economic rights: the right to own property, the right to make a profit, the right to make free choices, and the right to compete. The right to own property is central to a market economy. The main incentive in this system is profit, which encourages entrepreneurship. Profit is also necessary for producing goods and services, building plants, paying dividends and taxes, and creating jobs. The freedom to choose whether to become an entrepreneur or to work for someone else means that people have the right to decide what they want to do on the basis of their own drive, interest, and training. The government does not create job quotas for each industry or give people tests to determine what they will do.

In a market economy, competition is viewed as being good for both businesses and consumers. It leads to better and more diverse products, keeps prices stable, and increases the efficiency of producers. Producers try to produce their goods and services at the lowest possible cost and sell them at the highest possible price. But when profits are high, more firms enter the market to seek those profits. The resulting competition among firms tends to lower prices. Producers must then find new ways of operating more efficiently if they are to keep making a profit—and stay in business.

The Command Economy

command economy
An economic system characterized by government ownership of virtually all resources and economic decision making by central government planning; also known as a *planned economy*.

The opposite of the market economy is a command economy. A **command economy** is characterized by government ownership of virtually all resources and economic decision making is characterized by central government planning. The government decides what will be produced, where it will be produced, how much will be produced, where the raw materials and supplies will come from, and who will get the output.

Before the Soviet Union collapsed in 1991, it had a command economy, but even so it relied to some extent on market-determined prices and allowed some private ownership. Recent reforms in Russia, China, and most of the Eastern European nations have moved these economies toward more capitalistic, market-oriented systems. North Korea and Cuba are two examples of remaining command economies.

Socialism

socialism
An economic system in which the basic industries are owned either by the government itself or by the private sector under strong government control.

Socialism is a type of command economic system in which the basic industries are owned by the government or by the private sector under strong government control. A socialist state controls critical, large-scale industries such as transportation, communications, and utilities. Smaller businesses may be privately owned. To varying degrees the state also determines the goals of businesses, the prices and selection of goods, and the rights of workers. Socialist countries typically provide their citizens with a higher level of services, such as health care and unemployment benefits, than do most capitalist countries. As a result, taxes and unemployment may also be quite high in socialist countries.

The Mixed Economy

mixed economies
Economies that combine several economic systems; for example, an economy where the government owns certain industries but others are owned by the private sector.

The pure market economy and the pure command economy are both extremes; real-world economies fall somewhere between the two. In Canada our economy is classified as a **mixed economy** (i.e., a combination of other economic systems), where most industries are privately owned, but government policies are used to promote economic stability and growth. Also, through policies and laws, the government transfers money to the poor, the unemployed, and the elderly (e.g., Old Age Security Payments, Government Pension Plans, and Child Tax Credits).

concept check

- What is a market economy and why is it growing?
- Explain the concept of a command economy.
- What is socialism?
- Why are most economies mixed?

 **lg 2**

economics
The study of how a society uses scarce resources to produce and distribute goods and services.

How Businesses and Economies Work

Economics is the study of how a society uses scarce resources to produce and distribute goods and services. The resources of a person, a firm, or a nation are limited. Hence, economics is the study of choices—what people, firms, or nations choose from among the available resources. Every economy is concerned with what types and amounts of goods and services should be produced, how they should be produced, and for whom. These decisions are made by the marketplace, the government, or both. In Canada, the government and the free market system together guide the economy.

You probably know more about economics than you realize. Every day many news stories deal with economic matters: a union wins wage increases at General Motors; the Bank of Canada lowers interest rates; the Toronto Stock Exchange (TSX) has a record day; the Minister of Finance proposes a cut in income taxes; consumer spending rises as the economy grows; or retail prices are on the rise, to mention just a few examples.

Macroeconomics and Microeconomics

The state of the economy affects both people and businesses. How you spend your money (or save it) is a personal economic decision. Whether you continue in school and whether you work part-time are also economic decisions. Every business also operates within the economy. Based on their economic expectations and external factors, businesses decide what products to produce, how to price them, how many people to employ, how much to pay these employees, how much to expand the business, and so on.

Economics has two main subareas. **Macroeconomics** is the study of the economy as a whole. It looks at aggregate data for large groups of people, companies, or products considered as a whole. In contrast, **microeconomics** focuses on individual parts of the economy, such as households or firms.

Both macroeconomics and microeconomics offer a valuable outlook on the economy. For example, Ford might use both to decide whether to introduce a new line of cars, like the Smart car, from Europe. The company would consider such macroeconomic factors as the national level of personal income, the unemployment rate, interest rates, fuel costs, and the national level of sales of imported cars. From a microeconomic viewpoint, Ford would judge consumer demand for new cars versus the existing supply, competing models, labour and material costs and availability, and current prices and sales incentives.

macroeconomics
The subarea of economics that focuses on the economy as a whole by looking at aggregate data for large groups of people, companies, or products.

microeconomics
The subarea of economics that focuses on individual parts of the economy such as households or firms.

Economics as a Circular Flow

Another way to see how the sectors of the economy interact is to examine the **circular flow** of inputs and outputs among households, businesses, and governments as shown in Exhibit 1-1. The exchanges are reviewed by following the purple circle around the inside of the diagram. Households provide inputs (natural resources, labour, capital, entrepreneurship) to businesses, which convert these inputs into outputs (goods and services) for consumers. In return, consumers receive income from rent, wages, interest, and ownership profits (green circle). Businesses receive income from consumer purchases of goods and services.

The other important exchange in Exhibit 1-1 takes place between governments (federal, provincial, and local) and both individuals and businesses. Governments supply many types of publicly provided goods and services (highways, schools, police, courts, health services, employment insurance, etc.) that benefit individuals and businesses. Government purchases from businesses also contribute to business profits. A contractor who repairs a local stretch of highway, for example, is paid by the government for the work. As the diagram shows, government receives taxes from individuals and businesses to complete the flow.

Changes in one flow affect the others. If government raises taxes, households have less to spend on goods and services. Lower consumer spending causes businesses to reduce production, and economic activity declines; unemployment may rise. In contrast, cutting taxes can stimulate economic activity. Keep the circular flow in mind as we continue our study of economics. The way economic sectors interact will become more evident as we explore macroeconomics and microeconomics.

circular flow
The movement of inputs and outputs among households, businesses, and governments; a way of showing how the sectors of the economy interact.

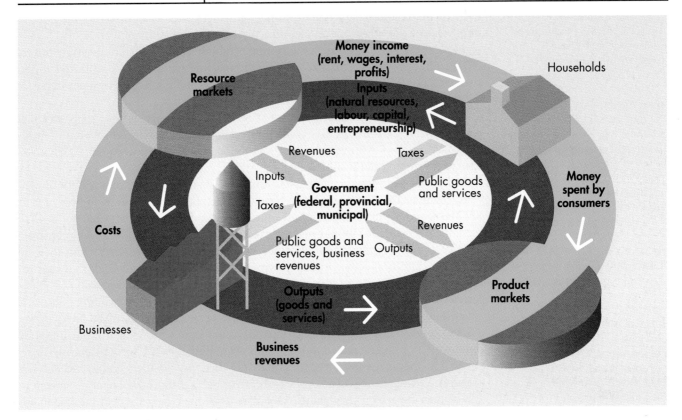

concept check

- What is economics?
- What is the difference between macroeconomics and microeconomics?
- How do resources flow among the household, business, and government sectors?

→ **lg 3**

HOT Links

The Canadian Government follows national and regional economic statistics, including the GDP. For the latest economic overview of the Canadian economy, visit

www.canadianeconomy.gc.ca

economic growth
An increase in a nation's output of goods and services.

Macroeconomics: The Big Picture

Have you ever looked at a news service on the Internet or turned on the radio or television and heard something like "Today Statistics Canada reported that for the second straight month unemployment declined"? Statements like this are macroeconomic news. Understanding the national economy and how changes in government policies affect households and businesses is a good place to begin our study of economics.

Let's look first at macroeconomic goals and how they can be met. Canada and most other countries have three main macroeconomic goals: economic growth, full employment, and price stability. A nation's economic well-being depends on carefully defining these goals and choosing the best economic policies to reach them.

Striving for Economic Growth

Perhaps the most important way to judge a nation's economic health is to look at its production of goods and services. The more the nation produces, the higher its standard of living. An increase in a nation's output of goods and services is **economic growth**.

gross domestic product (GDP)
The total market value of all final goods and services produced within a nation's borders each year.

gross national product (GNP)
The total market value of all final goods and services produced by a country regardless of where the factors of production are located.

business cycles
Upward and downward changes in the level of economic activity.

recession
A decline in GDP that lasts for at least two consecutive quarters.

full employment
Situation when the economy is producing to its maximum sustainable capacity, using labour, technology, land, capital, and other factors of production to their fullest potential.

Economic growth is usually a good thing, but it also has a bad side. Increased production yields more pollution. Growth may strain public facilities, such as roads, electricity, schools, and hospitals. Thus, the government tries to apply economic policies that will keep growth to a level that does not reduce the quality of life.

The most basic measure of economic growth is the **gross domestic product (GDP)**. GDP is the total market value of all final goods and services produced within a nation's borders each year. It is reported quarterly and is used to compare trends in national output. When GDP rises, the economy is growing.

Another measurement that is often used by economist is the **gross national product (GNP)**. Unlike the GDP, which calculates what is produced within the countries borders, the GNP measures what is produced by the nation regardless of where the factors of production are located.

The level of economic activity is constantly changing. These upward and downward changes are called **business cycles**. Business cycles vary in length, in how high or low the economy moves, and in how much the economy is affected. Changes in GDP trace the patterns as economic activity expands and contracts. An increase in business activity results in rising output, income, employment, and prices. Eventually, these all peak, and output, income, and employment decline. A decline in GDP that lasts for two consecutive quarters (each a three-month period) is called a **recession.** It is followed by a recovery period when economic activity once again increases.

Businesses must monitor and react to the changing phases of business cycles. When the economy is growing, companies often have a difficult time hiring good employees and finding scarce supplies and raw materials. When a recession hits, many firms find they have more capacity than the demand for their goods and services requires. During the recession of the early 1990s, many firms operated at 75 percent or less of their capacity. When plants use only part of their capacity, they operate inefficiently and have higher costs per unit produced. Let's say that Magna Corp. has a plant that can produce 100 Smartcar bodies a month, but because of a recession, DaimlerChrysler AG requires only 50 per month. Magna has a huge plant with large, expensive machines designed to produce 100 Smartcar bodies a month. Producing Smart car bodies at 50 percent capacity does not efficiently utilize Magna's investment in the plant and equipment.

Keeping People on the Job

Another macroeconomic goal is **full employment**, or having jobs for all who want to and can work. Full employment doesn't actually mean 100 percent employment. Some people choose not to work for personal reasons (attending school, raising children) or are temporarily unemployed while they wait to start a new job. Thus, the government defines full employment as the situation "when the economy is producing to its maximum sustainable capacity, using labour, technology, land, capital, and other factors of production to their fullest potential."[3]

The housing industry is a leading economic indicator. A rise in new home construction typically translates into a robust economy.

Measuring Unemployment

To determine how close we are to full employment, the government measures the **unemployment rate.** This rate indicates the percentage of the total labour force that is not working but is actively looking for work. It excludes "discouraged workers," those

During busy summer months, theme parks like Paramount Canada's Wonderland hire many young people and adults—a group of employees subject to seasonal employment.

➡ **lg 4**

unemployment rate
The percentage of the total labour force that is not working but is actively looking for work.

frictional unemployment
Short-term unemployment that is not related to the business cycle.

structural unemployment
Unemployment that is caused by a mismatch between available jobs and the skills of available workers in an industry or region; not related to the business cycle.

cyclical unemployment
Unemployment that occurs when a downturn in the business cycle reduces the demand for labour throughout the economy.

not seeking jobs because they think no one will hire them. Each month the Canadian government releases statistics on employment. These figures help us understand how well the economy is doing.

Types of Unemployment

Economists classify unemployment into four types: frictional, structural, cyclical, and seasonal. The categories are of small consolation to someone who is unemployed, but they help economists understand the problem of unemployment in our economy.

Frictional unemployment is short-term unemployment that is not related to the business cycle. It includes people who are unemployed while waiting to start a better job, those who are re-entering the job market, and those entering for the first time such as new college graduates. This type of unemployment is always present and has little impact on the economy.

Structural unemployment is also unrelated to the business cycle but is involuntary. It is caused by a mismatch between available jobs and the skills of available workers in an industry or a region. For example, if the birthrate declines, fewer teachers will be needed. Or the available workers in an area may lack the skills that employers want. Retraining and skill-building programs are often required to reduce structural unemployment.

Cyclical unemployment, as the name implies, occurs when a downturn in the business cycle reduces the demand for labour throughout the economy. In a long recession, cyclical unemployment is widespread, and even people with good job skills can't find jobs. The government can partly counteract cyclical unemployment with programs that boost the economy.

The last type is **seasonal unemployment**, which occurs during specific seasons in certain industries. Employees subject to seasonal unemployment include retail workers hired for the Christmas buying season, road construction workers, park maintenance workers, and so on.

Keeping Prices Steady

The third macroeconomic goal is to keep overall prices for goods and services fairly steady. The situation in which the average of all prices of goods and services is rising is called **inflation**. Inflation's higher prices reduce **purchasing power**, the value of what money can buy. If prices go up but income doesn't rise or rises at a slower rate, a given amount of income buys less. For example, if the price of a bag of groceries rises from $30 to $40 but your salary remains the same, you can buy only 75 percent as many groceries ($30 ÷ $40). Your purchasing power declines by 25 percent ($10 ÷ $40).

Inflation affects both personal and business decisions. When prices are rising, people tend to spend more—before their purchasing power declines further. Businesses that expect inflation often increase their supplies, and people often speed up planned purchases of cars and major appliances.

Types of Inflation

There are two types of inflation. **Demand-pull inflation** occurs when the demand for goods and services is greater than the supply. Would-be buyers have more money to spend than the amount needed to buy available goods and services. Their demand,

seasonal unemployment
Unemployment that occurs during specific seasons in certain industries.

inflation
The situation in which the average of all prices of goods and services is rising.

purchasing power
The value of what money can buy.

demand-pull inflation
Inflation that occurs when the demand for goods and services is greater than the supply.

cost-push inflation
Inflation that occurs when increases in production costs push up the prices of final goods and services.

consumer price index (CPI)
A measure of retail price movements that compares a representative "shopping basket" of goods and services.

HOT Links

Want to know where the consumer price index stands today? Go to Statistics Canada's Web site at
www.statcan.ca

➡ **lg 5**

HOT Links

For more information on the Bank of Canada and its importance see
www.bankofcanada.ca

monetary policy
The measures taken by the Bank of Canada to regulate the amount of money in circulation to influence the economy.

which exceeds the supply, tends to pull prices up. This situation is sometimes described as "too much money chasing too few goods." The higher prices lead to greater supply, eventually creating a balance between demand and supply.

Cost-push inflation is triggered by increases in production costs, such as expenses for materials and wages. These increases push up the prices of final goods and services. Wage increases are a major cause of cost-push inflation, creating a "wage-price spiral." For example, assume the Canadian Auto Workers union negotiates a three-year labour agreement that raises wages 3 percent per year and increases overtime pay. Automakers will then raise car prices to cover their higher labour costs. Also, the higher wages will give workers more money to buy goods and services, and this increased demand may pull up other prices. Workers in other industries will demand higher wages to keep up with the increased prices, and the cycle will push prices even higher.

How Inflation Is Measured

The rate of inflation is most commonly measured by looking at changes in the **consumer price index (CPI)**, an index that measures the retail price movements by comparing a representative "shopping basket" of goods and services. It is published monthly by Statistics Canada.

The Impact of Inflation

Inflation has several negative effects on people and businesses. For one thing, inflation penalizes people who live on fixed incomes. Let's say that a couple receives $1000 a month retirement income beginning in 2003. If inflation is 10 percent in 2004, then the couple can buy only 90 percent of what they could purchase in 2003. Similarly, inflation hurts savers. As prices rise, the real value, or purchasing power, of a nest egg of savings deteriorates.

c o n c e p t c h e c k

- What is a business cycle? How do businesses adapt to periods of contraction and expansion?
- Why is full employment usually defined as a target percentage below 100 percent? How is unemployment measured?
- What is the difference between demand-pull and cost-push inflation?

Achieving Macroeconomic Goals

To reach macroeconomic goals, countries must often choose among conflicting alternatives. Sometimes political needs override economic ones. For example, bringing inflation under control may call for a politically difficult period of high unemployment and low growth. Or, in an election year, politicians may resist raising taxes to curb inflation. Still, the federal government and the Bank of Canada must try to guide the economy to a sound balance of growth, employment, and price stability. The two main tools used are the fiscal policy and monetary policy. By having a separation of fiscal and monetary policymakers (i.e., the federal government and the Bank of Canada), Canada has separated the power to spend money (i.e., fiscal policy) from the power to create money (i.e., monetary policy).

Monetary Policy

Monetary policy refers to the Bank of Canada's programs for controlling the amount of money circulating in the economy and interest rates. Changes in the money supply affect both the level of economic activity and the rate of inflation. According to the

The interest rate set by the Bank of Canada is passed on to consumers and businesses by the banking system.

Bank of Canada
Canada's central bank whose objective is to "promote the economic and financial well-being of Canada."

contractionary policy
The use of monetary policy by the Bank of Canada to tighten the money supply by selling government securities or raising interest rates.

expansionary policy
The use of monetary policy by the Bank of Canada to increase the growth of the money supply.

fiscal policy
The government's use of taxation and spending to affect the economy.

Bank of Canada Act of 1934, the **Bank of Canada** is the central banking system that prints money and controls how much of it will be in circulation to "promote the economic and financial well-being of Canada."

When the Bank of Canada increases or decreases the amount of money in circulation, it affects interest rates (the cost of borrowing money and the reward for lending it). The Bank of Canada can change the interest rate on money it lends to banks, signalling to the banking system and financial markets that it has changed its monetary policy. Banks, in turn, may pass along this change to consumers and businesses that receive loans from the banks. If the cost of borrowing increases, the economy slows because interest rates affect consumer and business decisions to spend or invest. The housing industry, business, and investments react most to changes in interest rates.

As you can see, the Bank of Canada can use monetary policy to contract or expand the economy. With **contractionary policy**, the Bank of Canada restricts, or tightens, the money supply by selling government securities or raising interest rates. The result is slower economic growth and higher unemployment. Thus, contractionary policy reduces spending and, ultimately, lowers inflation. With **expansionary policy**, the Bank of Canada increases, or loosens, growth in the money supply. An expansionary policy stimulates the economy. Interest rates decline, so business and consumer spending go up. Unemployment rates drop as businesses expand. But increasing the money supply also has a negative side: more spending pushes prices up, increasing the inflation rate.

Fiscal Policy

The other economic tool used by the government is **fiscal policy**, its program of taxation and spending. By increasing government spending or by cutting taxes, the government can stimulate the economy. Look again at Exhibit 1-1 on page 13. The more government buys from businesses, the greater business revenues and output are. Likewise, if consumers or businesses have to pay less in taxes, they will have more income to spend for goods and services. Tax policies in Canada therefore affect business decisions. High corporate taxes can make it harder for Canadian firms to compete with companies in countries with lower taxes. As a result, companies may choose to locate facilities in other countries to reduce their tax burden.

If the government spends more for programs (social services, education, etc.) than it collects in taxes, the result is a **federal budget deficit**. To balance the budget, the government can cut its spending, increase taxes, or do some combination of the two. When it cannot balance the budget, the government must make up any shortfalls by borrowing (just like any business or household). The accumulated total of all of the federal government's annual budget deficits is known as the **national debt.**

Since 1991 the Government of Canada and the Bank of Canada have jointly been fighting inflation. In that year, they agreed to target inflation to a long-term objective of a 2 percent midpoint. By December of 1993, they were successful and this focus is needed in the short and medium term to maintain a relatively stable price environment. By keeping inflation between 1 and 3 percent, the Canadian economy should see an economic growth at a sustainable pace and avoid the "boom-and-bust" periods seen in the 1980s and 1990s.

federal budget deficit
The condition that occurs when the federal government spends more for programs than it collects in taxes.

national debt
The accumulated total of all of the federal government's annual budget deficits.

HOT Links

Want to know the current public deficit and debt? Head to www.fin.gc.ca

concept check

- What is a monetary policy? Who is responsible for this policy in Canada? What are its main objectives?
- What is fiscal policy? What fiscal policy tools can the government use to achieve its macroeconomic goals?
- What problems can a large national debt present?

Governments' Other Roles in the Economy

It has been mentioned that the government uses its fiscal policy to determine public spending and taxation, but it has other roles within our economy. The three levels of governments (federal, provincial, and local) use their many roles to influence businesses and the Canadian economy. Briefly, some of the more important roles are the following:

- *Customer.* Governments purchase thousands of products and services to carry out their functions. Some businesses (e.g., road construction companies) rely on governments for most if not all of their revenues.
- *Competitor.* Through Crown corporations, governments compete directly with private companies.
- *Provider of incentives.* Governments use many programs to stimulate economic growth, development, and employment. "Team Canada" (as illustrated in Chapter 2) is just one example.
- *Provider of essential services.* Governments have traditionally supplied and continue to supply services that private enterprises do not. The Canadian Armed Forces and Statistics Canada are two examples.
- *Regulator.* Governments are responsible for the safety and well-being of the citizens of Canada. This includes the protection of consumers (e.g., consumer rights, as discussed in Chapter 3), protecting businesses and competition (e.g., tariffs and quotas), protection of social goals (e.g., Canadian content laws), environmental protection (e.g., the Fisheries Act and anti-pollution laws), and so on.
- *Taxation agent.* Taxes are necessary for governments to employ people to provide goods and services. Taxes are not only the responsibility of individuals, but also of businesses.

→ **lg 6**

Microeconomics: Zeroing In on Businesses and Consumers

Now let's shift our focus from the whole economy to *microeconomics*—the study of households, businesses, and industries. This field of economics is concerned with how prices and quantities of goods and services behave in a free market. It stands to reason that people, firms, and governments try to get the most from their limited resources. Consumers want to buy the best quality at the lowest price. Businesses want to keep costs down and revenues high to earn larger profits. Governments also want to use their revenues to provide the most effective public goods and services possible. These groups choose among alternatives by focusing on the prices of goods and services.

As consumers in a free market, we influence what is produced. If Mexican food is popular, the high demand attracts entrepreneurs who open more Mexican restaurants. They want to compete for our dollars by supplying Mexican food at a lower price, of better quality, or with different features such as Santa Fe Mexican food rather than Tex-Mex. This section explains how business and consumer choices influence the price and availability of goods and services.

The Nature of Demand

demand
The quantity of a good or service that people are willing to buy at various prices.

demand curve
A graph showing the quantity of a good or service that people are willing to buy at various prices.

Demand is the quantity of a good or service that people are willing to buy at various prices. The higher the price, the lower the quantity demanded, and vice versa. A graph of this relationship is called a **demand curve**.

Let's assume you own a store that sells jackets for snowboarders. From past experience you know how many jackets you can sell at different prices. The demand curve in Exhibit 1-2 depicts this information. The x-axis (horizontal axis) shows the quantity of jackets, and the y-axis (vertical axis) shows the related price of those jackets. For example, at a price of $60, customers will buy (demand) 500 snowboard jackets.

In the graph the demand curve slopes downward and to the right. This means that as the price falls, people will want to buy more jackets. Some people who were not going to buy a jacket will purchase one at the lower price. Also, some snowboarders who already have a jacket will buy a second one. The graph also shows that if you put a large number of jackets on the market, you will have to reduce the price to sell all of them.

The Nature of Supply

supply
The quantity of a good or service that businesses will make available at various prices.

supply curve
A graph showing the quantity of a good or service that a business will make available at various prices.

Demand alone is not enough to explain how the market sets prices. We must also look at **supply**, the quantity of a good or service that businesses will make available at various prices. The higher the price, the greater the amount a jacket manufacturer is willing to supply, and vice versa. A graph of the relationship between various prices and the quantities a manufacturer will supply is a **supply curve**.

We can again plot the quantity of jackets on the x-axis and the price on the y-axis. As Exhibit 1-3 shows, 900 jackets will be available at a price of $60. Note that the supply curve slopes upward and to the right, the opposite of the demand curve. If snowboarders

e x h i b i t   1 - 2 | Demand Curve for Jackets for Snowboarders

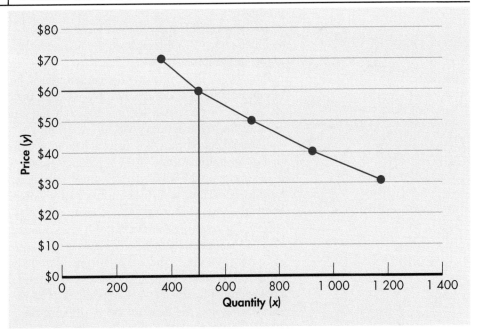

| e x h i b i t   1 - 3 | Supply Curve for Jackets for Snowboarders |

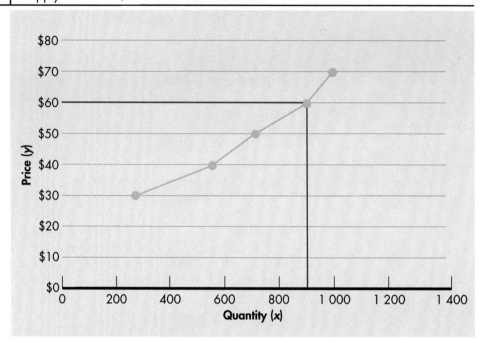

are willing to pay higher prices, manufacturers of jackets will buy more inputs (Goretex, dye, machinery, labour) and produce more jackets. The quantity supplied will be higher at higher prices, because producers can earn higher profits.

How Demand and Supply Interact to Determine Prices

In a stable economy, the number of jackets that snowboarders demand depends on the jackets' price. Likewise, the number of jackets that suppliers provide depends on price. But at what price will consumer demand for jackets match the quantity suppliers will produce?

To answer this question, we need to look at what happens when demand and supply interact. By plotting both the demand curve and the supply curve on the same graph in Exhibit 1-4, we see that they cross at a certain quantity and price. At that point, labelled E, the quantity demanded equals the quantity supplied. This is the point of **equilibrium**. The equilibrium price is $50; the equilibrium quantity is 700 jackets. At that point there is a balance between the amount consumers will buy and the amount the manufacturers will supply.

equilibrium
The point at which quantity demanded equals quantity supplied.

Market equilibrium is achieved through a series of quantity and price adjustments that occur automatically. If the price increases to $70, suppliers produce more jackets than consumers are willing to buy, and a surplus results. To sell more jackets, prices will have to fall. Thus, a surplus pushes prices downward until equilibrium is reached. When the price falls to $40, the quantity of jackets demanded rises above the available supply. The resulting shortage forces prices upward until equilibrium is reached at $50.

The number of snowboarder jackets produced and bought at $50 will tend to rest at equilibrium unless there is a shift in either demand or supply. If demand increases, more jackets will be purchased at every price, and the demand curve shifts to the right (as illustrated by line D_2 in Exhibit 1-5). If demand decreases, less will be bought at every price, and the demand curve shifts to the left (D_1). When demand decreased, snowboarders bought 500 jackets at $50 instead of 700 jackets. When demand increased, they purchased 800.

| Equilibrium Price and Quantity

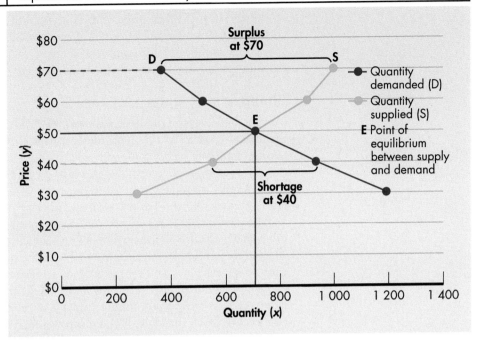

Changes in Demand

A number of things can increase or decrease demand. For example, if snowboarders' incomes go up, they may decide to buy a second jacket. If incomes fall, a snowboarder who was planning to purchase a jacket may wear an old one instead. Changes in fashion or tastes can also influence demand. If snowboarding were suddenly to go out of fashion, demand for jackets would decrease quickly. A change in the price of related products can also influence demand. For example, if the average price of a snowboard rises to $1000, some people will quit snowboarding and jacket demand will fall.

| Shifts in Demand

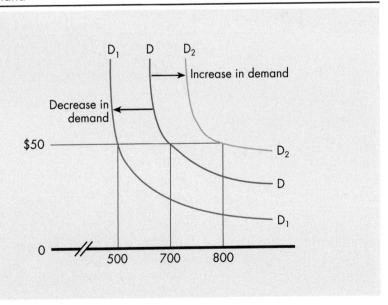

Another factor that can shift demand is expectations about future prices. If you expect jacket prices to increase significantly in the future, you may decide to go ahead and get one today. If you think prices will fall, you will postpone your purchase. Finally, changes in the number of buyers will affect demand. Snowboarding is a young person's sport. The number of teenagers will increase in the next few years. Therefore, the demand for snowboarding jackets should increase.

Changes in Supply

New technology typically lowers the cost of production. For example, North Face, a manufacturer of ski and snowboarder jackets, has just purchased laser-guided pattern-cutting equipment and computer-aided pattern-making equipment. Each jacket is now cheaper to produce, resulting in a higher profit per jacket. This becomes an incentive to supply more jackets at every price. If the price of resources such as labour or fabric goes up, North Face will earn a smaller profit on each jacket, and the amount supplied will decrease at every price. The reverse is also true. Changes in the prices of other goods can also affect supply. Let's say that snow skiing becomes a really hot sport. The number of skiers jumps dramatically and the price of ski jackets soars. North Face can use its machines and fabrics to produce either ski or snowboard jackets. If the company can make more profit from ski jackets, it will produce fewer snowboarding jackets at every price. Also, simply a change in the number of producers will shift the supply curve. If the number of manufacturers increases, more jackets will be placed on the market at every price and vice versa. Taxes can also affect supply. If the government decides, for some reason, to tax the manufacturer for every snowboard jacket produced, then profits will fall and fewer jackets will be offered at every price. Exhibit 1-6 summarizes the factors that can shift demand and supply curves.

concept check

- What is the relationship between prices and demand for a product?
- How is market equilibrium achieved?
- Draw a graph that shows an equilibrium point.

e x h i b i t   1 - 6 | Factors That Cause Demand and Supply Curves to Shift

Factor	Shift Demand	
	To the Right if:	**To the Left if:**
Buyers' incomes	increase	decrease
Buyers' preferences/tastes	increase	decrease
Prices of substitute products	increase	decrease
Expectations about future prices	will rise	will fall
Number of buyers	increases	decreases
	Shift Supply	
Technology	lowers costs	increases costs
Resource prices	fall	increase
Changes in prices of other products that can be produced with the same resources	profit of other product falls	profit of other product increases
Number of suppliers	increases	decreases
Taxes	lowered	increased

Competing in a Free Market

→ **lg 7**

market structure
The number of suppliers in a market.

One of the characteristics of a free market system is that suppliers have the right to compete with one another. The number of suppliers in a market is called **market structure**. Economists identify four types of market structures: (1) perfect competition, (2) pure monopoly, (3) monopolistic competition, and (4) oligopoly.

Perfect Competition

perfect (pure) competition
A market structure in which a large number of small firms sell similar products, buyers and sellers have good information, and businesses can be easily opened or closed.

Characteristics of **perfect (pure) competition** include:

- A large number of small firms are in the market.
- The firms sell similar products; that is, each firm's product is very much like the products sold by other firms in the market.
- Buyers and sellers in the market have good information about prices, sources of supply, and so on.
- It is easy to open a new business or close an existing one.

In a perfectly competitive market, firms sell their products at prices determined solely by forces beyond their control. Because the products are very similar and because each firm contributes only a small amount to the total quantity supplied by the industry, price is determined by supply and demand. A firm that raised its price even a little above the going rate would lose customers.

Pure Monopoly

pure monopoly
A market structure in which a single firm accounts for all industry sales and in which there are barriers to entry.

barriers to entry
Factors, such as technological or legal conditions, that prevent new firms from competing equally with a monopoly.

At the other end of the spectrum is **pure monopoly**, the market structure in which a single firm accounts for all industry sales. The firm *is* the industry. This structure is characterized by **barriers to entry**—factors that prevent new firms from competing equally with the existing firm. Often the barriers are technological or legal conditions. Polaroid, for example, has held major patents on instant photography for years. When Kodak tried to market its own instant camera, Polaroid sued, claiming patent violations. Polaroid collected millions of dollars from Kodak. Another barrier may be one firm's control of a natural resource. DeBeers Consolidated Mines Ltd., for example, controls most of the world's supply of uncut diamonds.

Public utilities such as natural gas and water are pure monopolies (although there are many public utilities being privatized and competition is being encouraged). Some monopolies have been created by government regulations that prohibit competition. Canada Post Corporation's direct mail service is one such monopoly.

Monopolistic Competition

monopolistic competition
A market structure in which many firms offer products that are close substitutes and in which entry is relatively easy.

Three characteristics define the market structure known as **monopolistic competition**:

- Many firms are in the market.
- The firms offer products that are close substitutes but still differ from one another.
- It is relatively easy to enter the market.

Under monopolistic competition, firms take advantage of product differentiation. Industries where monopolistic competition occurs include clothing, food, and similar consumer products. Firms under monopolistic competition have more control over pricing than do firms under perfect competition because consumers do not view the

Each motel offers essentially the same product with information about pricing easily accessible. Entry into the motel market is relatively simple and competition can change with the entry of a new operation.

products as exactly the same. Nevertheless, firms must demonstrate those product differences to justify their prices to customers. Consequently, companies use advertising to distinguish their products from others. Such distinctions may be significant or superficial. For example, Nike says "Just Do It," and Tylenol is advertised as being easier on the stomach than aspirin.

Oligopoly

oligopoly
A market structure in which a few firms produce most or all of the output and in which large capital requirements or other factors limit the number of firms.

An **oligopoly** has two characteristics:
- A few firms produce most or all of the output.
- Large capital requirements or other factors limit the number of firms.

Boeing and McDonnell Douglas (aircraft manufacturers) and Stelco Inc. (Canada's largest and most diversified Canadian steel producer) are major firms in different oligopoly industries.

With so few firms in an oligopoly, what one firm does has an impact on the other firms. Thus, the firms in an oligopoly watch one another closely for new technologies, product changes and innovations, promotional campaigns, pricing, production, and other developments. Sometimes they go so far as to coordinate their pricing and output decisions, which is illegal. Many antitrust cases—legal challenges arising out of laws designed to control anticompetitive behaviour—occur in oligopolies. Exhibit 1-7 summarizes the primary types of market structures.

concept check

- What is meant by market structure?
- Describe the four types of market structure.

---

e x h i b i t   1 - 7 | Types of Market Structures

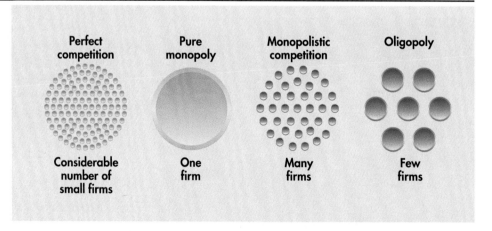

| Perfect competition | Pure monopoly | Monopolistic competition | Oligopoly |
| Considerable number of small firms | One firm | Many firms | Few firms |

➡ **lg 8**

CAPITALIZING ON TRENDS IN BUSINESS

Trends in business occur at both the macroeconomic and the microeconomic level. We will begin by taking a look at some microeconomic trends.

Delivering Value and Quality

Companies today are facing accelerating change in many areas, including better-educated and more demanding consumers, new technology, and the globalization of markets. As a result, competition is the toughest it has ever been. More and more, the key to building and sustaining a long-range advantage is a commitment to delivering superior customer value.

customer value
The customer's perception of the ratio of benefits (functionality, performance, durability, design, ease of use, and serviceability) to the sacrifice (of money, time, and effort) necessary to obtain those benefits.

Customer value is the customer's perception of the ratio of benefits to the sacrifice necessary to obtain those benefits. Customers receive benefits in the form of functionality, performance, durability, design, ease of use, and serviceability. To receive those benefits, they give up money, time, and effort.

Customer value is not simply a matter of high quality. A high-quality product that is available only at a high price will not be perceived as a value. Nor will bare-bones service or low-quality goods selling for a low price. Instead, customers value goods and services of the quality that they expect, sold at prices they are willing to pay. Value marketing can be used to sell a $150 000 Rolls Royce as well as a $3 bag of McCain frozen French fries.

Businesses provide customer value by:

- *Offering products that perform.* This is the bare minimum. Consumers have lost patience with shoddy merchandise.
- *Giving consumers more than they expect.* Soon after Toyota launched Lexus, the company had to order a recall. The weekend before the recall, dealers personally phoned all the Lexus owners that were affected and arranged to pick up their cars and provide replacement vehicles.
- *Avoiding unrealistic pricing.* Consumers couldn't understand why Kellogg's cereals commanded a premium over other brands, so Kellogg's market share fell 5 percent.
- *Giving the buyer facts.* Today's sophisticated consumer wants informative advertising and knowledgeable salespeople.

In today's business world, if a firm doesn't deliver customer value it doesn't survive. Firms that provide customer value end up with satisfied customers. Exhibit 1-8 lists some companies that are especially good at satisfying customers.

Creating Long-Term Relationships

relationship management
The practice of building, maintaining, and enhancing interactions with customers and other parties in order to develop long-term satisfaction through mutually beneficial partnerships.

Customer satisfaction helps build long-term relationships between a company and its clients. Today, companies are focusing on **relationship management**, which involves building, maintaining, and enhancing interactions with customers and other parties so as to develop long-term satisfaction through mutually beneficial partnerships. In general, the longer a customer stays with a company, the more that customer is worth. Long-term customers buy more, take less of a company's time, are less sensitive to price, and bring in new customers. Best of all, they require no acquisition or start-up

| e x h i b i t   1 - 8 | Some Companies and Products That Deliver Satisfaction |

Company or Division

McCain	Mars (food processing)
Irving	Maytag
Tim Hortons	Quaker Oats
Magna International	Cadillac
Bombardier	Hershey Foods
Shaw Communications	Coca-Cola
Mercedes-Benz	Toyota
H. J. Heinz (food processing)	

costs. Good long-standing customers are worth so much that in some industries, reducing customer defections by as little as five points—from, say, 15 percent to 10 percent per year—can double profits.

The Royal Bank of Canada practises relationship management by launching the Royal Rewards Program. The program thanks users of their Visa card by giving the cardholder one reward point for each dollar spent on the Visa card. These reward points can be used to purchase merchandize such as trips, dinnerware, televisions, DVD players, and so forth.

Relationship management also means creating long-term relationships with suppliers. Suppliers are making major adjustments in their thinking, management styles, and methods of responding to purchasers' standards and operational requirements. A satisfied customer is one of the best sources of new business because the customer already knows that the supplier can meet expectations and deliver on its promises. Thus, the supplier has created trust, and trust is the foundation of most successful relationships.

strategic alliance
A cooperative agreement between business firms; sometimes called a *strategic partnership*.

A **strategic alliance**, sometimes called a strategic partnership, is a cooperative agreement between business firms. The trend toward forming strategic alliances is accelerating rapidly, particularly among high-tech firms. These companies have realized that strategic partnerships are more than just important—they are critical. Xerox management, for example, has decided that to maintain its leadership position in the reprographics industry, the company must "include suppliers as part of the Xerox family." This strategy often means reducing the number of suppliers, treating those that remain as allies, sharing strategic information freely, and drawing on supplier expertise in developing new products that can meet the quality, cost, and delivery standards of the marketplace.

Creating a Competitive Work Force

Creating customer value and building long-term relationships require a world-class work force. The goal of leading companies such as McCain Foods Limited and Mark's Work Wearhouse is for all workers to add value to every job they do every day. Such firms place a strong emphasis on training and the use of technology to improve worker productivity. Mark's Work Wearhouse, for example, values the investment in the training of its workers and enjoys significant savings to the company (see Chapter 4).

Entrepreneurial Spirit in Former Command Economies

A key trend in macroeconomics is the surprising entrepreneurial spirit among many citizens of former command economies.

Russia and China have inched away from planned economies. Today, China has a population of 1.3 billion and they all want more and better goods and services.[4] Already there are 21 million *ge-ti-hu* (entrepreneurs) in China.

One entrepreneur, Robert Kuok, helped bring Coca-Cola to China. Kuok grew up in Hong Kong, where he started a chain of hotels. When Coca-Cola decided to enter mainland China, the company realized that careful handling would be needed to sell the most American product in the world (Coca-Cola) to the Chinese. Every entrepreneur in Asia coveted

By building strong customer relationships, retailers can turn a one-time buyer into a loyal, long-term customer.

the opportunity to license Coke in China, a deal that could in time be worth US$8 billion.[5] Coke chose Robert Kuok. "I thought, 'My God, this is a gift from Heaven,'" Kuok recalls. Kuok is being modest. It was not a gift. Coke knew what it was doing. Soft drinks were not Kuok's business, but Coke didn't need expertise in soft drinks. It needed a smart guy with contacts. And that's Kuok, a 73-year-old hotel owner, commodities trader, investor, and cosmopolite. Keeping 12.5 percent of the bottling venture, Coke granted 87.5 percent to Kerry Group, Kuok's Hong Kong-based conglomerate.[6]

Another example of an entrepreneur is Russia's Konstantin Borovoi. Borovoi was a math professor until he made a small fortune selling his knowledge of computer software. When the floodgates opened for capitalism, he started the Russian Commodities and Raw Materials Exchange and ended up indirectly controlling about 12 percent of Russia's economy.[7] The Russian economy is divided into two parts—the very profitable part and the rest. The very profitable part is under the patronage of the state, which has created a host of privileges that favour tycoons such as Borovoi. "Without these privileges," says Olga Kryshtanovska, a specialist on Russian elites, "all the other enterprises experience all the difficulties that exist in this country. No one helps them. They are completely defenseless."[8]

The entrepreneurial spirit is not limited to the evolving old command economies. Struggling developing countries are also creating their own share of entrepreneurs.

concept check

- How do businesses provide customer value?
- How does relationship management make a business more competitive?
- Explain the entrepreneurial movement in former command economies.

APPLYING THIS CHAPTER'S TOPICS

This chapter has been about micro- and macroeconomics. Economics is not something you should learn for an exam and then forget. Economics is an analytical science that will help you understand the world around you. It can help you be more imaginative and insightful in everyday life. You should now better understand why prices are going up or down, when interest rates will fall, and when and why the unemployment rate will fall. Understanding these basic economic concepts can help you decide whether to change jobs (and how much money to ask for) and whether to buy a car now or wait until next year. When you hear that Ford Motor Co. has 115 days of inventory, understanding supply and demand will tell you that now may be the time to buy that new car.

Similarly, economics will help you become a better-informed citizen. Almost every political issue is, in some way, grounded in economic concepts. You should now know what it means to balance the budget and what problems occur with monopoly power. In short, economics can help you make more thoughtful and informed decisions.

Economics can also help you understand what is happening in other countries and can help you become aware of opportunities there. As more and more countries have moved away from command economies, Canadian and foreign multinational firms are moving in to take advantage of ground-floor opportunities. Consider accepting a foreign assignment. It's a wonderful way to experience other cultures and, at the same time, get ahead in your career. More and more large organizations are requiring that their middle and upper-level managers have foreign field experience. When you have an opportunity for a foreign assignment, don't let it slip by.

TRY IT NOW!

1. **Understand Your Tax Commitment** Soon you will enter the permanent job market, if you are not there already. Typically, your earnings will rise over the next 35 years, but as your earnings increase, so will your taxes. The average Canadian works six months out of every year just to cover taxes. Are taxes too high in our country? Since taxes will be a major part of your financial life for the next 35 to 45 years, you need to be informed. Visit a few organizations that advocate tax reform such as the Canadian Taxpayers Federation (www.taxpayer.com).

2. **Public–Private Partnerships** What benefits are there for Canadians when the government and business interact to provide goods and services? See how the Canadian Council for Public–Private Partnerships organization conducts research, publishes the findings, and facilitates discussion between the public and private sectors as an alternative to government being the sole provider of traditionally government services. Go to www.pppcouncil.ca.

>looking ahead
at DaimlerChrysler AG

Consider the opening story about the Smart car. The two basic determinants of price for the Smart car are demand and supply: the number of people who want to purchase the car at various prices, and the number of cars DaimlerChrysler AG is willing to produce at various price points. DaimlerChrysler AG competes in a market with a few large competitors. What one auto manufacturer does will have an impact on the others. Therefore, DaimlerChrysler AG competes in an oligopolistic market. How will changes in the economy such as a recession or inflation affect the Smart car? During a recession, demand for the Smart car might decline, but it could also increase if people look for a low-price alternative to a traditional car. With inflation, prices of resources used to produce the Smart car will increase, so DaimlerChrysler AG would probably raise the price of the car.

SUMMARY OF LEARNING GOALS

➡lg 1 **What is an economic system and what economic systems are prevalent in the world today?**
An economic system is the combination of policies, laws, and choices made by a nation's government to establish the systems that determine what goods and services are produced and how they are allocated. The main economic systems in the world today include market economies (capitalism), command (planned) economies, socialism, and mixed economies.

➡lg 2 **What is economics, and how are the three sectors of the economy linked?**
Economics is the study of how individuals, businesses, and governments use scarce resources to produce and distribute goods and services. The two major areas in economics are macroeconomics, the study of the economy as a whole, and microeconomics, the study of particular markets. The individual, business, and government sectors of the economy are linked by a series of two-way flows. The government provides public goods and services for the other two sectors and receives income in the form of taxes. Changes in one flow affect the other sectors.

KEY TERMS

➡lg 3 **How do economic growth, full employment, and price stability indicate a nation's economic health?**

A nation's economy is growing when the level of business activity, as measured by gross domestic product, is rising. GDP is the total value of all goods and services produced in a year. The goal of full employment is to have a job for all who can and want to work. How well a nation is meeting its employment goals is measured by the unemployment rate. There are four types of unemployment: frictional, structural, cyclical, and seasonal. With price stability, the overall prices of goods and services are not moving very much either up or down.

➡lg 4 **What is inflation, how is it measured, and what causes it?**

Inflation is the general upward movement of prices. When prices rise, purchasing power falls. The rate of inflation is measured by changes in the consumer price index (CPI). There are two main causes of inflation. If the demand for goods and services exceeds the supply, prices will rise. This is called demand-pull inflation. With cost-push inflation, higher production costs, such as expenses for materials and wages, increase the final prices of goods and services.

➡lg 5 **How does the Bank of Canada and the government use monetary policy and fiscal policy to achieve their macroeconomic goals?**

Monetary policy refers to actions by the Bank of Canada to control the money supply. When the Bank of Canada restricts the money supply, interest rates rise, the inflation rate drops, and economic growth slows. By expanding the money supply, the Bank of Canada stimulates economic growth.

The government uses fiscal policy—changes in levels of taxation and spending—to control the economy. Reducing taxes or increasing spending stimulates the economy; raising taxes or decreasing spending does the opposite. When the government spends more than it receives in tax revenues, it must borrow to finance the deficit. Some economists favour deficit spending as a way to stimulate the economy; others worry about our high level of national debt.

➡lg 6 **What are the basic microeconomic concepts of demand and supply, and how do they establish prices?**

Demand is the quantity of a good or service that people will buy at a given price. Supply is the quantity of a good or service that firms will make available at a given price. When the price increases, the quantity demanded falls but the quantity supplied rises. A price decrease leads to increased demand but a lower supply. At the point where the quantity demanded equals the quantity supplied, demand and supply are in balance. This equilibrium point is achieved by market adjustments of quantity and price.

➡lg 7 **What are the four types of market structure?**

Market structure is the number of suppliers in a market. Perfect competition is characterized by a large number of buyers and sellers, very similar products, good market information for both buyers and sellers, and ease of entry and exit into the market. In a pure monopoly, there is a single seller in a market. In monopolistic competition, many firms sell close substitutes in a market that is fairly easy to enter. In an oligopoly, a few firms produce most or all of the industry's output. An oligopoly is also difficult to enter and what one firm does will influence others.

➡lg 8 **Which trends are reshaping the micro- and macroeconomic environments?**

One micro trend is that firms are placing more emphasis on delivering value and quality to the customer. Companies are also establishing long-term relationships with both customers and suppliers. To compete in today's environment, companies and industries must build a competitive work force. At the macro level, budding entrepreneurial spirit in former command economies is sparking wealth among individual business owners and fuelling the growth of capitalism.

WORKING THE NET

1. Point your cursor toward Statistics Canada at **www.statcan.ca**. Find the historical information for your province's gross domestic product (GDP). What trends do you see? Can you think of reasons for these trends? How does your province's GDP compare with the Canadian GDP overall?

2. Read more about how the consumer price index (CPI) is computed at **www.bankofcanada.ca**. Look at the relative importance of each category included in the CPI. How well do these weightings match your own expenditures on each of these categories? What are some of the drawbacks of computing the CPI this way? Do you think these categories give a realistic picture of how most Canadians spend their money? Why or why not?

CREATIVE THINKING CASE

Black Forest Motors: The Mercedes-Benz Strategy in Action

Mercedes-Benz (**www.mercedescenter.com**), a manufacturer headquartered in Germany, produces luxury and near-luxury automobiles for distribution in Germany, Canada, the United States, and elsewhere. To increase its sales and perceived customer value in the Canadian market, Mercedes-Benz decided to pursue a corporate strategy called the "Customer Value Triad." This strategy had three components: goods quality, service quality, and value-based pricing. While goods quality and value-based pricing are established by the manufacturer, dealerships are the key element in service quality.

Dealerships in Canada are a prime example of the Mercedes-Benz corporate strategy in action, particularly the service quality component of the Customer Value Triad. The dealerships pride themselves on exceeding customers' expectations of product quality, price, and service. As a result, their customer base, fondly referred to as its "family of owners," has continued to grow.

Some employees have been with dealerships since their founding and they view this as evidence that the dealerships are also a great place to work. This translates directly into quality customer service and helps the dealerships to be a great place to purchase a vehicle.

The sales, service, and parts departments powerfully demonstrate commitment to service quality, as well as to goods quality and value-based pricing. The sales departments' sole purpose is to exceed customer expectations from test drive to delivery of the vehicle. This commitment begins with the test drive, which customers can schedule online through dealerships' Web sites. The sales personnel are dedicated to providing the information that customers need to make an educated buying decision. Each dealership wants all of its customers to drive away in a Mercedes-Benz that they feel has been the perfect choice.

The service departments have a state-of-the-art facility, featuring the latest diagnostic and repair equipment used by highly trained factory technicians. The departments' operations are based on the premise that "you and your vehicle deserve only the best of care." Goods quality and service quality are also emphasized in the parts department. They are stocked with a large inventory of the same high-quality parts used in manufacturing Mercedes-Benz vehicles.

With its commitment to the Customer Value Triad of goods quality, service quality, and value-based pricing, Mercedes-Benz asks only one thing of its clients: "If you were treated well, your expectations met, and the service was good, please tell others."[9]

Critical Thinking Questions

1. Do you think the Mercedes-Benz Customer Value Triad is an effective way to formulate a corporate strategy?
2. How might a strategy based on the Customer Value Triad help Mercedes-Benz and its dealerships to compete effectively in the Canadian marketplace?
3. Why are product and service quality important elements of operating a successful business? What is the impact on the price of the cars?
4. Does Mercedes-Benz operate in an oligopolistic marketplace?

CHAPTER 2

The Global Marketplace and Governments' Roles

In Chapter 1 we looked at economic systems and competition as one factor in the external economic environment of a business. In this chapter you will learn about global trade and the role of the government in promoting global trade as well as protecting domestic trade. This chapter deals directly with the interrelationship between the *political* environment (the government's role) and the *economic* environment (the global marketplace), two factors in our PEST model. As we saw in Chapter 1, and will see again in this chapter, these two factors are related to each other and they impact on the success of the business.

For example, the external environment presents opportunities and threats for a business. These opportunities and threats are considered by the business in determining its *strategy* for the future. This chapter discusses Team Canada—a partnership between government and industry to promote global trade. Team Canada is an initiative of the political environment that presents opportunities for Canadian business to gain access to international markets. This opportunity is one that many businesses have capitalized on to develop and expand exposure for their products in global markets. Expanding their businesses globally is one strategy that these companies have chosen to meet their growth objectives.

Free trade zones are also discussed. This is another way that government helps to create opportunities for business to expand. How business capitalizes on these political initiatives is its strategy. Different strategies for expanding in the global marketplace—such as exporting, licensing, joint ventures, and so on—are explored in the chapter.

Other political initiatives result in threats to business. Tariff and nontariff barriers are obvious examples. In an attempt to protect domestic trade, governments create threats for foreign competition by making foreign goods more expensive through tariffs, or by restricting the import of foreign goods through quotas. These barriers are meant to create opportunities for domestic companies to grow within a protected domestic environment; however, they may very well stifle the companies because they

don't have to *innovate* (one of the critical success factors) and improve their operations to compete with this foreign competition.

These opportunities and threats exist in the economic environment as well. The chapter discusses the need for companies to have a global vision in order to recognize and react to international business opportunities, as well as remain competitive at home. In relation to our model of a successful business, what this means is that the *vision* that is created for the company must take the global economic environment that it operates in into account in order to survive and prosper. The environment affects the business. Opportunities exist in the global economic environment; that is sure. But if a business decides not to pursue a strategy that involves selling in the global marketplace, it cannot ignore that foreign firms may and will still compete in the domestic marketplace. This foreign competition presents a threat to business—one that, if ignored, can easily put it out of business.

This chapter also gives several examples of how the other aspects of the external environment are affected by or affect global trade. For example, McCain Foods Limited used its advanced *technology and agronomy* (field crop production and soil management) to become a leader in the global marketplace selling frozen French fries (among other products). Other technological factors, such as transportation improvements and the use of the Internet, make physical distances less of a barrier to global trade. Language and cultural differences are natural barriers to trade with foreign countries. These differences are part of the *social* environment of these countries that must be considered in terms of the products that are sold and the way business is conducted.

All of these external environmental factors interact when a business enters the global marketplace. They affect the vision for the company and its strategy for competing. They also affect the internal environment. The *marketing* department must consider the different needs of customers in different countries in which a company's products are sold. The *operations* department must consider the logistics of operating in a global environment depending on the strategic option chosen—exporting to the country or investing in its own facilities in that country, for example. The *human resource* department must consider the skills needed of its employees to do business effectively in foreign countries, language being an obvious example. And the *finance* department must consider differences in exchange rates in order to remain profitable.

If a company considers its external environment carefully and develops a global vision for doing business, it can work toward achieving the critical suc-cess factors. It can *achieve financial performance* by *meeting the needs of* foreign *customers* with *products of value* to their unique tastes and circumstances. And whether its strategy is to expand into foreign markets or not, it will be forced to innovate to stay ahead of foreign competition. These critical factors of success are of course achieved through a *committed work force.*

The Global Marketplace and Governments' Roles

CHAPTER 2

Learning Goals

→ **lg 1** Why is global trade important to Canada?
→ **lg 2** How is global trade measured?
→ **lg 3** Why do nations trade?
→ **lg 4** What are the barriers to international trade?
→ **lg 5** How do governments and institutions foster world trade?
→ **lg 6** What are the international economic communities?
→ **lg 7** How do companies enter the global marketplace?
→ **lg 8** What threats and opportunities exist in the global marketplace?
→ **lg 9** What are the trends in the global marketplace?

One World, One Fry: The Story of McCain Foods Limited

What was started by the McCain brothers of Florenceville, New Brunswick, is now the world's largest supplier of frozen French fries, with approximately 32 percent of the international market. Canada is not only the birthplace of McCain, but it still plays a leading role in the McCain family of companies worldwide. In Canada, the McCain name is one of the most popular and trusted brands in the food and retail industries. What has made McCain so successful? It is hard to pinpoint one critical success area, but it is easy to identify numerous success areas.

After several years with Irving Oil Ltd., another Atlantic Canada success story, Harrison McCain along with his younger brother, Wallace, founded McCain Foods Limited with the support of other family members in 1956. In 1957 the 30 employees produced about 600 kilograms of product per hour, resulting in $152 678 of sales for the year. The company has grown to $6.1 billion in international consolidated sales (year ended in June 2002), with over 18 000 employees in about 55 production facilities on six continents. Today, McCain can produce more than 408 000 kilograms of potato products every hour in its 30 potato-processing plants around the world. Although initially built on the frozen French fry, McCain produces many other fine food products, including juices and drinks, desserts, pizzas, and oven-ready entrées. In fact, if you look in the freezers of homes and restaurants in Canada, you will probably find several McCain products. McCain also exports to more than 100 countries worldwide.

McCain is a private corporation (see Chapter 5) and its success can be primarily attributed to its past and present visionary leadership. Proudly Canadian, the company has been successful in introducing new products, supporting its operations with aggressive marketing, and offering consistently high quality of products. Besides new product development, the company is a leader in agronomy (field crop production and soil management), technology, and innovation.

McCain's agricultural research teams work with the local farmers and governments in different regions to develop new varieties of potatoes and new methods of handling and processing them to assure dependability of supply and an excellent product every time. With over 100 McCain agronomists and potato specialists around the world, McCain helps growers to produce the best potatoes for their region, climate, and growing conditions, while focusing on their customers' taste preferences and top-quality products: "We pay special attention to satisfying the taste preferences of consumers—wherever they live."

Not only does McCain have more plants in more locations in more countries than any of its competitors, the company claims to set

CRITICAL THINKING QUESTIONS

As you read this chapter, consider the following questions as they relate to McCain Foods Limited:

- What are several factors that can make Canadian companies successful in the global marketplace?
- What are some of the factors that can make success difficult in the global marketplace?
- What can governments do to protect domestic competitors?
- What cultural differences should Canadian companies consider when entering international markets?

the pace in diversity, growth, and food industry leadership around the world. They stay on the leading edge of technology by constantly upgrading production processes, testing new methods and machinery, and maximizing engineering efficiencies.

McCain recognizes that they owe their world leadership not only to management, technology, and agronomy but mostly to their global team of outstanding individuals who are deeply committed to high ethical standards (see Chapter 3) and core values of honesty, integrity, respect, and fairness in their dealings.

"McCain is a family business, committed to building wealth through and for their people and the communities where they live and work. They encourage entrepreneurship through autonomous, hands-on local management." Their success is admired by those that have studied the company and its operations.[1]

HOT Links

Search the McCain Web site for more information about this exciting Canadian company at www.mccain.com

BUSINESS IN THE 21ST CENTURY

Today, global revolutions are under way in many areas of our lives: management, politics, communications, technology, and so forth. The word *global* has assumed a new meaning, referring to a boundless mobility and competition in social, business, and intellectual arenas. No longer just an option, having a global vision has become a business imperative. Having a **global vision** means recognizing and reacting to international business opportunities, being aware of threats from foreign competitors in all markets, and effectively using international distribution networks to obtain materials and move finished products to the customer.

global vision
The ability to recognize and react to international business opportunities, be aware of threats from foreign competition, and effectively use international distribution networks to obtain materials and move finished products to customers.

Canadian managers must develop a global vision if they are to recognize and react to international business opportunities, as well as remain competitive at home. Often a Canadian firm's toughest domestic competition comes from foreign companies. Moreover, a global vision enables a manager to understand that customer and distribution networks operate worldwide, blurring geographic and political barriers and making them increasingly irrelevant to business decisions. Sometimes, due to the dynamics of business, political arenas, and so on, that global vision must be fine-tuned. The purpose of this chapter is to explain how global trade is conducted and its importance to Canada. We also discuss the barriers to international trade and the organizations that foster global trade. The chapter concludes with trends in the global marketplace.

➡ **lg 1**

Canada Goes Global

Over the past two decades, world trade has climbed from $300 billion a year to more than $6 trillion. Countries and companies that were never considered major players in global markets are now contributing to this growth in world trade. In 2001, Canada exported over $400 billion and imported over $350 billion in goods and services.[2]

Global business is not a one-way street, where only Canadian companies sell their wares and services throughout the world. Foreign competition in the domestic market used to be relatively rare but now occurs in almost every industry. Nevertheless, the global market has created vast new business opportunities for many Canadian firms.

The Importance of Global Business to Canada

One reason the United Nations has ranked Canada as one of the best countries in which to live is because of our ability to do business with the "outside world." According to the Department of Foreign Affairs and International Trade, "trade enhances the quality of Canadian life" and helps give Canadians the economic energy we need to create the nation we want.[3]

Just how important is international trade to Canada? Canada's population, at approximately 31 million, is relatively small versus the 6 billion worldwide. This translates into roughly 200 times more potential customers for Canadian business. Canada exports approximately 45 percent of what Canadians produce. In terms of a dollar value, we export more than $15 000 in goods and services of what we produce for each Canadian resident. Every $1 billion increase in Canada's exports translates into more than 10 000 jobs. Approximately 33 percent of all jobs rely on exports.[4] We can see that exports are vital to the Canadian economy.

But can we maintain this advantage and keep our economy growing? The simple answer is no—not unless we continue to develop outside markets. Canada has seen international trade increase, in part, by its proactive partnership between government and industry known as "Team Canada." Together with the Minister of International Trade, provincial premiers, and territorial government leaders, the prime minister leads these missions in order to increase international trade and create or sustain jobs for Canadians.

The prime minister has led such successful international trade missions to Russia and European Union countries, China, Japan, Thailand, and Mexico, among other countries. These Team Canada missions have helped more than 2800 representatives of Canadian businesses and organizations gain access to international markets. Approximately $30.6 billion in new business can be directly attributed to these missions.[5]

The focus of the Team Canada missions is to emphasize Canadian commercial, political, educational, and cultural links with the countries visited. The presence and support of the prominent government leaders facilitates access to crucial economic decision-makers for Canadian firms and provides a much greater public profile for the business participants, helping them network with the international business community.[6]

"Team Canada missions send a strong message to prospective partners that Canada is committed to doing business with them. The missions help build prestige and credibility for Canada, while helping new exporters, particularly small- and medium-sized firms, to position themselves in markets where competition is fierce. This is important when you consider that most new jobs in Canada are created by smaller businesses and only about 10 percent of smaller businesses are currently involved in international markets."[7]

Former Canadian Prime Minister Jean Chretien and the then provincial premiers and territorial leaders, members of Team Canada's trade mission to Russia, stop for a photograph at Red Square in front of St. Basil's Cathederal in Moscow, Thursday, Febuary 14, 2002.

International trade refers to imports as well as exports. If we expect countries to purchase our products, they will need the dollars that are generated by their exports to do so. Imports offer Canadians a wider range and choice of products and services to purchase. Our economy (see Chapter 1) has become more sophisticated in recent decades, developing into a knowledge-based economy. Canada's technological potential is ranked first among nations according to the *Global Competitiveness Report*.[8] If Canada is to capitalize on its technical potential, we must convert this potential into global success.

Not only does international trade affect the Canadian economy and provide employment for Canadians, other benefits have been identified. These include:

HOT Links

The Canadian government's Department of Foreign Affairs and International Trade helps new and experienced companies to compete in foreign markets. Through the Canadian Trade Commissioner Service, it provides six core services. To understand better what it takes to do business in hundreds of countries, visit the Canadian Trade Commissioner Service at
www.dfait-maeci.gc.ca/trade/intl_bus_dev-en.asp

- Economies of scale in production and marketing.
- Ease of the transfer of experience, technology, and know-how across borders.
- Global recognition of products and brand names, allowing for easier introduction of new products and services.
- The possibility of a uniform global image for the companies.

concept check

- What is a global vision, and why is it important?
- What impact does international trade have on the Canadian economy and Canadians?

Measuring Trade between Nations

International trade improves relationships with friends and allies, helps ease tensions among nations, and—economically speaking—bolsters economies, raises standards of living, provides jobs, and improves the quality of life. The value of international trade is over $6 trillion a year and growing. This section takes a look at some key measures of international trade: exports and imports, the balance of trade, the balance of payments, and exchange rates.

Exports and Imports

exports
Goods and services produced in one country and sold in other countries.

imports
Goods and services that are bought from other countries.

The developed nations (those with mature communication, financial, educational, and distribution systems) are the major players in international trade. They account for about 70 percent of the world's exports and imports. **Exports** are goods and services made in one country and sold to others. **Imports** are goods and services that are bought from other countries. Canada is both an exporter and importer. The main countries (based on dollar amounts) that Canada trades with are listed in Exhibit 2-1.

As Exhibit 2-1 illustrates, approximately 84 percent of our exports are to the United States and approximately 72 percent of imports come from the United States. In contrast, only 19 percent of American imports originate in Canada, and 22.4 percent of their exports are destined here. This heavy reliance that Canada has on the United States for trade is another rationale for Canada seeking other international trading partners. For the most part, Canada increases its exports and imports each year. (One recent exception occurred in the years 2000 and 2001, resulting mainly from the recessions of many of our trading partners.) Exhibit 2-2 on page 40 shows the value, share, and growth of Canada's trade of its exports and imports by industry. We can see that machinery and equipment accounted for 24 percent of exports and 32 percent of imports in 2001. This industry is the most important among all major groups of exports and imports. Second most important is the automotive industry (22.5 percent of exports and 20.7 percent of imports). Of the industrial categories, agricultural and fishing products saw the most drastic increase (12.6 percent), reflecting gains in live animals, meat products, beverages, food, and so forth. One interesting statistic from Exhibit 2-2 is that consumer goods represent just 3.8 percent of Canadian exports but 12.2 percent of our imports.

Many Canadian exports and imports are transported between Canada and the US by the rail systems

exhibit   2 - 1 | Chart of Canada's Main Trading Partners Based on Dollar Amounts

	1997	1998	1999	2000	2001	2002
				$ millions		
Exports	**303 378.2**	**327 161.5**	**369 034.9**	**430 033.1**	**421 518.8**	**414 305.1**
United States[1]	242 542.3	269 318.9	309 116.8	359 000.9	352 081.7	346 990.6
Japan	11 915.5	9 745.8	10 125.9	11 386.0	10 227.9	10 291.6
United Kingdom	4 689.5	5 323.3	6 002.9	7 326.3	6 984.7	6 239.4
Other European Economic Community countries	13 260.4	14 000.5	14 383.8	16 982.2	16 887.5	16 496.4
Other OECD[2]	8 849.0	9 120.9	9 947.2	12 246.4	12 369.2	12 341.9
Other countries[3]	22 111.6	19 652.2	19 458.4	23 091.4	22 967.8	21 945.3
Imports	**277 726.5**	**303 398.6**	**327 026.0**	**362 206.5**	**350 631.9**	**356 459.3**
United States[1]	211 450.8	233 777.6	249 485.3	266 514.5	254 952.6	254 929.0
Japan	8 711.0	9 671.8	10 592.2	11 729.3	10 571.7	11 732.2
United Kingdom	6 126.5	6 083.1	7 685.4	12 289.7	11 947.9	10 312.4
Other European Economic Community Countries	18 112.9	19 141.2	20 765.8	21 178.9	23 218.0	25 863.3
Other OECD[2]	11 376.7	11 398.8	13 257.2	18 945.0	18 636.7	19 670.3
Other countries[3]	21 948.7	23 326.1	25 240.1	31 549.0	31.305.0	33 952.1
Balance	**25 651.7**	**23 762.9**	**42 008.9**	**67 826.6**	**70 886.9**	**57 845.8**
United States[1]	31 091.5	35 541.3	59 631.5	92 486.4	97 129.1	92 061.6
Japan	3 214.5	74.0	–466.3	–343.3	–343.8	–1 440.6
United Kingdom	–1 437.0	–759.8	–1 682.5	–4 963.4	–4 963.2	–4 073.0
Other European Economic Community countries	–4 852.5	–5 140.7	–6 382.0	–4 196.7	–6 330.5	-9 366.9
Other OECD[2]	–2 527.7	–2 277.9	–3 310.0	–6 698.6	–6 267.5	–7 328.4
Other countries[3]	162.9	–3 673.9	–5 781.7	–8 457.6	–8 337.2	–12 006.8

1. Includes also Puerto Rico and Virgin Islands.
2. Organization for Economic Co-operation and Development excluding the United States Japan United Kingdom and the other European Economic Community.
3. Countries not included in the European Economic Community or the OECD.

SOURCE: Statistics Canada "Canadian Statistics—Imports and exports of goods on a balance-of-payment basis." Adapted from Statistics Canada Web site www.statscan.ca/English/Pgdb/glec02a.html, accessed July 2, 2003.

 lg 2

balance of trade
The differences between the value of a country's exports and the value of its imports during a certain time.

trade surplus
A favourable balance of trade that occurs when a country exports more than it imports.

trade deficit
An unfavourable balance of trade that occurs when a country imports more than it exports.

Balance of Trade

The difference between the value of a country's exports and the value of its imports during a certain time is the country's **balance of trade**. A country that exports more than it imports is said to have a favourable balance of trade, called a **trade surplus**. A country that imports more than it exports is said to have an unfavourable balance of trade, or a **trade deficit.** When imports exceed exports, more money flows out of the country than flows into it.

Balance of trade, trade surpluses, and trade deficits are usually stated in the **balance of payments** method. The balance of payments includes imports and exports, long-term investments in overseas plants and equipment, government loans to and from other countries, gifts and foreign aid, military expenditures made in other countries, and money transfers in and out of foreign banks.

Although Canada has a favourable balance of trade, it is due to our trade with the United States (i.e., if we exclude our trade with the United States, Canada would have an unfavourable balance of trade). The lower section of Exhibit 2-1 shows that our overall favourable balance of trade is increasing. But as the United States increases its trade with other countries, Canada's balance of trade may become unfavourable.

e x h i b i t   2 - 2 | Value, Share, and Growth of Canada's Goods Trade (Balance of Payments Basis)

balance of payments
A summary of a country's international financial transactions
showing the difference between
the country's total payments to
and its total receipts from other
countries.

Industry	Level ($ billions)			Growth 2000–2001 (percent)
	1989	2002	2001	
Exports				
Total	147.0	422.6	412.5	–2.4
Agricultural & fishing	11.6	27.4	30.8	12.6
Energy	13.7	52.9	55.3	4.5
Forestry	21.5	41.8	38.6	–7.5
Industrial	32.3	65.9	66.3	0.5
M&E	24.0	106.9	98.8	–7.6
Automotive	34.0	97.9	92.7	–5.3
Consumer goods	2.6	14.8	15.8	6.7
Imports				
Total	139.2	363.3	351.0	–3.4
Agricultural & fishing	8.3	18.6	20.4	9.7
Energy	6.2	17.9	17.7	–0.9
Forestry	1.4	3.1	2.9	–5.8
Industrial	26.9	70.5	68.5	–2.9
M&E	43.3	122.7	112.4	–8.4
Automotive	31.9	77.4	72.5	–6.3
Consumer goods	15.0	40.1	42.9	7.1

SOURCE: Statistics Canada, adapted from "Canadian International Merchandise Trade." Catalogue no. 65-001-XPB, December 2001. Note: Sums may not add up to 100 because special transactions and inland freight and other balance of payments adjustments figures, which are part of the merchandise trade account, are not included.

The Changing Value of Currencies

The exchange rate is the price of one country's currency in terms of another country's currency. If a country's currency appreciates (i.e., becomes more valuable), then it would take less of the appreciated currency to purchase the other currency. If a country's currency depreciates (i.e., becomes less valuable), more of that currency will be needed to buy the other country's currency.

How does appreciation and depreciation affect the prices of a country's goods? If the Canadian dollar depreciates relative to the Japanese yen, Canadian residents have to pay more dollars to buy Japanese goods. To illustrate, suppose the dollar price of a yen is $0.012 and that a Toyota is priced at 2 million yen. At this exchange rate, a Canadian resident pays $24 000 for a Toyota ($0.012 × 2 million yen = $24 000). If the dollar depreciates to $0.018 to one yen, then the Canadian resident will have to pay $36 000 for a Toyota.

As the dollar depreciates, the prices of Japanese goods rise for Canadian residents, so they buy fewer Japanese goods—thus, Canadian imports decline. At the same time, as the dollar depreciates relative to the yen, the yen appreciates relative to the dollar. This means prices of Canadian goods fall for the Japanese, so they buy more Canadian goods—and Canadian exports rise.

Currency markets operate under a system called **floating exchange rates**. Prices of currencies "float" up and down based upon the demand for and supply of each currency. Global currency traders create the supply of and demand for a particular currency based on that currency's investment, trade potential, and economic strength.

floating exchange rates
A system in which prices of currencies move up and down based
upon the demand for and supply
of the various currencies.

If a country decides that its currency is not properly valued in international currency markets, the government may step in and adjust the currency's value. When a nation lowers the value of its currency relative to other currencies, it is said to have seen

devaluation
A lowering of the value of a nation's currency relative to other currencies.

a **devaluation** of its currency. In August 1998, Russia devalued the ruble by 34 percent.[9] A month later, Colombia and Ecuador also devalued their currencies but by much less than Russia. Russia not only devalued its currency but also restructured government short-term debt to long term and imposed strict financial controls on Russian banks and companies. As a result, companies and banks could not meet their foreign debt obligations. In 2000, Ecuador "dollarized" (i.e., made the United States dollar the official currency) its economy due to the banking sector collapse and the economic instability that drove a 70 percent devaluation of its currency in 1999.[10]

concept check

- Describe the position of Canada in world trade.
- Explain the importance of the United States to our balance of trade. How can we minimize our reliance on the United States for our exports?
- Explain the impact of a currency devaluation.

→ **lg 3**

Why Nations Trade

One might argue that the best way to protect workers and the domestic economy is to stop trade with other nations. Then the whole circular flow of inputs and outputs would stay within our borders. But if we decided to do that, how would we get resources such as cotton and coffee beans? Canada simply can't produce some things, and it can't manufacture some products, such as steel and most clothing, at the low costs we're used to. The fact is that nations—like people—are good at producing different things: you may be better at developing a Microsoft Excel spreadsheet than repairing a car. In that case you benefit by "exporting" your bookkeeping services and "importing" the car repairs you need from a good mechanic. Economists refer to specialization like this as *advantage*.

Absolute Advantage

absolute advantage
The situation when a country can produce and sell a product at a lower cost than any other country or when it is the only country that can provide the product.

A country has an **absolute advantage** when it can produce and sell a product at a lower cost than any other country or when it is the only country that can provide a product. Canada, for example, has an absolute advantage in softwoods and certain technologies.

Suppose that Canada has an absolute advantage in air traffic control systems for busy airports and that Brazil has an absolute advantage in coffee beans. Canada does not have the proper climate for growing coffee, and Brazil lacks the technology to develop air traffic control systems. Both countries would gain by exchanging air traffic control systems for coffee beans.

Comparative Advantage

principle of comparative advantage
The concept that each country should specialize in the products that it can produce most readily and cheaply and trade those products for those that other countries can produce more readily and cheaply.

Even if Canada had an absolute advantage in both coffee and air traffic control systems, it should still specialize and engage in trade. Why? The reason is the **principle of comparative advantage**, which says that each country should specialize in the products that it can produce most readily and cheaply and trade those products for goods that foreign countries can produce most readily and cheaply. This specialization ensures greater product availability and lower prices.

For example, Mexico and China have a comparative advantage in producing clothing because of low labour costs. Japan has long held a comparative advantage in consumer electronics because of technological expertise. Canada has an advantage in computer software, some agricultural products, oil exploration, and related activities.

free trade
The policy of permitting the people of a country to buy and sell where they please without restrictions.

protectionism
The policy of protecting home industries from outside competition by establishing artificial barriers such as tariffs and quotas.

Thus, comparative advantage acts as a stimulus to trade. When nations allow their citizens to trade whatever goods and services they choose without government regulation, free trade exists. **Free trade** is the policy of permitting the people of a country to buy and sell where they please without restrictions. The opposite of free trade is **protectionism**, in which a nation protects its home industries from outside competition by establishing artificial barriers such as tariffs and quotas. In 1947, the Canadian government enacted the Export and Import Controls Bureau to control the free-flow of certain imports and exports. Some examples are textiles and clothing, agricultural products, weapons and munitions, nuclear energy materials, and technology.[11] In the next section, we'll look at the various barriers, some natural and some created by governments, that restrict free trade.

concept check

- Explain the difference between absolute advantage and comparative advantage.
- Describe the principle of comparative advantage.
- Describe the policy of free trade and its relationship to comparative advantage.

➡ **lg 4**

Barriers to Trade

International trade is conducted by both businesses and governments—as long as there are no trade barriers. In general, trade barriers keep firms from selling to one another in foreign markets. The major obstacles to international trade are natural barriers, tariff barriers, and nontariff barriers.

Natural Barriers

Natural barriers to trade can be either physical or cultural. For instance, even though raising beef in the relative warmth of Argentina may cost less than raising beef in the bitter cold of Siberia, the cost of shipping the beef from South America to Siberia might drive the price too high. Distance is thus one of the natural barriers to international trade. Jet airplanes cut the time needed to ship goods long distances, but weight is a factor. Thus, air cargo is limited to products with a high value per kilogram. For example, it would not make sense to ship coal or gravel by air, although orchids, seafood, computers, and replacement parts for machinery are often moved this way. With advances in technology, liquefied natural gas, asphalt, and other hard-to-transport products can now be moved by ship or barge—something not feasible 15 or 20 years ago. Further improvements in technology should help lower other distance barriers as well.

Some other natural barriers include:
- *Language differences.* People who can't communicate effectively may not be able to negotiate trade agreements or may ship the wrong goods.
- *Cultural differences.* Companies that wish to pursue business with countries whose culture is different from theirs, must consider these differences and adjust their operations, products, services, and so on, to account for the differences.
- *Legal and regulatory differences.* Canadian companies do not only have to consider Canadian laws and regulations, but also the laws and regulations of the host country.

Tariff Barriers

tariff
A tax imposed on imported goods.

A **tariff** (also known as *customs duties*) is a tax imposed by a nation on imported goods. It may be a charge per unit, such as per barrel of oil or per new car; it may be a percentage of the value of the goods, such as 5 percent of a $500 000 shipment of shoes;

Tariffs on the imported goods arriving on this foreign ship make the products more expensive than those of Canadian competitors.

protective tariffs
Tariffs that are imposed in order to make imports less attractive to buyers than domestic products are.

or it may be a combination. No matter how it is assessed, any tariff makes imported goods more costly, so they are less able to compete with domestic products. Whenever a trade negotiation includes tariffs, the Canadian government's objective is to improve access for Canadian exports (by eliminating tariffs abroad) or to protect the domestic industry (by applying protective tariffs).

Protective tariffs make imports less attractive to buyers than domestic products are. The United States, for instance, has protective tariffs on imported softwood from Canada. The Americans contend that Canada subsidizes its softwood industry and this produces unfair competition for the American forestry industry (approximately 30 percent of all softwood used in the United States is imported from Canada).[12] Canada, interestingly, imposed a provisional duty on tomato imports from the United States of 71 percent.[13]

Arguments for and against Tariffs

Tariffs are not a new concept. For centuries industries have tried to protect their products and services and countries have used tariffs to protect employment. The main argument against tariffs is that they discourage free trade, and free trade lets the principle of comparative advantage work most efficiently. The main argument for tariffs is that they protect domestic businesses and workers.

One of the oldest arguments in favour of protectionism is the *infant-industry argument.* By protecting new domestic industries from established foreign competitors, so this argument goes, a tariff can give a struggling industry time to become an effective competitor.

A second argument for tariffs is the *job-protection argument.* Supporters—especially unions—say we should use tariffs to keep foreign labour from taking away Canadian jobs. Canadian jobs are lost, they say, when low-wage countries sell products at lower prices than those charged in Canada. The higher prices charged by the Canadian firms help pay the higher wages of Canadian workers.

An argument against tariffs is that they cause an increase in prices, thereby decreasing consumers' purchasing power. Over the long run, tariffs may also be too protective if they cause domestic companies to stop innovating and fall behind technologically. An example is the Italian car builder Fiat. Protective tariffs helped keep Fiat's Italian market share very high. As Europe's trade barriers fell, foreign competitors moved in with cars that Italian drivers preferred. Fiat is now desperately spending billions of dollars to revamp its factories and design new models.

Nontariff Barriers

Governments also use other tools in addition to tariffs to restrict trade. Among them are import quotas, embargoes, buy-national regulations, custom regulations, and exchange controls.

Import Quotas

import quota
A limit on the quantity of a certain good that can be imported; also known as a *quantitative restraint.*

One type of nontariff barrier is the **import quota,** or limits on the quantity of a certain good that can be imported. The goal of setting quotas is to limit imports to the optimum amount of a given product. Canada protects its textile and clothing industries with quotas. These quotas are being slowly eliminated over a 10-year period and on January 1, 2005, the remaining quotas are to be eliminated.[14]

Embargoes

embargo
A total ban on imports or exports of a product.

A complete ban against importing or exporting a product is an **embargo**. For instance, Canada does not allow the export of "military goods to countries that threaten Canada's security, are under UN sanction, are threatened by internal or external conflict, and/or abuse the human rights of their citizens."[15]

Custom Regulations

custom regulations
Regulations on products that are different from generally accepted international standards.

In a more subtle move, a country may make it hard for foreign products to enter its markets by establishing **custom regulations** that are different from generally accepted international standards, such as requiring bottles to be litre size rather than quart size. The French seem most adept at using this tactic. For example, to reduce imports of foreign VCRs, at one time France ruled that all VCRs had to enter through the customs station at Poitiers. This customs house was located in the middle of the country, was woefully understaffed, and was open only a few days each week. What's more, the few customs agents at Poitiers opened each package separately to inspect the merchandise. Within a few weeks, imports of VCRs in France came to a halt.

Exchange Controls

exchange controls
Laws that require a company earning foreign exchange (foreign currency) from its exports to sell the foreign exchange to a control agency, such as a central bank.

Exchange controls are laws that require a company earning foreign exchange (foreign currency) from its exports to sell the foreign exchange to a control agency, usually a central bank. For example, assume that Rolex, a Swiss company, sells 300 watches to a Canadian retailer for $120 000. If Switzerland had exchange controls, Rolex would have to sell its Canadian dollars to the Swiss central bank and would receive Swiss francs.

concept check

• Discuss the concept of natural trade barriers.
• Describe several tariff and nontariff barriers to trade.

➡ lg 5

Fostering Global Trade

From our discussion so far, it might seem that governments act only to restrain global trade. On the contrary, as discussed earlier (in the case of Team Canada), governments and international financial organizations also work hard to increase global trade.

Antidumping Laws

dumping
The practice of charging a lower price for a product in foreign markets than in the firm's home market.

Canadian firms don't always get to compete on an equal basis with foreign firms in international trade. To level the playing field, the federal government has passed antidumping laws. **Dumping** is the practice of charging a lower price for a product (perhaps below cost) in foreign markets than in the firm's home market. The company might be trying to win foreign customers, or it might be seeking to get rid of surplus goods. Sometimes, too, to help create an export market, a government will subsidize certain industries so that they can sell their goods for less. In the past, Japanese steel was sold below cost in world markets, and the losses were covered by government subsidies.

When the variation in price can't be explained by differences in the cost of serving the two markets, dumping is suspected. Most industrialized countries have antidumping regulations. They are especially concerned about *predatory dumping*, the attempt to gain control of a foreign market by destroying competitors with impossibly low prices. Many businesspeople feel that Japan has engaged in predatory dumping of semiconductors in the Canadian market.

The legal test for product dumping is based on two criteria. First, the product must be priced unfairly low—either below its production costs or below the selling price in the home country. Second, the imported product must harm the domestic industry.

The Uruguay Round and the World Trade Organization

Uruguay Round
A 1994 agreement by 117 nations to lower trade barriers worldwide.

The **Uruguay Round** of trade negotiations is an agreement to dramatically lower trade barriers worldwide. Adopted in 1994, the agreement was signed by 117 nations in Marrakech, Morocco. The most ambitious global trade agreement ever negotiated, the Uruguay Round reduced tariffs by one-third worldwide, a move that is expected to increase global income by US$235 billion annually by 2005. Perhaps the most notable aspect of the agreement is its recognition of new global realities. For the first time, an agreement covers services, intellectual property rights, and trade-related investment measures such as exchange controls.

The Uruguay Round made several major changes in world trading practices:

- *Entertainment, pharmaceuticals, integrated circuits, and software.* Under the new rules, patents, copyrights, and trademarks are protected for 20 years. Computer programs are protected for 50 years and semiconductor chips for 10 years. Many developing nations will have a decade to phase in patent protection for drugs. However, France, which limits the number of U.S. movies and television shows that can be shown, refused to liberalize market access for the U.S. entertainment industry.
- *Financial, legal, and accounting services.* Services were brought under international trading rules for the first time, potentially creating a vast opportunity for these competitive Canadian industries. Now it is easier to admit managers and key personnel into a country.
- *Agriculture.* Europe will gradually reduce farm subsidies, opening new opportunities for such Canadian farm exports as wheat and other grains. Japan and Korea will begin to import rice.
- *Textiles and clothing.* As mentioned before, strict quotas limiting imports from developing countries are being phased out over 10 years, potentially causing further job losses in the Canadian clothing industry. But retailers and consumers will be the big winners because quotas now add substantial costs that are ultimately passed on to the consumers.
- *A new trade organization.* The new **World Trade Organization (WTO)** replaces the old General Agreement on Tariffs and Trade (GATT), which was created in 1948. The GATT contained extensive loopholes that enabled countries to evade agreements to reduce trade barriers. Today, all WTO members must fully comply with all agreements under the Uruguay Round. The WTO also has an effective dispute settlement procedure with strict time limits to resolve disputes.

World Trade Organization (WTO)
An organization established by the Uruguay Round in 1994 to oversee international trade, reduce trade barriers, and resolve disputes among member nations.

The WTO has emerged as the world's most powerful institution for reducing trade barriers and opening markets. With more than 140 nations now belonging to the organization, it represents 97 percent of world trade. The advantage of WTO membership is that member countries lower trade barriers among themselves. Countries that don't belong must negotiate trade agreements individually with all their trading partners. Presently, more than 30 other countries are negotiating membership within the WTO.[16]

HOT Links

The World Trade Organization tracks the latest trade developments between countries and regions around the world. For the most recent global trading news, visit the WTO's site at www.wto.org

The World Bank and the International Monetary Fund

World Bank
An international bank that offers low-interest loans, as well as advice and information, to developing nations.

Two international financial organizations are instrumental in fostering global trade. The **World Bank** offers low-interest loans to developing nations. Originally, the purpose of the loans was to help these nations build infrastructure such as roads, power plants, schools, drainage projects, and hospitals. Now the World Bank offers loans to

International Monetary Fund (IMF)
An international organization, founded in 1945, that promotes trade, makes short-term loans to member nations, and acts as a lender of last resort for troubled nations.

HOT Links

Gain additional insight into the workings of the International Monetary Fund at www.imf.org

help developing nations relieve their debt burdens. To receive the loans, countries must pledge to lower trade barriers and aid private enterprise. In addition to making loans, the World Bank is a major source of advice and information for developing nations.

The **International Monetary Fund (IMF)** was founded in 1945, one year after the creation of the World Bank, to promote trade through financial cooperation and eliminate trade barriers in the process. The IMF makes short-term loans to member nations that are unable to meet their budgetary expenses. It operates as a lender of last resort for troubled nations. In exchange for these emergency loans, IMF lenders frequently extract significant commitments from the borrowing nations to address the problems that led to the crises. These steps may include curtailing imports or even devaluing the currency.

In the late 1990s, South Korea, Thailand, Malaysia, and Indonesia were hit by a severe recession. IMF intervention to rescue these economies did not seem to work as unemployment and interest rates soared. The crisis also hit Russia and several countries of Latin America including Brazil. Private money for economic development simply quit flowing into these economies. The basic problem was that capital (money) had flowed into these emerging economies with little attention paid to the creditworthiness of the borrowers. With easy money, borrowers took on more debt than they could repay. To make matters worse, banks and other financial institutions were so closely intertwined with governments that decisions were made for political reasons and not based on sound economics.

Such global financial problems do not have a simple solution. One option would be to pump a lot more funds into the IMF, giving it enough resources to bail out troubled countries and put them back on their feet. In effect, the IMF would be turned into a real lender of last resort for the world economy.

The danger of counting on the IMF, though, is the "moral hazard" problem. Investors would assume that the IMF would bail them out and would therefore be encouraged to take bigger and bigger risks in emerging markets, leading to the possibility of even deeper financial crises in the future.

concept check

- Describe the purpose and role of the WTO.
- What are the roles of the World Bank and the IMF in world trade?

→ lg 6

International Economic Communities

preferential tariff
A tariff that is lower for some nations than for others.

free-trade zone
An area where the nations allow free, or almost free, trade among each other while imposing tariffs on goods of nations outside the zone.

Nations that frequently trade with each other may decide to formalize their relationship. The governments meet and work out agreements for a common economic policy. The result is an economic community or, in other cases, a bilateral trade agreement (an agreement between two countries to lower trade barriers). For example, two nations may agree upon a **preferential tariff**, which gives advantages to one nation (or several nations) over others. For instance, when members of the British Commonwealth trade with Great Britain, they pay lower tariffs than do other nations. In other cases, nations may form free-trade associations. In a **free-trade zone**, few, if any, duties or rules restrict trade among the partners, but nations outside the zone must pay the tariffs set by the individual members. A *customs union* sets up a free-trade area and specifies a uniform tariff structure for members' trade with nonmember nations. In a *common market*, or economic union, members go beyond a customs union and try to bring all of their government trade rules into agreement.

North American Free Trade Agreement (NAFTA)

Launched in January 1994, the **North American Free Trade Agreement (NAFTA)** created one of the world's largest free-trade zone. It includes Canada, the United States, and Mexico, with a combined population of 360 million and an economy of more than $9 trillion.

Canada, the largest U.S. trading partner, entered a free-trade agreement with the United States in 1988. Thus, most of the new long-run opportunities opened for Canadian business under NAFTA are in Mexico, Canada's fifth largest trading partner. Since NAFTA came into effect, exports to Mexico have increased fivefold to $2.5 billion in 2001.[17]

As well, the Canadian economy has grown by an annual average of 3.8 percent since 1994, making the Canadian economy one of the healthiest in the world. This healthy growth has translated into approximately 2 million jobs for Canadians. Under NAFTA, Canadians have experienced this growth primarily by being able to operate in a more integrated and larger North American economy.[18]

The real test of NAFTA will be whether it can maintain delivery of rising prosperity to its three members. Ultimately, some Canadian politicians would like to expand NAFTA to include other Latin American countries. In March 2000, the Canadian International Trade Minister presented to Parliament, Canada's priorities for negotiating a **Free Trade Area of the Americas (FTAA)**. The FTAA will be the world's largest free-trade region, with approximately 800 million people.

In April 2001, Canada hosted 34 countries of the Americas (the third Summit of the Americas to take place) in Quebec City. The heads of state and government of the various countries strengthened their commitment to the process and the establishment the FTAA by 2005.[19] The current timetable for the FTAA is to conclude the negotiations by January 2005 and implement the FTAA by December of that same year.[20]

The largest new trade agreement is **Mercosur**, which includes Brazil, Argentina, Uruguay, and Paraguay. The elimination of most tariffs among the trading partners has resulted in trade revenues that currently exceed US$16 billion annually.[21] The economic boom created by Mercosur will undoubtedly cause other nations to either seek trade agreements on their own or enter Mercosur. The European Union, discussed next, hopes to have a free-trade pact with Mercosur by 2005.

The European Union (EU)

In 1993, the member countries of the European Community (EC) ratified the **Maastricht Treaty**, which proposed to take the EC further toward economic, monetary, and political union. Officially called the Treaty on **European Union**, the document outlined plans for tightening bonds among the member states and creating a single market. There are presently 15 member countries with many candidate countries anxious to become members. Exhibit 2-3 shows the members and candidate countries of the EU.

Although much of the treaty deals with developing a unified European market, Maastricht is also intended to increase integration among the EU members in areas much closer to the heart of national sovereignty. The treaty called for economic and monetary coordination, including a common currency and an independent central bank. In addition, EU members will eventually share foreign security and defence policies as well as European citizenship—any EU citizen will be able to live, work, vote, and run for office in any member country. The treaty also coordinated health and safety regulations and standardized trade rules, duties, customs procedures, and taxes. A driver hauling cargo from Amsterdam to Lisbon can now clear four border crossings by showing a single piece of paper. Before the Maastricht Treaty, a driver had to carry nearly a kilogram of paper to cross the same borders. By setting uniform standards, the treaty's goal is to eliminate the need for manufacturers to produce a separate product

---

North American Free Trade Agreement (NAFTA)
An agreement, launched in 1994, creating a free-trade zone including Canada, the United States, and Mexico.

HOT Links

Want to learn the latest info about NAFTA? Go to
www.nafta-customs.org

Free Trade Area of the Americas (FTAA)
A proposed free-trading area encompassing 34 democratic nations of the Americas.

HOT Links

See how the negotiations for FTAA are progressing and what will become of the existing trade communities when FTAA is completed at
www.ftaa-alca.org

Mercosur
A trade agreement among Argentina, Brazil, Paraguay, and Uruguay that eliminates most tariffs among the member nations.

Maastricht Treaty
A 1993 treaty concluded by the members of the European Community (now the European Union) that outlines plans for tightening bonds among the members and creating a single market; officially called the Treaty on European Union.

European Union (EU)
An organization of 15 European nations (as of early 2004) that works to foster political and economic integration in Europe; formerly called the European Community.

e x h i b i t   2 - 3 | Member Countries and Candidates of the European Union

for each country—one Braun electric razor for Italy, a slightly different one for Germany, and a third one for France, for example. Goods marked GEC (goods for EC) can be traded freely without being retested at each border.

It is an attractive market, with 380 million consumers with a purchasing power almost equal to that of the United States. But, the EU has many obstacles to overcome because of the uniqueness of the 15 member countries. For one thing, even in a united Europe, businesses will not be able to produce a single Europroduct for a generic Euroconsumer. With nine languages and different national customs, Europe will always be far more diverse than Canada. Thus, product differences will continue. It will be a long time, for instance, before the French begin drinking the same instant coffee that Britons enjoy. Even preferences for washing machines differ: British homemakers want front-loaders, and the French want top-loaders; Germans like lots of settings and high spin speeds, while Italians like lower speeds.

An entirely different type of problem facing global businesses is the possibility of a protectionist movement by the EU against outsiders. For example, European automakers have proposed holding Japanese imports at roughly their current 10 percent market share. The Irish, Danes, and Dutch don't make cars and have unrestricted home markets; they are unhappy at the prospect of limited imports of Toyotas and Hondas. Meanwhile France has a strict quota on Japanese cars to protect its own Renault and Peugeot. These local automakers could be hurt if the quota is raised at all.

The eurodollar replaces the individual currencies of 12 European Union nations. The new common currency enables the countries to do business as a single trading bloc.

The Euro

Twelve of the 15 members of the European Union have converted their currencies to the eurodollar, or "euro" for short, the new currency that is circulated in all 12 nations. Due to internal policies, Great Britain, Denmark, and Sweden have not converted to the euro; the currencies that will become obsolete are listed in Exhibit 2-4. The conversion began on January 1, 1999, and euro notes and coins were introduced on January 1, 2002. With the conversion, the participating European nations will be doing business as a single trading bloc, which will become the largest economy in the world in terms of percentage of world GDP (see Chapter 1).

In addition to the aforementioned trading agreements, there are others that are being developed and modified on an ongoing basis.

concept check

- Explain the pros and cons of NAFTA.
- What is the European Union? What are the benefits to its members?
- Discuss the concept of the euro.

→ lg 7

Participating in the Global Marketplace

Companies decide to "go global" for a number of reasons. Perhaps the most urgent reason is to earn additional profits. If a firm has a unique product or technological advantage not available to other international competitors, this advantage should result in major business successes abroad. In other situations, management may have exclusive market information about foreign customers, marketplaces, or market situations not known to others. In this case, although exclusivity can provide an initial motivation for going global, managers must realize that competitors will eventually catch up. Finally, saturated domestic markets, excess capacity, and potential for cost savings can also be motivators to expand into international markets. A company can enter global trade in several ways, as this section describes.

e x h i b i t　2 - 4	Converting to the Eurodollar Means That Twelve Currencies Will Eventually Disappear

Countries That Have Converted to the Eurodollar/Currency Replaced

Austria/Schilling	Ireland/Pound
Belgium/Franc	Italy/Lira
Finland/Markka	Luxembourg/Franc
France/Franc	Netherlands/Guilder
Germany/Deutsche mark	Portugal/Escudos
Greece/Drachma	Spain/Pesetas

SOURCE: Eupora, "Economic and Financial Affairs—Euro Essentials," Europa Web site, europa.eu.int/comm...euro/participating_member_states_en.htm, accessed July 2, 2003.

IBM's entry into global markets includes exporting, which helps the company to expand the global distribution of products to businesses and consumers in Japan.

exporting
The practice of selling domestically produced goods to buyers in another country.

licensing
The legal process whereby a firm agrees to allow another firm to use a manufacturing process, trademark, patent, trade secret, or other proprietary knowledge in exchange for the payment of a royalty.

HOT Links

Find out more about the Canadian Franchise association at www.cfa.ca

contract manufacturing
The practice in which a foreign firm manufacturers private-label goods under a domestic firm's brand name.

Exporting

When a company decides to enter the global market, usually the least complicated and least risky alternative is **exporting**, or selling domestically produced products to buyers in another country. A company, for example, can sell directly to foreign importers or buyers. Exporting is not limited to large corporations.

Licensing

Another effective way for a firm to move into the global arena with relatively little risk is to sell a licence to manufacture its product to a firm in a foreign country. **Licensing** is the legal process whereby a firm (the *licensor*) agrees to let another firm (the *licensee*) use a manufacturing process, trademark, patent, trade secret, or other proprietary knowledge. The licensee, in turn, agrees to pay the licensor a royalty or fee agreed on by both parties.

U.S. companies have eagerly embraced the licensing concept. For instance, Philip Morris licensed Labatt Brewing Company to produce Miller High Life in Canada. The Spaulding Company receives more than US$2 million annually from licence agreements on its sporting goods. Fruit-of-the-Loom lends its name through licensing to 45 consumer items in Japan alone, for at least 1 percent of the licensee's gross sales.

The licensor must make sure it can exercise sufficient control over the licensee's activities to ensure proper quality, pricing, distribution, and so on. Licensing may also create a new competitor in the long run, if the licensee decides to void the licence agreement. International law is often ineffective in stopping such actions. Two common ways that a licensor can maintain effective control over its licensees are by shipping one or more critical components from Canada and by locally registering patents and trademarks in its own name.

Franchising, which we'll discuss in Chapter 5, is a form of licensing that has grown rapidly in recent years. The Canadian Franchise Association publishes a bimonthly magazine for entrepreneurs wanting to establish a successful franchise and an annual comprehensive directory listing franchises available in Canada.

Contract Manufacturing

In **contract manufacturing**, a foreign firm manufactures private-label goods under a domestic firm's brand. Marketing may be handled by either the domestic company or the foreign manufacturer. Levi Strauss, for instance, entered into an agreement with the French fashion house of Cacharel to produce a new Levi's line called "Something New" for distribution in Germany.

The advantage of contract manufacturing is that it lets a company "test the water" in a foreign country. By allowing the foreign firm to produce a certain volume of products to specification, and put the domestic firm's brand name on the goods, the domestic firm can broaden its global marketing base without investing in overseas plants and equipment. After establishing a solid base, the domestic firm may switch to a joint venture or direct investment, as explained below.

joint venture
An agreement in which a domestic firm buys part of a foreign firm to create a new entity.

HOT Links

Find out more about Suzuki's international joint ventures at **www.suzuki.co.ip/cpd/ koho_e/kaigai**

Joint Ventures

Joint ventures are somewhat similar to licensing agreements. In a **joint venture**, the domestic firm buys part of a foreign company or joins with a foreign company to create a new entity. A joint venture is a quick and relatively inexpensive way to enter the global market. It can also be very risky. Many joint ventures fail. Others fall victim to a takeover, in which one partner buys out the other.

In a successful joint venture, both parties gain valuable skills from the alliance. In the General Motors–Suzuki joint venture in Canada, for example, both parties have contributed and gained. The alliance, CAMI Automotive, was formed to manufacture low-end cars for the U.S. market. The plant, which is run by Suzuki management, produces the Geo Metro/Suzuki Swift—the smallest, most fuel-efficient GM car sold in North America—as well as the Geo Tracker/Suzuki Sidekick sport utility vehicle. Through CAMI, Suzuki has gained access to GM's dealer network and an expanded market for parts and components. GM avoided the cost of developing low-end cars and obtained models it needed to revitalize the lower end of its product line and its average fuel economy rating. The CAMI factory may be one of the most productive plants in North America. There GM has learned how Japanese automakers use work teams, run flexible assembly lines, and manage quality control.

direct foreign investment
Active ownership of a foreign company or of manufacturing or marketing facilities in a foreign country.

Direct Foreign Investment

Active ownership of a foreign company or of overseas manufacturing or marketing facilities is **direct foreign investment**. Direct investors have either a controlling interest or a large minority interest in the firm. Thus, they stand to receive the greatest potential reward but also face the greatest potential risk. A firm may make a direct foreign investment by acquiring an interest in an existing company or by building new facilities. It might do so because it has trouble transferring some resources to a foreign operation or obtaining that resource locally. One important resource is personnel, especially managers. If the local labour market is tight, the firm may buy an entire foreign firm and retain all its employees instead of paying higher salaries than competitors. Sometimes firms make direct investments because they can find no suitable local partners. Also, direct investments avoid the communication problems and conflicts of interest that can arise with joint ventures. IBM, for instance, insists on total ownership of its foreign investments because it does not want to share control with local partners.

Kodak paid more than US$1 billion to acquire and upgrade three government-owned film manufacturers in China. In return, the Chinese government granted Kodak a virtual monopoly to manufacture film in the country. In the past, the Chinese government would simply erect more trade barriers to keep companies like Kodak and Fuji out. In a more pragmatic move, the government decided to sell the debt-ridden, inefficient plants to outside investors and exit the film manufacturing business.[22]

concept check

- Discuss several ways that a company can enter international trade.

➡ **lg 8**

Threats and Opportunities in the Global Marketplace

To be successful in a foreign market, companies must fully understand the foreign environment in which they plan to operate. Politics, cultural differences, and the economic environment can represent both opportunities and pitfalls in the global marketplace.

Political Considerations

We have already discussed how tariffs, exchange controls, and other governmental actions threaten foreign producers. The political structure of a country may also jeopardize a foreign producer's success in international trade.

Intense nationalism, for example, can lead to difficulties. **Nationalism** is the sense of national consciousness that boosts the culture and interests of one country over those of all other countries. Strongly nationalistic countries, such as Iran and New Guinea, often discourage investment by foreign companies. In other, less radical forms of nationalism, the government may take actions to hinder foreign operations. France, for example, requires that pop music stations play at least 40 percent of their songs in French. This law was enacted because the French love American rock and roll. Without airtime, American CD sales suffer. Coca-Cola recently attempted to purchase Orangina, France's only domestically owned and distributed soft drink. The French government blocked the sale saying that it would be "anticompetitive."[23] The real reason was nationalism.

In a hostile climate, a government may expropriate a foreign company's assets, taking ownership and compensating the former owners. Even worse is confiscation, when the owner receives no compensation. This happened during rebellions in several African nations during the 1990s.

nationalism
A sense of national consciousness that boosts the culture and interests of one country over those of all other countries.

Cultural Differences

Central to any society is the common set of values shared by its citizens that determine what is socially acceptable. Culture underlies the family, educational system, religion, and social class system. The network of social organizations generates overlapping roles and status positions. These values and roles have a tremendous effect on people's preferences and thus on marketers' options. Inca Kola, a fruity, greenish-yellow carbonated drink, is the best-selling soft drink in Peru. Despite being described as "liquid bubble gum," the drink has become a symbol of national pride and heritage. The drink was invented in Peru and contains only fruit indigenous to the country. A local consumer of about a six-pack a day says, "I drink Inca Kola because it makes me feel like a Peruvian." He tells his young daughter, "This is our drink, not something invented overseas. It is named for your ancestors, the great Inca warriors."

Language is another important aspect of culture. Marketers must take care in selecting product names and translating slogans and promotional messages so as not to convey the wrong meaning. For example, Mitsubishi Motors had to rename its Pajero model in Spanish-speaking countries because the term refers to a sexual activity. Toyota Motors' MR2 model dropped the number 2 in France because the combination sounds like a French swearword. The literal translation of Coca-Cola in Chinese characters means "bite the wax tadpole."

Each country has its own customs and traditions that determine business practices and influence negotiations with foreign customers. In many countries, personal relationships are more important than financial considerations. For instance, skipping

DO:

- **Read up** on the culture of the country where you will be doing business. Pointing or beckoning with the forefinger is considered rude in some Asian countries, for example; pointing your foot at another person is considered rude in Thailand.
- **Remember** that pleasure and personal relationships are often a determining factor when Latin Americans and Asians do business.
- **Treat business cards** seriously almost everywhere. In many cultures, a business card is as important as a résumé. Don't glance at the card and shove it in your pocket. Take the card in your right hand, carefully examine it, and memorize the person's name, title, and company and the company's address. You may be tested later.
- **Be aware** of dietary taboos. Pork is considered unclean, for example, by Muslims. Nor should you offer a Hindu a meal containing beef; the cow is considered a sacred animal in the Hindu religion.

DON'T:

- **Dress too casually**. Canadians view casual as comfortable or even as part of the breakdown of phoney corporate hierarchical rules. In many Asian and Latin American countries, though, casual equals sloppy.
- **Use your left hand** to eat, or to give or receive objects, unless you are certain it is acceptable. In many Asian, Middle Eastern, and African cultures, the left hand is used for personal hygiene and is considered unclean.

Some Examples of Cultural Differences That Can Affect Business Dealings

- The Japanese do not like to say no. If your Japanese business partner tells you that your proposition would "be very difficult," she means "no, we don't want to do it that way."
- In Asia, companies usually do not provide employee evaluations, or performance reviews, unless the employee is about to be fired.
- A powerful Chinese buyer will buy the highest-quality product. He doesn't care about marketing or advertising pitches.
- In many parts of Latin America, the business day begins at about 11 a.m., and proceeds until about 3 p.m., when there is a two-to-three-hour break; the last part of the work day runs from about 6 to 9 p.m.
- Hype doesn't sell in many countries, such as Germany and China. A good product stands on its own merits. If you have to hype a product, people believe that something must be wrong with it.
- European and Asian résumés include only the facts: a complete professional history and a copy of every degree, certificate, or award earned. Expressions of professional accomplishment on the job are frowned on.
- Cultural norms vary from culture to culture. You might have to turn your head to avoid being kissed on the lips by another man in Russia, for example, as a sign of affection or expression of celebration. But a Chinese businessperson, even one who is a close friend, would generally be uncomfortable with physical contact beyond a handshake.

SOURCE: Bill Bowen, "Culture Clash," *Fort Worth Star Telegram* (September 28, 1998), pp. 14–15.

social engagements in Mexico may lead to lost sales. Negotiations in Japan often include long evenings of dining, drinking, and entertaining; only after a close personal relationship has been formed do business negotiations begin. Exhibit 2-5 presents some cultural "dos and don'ts."

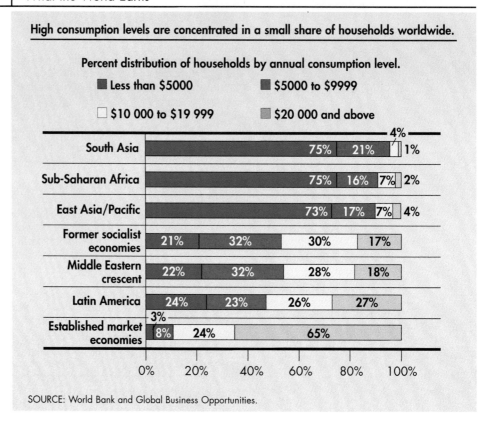

High consumption levels are concentrated in a small share of households worldwide.

Percent distribution of households by annual consumption level.

■ Less than $5000   ■ $5000 to $9999

□ $10 000 to $19 999   ■ $20 000 and above

	Less than $5000	$5000 to $9999	$10 000 to $19 999	$20 000 and above
South Asia	75%	21%	4%	1%
Sub-Saharan Africa	75%	16%	7%	2%
East Asia/Pacific	73%	17%	7%	4%
Former socialist economies	21%	32%	30%	17%
Middle Eastern crescent	22%	32%	28%	18%
Latin America	24%	23%	26%	27%
Established market economies	3% / 8%	24%	65%	

SOURCE: World Bank and Global Business Opportunities.

Economic Environment

The level of economic development varies considerably, ranging from countries where everyday survival is a struggle, such as the Sudan and Eritrea, to countries that are highly developed, such as Switzerland and Japan. In general, complex, sophisticated industries are found in developed countries, and more basic industries are found in less developed nations. Average family incomes are higher in the more developed countries than in the least developed markets. Larger incomes mean greater purchasing power and demand not only for consumer goods and services but also for the machinery and workers required to produce consumer goods. Exhibit 2-6 provides a glimpse of what families earn throughout the world.

Business opportunities are usually better in countries that have an economic infrastructure in place. **Infrastructure** is the basic institutions and public facilities upon which an economy's development depends. When we think about how our own economy works, we tend to take our infrastructure for granted. It includes the money and banking system that provides the major investment loans to our nation's businesses; the educational system that turns out the incredible varieties of skills and basic research that actually run our nation's production lines; the extensive transportation and communications systems—interprovincial highways, railroads, airports, canals, telephones, Internet sites, postal systems, television stations—that link almost every piece of our geography into one market; the energy system that powers our factories; and, of course, the market system itself, which brings our nation's goods and services into our homes and businesses.

infrastructure
The basic institutions and public facilities upon which an economy's development depends.

concept check

- Explain how political factors can affect international trade.
- Describe several cultural factors that a company involved in international trade should consider.
- How can economic conditions affect trade opportunities?

➡ **lg 9**

CAPITALIZING ON TRENDS IN BUSINESS

In this section we will examine several underlying trends that will continue to propel the dramatic growth in world trade. These trends are market expansion, resource acquisition, competition, technological change, and governmental actions.

Market Expansion

The need for businesses to expand their markets is perhaps the most fundamental reason for the growth in world trade. The limited size of domestic markets often motivates managers to seek markets beyond their national frontiers. The economies of large-scale manufacturing demand big markets. Domestic markets, particularly in less populated countries like Canada and the Netherlands, simply can't generate enough demand. Nestlé was one of the first businesses to "go global" because its home country, Switzerland, is so small. Nestlé was shipping milk to 16 different countries as early as 1875. Today, hundreds of thousands of businesses are recognizing the potential rich rewards to be found in international markets.

Resource Acquisition

More and more companies are going to the global marketplace to acquire the resources they need to operate efficiently. These resources may be cheap or skilled labour, scarce raw materials, technology, or capital. Nike, for example, has opened manufacturing facilities in many Asian countries in order to use cheap labour. Honda opened a design studio in southern California to put that "California flair" into the design of some of its vehicles. Many of the larger Canadian public corporations are not only listed on the Toronto Stock Exchange but also on foreign stock exchanges in order to attract capital from around the globe.

Competition

As firms continue to enter new markets, their competitors will often do the same to maintain their competitive position. Starbucks, for example, recently entered Great Britain. Nestlé quickly developed Starbucks-type stores and moved into London shortly after Starbucks. Mazda has struggled for years in Japan because it lacked the resources of its larger domestic competitors—Toyota and Nissan. It entered the Canadian market in an effort to keep pace with its Japanese rivals by gaining market share and profitability. With the opening of Eastern Europe and China, thousands of businesses are racing to capture new customers. Each realizes that if it falls behind its competitors, it may have a difficult time catching up.

Technological Change

New technology (which we'll discuss in more detail in Chapter 4), particularly the Internet, transportation systems, and information processing, fosters continued growth in international trade. Transportation improvements from computerized container ships to cargo jetliners have dramatically improved the efficiency of distribution throughout the world. Moreover, Federal Express and other shippers use advanced computerized tracking software to tell shippers where their packages are at any point in time. Shippers can use special software that enables them to enter FedEx's database and track the packages themselves, if they so desire. It's a far cry from the sailing ships of yesteryear when voyages took weeks or months, and there was no way to communicate with the ship once it left port.

The Internet opens up the world to any seller with a Web site. Markets no longer have geographic boundaries. E-mail enables a manager in London to receive reports from Toronto, Moscow, Cape Town, and Tokyo in a matter of minutes rather than days. Thus, coordinating global business strategies is now a workable reality.

Government Actions

Governments around the globe, working with the WTO, have significantly lowered barriers to world trade. Sellers in the global marketplace have a more level playing field than ever before. Regional trade organizations, such as the European Union, NAFTA, and Mercosur, also have reduced trade barriers in large geographic areas. As these governmental actions continue to make it easier to "go global," world trade will continue to grow.

These government actions of trade liberalization and political changes have presented numerous opportunities for Canadian companies as markets become more attractive.

concept check

- What trends will foster continued growth in world trade?
- Describe some of the ways businesses can take advantage of these trends to "go global."

APPLYING THIS CHAPTER'S TOPICS

Continue Your Education

The handwriting is on the wall. Low-skilled jobs are rapidly disappearing in Canada. Canadian businesses know that to compete globally, they must find cheap labour for labour-intensive businesses. This means establishing plants in Mexico, Asia, or other places in the world where labour is inexpensive. It also means that unskilled or low-skilled Canadian workers will find it increasingly difficult to secure a permanent job. By continuing your education, you won't fall into this very undesirable trap.

Study the Role of a Global Manager

As business becomes more global, chances are that you may become a global manager. Start learning right now what this means and if it's right for you. The life of a global manager can be hectic, as these examples illustrate:

> As president of DoubleClick International, a unit of the New York Internet advertising company, Barry Salzman spends about 75% of his time traveling. He takes a laptop and four battery packs so he can wade through the 200 e-mail messages he averages daily. Welcome to the world of global management. It's a punishing pace, but it's the only way Mr. Salzman knows how to manage his network of 13 offices world-wide.
>
> Global managers spend proportionately more of their energy combating the sense of isolation that tends to gnaw at employees in remote offices. Mr. Salzman conducts a conference call every Monday morning for international managers in Canada, Europe and Asia. Only those who are flying somewhere are excused. "We try to maintain voice contact," he says. "We lose that with computers and e-mail."
>
> Top overseas performers at Secure Computing, a San José, California, software developer, are treated to a dinner for two by Christine Hughes, senior vice president of marketing and business development. Ms. Hughes supervises a 24-person staff in North and South America and Asia. One of her missions on trips is to combat the tendency of foreign-based employees to think the organization is "U.S.-centric," she says. Because they take much longer flights than the typical corporate road warrior, global managers wind up turning airplanes into offices. When she is overseas, Ms. Hughes has her office ship her a package of paperwork overnight, so she can work on the flight home. Mr. Salzman considers flight time some of his most productive; he uses it to answer e-mail and review contracts.
>
> Indeed, a global manager's workday never really ends. Wherever they are, it's still business hours somewhere else. When she's working in Australia, Ms. Hughes usually ends her day in a hotel room, talking with someone at the home office. "I'm on the phone until two in the morning dealing with issues," she says. "You just have to accept that."[24]

Your position may not be as hectic as that of Salzman or Hughes, but you can easily see the differences between a person who is a global manager and one who is not. Is this the life for you? Would you enjoy living abroad? Can you adapt easily to other cultures?

One way to see if you might be cut out to be a global manager is to spend some time abroad. The ideal situation is to find a job overseas during the summer months. This experience will help you decide if you want to be a global manager. Also, it will look good on your résumé. One source of international jobs information is **www.internationaljobs.org/**.

If you can't find a job overseas, save your money and travel abroad. Seeing how others live and work will broaden your horizons and give you a more enlightened view of the world. Even international travel can help you decide what you want to do in the global marketplace.

TRY IT NOW!

Changing Money Abroad If you travel, work, or study abroad, you are going to need to change Canadian dollars to foreign currency. Making mistakes when changing money can cost you 10 to 20 percent of your bankroll. Here are a few tips about changing money abroad.

1. Know the exchange rate between Canadian dollars and the currencies of the countries you plan to visit before you go. Go to www.xe.com/ucc/ for the latest quotations. Keep up with the changing rates by reading the business section of your local newspaper (or any of the national papers).

2. Avoid changing money at airports, train stations, and hotels. These places usually have the least attractive rates. Ask local people where they change money. Locals know where the best rates are.

3. Try to bargain with the clerk. Sometimes you can do better than the posted rate simply by asking.

4. Rather than making several small transactions, make one large exchange. This will often get you a better rate.

5. Don't change more than you will need. You'll pay another fee to change the foreign currency back to Canadian dollars.

6. Use a bank or credit card. Typically, any major bank or credit card will give you a better rate than a change booth or bank. Sometimes the spread is substantial, so minimize cash and use credit.

7. Traveller's cheques usually have a worse exchange rate than cash. In other words, a $100 American Express traveller's cheque will give you less in exchange than a $100 bill. If your traveller's cheques are lost or stolen, however, they will be replaced, so the peace of mind is usually worth the added expense.

>looking ahead

at McCain Foods Limited

Look back at the opening story about McCain Foods Limited and its influence. Cultural factors, domestic competition, economic conditions, government actions, and regional trade agreements can all make selling in the global marketplace more difficult. Governments can take a number of actions to protect domestic competitors. Some common tactics are tariffs, quotas, embargoes, exchange controls, and buy-national regulations.

There are a number of cultural factors that Canadian companies should consider when entering a foreign market. For example, many Europeans shop for groceries every day; there is always an emphasis on freshness. Also, Europeans are not used to shopping at night or on Sundays. Offering late hours will probably not create an immediate rush of business.

SUMMARY OF LEARNING GOALS

➡lg 1   **Why is global trade important to Canada?**

International trade improves relations with friends and allies, eases tensions among nations, helps bolster economies, raises people's standard of living, gives Canadians more options, and improves the quality of life. International trade enhances our quality of life and helps us to create the nation we want. Canada produces much more of some products that we export and cannot produce others, that we need to import. Approximately one-third of all jobs in Canada are directly related to international trade.

➡lg 2   **How is global trade measured?**

Two concepts important to global trade are the balance of trade (the difference in value between a country's exports and its imports over some period) and the balance of payments (the difference between a country's total payments to other countries and its total receipts from other countries). Canada now has both a positive balance of trade and a positive balance of payments.

Another important concept is the exchange rate, which is the price of one country's currency in terms of another country's currency. Currencies float up and down based upon the supply of and demand for each currency. Sometimes a government steps in and devalues its currency relative to the currencies of other countries.

➡lg 3   Why do nations trade?

Nations trade because they gain by doing so. The principle of comparative advantage states that each country should specialize in the goods it can produce most readily and cheaply and trade them for those that other countries can produce most readily and cheaply. The result is more goods at lower prices than if each country produced by itself everything it needed. Free trade allows trade among nations without government restrictions.

➡lg 4   What are the barriers to international trade?

The three major barriers to international trade are natural barriers, such as distance and language; tariff barriers, or taxes on imported goods; and nontariff barriers. The nontariff barriers to trade include import quotas, embargoes, buy-national regulations, customs regulations, and exchange controls. The main argument against tariffs is that they discourage free trade and keep the principle of comparative advantage from working efficiently. The main argument for using tariffs is that they help protect domestic companies, industries, and workers.

➡lg 5   How do governments and institutions foster world trade?

The World Trade Organization created by the Uruguay Round has dramatically lowered trade barriers worldwide. For the first time a trade agreement covers services, intellectual property rights, and exchange controls. The World Bank makes loans to developing nations to help build infrastructures. The International Monetary Fund makes loans to member nations that cannot meet their budgetary expenses.

➡lg 6   What are international economic communities?

International economic communities reduce trade barriers among themselves while often establishing common tariffs and other trade barriers toward nonmember countries. The best-known economic communities are the European Union, NAFTA, and Mercosur.

➡lg 7   How do companies enter the global marketplace?

There are a number of ways to enter the global market. The major ones are exporting, licensing, contract manufacturing, joint ventures, and direct investment.

➡lg 8   What threats and opportunities exist in the global marketplace?

Domestic firms entering the international arena need to consider the politics, economies, and culture of the countries where they plan to do business. For example, government trade policies can be loose or restrictive, countries can be nationalistic, and governments can change. In the area of culture, many products fail because companies don't understand the culture of the country where they are trying to sell their products. Some developing countries also lack an economic infrastructure, which often makes it very difficult to conduct business.

➡lg 9   What are the trends in the global marketplace?

Global business activity will continue to escalate due to several factors. Firms that desire a larger customer base or need additional resources will continue to seek opportunities outside their country's borders. When an organization moves into a new global market, competitors typically follow its lead and enter the same new market. In addition, technological improvements in communication and transportation will continue to fuel growth in global markets by making it easier to sell and distribute products internationally.

WORKING THE NET

1. As a leader in such areas as peacekeeping, technology, and innovation, Canada has much to offer its global partners. Go to the Department of Foreign Affairs and International Trade Web site at **www.dfait-maeci.gc.ca/menu-en.asp** to learn more about our imports and exports with our international trading partners. Choose a country that interests you and find out more about the country (see the fact sheet), the country overview, and information on doing business in that country (including cultural issues). Think of various business opportunities for Canadians and Canadian companies in this country. What are the main barriers to trade Canadian companies might face in doing business with this country?

2. Review the historical data about exchange rates between the Canadian dollar and the currency of the country you chose in question 1 at **www.x-rates.com/**. What are the trends? How do these trends affect the imports to Canada and exports from Canada?

3. Pretend that you are the president of a mid-sized Canadian software company who is trying to decide whether to export. Explore your opportunities for exporting your products at **www.edc.ca/index_e.htm**. What opportunities might exporting hold for your firm? What barriers might you face?

4. Visit *Export Today* magazine's online site at **www.exporttoday.com**. Read one of the articles from the current issue. Make a list of additional information you would need if you were the owner of a business affected by the events described in the article. Do a search on the search engine Alta Vista, **www.altavista.com**, to uncover additional Internet sites related to the topic. Pick one site and write a review of the information and resources available on it. Rate the usefulness of the site and the information it offers.

CREATIVE THINKING CASE

Adaptive Eyecare Limited

Professor Joshua Silver is a physicist at Oxford University who spends much of his time exploring the mysteries of subatomic particles. But for the last 13 years he has quietly pursued a more earthly passion: to devise low-cost adjustable spectacles for the one billion people in the world who need glasses, but don't have them. He also hopes to turn some of these people into paying customers.

The lenses of Silver's glasses are made from pairs of transparent plastic membranes, filled with a colourless silicone fluid. Attached to the spectacle frame are two circular "focus adjusters," which contain the fluid. A user can adjust the power of the lenses by twirling the adjusters. This injects fluid through a tiny hole in the frame.

A fatter lens increases magnification, helping those who are nearsighted; a thinner lens reduces magnification, helping the farsighted. Once each eye has been properly focused, the adjusters are snapped off, sealing the holes, and the spectacles are ready for use.

A pair could cost as little as $10. There is no need for a vision test, a visit to an optician, or an expensive prescription. "There's a strong argument to get these specs out to the millions of people who need them," says Bjorn Thylefors, who heads the World Health Organization's campaign to prevent blindness and has seen Silver's glasses. He calls the lack of spectacles "a sizable health problem in the developing world, with economic and educational repercussions."

Silver's start-up, Adaptive Eyecare Ltd., hopes to sell the glasses, for a profit, in developing countries. It has assembled a management group, including two manufacturing optometrists and a business consultant.[25]

Critical Thinking Questions
1. Should Professor Silver "go global"?
2. If so, how should he enter the global marketplace?
3. What are several threats and opportunities Adaptive Eyecare may face?
4. Will the product be successful in the Canada? Elsewhere?

CHAPTER 3

Trends, Social Responsibility, and Ethics

In this chapter you'll be learning about some very important trends in the *social* environment: for example, the changing demographic composition of the Canadian population and the changing lifestyles in the work force, as well as one of the most important and newsworthy trends in the social environment—the trend toward better ethics and increased corporate responsibility.

Just as the other trends in the PEST environment model affect and are affected by each other, so are these trends. For example, demographic changes in the population lead to changing consumer wants and needs (another social trend), but also to changes in government/*political* policy (perhaps to extend the mandatory retirement age to hold off the damage to the Canada Pension Plan that is inevitable as the large bulge of boomers retire), and changes in *technology* (as businesses look for ways to make up for a shrinking labour force). This trend has even helped lead to the *economic* trend toward entrepreneurship (which we'll discuss in Chapter 6) as baby boomers born at the latter part of the boom have difficulty finding jobs at higher levels in companies because the early boomers have taken all those jobs.

Acting ethically and in a responsible manner is so integrative because it creeps into everything we do, both inside and outside the business. As the chapter indicates, people who seldom consider the ethical implications of daily activities won't have the coordination to work through the more difficult times in their lives, particularly when such issues come up in a business context. For the business specifically, the chapter shows how economic factors relate to ethics and corporate responsibility by discussing how market forces and market failures have motivated greater corporate responsibility for organizations wishing to promote consumer confidence. The chapter also discusses how technology is related, as the Internet often creates a perception of anonymity prompting less than ethical behaviour in some businesspeople because they have less fear of getting caught. And the political factor is always looming because if business does not act ethically and take its social responsibility voluntarily, governments are likely to step in and increase legislation, as we have seen in response to the Enron and WorldCom scandals in the United States.

Using research done by the Canadian Centre for Social Performance and Ethics at the University of Toronto, this chapter also shows how a company's commitment to ethical and responsible behaviour affects the success of the company, or helps it meet the critical success factors in our model. For example, it leads to reduced operating costs (helping *achieve financial success*); enhanced brand and image reputation and increased sales and customer loyalty (both helping to achieve financial success because the company gains the trust of customers and better *meets their needs* long term); and increased ability to attract and retain employees (helping to *gain employee commitment*).

An interesting piece of evidence to support that ethical and socially responsible corporate behaviour improves the financial performance of a company can be found in the first issue of the magazine *Corporate Knights*. The *Corporate Knights* organization undertook the first-ever ranking of the 50 best corporate citizens in Canada in 2002. Their research shows that when you compare the historical returns of the 50 best corporate citizens in Canada against the TSE 300 Composite Index, the more socially responsible companies come out on top by a margin of 21.6 percent for the year ended December 31, 2001, 10.8 percent for the past three years, and 14.9 percent for the past five years.

Thus, acting in an ethical and responsible fashion creates a key opportunity for businesses to be more financially successful, and not doing so creates enormous threats to the survival of the business—just look at WorldCom and Enron. In fact, all environmental trends create both threats and opportunities. The environment does change constantly and uncontrollably, but if seen early enough and handled proactively, these changes can be exploited as opportunities. Look for examples discussed in this chapter, such as Levi Strauss taking advantage of the social trend toward casual office dress with its Dockers brand, as well as the social trend toward working women having a direct economic effect on dual-income families and the opportunities this trend creates (for child-care and elder-care, home cleaning services, and other convenience items and services).

One of the more interesting and challenging opportunities discussed in the chapter is the trend toward component lifestyles. This makes meeting customer needs very difficult but full of opportunities. It makes it necessary to use technology to track customer needs, and then to focus on *innovation* and developing products of *value* to customers, while keeping *operations* extremely flexible to meet changes as they occur and adjust to the differing demands of the consumer.

One of the major social trends discussed in this chapter is the shift in the demographic composition of the Canadian population created by the baby boom. Pay close attention to the impact of this trend as it has definite implications for business. (A good reference to understanding the impact of demographics is David Foot's book *Boom, Bust and Echo.*) As the chapter indicates, demographic changes definitely affect the market for products, as well as the size and composition of the work force. So shifts in demographics have implications for the overall *strategy* of a business as well as its functional areas. Some products will find demand declining, while others experience increased demand as demographics shift—important concerns for *marketing*. The size and composition of the work force will change, and that's important for *human resources to* understand and plan for. This changing composition of the work force may necessitate moving operations to other countries in search of labour with the required skills. For the *finance* area, clearly all of these implications have an impact, but also the demographic shifts we are experiencing in Canada, coupled with a declining birth rate, causes the government to respond with changes in economic policy, which inevitably affects the finance area of the business.

Without a doubt, there is also a connection between functional areas and ethical and responsible corporate behaviour. According to Canadian Business for Social Responsibility (CBSR), companies that practise corporate social responsibility develop and practise policies and programs in areas such as employee relations (human resources), international relations (operations), marketplace practices (marketing), and fiscal responsibility and accountability (finance). In fact, in order to be truly responsible, commitment must come from the top, be part of the *mission* and culture of the company, and therefore be part of the decisions made within all functional areas.

Add to this list community development and environmental stewardship and you've covered the major *stakeholder* groups. Clearly, being ethical and responsible involves operating in a manner that recognizes and balances the competing expectations of all the different stakeholders of the business, and building a relationship of trust with them. And meeting the company's obligations to its stakeholders also helps the company achieve its critical success factors. For example, meeting its responsibility to employees helps gain employee commitment, meeting its responsibility to customers helps meet customer needs, and meeting its responsibility to investors helps achieve financial performance by providing needed capital. In fact, social investing would suggest that this is a very big factor. More and more investment funds are moving toward socially responsible companies, and as we can see in the *Corporate Knights* survey, they are doing very well.

Trends, Social Responsibility, and Ethics

CHAPTER 3

Learning Goals

→ **lg 1** How is the trend of changing lifestyles affecting business?

→ **lg 2** How are changing demographic trends creating more opportunities for business?

→ **lg 3** Why is an understanding of demographic trends important for the marketing of goods and services?

→ **lg 4** What philosophies and concepts shape personal ethical standards, and what are the stages of ethical development?

→ **lg 5** How can organizations influence organizational ethics?

→ **lg 6** What are the techniques for creating employee ethical awareness?

→ **lg 7** What is social responsibility?

→ **lg 8** How do businesses meet their social responsibilities to various stakeholders?

→ **lg 9** What are the global and domestic trends in ethics and social responsibility?

Business Integrity at Nexen, Inc.

Dr. Randall Gossen is the vice president of safety, environment, and social responsibility for Nexen, Inc., and the current chairman of the International Petroleum Industry Environmental Conservation Association. Randy describes business integrity as "the human face of business." He suggests that the term *business integrity* tends to be more palatable to business than the more commonly used *corporate responsibility*. Nexen supports five pillars of corporate social responsibility: business practices, employee relations, community investment, safety and environment, and supplier and customer relations. The figure below illustrates the five pillars.

Nexen operates internationally and several locations would be considered high risk. Many of the risks faced by Nexen include the obvious social, environmental, political, legal, economic, and security risks, but there are also problems with drug cartels, terrorists, corruption, and kidnapping. The approach taken by Nexen is to improve the quality of life in the communities and the societies of the host countries. With reference to their operations in Columbia, Randy says, "Community support is the cornerstone of our security program." Nexen designs

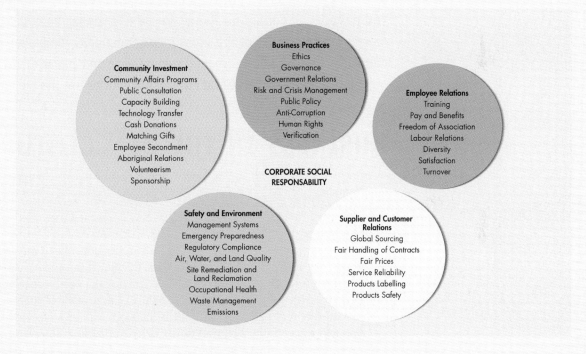

The Five Pillars of Corporate Responsibility

CRITICAL THINKING QUESTIONS

As you read this chapter consider the following questions as they relate to Nexen:

- How have trends affected Nexen and what opportunities and threats have these trends offered Nexen?
- How has Nexen shown that they are socially responsible, and how does this impact their profits in the short and long terms?
- Why is ethical behaviour important to companies such as Nexen?

and implements programs such as developing computer literacy in the local schools, protecting the water supplies, and training local leaders in formulating projects. In Yemen, Nexen has steadily increased the number of locals employed by the company. The company provides English-language and technical training and a scholarship program for Yemeni students to study in Canada at postsecondary institutions. "In order to operate in this way, we need the management structure and system to support it," explains Randy. This structure includes knowledgeable employees, who are prepared to "walk the talk." Nexen's continuous improvement model for business integrity involves "(1) knowing what we stand for, (2) taking action, (3) measuring performance, (4) verifying." With respect to "knowing what we stand for," Nexen's statement of vision, beliefs, values, and principles is made available to employees and any member of the general public who wishes to read it. "How can a company practise business integrity without transparency?" asks Randy. Take a look at Nexen's code of ethics in Exhibit 3-3 on page 77.

Randy explains that Nexen believes there is a strong business case for practising business integrity and behaving in a socially responsible manner. The rewards, according to Randy, include "stronger financial performance, meeting expectations of the investment community, employee commitment, motivation and morale, decreased vulnerability, and improved reputation." The bottom line for Nexen is "Good business practices are the best insurance."[1]

BUSINESS IN THE 21ST CENTURY

Consider an example of how a company has responded to changes in the business environment:

> The social trend toward casualness has finally reached the office. Many firms now have a "dress-down" day on Fridays, when jackets and ties aren't required. When Charles Schwab, the discount stockbroker, considered offering a "dress-down" day, it called Levi Strauss and Co., the blue jeans and casual wear manufacturer, for a little fashion advice. Recognizing the significance of this trend, Levi Strauss responded with more than advice. It provided brochures showing how dress could be casual without being sloppy, names of other companies that had successfully shed traditional attire, and studies that showed how the apparel shift had improved workers' productivity and morale. By capitalizing on a new social trend, Levi's Dockers now capture one-third of all department store pants sales.[2]

No one business is large or powerful enough to create major changes in the external environment. Thus, managers are basically adapters to rather than agents of change. For example, despite the huge size of General Motors, Ford, and DaimlerChrysler, these companies have only recently been able to stem the competitive push by the Japanese for an ever-growing share of the North American automobile market. Global competition is basically an uncontrollable element in the external environment, as discussed in Chapter 2. This chapter examines the social trends in the business environment that are reshaping today's business landscape. Most important are the trends for companies to consider their social responsibility and the expectation that they will act in an ethical manner.

➡ **lg 1**

Trends in Canada Today

Social change is perhaps the most difficult environmental factor for owners and managers to forecast, influence, or integrate into business plans. Social factors include our attitudes, values, and lifestyles. Social factors influence the products people buy, the prices paid for products, the effectiveness of specific promotions, and how, where, and when people expect to purchase products.

The Growth of Component Lifestyles

component lifestyle
A lifestyle made up of a complex set of interests and choices.

People in North America today are piecing together component lifestyles. A lifestyle is a mode of living; it is the way people decide to live their lives. A **component lifestyle** is a lifestyle made up of a complex set of interests and choices. In other words, people are choosing products and services that meet diverse needs and interests rather than conforming to traditional stereotypes.

In the past, a person's profession—for instance, banker—defined that person's lifestyle. Today a person can be a banker, gourmet, fitness enthusiast, dedicated single parent, and conservationist—all at once. Each of these lifestyles is associated with different goods and services and represents a unique market. For example, businesses advertise cooking utensils, wines, and exotic foods through magazines like *Bon Appetit* and *Gourmet* for the gourmets. The fitness enthusiast buys Adidas equipment and special jogging outfits and reads *Runner's World* magazine. Component lifestyles increase the complexity of consumers' buying habits. The banker may own a BMW but change the oil herself. She may buy fast food for lunch but French wine for dinner, own sophisticated photographic equipment and a low-priced home stereo, and shop for stockings at Zellers or Wal-Mart and suits at Holt Renfrew.

The Changing Role of Families and Working Women

Component lifestyles have evolved because consumers can choose from a growing number of goods and services, and most have the money to exercise more options. Increased purchasing power is largely a result of the growth of dual-income families. The phenomenon of working women has had a greater effect on business than any other social change. The demand for child-care, elder-care, and home cleaning services are all affected, to name just a few examples.

As women's earnings grow, so do their levels of expertise, experience, and authority. The word *handyman* may no longer be politically correct—or correct at all—as women become a more potent force in buying tools and hardware for both inside and outside the home. From simply using more "feminine" colours to designing tools especially for women do-it-yourselfers, companies are responding by creating products with women in mind. "Our research shows more females are the primary decision-makers and buyers of home items," says Lorrie Crum, a spokeswoman for Rubbermaid, Inc.[3]

Other hardware companies have assembled "kits" for customers tackling a specific home project for the first time. The Miracle Restoration Kit includes a Miracle Eraser pumice stone sander and rejuvenation oil for refinishing furniture. "The stores say that women are the people who refinish furniture, and we came up with a product that doesn't take any pressure at all and doesn't get clogged up like sandpaper," said Hank Greenfield, who makes the kits.

Health and Other Lifestyle Trends

A general trend toward a healthier lifestyle has implications for businesses that cannot be overlooked. For many business owners, the trend toward non-smoking workplaces can represent a threat to those that operate businesses associated with a smoking environment (e.g., night clubs). The trend towards healthier eating provides opportunities for many business owners (e.g., organic food restaurants). As well, the trend toward a more active lifestyle has led to many business opportunities such as low-risk, yet exciting and active vacation packages, more recreational facilities at work, and more active leisure pursuits. However, it should be noted that trends are different in different regions of Canada, and scanning one's specific environment for relevant trends is an important component of the planning process for any business. As more value is attached to being environmentally and socially responsible, firms must assess the importance of these trends to their overall strategy.

concept check

- Why are social changes the most difficult environmental factor to predict?
- How do component lifestyles make it more difficult to predict a consumer's buying habits?
- What social change has had the greatest impact on business?

demography
The study of people's vital statistics, such as their age, race and ethnicity, and location.

Demographic Trends

Demographic trends—another uncontrollable factor in the business environment—are also extremely important to managers. **Demography** is the study of people's vital statistics, such as their age, race and ethnicity, and location. Demographics are significant because the basis for any market is people. Demographics also determine the size and composition of the work force. Below is a discussion of the some of the key age groups.

Generation Y—Born to Shop

Generation Y
People born from the early 1980s to the mid-1990s.

People born from the early 1980s to the mid-1990s make up **Generation Y** (also called the echo generation). Its numbers are smaller than some other past generations (e.g., baby boomers, discussed below) but plentiful enough to put their own footprints on society.

The marketing impact of Generation Y has been immense. Companies that sell toys, videos, software, and clothing to this group have boomed in recent years. Nine of the ten best-selling videos of all time are animated films from Walt Disney Co. Club Med, the French vacation company, now earns half its U.S. revenues from family resorts. The members of Generation Y were born into a world vastly different from the one their parents entered. The changes in families, the work force, technology, and demographics in recent decades will no doubt affect their attitudes, but in unpredictable ways.

Generation Y is also driving the educational software industry, which has grown to an almost $1 billion business in North America from practically nothing in 1990. Titles like Baby-ROM from Byron Preiss Multimedia Co. are designed to help infants as young as six months learn to identify numbers, shapes, colours, and body parts.

Members of Generation Y love to shop. Born into a world of technology, they're big consumers of high-tech products like cellular phones.

Generation X—Savvy and Cynical

Those born between the mid-1960s and the late 1970s have been labelled **Generation X**. They are the first generation of latchkey children—products of dual-career households or, in roughly half the cases, of divorced or separated parents. The

Generation X
Those born between the mid-1960s and the late 1970s.

members of Generation X began entering the work force in the era of downsizing, so they are more likely than the previous generation to be unemployed, underemployed, and living at home with mom and dad. As a generation that's been bombarded by multiple media since their cradle days, they're savvy and cynical consumers.

For decades, Ford marketed its light-duty pickups by emphasizing their roughness and toughness. Advertisements featured trucks climbing rugged mountains or four-wheeling through mud. But Ford quickly realized that this approach was not going to work with the Generation Xers. Instead, Ford chose to lead with a new product. The company created a new version of its popular Ranger pickup, giving it flares on the fenders, jazzy graphics and a youthful new name—Splash. The promotion campaign attempted to infuse the vehicle with personality by combining the truck with adventuresome sports.

Baby Boomers—Canada's Mass Market

baby boomers
People born between the late 1940s (after World War II) and the mid-1960s.

People born between the late 1940s (after World War II) and the mid-1960s are called **baby boomers**. Many baby boomers are now over 50, but they still cling to their youth. Most continue to live a very active life. This group cherishes convenience, which has resulted in a growing demand for home delivery of large appliances, furniture, groceries, and other items. In addition, the spreading culture of convenience explains the tremendous appeal of prepared take-out foods, VCRs, DVDs, cordless telephones, and the Internet.

Baby boomers' parents raised their children to think for and of themselves. Studies of child-rearing practices show that parents of the 1950s and 1960s consistently ranked "to think for themselves" as the number-one trait they wanted to nurture in their children. Postwar affluence also enabled parents to indulge their children as never before. They invested in their children's skills by sending them to university. They encouraged their children to succeed in a job market that rewarded competitive drive more than cooperative spirit and individual skills more than teamwork.

In turn, the sheer size of the generation encouraged businesses to play to the emerging individuality of baby boomers. Even before the oldest baby boomers started earning a living more than three decades ago, astute businesspeople anticipated the profits that could come from giving millions of young people what they wanted. Businesses offered individualistic baby boomers a growing array of customized products and services—houses, cars, furniture, appliances, clothes, vacations, jobs, leisure time, and even beliefs.

Older Consumers—Not Just Grandparents

The oldest baby boomers have already crossed the 50-year threshold that many demographers use to define the "mature market." Yet today's mature consumers are wealthier, healthier, and better educated than those of earlier generations.[4] These consumers that are 50-plus buy half of all domestic cars, half of all silverware, and nearly half of all home remodelling. As the birthrate decreases and the Canadian life expectancy increases, this group will continue to be an increasingly important consumer group.

Businesspeople who want to actively pursue the mature market must understand it. Aging consumers create some obvious opportunities.

Growing Ethnic Markets

Canada is a society composed of people from multiple cultures. Over the next decades, Canada will shift further away from a society dominated by whites and rooted in Western culture toward a society characterized by many racial and ethnic minorities. All minorities will grow in size and in share of the population, while the white majority declines as a percentage of the total. First Nations people and people with roots in Australia, the Middle East, the former Soviet Union, and other parts of the world will further enrich the fabric of Canadian society.

➡ **lg 3**

multiculturalism
The condition when all major ethnic groups in an area, such as a city, county, or province, are about equally represented.

Doug Dokis, a member of the Ojibwe Nation of Ontario, acts as a liaison between a large college and the Native community in the area. According to Doug, the growth rate in the Native population is the largest of any population segment. This has tremendous implications for business and to take advantage of the opportunity, businesses must respond to the demands of this sector. Many Native entrepreneurs are emerging to fill the demand for goods and services, such as Cree-ative Imaging of Calgary.

Multiculturalism exists when all major ethnic groups in an area—such as a city, county, or province—are roughly equally represented. Because of the current demographic transition, the trend in Canada is toward greater multiculturalism, although the degree varies in different parts of the country.

Changing demographics affect the marketing of our goods and services. As Canadians are becoming more health conscious, for instance, our companies should promote the "healthiness" of our goods and services. As our population ages and becomes more technically sophisticated, we need to search for new marketing streams that will encourage our target market to purchase our goods and services.

Organizations need to be responsive to the customers, and as they change, the organizations need to change their marketing efforts. This includes the goods and services that they are providing, the price at which they offer them, the place where the customer can have access to them, and how the organizations promote the goods and services.

If organizations fail to monitor the changing demographics of their customers, they will not be able to respond to these changes and will most likely lose sales.

concept check

• How has the changing role of women affected business?
• Explain how Generation X, Generation Y, and baby boomers differ.
• How is multiculturalism changing business?

➡ **lg 4**

ethics
A set of moral standards for judging whether something is right or wrong.

Ethics and Business

Every day, managers and business owners make business decisions based on what they believe to be right and wrong. Through their actions, they demonstrate to their employees what is and is not acceptable behaviour and shape the moral standard of the organization. **Ethics** is a set of moral standards for judging whether something is right or wrong. As shown in this chapter, personal and professional ethics are important cornerstones of an organization and shape its ultimate contributions to society. Let's now consider how individual business ethics are formed.

Individual Business Ethics

Individual business ethics are shaped by personal choices and the environments in which we live and work. In addition, the laws of our society are guideposts for choosing between right and wrong. This section describes personal philosophies and legal factors that influence the choices people make when confronting ethical dilemmas.

utilitarianism
A philosophy that focuses on the consequences of an action to determine whether it is right or wrong; holds that an action that affects the majority adversely is morally wrong.

Utilitarianism

One of the philosophies that may influence choices between right and wrong is **utilitarianism,** which focuses on the consequences of an action taken by a person or organization. The notion that "people should act so as to generate the greatest good for the greatest number" is derived from utilitarianism. When an action affects the majority adversely, it is morally wrong. One problem with this philosophy is that it is nearly impossible to accurately determine how a decision will affect a large number of people. Another problem is that utilitarianism always involves both winners and losers. If sales are slowing and a manager decides to fire five people rather than putting everyone on a 30-hour workweek, the 20 people who keep their full-time jobs are winners, but the other five are losers.

A final criticism of utilitarianism is that some "costs," although small relative to the potential good, are so negative that some segments of society find them unacceptable. For example, animal testing that may injure or cause death to the animal for medical research is seen by many as too high of a price to pay for this type of research to continue.

Individual Rights

In our society, individuals and groups have certain rights that exist under certain conditions regardless of any external circumstances. These rights serve as guides when making individual ethical decisions. The term *human rights* implies that certain rights are conveyed at birth and cannot be arbitrarily taken away. Denying the rights of an individual or group is considered to be unethical and illegal in most, though not all, parts of the world. Certain rights are guaranteed by the various levels of government and their laws, and these are considered legal rights. The **Canadian Charter of Rights and Freedoms** was enacted in 1982 to guarantee the rights and freedoms of Canadians and is superordinate to any other laws that affect Canadians' rights and freedoms.

Some of the freedoms listed in the Charter include:
- The freedom of conscience and religion.
- The freedom of thought, belief, opinion, and expression (e.g., press and other media of communication).
- The freedom of peaceful assembly.
- The freedom of association.

Charter rights include:
- Democratic rights (right to voting at the age of majority).
- Mobility rights (the right to enter, remain in, and leave Canada).
- Legal rights (the right to life, liberty, and security).
- Equality rights (everyone is equal under the law).
- Minority language educational rights (the right to be educated in either English or French).

Justice—The Question of Fairness

Another factor influencing individual business ethics is **justice**, or what is fair according to prevailing standards of society.[5] We all expect life to be reasonably fair. You expect your exams to be fair, the grading to be fair, and your wages to be fair, based on the type of work being done.

In the 21st century, we take *justice* to mean an equitable distribution of the burdens and rewards that society has to offer. The distributive process varies from society to society. Those in a democratic society believe in the "equal pay for equal work" doctrine, in which individuals are rewarded based on the value that the free market places on their services. Because the market places different values on different occupations, the rewards, such as wages, are not necessarily equal. Nevertheless, many regard the rewards as just. At the other extreme, communist theorists have argued that justice would be served by a society in which burdens and rewards were distributed to individuals according to their abilities and their needs, respectively.

Canadian Charter of Rights and Freedoms
Legislation that guarantees the rights and freedoms of Canadians.

HOT Links

For more about the Canadian Charter of Rights and Freedoms and other Canadian legislation, go to
www.canada.justice.gc.ca

justice
What is considered fair according to the prevailing standards of society; in the 21st century, an equitable distribution of the burdens and rewards that society has to offer.

Stages of Ethical Development

preconventional ethics
A stage in the ethical develop-ment of individuals in which people behave in a childlike manner and make ethical deci-sions in a calculating, self-cen-tred, selfish way, based on the possibility of immediate punish-ment or reward; also known as self-centred ethics.

conventional ethics
The second stage in the ethical development of individuals in which people move from an ego-centric viewpoint to consider the expectations of an organization of society; also known as social ethics.

postconventional ethics
The third stage in the ethical development of individuals in which people adhere to the eth-ical standards of a mature adult and are less concerned about how others view their behaviour than about how they will judge them-selves in the long run; also known as principled ethics.

We can view an individual's ethical development as having reached one of three levels: preconventional, conventional, or postconventional. The behaviour of a person at the level of **preconventional ethics** is childlike in nature; it is calculating, self-centred, and even selfish, and is based on the possibility of immediate punishment or reward. Thus, a student may not cheat on an exam because he or she is afraid of getting caught and therefore receiving a failing grade for the course. The student's behaviour is based not on a sense of what's right or wrong, but instead on the threat of punishment.

Conventional ethics moves from an egocentric viewpoint toward the expectations of society. Loyalty and obedience to the organization (or society) become paramount. At the conventional ethics level, a businessperson might say, "I know that our adver-tising is somewhat misleading, but as long as it will increase sales we should continue the campaign." Right or wrong is not the issue; the only question is whether the cam-paign will benefit the organization.

Postconventional ethics represents the ethical standards of the mature adult. At the postconventional level, businesspeople are concerned less about how others might see them and more about how they see and judge themselves over the long run. A person who has attained this ethical level might ask, "Even though this action is legal and will increase company profits, is it right in the long run? Might it do more harm than good in the end?" A manager at a fast food restaurant may refuse to offer Styrofoam cups because they are nonbiodegradable. An advertising agency manager might refuse a tobacco account because of the health hazards of smoking. A lab tech-nician might refuse to recommend a new whitener for a detergent because it could harm the environment. All of these individuals are exhibiting postconventional morality.

Many people believe that the Internet is a vast anonymous place where they can say and do just about anything. When they think that they can't be caught, they some-times revert to preconventional ethics. Yet e-mail servers owned by businesses and governmental agencies can quickly tell what is being sent and to whom. The Computer Ethics Institute proposes the "Ten Commandment of Computer Ethics" shown below.

Computers and Ethics

The Computer Ethics Institute (CEI) is a research, education, and policy study organ-ization focusing on the interface of information technologies, ethics, and corporate and public policy. Its objective is to undertake research about the actual and potential effects of information technology, and provide advice to various interested parties (individuals, organizations, communities, etc.) regarding ethical and social responsi-bilities.

There has been a very laissez-faire approach to ethics when it comes to cyberspace and there has been great reluctance to restrict information on the Internet, but this is changing in the 21st century. The increased use of the information highway has encouraged more policing. First presented in Dr. Ramon C. Barquin's paper, "In Pursuit of a 'Ten commandments' for Computer Ethics," the CEI has created the "Ten Commandments of Computer Ethics" shown in Exhibit 3-1.

concept check

- Define ethics.
- What is utilitarianism?
- Discuss the stages of ethical development.

exhibit 3-1 | Ten Commandments of Computer Ethics

1. Thou shalt not use a computer to harm other people.
2. Thou shalt not interfere with other people's computer work.
3. Thou shalt not snoop around in other people's computer files.
4. Thou shalt not use a computer to steal.
5. Thou shalt not use a computer to bear false witness.
6. Thou shalt not copy or use proprietary software for which you have not paid.
7. Thou shalt not use other people's computer resources without authorization or proper compensation.
8. Thou shalt not appropriate other people's intellectual output.
9. Thou shalt think about the social consequences of the program you are writing or the system you are designing.
10. Thou shalt always use a computer in ways that ensure consideration and respect for your fellow humans.

SOURCE: Computer Ethics Institute, The Brookings Institution, "Then Commandments Of Computer Ethics," www.brook.edu/its/cei/overview/Ten_Commandments_of_Computer_Ethics.htm, accessed July 3, 2003. Reprinted by permission of The Computer Ethics Institute.

→ lg 5

How Organizations Influence Ethical Conduct

People choose between right and wrong based on their personal code of ethics. Ethical behaviours (or unethical behaviours) are also influenced by the ethical environment created by their employers. Consider the following newspaper headlines that announce legal claims against organizations that failed to manage their employees ethically:

- "Home Depot Pays $87.5 Million for Not Promoting More Women"
- "Home Depot's Agreement to Settle Suit Could Cut 3rd-Quarter Earnings by 21%."[6]

As these headlines illustrate, poor business ethics can be very expensive for a company. Organizations can reduce the potential for these types of liability claims by educating their employees about ethical standards through various informal and formal programs. The first step, however, in making a good ethical decision is to recognize unethical business activities when they occur.

Recognizing Unethical Business Actions

Researchers from Brigham Young University tell us that all unethical business activities will fall into one of the following categories:

1. *Taking things that don't belong to you.* The unauthorized use of someone else's property or taking property under false pretences is taking something that does not belong to you. Even the smallest offence, such as using the postage meter at your office for mailing personal letters or exaggerating your travel expenses, belongs in this category of ethical violations.
2. *Saying things you know are not true.* Often, when trying for a promotion and advancement, fellow employees discredit their co-workers. Falsely assigning blame or inaccurately reporting conversations is lying. Although "This is the way the game is played around here" is a common justification, saying things that are untrue is an ethical violation.
3. *Giving or allowing false impressions.* The salesperson who permits a potential customer to believe that cardboard boxes will hold the customer's tomatoes for long-distance shipping when the salesperson knows the boxes are not strong enough has given a false impression. A car dealer who fails to disclose that a car has been in an accident is misleading potential customers.

4. *Buying influence or engaging in a conflict of interest.* A conflict of interest occurs when the official responsibilities of an employee or government official are influenced by the potential for personal gain. Suppose a company awards a construction contract to a firm owned by the father of the provincial attorney general while the provincial attorney general's office is investigating that company. If this construction award has the potential to shape the outcome of the investigation, a conflict of interest has occurred.

5. *Hiding or divulging information.* Failing to disclose the results of medical studies that indicate your firm's new drug has significant side effects is the ethical violation of hiding information that the product could be harmful to purchasers. Taking your firm's product development or trade secrets to a new place of employment constitutes the ethical violation of divulging proprietary information.

6. *Taking unfair advantage.* Many current consumer protection laws were passed because so many businesses took unfair advantage of people who were not educated or were unable to discern the nuances of complex contracts. Credit disclosure requirements, truth-in-lending provisions, and new regulations on auto leasing all resulted because businesses misled consumers who could not easily follow the jargon of long, complex agreements.

7. *Committing improper personal behaviour.* Although the ethical aspects of an employee's right to privacy are still debated, it has become increasingly clear that personal conduct outside the job can influence performance and company reputation. Thus, a company driver must abstain from substance abuse because of safety issues. Even the traditional company Christmas party and picnic have come under scrutiny due to the possibility that employees at and following these events might harm others through alcohol-related accidents.

8. *Abusing another person.* Suppose a manager sexually harasses an employee or subjects employees to humiliating corrections in the presence of customers. In some cases, laws protect employees. Many situations, however, are simply interpersonal abuse that constitutes an ethical violation.

9. *Permitting organizational abuse.* Many companies with operations outside of their own country have faced issues of organizational abuse. The unfair treatment of workers in international operations appears in the form of child labour, demeaning wages, and excessive work hours. Although a business cannot change the culture of another country, it can perpetuate—or stop—abuse through its operations there.

10. *Violating rules.* Many organizations use rules and processes to maintain internal controls or respect the authority of managers. Although these rules may seem burdensome to employees trying to serve customers, a violation may be considered an unethical act.

11. *Condoning unethical actions.* What if you witnessed a fellow employee embezzling company funds by forging her signature on a cheque that was to be voided? Would you report the violation? A winking tolerance of others' unethical behaviour is itself unethical.[7]

lg 6

Resolving Ethical Problems in Business

In many situations, there are no right or wrong answers. Instead, organizations must provide a process to resolve the dilemma quickly and fairly. Two approaches for resolving ethical problems are the "three-questions test" and the newspaper test.

HOT Links

Visit the Canadian Resources for Business Ethics site at
www.businessethics.ca

The Three-Questions Test

In evaluating an ethical problem, managers can use the three-questions test to determine the most ethical response: "Is it legal?" "Is it balanced?" and "How does it make me feel?" Many companies rely on this test to guide employee decision-making. If the answer to the first question is "no," then don't do it. Many ethical dilemmas, however, involve situations that aren't illegal. For example, the sale of tobacco is legal in Canada. But, given all the research that shows that tobacco use is dangerous to one's health, is it an ethical activity?

The second question, "Is it balanced?" requires you to put yourself in the position of other parties affected by your decision. For example, as an executive, you might not favour a buyout of your company because you will probably lose your job. Shareholders, however, may benefit substantially from the price to be paid for their shares in the buyout. At the same time, the employees of the business and their community may suffer economically if the purchaser decides to close the business or focus its efforts in a different product area. The best situation, of course, is when everybody wins or shares the burden equally.

The final question, "How does it make me feel?" asks you to examine your comfort with a particular decision. Many people find that after reaching a decision on an issue they still experience discomfort that may manifest itself in a loss of sleep or appetite. Those feelings of conscience can serve as a guide in resolving ethical dilemmas.

Front Page of the Newspaper Test

Many managers use the "front page of the newspaper test" for evaluating ethical dilemmas. The question to be asked is how a critical and objective reporter would report your decision in a front-page story. Some managers rephrase the test for their employees: How will the headline read if I make this decision? This test is helpful in spotting and resolving potential conflicts of interest. When Salomon Brothers experienced difficulties with federal regulators over securities transactions, its new CEO explained to employees that before making any choice or decision they should reflect on whether they would be willing to see it reported in a newspaper that their family, friends, and communities would read.[8]

Leading by Example

Employees often follow the examples set by their managers. That is, leaders and managers establish patterns of behaviour that determine what's acceptable and what's not within the organization. While Ben Cohen was president of Ben & Jerry's ice cream, he followed a policy that no one could earn a salary more than seven times the lowest-paid worker. He wanted all employees to feel that they were equal (remember the "balance question"). At the time he resigned, company sales were US$140 million and the lowest-paid worker earned US$19 000 per year. Ben Cohen's salary was US$133 000 based on the "seven times" rule. A typical top executive of a similar company might have earned ten times Cohen's salary. Ben Cohen's actions helped shape the ethical values of Ben & Jerry's.

Employees of Ben & Jerry's are influenced by the ethical values of company founders Ben Cohen and Jerry Greenfield, who created an environment of equity in compensating employees.

HOT Links

Ben & Jerry's recently announced that it would no longer use bleached paper for its ice cream cartons because the chemicals used in the bleaching process pollute the environment. For other environmentally friendly practices at Ben & Jerry's, go to www.benjerry.com/ our_company/about_us/ environment/2001/ page10.cfm

code of ethics
A set of guidelines prepared by a firm to provide its employees with the knowledge of what the firm expects in terms of their responsibilities and behaviour toward fellow employees, customers, and suppliers.

HOT Links

Discover what Texas Instruments' "Ethics Quick Test" includes at www.ti.com/corp/docs/ ethics/quicktest.html

Ethics Training

In addition to providing a system to resolve ethical dilemmas, organizations also provide formal training to develop an awareness of questionable business activities and to practise appropriate responses. The most effective ones begin with techniques for solving ethical dilemmas such as those discussed earlier. Next, employees are presented with a series of situations and asked to come up with the "best" ethical solution. One of these ethical dilemmas is shown in Exhibit 3-2.[9] Some companies have tried to add a bit of excitement and fun to their ethics training programs by presenting them in the form of games. Citigroup, for example, has created *The Work Ethic*, a board game in which participants strive to correctly answer legal, regulatory, policy-related, and judgment ethics questions.

Establishing a Formal Code of Ethics

Most large companies and thousands of smaller ones have created, printed, and distributed codes of ethics. In general, a **code of ethics** provides employees with the knowledge of what their firm expects in terms of their responsibilities and behaviour toward fellow employees, customers, and suppliers. Some ethical codes offer a lengthy and detailed set of guidelines for employees. Others are not really codes at all but rather summary statements of goals, policies, and priorities. Some companies have their codes framed and hung on office walls or printed on cards to be carried at all times by executives. The code of ethics for Nexen, Inc., is shown in Exhibit 3-3.

Do codes of ethics make employees behave in a more ethical manner? Some people believe that they do. Others think that they are little more than public relations gimmicks.

Fortunately, most workers only rarely face an ethical dilemma. A survey of 1002 adults found that 75 percent had never been asked or told to do something that they thought was unethical on the job.[10] Of those who were asked to do something unethical, four out of ten people did the unethical act. When asked what they would do if they found their boss doing something unethical, most (78 percent) said that they would try to talk to the boss or otherwise try to resolve the situation without losing their jobs. Nine percent said that they would "look the other way" and 5 percent claimed that they would quit. The rest weren't sure what they would do.

e x h i b i t 3 - 2	An Ethical Dilemma Used for Employee Training

Donations and Vendors

As CEO of a large Montreal hotel, you and your purchasing manager are in the midst of the annual review of several vendors' contracts. One of the suppliers is Sherman Distributors, a restaurant supply company that furnishes straws, salt, pepper, condiments, and related items for the restaurants and room service in your hotel. Your spouse, an associate dean at a local university's business school, has informed you that Sherman's CEO, who serves on the school's council of advisers, has mentioned Sherman's supply contract and a willingness to endow a scholarship fund. Your spouse's primary area of responsibility at the school is fund-raising.

Discussion Questions

1. What ethical issues does the situation raise?
2. Would it make a difference if Sherman's bid were the lowest?
3. Would renewing Sherman's contract create an appearance of impropriety?
4. What would you do to avoid negative perceptions?
5. Should the university be concerned about perceptions?

| Nexen's Code of Ethics

International Code of Ethics for Canadian Business[1]

Nexen helped develop this code in 1997 as a template for Canadian businesses to follow when conducting business at home and abroad. Since then, many businesses have adopted the code to ensure they operate ethically.

Vision

Canadian business has a global presence that is recognized by all stakeholders[2] as:

- economically rewarding to all parties,
- acknowledged as being ethically, socially and environmentally responsible,
- welcomed by the communities in which we operate, and
- facilitates economic, human resource and community development within a stable operating environment

We believe that:

- we can make a difference within our sphere of influence (stakeholders);
- business should take a leadership role through establishment of ethical business practices;
- national governments have the prerogative to conduct their own government and legal affairs in accordance with their sovereign rights;
- all governments should comply with international treaties and other agreements that they have committed to, including the areas of human rights and social justice;
- while reflecting cultural diversity and differences, we should do business throughout the world consistent with the way we do business in Canada;
- the business sector should show ethical leadership;
- we can facilitate the achievement of wealth generation and a fair sharing of economic benefits;
- our principles will assist in improving relations between the Canadian and host governments;
- open, honest and transparent relationships are critical to our success;
- local communities need to be involved in decision-making for issues that affect them;
- multi-stakeholder processes need to be initiated to seek effective solutions;
- confrontation should be tempered by diplomacy;
- wealth maximization for all stakeholders will be enhanced by resolution of outstanding human rights and social justice issues; and
- doing business with other countries is good for Canada and vice versa.

We value:

- human rights and social justice;
- wealth maximization for all stakeholders;
- operation of a free market economy;
- public accountability by governments;
- a business environment that militates against bribery and corruption;
- equality of opportunity;
- a defined code of ethics and business practice;
- protection of environmental quality and sound environmental stewardship;
- community benefits;
- good relationships with all stakeholders; and
- stability and continuous improvement within our operating environment.

Principles

A. Concerning community participation and environmental protection, we will:
- strive within our sphere of influence to ensure a fair share of benefits to stakeholders impacted by our activities;

continued

e x h i b i t   3 - 3 | continued

- ensure meaningful and transparent consultation with all stakeholders and attempt to integrate our corporate activities
- ensure our activities are consistent with sound environmental management and conservation practices; and
- provide meaningful opportunities for technology cooperation, training and capacity building within the host nation.

B. Concerning human rights, we will:
- support and respect the protection of international human rights within our sphere of influence;
- not be complicit in human rights abuses.

C. Concerning business conduct, we will:
- not make illegal and improper payments and bribes and will refrain from participating in any corrupt business practices;
- comply with all applicable laws and conduct business activities with integrity; and
- ensure contractors,' suppliers' and agents' activities are consistent with these principles.

D. Concerning employee rights and health and safety, we will:
- ensure health and safety of workers is protected;
- strive for social justice and respect freedom of association and expression in the workplace; and
- ensure consistency with other universally accepted labour standards related to exploitation of child labour, forced labour and non-discrimination in employment.

Footnotes
1. The Code is a statement of values/principles designed to facilitate and assist individual firms in developing their policies and practices that are consistent with the visions, beliefs, and principles contained herein.
2. Should include local communities, Canadian and host governments, local governments, shareholders, the media, customers and suppliers, interest groups and international agencies.

SOURCE: Reprinted by permission of Nexen, Inc.

concept check

- Discuss two approaches to resolving ethical problems.
- What is the role of top management in organizational ethics?
- What is a code of ethics?

➡ **lg 7**

Managing to Be Socially Responsible

Founded in 1995, Canadian Business for Social Responsibility (CBSR) is the reference point for responsible business in Canada. According to its mission statement, "CBSR defines, promotes and educates responsible business policies and practices that benefit our society, our economy, and our environment."[11] As a national not-for-profit membership organization, CBSR's mandate is to help businesses integrate financial, social, and environmental performance into their business practices. Over the past several years, market forces and market failures have motivated greater corporate responsibility for organizations wishing to promote consumer confidence. "Consumers today want proof that a company deserves their trust—and their investment."[12] Today corporations are recognized as being an integral part of the community, and organizational sustainability and community health have never been more important. Companies that are perceived to be socially responsible are also perceived to be better able to offer the consumers and communities real value for the goods and services that they provide without harming people or the environment.[13]

According to its Web site, CBSR and its members are committed to implementing those policies that demonstrate their social responsibilities. Each of its members is committed to "ensuring shared prosperity of shareholders, staff, the environment, as well as local and international communities; and fostering an exchange of ideas and information within the business community."[14] Some of the programs and services that the CBSR provides are the tracking of emerging issues and trends, providing information on corporate best practices, conducting research and educational workshops, and developing practical business tools, technical assistance, and consulting services to help the member companies implement more responsible policies into their own business.[15]

Many people and businesses assume that corporate social responsibility and regular good works are the same thing. But according to the CBSR, corporate social responsibility goes beyond such good works as volunteerism and charity. Companies that practise corporate social responsibility develop and practise policies and programs in areas such as "employee relations, community development, environmental stewardship, international relations, marketplace practices, fiscal responsibility and accountability."[16]

CBSR defines social responsibility as "a company's commitment to operating in an economically and environmentally sustainable manner while recognizing the interests of its stakeholders."[17] As we will see later in this chapter, stakeholders include anyone or any organization that has an interest in the organization. Stakeholders include the investors or shareholders (those with a financial interest), employees, customers, suppliers (business partners), governments, local communities, the environment, and society as a whole.

"Many of today's successful companies are operating with their stakeholders in mind. Their progressive corporate social performance contributes to their long-term financial viability, which further promotes healthy communities and stable economies."[18] Research conducted at the Canadian Centre for Social Performance and Ethics at the University of Toronto indicates that over the longer term, companies that are most profitable also rate highest on ethics and corporate social responsibility.[19] Just how does corporate social responsibility positively affect the bottom line? Some examples include:

- Reduced operating costs.
- Enhanced brand and image reputation.
- Increased sales and customer loyalty.
- Increased ability to attract and retain employees.
- Publicity and increased public image from good works.[20]

Just how can a company become more socially responsible? The CBSR has developed ten steps to corporate social responsibility, as shown in Exhibit 3-4.

Acting in an ethical manner is one of the four components of the pyramid of corporate social responsibility. **Social responsibility** is the concern of businesses for the welfare of society as a whole. It consists of obligations beyond those required by law or union contract. This definition makes two important points. First, social responsibility is voluntary. Beneficial action required by law, such as cleaning up factories that are

social responsibility
The concern of businesses for the welfare of society as a whole; consists of obligations beyond those required by law or contracts.

e x h i b i t   3 - 4 | Ten Steps to Corporate Social Responsibility

1. Involve employees in decision-making.
2. Create opportunities for employee ownership and profit sharing.
3. Promote from within and institute fair and open performance management practices.
4. Develop an employee volunteer program.
5. Practise the three R's—reduce, reuse and recycle.
6. Develop an ethical purchasing policy.
7. Donate 1 percent of pre-tax profits back to the community.
8. Work in partnership with community groups to achieve mutual goals.
9. Audit social and environmental performance.
10. Be profitable!

SOURCE: Canadian Business for Social Responsibility, "10 Steps to CSR," www.cbsr.bc.ca/what_is_csr/10steps.cfm, accessed May 23, 2002.

HOT Links

Find out what's new at Canadian Business for Social Responsibility at www.cbsr.ca

stakeholders
Individuals or groups (including organizations) to whom the business has a responsibility; including the investors or shareholders (those with a financial interest), employees, customers, suppliers (business partners), governments, local communities, the environment, and society as a whole.

polluting air and water, is not voluntary. Second, the obligations of social responsibility are broad. They extend beyond investors (those with a financial interest in the company) to include all stakeholders. **Stakeholders** are individuals or groups (including organizations) to whom the business has a responsibility, including the investors or shareholders, employees, customers, suppliers (business partners), governments, local communities, the environment, and society as a whole.

Exhibit 3-5 portrays economic performance as the foundation for the other three responsibilities. At the same time that a business pursues profits (economic responsibility), however, it is expected to obey the law (legal responsibility); to do what is right, just, and fair (ethical responsibility); and to be a good corporate citizen (philanthropic responsibility). These four components are distinct but together constitute the whole. Still, if the company doesn't make a profit, then the other three responsibilities are moot.

Understanding Social Responsibility

Peter Drucker, a management expert, said that we should look first at what an organization does to society and second at what it can do for society. This idea suggests that social responsibility has two basic dimensions: legality and responsibility.

Illegal and Irresponsible Behaviour

The idea of social responsibility is so widespread today that it is hard to conceive of a company continually acting in illegal and irresponsible ways. Nevertheless, such actions do sometimes occur. For example, Royal Caribbean Cruise Lines, the world's second-largest cruise line, had to pay a US$9 million fine for dumping oily bilge waste into the ocean and then lying about it.[21] Federal, provincial, and local laws determine whether an activity is legal or not.

Irresponsible but Legal Behaviour

Sometimes companies act irresponsibly, yet their actions are legal. For example, if a company knows that certain standards are not safe for a product, but the legislation has not been changed to reflect newer standards, and the company continues to produce a product with the old standards as their guideline, such actions could be considered irresponsible.

| The Pyramid of Corporate Social Responsibility

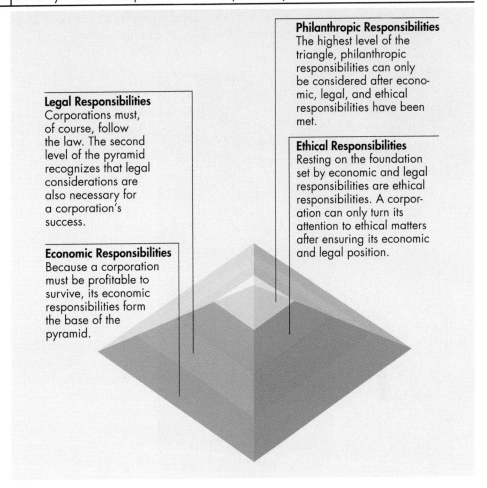

Philanthropic Responsibilities
The highest level of the triangle, philanthropic responsibilities can only be considered after economic, legal, and ethical responsibilities have been met.

Legal Responsibilities
Corporations must, of course, follow the law. The second level of the pyramid recognizes that legal considerations are also necessary for a corporation's success.

Ethical Responsibilities
Resting on the foundation set by economic and legal responsibilities are ethical responsibilities. A corporation can only turn its attention to ethical matters after ensuring its economic and legal position.

Economic Responsibilities
Because a corporation must be profitable to survive, its economic responsibilities form the base of the pyramid.

Legal and Responsible Behaviour

The vast majority of business activities fall into the category of behaviour that is both legal and responsible. Most firms act legally, and most try to be socially responsible. This would be the case of most companies' employment practices.

Making Ethical Choices

Should business be socially responsible? Can business be socially responsible? Some executives, such as Randall Gossen of Nexen, believe that business can and should be socially responsible. Some executives say that the marketplace alone is insufficient for achieving social responsibility. These executives are calling "faith in value-free, self-regulating markets a dangerous illusion and urging governments to protect people and the planet before it's too late." Other people, however, believe that business should be ethically neutral and focus on profit as the primary measure of corporate success. They argue that the most socially responsible thing a business can do is to make as much profit as possible.

concept check

- What are the four components of social responsibility?
- Give an example of legal but irresponsible behaviour.

→ lg 8

Responsibilities to Stakeholders

What makes a company admired or perceived as socially responsible? Such a company meets its obligations to its stakeholders.

CIBC's sponsorship of the Run for the Cure represents a legal and socially responsible activity that also serves to enhance the image of the bank in the eyes of many consumers.

consumer fraud
The practice of deceiving customers by such means as failing to honour warranties or other promises or selling goods or services that do not meet advertised claims.

Responsibility to Employees

An organization's first responsibility is to provide a job to employees. Keeping people employed and letting them have time to enjoy the fruits of their labour is the finest thing business can do for society. Beyond this fundamental responsibility, employers must provide a clean, safe working environment that is free from all forms of discrimination. Companies should also strive to provide job security whenever possible.

Enlightened firms are also empowering employees to make decisions on their own and suggest solutions to company problems. Empowerment contributes to an employee's self-worth, which, in turn, increases productivity and reduces absenteeism. The Ritz Carlton hotel chain, for example, empowers all employees to solve any guest problem on the spot. Dana Corp., an automotive-components manufacturer, has created a culture where empowerment has become a reality. The company has implemented a number of programs and practices that encourage and recognize individual contributions. These include a commitment to 40 hours of education for each employee every year, an internal promotion policy in which the people who help create the company's success share in the rewards, a suggestion system in which each employee is encouraged to submit two ideas per month and the company strives for 80 percent implementation of those ideas, an organizational structure that supports individual responsibility, a retirement program that encourages longevity, and a stock-purchase program that encourages eligible employees to own a share of the company.

Responsibility to Customers

A central theme of this text is that to be successful in the new millennium a company must satisfy its customers. Satisfied customers lead to long-term relationships and a long-term stream of revenue and profits for the firm. Poor customer service or shoddy products will drive customers away. However, nothing drives customers away faster or breaks the bonds of a long-term relationship more quickly than failure to treat a customer fairly or honestly.

Iomega Corp. learned this lesson the hard way. Recently, the company agreed to provide free customer support via the Internet or by telephone as part of a settlement of a **consumer-fraud** lawsuit. The lawsuit accused the disk drive maker of not honouring product warranties and failing to provide adequate technical support. Customers said they had trouble installing Iomega products despite packaging claims that installation was easy. When they tried to call Iomega, they learned the company charged up to US$19.99 for the help. Even then, they had trouble getting help because technical-support lines were severely understaffed. Customers were often left waiting on hold for an hour or more.[22]

HOT Links

Levi Strauss's unique corporate culture rewards and recognizes employee achievements. To learn about working for a company that values employees' efforts, go to the Levi Strauss home page at www.levistrauss.com

Responsibility to Suppliers

As noted in Chapter 2, many companies rely on other companies for their survival. Often companies hire other companies to provide products or perform services for them. These suppliers (or business partners) are usually contracted because they can provide the products or perform the service cheaper. Mark's Work Wearhouse, for example does not produce its own line of clothing for resale, but contacts it out to its suppliers. These suppliers are employing people, in turn providing more money to fuel the economy. It is important that businesses support their suppliers (e.g., giving contracts, paying supplier invoices, etc.). As we will see in Chapter 4, many companies are tying the e-business technology to their suppliers to realize many of the efficiencies that this can provide.

Responsibility to the Governments

Governments in Canada rely on tax dollars in order to operate and provide their services to Canadians. Much of the tax revenue that the governments collect is in the form of corporate taxes (see Chapter 7). Corporations are responsible for accurately reporting their earnings and fulfilling their tax obligations.

Responsibility to the General Public

Businesses must also be responsible to the general public. A business provides a community with jobs, goods, and services. It must accurately report its earnings and tax responsibilities to the government (and pay tax obligations) to help pay to support schools, hospitals, better roads, and so on.

To preserve the environment, businesses as well as the general population must become more environmentally responsible.

corporate philanthropy
The practice of charitable giving by corporations; includes contributing cash, donating equipment and products, and supporting the volunteer efforts of company employees.

Environmental Protection

Business is also responsible for protecting and improving the world's fragile environment. The world's forests are being destroyed fast. Every second, an area the size of a football field is laid bare. Plant and animal species are becoming extinct at the rate of 17 per hour. A continent-size hole is opening up in the earth's protective ozone shield.

To slow the erosion of the world's resources, many companies are becoming more environmentally responsible. Canadian Tire, for example, strives to divert as much waste as possible from landfills. Since 1990 it has implemented aggressive pallet reuse and packaging recycling programs.[23]

Corporate Philanthropy

Companies also display their social responsibility through corporate philanthropy. **Corporate philanthropy** includes cash contributions, donations of equipment and products, and support for the volunteer efforts of company employees. General Motors of Canada Limited (GMCL) has an impressive record of responding to the needs of the community. GMCL's donations of cash, in-kind donations, and, the most precious of all, volunteerism of its employee's time demonstrate the company's commitment to the communities it serves.

More and more companies are donating products and research findings rather than cash. IBM, for example, donates about US$100 million a year to various organizations. About US$70 million of IBM's donations are in non-cash items. Recently, Merck, the giant pharmaceutical firm, donated US$5 million in cash and US$116 million in non-cash items to various charitable causes.[24] Such giving makes business sense because companies can value their donations at fair-market prices, rather than the cost

HOT Links

Find out more about General Motors of Canada Limited's commitment to the environment and the communities it serves at

www.gmcanada.com

social investing
The practice of limiting investments to securities of companies that behave in accordance with the investor's beliefs about ethical and social responsibility.

to produce them. Better yet, a generous tax law allows corporations to write off the cost of producing the donation as well as the difference between the cost and retail value. In contrast, a business that donates $1 million in cash can write off only that amount.

Responsibilities to Investors (Shareholders)

Companies' relationships with investors also entail social responsibility. Although a company's economic responsibility to make a profit might seem to be its main obligation to its shareholders, many investors increasingly are putting more emphasis on other aspects of social responsibility.

Some investors are limiting their investments to securities that fit within their beliefs about ethical and social responsibility. This is called **social investing.** For example, a social investment fund might eliminate from consideration the securities of all companies that make tobacco products or liquor, manufacture weapons, or have a history of polluting.

When investors are dissatisfied with corporate managers, they are less passive than in the past. They are pressuring corporations with tactics such as exposés on television and other media and calling government attention to perceived wrongdoings. Groups of owners are pressuring companies to increase profits, link executive pay to performance, and oust inefficient management. Consequently, executives and managers are giving more weight to the concerns of owner stakeholders in the decision-making process.

concept check

- How do businesses carry out their social responsibilities to consumers?
- What is corporate philanthropy?
- Is a company's only responsibility to its investors to make a profit? Why or why not?

➡ lg 9

CAPITALIZING ON TRENDS IN BUSINESS

Three important trends related to ethics and social responsibility for the new millennium are changes in corporate philanthropy, a new social contract between employers and employees, and the growth of global ethics and social responsibility. This section will examine each trend in turn.

Trends in Corporate Philanthropy

strategic giving
The practice of tying philanthropy closely to the corporate mission or goals and targeting donations to regions where a company operates.

Corporate philanthropy has typically involved seeking out needy groups and then giving them money or company products. Today, the focus is shifting to **strategic giving,** which ties philanthropy more closely to the corporate mission or goals and targets donations to regions where a company operates.

Thomas Kimble is the chairman of the General Motors Foundation, which is General Motor's philanthropic organization. Kimble notes, "Prior to 1997 our giving was simply for unselfish purposes. Now our thinking is that we need to balance unselfish giving with strategic donations to target groups." Most of the foundation's gifts now go to areas such as education, health and human services, and public policy

Computer firms that link their product donations to schools with their corporate goals represent the corporate philanthropy trend of strategic giving.

that are related to GM's corporate goals such as lowering costs. Funding for research on a major health threat such as cancer makes both social and economical sense, GM believes. "Health care was the company's highest cost, so funding health, especially cancer-related research, became a priority," explains Kimble.[25]

IBM Canada Ltd, headquartered in Markham, Ontario, with many operations throughout Canada, combines its technology and its people to bring solutions to problems that impact society, business, and quality of life. IBM's focus is primarily kindergarten to Grade 12 and preschool education, and work force development. IBM also supports other areas including health, human welfare, and the arts. Corporate contributions valued at more than $2.2 million (in the form of IBM technology and cash) in 2001, have benefited Canadian communities.

In addition, IBM employees and its retirees pledged $2.9 million in personal donations to more than 1000 registered charities across Canada through its Employee Charitable Fund Campaign. "More than 40 IBM employees volunteered their time for a number of new Women in Technology initiatives (Exploring Interests in Technology and Engineering—EXITE summer camp; e-Mentoring) for Grade 7 and 8 girls, designed to stimulate their ongoing interest in maths and sciences. In total, IBMers volunteered more than 400 000 hours of their personal time supporting their communities."[26]

A New Social Contract Trend between Employer and Employee

Another trend in social responsibility is the effort by organizations to redefine their relationship with their employees. Many people have viewed social responsibility as a one-way street that focuses on the obligations of business to society, employees, and others. Now, companies are telling employees that they also have a responsibility when it comes to job security. The new contract goes like this: "There will never be job security. You will be employed by us as long as you add value to the organization, and you are continuously responsible for finding ways to add value. In return, you have the right to demand interesting and important work, the freedom and resources to perform it well, pay that reflects your contribution, and the experience and training needed to be employable here or elsewhere." Coca-Cola, for example, requires extensive employee retraining each year. The idea, according to a Coke executive, is to become a more valuable employee by adding 25 percent to your existing knowledge every year.

Trends in Global Ethics and Social Responsibility

As Canadian businesses expand into global markets, their corporate codes of ethics and policies on social responsibility must travel with them. As a citizen of several countries, a multinational corporation has several responsibilities. These include respecting local practices and customs, ensuring that there is harmony between the organization's staff and the host population, providing management leadership, and developing a cadre of local managers who will be a credit to their community. When a multinational makes an investment in a foreign country, it should commit to a long-term relationship. That means involving all stakeholders in the host country in decision-making.

If consumers believe a firm is acting unethically in their dealings with offshore manufacturers, the consumers may boycott the company's products.

Finally, a responsible multinational will implement ethical guidelines within the organization in the host country. By fulfilling these responsibilities, the company will foster respect for both local and international laws.

Canada is a member of the Organization for Economic Cooperation and Development (OECD) and has signed the OECD Guidelines for Multinational Enterprises. These guidelines present voluntary principles for responsible business conduct. The guidelines encourage operations of the enterprises that are consistent with government policies, mutual confidence between the enterprises and the society in which they are operating in, improvement of the foreign investment climate, and enhancement of the enterprises' contribution to sustainable development.[27]

HOT Links

For further study of OECD and its guidelines, visit the Web site at www.ncp-pcn.gc.ca

concept check

- Describe strategic giving.
- What role do employees have in improving their job security?

APPLYING THIS CHAPTER'S TOPICS

Are you at the preconventional, conventional, or postconventional stage of ethical development? If you determine that you are at the preconventional level, you should begin striving for a more mature ethical outlook. This may mean taking an ethics course, reading a book on ethics, or engaging in a lot of introspection about yourself and your values. A person with preconventional ethics will probably have a difficult time succeeding in today's business world.

Ethics Are Part of Everyday Life

Realize that ethics play a part in our lives every day. We all must answer questions such as these:

- How do I balance the time and energy obligations of my work and my family?
- How much should I pay my employees?
- What should I do with the child of my husband's first marriage who is disrupting our new family?
- How am I spending my money?
  Should I "borrow" a copy of my friend's software?
- If I know my employee is having troubles at home, should I treat her differently?
- What should I do if I know a neighbour's child is getting into serious trouble?
- How do I react to a sexist or racist joke?

Too many people make decisions about everyday questions without considering the underlying moral and ethical framework of the problems. They are simply swept along by the need to get through the day. Our challenge to you is to always think about the ethical consequences of your actions. Make doing so a habit.

Waiting for dramatic events before consciously tackling ethical considerations is like playing a sport only on the weekend. Just as a weekend warrior often ends up with pulled muscles and poor performance, people who seldom consider the ethical implications of daily activities won't have the coordination to work through the more difficult times in their lives. Don't let this happen to you.

Work for a Firm That Cares about Its Social Responsibilities

When you enter the job market, make certain that you are going to work for a socially responsible organization. Ask a prospective employer how the company gives back to society. Do your research! Not only can you ask your prospective employer, but check with other people and Web sites that offer information about the company.

at Nexen

Nexen has demonstrated social responsibility through such projects as education provided for members of the local communities in which they operate and other community-based projects. Read about Nexen's experience in Yemen on their Web site at **www.nexeninc.com**.

As Nexen continues its exploration for oil and gas in other parts of the world, how else can they demonstrate socially responsible behaviours to enhance the lives of the people in the host countries?

1. **Support a Good Cause** You don't have to wait until graduation to start demonstrating your social responsibility. Look in your community for organizations that use volunteers that interest you. Donate your time, energies, money, and so forth, to help to make a difference to your community. Here are some suggestions:

   - Check with a local school that offers classes (any grade range from kindergarten to Grade 12) that uses volunteers and get involved.

   - Look for charitable organizations in your area that are in need of volunteers and get involved.

2. **Know Your Ethical Values** To get a better idea of your own level of ethical development, take an ethics test. Go to www.ethicsandbusiness.org/stylequiz.htm. This test will give you better insight into yourself.

3. **Find Out More** Check out the following Web sites for relevant and useful information on ethics in business:

   - www.transparency.ca (Transparency International in Canada)

   - www.wbcsd.ch (World Business Council for Sustainable Development)

   - www.traceinternational.org (Transparent Agents and Contracting Entities)

SUMMARY OF LEARNING GOALS

➡️ **lg 1 How is the trend of changing lifestyles affecting business?**

The business environment consists of social, demographic, economic, technological, and competitive trends. Managers cannot control environmental trends. Instead, they must understand how the environment is changing and the impact of those changes on the business. Several trends are currently influencing businesses. First, people of all ages have a broader range of interests and are defying traditional consumer profiles. Second, changing gender roles are bringing more women into the work force. This trend is increasing family incomes, heightening demand for time-saving goods and services, and changing family shopping patterns.

➡️ **lg 2 How are changing demographic trends creating more opportunities for business?**

Businesses today must deal with the unique shopping preferences of Generations X and Y and the baby boomers. Each must be appealed to in a different way with different goods and services. Generation Y, for example, is the most computer literate and the most interested in computers and accessories. And because the population is growing older, businesses are offering more products that appeal to middle-aged and elderly markets. As we continue to become a multicultural marketplace, new opportunities for business are being created.

➡️ **lg 3 Why is an understanding of demographic trends important for the marketing of goods and services?**

Changing demographics affect the marketing of our goods and services. As Canadians are becoming more health conscious, for instance, companies should promote the "healthiness" of our goods and services. As our population ages and becomes more technically sophisticated, we need to search for new marketing streams that will encourage our target market to purchase our goods and services.

➡️ **lg 4 What philosophies and concepts shape personal ethical standards, and what are the stages of ethical development?**

Ethics is a set of moral standards for judging whether something is right or wrong. A utilitarianism approach to setting personal ethical standards focuses on the consequences of an action taken by a person or organization. According to this approach, people should act so as to generate the greatest good for the greatest number. Every human is entitled to certain rights such as freedom and the pursuit of happiness. Another approach to ethical decision making is justice, or what is fair according to accepted standards.

There are three stages of ethical development. At the level of preconventional ethics, behaviour is childlike in nature and self-centred. Conventional ethics moves from an egocentric point of view toward the expectations of society or an organization. Postconventional ethics represents the ethical standards of the mature adult.

➡️ **lg 5 How can organizations influence organizational ethics?**

The first step management should take is to recognize the categories of unethical business actions. Managers should educate employees to use the three-questions test or the front page of the newspaper test when faced with ethical dilemmas. Top management must shape the ethical culture of the organization. They should lead by example.

➡️ **lg 6 What are the techniques for creating employee ethical awareness?**

The most common way companies raise employee ethical awareness is through ethics training. Typically, this involves analyzing and discussing ethical dilemmas. Companies also create and distribute codes of ethics to heighten ethical awareness.

➡ lg 7 **What is social responsibility?**

Social responsibility is the concern of businesses for the welfare of society as a whole. It consists of obligations beyond just making a profit. Social responsibility also goes beyond what is required by law or union contract. Companies may engage in illegal and irresponsible behaviour, irresponsible but legal behaviour, or legal and responsible behaviour. The vast majority of organizations act legally and try to be socially responsible.

➡ lg 8 **How do businesses meet their social responsibilities to various stakeholders?**

Stakeholders are individuals or groups to whom business has a responsibility. Businesses are responsible to employees. They should provide a clean, safe working environment. Organizations can build employees' self-worth through empowerment programs. Businesses also have a responsibility to customers to provide good, safe products and services. Organizations are responsible to the general public to be good corporate citizens. Firms must help protect the environment and provide a good place to work. Companies also engage in corporate philanthropy, which includes contributing cash, donating goods and services, and supporting volunteer efforts of employees. Finally, companies are responsible to investors. They should earn a reasonable profit for the owners.

➡ lg 9 **What are the global and domestic trends in ethics and social responsibility?**

Today, corporate philanthropy is shifting away from simply giving to any needy group and is focusing instead on strategic giving, in which the philanthropy relates more closely to the corporate mission or goals and targets donations to areas where the firm operates. Corporate philanthropy is coming under increasing attacks from special-interest groups, however.

A second trend is toward a new social contract between employer and employee. Instead of the employer having the sole responsibility for maintaining jobs, now the employee must assume part of the burden and find ways to add value to the organization.

As the world increasingly becomes a global community, multinational corporations are now expected to assume a global set of ethics and responsibility. Global companies must understand local customs. They should also involve local stakeholders in decision making. Multinationals must also make certain that their suppliers are not engaged in human rights violations.

WORKING THE NET

1. Visit the Web site of the People for the Ethical Treatment of Animals (PETA) at **www.furisdead.com**. Read about PETA's view of the fur industry. Do you agree or disagree with this view? Why? How do you think manufacturers who make fur clothing would justify their actions to someone from PETA? Would you work for a store that offered fur-trimmed clothing in addition to other items? Explain your answer.

2. Use a major search engine such as Yahoo (**www.yahoo.com**) or Lycos (**www.lycos.com**) to look for several examples of corporate codes of ethics. What common elements appear in the examples you found? Suggest how one of the codes could be improved.

3. At **www.goodmoney.com/wpubco.htm**, you will find a list of public companies that have been identified as being socially responsible. Pick one of the companies and find its Internet home page (Yahoo at **www.yahoo.com** is one way to find this). Read about the firm's operations and marketing efforts. Do you agree or disagree that this firm is socially responsible? Give specific examples from the company's Web site to support your answer.

CREATIVE THINKING CASE

Geekcorps: From Dot.com to Dot.org

What would you do if you helped start a successful Internet company and made your first million before you turned 30? If you're Ethan Zuckerman, you found Geekcorps (**www.Geekcorps.org**), a nonprofit organization with the goal of spreading electronic commerce to developing nations.

Zuckerman, a 1993 graduate of Williams College, made his fortune as vice president of research and development at Tripod, an online personal publishing site. When Lycos bought Tripod in 1999, Zuckerman became an instant millionaire. With $100 000 of his own money, Zuckerman started Geekcorps in 2000. Geekcorps hopes to send techno-savvy volunteers to countries like Ghana, Nicaragua, and Bolivia, where Internet technology is limited. The volunteers, on sabbaticals from their current jobs, will spend three months in each country helping local firms and governments develop and implement electronic commerce initiatives.

Zuckerman says he has no lack of volunteers interested in joining Geekcorps. "My generation has made a lot of money at a very young age," says Zuckerman. "Rather than the Yuppie boom of the '80s and '90s where wealth led to excess, I believe we'll see people interested in building things intelligently."

Sending Geekcorps volunteers abroad, however, will take more capital than Zuckerman's initial investment. It will cost about $10 000 for each three-month volunteer stint. Zuckerman has already secured some contributions, including $250 000 from Tripod's founder Bo Peabody. Zuckerman hopes to convince more private and corporate donors to contribute. "If I can give $100 000 just with my modest net worth, others in the industry can give a lot more," he says.

To raise the needed funds, Zuckerman says Geekcorps needs to get creative. He arranged a partnership with Dewar's, the whisky brand, that will feature Geekcorps in Dewar's ads. He hopes to convince emerging high-technology firms to place a small percentage of their initial stock in Geekcorps's name. As these firms mature, Geekcorps would receive dividends from the stock. Zuckerman is considering other plans as well, such as starting a for-profit consulting arm of Geekcorps.[28]

Critical Thinking Questions

1. If you were Ethan Zuckerman, how would you explain to high-technology firms why contributing to Geekcorps would be a strategic giving choice?
2. Do you think other consumer goods firms like Dewar's would see this as an opportunity to meet their social responsibilities to employees, customers, or investors? Explain.
3. Do you agree with Zuckerman's assessment that the generation building their wealth from electronic commerce will be more likely to take on social causes?

CHAPTER 4

Technology, the Internet, and Business Success

In this chapter you'll learn about the last piece of our PEST model puzzle—the *technological* environment.

This is a wonderful example of the integrative nature of business because technology permeates just about every aspect of our model. To begin with, it affects a company's ability to meet its critical success factors. *Financial performance* is affected by technology because a firm can operate more efficiently and, therefore, increase its bottom line using technology. Technology also gives businesses quicker and better access to information on customer needs. And *customer needs* are better met through the speed with which technology helps us deliver on our promises and provide customer service. In fact, even greater needs can be met with expanded product offerings because the Internet does not have the physical limits of a typical store—any number of items can be sold through a single Web site. *Quality* is also enhanced through the use of technology. In fact, *innovations* have allowed us to make quality a priority at all levels of an organization. The rate of these and other innovations has been sped up to "warp speed" due to technology. And finally, *employees are more committed* to meeting company goals because companies can make their jobs more interesting by having the most repetitive and monotonous jobs completed through the use of technology instead of valuable human resources. So technology can definitely help a business be more successful, and given that the rapid pace of technological change is a reality for today's business, it is in fact a necessity for success.

Technology as an environmental factor affects the other factors in our PEST model also. For example, in the *political* environment, the government issues patents on new technology preventing other firms from copying that technology. This gives a company an advantage over other firms for years to come. *Economically*, we have seen recently how the rapid growth of technological firms can fuel the stock market to the point of overvalue and then rapid adjustment, to the shock of many investors. Technology also changes the nature of competition. As you'll read in the chapter, the Internet has removed the geographic and time-related limits to doing business. Customers no longer have to visit a store during business hours—companies don't even have to have a store! And the traditional relationship between manufacturers, distributors, and retailers has changed because companies can bypass these channels by selling directly over the Internet. *Socially*, it is clear that technology has changed how we as consumers see the world—it has given us much more access to information, making us better equipped to make buying decisions and more demanding in terms of the speed with which we expect our needs to be met. It is also important to understand, as the chapter explains, that as new technologies are adopted they "promote another wave of technological innovation." So technology enhances our ability to create more technology.

Technology also affects how companies operate. It affects the way businesses communicate and share information in all areas of the company. It also affects each specific functional area. For example, *operationally* it affects how products are built (using computers to design products and guide manufacturing), as well as what products are built (as technology allows for greater customization to meet customer needs). It affects how products are *marketed* (such as through the Internet using e-commerce). It also affects how products are *financed*. Technology has had such an impact on capital markets that it's becoming very difficult for new technology firms to sell their stock to the public and generate much-needed funds for expansion to raise money. Even the *human resource* function is affected by technology because computers can take over many tasks done by humans, and companies have the added demand of finding the best people with the necessary skills to use technology and manage technology workers.

The very nature of business has changed dramatically with technology. E-business has revolutionized the way business is done. It has affected the overall *strategies* of many organizations as it has created a new paradigm for business. As the chapter indicates, we have moved beyond the individual enterprise to an interconnected economy. As businesses become more interconnected between suppliers, manufacturers, and retailers, they operate more as one company. This allows them to better meet the needs of the customer, providing a seamless integration from the beginning of the business chain to the ultimate consumer.

Technology, the Internet, and Business Success

CHAPTER 4

Learning Goals

➡ **lg 1** What is the Internet, and how does it work?

➡ **lg 2** Who uses the Internet, and for what purpose?

➡ **lg 3** How has the Internet economy changed the business environment?

➡ **lg 4** How can companies incorporate e-business and e-commerce into their overall business strategies?

➡ **lg 5** What benefits do businesses achieve through e-business and e-commerce?

➡ **lg 6** What steps are involved in launching an e-business and e-commerce venture?

➡ **lg 7** What lies ahead for the Information Superhighway?

Mark's Work Wearhouse: An E-Business Success Story

According to Robin Lynas, the chief information officer for Mark's Work Wearhouse (MWW), the company's e-business strategy is to "build an integrated multichannel retailing environment." This strategy is based on the key customer requirements of convenience, access to products, brand loyalty, selection, and information. The main challenges for MWW are the dynamic retail environment and rapidly changing technologies. With over 320 stores and sales exceeding $525 million per year, these challenges require a comprehensive understanding of the organization and its strategies.

MWW is one of Canada's largest retail clothing chains whose customers include both individuals and corporations. Its target market is defined as "anyone who typically does not wear a suit and tie to work and those customers who have needs for casual outdoor clothing and footwear." The company has been successful, in part, by developing computer applications that put timely customer information in the hands of its sales force. Every MWW store is linked to a database that provides information on sales and inventory levels, replenishes inventories at the SKU (stock-keeping unit—the bar code attached to each product) level by store, and reports gross margins as well as expenses by individual store.

"We have become less 'techie' and much more strategic in our approach to e-business and have become very successful," says Lynas. E-commerce (the actual exchange of transactions using electronic technology and part of e-business) accounts for less than 10 percent of their e-business. "Our philosophy has been to understand our business, including our customers, and develop an infrastructure that responds to the needs of our stakeholders."

The electronic culture (or e-culture) at MWW incorporates three primary focuses: business-to-business (B2B), business-to-consumer (B2C), and business-to-enterprise (B2E), as shown in the model on the following page.

B2B incorporates both its suppliers and corporate customers. Each of the stores maintains its minimal level of stock according to product and size. Once the inventory of a particular product reaches its minimal level in the store, an automatic message is sent to the supplier for replenishing (60 percent of suppliers are domestic and concentrated in the Toronto–Montreal corridor). The supplier completes the order, and all stock for each particular store is then packaged together and transported to the distribution centre where the packages are sorted and sent to the appropriate stores. (MWW picks up the orders from its domestic suppliers twice a week.) This procedure ensures that stock levels are maintained (therefore, maximizing sales) and markdowns are kept to a minimum.

MWW has been very responsive to its corporate customers. The "Product Knowledge Database" and catalogues specific to a particular customer have been

CRITICAL THINKING QUESTIONS

As you read this chapter, consider the following questions as they relate to Mark's Work Wearhouse:

- What is the difference between e-business and e-commerce? How does MWW use each to satisfy customers' requirements?
- What are the advantages and disadvantages to the company and the customer of online retailing?
- Identify some of the reasons why MWW has been successful in the retail market.
- Are clothes and footwear well-suited for Web sales? Why or why not?

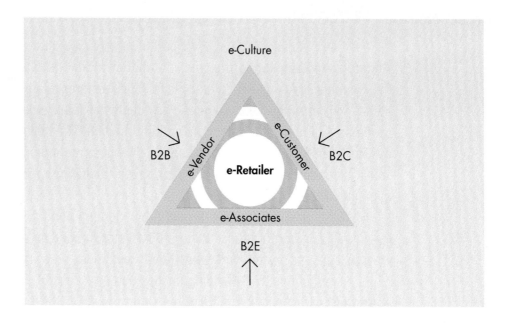

very successful. The applications allow the customers (i.e., the corporations) to manage their own programs online and track employee purchases. Since each employee of the corporate customer is registered and purchases are recorded, it is impossible for the employee to purchase more than the authorized amount.

B2C has given customers the ability to browse online catalogues, obtain product information, place orders, and get company information. Typically, MWW has developed brand loyalty with the individual customer who would purchase products online. The system is customer-focused and turnaround time is typically less than 48 hours. The customer simply chooses a product, and provides his or her name, address, and credit card information. The system then locates the closest store that has the product (using the customer's postal code) and sends the order to that store. The order is then processed by the store and couriered to the customer.

MWW has incorporated the Lotus Domino AS/400 that has also allowed the company to handle the day-to-day activities and the new applications that it is developing to stay competitive within the industry. The B2E incorporates the internal messaging system and the dynamic sales force automated training system (these are part of the intranet, as discussed in Chapter 17). B2E connects all employees with the information that is necessary to be successful.

As part of the strategy group at MWW, Robin Lynas has ensured that the use of technology and information has been successful. The mandate for the technical infrastructure requirements is standardization (build it once), scalability (ability to grow), and efficiency (both in the ease of use and the amount of resources required). The e-business strategy at MWW requires that it appears seamless to both the customer and the employee regardless of where the purchase is made.[1]

BUSINESS IN THE 21ST CENTURY

information technology (IT)
The equipment and techniques used to manage and process information.

Information technology (IT), the equipment and techniques used to manage and process information, has changed the way people make business decisions today. Only 30 years ago, well within the careers of many of today's top executives, few companies used computers. Today, IT is one of the fastest-growing industries and includes not only computers but also telecommunications and Internet-related products and services. Computers now reside on almost every employee desktop and provide vast stores of information for decision-making—some of it is useful and some is not. (See Chapter 9 for more information of the effective use of information in business decision-making.)

Many technology trends have a major impact on businesses that require them to restructure the business process. The increasing speed and capacity of electronic components, the increased amount of digitized information, the portability of electronic devices, greater connectivity, and the ease of use are probably the most significant. In fact, most major restructuring in business processes of Canadian companies include "electronic messaging, collection of data on customer spending patterns, the centralization of the vast amounts of information, supply-chain management, and automated manufacturing plants."[2]

Many business trends have also been identified that require businesses to restructure. These include, but are not limited to, new forms of organizations and management, faster pace of business, increasing globalization and, probably the most important, the acceptance of global standards.

As we saw in the MWW illustration, it is necessary to understand the business environment that the company is working in. Companies need to choose the right target environment and match this with the right technology. When a company is introducing new technologies, it is important that there is an infrastructure in place that allows the company to take advantage of the new technology. It is also important for the company to focus on the timeline and budget considerations for the implementation.

In addition, the Internet has changed the way most businesses operate and has forced companies and even whole industries to change their business models. The Internet creates new opportunities for growth through new products, greater speed to market, and enhanced cost competitiveness.

Clearly, the Internet has transformed the business landscape in the same way that railroads and automobiles triggered earlier revolutions. The computerization of businesses initiated the first stage of the Information Revolution. Now the Internet is a driving force in the second stage, moving us beyond the individual enterprise to an interconnected economy. In the virtual world of cyberspace, companies transact business without regard to traditional boundaries and constraints.

To succeed in business in the new millennium, you must understand how this relatively new communication and transaction medium is shaping business and society, as well as how to use the Internet to your advantage. First, this chapter explores the Information Superhighway with some background on the Internet: how it works, its size, and how people use it. Next the chapter looks at the impact of the Internet on business operations and industry dynamics, examines the growth of electronic commerce in both the business-to-business and the business-to-consumer markets (as well as consumer-to-consumer and consumer-to-business), and describes the steps required for successful e-business and e-commerce. The chapter ends with a look at what lies ahead for the Internet.

➡ lg 1

The Internet

Hard to believe, but in the early 1990s, hardly anyone knew what the Internet was. With unprecedented speed, the Internet has become a mainstay for businesses and individuals. Whereas radio took 38 years to gain 50 million users, television took

13 years, and PCs needed 16 years, the Internet took just four years.[3] The Internet is a fixture in our lives at home and work. Consider the following statistics about Internet users from several recent studies:

- Approximately 43 percent of all Canadians have Internet access.[4]
- Canadians are using the Internet more often and for longer periods of time. Almost two-thirds access the Internet every day and more than two-thirds spend at least ten hours per month using the Internet from home.[5]
- Ninety-two percent of Internet users use it for e-mailing purposes.[6]

Just what is this phenomenon? The **Internet** represents the convergence of the computer's high-speed processing power with telecommunications networks' capability to transmit information around the world almost instantaneously. It is the world's largest computer network, essentially a worldwide "network of networks." All of the commercial and public networks that make up the Internet use **transmission control protocol/Internet protocol (TCP/IP)**, a communications technology that allows different computer platforms to communicate with each other to transfer data. The Internet is a truly unique entity—a decentralized, open network that almost anyone can access. It has no beginning or end. Networks can be added or removed at any time.

The Internet began life in 1969 as ARPAnet, a U.S. Defense Department network connecting various types of computers at universities doing military research. It subsequently developed into a larger system of networks for academic and research sites managed by the National Science Foundation (NSF). A major growth spurt began around 1993, when the introduction of browser technology made it easy to access graphics and sound as well as text over the World Wide Web. The **World Wide Web (WWW)**, a subsystem of the Internet, is an information retrieval system composed of **Web sites.** Each Web site contains a *home page*, the first document users see when they enter the site. The site might also contain other pages with documents and files. **Hypertext**, a file or series of files within a Web page, links users to documents at the same or other Web sites.

By April 1995, the Internet was so large that the NSF turned over its backbone—the major long-distance, high-speed, high-capacity transmission networks—to a group of commercial carriers. However, no one "owns" the Internet. Each private company operates its own networks. In addition to network administrators and users, the Internet also includes several thousand **Internet service providers (ISPs),** commercial services that connect companies and individuals to the Internet. All these players create a shared resource that becomes more useful as the number of networks expands.

Today, the terms *World Wide Web* and *Internet* are used interchangeably by most users. However, the Internet offers users other capabilities, including e-mail, file transfer, online chat sessions, and newsgroups (discussion groups on just about any topic). Thanks to **browsers,** software that allows users to access the Web with a graphical point-and-click interface, the Web has become the centre of Internet activity, with the largest collection of online information in the world. As new technology makes it possible to send audio, video, voice (including telephone calls), 3-D animations, and videoconferencing over the Net, the Web is also becoming a multimedia delivery system.

How the Internet Works

To users around the world, the Internet operates as a single seamless network enabling them to send and receive text, graphics, movies, and sound files. With TCP/IP, the Internet's interconnected local and long-distance networks work together, regardless of the underlying hardware or software, to send and receive information. For example, suppose that you type in the address of a Web page for a company you are researching

Internet
A worldwide computer network that includes both commercial and public networks and offers various capabilities, including e-mail, file transfer, online chat sessions, and newsgroups.

transmission control protocol/Internet protocol (TCP/IP)
A communications technology that allows different computer platforms to communicate with each other to transfer data.

World Wide Web (WWW)
A subsystem of the Internet that consists of an information retrieval system composed of *Web sites.*

Web sites
Locations on the World Wide Web consisting of a *home page* and, possibly, other pages with documents and files.

hypertext
A file or series of files within a Web page that links users to documents at the same or other Web sites.

Internet service provider (ISP)
A commercial service that connects companies and individuals to the Internet.

browser
Software that allows users to access the Web with a graphical point-and-click interface.

exhibit 4 - 1 | Diagram of Internet Networks

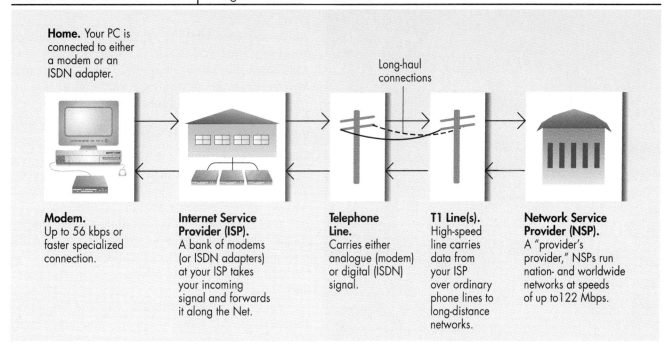

Home. Your PC is connected to either a modem or an ISDN adapter.

Long-haul connections

Modem. Up to 56 kbps or faster specialized connection.

Internet Service Provider (ISP). A bank of modems (or ISDN adapters) at your ISP takes your incoming signal and forwards it along the Net.

Telephone Line. Carries either analogue (modem) or digital (ISDN) signal.

T1 Line(s). High-speed line carries data from your ISP over ordinary phone lines to long-distance networks.

Network Service Provider (NSP). A "provider's provider," NSPs run nation- and worldwide networks at speeds of up to 122 Mbps.

---

host computer
The central computer for a Web site that stores services and data used by other computers on the network.

and hit the enter key. Exhibit 4-1 shows the route that these data might travel from your PC to the Web site's host computer and back again. A **host computer** stores services and data used by other computers on the network.

The message travels from your computer to a bank of modems at your ISP (either by telephone or cable lines). Then the request travels along a succession of interconnected national backbones to the network of the ISP that hosts the company's Web site. These national and international networks are run by network service providers (NSPs), the major telecommunications companies that operate the high-speed long-distance networks. ISPs interconnect and share information at specific interchange points. Finally, your request reaches the company's Web server that stores the actual content of the Web site. **Servers** are computers that store data and "serve" information to other computers, called *clients*, upon request. Internet servers run specialized software for different applications, like the World Wide Web, e-mail, and Usenet (newsgroups). Each organization on the Web also has its own server with a unique site, or domain, name. The desired information then makes its way back to you over a similar route.

servers
Computers that store data and "serve" information to other computers called clients, upon request.

 lg 2

The Who, What, and Where of the Internet

The Internet's explosive growth is unparalleled. There were 13.3 million Canadians online in 2000.[7] It is important for Canadian companies to understand who these Canadians are and the opportunities that they present to their marketing efforts.

Who's Online?

According to surveys of Internet usage, higher-income households are more likely to be connected, as are households with higher levels of education. While Quebec is experiencing the highest rate of growth, the provinces of Alberta, British Columbia, and Ontario are the most connected. Households in urban centres are more likely to be connected than in other geographical areas. In 1999 more than one-third of all households with heads of the homes under 55 used the Internet from home, compared with

SENIORS: 10%

As characteristics of Internet users change, businesses must rethink the type of services they offer over the Net.

one-quarter for households with heads between 55 and 64 years of age and less than 10 percent for the over-65 group.[8]

As the characteristics of Internet users change, businesses must rethink the type of services they offer and change marketing campaigns to reach new groups. Merchants are simplifying their Web sites to make it easier for new users to find their way around.

What Attracts Web Surfers

Using the Hot Links in each chapter of this book, you can discover the wealth of resources available on the World Wide Web. From the five-day weather forecast for any city in the world to statistics on steel production in Russia to the best-selling CD albums of the week—it's all on the Web. The most visited Web sites are the ones offering news, travel, entertainment, government, health/medicine, product information, sports, music, and games.

What do people do when they log on to the Internet? Sending e-mail is the most popular activity (92 percent), followed closely by accessing the Web for information. Once on the Web, people pursue a variety of interests, as summarized in Exhibit 4-2.

---

e x h i b i t   4 - 2 | Most Popular Reasons to Use the Internet

Proportions of Households Using the Internet from Home, by Purpose of Use	All Households				Regular Home-Use Households*		
	1997	1998	1999		1997	1998	1999
E-mail	13.3	19.3	26.3	%	83.1	85.6	91.7
Electronic banking	3.1	5.5	8.0		19.6	24.4	27.7
Purchasing goods/services	1.5	2.5	5.5		—	10.9	19.0
Medical/health information	—	9.6	15.6		—	42.5	54.2
Formal education/training	—	6.8	9.2		—	30.0	32.0
Government information	—	8.2	12.7		—	36.4	44.1
Other specific information	—	15.3	24.4		—	67.9	85.1
General browsing	13.5	17.6	24.3		84.7	78.1	84.7
Playing games	—	7.8	12.3		—	34.4	42.7
Chat groups	—	5.7	7.5		—	25.4	26.2
Obtaining/saving music	—	—	7.8		—	—	27.1
Listening to radio	—	—	5.0		—	—	17.5
Other Internet services	2.2	2.6	10.0		10.0	11.6	34.7

* Regular-use households are those that responded yes to the question: "In a typical month, does anyone in the household use the Internet—from any location?"

Note: "—" indicates a category of use not asked in that year's survey.

SOURCE: Adapted from Statistics Canada, "Canadian Economic Observer," Catalogue 11-10, January 2001.

How Businesses Tap the Net's Resources

Corporations and business users are also active Web participants. In a recent study of major corporations, 89 percent of the respondents had a Web site. Of those, 56 percent offered customer service and 37 percent allowed visitors to make purchases online.[9] In addition to purchasing supplies and materials and selling products online, businesses use the Internet's vast resources to:

- Collect information on the latest economic conditions, competitors, industry trends, technology, and other developments.
- Gather information on customers.
- Allow employees in different locations to collaborate on projects.
- Provide customer service.
- Communicate with suppliers and customers.
- Market their products.
- Recruit and train employees.
- Hold virtual meetings and conferences.

Exhibit 4-3 lists the top five responses of Inc. 500 executives when asked what their company's Web page helped them to achieve.

concept check

- How did the Internet develop into a global "network of networks"?
- Describe briefly how the Internet works.
- Who are today's Web users, and how will Web demographics change over the next five years?
- How can managers use the Internet to improve business operations?

➡ lg 3   The New Internet Economy

The Internet has significantly changed today's global economic framework. As companies rush to adapt Net technology to different tasks and industries, they promote another wave of technological innovation. In addition, the Internet has taken off in ways that its originators probably never imagined. It is more than just a communication tool, as first envisioned, or another way to get traditional information.

We are in the midst of a shift to a new Internet-centred economy. Existing companies must reinvent themselves to take advantage of Internet technology. Old business models no longer apply as the Net changes the rules of doing business. Many established companies waited for the Internet market to develop before moving online.

e x h i b i t 4 - 3	Advantages of Corporate Web Site	
More widespread marketing		84%
Increased sales		36
Improved customer service		31
Identify product improvements		24
Reduce costs		13

SOURCES: A.T. Kearny, CEO Survey cited in NUA Internet Surveys (July 24, 2000), downloaded from www.nua.com; Shane McLaughlin, "Web Sites We Love," *1998 Inc. 500* (October 20, 1998), p. 181.

Businesses are designing more Web sites that target women, one of the fastest-growing groups of Internet users. Women shown here using the Internet at a cybercafé can visit sites like iVillage that cater to their interests and tastes.

HOT Links

Check out the latest on eBay "The World's Online Marketplace"™ at
www.ebay.ca

HOT Links

Check out Air Canada's Web saver deals at
www.aircanada.ca/websaver/

Confident that their size would allow them to push the entrepreneurial upstarts out of the way, they were surprised to find themselves left in the dust. The Internet moved so quickly that they lost the advantage of being first to the Amazon.coms, Yahoo!s, and so on. Let's now consider how the Internet affects competition, channel relationships, and marketing.

The New Face of Competition (Click versus Brick)

The Internet is redefining the nature of competition by blurring the traditional barriers of geography and time. Store location and hours were once key factors in attracting customers. Your competition was located within easy driving distance. Now the competitive universe is unlimited. It doesn't matter whether a company is physically located in Vancouver or Kitchener-Waterloo. On the Web, competitors are just a click away.

In addition, new Internet businesses encounter fewer barriers than traditional businesses when entering a new market. To expand geographically or add new products, traditional retailers must incur substantial costs for a physical storefront and distribution. Once a company has a Web site, the cost to acquire a customer in Newfoundland is the same as adding one in New Zealand. Online companies find it easier to enter new markets than traditional companies. Amazon.com started with books but now offers CDs, videos, gifts, and other products. In its quest to become a one-stop online transaction company, Amazon developed its own auction site to compete with eBay and is investing in other online retailers such as Pets.com and Homegrocer.com.[10]

Going Direct

The Internet is changing relationships among all channel members: manufacturers, distributors, retailers/service providers, and customers (see Chapter 10). No longer do companies have to rely on intermediaries to connect with other participants in the supply chain. They can go directly to customers, bypassing traditional channels and displacing some intermediaries.

Take the domestic travel industry, for example, which accounted for over $54.6 billion of consumer spending in 2001.[11] Travel agents are becoming less important as *cybertravellers* can now access much of the same information on the Web. Travellers can easily check airplane schedules, find the lowest fares and room prices, view panoramic photos of hotel rooms, obtain maps showing the best route between cities, get advice from experienced travellers in discussion groups, and then make their own reservations. The percentage of airline tickets sold by agents is dropping rapidly, as more travellers buy tickets over the Web. Some airlines are encouraging this self-service by giving discounts for Web ticket purchases.

Manufacturers with strong brands can also sell directly on the Web. To the dismay of wholesalers and traditional retailers, Levi Strauss has begun selling direct. Iomega, makers of the popular Zip and Jaz hard drives, and Polaroid started selling directly to consumers in 1999. Manufacturers with brands carrying more weight than the retailers—Estée Lauder and Tommy Hilfiger are two—may be able to bypass retailers entirely.

Most manufacturers, however, don't have the breadth of product to sell exclusively on the Web and will use it to provide information to support sales and refer customers to dealers. A retailer such as The Bay can use the Web's interactivity to combine apparel

The Internet is changing channel relationships in the travel industry, as more consumers purchase tickets directly from airlines and reserve rooms at hotels over the Web rather than using the services of travel agents.

and accessory products from several manufacturers to show consumers an outfit that they will want to buy. Nor is it economically feasible for most manufacturers to fill small orders for individual customers. These limitations, along with the risk of alienating business partners, have discouraged many manufacturers from selling direct. They will continue to sell in large quantities to resellers.[12]

Distributors are using their customers' move to the Web to their advantage. They are providing warehousing, logistics, and e-commerce services to retailers and manufacturers. Distributors offer economies of scale to small retailers that want to set up Web shops. A new category of virtual merchant is emerging. Buy.com, for example, outsources order fulfillment and focuses only on selling products at extremely low prices to consumers. Merisel, a leading computer products distributor, expects the Internet to make distributors more important to retail customers because they will take on a larger share of retailers' expenses.[13]

In some industries, going direct takes on additional meaning. Customers no longer have to wait to get boxed software from many developers. They can download programs directly from a Web site, using a special password to unlock the software for their use. New technology to deliver music over the Web is changing the dynamics of the music industry.

Power to the Consumer

The radical shift in bargaining power from sellers to buyers is probably the most fundamental development being shaped by electronic commerce. As John Hagel III, author of *Net Gain* and *Net Worth*, says, "Information has been the key driver of negotiating power in economics for a long time, and electronic commerce is giving information to the customer, which in turn will dramatically enhance their bargaining power as they deal with vendors." All customers, from corporate purchasing agents to individuals, can search sites of various providers to compare products and prices. They can find the best products for their needs, rather than simply accepting what retailers offer. Vendors have a huge opportunity to build relationships by providing assistance in finding the right goods and services.[14]

The availability of neutral sources of product information gives consumers greater freedom of choice and control. For example, about 45 percent of car buyers use the Web to shop for their cars, gathering information on dealer costs, options, and financing plans. They arrive at the dealership armed with the facts and ready to drive a hard bargain.

New types of "infomediaries" make it even easier for buyers by pulling together product information from many vendors. Thanks to *intelligent agents* that scour the Web's many databases, consumers no longer have to go from site to site to compare prices and obtain information. For example, CompareNet offers product reviews and online discussion forums as well as price and feature comparisons for a wide range of products. *Portals* are also becoming popular. These Web sites gather many resources into one convenient gateway to the Web. Some like Yahoo! are general portals with links to popular destination sites. Specialized portals like Intuit's financial services site also compete for viewer attention.

Service industries are also noticing a change in consumer buying patterns. In financial services, for example, customers can now comparison shop in a way never before possible for financial products such as personal loans, mortgages, auto insurance, and credit cards. Online banking services and stock brokerages attract more users daily. The Internet's impact on financial institutions and markets is discussed further in Chapter 14.

HOT Links

See how CompareNet takes the hassle out of comparison shopping. Search the site for the lowest price on one of your favourite products at
www.compare.com

HOT Links

See how Intuit Canada is revolutionizing the way Canadians manage their financial lives at
www.intuit.com/canada

Keep these fundamental changes in mind as we now look at how companies in different industries are using e-business strategies.

concept check

- Describe the impact of the Internet on competition.
- How does the Internet change channel relationships among manufacturers, distributors, and retailers?
- Why does John Hagel III consider the increasing power of the consumer the most important effect of the Internet on the business environment? Do you agree?

➡ **lg 4**

electronic business (e-business)
The entire process that involves the full value chain (the entire value-adding process, from the raw materials to the eventual end user, including the disposing of the packaging after use) and how all units of a business operate.

electronic commerce (e-commerce)
The actual transaction of selling a product or service via the Internet.

business-to-business (B2B) e-commerce
Electronic commerce that involves transactions between companies.

business-to-consumer (B2C) e-commerce
Electronic commerce that involves transactions between businesses and the end user of the goods or services; also called *e-tailing*.

consumer-to-consumer (C2C) e-commerce
Electronic commerce that involves transactions between consumers.

consumer-to-business (C2B) e-commerce
Electronic commerce that involves transactions between consumers and businesses initiated by the consumer.

business-to-enterprise (B2E)
Electronic collecting, storing, updating, and using of information within the business.

Capitalizing on E-Business

Many people use the terms *e-business* and *e-commerce* interchangeably, but for this discussion, we need to differentiate them. **Electronic business (e-business)** involves the full value chain (the entire value-adding process, from the raw materials to the eventual end user, including the disposing of the packaging after use)[15] and how all units of a business operate. The actual transaction of selling a product or service via the Internet is called **electronic commerce (e-commerce)**. Therefore, e-commerce is a subset of e-business. E-business goes beyond selling products through an electronic catalogue, however. Among the benefits of the Web's interactivity are convenience and increased efficiency, better customer service, lower transaction costs, and new relationship-building strategies.

E-commerce has moved into the business mainstream. More and more corporate and individual purchasers now go first to the Web to buy products ranging from diesel engine parts to consulting services to baby clothes. Although e-commerce barely existed in 1995, in 2000, 1.5 million Canadian households placed 9.1 million orders.[16] Many others, if not purchasing orders over the Internet, are obtaining product/service information and comparison-shopping.

E-commerce includes four distinct market segments. **Business-to-business (B2B) e-commerce** involves transactions between companies—for example, purchasing raw materials to manufacture products or supplies. **Business-to-consumer (B2C) e-commerce**, also known as "e-tailing," involves transactions between businesses and the end user of the goods or services. **Consumer-to-consumer (C2C) e-commerce** refers to non-business selling to others (e.g., eBay), and **consumer-to-business (C2B) e-commerce** involves consumers offering prices to businesses (e.g., Priceline.com).

Each of the above four segments are between two separate entities, but within a business there are also exchanges via electronics. This is known as **business-to-enterprise (B2E)**. The concept of B2E has been gaining more popularity and focus because of its importance to e-business. Companies use many different types of information to make decisions (see Chapter 9). Some examples of these internal electronic exchanges (B2E) are intranets or other electronic messaging systems, inventory controls, and consumer demographics.

New E-Business Models Emerge

In the early days of e-business, companies could choose from three basic models:
- Selling merchandise or services on the Internet.
- Providing entertainment or information on a fee-for-service or subscription basis.
- Providing advertising or referral-supported entertainment or information sites.

With the vast amount of free information on the Internet, the subscription model has not proved successful in most cases. Already new types of business models are emerging that use the Web to create more efficient marketplaces, especially in the business-to-business sector:[17]

- *Auctions to sell merchandise to businesses and consumers.* Examples of online auctions include eBay, the leading person-to-person auction site; OnSale, a merchant-to-buyer auction service; and Freemarkets, a business-to-business auction service for qualified buyers of industrial materials and components.
- *E-service providers that help other firms establish e-business and e-commerce operations.* The e-services market—from consultants to technology outsourcing companies—is poised for growth, from US$22 billion in 1999 to a projected US$220 billion by 2003. Services are driving revenue growth at IBM.
- *Industry exchanges and other information gatherers that serve as "infomediaries."* Industry exchanges bring together multiple buyers and sellers within one industry: Chemdex.com allows scientists to locate over 250 000 laboratory chemicals from 120 suppliers. Other infomediaries gather together vendors in many industries. SupplyBase brings together over 30 000 online supplier directories. Users can search a central database by geography, industry, technology, or other criteria.
- *Consumer infomediaries and portal sites.* These sites simplify the online experience by bringing together a combination of information, goods, and services from many individual companies. CatalogCity.com and Shopping.com are two examples of shopping sites, while Intelihealth is a specialized portal offering medical data, health tips, and services such as online pharmacies and health insurance.

Companies often incorporate more than one business model into their e-business strategy. Yahoo!, for example, began as an advertising-supported Internet directory. It is now a leading portal where visitors can make travel reservations, shop, and bid at its own auction site.

The Business-to-Business Boom

Fortune 500 corporations and small businesses alike are embracing business-to-business e-business and e-commerce to save hundreds of millions of dollars through lower costs and reduced inventories. B2B includes all aspects of the supply chain, from product information to order, invoice, fulfillment, payment, and customer service. About 60 percent of purchasing managers rely on the Web to find supplies, and that number is quickly climbing. Companies without a Web site will lose business opportunities. In addition to Web-based e-business and e-commerce, many electronic data interchange (EDI) networks are moving to the Internet, replacing expensive proprietary networks.

It is no surprise that high-technology companies were early adopters of e-business. IBM purchases over US$4 billion of goods and services per year over the Internet, citing significant cost savings and improved connections with customers and business partners as clear benefits.

E-business is no longer limited to the high-tech companies; in fact, most companies are becoming active participants. As illustrated in the Mark's Work Wearhouse vignette, all aspects of the company are now involved in e-business. Not only does this provide better customer satisfaction, but the company is realizing increasing cost savings as well.

Extranets are becoming a popular business-to-business e-business tool for such activities as purchasing, inventory management, order fulfillment, information transmission, training, and sales presentations. Like an intranet, an **extranet** is a private network that uses Internet technology and a browser interface. Extranets, however, are accessible only to authorized outsiders with a valid user name and password. Companies can easily designate specific portions of their Web sites to share specific information and processes with suppliers, vendors, partners, customers, and other businesses at remote locations. For example, customers can find account balances and customized catalogues with account-specific pricing.

HOT Links

ITBusiness.ca is an electronic publishing subsidiary of Plesman Communications that provides recent news, product information, and useful links in the IT industry. Find the latest news at

www.itbusiness.ca

---

extranet
A private computer network that uses Internet technology and a browser interface but is accessible only to authorized outsiders with a valid user name and password.

Extranets are a very efficient format for business-to-business e-commerce and could handle the majority of these transactions in the near future. Marine Power Europe, a manufacturer of boat parts, saves US$1 million a year in order placement and processing costs. Thanks to a special multilingual extranet application, Marine Power's international distributors and dealers can get product information and transact business in their native languages. Multiple users from around the globe can even view the same live document in their native language.[18]

E-Commerce Hits Its Stride

Since Amazon.com turned the retailing world on its head in 1994, selling consumer goods over the Internet has become big business. In 2001, more than 70 percent of Canadian businesses were connected to the Internet and approximately 29 percent of businesses had their own Web sites. The value of sales over the Internet has grown from $4.2 billion in 1999 to $10.4 billion in 2001 (see Exhibit 4-4).

What do e-shoppers buy? Travel accounts for by far the most revenues, as Exhibit 4-5 shows, followed by computer hardware and software, financial brokerage, and collectibles (person to person auctions). In general, computer services, electronics, and low-risk, low-cost items sell best.

What makes a successful cybermerchant? The answer is convenience, selection, community service, and pricing. Consumers love the convenience of Web shopping. They can get more product choice and information in the same or less time. Chats and online discussion groups create a sense of community among shoppers with similar interests. Bargains are easy to find as intelligent agent software learns customer preferences and quickly scouts the Web for the best products and lowest prices.

Cyberspace also gives retailers a chance to break out of the size constraints of a physical store. A store might support 10 000 items, but on the Internet a retailer can offer millions of them without adding expensive shelf space (click versus brick). In

HOT Links

Discover what's in style at The Gap and learn how a successful retailer uses the Web to its advantage at

www.gapinc.com

e x h i b i t   4 - 4 | Electronic Commerce and Technology, 1999, 2000, and 2001

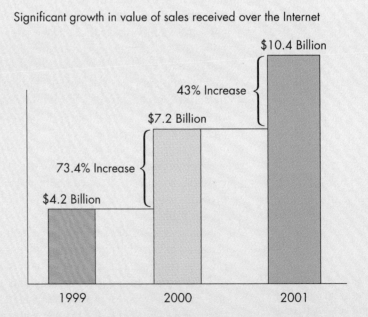

Significant growth in value of sales received over the Internet

$10.4 Billion

43% Increase

$7.2 Billion

73.4% Increase

$4.2 Billion

1999   2000   2001

SOURCE: Adapted from Statistics Canada website, www.statcan.ca/english/research/56F0004MIE/ 56F0004MIE2001005.pdf and www.statcan.ca/Daily/English/020402/d020402a.htm.

e x h i b i t   4 - 5 | Most Popular Categories of Online Purchases

Travel
Computer hardware and software
Financial brokerage
Collectibles (person to person auctions)
Books, music, and entertainment
Automobiles (direct to consumer and referral fees)
Apparel/sporting
Event tickets
Flowers/cards/gifts
Consumer electronics
Home/garden
Toys
Food/beverage
Health/beauty

SOURCE: Shop.org and Boston Consulting Group, cited in "The E-Commerce Battleground," *The Wall Street Journal* (July 17, 2000), p. R4.

addition to selling a broader merchandise mix, retailers can also use their Web sites for special promotions, merchandise that may be out of season in their regular stores, and excess inventory.

Where's the Profit?

Despite the increasing popularity of e-shopping, less than 5 percent of e-tailers are expected to show profits in the near term. Currently, the most profitable Internet-related companies are not the e-tailers, but rather the companies that provide infrastructure—computer, networking, and telecommunications equipment providers and telecommunications carriers. In these first stages of e-business, businesses are finding that they must focus on developing a solid infrastructure and building online relationships and brands, not on generating short-term profits.[19] It will take time for the financial benefits of e-business, such as reduced overhead, to reach the bottom line.

In the meantime, e-tailers are finding it hard to achieve a profit for several reasons:
- *Pricing.* It's so easy for shoppers to make price comparisons on the Internet that merchants get into price wars that cut margins considerably.
- *Cannibalization.* Online sales may cannibalize higher-margin sales from traditional retail stores.
- *Unexpected costs.* Although the Web can reduce brick-and-mortar costs, operating expenses are higher than anticipated. As the cost comparison in Exhibit 4-6 shows, online merchants must offer lower prices—but still incur higher expenses than a competing superstore. Online "real estate" (renting space at other sites through ads or other placements) and marketing are expensive. Barnes & Noble paid AOL, the most popular online shopping mall, US$40 million to be its exclusive bookseller for four years. In addition, online customer support hasn't eliminated the need for telephone support. Online shoppers jammed phone lines during the 1998 holiday season. Shopping.com had to double its call centre support staff because of waits as long as an hour.[20]
- *Aggressive growth.* Companies that want to grab a beachhead on the e-business shores have to grow quickly, and this growth is expensive. To build a brand name, market share, and a loyal customer base, companies make large investments in marketing and improved technology. Even as revenues soar, leaders such as Amazon.com continue to post losses. Industry analysts support this hypergrowth strategy and predict that profitability will follow.

exhibit 4 - 6 | Cost Comparison: Superstore versus Online Store

	Superstore	Online
Average sale	$100	$100
Less: Discount	–10	–20
Shipping & handling (S&H)	—	11
Provincial sales tax	7	—
Customer pays	$ 97	$ 91
Cost of sales, S&H	70	68
Gross profit	$ 27	$ 23
Operating expenses:		
Rent	1	5
Labour and store	11	—
Web site development	—	3
Marketing	3	17
Total	$ 15	$ 25
Operating profit per order	$ 12	–$2

SOURCE: Adapted from Mary Beth Grover, "Lost in Cyberspace." Reprinted by permission of *Forbes* Magazine ©2003 Forbes Inc.

Although e-tailers want to make money from their Web sites, most firms must also look beyond the bottom line. As the following section explains, e-business brings many other worthwhile benefits, such as substantial savings in costs and time, improved quality of service, and better customer relationships.

➡ **lg 5**

Benefiting from E-Business and E-Commerce

Online shopping appeals to consumers because it's convenient and offers them an enormous selection of merchandise at competitive prices.

As the Mark's Work Wearhouse example from the beginning of this chapter demonstrates, a company that uses the Internet effectively can gain clear advantages. Among the attractions of incorporating e-business into corporate strategies are the following:

1. *Lower prices.* Competition among online vendors leads to lower prices, for both businesses and individual consumers.

2. *Greater selection of products and vendors.* The Web makes it possible for corporate purchasing agents and individuals to find numerous vendors and retailers for almost any product.

3. *Access to customer and product sales data.* Companies can develop customer lists and learn their buying characteristics. They can also immediately learn which products are selling best.

4. *Around-the-clock ordering and customer service.* Company Web sites provide extensive product information for prospective customers around the world on a "24/7" basis, thereby expanding markets and facilitating more transactions—without hiring additional personnel. Customers themselves decide how much information they require by clicking on site links. Well-designed sites offer solutions to customer problems and make product suggestions.

5. *Lower costs.* As many companies and their customers have learned, cost savings are a major benefit of e-business. These can take many forms, from the distribution savings shown in Exhibit 4-7 to staff reductions and lower costs of purchasing supplies. A report by the Organization for Economic Cooperation and Development (OECD) indicates that companies can reduce customer service costs by 10 to 50 percent and order processing time by 50 to 96 percent, depending on the type of business.[21]

| exhibit 4 - 7 | How E-Commerce Lowers Distribution Costs |

Category	Traditional System	Internet	Percent Savings
Airline tickets	$ 8.00	$ 1.00	87 %
Banking	1.08	0.13	89
Bill payment	2.22–3.32	0.65–1.10	67–71
Term life insurance policy	400–700	200–350	50
Software	15	0.20–0.50	97–99

SOURCE: "Spotlight: The Economic Impact of E-commerce" by Maryann Jones Thompson. Copyright April 26, 1999 by *The Industry Standard*. Reproduced with permission of The Industry Standard in the format Textbook via Copyright Clearance Center.

6. *Customized products.* The Internet is revolutionizing product design and manufacturing. No longer do companies have to design and build products well in advance of the sale, basing product decisions on market research. They can use the Internet to take orders for products tailored to customer specifications. Dell Computers was one of the first to allow computer buyers to configure their ideal computer from menus at Dell's Web site. Even though Dell's build-to-order procedures were remarkably efficient when customers phone in their orders, the Web has increased its efficiency and profitability. Warehouses receive supply orders via Internet messages every two hours instead of daily faxes. Suppliers know about the company's inventory and production plans and get feedback on their performance in meeting shipping deadlines. Inventory on hand is a low eight days, versus competitor Compaq's 26, and revenue is up 55 percent.[22]

Roadblocks on the E-Business Highway

Despite the increasing acceptance of e-business and e-commerce, companies are encountering some barriers along the Information Superhighway. Some of the problems include the following:

Michael Dell (right), chief executive of Dell Computer, uses the Internet to allow customers to design their own computer systems, which has increased the company's efficiency and profitability.

1. *Disruptions in channel relationships.* For example, manufacturers that start to sell directly to customers can jeopardize relationships with distributors.
2. *Poor customer service.* Although more consumers are venturing online to shop, they easily become frustrated when technology doesn't perform flawlessly. The top three reasons for dissatisfaction were product availability problems, high shipping and handling costs, and slow Web site performance. Customer service has

improved, but during the busy 1999 holiday shopping season 53 percent of shoppers responding to a survey didn't receive a product in time, and 30 percent had to pay extra for on-time delivery.[23]

3. *Payment problems.* Because of a lack of standards for electronic payment methods, customers must enter personal information and credit card data at each online store. About 27 percent of Net shoppers find this enough of a nuisance to leave a site before completing their orders. Electronic commerce modelling language (ECML), a standard technology endorsed by a consortium of major technology companies and by Visa and MasterCard, may solve this problem. With ECML, shoppers enter information into their "digital wallet" just once, accessing it when they want to make a purchase.[24]

4. *Security and privacy issues.* Many consumers remain reluctant to order merchandise over the Web, even though they readily give out credit card numbers over the telephone or in retail stores. The increasing availability of special secure sites that encrypt personal data is solving this problem. We'll discuss privacy issues later in the chapter.

concept check

- Why are businesses incorporating e-business and e-commerce into their overall business strategies?
- Differentiate between the four major e-commerce market segments.
- Why do most businesses find it hard to show a profit on e-business? What barriers to success still exist?

➡ **lg 6**

Launching a Successful E-Business

E-business involves more than building a flashy Web site to attract customers. It's also about adding value. Internet shoppers don't just want to duplicate the in-store experience when they visit a company's Web site—they want a *better* experience than they can get in their local store. In addition, e-business requires the right infrastructure to retain customers and encourage repeat purchases. In and of itself, e-business cannot make a company a winner. "If you don't have the right product, the right timing, and the right distribution channels, the Internet won't change that," says Bruce Temkin of Forrester Research.[25]

Businesses can get involved with e-business in stages, as Exhibit 4-8 illustrates. A company might start with a simple promotional Web site (Level 1) or go a step further and add marketing and interactive capabilities that enhance the ability to get and keep customers (Level 2). Next, it can totally integrate its Web activities into its existing business structure (Level 3). These three levels supplement rather than replace business procedures that can be performed offline. At Level 4, the highest level of strategic value, the company is transformed as it creates new business and shifts traditional business to the Internet.

As the potential benefits from the site increase, so do the costs. Developing a successful e-business strategy also takes time. Companies may not achieve positive returns on their Internet investment until they reach Level 3. Moving up the learning curve by working through the first levels before implementing more sophisticated technology is more likely to lead to success than attempting to transform the business in one step.[26]

Once a company decides to roll out or expand an e-business strategy, it faces a series of high-level decisions involving merchandising, Web site design, marketing, customer service and order fulfillment, Web site operations, and infrastructure. These decisions, summarized in Exhibit 4-9, form a road map leading to an Internet strategy that complements the firm's overall business strategy.

exhibit   4 - 8 | Four Stages of E-Business

Level 1: Basic Presence

Basic site with corporate information, marketing materials. Updated at regular intervals.

Cost: $30 000–$100 000 for design and hosting

Example: Thomson Publishing Group, **www.thomson.com**

Level 2: Prospecting

Interactive, marketing-focused site with more corporate, product, and service information. Personalized content and e-mail customer support enhance the ability to get and keep customers.

Cost: $400 000– $900 000

Example: Yahoo!, **www.yahoo.com**

Level 3: Business Integration

More sophisticated sites with increased customer interaction. Greater process efficiencies, targeted marketing, self-service support, advanced search capabilities, online communities. Achieve profitability.

Cost: $1 million and up

Example: Charles Schwab & Co., **www.schwab.com**

Level 4: Business Transformation

Total integration with back-office systems; more efficient supplier and customer communications; electronic transactions replace paper. Improved profitability from reduced operating costs, greater depth and breadth of sales channels.

Cost: $2 million and up

Example: Mark's Work Wearhouse, **www.marks.com**

SOURCE: Adapted from Jane Asteroff and Maureen Fleming, "Four Ways to Increase a Web Site's Strategic Value," *Executive Edge* (September 1998), p. 7.

Merchandising

Many companies underestimate the effort required to effectively merchandise products on the Internet. First they must decide which products to sell and how to price them. Not all products can be sold successfully online. And slapping a picture of a product on a site with a basic description isn't sufficient. Successful sites provide

exhibit   4 - 9 | Key Issues in Developing an E-Business Strategy

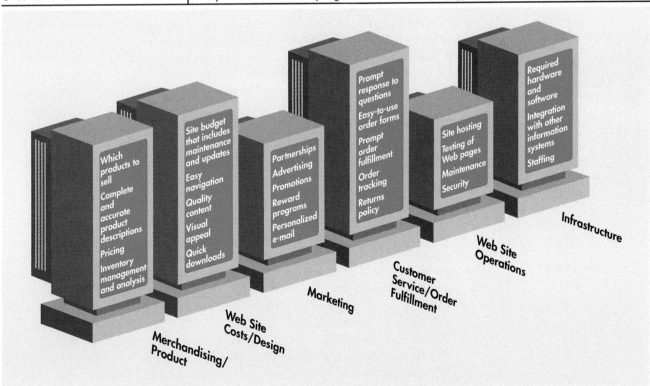

guidance and have accurate and lively product descriptions. Other merchandising issues include testing to make sure links to product pictures and descriptions are correct and designing easy-to-use order forms.

Site Costs and Design

Establishing an e-business Web site has become much easier over the past few years. Off-the-shelf software packages costing as little as $100 provide templates for sales-oriented Web sites. Packages with more sophisticated features like search engines and databases to manage inventory cost about $2000 to $5000. Companies can also hire a Web designer or outsource Web site development to a specialist. As Exhibit 4-8 shows, the cost of a corporate Web site ranges from $30 000 to over $2 million and includes not only the design and equipment but also updates to site content and technology and maintenance. On average, however, corporate Web sites cost about $250 000 to develop and $180 000 to maintain. For sites with online purchasing capabilities, the averages rise to $370 000 and $275 000, respectively.[27]

Regardless of who develops a site, managers responsible for the company's e-business strategy must plan carefully to ensure that the site meets the company's e-business objectives, in terms of both content and budget. Among the most important design considerations for e-business sites are simplicity, ease of navigation, visual appeal, download speed, and good product information. (For tips on creating an effective Web site, see Applying This Chapter's Topics.)

Marketing

Building brand equity is critical for e-business marketing. The first companies to build a successful online relationship with the consumer have a large advantage. But a challenge for new e-business is for the business to attract existing and new shoppers to the Web site. Print and television ads are an important way to attract shoppers to a Web site. And other traditional marketing efforts (e.g., flyers) are also used.

One of the underlying differences between Internet marketing and traditional marketing is the difficulty of turning shoppers into buyers. An estimated 12.3 percent of Canadian households placed an order over the Internet and an additional 9.6 percent were window shoppers on the Internet in 2000.[28] To increase the profitability of a Web site, e-businesses must encourage a higher percentage of Canadian households using the Internet to purchase products. This requires marketing strategies that create "stickiness," an increase in the amount of time visitors spend at a Web site, and bring visitors back to the site.

Companies use a variety of strategies to achieve these marketing objectives, including:

- *Partnerships* with other organizations, such as alliances with consumer providers like AOL or with complementary retailers for placement of banner ads.
- *Advertising* in both electronic and traditional media. In addition to banner ads, companies can buy sponsorships on Web pages that put their message into the content of the other Web sites.
- *Promotions, contests, and sweepstakes* at the Web site or through e-mail—for example, e-mail newsletters with notices of sale items, an e-mail dollars-off coupon for customers who haven't ordered for a while, and sweepstakes giving away trips and popular products.
- *"Frequent buyer" programs* for Internet retail sites, sponsored by individual merchants or companies like ClickRewards that offer awards for purchases at member sites.
- *Personalized e-mail* with links to Web sites, which increases sales by driving traffic to Web sites and improving customer retention. This type of e-mail marketing costs less than banner advertising and has a much higher "click-through" rate—an average of 18 percent, compared to 0.65 percent on banner ads.

HOT Links

Learn how you can earn "ClickMiles" from many different merchants at
www.clickrewards.com

What brings site visitors back? For 75 percent of Web surfers, high-quality content is the key. Other criteria include ease of use, fast download time, and frequent updates.

Customer Service and Order Fulfillment

On the Internet, disgruntled shoppers usually don't wait around. Slow service? Poor information? Difficult ordering process? With just a click of the mouse, consumers find another site that makes shopping easier. Therefore, good customer service and order fulfillment are critical to gaining a competitive edge on the Internet.

With few exceptions, Internet customer service currently falls far below consumer expectations. A recent Jupiter Research study, for instance, found that 51 percent of Internet sites failed to respond to customer service questions within five days. Companies must set up an effective system and train customer service representatives to provide quick responses to customer questions about orders and products.

Web merchants must add more customer service staff and train them to sell and to advise online customers. Another option is to automate the process where possible. Customers see the Web as a way to speed up the entire buying process. Companies must be quick to learn from and adapt to this new selling medium.

Order fulfillment strategies are just as critical. Companies need new procedures to fill orders from the Web site without loss of data. Inventory management is critical for e-business sites. Many businesses are unprepared for the influx of new customers and do not have adequate inventory to fill customer orders. Whenever products are out of stock, it is a major complaint of consumers and decreases their confidence in e-business. Mark's Work Wearhouse has minimized this problem by having the information systems search for the closest store to the customer (using the postal code) that has the desired product (B2C) and using the SKU to fulfill inventories in the stores when they reach their minimal levels (B2B).

Companies are re-evaluating operational strategies in response to the realities of e-business. Companies like MWW are outsourcing parts of the distribution process to reduce warehouse and inventory holding costs. As noted in the opening vignette on MWW, once inventory levels reach their minimal level for that store, an automatic message is sent to their supplier for immediate replenishing that is then packaged and sent to the outsourced distribution centre.

Web Site Operations and Infrastructure

When planning an Internet strategy, managers must develop a plan for Web site operations and infrastructure. This involves first understanding their business. Then some of the questions they need to ask include:

1. What hardware and software will we need?
2. Will design and operations, such as hosting the Web site on a server and distribution, be handled in-house or outsourced?
3. How will sales be integrated with the financial, accounting, and manufacturing systems?
4. What are our staffing needs?
5. Is the Web site secure so that customers feel comfortable ordering online? Have we created firewalls to protect internal company data from unauthorized access?

Once the Web site is online, managers must have a way to evaluate its effectiveness. They also need to know whose sites are best for their ads and promotions.

Measuring the return on an Internet investment is no easy task, however. As yet, the Web offers no standard measurement procedures. Auditing services use different methods to analyze Web-traffic data, often with conflicting results. Some common measurements include page impressions (number of times a page is seen), reach (number of unique visitors to a site), total number of site visits, time online, and click-throughs on linked ads. Companies must use caution in interpreting these results, however. A service that tells a company how many times its site is seen may not know if the visitor spends time on a page or quickly links to another site.

concept check

- What are the four stages in developing an e-business strategy?
- How can a business increase the time visitors spend at its Web site?
- Describe several ways to ensure superior Internet customer service.

➡ lg 7   CAPITALIZING ON TRENDS IN BUSINESS

Predictions of a *Jetsons*-like future for the Internet abound. Within ten years, we could live in a world where everything is interconnected through the Net. An in-home network would know to turn the coffeemaker on at a different time during the week and on weekends. Sprinkler systems would check the Web's weather reports and turn off if rain is expected. Manufacturers will use built-in Net links to diagnose and perhaps even fix problems with your kitchen appliances. Your refrigerator may be able to tell when supplies run low and generate orders from online grocers.[29] As we'll discuss in Chapter 9, information appliances from Web-browsing phones to wireless handheld units bring a wider range of services to consumers. Faster and more reliable Internet access will improve the quality of the Internet experience and make software and music downloads easier. Other trends include one-to-one marketing, better privacy policies, and industry consolidation.

Let's Get Personal

The Internet's ability to provide companies with a new, more effective link with customers could make it the most powerful direct marketing tool yet. Already it is creating new types of one-to-one marketing models. The Web's unique ability to provide immediate communication with and feedback from customers will allow merchants to meet customer demands on an individual basis. One year after implementing customized services, sites reported 47 percent growth in new customers and a 52 percent increase in sales.[30]

With the Internet, companies can:
- Target and deliver messages geared to a specific market segment based on demographics and interests.
- Create communities through chat sessions, newsgroups, and electronic personal shopping to build loyalty and enhance customer connections.
- Collect, track, and analyze customer data to identify consumer behaviour and buying patterns.
- Convert online advertisements to sales transactions by allowing customers to link from the ad to the purchasing site.

Many different types of sites use personalization to create customer loyalty and increase purchases. Portal sites like Yahoo! and Excite let users create personalized pages with an e-mail box, news on specific topics, weather for their hometown, sports scores, and reminders of upcoming events like birthdays. Air Canada sends e-mail informing customers of special fares on designated routes. CDNow's customers get personalized pages that recommend music according to past purchases, stated preferences, and ratings on performers and CDs. "It really is a music store for each of our 600 000-plus customers," says Jason Olim, CDNow's co-founder and CEO.[31]

Privacy Policies Go Public

The Web's ability to provide personalized service comes at a price. Consumers have to supply personal information, raising concerns about privacy. The Web site's ability to follow an electronic trail is another issue.

HOT Links

Discover what new initiatives the Office of Consumer Affairs has developed to protect Canadian consumers at strategis.ic.gc.ca/oca

In response to consumer concerns, companies are posting their privacy policies on their Web sites. These policies tell consumers what information the site collects and how it will be used. To reduce consumer fears and prevent possible future government regulation, companies are taking a strong privacy stance and leading a voluntary industry effort to protect customer privacy. Many of these companies have announced that they will not advertise on Web sites that don't clearly state their privacy policies. As well, many companies are encouraging Web sites on which they advertise to allow visitors to prevent their personal information from being sold to outside marketers.

Industry Canada's Office of Consumer Affairs has numerous initiatives that are intended to protect consumers, and as e-business and e-commerce become more prevalent in our economy, the Office of Consumer Affairs has developed guidelines for companies to earn consumers' trust.

concept check

- How can companies use the Internet to build customer relationships?
- What can online merchants do to lessen consumers' privacy concerns?

APPLYING THIS CHAPTER'S TOPICS

One of the biggest challenges you will face in your business career is keeping up with the Internet industry. By the time you read this chapter, new developments in access speed, voice and data transmission, and e-business will be making even more remarkable headlines. Just as in other areas of information technology, acquiring and maintaining Internet-related skills will serve you well in the future.

You may be called on to help your company go online or make its Web site more effective. A study found that about only 29 percent of Canadian businesses had a Web site in 2001 (up from 22 percent in 1999).[32] And often small and medium-sized companies that are online do not know how to use the Internet to improve their business. For some, "the Web site is more of a toy than a business tool."[33]

Creating a Successful Web Site

What makes a Web site a winner? According to four Web experts interviewed by *The Wall Street Journal Interactive Edition,* a site's overall look and "feel," layout, content, and ease of use are among the most important features. Simple, visually appealing layouts won praise. But the best Web sites have more than attractive design elements. The Web designers also included good prices and service in their list of "must-haves."[34]

Even the most attractive Web site will fail if the company doesn't fill orders promptly and provide good customer service. Here are some guidelines for creating effective Web sites:

- *Know what you want to accomplish.* Is the site mainly informational, or is it interactive, with searching and ordering capabilities?
- *Follow the 30-second rule.* Viewers have a short attention span and will move on to one of the millions of other sites unless they can see what the site is within 10 seconds, what it's about within the next 10 seconds, and how it's organized and what links it has in 10 more seconds.
- *Keep the design appropriate to the company.* The no-frills Cheap CDs site (**www.cheap-cds.com**) gives the customer the impression that this company offers the lowest prices—even if it doesn't always have the cheapest CDs.
- *Create strong content and update it regularly.* Quality content is the number one reason that users return to Web sites. Provide complete and accurate product information. Regular updates give visitors a reason to return to your site.
- *Flashy is not necessarily better.* Too many colours or graphic elements can be distracting. Strive for clarity, not clutter.
- *Make navigation easy.* Users want to move around a site as quickly as possible. Two common navigational tools are tabs along the top of the screen and a navigation bar on the left side. Search features also help visitors find what they need. Make sure links work.
- *Keep download times short.* Users like speedy sites. Multimedia effects can make pages slow to load. Customers quickly become frustrated and will leave a site without ordering if they have to wait for images to appear. Offering a text-only version of your site makes it easier for visitors with slower modems to access information.
- *Avoid long blocks of text.* Reading lots of text is difficult on the small screen. Users prefer to see headlines and article summaries, with links to the complete article for those who want more information.[35]

Gearing Up for E-Business and E-Commerce

Suppose your company wants to start an online business venture. If you want your Web site to generate sales and repeat visits, you should start by analyzing the company's readiness for e-business (i.e., its infrastructure). Here are some critical questions to ask:

1. Which customers are we trying to reach through the Internet: current customers, new customers, or a combination of both?
2. Will we offer a deep range of merchandise or only selected products?
3. Will we design our Web site in-house or outsource it?
4. How will we attract customers to our Web site?
5. How will we encourage purchases and repeat visits at our Web site?
6. How will we ensure that customers receive quality customer service?
7. What percentage of total sales do we hope to achieve through the Internet?
8. What internal operational changes do we need to make to support our Internet strategy?
9. Does our current technological infrastructure support our goals? If not, will we upgrade or outsource?
10. How will we mine customer information and purchases to improve service and profits?

You can also use similar questions to evaluate the success of an existing operation. In addition, you would determine the number of visitors, the percentage who buy, how well the order fulfillment and customer service procedures work, and what improvements and upgrades are necessary.

TRY IT NOW!

1. **Create Your Own Web Site** Many ISPs now offer customers the chance to have their own Web site. Develop a proposal for a personal or business Web site, including the purpose, features, estimated cost, maintenance, update plan, and similar details. Refer to the guidelines in the "Applying This Chapter's Topics" section. For more help, visit Jakob Nielsen's Alertbox site (www.useit.com) for his biweekly columns on improving Web site usability. Check out his column "The Top Ten Mistakes of Web Design," which he recently updated. If possible, create and test the Web site.

2. **Build an E-Business Site** If you're thinking of setting up a Web site to market products on the World Wide Web, check out the online e-commerce tutorial at www.hotwired.com/webmonkey/e-business/tutorials/tutorial3.html. You'll find five lessons that describe how to generate a realistic e-business plan, create an appropriate site design, market the site, handle payments, set up shipping procedures, and establish adequate security. With links to related articles on the HotWired site, this series guides you through the whole process, including whether to build your e-business site in-house or use outside experts.

>looking ahead

at Mark's Work Wearhouse

The fast-paced world of Web retailing doesn't let a company rest on its laurels. Mark's Work Wearhouse is working hard to hold on to its position using e-business. Many new initiatives and technologies have been developed and will be developed that will decrease costs, increase profits, and increase customer satisfaction. According to Robin Lynas, CIO of MWW, "the future is unlimited, and at MWW we are convinced to provide a reasonable return to the shareholders and maintain customer satisfaction, our business must first understand our business (including customers) and implement technology that will achieve our organizational goals."

Globalization of trade has been crucial to the Canadian economy. The increase in global trade is due in part to the international trading communities (e.g., the North American Free Trade Agreement) but, more importantly, technology has facilitated the increasing global trade (e.g., through standardization of products and their quality and telecommunications such as the Internet). The challenges for companies are to recognize the changes that are occurring and capitalize on them.

SUMMARY OF LEARNING GOALS

➡lg 1 **What is the Internet, and how does it work?**
The Internet is a global "network of networks" that is revolutionizing how businesses operate. It combines high-speed communications and computing power to transmit information immediately. All networks in the Internet use TCP/IP, a special language that allows different types of computers to communicate. In addition to the resources of the World Wide Web, the Internet provides file transfer capabilities, e-mail, chat sessions, and newsgroups. Data travel from the user's access point to the Internet service provider and then through a series of interlinked national backbones to the recipient's ISP.

KEY TERMS

browser 96
business-to-business (B2B)
    e-commerce 102
business-to-consumer (B2C)
    e-commerce 102
business-to-enterprise (B2E)
    102
consumer-to-business (C2B)
    e-commerce 102
consumer-to-consumer (C2C)
    e-commerce 102
electronic business (e-business)
    102
electronic commerce (e-com-
    merce) 102
extranet 103
host computer 97
hypertext 96
information technology (IT)
    95
Internet 96
Internet service provider (ISP)
    96
servers 97
Transmission control pro-
    tocol/Internet protocol
    (TCP/IP) 96
Web sites 96
World Wide Web (WWW)
    96

➡ lg 2 **Who uses the Internet, and for what purpose?**

About 378 million people worldwide use the Internet. About 43 percent of all Canadians are regular users. Although adopters of the technology were younger, more affluent, and better educated than the general population, the profile of the Net user is moving closer to the national averages in these areas. Among the most popular Web sites are those with company and product information, news, reference materials, periodicals, financial quotes, and entertainment. Businesses use the Internet to research economic trends; gather industry information; learn about competitors; provide customer service; communicate with employees, vendors, and customers; market and sell products; and purchase supplies.

➡ lg 3 **How has the Internet economy changed the business environment?**

New types of companies provide enabling technology and services. The competitive arena is expanding as the Internet eliminates barriers of time and place and reduces barriers to entry. Channel relationships are changing as well. The Internet allows companies to sell directly to consumers without using distributors. Some distributors are finding new roles by providing services to online merchants who want to outsource order fulfillment. The Internet also empowers consumers by increasing access to information and making it easy to compare prices.

➡ lg 4 **How can companies incorporate e-business and e-commerce into their overall business strategies?**

E-business (the entire process of adding value from the raw materials to the eventual end user and how all units of a business operate) and e-commerce (selling a product or service via the Internet) have four primary market segments: business-to-business, business-to-consumer, consumer-to-consumer, and consumer-to-business. Also, e-business incorporates business-to-enterprise (the internal exchanges). It is important to understand the entire business, its strategies and objectives, to incorporate a successful e-business. In addition, the infrastructure must be able to support e-business.

The business-to-business market accounts for about 75 percent of all e-commerce revenue. Among the many models for e-commerce are selling goods and services over the Web, providing information for a fee, supporting an information or entertainment site with advertising or referral fees, facilitating sales through auctions, providing e-business-enabling services, and gathering industry or consumer information into "infomediary" sites.

➡ lg 5 **What benefits do businesses achieve through e-business and e-commerce?**

E-business and e-commerce reduce costs by streamlining the company's operating procedures. They offer the convenience of lower prices, greater selection of products and vendors, around-the-clock ordering and customer service availability (increasingly important in the global economy), ease of updating and distributing of product catalogues without incurring printing costs, and the ability to track customer and product sales data. Companies can eliminate intermediaries and sell directly to consumers and can offer customized products. The increased efficiency results in better customer service, lower transaction costs, and new relationship-building strategies.

➡ lg 6 **What steps are involved in launching an e-business and e-commerce venture?**

Companies can choose from several levels of e-commerce, starting with a basic promotional Web site and then adding order-taking and customer service features. More sophisticated strategies integrate Web activities into the company's existing business structure. To implement an e-business and e-commerce strategy, companies must consider merchandising, Web site costs and design, marketing, customer service and order fulfillment, operations, and infrastructure.

➡lg 7   **What lies ahead for the Information Superhighway?**

One-to-one marketing is on the rise as e-business companies recognize the added value of personalization. Government, industry, and consumer groups are developing solutions to protect customer privacy. Industry leaders are taking steps to protect their turf by acquiring other companies.

WORKING THE NET

1. Compare the features of two Web-based grocery services such as Webvan (**www.webvan.com**), Peapod (**www. peapod.com**), NetGrocer (**www.netgrocer.com**), and ShopLink (**www.shoplink.com**). Which do you prefer, and why? How easy is it for consumers to shop at the site? Pick five items you regularly buy and compare the prices with those at your local market. Do you think consumers will eventually do more of their grocery shopping online?

2. Use the NUA Internet Surveys site at **www.nua.ie** to track the latest statistics and demographics on Internet users and to research the latest studies on e-commerce and business use. Summarize your findings in a brief report on key trends.

3. To avoid government intervention, Internet industry organizations are working toward self-regulation to protect consumer privacy. Visit the sites for the Online Privacy Alliance (**www.privacyalliance.org**) and TrustE (**www.truste.org**), and evaluate what they are doing. What criteria must firms meet to win the right to display the TrustE seal of approval?

4. What makes a good Web site? Check out the site for the Webby Awards, **www.webbyawards.com**. Then compare the winning sites to the winners of the Muddies Awards for worst Web sites, **www.netstudio.com/mudbrick/**. Summarize the differences.

5. How good are "prebuilt" Web site templates for e-commerce? Compare the features and pricing offered by such companies as QuickSite (**www.quicksite.com**), VersaCheck Web Commerce (**www.mipsdla.com**), Maestro Commerce Suite (**bitsoftware.com**), Net.Commerce Start (**www.software.ibm.com/commerce/net.commerce**), and iCat (**www.icat.com**). If you were starting an online retail business, would you use one of these or hire an outside site designer?

CREATIVE THINKING CASE

Ticketmaster on the Web

Unlike many companies, Ticketmaster probably didn't need a Web presence to survive. With its automated phone sales system, it already had a near monopoly in the ticket services industry. It embraced the Internet in a big way, however, and became the leading ticket seller online and off, selling a total of about 75 million tickets a year for about 3750 clients under exclusive distribution agreements.

Ticket sales are only one part of Ticketmaster.com's (**www.ticketmaster.com**) e-commerce strategy. The company wants to take a greatly expanded role in its customers' lives. To create an entertainment portal—the only place people need to visit for their event and live entertainment needs—Ticketmaster acquired CitySearch, an online directory of local information, in 1998, and MSN Sidewalk, a similar service, in 1999. Just log on to the Ticketmaster.com site to access local information on entertainment, business, and news in one of the numerous markets in the world. Once you've found a concert, play, or sporting event you like, you can immediately select seats, order tickets online, and even print them out at home, complete with bar codes for verification and coupons for nearby restaurants and parking lots. Need a date for the concert? Ticketmaster.com can even help with that! The company also owns Match.com, the leading online matchmaking and dating service.

In addition to service charges on its ticket sales, Ticketmaster.com generates revenues from advertising on the site and partnerships with other dot-com companies. For example, local delivery service Kozmo.com pays Ticketmaster.com a fee for referrals for video rentals or food delivery. To broaden its entertainment listings, it formed a partnership with CultureFinder.com. Restaurant-reservations site foodline.com Inc. is another partner. Alliances with wireless providers make Ticketmaster.com services mobile as well.

Ticketmaster.com takes the parent company's original idea of direct ticket sales many steps further. Its phone service is passive; buyers come to it when they want tickets. The Web site is proactive; soon after you attend a concert, you'll receive an e-mail with the play list from the concert and an offer for promotional items like concert t-shirts. Register for MyTicketmaster and you'll get newsletters with events that match your interests. Whereas Ticketmaster's phone service focuses on major events in big stadiums, Ticketmaster.com offers tickets to events at much smaller venues through its TicketWeb subsidiary.[36]

Critical Thinking Questions

1. Describe Ticketmaster.com's e-commerce strategy. How is it using the power and unique capabilities of the Web to its advantage?
2. Based on the information in the case and a visit to Ticketmaster.com's Web site, in what stage of e-commerce (see Exhibit 4-8 on page 109) would you place Ticketmaster.com currently?
3. What problems might Ticketmaster.com face as its services increase in popularity?

E-Mail Alert

How would you feel if the contents of your entire hard drive were open to public scrutiny? Is there anything on it that might be incriminating? Over 5 million e-mails are sent every day in North America and each and every one of these could be called into evidence if warranted in a court of law. A huge business opportunity exists in the field of e-evidence and Kroll Ontrack of Minnesota, an e-evidence processing centre, is planning to enter the Canadian market.

It seems that the public does not recognize the risk in writing damaging detail in everyday e-mail correspondence. Indiscriminate e-babble can end up costing your employer hundreds of thousands of dollars. The e-evidence from one hard drive can be the key to a successful litigation. One of the reasons we tend to put things in e-mail that we might not verbalize is the vast number of e-mails many people receive every day. The inclination is to get it off your incoming mail and onto someone else's as quickly as possible. Unfortunately, this leads to minimal, if any, thought being put into the response. Many of us believe that by deleting and emptying our trash, the e-mail is gone. It is definitely not. Not only can an e-evidence company search for an e-mail on your hard drive, it can search your Internet provider's files as well.

The implications for risk to employers are massive, and experts believe that the general public still does not take this matter seriously. If, as a conscientious employee, you wish to consider the risk, what does this mean? Basically, it forces us to be more open and honest in our business dealings. If you are planning to send an e-mail to a co-worker, think how you would feel if that e-mail were to appear on the front page of the *Globe and Mail*. In other words, no matter how busy you are, think before you press "send."

Critical Thinking Questions

1. To what extent do you feel your classmates or co-workers have considered the issue of indiscreet e-mail communication?
2. What are the implications for employers if employees do not see the risk of this sort of behaviour?
3. To what extent do you apply standards of confidentiality, honesty, privacy, and nondisclosure of information to your own communication with others?

Mohair Socks

Theresa Bergeron is an entrepreneur who has recognized the possibilities in the global marketplace and has business dealings that span half the globe. From her home in South Mountain, Ontario, a small town just one hour south of Ottawa, she conducts her business. Theresa buys kid mohair wool from Texas and South Africa, has it spun in England, has the socks knit in Georgetown, Ontario, and labels and packages the socks at her own home with the help of her family. Her previous year's sales were approximately one quarter of a million dollars, with sales approaching half a million dollars expected in the next year.

The socks are a high-quality specialty item made from the first shearing of a baby goat, which is processed into a fibre called kid mohair. The mohair is very strong and long-wearing and feels like cashmere. Theresa would like to break into the U.S. market, but with a wholesale price of $12.00 and a retail price of $30.00, the socks are not for everyone. Efforts to contact the appropriate people in the U.S. firms sometimes lead to frustration. Theresa uses personal selling techniques to attempt to place her products in local retail establishments. She also attends trade shows in order to contact shop owners. A new advertising effort, with a new logo and catchy language, is expected to attract additional attention. Once the orders start flowing in, however, there is still the problem of supplying enough socks. Due to the nature of her product, many factors are out of her control. The number of goat farmers in Texas is dwindling, the droughts in Africa cause reduced availability of wool, and problems at the weaving facility in England cause additional delays in getting the wool to the knitter.

Nevertheless, Theresa looks forward to a successful year and is planning her next move to expand her business.

Critical Thinking Questions

1. Using the PEST model, discuss the impact of environmental factors on Theresa's business decisions.
2. How has Theresa successfully taken advantage of the global marketplace?
3. What else might she do to expand her business?

CHAPTER 5

Forms of Business Ownership

In this chapter you'll learn about the different forms of organization taken by business owners. How does an owner set the business up legally, and what does this imply for the business and its owner(s)? This is related directly to our *political* environment in the PEST model because the government regulates the options for business ownership and the rules to follow. However, you will see that the form of business ownership has implications on all aspects of the integrative business model and thus ultimately on the success of the business.

Let's look at the critical success factors. First, the form of business ownership chosen will affect the *financial performance* of the company because it affects its costs (costs of setting up the organization, for example) and the level of taxes that it must pay. It also affects how much profit is available or distributed to the owner(s). The form of business ownership can also indirectly affect the business's ability to *meet customer needs* as the degree of flexibility and control for the owner(s) tends to decrease as the business grows larger, which is often when the form of ownership is changed. More directly, the owner is restricted in terms of how to meet the needs of the customer if he or she is under a franchise agreement, for example. This in turn will also affect the degree of *innovation and creativity* that is possible. Finally, it is perhaps easier to *gain employee commitment* in some forms of business organization, as they offer the possibility of direct ownership beyond purchasing a minority interest in the company's stock.

So the form of business ownership, like all the decisions made in a business, has an integrative impact. It must be chosen with the company's overall goals and *strategy* in mind; for example, it would be difficult for a sole proprietorship to raise sufficient capital to build a chain of hotels worldwide. It affects how the external environment treats the business and how that business affects the environment in turn, and it also affects the decisions that are made internally.

Looking back at our PEST model of the external environment, we can examine the effect that the form of business ownership has with regard to those dealing with the business from the outside. For example, within the political environment, the government tends to regulate larger businesses more heavily, especially large public corporations that have a greater impact on society. The amount of legal liability that the owners have for business debts depends on the form of ownership. This can lead to a situation where a loan may be turned down because the lender doubts the debt can be satisfied out of business assets, and yet the form of ownership chosen (namely, incorporation) does not allow for the debt to be satisfied from the personal assets of the owner(s) unless they are specifically used as collateral. The form of business ownership chosen affects the amount of taxes paid to the government as well, which in turn affects the *economic* environment: paying less tax allows for greater spending to grow the business. Within the *social* environment, society is becoming increasingly demanding of businesses to be socially responsible and act ethically. This extends to all forms of business organization, but perhaps the highest expectations rest on the larger public corporations because of their visibility and resources. The *technological* environment is perhaps the only area not directly impacted by the form of business organization. Small and large organizations, whether sole proprietorships, partnerships, or corporations, have equal access to technology. However, this access to technology has allowed different forms of business to compete on more of a level playing field, leading to the creation of many new businesses. These new businesses usually start small as sole proprietorships, partnerships, or small private corporations—creating a trend that we will discuss in Chapter 6.

When looking at the advantages and disadvantages of each form of ownership, you will see many examples of the integration of the form of ownership and the decisions made within the functional areas. For example, in the *finance* area, the form of ownership directly affects the degree of capital that the business has access to, and the options it has to raise that capital. This in turn will affect the size of its *operations*. In the *human resource* area, taking the large corporation as an example, this form of ownership affects the ability to find and keep quality employees as well as the incentives available to them—as the larger the company the greater the opportunities for employees to advance and the greater the resources to attract and hold on to them.

In a broader sense, the form of ownership affects the ability of the business to make good decisions in all areas. It is very unlikely for a sole proprietor, for example, to be an expert at every function, and thus the business will be weak where he or she is weak unless expert assistance is brought in. This is often why businesses develop partnerships, preferably with people who have complementary skills, and/or create corporations that can, as they grow larger, attract professional talent to round out the company's needs. A good example is Research In Motion (RIM), the maker of the famous BlackBerry pager. The company was built on the strength of its technology, but a major weakness early on was in the area of marketing. Due to the success and visibility of this publicly traded corporation, it was able to attract very strong talent in that area to continue the success of the company. A sole proprietorship would have had more difficulty.

This issue is the same with respect to the basic tasks of a manager in any of the functional areas or levels of the company. A sole proprietor may be good at *planning*, but bad at executing (*organizing*, *leading*, and *controlling*), or vice versa. Bringing other people into the company to balance those needs is important to the success of the company, and it is easier as the business grows, which often necessitates a change in the form of ownership.

Forms of Business Ownership

CHAPTER 5

Learning Goals

➡ **lg 1** What are the three main forms of business organization? What factors should a company's owners consider when selecting a form?

➡ **lg 2** What are the advantages and disadvantages of sole proprietorships?

➡ **lg 3** Why would a new business venture choose to operate as a partnership, and what downside would the partners face?

➡ **lg 4** How does the corporate structure provide advantages and disadvantages to a company and its owners.

➡ **lg 5** Does a company have any business organization options besides sole proprietorship, partnership, and corporation?

➡ **lg 6** Why is franchising growing in importance?

➡ **lg 7** Why would a company use mergers and acquisitions to grow?

➡ **lg 8** What trends will affect business organization in the future?

The Freedom of Ownership

For six years, Christopher Halpin, owner of Manna Catering Services, was frustrated by what he describes as "the lack of respect for employees and lack of choices for the customers." During these six years, Christopher worked for numerous catering companies to supplement his art consulting business. The frustration that Christopher felt convinced him that he could become a successful business owner and demonstrate respect for his employees all the while delivering professional service and products to his customers.

His philosophy is simple: "create the right atmosphere and allow the customers to feel comfortable. The customers must see that the events are flexible, creative, unique, remarkable, and memorable." He says that our culture is generally not comfortable with being "served" so this has been his major challenge.

Since Christopher started Manna Catering Services in 1995, he has used his prior knowledge of the industry and has learned some valuable lessons along the way. From what he saw while working for other people, he did not believe that the catering industry was viewed as being professional or "white collared." Since opening the business, his approach has been "treat the industry from a professional aspect and others will see it as being professional."

First he had to design flexible menu choices for the customers. "Not all customers want the same experience. By offering a variety of menus and a unique atmosphere around these menus, each event is seen as special and memorable," he says. He was also very aware that it was important to keep his costs to a minimum, without sacrificing quality, so that these savings could be passed on to the customer. With the combination of a variety of experiences and savings to the customers, Christopher ensures that they are receiving the quality and service they want.

Christopher also believes that to be truly customer-focused he must also be considerate of his employees and their needs. "Employees must enjoy their job and the customer must be made to realize that it is okay to be served." Christopher continued to share his philosophy about employees: "Typically, employees in the small catering businesses are part-time, supplementing their regular income. This often results in employees being very transient. I wanted to have a more secure and stable part-time group. I pay well (about 50 percent more than the standard), I allow the staff to eat the same food as the clients (therefore there is no thieving), they dress professionally (basic black, and of course, the Manna Catering signature natural linen apron—always freshly laundered), I provide training to ensure consistency in the service and to respect the customers and make them feel comfortable and, most importantly, I respect my employees." Because of his

CRITICAL THINKING QUESTIONS

As you read this chapter, consider the following questions as they relate to Christopher Halpin and Manna Catering Services:

- What factors did Christopher consider when selecting a form of business organization?
- What are some of the pros and cons of operating the business as a sole proprietorship? If Christopher decided to include a partner, what should that partner bring to the business?
- What would be the benefits to incorporating the business?

respect for his employees and the fair and equitable treatment of them, the turnover rate of his staff has been very low and they do not work for other caterers.

Being customer-focused has been a very valuable and profitable lesson for Christopher. He warns those who are considering starting their own business not to forget to do their homework. He recommends that after you decide to start a business and determine what the business focus is, you should think about what the legal structure of your company is going to be. "I researched the various types of business ownership and decided to form the simplest, the sole proprietorship, for many reasons," says Christopher.

"I looked into incorporating," he says, "but did not think the added expense and regulations were worth the investment; I could do better things with the money. The limited liability appealed to me, but in this business if you are customer-focused and careful (e.g., handling of food), there is little risk."

Also, the partnership form had very little interest for him. He sat down and wrote out his qualifications for the catering business. From the day-to-day operations, there were no skills that he felt he did not possess or could not learn quickly, so there was no need to have a partner from that perspective. He did acknowledge that he was weak in the accounting and financial management area, but to overcome this situation, he found an accounting firm to help with financial and tax advice. Christopher sums up his sense about the possibility of forming a partnership: "Besides, I had no interest in sharing the profits with anyone."

"The sole proprietorship appealed to me the best. I am able to make the decisions by myself and control the growth of the company. I don't ever think that I will take on a partner, but I can see the day that if I want the company to grow to a certain point, I will have to incorporate it."

Today, Chris enjoys a successful business, the flexibility it offers him, and the respect from both his employees and his customers. He is happy in his venture and suggests that if you want to start a business—"Do your homework."[1]

BUSINESS IN THE 21ST CENTURY

As a business novice, Christopher Halpin knew very little about choosing a form of business organization for his new venture. He was fortunate to have good advisers who helped him understand the pros and cons of sole proprietorships, partnerships, and corporations. He also learned that a company might need to change its legal form as it grows.

If you, like Christopher, dream of owning your own business, you are not alone. Most of you probably know someone who has started a business (or perhaps you yourself have done so). New businesses, especially small businesses, play a very important role in the Canadian economy. Most new job creations result from the small business sector, and particularly from new businesses.[2]

Regardless of size, every new business must choose a form of business organization that reflects its goals. In this chapter we will look at the different ways to organize a business. The three main types of business organization—sole proprietorships, partnerships, and corporations—all have advantages and disadvantages. Other business structures, such as cooperatives, joint ventures, and franchising, are appropriate for special situations. Next we will explore how corporations use mergers and acquisitions to grow. Finally, we'll look ahead at trends shaping business organization in the future.

→ **lg 1**

Types of Business Organization

Congratulations! You've decided to start a company. You've got a great idea and some start-up funding. Before you go any further, however, you must set up your business entity. Which form of business organization best suits the needs of your particular business?

To choose wisely, you must ask several key questions: Do you want to own the business alone or with other participants? What skills does each of the owners bring to the business? How much operating control do the owners want? Who will be liable for the firm's debts and taxes? Can the firm attract employees? What costs are associated with the chosen ownership structure? How easy will it be to find financing? How will the business be taxed? The answers determine the legal ownership structure you will select.

Most businesses fall into one of three major ownership categories: sole proprietorships, partnerships, or corporations. Most sole proprietorships and partnerships remain small; however, corporations can be small, medium, or large (i.e., the size of the company does not determine the type of ownership). Each form of business ownership has advantages and disadvantages. As we will discover in the following sections, the form that offers the most advantages in the early stages of a company's life may no longer meet its needs as it grows.

→ **lg 2**

Sole Proprietorships

Starting Hot Pots, a company that specializes in container gardens for small spaces, gave owner Gail Cecil the chance to combine her love of gardening with her desire to bring beauty into people's homes. All she needed to get started was her expertise in horticulture, a business licence, and the money for business cards, plants, pots, and related materials. "I love being my own boss and the challenge of creating new designs for each location," she says. At the same time, Gail has no guaranteed paycheque, and the work can be lonely: "It's hard to stay motivated. Some days I really have to push myself to look for new clients."[3]

sole proprietorship
A business that is established, owned, and often financed by one person.

Gail Cecil formed Hot Pots as a **sole proprietorship**, a business that is established, owned, operated, and often financed by one person. Your neighbourhood florist, shoe repair shop, babysitters, and hair stylists are usually sole proprietorships. Most small service businesses often operate as sole proprietorships.

Advantages of Sole Proprietorships

Sole proprietorships have several advantages that make them popular:
- *Easy and inexpensive to form.* As Gail Cecil discovered, sole proprietorships have few legal requirements, and forming one doesn't cost much. Once the owner obtains the start-up funds (if needed) and necessary local licences and permits, he or she can start the business.
- *Profits that all go to the owner.* The owner of a sole proprietorship gets all the profits the business earns. The more efficiently the firm operates, the higher the profits will be.

As the sole proprietor of two successful small businesses, a high-end fashion boutique and a women's bookstore, Carolyn Anderson enjoys having direct control over business decisions.

- *Direct control of the business.* Successful sole proprietors like Gail Cecil thrive on their independence and the freedom in decision-making. They like being their own boss and controlling all business decisions without having to consult anyone else. It's easy to respond quickly to changing business conditions and customers' needs.
- *Freedom from government regulations.* Although all businesses are subject to some government controls, generally speaking, sole proprietorships have more freedom than other forms of business.
- *No special taxation.* Proprietorships do not pay corporate taxes. Their profits are treated as personal income of the owner and reported on the owner's individual tax return. Business income is combined with all other personal income and taxed at the personal rate. Combining business and personal income *may* provide a tax break.
- *Ease of dissolution.* With no co-owners or partners involved, the proprietor can close or sell the business at any time. Thus, sole proprietorships are an ideal way to test new business ideas.

Disadvantages of Sole Proprietorships

Along with the freedom to operate the business as they wish, sole proprietors face several disadvantages:

- *Unlimited liability.* In the eyes of the law, the sole proprietor and the business are identical (i.e., the sole proprietor is the business). Thus, the owner is personally responsible for all the debts of the business—even when they are more than the company is worth. The owner may have to sell personal property, such as a car, house, or investments, to satisfy claims against the business.
- *Difficulty in raising capital.* Financial resources are more limited for sole proprietorships. Business lenders view the owner's unlimited liability as a high risk. Business assets are not protected from claims of personal creditors. Owners must often use personal funds—borrowing on credit cards, taking second mortgages on their homes, and selling investments—to finance the business. Inability to raise additional funding may curtail expansion plans or even to ensure the "ongoing-concern" of the business.
- *Limited managerial expertise.* The success of a sole proprietorship depends entirely on the owner's skills and talents. The owner is fully responsible for all business decisions and must be a "jack-of-all-trades." Not all owners are equally skilled in all areas. For example, an inventor who creates a new potentially profitable product may not be a good salesperson, production manager, or accountant.
- *Trouble finding qualified employees.* Sole proprietors have difficulty finding and keeping good employees. Small firms cannot offer the same fringe benefits and opportunities for advancement as larger companies.
- *Personal time commitment.* Running a sole proprietorship requires a considerable time commitment and often dominates the owner's life. The owner must be willing to make sacrifices, often working 12 or more hours a day, six or even seven days a week.
- *Unstable business life.* The life span of a sole proprietorship is uncertain. If the owner loses interest, retires, or dies, the business will cease to exist unless the owner finds a buyer.
- *Losses that all go to the owner.* The sole proprietor is responsible for all losses. However, tax law allows the proprietor to deduct these losses from other types of personal income.

The sole proprietorship may be a suitable choice for a one-person start-up operation that has no employees and little risk of liability exposure, like Hot Pots. For many sole proprietors, however, this is a temporary choice. As the business grows, the owner may not have the managerial and financial resources to operate alone. At this point she or he may decide to go into partnership with one or more co-owners.

concept check

- What is a sole proprietorship?
- Why do so many businesspeople choose this form of business organization?
- What are the positive aspects and the drawbacks to being a sole proprietor?

→ lg 3

Partnerships

Brett Cosor had an idea for a company that provides big-screen multimedia installations for special events. However, he realized that his strengths were in the creative vision rather than the nuts-and-bolts details of the business. In 1988 he recruited his cousin Jeff Studley to handle the operational side of CPR MultiMedia Solutions. The cousins' abilities were complementary. "Brett is a goal-oriented guy; I'm a task-oriented guy," explains Studley. Within ten years, their partnership had grown into a business with two divisions, 47 employees, and revenues of $10 million.[4]

For those like Brett Cosor who don't want to "go it alone," the partnership offers another form of business ownership. A **partnership** is an association of two or more persons who agree to operate a business together for profit.

Forming a partnership is simple. The parties agree, either orally or in writing, to share in the profits and losses of a joint enterprise. Written partnership agreements that spell out the terms and conditions of the partnership can prevent later conflicts between the partners. These agreements typically include the name and purpose of the partnership, contributions of each partner (financial, talent, equipment, etc.), management responsibilities and duties of each partner, compensation arrangements (salaries and shares of profits), provisions covering the addition of new partners and sale of partnership interests, and procedures for resolving conflicts, dissolving the business, and distributing assets.

There are two basic types of partnerships: general and limited. In a **general partnership**, all partners share in the management and profits. They co-own assets, and each can act on behalf of the firm. Each partner has unlimited liability for all the business obligations of the firm. A **limited partnership** has two types of partners: one or more **general partners**, who have unlimited liability, and one or more **limited partners**, whose liability is limited to the amount of their investment. In return for limited liability, limited partners agree not to take part in the day-to-day management of the firm. They help to finance the business and/or promote the business, but the general partners maintain operational control.

Advantages of Partnerships

Some advantages of partnerships come quickly to mind:

- *Ease of formation.* Like sole proprietorships, partnerships are easy to form. The partners agree to do business together and develop a partnership agreement. For most partnerships, applicable laws are not complex.
- *Availability of capital.* Because two or more people contribute financial resources, partnerships can raise funds more easily for operating expenses and business expansion than can a sole proprietorship. The partners' combined financial strength also increases the firm's ability to raise funds from outside sources.

partnership
An association of two or more persons who agree to operate a business together for profit.

general partnership
A partnership in which all partners share in the management and profits. Each partner can act on behalf of the firm and has unlimited liability for all its business obligations.

limited partnership
A partnership with one or more general partners, who have unlimited liability, and one or more limited partners, whose liability is limited to the amount of their investment.

general partners
Partners who have unlimited liability for all of the firm's business obligations and who control its operations.

limited partners
Partners whose liability for the firm's business obligations is limited to the amount of their investment. They help to finance the business and/or promote the business, but do not participate in the firm's day-to-day operations.

- *Diversity of skills and expertise.* Partners share the responsibility for managing and operating the business. Ideal partnerships bring together people with complementary backgrounds, rather than those with similar experience. Combining partner skills to set goals, manage the overall direction of the firm, and solve problems increases the likelihood of the partnership's success. Finding the right partner entails looking at your own strengths and weaknesses and examining what you're looking for in a partner. In Exhibit 5-1 you'll find some advice on choosing a partner.
- *Flexibility.* General partners take an active role in managing their firm and can respond quickly to changes in the business environment and to customers' needs.
- *No special taxes.* Partnerships pay no income taxes. Each partner's profit or loss is reported on the partner's personal income tax return, with profits taxed at personal tax rates.
- *Relative freedom from government control.* Except for rules for licensing and permits, the government has little control over partnership activities (i.e., generally, less government control than corporations).

Disadvantages of Partnerships

Despite their advantages, partnerships also have their downside:
- *Unlimited liability.* All general partners have unlimited liability for the debts of the business. In fact, any one partner can be held personally liable for all partnership debts and legal judgments (such as failing to fulfill a contract)—regardless of who caused them. As with sole proprietorships, business failure can lead to a loss of the general partners' personal assets.

---

e x h i b i t   5 - 1 | Picking the Right Partner

Picking a partner is an art, not a science. Be prepared to talk, talk, talk—about everything. On paper someone may have all the right business credentials. But does that person share the ideas you have for your company? And honesty, integrity, and ethics are equally, if not more, important. After all, you may be liable for what your partner does. Be willing to trust your intuition. "Trust those gut feelings—they're probably right," advises Irwin Gray, author of *The Perils of Partners*. First, ask yourself the following questions. Then ask a potential partner and see how well your answers match.

1. Why do you want a partner?
2. What characteristics and talents does each person bring to the partnership?
3. How will you divide partnership responsibilities? Consider every aspect of the business, from long-range planning to daily operations. Who will handle marketing, sales, accounting, customer service?
4. What is your long-term vision for the business (size, life span, financial commitment, etc.)?
5. What are your personal reasons for forming this company—for example, steady paycheque, independence, creating a company that stays small, building a large company?
6. Are all parties willing to put in the same amount of time, and if not, is there an alternative arrangement that is acceptable to everyone?
7. Do you have similar work ethics and values on how to run the company? Is the person honest?
8. What requirements should be included in the partnership agreement?

SOURCES: Julie Bawden Davis, "Buddy System," *Business Start Ups* (June 1998), downloaded from www.entrepreneurmag.com; Azriela Jaffe, "'Till Death Do Us Part' Is No Way to Start a Business," *Business Week Online* (October 23, 1998), downloaded from www.businessweek.com/smallbiz; Jerry Useem, "Partners on the Edge," *Inc.* (August 1998), pp. 54, 59.

Selecting the corporate form of business ownership allows JobDirect to attract the investors it needs to finance the company's growth in the fast-paced Internet environment.

- *Potential for conflicts between partners.* Partners may have different ideas—personal or business—about such matters as how and when to expand the business, which employees to hire, and how to allocate responsibilities. As many partnerships grow, so do the strains of managing a larger company. Differences in the personalities and work styles can cause major clashes and a communications breakdown between partners.

- *Sharing of profits.* Dividing the profits is relatively easy if all partners contribute about the same amount of time, expertise, and capital. But if one partner provides more money and the other puts in more time, it is more difficult to arrive at a fair profit-sharing formula.

- *Difficulty in leaving or ending a partnership.* Partnerships are easier to form than to leave. Suppose one partner wants to leave. How much is that partner's share worth? Is there a buyer who is acceptable to the other partners? If a partner withdraws, dies, or becomes disabled, the partnership can legally dissolve or can reorganize. To avoid these problems, most partnership agreements include specific guidelines for transfer of partnership interests and buy-sell agreements so that surviving partners can buy a deceased partner's interest. Partners often buy special life insurance policies on each partner that fund this purchase.

Choosing the right partner is critical. If you're considering forming a partnership, allow plenty of time to evaluate both your own and your potential partner's skills, goals, personalities, business values, and work habits.

concept check

- How does a partnership differ from a sole proprietorship?
- Describe briefly the three types of partnerships and explain the difference between a general partner and a limited partner.
- What are the main advantages and disadvantages of partnerships, and how do they compare to sole proprietorships?

Corporations

When people think of corporations, they typically think of major, well-known corporations such as Air Canada, Petro-Canada, Hudson Bay Corporation, Bank of Montreal, and so on. Corporations range in size from large multinational corporations such as these, with sales in the billions of dollars and thousands of employees, to small firms with a few employees and considerably smaller revenues.

corporation
A legal entity with an existence and life separate from its owners, who therefore are not personally liable for the entity's debts. A corporation has many of the same legal rights and responsibilities as that of a person: it can own property, enter into contracts, sue and be sued, and engage in business operations.

A **corporation** is a legal entity with an existence and life separate from its owners. Because of this separation, the owners are not personally liable for the corporation's debts. A corporation is subject to the laws in the jurisdiction in which it is incorporated. A corporation can own property, enter into contracts, sue and be sued, and engage in business operations. Unlike sole proprietorships and partnerships, corporations are taxable entities.

Corporations play an important role in the Canadian economy. Exhibit 5-2 shows the ten largest Canadian companies based on sales and Exhibit 5-3 shows the ten largest Canadian corporations based on the number of employees.

| exhibit 5-2 | Ten Largest Canadian Companies Based on Sales/Revenues (2002) |

Name	Sales/Revenues (in millions of dollars)
Weston (George) Ltd.	27 446
Royal Bank of Canada	23 234
Sun Life Financial SVSC Canada	23 101
Loblaw Companies Ltd.	23 082
Onex Corporation	22 653
Bombardier Inc.	21 815
Magna International Inc.	20 364
BCE Inc.	19 768
Power Corp of Canada	19 017
Power Financial Corp.	18 620

SOURCE: Bloomberg LP. (March 10, 2003) Sales/Revenue/Turnover (December 31, 2002) S&P/TSX Composite Index RV.

| exhibit 5-3 | Ten Largest Canadian Companies Based on the Number of Employees (2002) |

Company Name	Number of Employees
Weston (George) Ltd.	139 000
Bombardier Inc.	60 000
Hudson's Bay Co.	70 000
BCE Inc.	66 000
Magna International Inc.	64 200
Royal Bank of Canada	57 568
Quebecor Inc.	54 000
Nortel Networks Corp.	52 600
Alcan Inc.	51 800
Sears Canada Inc.	50 552

SOURCE: Bloomberg LP. (March 10, 2003) Number of Employees (December 31, 2002) S&P/TSX Composite Index RV.

Types of Corporations

public corporation
Corporation that has the right to issue shares to the public.

private corporation
Corporation that does not trade publicly and, therefore, is not listed on a stock exchange.

Corporations can be either public or private. A **public corporation** has the right to issue shares to the public. This means that the company is listed on a stock exchange. A **private corporation** does not trade publicly; therefore, it is not listed on a stock exchange. Most of the smaller corporations are private and most large companies are public.

The Incorporation Process

Setting up a corporation is more complex than starting a sole proprietorship or partnership. If the business activity is primarily only in one province, it is necessary to incorporate only as a provincial company under that province's Companies Act (or other similarly named act). A corporation can also be set up under the Canada Business Corporations Act if it is to operate in more than one province or across Canada. Either route of incorporation requires more steps than setting up a sole proprietorship or partnership.

Incorporating a company involves five main steps:

1. Selecting the company's name (including searching existing company names, to confirm that you can use the name).
2. Writing the articles of incorporation (see Exhibit 5-4) and filing them with the appropriate government office.
3. Paying required fees and taxes.

exhibit 5 - 4 | Articles of Incorporation

Articles of incorporation are prepared on a form authorized or supplied by the province or the federal government, if the corporation incorporated federally. Although they may vary slightly from province to province, all articles of incorporation include the following key items:

- Name of the corporation.
- The province where the registered office is to be situated.
- The classes and any maximum number of shares that the corporation is authorized to issue.
- If the issue, transfer, or ownership of shares is to be restricted, a statement that clearly sets out the restrictions.
- The number of directors, or the minimum and maximum number of directors.
- Any restriction on the business that the corporation may carry on.

4. Holding an organizational meeting.
5. Adopting bylaws, electing directors, and passing the first operating resolutions.

The province or federal government issues the corporate charter based on the information in the articles of incorporation. Once the corporation has its charter, it holds an organizational meeting to adopt bylaws, elect directors, and pass initial operating resolutions. Bylaws provide the legal and managerial guidelines for operating the firm.

The Corporate Structure

shareholders
The owners of a corporation, who hold shares of stock that provide certain rights; also known as *stockholders*.

As Exhibit 5-5 shows, corporations have their own organizational structure with three important components: shareholders, directors, and officers.

The owners of a corporation are its **shareholders**, or *stockholders*, who hold shares of stock that provide certain rights. They may receive a share of the corporation's profits in the form of dividends, and they can sell or transfer their ownership in the

exhibit 5 - 5 | Organizational Structure of Corporations

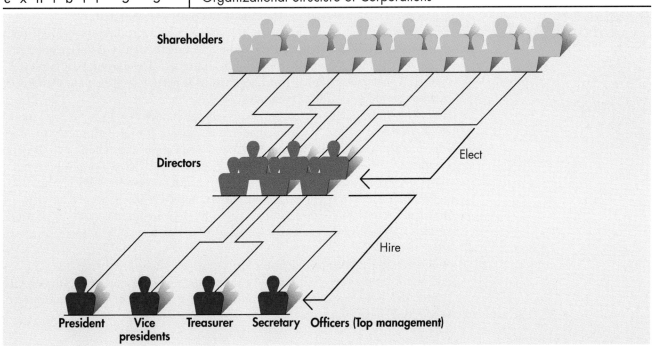

Shareholders

Directors

Elect

Hire

President   Vice presidents   Treasurer   Secretary   Officers (Top management)

corporation (the shares of stock) at any time. Shareholders can attend annual meetings, elect the board of directors, and vote on matters that affect the corporation, as the charter and bylaws specify. They generally have one vote for each share of stock they own.

It is possible for one person to own all the shares of a corporation. In some cases, corporations issue various classes of stock to be able to retain control on one hand and attract capital on the other, such as Canadian Tire Corporation Limited and Magna International Inc. Also, some corporations issue multiple voting shares (more than one vote per share), such as Four Seasons Hotels Inc., to retain control.

Shareholders elect a **board of directors** to govern the corporation. The directors handle overall management of the corporation. They are responsible to ensure that the business is managed with the corporation's best interest in mind (see Chapter 7 for a discussion of corporate governance). They set major corporate goals and policies, hire corporate officers, and oversee the firm's operations and finances. The number of directors will vary depending on the limitations as set out in the "articles of incorporation." Large corporations typically include both corporate executives and outside directors (not employed by the organization) chosen for their professional and personal expertise. Because they are independent of the firm, outside directors can bring a fresh view to the corporation's activities.

The *officers* of a corporation are its top management. Hired by the board, they include the president and chief executive officer (CEO), vice-presidents, treasurer, and secretary, and are responsible for achieving corporate goals and policies. Besides the CEO, other common titles of offices of a corporation include chief financial officer (CFO), chief investment officer (CIO), and chief operating officer (COO). Officers may also be board members and shareholders.

board of directors

A group of people elected by the shareholders to handle the overall management of a corporation, such as setting corporate goals and policies, hiring corporate officers, and overseeing the firm's operations and finances.

➡ **lg 4**

Advantages of Corporations

Certain features enable corporations to merge financial and human resources into enterprises with great potential for growth and profits:

- *Limited liability.* This is one of the key advantages of corporations. Because a corporation is a legal entity that exists apart from its owners, a shareholder's liability for the debts of the firm is limited to the amount of the stock owned. If the corporation goes bankrupt, creditors can look only to the assets of the corporation for payment (i.e., the personal assets of the shareholder are protected).
- *Ease of transferring ownership.* Shareholders of public corporations can sell their shares to someone else at any time without affecting the status of the corporation.
- *Unlimited life.* The life of a corporation is unlimited. The corporation is separate from its owners, so unlike a sole proprietorship or partnership, death or withdrawal of an owner does not affect its existence.
- *Ability to attract financing.* Corporations can raise money by selling new shares of stock. Dividing ownership into smaller units makes it more affordable to more investors, who can purchase one share or several thousand. The larger size and stability of corporations also help them get bank loans. These financial resources allow corporations to invest in facilities and human resources and grow much larger than sole proprietorships and partnerships. Clearly, it would be virtually impossible to make automobiles, provide nationwide telecommunications services, or build major oil or chemical refineries as a sole proprietorship or partnership.
- *Ability to attract potential employees.* Corporations often offer better benefit plans and opportunities that allow them to attract more potential employees. Larger companies also have the advantage of professional management opportunities (e.g., accounting managers).

Disadvantages of Corporations

Although corporations offer businesses many benefits, they also have several disadvantages:

- *Double taxation of profits.* Corporations must pay federal and provincial income taxes on their profits. In addition, any profits paid to shareholders as dividends are also taxed as personal income.
- *Cost and complexity of formation.* As discussed earlier, forming a corporation takes several steps. These incorporation costs can run into thousands of dollars.
- *More government regulations and restrictions.* Unlike sole proprietorships and partnerships, corporations are subject to many regulations and reporting requirements.

A Special Type of Corporation: The Crown Corporation

Crown corporations
Companies that only the provincial and federal governments can set up.

Corporations that are owned either by a provincial or the federal government are called **Crown corporations**. Some of the more recognizable Crown corporations are Canada Post Corporation, the Canadian Broadcasting Corporation (CBC), the Bank of Canada, and the National Museum of Science and Technology. Exhibit 5-6 lists the top ten federal Crown corporations and Exhibit 5-7 lists the top ten provincial Crown corporations based on revenues.

exhibit 5-6 | The Top Ten Federal Crown Corporations Based on Revenues

Federal Crown Corporations	Revenues (in thousands of dollars)
Canada Post (Dec. 2001)	4 460 000
Canada Mrtg. & Housing (Dec. 2001)	4 064 000
Export Development Canada (Dec. 2001)	1 882 000
Canadian Broadcasting Corp. (May 2001)	1 478 809
Business Development Bank Canada (May 2001)	668 290
Atomic Energy of Canada (May 2001)	621 609
Farm Credit Canada (May 2001)	583 107
Via Rail Canada (Dec. 2000)	461 155
Marine Atlantic (Dec. 2001)	118 850
Vancouver Port Authority (Dec. 2000)	83 239

SOURCE: globeinvestor.com, "The Top 1000: Canada's Power Book," top1000.globeandmail.com/2002/crown/crowns.htm, accessed March 10, 2003. Reprinted with permission from *The Globe and Mail.*

exhibit 5-7 | The Top Ten Provincial Crown Corporations Based on Revenues

Provincial Crown Corporations	Revenue (in thousands of dollars)
Hydro-Quebec (Dec. 2001)	12 629 000
B.C. Hydro & Power (May 2001)	8 007 000
Ontario Power Generation (Dec. 2001)	6 239 000
Caisse de depot et placement (Dec. 2001)	3 817 000
Epcor Utilities (Dec. 2001)	3 725 800
Hydro One (Dec. 2001)	3 471 000
Insurance Corp. of B.C. (Dec. 2001)	2 901 021
Manitoba Hydro Electric Board (May 2001)	1 903 000
Societe de l'assur Automobile (Dec. 2000)	1 412 406
Saskatchewan Power Corp. (Dec. 2000)	1 129 000

SOURCE: globeinvestor.com, "The Top 1000: Canada's Power Book," top1000.globeandmail.com/2002/crown/crowns.htm, accessed March 10, 2003. Reprinted with permission from *The Globe and Mail.*

Exhibit 5-8 summarizes the advantages and disadvantages of each form of business ownership.

e x h i b i t   5 - 8 | Advantages and Disadvantages of Major Types of Business Organization

Sale Proprietorship	Partnership	Corporation
Advantages		
Owner receives all profits.	More expertise and managerial skill available.	Limited liability protects owners from losing more than they invest.
Low organizational costs	Relatively low organizational costs.	Can achieve large size due to marketability of stock (ownership).
Income taxed as personal income of proprietor.	Income taxed as personal income of partners.	Ownership is readily transferable.
Independence	Fund-raising ability is enhanced by more owners.	Long life of firm (not affected by death of owners).
Secrecy		Can attract employees with specialized skills.
Ease of dissolution		Greater access to financial resources allows growth. Receives certain tax advantages.
Disadvantages		
Owner receives all losses.	Owners have unlimited liability; may have to cover debts of other, less financially sound partners.	Double taxation because both corporate profits and dividends paid to owners are taxed.
Owner has unlimited liability; total wealth can be taken to satisfy business debts.	Dissolves or must reorganize when partner dies.	More expensive and complex to form.
Limited fund-raising ability can inhibit growth.	Difficult to liquidate or terminate.	Subject to more government regulation.
Proprietor may have limited skills and management expertise.	Potential for conflicts between partners.	Financial reporting requirements make operations public.
Few long-range opportunities and benefits for employees.	Difficult to achieve large-scale operations.	
Lacks continuity when owner dies.		

c o n c e p t c h e c k

• What is a corporation? Describe how corporations are formed and structured.
• Summarize the advantages and disadvantages of corporations. Which features contribute to the dominance of corporations in the business world?

➡ **lg 5**

cooperatives
Legal entities typically formed by people with similar interests, such as customers or suppliers, to reduce costs and gain economic power. A cooperative has limited liability, an unlimited life span, an elected board of directors, and an administrative staff; all profits are distributed to the member-owners in proportion to their contributions.

Agricore is a cooperative formed by western farmers to reduce costs and gain economic power by linking farmers to domestic and international end-use customers.

HOT Links

For more information about cooperatives in Canada, visit the Canadian Co-operative Association's Web site at

www.coopcca.com

➡ **lg 6**

franchising
A form of business organization based on a business arrangement between a franchisor, which supplies the product concept, and the franchisee, who sells the goods or services of the franchisor in a certain geographic area.

Specialized Forms of Business Organization

In addition to the three main forms, several specialized types of business organization play a role in our economy. Two of these are cooperatives and joint ventures.

Cooperatives

Cooperatives in Canada are a vital component in our economy; there are approximately 10 000 cooperatives in the country, with over 15 million members.[5] **Cooperatives** are typically formed by people with similar interests, such as customers or suppliers, to reduce costs and gain economic power. The member-owners pay annual fees and share in any profits. Cooperatives may be organized to provide just about any good or service, such as business services, child-care, financial services, food, health-care, marketing of agricultural and other products, utilities, and cable television.

A cooperative is a legal entity with several corporate features, such as limited liability, an unlimited life span, an elected board of directors, and an administrative staff. Cooperatives distribute all profits to the members in proportion to their contributions. Because they do not keep any profits, cooperatives do not pay taxes. Mountain Equipment Co-op, Credit Union Central of Canada, and Federated Co-operatives Limited are just a few of the cooperatives in Canada.

Joint Ventures

In a *joint venture* (defined in Chapter 2), two or more companies form an alliance to pursue a specific project, usually for a specific time period. There are many reasons for joint ventures. The project may be too large for one party to handle on its own. By forming joint ventures, companies can gain access to new markets, products, or technology. Both large and small companies benefit from joint ventures. For example, Syncrude Canada Ltd. is a joint venture of oil-producing companies, including Nexen Inc. and Petro-Canada, that produces approximately 350 000 barrels of oil per day.[6] By creating the joint venture, infrastructure costs, production costs, and risks were spread out amongst the owners. Exhibit 5-9 shows the ownership percentages of Syncrude Canada Ltd.

Franchising

Franchises come in all sizes including McDonald's, with 23 000 franchises in over 100 countries, and new concepts still on the drawing boards. Chances are you deal with one of the more than 2100 franchise systems in Canada and the United States almost every day. When you have lunch at Taco Time or Papa John's Perfect Pizza, use the services of Mail Boxes Etc., take your car for servicing at AAMCO, buy candles at Buck or Two, or rent a car from Budget Rent-A-Car, in each case you are dealing with a franchised business. These and other familiar name brands have come to mean quality, consistency, and value to customers.

Franchising, one of the fastest growing segments of the economy, provides a way to own a business without starting it from scratch. **Franchising** is a form of business organization that involves a business arrangement between a **franchisor**, the company that supplies the product concept, and the **franchisee**, the individual or company that

e x h i b i t   5 - 9 | Ownership of Syncrude Canada Ltd.   *8 COMPANIES*

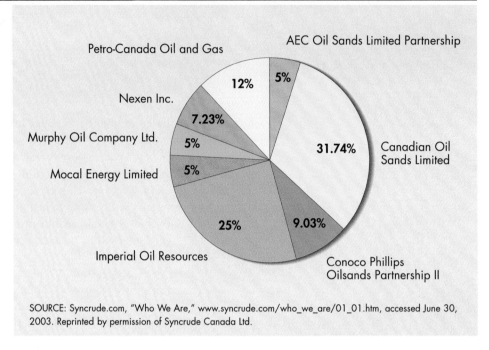

SOURCE: Syncrude.com, "Who We Are," www.syncrude.com/who_we_are/01_01.htm, accessed June 30, 2003. Reprinted by permission of Syncrude Canada Ltd.

franchisor
In a franchising arrangement, the company that supplies the product concept to the franchisee.

franchisee
In a franchising arrangement, the individual or company that sells the goods or services of the franchisor in a certain geographic area.

franchise agreement
A contract setting out the terms of a franchising arrangement, including the rules for running the franchise, the services provided by the franchisor, and the financial terms. Under the contract, the franchisee is allowed to use the franchisor's business name, trademark, and logo.

sells the goods or services in a certain geographic area. With a franchise, the business owner buys a package: a proven product, proven operating methods, and training in managing the business.

The **franchise agreement** is a contract allowing the franchisee to use the franchisor's business name and its trademark and logo. The agreement outlines the rules for running the franchise, the services provided by the franchisor, and the financial terms. The franchisee agrees to keep inventory at certain levels, buy a standard equipment package, keep up sales and service levels, follow the franchisor's operating rules, take part in the franchisor's promotions, and maintain a relationship with the franchisor. In return, the franchisor generally provides the use of a proven company name and symbols, building plans and help finding a site, guidance and training, management assistance, managerial and accounting procedures, employee training, wholesale prices on supplies, and financial assistance.

Advantages of Franchises

Like other forms of business organization, franchising offers some distinct advantages:
- *Increased ability for franchisor to expand.* Because franchisees finance their own units, franchisors can grow without making a major investment. Although franchisors give up a share of profits to their franchisees, they receive ongoing revenues in the form of royalty payments.
- *Recognized name, product, and operating concept.* The franchisee gets a widely known and accepted business with a proven track record, as well as operating procedures, standard goods and services, and national advertising. Consumers know they can depend on products from such franchises as Pizza Hut, Hertz, and Holiday Inn. As a result, the franchisee's risk is reduced and the opportunity for success rises.
- *Management training and assistance.* The franchisor provides a structured training program that gives the new franchisee a crash course in how to start and operate the business. Ongoing training programs for managers and employees are another plus. In addition, franchisees have a peer group to provide support and share ideas.

- *Financial assistance.* Being linked to a nationally known company can help a franchisee obtain funds from a lender. Also, the franchisor typically gives the franchisee advice on financial management, referrals to lenders, and help in preparing loan applications. Many franchisors also offer payment plans, short-term credit for buying supplies from the franchise company, and loans to buy real estate and equipment.

Disadvantages of Franchises

Franchising also has disadvantages, of course:

- *Loss of control.* The franchisor has to give up some control over operations and has less control over its franchisees than over company employees.
- *Costs of franchising.* Franchising can be a costly form of business. A recent Gallup survey reports that the average franchise start-up cost is about US$143 000. These costs vary, depending on the type of business, and may include expensive facilities and equipment. The franchisee also pays ongoing fees or royalties (usually a percentage of sales). Fees for national and local advertising and management advice may add to the franchisee's costs. Franchise fees are higher for better-known franchises, but even newer companies may charge $10 000 to $25 000 or more. Industry averages range from a low of US$12 000 for real estate franchises to US$36 000 in the lodging industry. Lodging franchises require the highest average total initial investment—US$1.8 million, excluding real estate.[7]
- *Restricted operating freedom.* The franchisee agrees to conform to the franchisor's operating rules and facilities design, as well as inventory and supplies standards. Some franchises require franchisees to purchase only from the franchisor or approved suppliers. The franchisor may restrict the franchisee's territory or site, which can limit growth. Failure to conform to franchisor policies can mean loss of the franchise.

HOT Links

Considering buying a franchise? Check out the opportunities and costs at

www.canadianfranchise.com

Franchise Growth

Many of today's major names in franchising, such as McDonald's and Kentucky Fried Chicken, started in the 1950s. Franchising grew rapidly in the 1960s and 1970s as more types of businesses—clothing, business services, convenience stores, and many others—used franchising to distribute their goods and services. The popularity of franchising continued as more business owners turned to franchising as a way to expand operations quickly and in new geographic areas, with limited capital investment.

Franchises offer a recognized name, product, and operating concept and, in many cases, management training and financial assistance.

International Franchising

Like other areas of business, franchising is part of the global marketplace. As mentioned in Chapter 2, the elimination of trade barriers and globalization has permitted many different types of businesses to operate outside their borders. This is also true for franchise companies; most franchise systems either operate units internationally already or plan to expand overseas as the demand for all types of goods and services grows. "Our research has shown us that this is an ideal time to move into the Korean market," says Doug Dwyer, president of Worldwide Refinishing Systems, a bath and kitchen remodelling franchise. "Because the average living standard now is fairly high in Korea, people not only desire but also can afford a better living environment that refinishing and restoring can provide."[8] Currently, among the most popular types of international franchises are restaurants, hotels, business services, educational products, car rentals, and nonfood retail stores.

Franchisors in foreign countries face many of the same problems as other firms doing business abroad. In addition to tracking the market and currency changes, franchisors must be aware of the local culture, language differences, and political risks.

Franchisors in foreign countries also face the challenge of aligning their business operations with the goals of their franchisees, who may be located half a globe away. Technology improves communication with the franchisee and unites worldwide suppliers and customers.

concept check

- Describe franchising and the main parties to the transaction.
- Summarize the major advantages and disadvantages of franchising.
- Why has franchising proved so popular?

➡ lg 7

Corporate Growth through Mergers and Acquisitions

merger
The combination of two or more firms to form a new company, which often takes on a new corporate identity.

acquisition
The purchase of a corporation by another corporation or by an investor group; the identity of the acquired company may be lost.

A **merger** occurs when two or more firms combine to form one new company, which often takes on a new corporate identity. In an **acquisition**, a corporation or an investor group buys a corporation, and the identity of the acquired company may be lost. (A company can also acquire divisions or subsidiaries of another firm.) Normally, an acquiring company finds a target company and, after analyzing the target carefully, negotiates with its management or shareholders.

Merger Motives

Although the headlines tend to focus on mega-mergers, the current "merger mania" affects small companies as well. The motives for undertaking mergers and acquisitions are similar regardless of size. Often the goal is strategic: improving the overall performance of the merged firms through cost savings, elimination of overlapping operations, improved purchasing power, increased market share, or reduced competition. Growth, widening of product lines, and the ability to quickly acquire technology or management skill are other motives. Acquiring a company is often faster, less risky, and less costly than developing products internally or expanding internationally.

Another motive for acquisitions is financial restructuring—cutting costs, selling off units, the laying off of employees, refinancing the company—to increase the value of the company to its shareholders. Financially motivated mergers are based not on the potential to achieve economies of scale, but rather on the acquirer's belief that the target has hidden value that can be unlocked through restructuring. Most financially motivated mergers involve larger companies.

In merging their companies, Chrysler and Daimler-Benz are combining the firms' two different cultures by building trust through team building and rewarding managers who can adapt to change.

Types of Mergers

The three main types of mergers are horizontal, vertical, and conglomerate. In a **horizontal merger,** companies at the same stage in the same industry merge to reduce

horizontal merger

A merger of companies at the same stage in the same industry; done to reduce costs, expand product offerings, or reduce competition.

vertical merger

A merger of companies at different states in the same industry; done to gain control over supplies of resources or to gain access to different markets.

conglomerate merger

A merger of companies in unrelated businesses; done to reduce risk.

leveraged buyout (LBO)

A corporate takeover financed by large amounts of borrowed money; can be done by outside investors or by a company's own management.

HOT Links

To learn more about the latest information technology industry mergers, explore the Broadview Associates site at www.broadview.com

costs, expand product offerings, or reduce competition. Many of the large mergers in the late 1990s were horizontal mergers to achieve economies of scale.

In a **vertical merger**, a company buys a firm in its same industry that is involved in an earlier or later stage of the production or sales process.

A **conglomerate merger** brings together companies in unrelated businesses to reduce risk. Combining with a company whose products have a different seasonal pattern or that respond differently to the business cycle can result in a more stable sales pattern. GE Capital Corp., the financial unit of General Electric Co., targets acquisitions that balance each other: risky companies whose performance fluctuates with changing financial markets and companies that perform consistently regardless of market conditions. GE Capital has 28 separate business lines in five major product groups: specialty insurance; consumer services such as credit card operations and auto and home financing; equipment leasing, ranging from aircraft to satellites to portable toilets; commercial financing; and financing for smaller businesses. Recently, it entered the rapidly growing information technology services market as well.[9]

A specialized financially motivated type of merger, the **leveraged buyout (LBO)**, became popular in the 1980s but is less common today. LBOs are corporate takeovers financed by large amounts of borrowed money—as much as 90 percent of the purchase price. LBOs can be started by outside investors or the corporation's management. Believing that the company is worth more than the value of all the stock, they buy the stock and take the company private. The purchasers expect to generate cash flow by improving operating efficiency or by selling off some units for cash that can be used to pay the debt. Although some LBOs did improve efficiency, many did not live up to investor expectations or generate enough cash to pay the debt.

Exhibit 5-10 shows the some of the largest transactions of acquisitions based on dollar amounts in Canada by Canadian companies acquiring other Canadian companies since 2001.

concept check

- Differentiate between a merger and an acquisition.
- What are the most common motives for corporate mergers and acquisitions?
- Describe the different types of corporate mergers.

e x h i b i t   5 - 1 0 | Major Acquisitions of Canadian Companies by Other Canadian Companies since 2001

Rank	Target Name	Acquirer Name
1	Alberta Energy Co Ltd.	Encana Corp.
2	AT&T Canada Inc.	Brascan Corporation
3	Clarica Life Insurance Co.	Sun Life Financial Services Canada
4	Bell Canada	BCE Inc.
5	Rio Alto Exploration Ltd.	Canadian Nautral Resources
6	Gerdau North American Operations	Gerdau Amersteel Corp.
7	Data Transmissions & Internet	Bell West Inc.
8	CPL Long Term Care Reit	Retirement Residences Reit
9	Mutual Fund Subsidiaries	CI Fund Management Inc
10	Electricity Transmission Lines	AltaLink

SOURCE: Bloomberg LP. (March 12, 2003) Mergers and Acquisitions search (December 31, 2002) Equity MA.

➡ **lg 8**

CAPITALIZING ON TRENDS IN BUSINESS

An awareness of trends in the business environment is a critical component of business success. Many of the social, demographic, and technology trends described Chapters 3 and 4 affect how businesses organize. When studying options for organizing a business or choosing a career path, consider the following trends in franchising and mergers and acquisitions.

Niche Markets

HOT Links

Learn more about Your Dollar Store With More Inc. and franchising opportunities at www.dollarstore.ca

More and more franchises are catering to niche markets. For example, Wild Birds Unlimited, Inc., started by Jim Carpenter in 1981, now has more than 280 units in Canada and the United States. The dollar store concept caters to customers that want convenient locations, value (including low pricing), variety, and so on. Few have grown as quickly and successfully in the past few years as *Your Dollar Store with More!* In May of 1998 the first store was opened in Merritt, British Columbia, by Dave Uzelman. He had so much success with his first store and the second one in Kelowna he decided to franchise the concept.[10]

The Big Get Bigger

As noted earlier, consolidation to achieve economies of scale is driving strategic mergers in industries such as automobiles, oil, telecommunications, utilities, and financial services. These and other industries overexpanded due to an abundance of investment capital, globalization, better information technology, deregulation, and privatization. The result was fierce price competition and a search for other ways to improve financial performance.[11] Consolidation is affecting companies of all sizes, from small businesses to industry leaders.

To boost its market share, Tim Hortons is expanding beyond coffee cafés by operating kiosks in airports and selling its coffee in supermarkets.

Hands across the Sea

Because size is also an advantage when competing in the global marketplace, cross-border mergers are also on the rise. In particular, Canadian, U.S., and European companies want new markets around the world. German automaker Daimler-Benz's 1998 acquisition of Chrysler, the number three U.S. automaker, created the world's third largest auto manufacturer based on revenues. Other trans-Atlantic acquisitions in recent years include the 2000 acquisition of Bestfoods by British-Dutch consumer firm Unilever for US$20 billion and the US$56 billion 1999 merger between Britain's Vodaphone Group and its joint venture partner AirTouch Communications to create the world's largest cellular phone company.

Cross-border mergers present special challenges for the combined entity. It must contend with differences in language and social and workplace cultures in addition to the usual complexities of merging two companies. Regulatory considerations also increase.

concept check

- What are the important trends in franchising?
- How will the performance of the stock market affect future merger activity?
- What are the important trends in mergers and acquisitions?

APPLYING THIS CHAPTER'S TOPICS

Clearly, you need to understand the benefits of different forms of business organization if you start your own company. If you decide to work for someone else, this information will help you match a business entity with your goals. Suppose you are considering two job offers for computer programming positions: a two-year-old consulting firm with ten employees owned by a sole proprietor or a publicly traded software developer with sales of $500 million. In addition to comparing the specific job responsibilities, consider the following:

- Which company offers the better training? Do you prefer the on-the-job training you'll get at the small company, or do you want formal training programs as well?
- Which position offers the chance to work on a variety of assignments?
- What are the opportunities for advancement? Employee benefits?
- What happens if the owner of the young firm gets sick or decides to sell the company?
- Which company offers a better work environment for you?

Answering these and similar questions will help you decide which job meets your particular needs.

Is Franchising in Your Future?

If the franchise route to business ownership interests you, begin educating yourself about the franchise process and investigate various types of franchise opportunities. You should research a franchise company thoroughly before making a financial commitment, because there are considerable differences among the more than 2100 franchise systems.

Would-be franchisees should check recent issues of small business magazines such as *Canadian Business Franchise Magazine, Canadian Business, Entrepreneur, Inc.,* and *Business Start Ups* for industry trends, ideas on promising franchise opportunities, and advice on how to choose and run a franchise. The International Franchise Association Web site at **www.franchise.org** has links to *Franchise World* magazine and other useful sites. (For other franchise-related sites, see the Try It Now box and the Working the Net questions.)

Is franchising for you? Assertiveness, desire to be your own boss, willingness to make a substantial time commitment, passion about the franchise concept, optimism, patience, and integrity rank high on franchisors' lists. Prior business experience is also a definite plus, and some franchisors prefer or require experience in their field. The information in Exhibit 5-11 can help you make a realistic self-assessment and increase your chances of success.

e x h i b i t 5 - 1 1 | Are You a Perfect Franchisee?

What traits do franchisors look for in a prospective franchisee? Specific preferences vary depending on the type of franchise company. For example, most lodging franchisors want prior experience in hotel management. The following questions are based on characteristics franchisors cited in a *Nation's Business* magazine survey:

- How long have you wanted to own a business?
- Are you willing to work hard and put in long hours?
- Do you have the required financial resources for your chosen franchise?
- Does the idea of running all aspects of a small business, from dealing with customers to bookkeeping and maintenance, appeal to you?
- Are you excited about the specific franchise concept?
- Do you have prior business experience? In what fields?
- Can you balance your entrepreneurial tendencies with the need to follow the franchisor's operating procedures?
- Are you competitive and a high achiever?
- Do your expectations and personal goals match the franchisor's?

SOURCE: Adapted from Thomas Love, "The Perfect Franchisee," *Nation's Business* (April 1, 1998), downloaded from business.elibrary.com.

Mergers and You

The high level of merger and acquisition activity changes the business environment for employees, business owners, and customers. You may work for an acquiring or a target company. What does this mean career-wise?

It's important in any job to take opportunities to develop a portfolio of transferable skills. This increases your chances of finding another job, either at the new company or at a new firm. Announcement of a merger increases the stress level for all employees. You will have to live with uncertainty for many months while the companies work out the details of integrating two operations. You may lose your job when overlapping departments are combined. Even if you keep your job, the corporate culture may change whether the acquirer is a Canadian company or one based overseas. The best approach is to keep the quality and quantity of your work at the highest levels and be flexible.

If you own a small company, you may become a target. Or your customers may disappear as they are acquired by other companies. Should the large number of mergers discourage you from starting your own company? Not at all! Even though size is an advantage in many industries, the worldwide economy still needs small, entrepreneurial firms. Despite consolidation trends, large corporations still prefer to outsource many projects to companies with specialized expertise in such areas as design and technology. Also, many niche markets exist where being small provides benefits such as personal service and quick, creative solutions to customer problems.

Mergers also affect vendors, competing firms, and customers. If you own or work for a supplier in an industry with lots of merger activity, increase your efforts to acquire new customers, perhaps in different sectors. Maintain and nurture customer contacts. Those employees often move to other companies where they can recommend your firm. As a customer, you may find that your local bank branch or supermarket disappears after a merger. If competition decreases as a result of a merger, you may face fewer choices and higher prices.

TRY IT NOW!

1. **Learn the Laws** Before starting your own company, you should know the legal requirements in your area. Check the Web sites of the appropriate municipal or provincial departments, such as licensing, health, and zoning, to find out what licences and permits you need and any other requirements you must meet. Do the requirements vary depending on the type of company? Are there restrictions on starting a home-based business? Then check your provincial Web site to get the information on how to incorporate a business.

2. **Study Franchise Opportunities** Franchising offers an alternative to starting a business on your own. Do you have what it takes to be successful? Start by making a list of your interests and skills, and do a self-assessment using some of the suggestions in the last section of this chapter. Next you need to narrow the field of thousands of different franchise systems. At *Franchise Handbook Online* (www.franchise1.com), you'll find articles with checklists to help you thoroughly research a franchise and its industry, as well as a directory of franchise opportunities. Armed with this information, you can develop a questionnaire to evaluate a prospective franchise.

>looking ahead
at Manna Catering Services

Choosing the company structure early in its life paid off for Christopher Halpin and Manna Catering Services. Despite competition from other catering companies, Manna has differentiated itself through its customer focus and the training and respect of its employees.

Recently, Christopher made the decision to start to utilize a new company in his area that provides Manna with serving staff, whereas before Christopher had to worry about this matter and is happy with their training and presentation. He has also hired an outside salesperson that actively promotes his company through various contacts that he and his outside salesperson have developed. Another innovation that Christopher has incorporated is having "guest chefs" who offer new variety to the menu.

Manna has become noted for its creative and distinctive menus and attention to service. This has placed a great demand on the services of Manna and Christopher is considering incorporating the company. He has been able to "control the growth" and by using a staffing agency and hiring an outside salesperson, he can concentrate on continuing to provide the service that has made Manna successful.

The ultimate tribute to Christopher's hard work and attention to detail is his reputation as both an accomplished chef and a fair and consistent employer and caterer. Christopher has not come directly from the catering business but from other sources. He has contributed to a new cookbook showcasing Canadian chefs entitled *Cooks in My Kitchen* (published by Whitecap Books). Christopher continues to teach cooking classes, appearing on television, and often being profiled in the print media.

SUMMARY OF LEARNING GOALS

➡ lg 1 **What are the three main forms of business organization? What factors should a company's owners consider when selecting a form?**

A sole proprietorship is a business owned and operated by an individual. A partnership is an association of two or more people who operate a business as co-owners. A corporation is a legal entity with an existence separate from its owners. When choosing a form of organization for a business, evaluate the owner's liability for the firm's debts, the ease and cost of forming the business, the ability to raise funds, the taxes, the degree of operating control the operator can retain, and the ability to attract employees.

➡ lg 2 **What are the advantages and disadvantages of sole proprietorships?**

The advantages of sole proprietorships include ease and low cost of formation, the owner's rights to all profits, the owner's control of the business, relative freedom from government regulation, absence of special taxes, and the ease of dissolution. Disadvantages include unlimited liability of the owner for debts, difficulty in raising capital, limited managerial expertise, large personal time commitment, unstable business life, difficulty in attracting qualified employees, and the owner's personal absorption of all losses.

➡ lg 3 **Why would a new business venture choose to operate as a partnership, and what downside would the partners face?**

Partnerships can be formed as either general partnerships or limited partnerships. In a general partnership, the partners co-own the assets and share in the profits. Each partner is individually liable for all debts and contracts of the partnership. The operations of a limited partnership are controlled by one or more general partners, who have unlimited liability. Limited partners are financial partners whose liability is limited to their investment; they do not participate in the firm's operations. The advantages of partnerships include ease of formation, availability of capital, diversity of managerial expertise, flexibility to respond to changing business conditions, and relative freedom from government control. Disadvantages include unlimited liability for general partners, potential for conflict between partners, limited life, sharing of profits, and difficulty in leaving a partnership.

➡ lg 4 **How does the corporate structure provide advantages and disadvantages to a company and its owners?**

A corporation is a legal entity chartered by a province. Its organizational structure includes shareholders, who own the corporation; the board of directors, who are elected by the shareholders and govern the firm; and officers who carry out the goals and policies set by the board. Shareholders can sell or transfer their shares at any time and are entitled to receive profits in the form of dividends.

Advantages of corporations include limited liability, ease of transferring ownership, stable business life, and ability to attract financing. Disadvantages are double taxation of profits, the cost and complexity of formation, and government restrictions.

➡ lg 5 **Does a company have any business organization options besides sole proprietorship, partnership, and corporation?**

Businesses can also organize as cooperatives, joint ventures, and franchises.

Cooperatives are collectively owned by individuals or businesses with similar interests that combine to achieve more economic power. Cooperatives distribute all profits to their members. Two types of cooperatives are buyer and seller cooperatives.

A joint venture is an alliance of two or more companies formed to undertake a special project. Joint ventures can be set up in various ways, such as through partnerships or special-purpose corporations. By sharing management expertise, technology, products, and financial and operational resources, companies can reduce the risk of new enterprises.

→lg 6 Why is franchising growing in importance?

Franchising is one of the fastest growing forms of business ownership. It involves an agreement between a franchisor, the supplier of goods or services, and a franchisee, the individual or company that buys the right to sell the franchisor's products in a specific area. With a franchise, the business owner does not have to start from scratch but buys a business concept with a proven product and operating methods. The franchisor provides management training and assistance; use of a recognized brand name, product, and operating concept; and financial assistance. Franchises can be costly to start, however, and restrict operating freedom because the franchisee must conform to the franchisor's standard procedures.

→lg 7 Why would a company use mergers and acquisitions to grow?

In a merger, two companies combine to form one company; in an acquisition, one company or investor group buys another. Companies merge for strategic reasons, such as growth, diversification of product lines, increased market share, and economies of scale. The other main motive for merging is financial restructuring—cutting costs, selling off units, laying off employees, refinancing the company—to increase the value of the company to its shareholders.

There are three types of mergers. In a horizontal merger, companies at the same stage in the same industry combine to have more economic power, to diversify, or to win greater market share. A vertical merger involves the acquisition of a firm that serves an earlier or later stage of the production or sales cycle, such as a supplier or sales outlet. In a conglomerate merger, unrelated businesses come together to reduce risk through diversification.

→lg 8 What trends will affect business organization in the future?

North Americans continue to open new businesses, from sole proprietorships to multi-unit franchise operations, at record rates. Niche markets are rapidly appearing that business can respond to. Key merger trends include increasing numbers of mergers between companies that wish to consolidate to achieve economies of scale domestically and internationally.

WORKING THE NET

1. Consult *Entrepreneur.com*'s guide to business start-ups (click on Start-Ups) at **www.entrepreneur.com/** and review the essentials. Summarize for the class the reasons that the entrepreneurs profiled chose a particular structure. Do you agree with their choices?

2. Research how to form a corporation in your province using a search engine to find relevant sites. Start by visiting your provincial government's Web site. What steps are necessary to set up a corporation in your province? How do the fees compare to other provinces? If you were incorporating a business, what province would you choose and why?

3. Select three franchises that interest you. Research them at sites that cater to franchises. Try Canadian Business Franchise (**www.cgb.ca**) and CanadianFranchise.com (**www.canadianfranchise.com**). Prepare a chart comparing them, including history, number and location of units, financial requirements (initial franchise fee, other start-up costs, royalty and advertising fees), and any other information that would help you evaluate the franchise.

4. Check out the latest merger trends at *Industry Week* (**www.industryweek.com**). Find examples of a horizontal merger and a merger that failed.

CREATIVE THINKING CASE

Should Jason Take the Subway?

Jason Collins's dream of starting and running a business in his hometown became reality when he inherited $35 000 from his grandfather. Jason, who wanted a low-risk venture that provided a decent income, decided that his town needed a sandwich store near two large office parks. Jason had worked during college at a Subway sandwich store and knew that designing the store, rent, and equipment and supply costs would quickly eat up his $35 000, leaving little for advertising or promotion. Jason also didn't know much about finding suppliers, setting up an accounting system, and hiring employees.

Jason contacted his former boss John Smart, who owned five Subway franchises. Mr. Smart was very positive about his experiences, telling Jason that Subway was one of the lowest-cost food franchises to start and pointing to his late-model sports car and house in an affluent neighbourhood as proof of the income potential.

Jason requested information about becoming a franchisee from Subway's corporate offices. He learned that his total initial investment was approximately $103 000. The company could help with financing for most of the costs and provide training to help him set up an efficient operation. The only cash down payment was the $20 000 franchise fee. After the store opened, out of weekly gross sales Jason would pay 8 percent royalties and 3.5 percent to Subway's fund for national advertising.

Jason had two other options. His parents would lend him $20 000 to open his own independent sandwich store or to buy a different type of franchise. His girlfriend said she'd contribute about $30 000, so they could pool their funds and go into business as partners. After all, they got along really well and this would give them a chance to spend more time together.[12]

Critical Thinking Questions

1. Should Jason purchase a Subway sandwich franchise? Defend your answer.
2. How could Jason minimize the potential risks of opening an independent sandwich shop? Would you recommend this course of action? Why?
3. What potential problems might Jason encounter if he goes into partnership with his girlfriend? How could they reduce these problems?
4. If you were Jason, which course of action would you take? Why?

Entrepreneurship: Starting and Managing Your Own Business

This chapter is an extension of Chapter 5, or put more correctly, this chapter involves the decision that comes before deciding on the form of business ownership—the decision to start the business in the first place. What motivates people to start businesses and what factors shape the business's success?

The first example in the chapter, of the Panucci brothers and their entrepreneurial ventures into hotels and nightclubs, gives you a taste of how integrative this decision is. Regardless of the amount of effort they put into their hotel in southeastern Alberta, the *economic* environment, one of our uncontrollable environmental factors, eventually led to their hotel's demise. As discussed in the chapter, economic factors, financial factors, and lack of experience in management are leading causes of small business failure. And they are interrelated. For example, poor management can create financial problems that make it difficult to respond proactively to downturns in the economic environment. But the Panuccis learned an important lesson from that first disappointment: to make sure that they put balance in their lives—to work hard, but to balance that with taking care of their families and their health. This is a critical lesson for entrepreneurs—the integrative nature of business extends beyond the business to you personally as well. It creeps into your life outside of work and therefore the interconnections need to be viewed on a much broader level. You can't get more integrative than that!

Individuals with a desire to start a business, whether they are people who simply want to start a small business of their own or they are entrepreneurs with a grander *vision*, need to see the big picture. Every business is affected by its external environment, all those environmental factors have an effect on each other, and they also affect whether or not the business meets its critical success factors. However, the decisions that these individuals make inside their businesses—whether marketing, finance, operations, or human resource decisions—will also affect and be affected by the environment and, in turn, affect the degree to which the business achieves the critical success factors. This is their business—the whole thing, in all its integrative glory!

This chapter is full of examples of trends in the external environment affecting entrepreneurs and small business owners. Just look at why people create their own businesses. For example, in the economic environment we see many corporations restructuring and downsizing their staff requirements, and so employees look to creating their own businesses for greater job security. (Let's face it, you aren't going to fire yourself, and at least if you fail it will be your responsibility as opposed to something outside your control.) A trend that is both *social* and economic is the fact that there simply aren't as many advancement opportunities for women and minorities as there should be, despite the advancements made in this area, and so many of these people are looking to create their own opportunities in their own businesses. You'll find as you read the chapter that this in turn has led to many *innovations* in the workplace, such as more flexible scheduling, family-like environments, and more socially responsible business practices—changes favoured by women and, therefore, incorporated into their own businesses. Also, advancements in the *technological* environment have given small business people the ability to compete in areas before inaccessible to them, giving rise to many new small businesses and entrepreneurial ventures. Interestingly, this trend in technology has in turn led to a *social* change in the demographics of small business owners and entrepreneurs—they are younger, as most technologically literate people are from a younger generation that grew up with this technology.

The external environment also presents numerous opportunities for business ideas. In fact, as a result of the restructuring mentioned above, many of these same corporations have begun to outsource various things they used to do in-house, thus creating an opportunity for small businesses to pick up the slack. Another example discussed in this chapter is Margaret Nemeth's organic food restaurants. This example illustrates how one entrepreneur capitalized on a trend in the social environment toward healthier eating to help her achieve one of the critical success factors—*meeting customer needs*, which she does also by decorating her restaurants and choosing her music to meet the needs of the particular market segment she is targeting.

Just as we see the technological environment today making it easier for small businesses to compete, the economic environment today actually improves the odds for entrepreneurs and small business owners. As the chapter states, "Today's global economy rewards innovative, flexible companies that respond quickly to changes in the business environment." Because our economy today is so global, we have much more competition and we need to be more concerned with *meeting customer needs*. Smaller, more entrepreneurial firms tend to be more flexible and innovative (one of our critical success factors, remember); therefore, they can respond more quickly to changing customer needs due to changes in the external environment. But larger businesses can also encourage innovation and creativity by simulating this entrepreneurial environ-

ment within the organization. This is called "intrapreneurship."

Thus *marketing* decisions made by small business owners and entrepreneurs tend to be innovative and responsive to customer needs, and *human resource* decisions are also innovative and are often made to rectify problems they saw in their previous jobs (remember Christopher Halpin of Manna Catering Services in Chapter 5?). But *financing* can be difficult for new businesses. However, with good ideas and well-thought-out business plans that see the whole business in an integrative way, funds can be generated to cover *operations* and growth.

Entrepreneurship: Starting and Managing Your Own Business

CHAPTER 6

Learning Goals

→ **lg 1** Why do people become entrepreneurs, and what are the different types of entrepreneurs?

→ **lg 2** Which characteristics do successful entrepreneurs share?

→ **lg 3** How do small businesses contribute to the Canadian economy?

→ **lg 4** What are the advantages and disadvantages facing owners of small businesses?

→ **lg 5** How does the Business Development Bank of Canada help small businesses?

→ **lg 6** What are the first steps to take if you are starting your own firm?

→ **lg 7** Why does managing a small business present special challenges for the owner?

→ **lg 8** What trends are shaping the small business environment?

The Excitement and Challenge of Running Your Own Nightclub

In 1979, Gino Panucci was a student in a public relations program at an Alberta college. Little did he realize how his life would change over the next few years. The college program was going well, but Gino's brother, Dominic, had bought a hotel in a small town in south-eastern Alberta and needed help running the business. He invited Gino to join him in the venture. Gino agreed and thus began his life as an entrepreneur. The hotel had a tavern downstairs, as well as 52 rooms to maintain and rent in order to survive. As Gino says, "It was a struggle, I was a young guy, we stuck it out through thick and thin. It was a seven-day-a-week job, opening at 11:00 A.M. and closing at one or so. Dealing with a combination of the farm community and the oil patch workers was a challenge but business was good until the economy took a dive in the mid-eighties." The brothers were also a casualty of the economic downturn and were unable to continue. Gino moved to Calgary and worked as a construction worker while helping his wife, Shelley, open two successful hairdressing salons. Dominic moved to Kelowna, BC, and worked in a liquor store, while scouting out another business opportunity. The desire to own their own business never left the brothers, even though the previous experience had drained them physically, mentally, and financially. They saw the hotel years as a learning experience and were anxious to leave the past in the past. They worked well together. As Gino says, "Dominic is the back end and I am the front end," meaning Gino is the people person and Dominic is the numbers guy. The brothers observed the "scene" in Kelowna and saw an opportunity to take over a nightclub from a previous owner. They invested every penny they could lay their hands on to start the business and have never looked back.

Today, Gotcha's is one of the most successful nightclubs in the Okanagan Valley. Dominic has left the partnership but Gino's brother-in-law, Bob, has joined the business. They have recently bought a second club and are continuing on the road to financial success and having fun doing it. "I will never forget the lessons we learned in the hotel business. One of the most important was to put some balance in your life ... you can't work all the time and ignore your family and your health. It's just not worth it. And then economic conditions can just come along and take you down anyway! You gotta have fun!"[1]

CRITICAL THINKING QUESTIONS

As you read this chapter, consider the following questions as they relate to the Panucci brothers:

- What type of entrepreneur is Gino? What were his motives in starting the nightclub Gotcha's?
- What personal characteristics contributed to Dominic and Gino's success?
- What opportunities and challenges did Dominic and Gino face as small business owners, and how did they overcome them?

BUSINESS IN THE 21ST CENTURY

The entrepreneurial spirit is capturing the interest of people from all backgrounds and age groups. Teenagers are starting fashion clothing and high-tech companies. Downsized employees and mid-career executives form another large group of small business owners. Retirees who worked for others all their lives may form the company they always wanted to own.

Canada has approximately 2 million small businesses, representing an increase of one third since 1982. Ninety-nine percent of all registered businesses have fewer than 100 employees. Small business is responsible for almost all new job creation and accounts for almost two-thirds of private sector employment and 60 percent of our economic output.[2]

Companies started by entrepreneurs and small business owners make significant contributions to the global economy. They are hotbeds of innovation, taking leadership roles in technological change and the development of new goods and services. In a 2003 survey of 2180 business owners conducted by the Canadian Federation of Independent Business, the respondents were optimistic about 2003, with 34 percent expecting a stronger business performance over the next three months and 53 percent expecting a higher performance over the next 12 months.[3]

You may be one of the millions of Canadians who's considering joining the ranks of business owners. As you read this chapter, you will get the information and tools you need to help you decide whether owning your own company is the right career path for you. You'll discover why entrepreneurship continues to be one of the hottest areas of business activity and learn the characteristics of a successful entrepreneur. Then we'll look at the importance of small businesses in the economy, their advantages and disadvantages, and the role of the Business Development Bank of Canada. Next, the chapter offers guidelines for starting and managing a small business. Finally, it explores the trends that will shape entrepreneurship and small business ownership in the 21st century.

Business owners and managers use their skills and resources to create goods and services that will satisfy customers and prospective customers. Owners and managers have a great deal of control over day-to-day business decisions such as which supplies are purchased, which employees are hired, what products are sold, and where they are sold. However, certain environmental conditions that affect a business cannot be controlled. These conditions are constantly changing and include social change and demographics (see Chapter 3), economic conditions (see Chapter 1), technology (see Chapter 4), and global competition (see Chapter 2). Successful owners and managers must continuously study these conditions and adapt their businesses, or they will lose their ability to compete.

HOT Links

Read all about the Canadian Federation of Independent Business at
www.cfib.ca

➡ **lg 1**

Entrepreneurship Today

Margaret Nemeth graduated from university with an engineering degree and became a petroleum "landman." While working for Dome Petroleum, Margaret had the opportunity to buy an apartment building. This became her first step into the small business environment. Margaret left the oil and gas industry and moved through various small business ventures, landing where she is today as owner of two very successful organic food restaurants. "You have to realize that when you own your own business, you don't just close the door and leave work at work. It is always with you," says Margaret. "You have to constantly watch the trends, hence the organic food to respond to the desire for healthier eating." Margaret also decorates her restaurants and chooses the music based on the likes and dislikes of the particular population segment she is targeting. She is aware of everything her competition is doing and tries to stay one step ahead. Why does she do this? "I like being the boss," says Margaret.

Canada is blessed with a wealth of entrepreneurs like Margaret. According to research by the Canadian Federation of Independent Business, the majority of members surveyed in December 2002 saw economic growth on the horizon for their business.[4] And their ranks continue to swell as up-and-coming entrepreneurs aspire to become the next Bill Gates.

Why has entrepreneurship remained a strong part of the foundation of the Canadian business system for so many years? Today's global economy rewards innovative, flexible companies that respond quickly to changes in the business environment. These companies are started by **entrepreneurs**, people with vision, drive, and creativity, who are willing to take the risk of starting and managing a business to make a profit.

entrepreneurs
People with vision, drive, and creativity who are willing to take the risk of starting and managing a new business to make a profit or of greatly changing the scope and direction of an existing firm.

Entrepreneur or Small Business Owner?

The term *entrepreneur* is often used in a broad sense to include most small business owners. But there is a difference between entrepreneurship and small business management. Entrepreneurship involves taking a risk, either to create a new business or to greatly change the scope and direction of an existing firm. Entrepreneurs typically are innovators who start companies to pursue their ideas for a new product or service. They are visionaries who spot trends.

While entrepreneurs may be small business owners, not all small business owners are entrepreneurs. They are managers or people with technical expertise who started a business or bought an existing business and made a conscious decision to stay small. For example, the proprietor of your local independent bookstore is a small business owner. Jeff Bezos, founder of Amazon.com, also sells books. But Bezos is an entrepreneur: he developed a new model—a Web-based book retailer—that revolutionized the world of book selling. In fact, he made e-commerce history with one of the largest sales and distribution events ever. Amazom.com teamed up with Federal Express and the U.S. Postal Service to deliver more than 789 000 copies of *Harry Potter and the Order of the Phoenix* to delighted Potter fans on the release date of the book.[5] The two groups share some of the same characteristics, and some of the reasons for becoming an entrepreneur or a small business owner are very similar. However, entrepreneurs are less likely to accept the status quo and generally take a longer-term view than the small business owner.

Types of Entrepreneurs

Entrepreneurs fall into several categories: classic entrepreneurs, multipreneurs, and intrapreneurs.

Classic Entrepreneurs

Classic entrepreneurs are risk takers who start their own companies based on innovative ideas. Some classic entrepreneurs are micropreneurs who start small and plan to stay small. They often start businesses just for personal satisfaction and the lifestyle. Albert Nasaar opened his small business in 1979 and is still the sole proprietor of the Isis Hair Salon. Albert enjoys the freedom, flexibility, and overall fun of being his own boss. Many of Albert's clients have been returning to him for over 20 years. When asked why he has never expanded, Albert replies, "Why would I? I do well. I have loyal clients and I have fun. Life is good!"

Albert Nasaar of Isis is an example of a classic entrepreneur who started his business on a small scale with the intention of remaining small and has been very successful for 24 years.

In contrast, *growth-oriented entrepreneurs* want their businesses to grow into major corporations. Most high-tech companies are formed by growth-oriented entrepreneurs. Jeff Bezos recognized that with Internet technology he could compete with large chains of traditional book retailers. Bezos's goal was to build his company into a high-growth enterprise—and he even chose a name that reflected this strategy: Amazon.com. Now he's moved beyond books to sell CDs, toys, and other products in an effort to make his company a one-stop shopping site.[6]

Multipreneurs

Then there are multipreneurs, entrepreneurs who start a series of companies. Jim Clark is the quintessential multipreneur, starting three high-tech companies with market values of more than US$1 billion each. A former Stanford professor, Clark founded Silicon Graphics, Inc., which makes powerful high-end graphics computers, in 1982. His next venture, Internet pioneer Netscape, was formed in 1994 and went public in 1995. While Clark was still Netscape's chairman, he shifted his attention to his newest company, Healtheon, which he founded in 1996 and took public in early 1999. Healtheon provides online medical data for physicians, insurers, and hospitals. A visionary who's better at creating companies, putting together a management team, and advising the company than at day-to-day management, Clark began looking for his next start-up before Netscape went public.[7]

Intrapreneurs

Some entrepreneurs don't own their own companies but apply their creativity, vision, and risk taking within a large corporation. Called **intrapreneurs**, these employees enjoy the freedom to nurture their ideas and develop new products, while their employers provide regular salaries and financial backing. Intrapreneurs have a high degree of autonomy to run their own mini-companies within the larger enterprise. They share many of the same personality traits as classic entrepreneurs but take less personal risk. According to Gifford Pinchot, who coined the term *intrapreneur* in 1985, corporations have lost billions of dollars by rejecting ideas from employees who then leave to start their own companies. Corporations that create supportive environments for intrapreneurship retain their most innovative employees—as well as ownership of the products they develop.[8] Xerox Technology Ventures (XTV) funds promising research projects that don't quite fit the overall corporate objectives until the projects are ready for outside financing. This gives them the chance to develop into profitable businesses, rather than be shunted aside.[9]

Why Become an Entrepreneur?

As the examples in this chapter show, entrepreneurs are found in all industries and have different motives for starting companies. The most common reason cited is the desire to control their own destiny. When Gino Panucci was asked why he preferred to own his own business despite the past difficulties, he replied, "I just want to be my own boss." Related to this is a desire for job security, now that large corporations regularly downsize staff and streamline operations. Other reasons, as Exhibit 6-1 shows, include making money and building a new company. Two other important basic motives mentioned in other surveys are feeling personal satisfaction with your work and creating the lifestyle that you prefer.

concept check

- What is an entrepreneur? Describe several types of entrepreneurs.
- What differentiates an entrepreneur from a small business owner?
- What are some major factors that motivate entrepreneurs to start businesses?

intrapreneurs
Entrepreneurs who apply their creativity, vision, and risk taking within a large corporation, rather than starting a company of their own.

Reason	Percentage Citing
To be my own boss or control my own life	41%
To make money	16
To create something new	12
To prove I could do it	9
Because I was not rewarded at my old job	6
Because I was laid off from my old job	5
Other	11

SOURCE: "Inc. 500 Almanac," *Inc. 500* (October 22, 1996), p. 24. Reprinted by permission of the *Inc. 500*.

➡ **lg 2**

Characteristics of Successful Entrepreneurs

Do you have what it takes to become an entrepreneur? Being an entrepreneur requires special drive, perseverance, passion, and a spirit of adventure in addition to managerial and technical ability. Having a great concept is not enough. An entrepreneur must also be able to develop and manage the company that implements the idea. In addition, entrepreneurs are the company; they cannot leave problems at the office at the end of the day. Most entrepreneurs tend to work longer hours and take fewer vacations once they have their own company. They also share other common characteristics, as described in the next section.

The Entrepreneurial Personality

Many of the studies of the entrepreneurial personality have found similar traits.[10] In general, entrepreneurs are:

- *Ambitious.* Entrepreneurs have a high need for achievement and are competitive.
- *Independent.* They are self-starters who prefer to lead rather than follow. They are also individualists. "I couldn't stand to have someone else tell me how to do my job. I like being the boss," says Gino Panucci.
- *Self-confident.* They understand the challenges of starting a business but are decisive and have faith in their abilities to resolve problems. Entrepreneurs trust their hunches and act on them. " I'm good at what I do," says Albert of the Isis Hair Salon, "and that's why my clients keep coming back."
- *Risk taking.* Though they are not averse to risk, most successful entrepreneurs prefer situations with a moderate degree of risk, where they have a chance to control the outcome of highly risky ventures that depend on luck.
- *Visionary.* Their ability to spot trends and act on them sets entrepreneurs apart from small business owners and managers.
- *Creative.* To compete with larger firms, entrepreneurs need to have creative product designs, marketing strategies, and solutions to managerial problems. Albert says, "I like to try different cuts and colours on my clients. Give them some pizzazz!"
- *Energetic.* Starting a business takes long hours. "While we had the hotel we worked seven days a week, 14 hours a day," says Gino.
- *Passionate.* Entrepreneurs love their work. "If you're not passionate about what you're doing, why bother?" says Margaret Nemeth.
- *Committed.* They make personal sacrifices to achieve their goals. Because they are so committed to their companies, entrepreneurs are persistent in seeking solutions to problems.

Margaret Nemeth, a successful entrepreneur, has operated several profitable small business ventures and still enjoys "being the boss."

The Hagberg Consulting Group, a leadership development consulting firm, studied over 2000 executives for 12 years. In addition to the characteristics already mentioned, the study found that in comparison to the average executive, entrepreneurs are much more opinionated, emotionally aloof, impatient, focused, and aggressive. They also tend to get upset when things don't go their way.[11]

A person with all the characteristics of an entrepreneur might still lack the business skills to run a successful business. As we'll discuss later in this chapter, entrepreneurs believe they can learn many of these technical skills.

Entrepreneurs need managerial ability to organize a company, develop operating strategies, obtain financing, and manage day-to-day activities. Good interpersonal and communication skills are also essential in dealing with employees, customers, and other businesspeople, such as bankers, accountants, and lawyers. They also need the technical knowledge to carry out their ideas. For instance, an entrepreneur may have a great idea for a new computer game and be a self-confident, hard-working, motivated person with good interpersonal skills. But without a detailed knowledge of computers, that entrepreneur would find it nearly impossible to produce a computer game that would sell.

concept check

- Describe the personality traits and other skills characteristic of successful entrepreneurs.
- What does it mean to say that an entrepreneur should work on the business, not in it?

→ lg 3

Small Business

Although large corporations dominated the business scene for many decades, in recent years small businesses have once again come to the forefront of the Canadian economy. As stated earlier, over 75 percent of the businesses in Canada have fewer than five employees and nearly 98 percent of all Canadian businesses have fewer than 50 employees.

Let's look at some of the main reasons behind the increase in small business formation:

- *Independence and a better lifestyle.* Large corporations no longer represent job security or offer as many fast-track career opportunities. Mid-career employees leave the corporate world in search of new opportunities. Many new college and business school graduates shun the corporate world altogether and start their own companies or look for work in small firms.
- *Personal satisfaction from work.* Many small business owners cite this as one of the primary reasons for starting their companies. They love what they do.
- *Best route to success.* Small businesses offer their owners the potential for profit. Also, business ownership provides greater advancement opportunities for women and minorities, as we discuss later in this chapter.

small business
A business that is independently owned, is owned by an individual or a small group of investors, is based locally, and is not a dominant company in its industry.

- *Rapidly changing technology.* Advances in computer and telecommunications technology, as well as the sharp decrease in the cost of this technology, have given individuals and small companies the power to compete in industries that were formerly closed to them. The arrival of the Internet and World Wide Web is responsible for the formation of many small businesses, as discussed in greater detail in Chapter 4.
- *Outsourcing.* As a result of downsizing, corporations often contract with outside firms for services they used to provide in-house. This outsourcing creates opportunities for smaller companies, many of which offer specialized goods and services.
- *Major corporate restructurings and downsizings.* These force many employees to look for other jobs or careers.

What Is a Small Business?

So what makes a business "small"? As we've seen, there are different interpretations, and the range is extremely broad. Generally, though, a **small business** has the following characteristics:
- Independently managed
- Owned by an individual or a small group of investors
- Based locally (although the market it serves may be widespread)
- Not a dominant company (thus it has little influence in its industry)

Small businesses in Canada can be found in almost every industry sector. See Exhibit 6-2 for a breakdown of employment in Canada by sector. Small businesses are found in all of the various sectors as suggested below:
- *Services.* Service firms are the most popular category of small businesses because they are easy and low cost to start. They are often small; very few service-oriented companies are national in scope. They include repair services, restaurants, specialized software companies, accountants, travel agencies, management consultants, and temporary help agencies.
- *Wholesale and retail trade.* Retailers sell goods or services directly to the end user. Wholesalers link manufacturers and retailers or industrial buyers; they assemble, store, and distribute products ranging from heavy machinery to produce. Most retailers also qualify as small businesses, whether they operate one store or a small chain.
- *Manufacturing.* This category is dominated by large companies, but many small businesses produce goods. Machine shops, printing firms, clothing manufacturers, beverage bottlers, electronic equipment manufacturers, and furniture makers are often small manufacturers. In some industries, small manufacturing businesses have an advantage because they can focus on customized products that would not be profitable for larger manufacturers.

e x h i b i t   6 - 2 | Types of Business by Industry Sector

Industry	Percentage Employment
Services	45.17%
Retail and wholesale trade	18.64
Construction	4.57
Finance, insurance, real estate	6.02
Wholesale trade	7.4
Manufacturing	16.44
Transportation, public utilities	7.45
Agriculture, mining, other	1.71

SOURCE: Statistics Canada, www.statscan.ca/english/Pgdb/economy/communications/trade03.htm.

- *Construction.* Firms employing fewer than 20 people account for many of Canada's construction companies. They include independent builders of industrial and residential properties and thousands of contractors in such trades as plumbing, electrical, roofing, and painting.
- *Agriculture.* Small businesses dominate agriculture-related industry, including forestry and fisheries.

→ **lg 4**

Advantages of Small Business

Small businesses have advantages directly related to their size:

- *Greater flexibility.* Because most small businesses are owner-operated, they can react more quickly to changing market forces. They can develop product ideas and market opportunities without going through a lengthy approval process.
- *More efficient operation.* Small businesses are less complex than large organizations. They have fewer employees doing things that are not directly related to producing or selling the company's product (such as accounting and legal work). Thus, they can keep their total costs down.
- *Greater ability to serve specialized markets.* Small businesses excel in serving specialized markets. Large firms tend to focus on goods and services with an established demand and the potential for high sales.
- *More personal service.* Another advantage of small businesses is their ability to give the personal touch. In businesses like gourmet restaurants, health clubs, fashion boutiques, and travel agencies, customers place a high value on personal attention. Through this direct relationship with customers, the owner-manager also gets feedback on how well the firm is meeting customer needs.

Disadvantages of Small Business

Small businesses also face several disadvantages:

- *Limited managerial skill.* Small business owners may not have the wide variety of skills they need to respond quickly to change. As noted earlier, they often lack knowledge in areas like finance, marketing, taxation, and business law. They may have experience in one area of business but not in the specific type of business they choose to start. Others have the technical skills but not the management ability. As Gino Panucci said, "I am the front end of the business and Dominic is the back end." Other entrepreneurs hire consultants to help them solve problems. Later in this chapter we'll discuss how these problems can be overcome when starting and managing a small business.
- *Fund-raising difficulty.* Another big problem for small businesses is obtaining adequate financing. Small firms must compete with larger, more established firms for the same pool of investment funds. Getting loans can be difficult because new businesses are obviously more risky than established ones. And the interest rates charged by banks and private investors are usually higher for small firms than for large ones. Sources of financing are examined in greater detail in the Chapter 12.
- *Burdensome government regulations.* The addition of new federal, provincial, and local regulations creates more compliance and reporting requirements for small businesses. Expanded federal, provincial, and local environmental regulations on water pollution and toxic wastes are especially burdensome. Local laws regulate noise pollution and traffic related to home-based businesses. With limited staff and financial resources, small firms may have to hire outside consultants to help prepare the many types of reports the government requires.
- *Extreme personal commitment of the owner.* Starting and managing a small business requires a major commitment by the owner. Long hours, the need for owners to do much of the work themselves, and the stress of being personally responsible for the success of the business are big disadvantages.

➡ **lg 5**

Business Development Bank of Canada (BDC)
Bank that provides small and medium-sized businesses with flexible financing, affordable consulting services, and venture capital.

The Business Development Bank of Canada

Many small business owners turn to the **Business Development Bank of Canada (BDC)** for assistance. The BDC's mission is to help people start and manage small businesses, help them win federal contracts, and speak on behalf of small business. Through its national network of local offices, the BDC advises and helps small businesses in the areas of finance and management.

Business Service Centres

Business service centres provide services for start-up and growing small businesses. They typically have both print material and databases that provide insight not only to industry and the competition but also for start-up regulations for each city and province. An interactive business planner is also available.

concept check

- What is a small business? Why are small businesses becoming so popular?
- Discuss the major advantages and disadvantages of small business ownership.
- What is the Business Development Bank of Canada?

➡ **lg 6**

HOT Links

What does it take to start up a business in your province or territory?
Alberta: www.cbsc.org/ alberta index.html
British Columbia: www.sb.gov.bc.ca/smallbus/ sbhome.html
Manitoba: www.cbsc.org. manitoba/index.html
Nunavut: www.cbsc.org/ nunavut/index.html
New Brunswick: www.csbc.org/ nb/index.html
Newfoundland: www.cbsc.org/ nf/index.html
Nova Scotia: www.cbsc.org/ ns/index.html
Ontario: www.cbsc.org/ontario
Prince Edward Island: www.cbsc.org/pe/index.html
Quebec: www.infoentrpreneurs. org/eng/index/html
Saskatchewan: www.cbsc.org/sask
Yukon: www.cbsc.org/yukon/ index.html

Starting Your Own Business

You may have decided that you'd like to go into business for yourself. If so, what's the best way to go about it? You can (1) start from scratch, (2) buy an existing business, or (3) buy a franchise.

Getting Started

The first step in starting your own business is a self-assessment to determine whether you have the personal traits you need to succeed and, if so, what type of business would be best for you. Finding the idea and choosing a form of business organization come next.

Finding the Idea

Entrepreneurs get ideas for their businesses from many sources. It is not surprising that 60 percent of *Inc.* 500 executives got the idea for their company while working in the same industry. Starting a firm in a field where you have experience improves your chances of success. Other sources of inspiration are hobbies and personal interests; suggestions from customers, family, and friends; and college courses or other education.

Ideas are all around you. Do you have a problem that you need to solve or a product that doesn't work as well as you'd like? Maybe one of your co-workers has a complaint. Raising questions about the way things are done is a great way to generate ideas. Many successful businesses get started because someone notices problems and needs and then finds a way to fill them.

Choosing a Form of Business Organization

Another key decision for a person starting a new business is whether it will be a sole proprietorship, partnership, corporation, or limited liability company. As discussed in Chapter 5, each type of business organization has advantages and disadvantages. The choice depends on the type of business, number of employees, capital requirements, tax considerations, and level of risk involved.

HOT Links

For tips on how to start, grow, or manage your business, check out Entrepreneur magazine's "Smart Tip of the Day" at www.entrepreneurmag.com/smarttip.hts

Developing the Business Plan

Once you have the basic concept for a product, you must develop a plan to create the business. The planning process is one of the most important steps in starting a business and helps minimize the risks involved. A good business plan can be a critical determinant of whether a firm succeeds or fails. A range of software is available for downloading from both government and industry sites. Some examples include:

- Business Development Bank of Canada: **www.bdc.ca/home/Default.asp**
- Canada Business Service Centres: **www.cbsc.org/main.html**
- Nova Scotia Economic Development: **www.gov.ns.ca.ecor.ced.busplan**

business plan
A formal written statement that describes in detail the idea for a new business and how it will be carried out; includes a general description of the company, the qualifications of the owner(s), a description of the product or service, an analysis of the market, and a financial plan.

A formal, written **business plan** that describes in detail the idea for the new business and how it will be carried out is essential. A well-prepared, comprehensive business plan helps business owners take an objective and critical look at their business venture and set goals that will help them manage the business and monitor its growth and performance.

Key features of a business plan are a general description of the company, the qualifications of the owner(s), a description of the product or service, an analysis of the market (demand, customers, competition), and a financial plan. It should focus on the uniqueness of the business and explain why customers will be attracted to it. Exhibit 6-3 is a brief outline of what a business plan should include.

e x h i b i t 6 - 3	Outline for a Business Plan

Title page: Provides names, addresses, and phone numbers of the venture and its owners and management personnel; date prepared; copy number; and contact person.

Table of contents: Provides page numbers of the key sections of the business plan.

Executive summary: Provides a one- to three-page overview of the total business plan. Written after the other sections are completed, it highlights their significant points and, ideally, creates enough excitement to motivate the reader to continue reading.

Vision and mission statement: Concisely describes the intended strategy and business philosophy for attaining the vision.

Company overview: Explains the type of company, such as manufacturing, retail, or service; provides background information on the company if it already exists; describes the proposed form of organization—sole proprietorship, partnership, or corporation. This section should be organized as follows: company name and location, company objectives, nature and primary product or service of the business, current status (start-up, buyout, or expansion) and history (if applicable), and legal form of organization.

Product and/or service plan: Describes the product and/or service and points out any unique features; explains why people will buy the product or service. This section should offer the following descriptions: product and/or service; features of the product or service providing a competitive advantage; available legal protection—patents, copyrights, trademarks—and dangers of technical or style obsolescence.

Marketing plan: Shows who the firm's customers will be and what type of competition it will face; outlines the marketing strategy and specifies the firm's competitive edge. This section should offer the following descriptions: analysis of target market and profile of target customer; methods of identifying and attracting customers; selling approach, type of sales force, and distribution channels; types of sales promotions and advertising; and credit and pricing policies.

Management plan: Identifies the key players—active investors, management team, and directors—citing the experience and competence they possess. This section should offer the following descriptions: management team, outside investors, and/or directors and their qualifications, outside resource people and their qualifications, and plans for recruiting and training employees.

Operating plan: Explains the type of manufacturing or operating system to be used; describes the facilities, labour, raw materials, and product processing requirements. This section should offer the following descriptions: operating or manufacturing methods, operating facilities (location, space, and equipment), quality-control methods, procedures to control inventory and operations, sources of supply, and purchasing procedures.

Financial plan: Specifies financial needs and contemplated sources of financing; presents projections of revenues, costs, and profits. This section should offer the following descriptions: historical financial statements for the last three to five years or as available; pro forma financial statements for three to five years, including income statements, balance sheets, cash flow statements, and cash budgets (monthly for first year and quarterly for second year); break-even analysis of profits and cash flows; and planned sources of financing.

Appendix of supporting documents: Provides materials supplementary to the plan. This section should offer the following descriptions: management team biographies, any other important data that support the information in the business plan, and the firm's ethics code.

SOURCE: From *Small Business Management, An Entrepreneurial Emphasis,* 11th edition, by Justin G. Longenecker and Carlos W. Moore. © 2000. Reprinted with permission of South-Western College Publishing, a division of Thomson Learning: www.thomsonrights.com. Fax 800 730-2215.

To successfully persuade lenders and investors to finance a venture, a solid business plan should be part of the proposal package.

HOT Links

See the Royal Bank Web site for a template of a business plan at www.royalbank.ca

debt
A form of business financing consisting of borrowed funds that must be repaid with interest over a stated time period.

equity
A form of business financing consisting of funds raised through the sale of stock in a business.

angel investors
Individual investors or groups of experienced investors who provide funding for start-up businesses.

venture capital
Financing obtained from investment firms that specialize in financing small, high-growth companies and receive an ownership interest and a voice in management in return for their money.

HOT Links

Check out the listing of venture capital firms at
www.cvca.ca

Writing a good business plan may take many months. Many businesspeople, in their eagerness to begin doing business, neglect planning. They immediately get caught up in day-to-day operations and have little time for planning. But taking the time to develop a good business plan pays off. Writing the plan forces you to analyze your concept carefully and make decisions about marketing, production, staffing, and financing. A venture that seems sound at the idea stage may not look so good after closer analysis. The business plan also serves as the first operating plan for the business.

The most common use of business plans is to persuade lenders and investors to finance the venture. The detailed information in the business plan helps them decide whether to invest. Even though the business plan may have taken months to write, it must capture the potential investor's interest in only a few minutes. For that reason, the basic business plan should be written with a particular reader in mind; it should be tailored to the type of investor you plan to approach and his or her investment goals.

The business plan should not be set aside once financing is obtained and the company is operational. Entrepreneurs who think the business plan is only for raising money make a huge mistake. Owners should review the plan on a regular basis—monthly, quarterly, or annually, depending on how fast their particular industry changes.

Financing the Business

Once the business plan is complete, the next step is to get the financing to set up the business. The amount required depends on the type of business and the entrepreneur's planned investment. Businesses started by lifestyle entrepreneurs require less financing than growth-oriented businesses. When Margaret Nemeth started her first business, she financed it partially using her Visa card. Of course, manufacturing and high-tech companies generally require a larger initial investment.

The two forms of business financing are **debt,** borrowed funds that must be repaid with interest over a stated time period, and **equity**, funds raised through the sale of stock in the business. Those who provide equity funds get a share of the profits. Lenders usually limit debt financing to no more than a quarter to a third of the firm's total needs. Thus, equity financing usually amounts to about 65 to 75 percent of total start-up financing.

Two sources of equity financing for young companies are angel investors and venture capital firms. **Angel investors** are individual investors or groups of experienced investors who provide funding for start-up businesses. Angels often get involved with companies at a very early stage. **Venture capital** is financing obtained from investment firms that specialize in financing small, high-growth companies and receive an ownership interest and a voice in management in return for their money. They typically invest at a later stage than angel investors. We'll discuss venture capital in greater detail in Chapter 12.

Who provides the start-up funding, whether debt or equity, for small companies? Most business owners contribute personal savings to their new companies.

Buying a Small Business

Another route to small business ownership is buying an existing business. Although this approach is less risky, it still requires careful and thorough analysis. Several important questions must be answered: Why is the owner selling? Does he or she want to retire or move on to another challenge, or are there some problems with the business?

Is the business operating at a profit? If not, can the problems be corrected? What are the owner's plans after selling the company? Depending on the type of business, customers may be more loyal to the owner than to the product or service. They could leave the firm if the current owner decides to open a similar business. To protect against this situation, a "non-compete clause" can be included in the contract of sale.

Many of the same steps for starting a business from scratch apply to buying an existing company. A business plan that thoroughly analyzes all aspects of the business should be prepared. Get answers to all your questions, and determine, via the business plan, that the business is a good one. Then you must negotiate the purchase price and other terms and get financing. This can be a difficult process, and it may require the use of a consultant. Ernst and Young offer a site with industry information and useful research information under its media publication address at **www.ey.com**.

Risks of Small Business Ownership

Running your own business may not be as easy as it sounds. Despite the many advantages of being your own boss, the risks are great as well. Many businesses fail each year. Businesses close down for many reasons. Here are the most common causes:

- Economic factors—business downturns and high interest rates
- Financial causes—inadequate capital, low cash balances, and high expenses
- Lack of experience—inadequate business knowledge, management experience, and technical expertise

Many of the causes of business failure are interrelated. For example, low sales and high expenses are often directly related to poor management.

Inadequate planning is often at the core of business problems. As described earlier, a thorough feasibility analysis, from market assessment to financial plan, is critical to business success. And even with the best plans, business conditions change and unexpected situations arise. An entrepreneur may start a company based on a terrific new product only to find that a large firm with more marketing and distribution clout introduces a similar item.

The stress of managing a business can take its toll. The business can consume your whole life. Owners may find themselves in over their heads and unable to cope with the pressures of business operations, from the long hours to being the main decision maker.

Even successful businesses may have to deal with many of these difficulties. For example, growing too quickly can cause as many problems as sluggish sales. Growth can strain a company's finances. Additional capital is required to fund the expanded operations, from hiring additional staff to purchasing more equipment. Successful business owners must respond quickly as the business changes and develop plans to manage growth.

concept check

- How can potential business owners find new business ideas?
- Why is it important to develop a business plan? What should such a plan include?
- What financing options do small business owners have?
- Summarize the risks of business ownership.

➡ lg 7

Managing a Small Business

Whether you start a business from scratch or buy an existing one, you must be able to keep it going. The main job of the small business owner is to carry out the business plan through all areas of the business—from personnel to production and maintenance. The small business owner must be ready to solve problems as they arise and move quickly when market conditions change. Hiring, training, and managing employees are other crucial responsibilities. Clearly, managing a small business is quite a challenge.

Over time, the owner's role will change. As the company grows, others will make many of the day-to-day decisions while the owner focuses on managing employees and making plans for the firm's long-term success. The owner must always watch performance, evaluate company policies in light of changing conditions, and develop new policies as required. She or he must nurture a continual flow of ideas to keep the business growing. The type of employees needed may also change as the firm grows. A larger firm may need more managerial talent and technical expertise.

Using Outside Consultants

One way to ease the burden of managing a business is to hire outside consultants. Most small businesses need a good accountant (e.g., CA, CMA, or CGA) who can help with financial record keeping, tax planning, and decision making. An accountant who works closely with the owner to help the business grow is a valuable asset. A lawyer who knows about small business law can provide legal advice and draw up essential documents. Consultants in other areas, such as marketing, employee benefits, and insurance, can be hired as needed. Outside directors with business experience are another way for small companies to get advice. Resources like these free the small business owner to concentrate on planning and day-to-day operations.

Some aspects of the business can be outsourced, or contracted out to specialists in that area. Many small businesses outsource at least one business function. For example, Employease is an Internet-based human resources system that manages benefits information for small and mid-size companies. At a secure Web site, a company's employees can review, change, or update benefits information. The company's personnel managers can analyze its benefits data to see how employees are using the benefits. The service costs less than buying the sophisticated software, which would be too expensive for most small firms.[12]

HOT Links

Want to know more about Employease? Read about its services at its Web site,

www.employease.com

Hiring and Retaining Employees

Attracting good employees can be hard for a small firm, which may not be able to match the salaries, benefits, and advancement potential offered by larger firms. Compounding the problem is the general labour shortage. With unemployment rates low, small companies are finding it even harder to compete for qualified workers.

Once they hire employees, small business owners must promote employee satisfaction to retain them. Comfortable working conditions, flexible hours, employee benefit programs, opportunities to help make decisions, and a share in profits and ownership are some of the ways to do this.

Later chapters of the book present detailed discussions of management, production, human resources, marketing, accounting, computers, and finance, all of which are useful to small business owners.

Many small businesses hire international trade specialists to get started selling overseas. They have the time, knowledge, and resources that most small businesses lack. Export trading companies buy goods at a discount from small businesses and resell them abroad. *Export management companies (EMCs)* act on a company's behalf. For fees of 5 to 15 percent of gross sales and multi-year contracts, they handle all aspects of exporting, including finding customers, billing, shipping, and helping the company comply with foreign regulations. Export Affairs and International Trade Canada (**www.infoexport.gc.ca**) offers an export information kit, a newsletter, and a directory of Canadian Foreign Trade representatives that may be contacted for export

HOT Links

Want a quick course on how to expand into global markets? Check out Deloitte & Touche's Expanding Your Business Globally at

www.dtonline.com, click on "services," go to "merger and acquisition services," and choose a country from those listed.

and import opportunities and country-specific information. You can also check out ExportCanada.com at **www.exportcanada.com** and the Export Development Corporation at **www.edc.ca**.

concept check

- How does the small business owner's role change over time?
- Explain strategies small business owners can use to acquire the expertise they need to help them run the business. Discuss both outside sources and employees.
- Why should a small business consider exporting?

➡ **lg 8**

CAPITALIZING ON TRENDS IN BUSINESS

Social and demographic trends, combined with the challenges of operating in the fast-paced technology-dominated business climate of the 21st century, have changed small business ownership. New ownership trends are emerging and more young people are choosing entrepreneurship over traditional career paths. The number of women and minority business owners also continues to grow. Finally, the Internet is creating numerous opportunities for new types of small businesses.

Home Is Where the Office Is

For an increasing number of business owners, their daily commute is a walk down the hall to their home office. In the year 2000, there were approximately 1 369 000 home-based businesses in Canada, with over 10 percent of those having preschool children in the home.[13] Technology has made it easier to start a home-based business by connecting home offices to customers through the Internet.

No longer does running a business from home carry a stigma. In fact, many home-based entrepreneurs who could afford outside offices choose to stay home. Two trends that contribute to the rising popularity of working at home are the availability of low-cost technology—from voice mail to powerful computers and the Internet—and the large number of former corporate executives who consult or start businesses from home.[14]

HOT Links

Considering starting a business at home? You'll find tips and advice for the home office as well as free software and links to financing opportunities at the Quicken Small Business Centre at www.quicken.ca/eng/soho/index.html

Ownership Trends

At one time, most entrepreneurs were career changers starting second or third careers and corporate executives deciding to go out on their own. Today, many young people are choosing entrepreneurship as their first career. Check out the Canadian Youth Business Foundation at **www.cybf.ca** for financing tips for young business owners as well as an online loan application. For women and minorities, entrepreneurship and small business ownership are a route to economic independence and personal and professional fulfillment. These groups are starting small businesses at rates far above the general population.

Women-owned businesses make a significant contribution to today's business environment. They favour such workplace innovations as flexible scheduling, employee autonomy, and a family-like work environment, and are more likely to commit to socially responsible business practices. Who are the top 100 women business owners? Find out at **www.profitguide.com/w100/2002/**. Also check out the Centre for Women in Business at **www.msvu.ca/cwb/**.

HOT Links

What services does the Women Business Owners of Canada Inc. provide for small business owners? Click over to www.wboc.ca

Doug Dokis, who works extensively with Native students and entrepreneurs, sees the Native population as an increasingly important group offering a wide range of products and services.

Similar to women business owners, today's minority entrepreneurs have more education and prior business experience than their predecessors and are branching out into new industries. Over the next few decades, Canada will shift further away from a society dominated by whites and rooted in Western culture toward a society characterized by many racial and ethnic minorities. All minorities will grow in size and in share of the population, while the white majority declines as a percentage of the total. First Nations people and people with roots in Australia, the Middle East, the former Soviet Union, and other parts of the world will further enrich the fabric of Canadian society.

Doug Dokis, a member of the Ojibwe Nation of Ontario, acts as a liaison between a large college and the Native community in the area. According to Doug, the growth rate in the Native population is the largest of any population segment: "This has tremendous implications for business and to take advantage of the opportunity, businesses must respond to the demands of this sector." Many Native entrepreneurs are emerging to fill the demand for goods and services, for example, Cree-ative Media (1999) Ltd. of Calgary.

The Internet Explosion

As noted earlier, advances in technology make it easier than ever to start a company and develop a loyal customer following. The Internet has opened new opportunities for small businesses, and research shows that small businesses are taking advantage of its benefits. Small businesses use the Internet for e-mail, to purchase goods and services, to conduct business research, and, of course, to sell their products and communicate with customers. See Chapter 4 for a more in-depth discussion of technology and business.

HOT Links

For an overview of services for Aboriginal entrepreneurs check out these links: Aboriginal Business Canada (www.abc.gc.ca), Aboriginal Youth Business Council (www.aybc.org), and National Aboriginal Business Association (www.nabacanada.com).

concept check

- What significant trends are occurring in small business management?
- How is the Internet affecting small business?

APPLYING THIS CHAPTER'S TOPICS

After reading Chapter 6, you may be ready to go into business. Perhaps you believe you have just the "better mousetrap" the world needs. Maybe you want to be your own boss or seek financial rewards. Job security or quality-of-life issues may be your primary motives.

Whatever your reasons, you'll have to do a lot of groundwork before taking the plunge. Do you know what you want from life and how the business fits into your overall goals? Do you have what it takes to start a business, from personal characteristics like energy and persistence to money to fund the venture? You'll also have to research the feasibility of your product idea and develop a business plan. No question about it, becoming an entrepreneur or small business owner is hard work.

Taking the First Steps

Maybe you know that you want to run your own business but don't know what type of business to start. In addition to the advice provided earlier in the chapter, here are some ways to gather possible ideas:

- Brainstorm with family and friends without setting any limits, and then investigate the best ideas, no matter how impossible they may seem at first.
- Look at products that don't meet your needs and find ways to change them.
- Focus on your interests and hobbies.
- Use your skills in new ways. Are you computer-savvy? You could start a business providing in-home consulting to novices who don't know how to set up or use their computers.
- Be observant—look for anything that catches your interest wherever you are, in your hometown or when you travel. What's special about it? Is there a niche market you can fill?
- Pay attention to the latest fads and trends.
- Surf the Web, especially the "What's New" or "What's Hot" sections of search engines.[15]

Working at a Small Business

Working for a small company can be a wonderful experience. Many people enjoy the less structured atmosphere and greater flexibility that often characterize the small business workplace. Several years' experience at a small company can be a good stepping-stone to owning your own company. You'll get a better understanding of the realities of running a small business before striking out on your own. Other potential benefits include:

- *More diverse job responsibilities.* Small companies may not have formal job descriptions, giving you a chance to learn a wider variety of skills to use later. At a large company your job may be strictly defined.
- *Less bureaucracy.* Small companies typically have fewer formal rules and procedures. This creates a more relaxed working atmosphere.
- *Your ideas are more likely to count.* You'll have greater access to top management and be able to discuss your ideas.
- *Greater sense of your contribution to business.* You can see how your work contributes to the firm's success.

However, you should also be aware of the disadvantages of being a small business employee:

- *Lower compensation packages.* Although the gap between large and small businesses is narrowing, salaries are likely to be lower at small businesses. In addition, there may be few, if any, employee benefits such as health insurance and retirement plans.
- *Less job security.* Small businesses may be more affected by changing economic and competitive conditions. A change in ownership can put jobs at risk as well.
- *Greater potential for personality clashes.* When two employees don't get along, their hostility really stands out. Such conflicts can affect the rest of the staff. Also, if you have a problem with your boss, you don't have anyone to go to if the boss owns the company.
- *Fewer opportunities for career advancement.* After a few years, you may outgrow a small firm. There may be no chances for promotion. And with fewer people within the firm with whom to network, you'll have to join outside organizations for these connections.

Evaluating these factors will help you decide whether working at a small business is the right opportunity for you.

TRY IT NOW!

1. **Explore the Possibilities** Starting a business at home is one of the easiest ways to become self-employed. Check out the networking site for young entrepreneurs at www.yea.ca or the Canadian Association of Family Enterprise at www.cafeuc.org.

2. **Learn from an Entrepreneur** What does it really take to become an entrepreneur? Find out by interviewing a local entrepreneur or researching an entrepreneur you've read about in this chapter or in the business press. Get answers to the following questions, as well as any others you'd like to ask:

   • How did you develop your vision for the company?

   • What are the most important entrepreneurial characteristics that helped you succeed?

   • Where did you learn the business skills you needed to run and grow the company?

   • How did you research the feasibility of your idea? Prepare your business plan?

   • What were the biggest challenges you had to overcome?

   • Where did you obtain financing for the company?

   • What are the most important lessons you learned by starting this company?

   • What advice do you have for would-be entrepreneurs?

3. **Check Out the Current Research** Gain an understanding of why many new firms fail while others experience incredible growth at the Entrepreneurship Research Alliance at www.era.commerce.ubc.ca/.

>looking ahead

at Gotcha's

Although Gino Panucci is now, once again, a successful businessperson, he is far from complacent. He is constantly looking for ways to improve the service he provides to his customers, whether it be non-smoking areas, outdoor patios, contests for trips and cars, and so on. "You never let yourself get too comfortable," says Gino. "That's when you'll get in trouble." Constantly scanning the business environment for new trends is a regular activity. Trips to Las Vegas to check out the latest in night club ideas is an annual expedition and regular trips to larger centres to check out what other clubs are doing successfully is a part of keeping in touch with the industry. Also, a good relationship with your suppliers is critical and Gino maintains strong ties with the distributors. It is important to have a sense of what the various levels of government might be planning as well. By scanning the environment in these ways, he stays more aware of the opportunities and threats for his business: "You have to know if a new club might be opening in the area and be ready for them if they do. When you run your own business, you don't want to get caught sleeping."

KEY TERMS

angel investors 163
Business Development Bank of
  Canada (BDC) 161
business plan 162
debt 163
entrepreneur 155
equity 163
intrapreneur 156
small business 159
venture capital 163

SUMMARY OF LEARNING GOALS

➡lg 1 **Why do people become entrepreneurs, and what are the different types of entrepreneurs?**

Entrepreneurship involves taking the risk of starting and managing a business to make a profit. Entrepreneurs are innovators who start firms either to have a certain lifestyle or to develop a company that will grow into a major corporation. People become entrepreneurs for four main reasons: the opportunity for profit, independence, personal satisfaction, and lifestyle. Classic entrepreneurs may be micropreneurs, who plan to keep their businesses small, or growth-oriented entrepreneurs. Multipreneurs start multiple companies, while intrapreneurs work within large corporations.

➡lg 2   Which characteristics do successful entrepreneurs share?

Successful entrepreneurs are ambitious, independent, self-confident, creative, energetic, passionate, and committed. They have a high need for achievement and a willingness to take moderate risks. They have good interpersonal and communication skills. Managerial skills and technical knowledge are also important for entrepreneurial success.

➡lg 3   How do small businesses contribute to the Canadian economy?

A small business is independently owned and operated, has a local base of operations, and is not dominant in its field. Small businesses play an important role in the economy. About 97 percent of Canadian businesses have fewer than 50 employees. Small businesses are found in every field, but they dominate the construction, wholesale, and retail categories. Most new private-sector jobs created in Canada over the past decade were in small firms. Small businesses also create about twice as many new goods and services as larger firms.

➡lg 4   What are the advantages and disadvantages facing owners of small businesses?

Small businesses have flexibility to respond to changing market conditions. Because of their streamlined staffing and structure, they can be efficiently operated. Small firms can serve specialized markets more profitably than large firms and provide a higher level of personal service. Disadvantages include limited managerial skill, difficulty in raising the capital needed for start-up and expansion, the burden of complying with increasing levels of government regulation, and the major personal commitment required on the part of the owner.

➡lg 5   How does the Business Development Bank of Canada (BDC) help small businesses?

The BDC is the main federal agency serving small businesses. It provides guarantees of private lender loans for small businesses. The BDC also offers a wide range of management assistance services, including courses, publications, and consulting.

➡lg 6   What are the first steps to take if you are starting your own firm?

After finding an idea that satisfies a market need, the small business owner should choose a form of business organization. The process of developing a formal business plan helps the business owner to analyze the feasibility of his or her idea. This written plan describes in detail the idea for the business and how it will be implemented. The plan also helps the owner obtain both debt and equity financing for the new business.

➡lg 7   Why does managing a small business present special challenges for the owner?

At first, small business owners are involved in all aspects of the firm's operations. Wise use of outside consultants can free up the owner's time to focus on planning and strategy in addition to day-to-day operations. Other key management responsibilities are finding and retaining good employees and monitoring market conditions.

➡lg 8   What trends are shaping the small business environment?

Many young people are choosing entrepreneurship as their first career. Women are starting businesses at a faster rate than any other group. Women often choose self-employment for lifestyle reasons and to overcome limited opportunities in large firms. For many business owners, the office is at home as the Internet is fuelling small business growth by making it easier to open Web-based businesses.

WORKING THE NET

1. Visit Sample Business Plans at **www.bplans.com/** to review sample plans for all types of businesses. Select an idea for a company in a field that interests you, and using information from this site, prepare an outline for its business plan.

2. Visit the Canadian Venture Capital Association site (**www.cvca.ca**) and find a business idea you like or dislike. Explain why you think this is a good business idea or not. List additional information the entrepreneur should have about starting this business and research the industry on the Web using a search engine.

3. Check out the international trade Web links at **www.exportCanada.com**. Pick two or three of the suggested global business Web sites. Compare them in terms of the information offered to small businesses that want to venture into overseas markets. Which is the most useful, and why?

4. Explore the Human Resources Development Canada site at **www.hrdc-drhc.gc.ca**. What resources are available to you locally? What services do they offer? What market trends and industry information are available?

CREATIVE THINKING CASE

Buzzing Around

For some entrepreneurs, success can overwhelm their abilities to manage. When they are very successful and are making large amounts of money, can the entrepreneur lose sight of what caused him or her to be successful in the first place?

Carman was an entrepreneurship student at a large college. As part of his program, he was required to complete two directed field studies components worth 15 credit hours each. During the field studies he was required to open and run his own business. He decided to build on his early teen experience of mowing lawns and open a landscaping business. During the first four-month field-study period, the business was a huge success. Carman was able to buy a truck and hire a crew to work with him. He hired other students from the college as well as friends and family. The work team arrived at the customer's house and with each member performing a different duty, completed the lawn care in under 15 minutes. Some members mowed, others used a weed eater, while others did edging and clean-up. Customers commented that it was like watching a herd of cattle disgorge from a barn, forage around, and then return as quickly as they left. Since the business was so successful, when Carman returned to college for his academic semester, he attempted to keep his business open. Then, when he entered his second field-study semester, the business would already be up and running.

As the academic semester progressed, Carman realized just what a huge commitment he had made. He was forced to drop a course in order to maintain service to his customers. Even at that, there were times when he was forced to send his team to a location without him. When this occurred, the quality and level of service dropped significantly. Slowly the number of full-time customers began to drop. Carman dropped another course so that he could spend more time at his business. He started to miss classes and ended up having to do an extra semester to finish his program.

Today, Carman has gone on to a master's program and has rethought his hiring practices while running his small business. "I guess I just hired any warm body who could handle a lawnmower," he says. "I guess that wasn't the best idea."[16]

Critical Thinking Questions
1. Why do you think Carman had trouble maintaining his customer base? Was there something he could have done differently?
2. With someone other than himself making the day-to-day decisions, did Carman's role change?

Corporate Governance, the Legal Environment, and Taxation

In this chapter we're back to our PEST model. Corporate governance, the legal environment, and taxes fit most directly in the *political* environment, as the government at all levels regulates business activity. It lays out the laws for business to follow, and taxes businesses in many different ways.

However, these laws are shaped not just by the political environment. The political environment responds to the changing needs of the social, economic, and technological environments, changing laws and creating new ones as appropriate. You'll read in this chapter, for example, about laws relating to the natural environment as the *social* environment becomes increasingly more aware of and protective of the natural environment, laws relating to employment equity as the work force becomes more diverse, laws relating to competition (the *economic* environment) to protect consumers from businesses engaging in anticompetitive behaviour, and laws relating to privacy issues and the Internet (the *technological* environment). An interesting integrative example is in the economic trend toward deregulation—removing regulations governing competition in certain industries, as opposed to creating new regulations. This practice has led to one of the major trends discussed in Chapter 6—the increase of new small and entrepreneurial businesses in the economy as opportunities have opened up in these industries. So business needs to see the whole of the external environment in an integrative and proactive way to

stay within the boundaries created by the legal system.

There are many examples in this chapter of how the legal system affects decisions made by business, and therefore ultimately the success of the business. For example, in the area of *operations* the law of negligence requires that "businesses comply with industry standards in the manufacture" of products or "liability to consumers may result." This makes it extremely critical to monitor product *quality* (one of our critical success factors) to prevent strict liability resulting from defective products or packaging. In the area of *human resources*, the Employment Standards Act covers minimum wage, hours of work, and other workplace regulations. In the area of *marketing*, the Trademarks Act applies to all businesses and affects the ability of the company to create a unique brand in the customer's mind. Patent law also affects the ability to create a competitive advantage and *meet customer needs* by protecting *innovations* from competitive threats (more critical success factors). And lastly, there is the tax system, which of course affects the *financial* area of business and cannot be ignored. If not managed correctly, the amount of taxes that a business is required to pay can severely affect its ability to *achieve financial success.*

Associations, industry, and governments are working closely together to protect the *stakeholders* of business. Clearly, as with the changes in the other areas of the external environment, the legal and tax environment of a business is a certain yet virtually uncontrollable factor that must be monitored and managed in an integrative way, in order for the business to achieve success in all areas.

Corporate Governance, the Legal Environment, and Taxation

CHAPTER 7

Learning Goals

→ **lg 1** What is corporate governance and why is it important?

→ **lg 2** How does the legal system govern business transactions and settle business disputes?

→ **lg 3** What are the required elements of a valid contract; and what are the key types of business law?

→ **lg 4** What are patents, copyright, and trademarks? How do these help businesses?

→ **lg 5** What are Employment Standards Acts?

→ **lg 6** What are the most common taxes paid by businesses?

A Basic Understanding of Canadian Business Law and the Tax System Adds Certainty

According to Sandra Malach, LLB, LLM, the law has an effect on how business is conducted in Canada because it sets standards, defines business risks, and defines business relationships. As an instructor of business law, securities, and corporate tax, as well as being a contributing author of legal issues in small business publications, Sandra believes that a business law course for management students is invaluable because it provides a background to areas that are not, in the strictest sense, day-to-day management issues but affect managers and the way they conduct their operations, both internally and externally. "Managers need to be aware of the laws that affect their day-to-day operations," she says. "And more importantly, that they can recognize legal issues and contact the appropriate professional to resolve the issue."

"Many businesspeople see the law as solely establishing rules regarding permissible and illegal business activities. But the law goes beyond dictating what can and what cannot be done. By understanding the basics of the laws as they affect business, it can add certainty to business activity, particularly with regard to activities that affect third parties. For example, the law of contract allows businesses to know when they have formed an enforceable contract allowing them to seek compensation if the contracting party does not fulfill its obligations." Sandra continues, "The law of negligence has established that businesses must comply with industry standards in the manufacture and inspection of their products or liability to consumers may result. Regulations establish standards for the import of certain products and the conduct of certain kinds of business."

"The Employment Standards Act is one of the most important areas for any employer. Each of the provinces has its own act that covers topics such as minimum wage, allowable deductions, hours of work, and so on. Without the knowledge of the act (or in some cases its existence) business owners may be violating laws that they are not aware of, which could amount to considerable costs if violations occur."

Another vital area, to have at least some knowledge of, is the tax system and the obligations of a corporation and its directors. "Often when businesses are having financial difficulties, they will not remit their payroll deduction amounts and the directors are often surprised to find out that they are personally responsible," she says.

In a final thought Sandra states, "As a result, it is important for businesspeople to become familiar with the laws, as it affects their business, so that they can minimize their risk exposure through proper conduct of the operational aspects of their business."[1]

CRITICAL THINKING QUESTIONS

As you read this chapter, consider Sandra Malach's thoughts of why it is important for employees, business owners, and corporations to have at least a basic understanding of Canadian business law and the tax system. Consider the following:

- Why are there laws that relate to external business practices?
- How do contracts help the parties to the contract?
- What laws apply to the business when it has employees?
- How are consumers protected by the laws?
- Why is the tax system important to Canada and its society?

➡️ **lg 1**

corporate governance
The way in which an organization is being governed, directed, and administered.

BUSINESS IN THE 21ST CENTURY

Corporate governance refers to the way in which an organization is being governed, directed, and administered.[2] As discussed in Chapter 5, the board of governors are responsible for the organization being managed in the best interest of the corporation. Recent experiences in Canada, the U.S, and around the world have highlighted the outcome of poor corporate governance on the organization's performance and survival. Increasingly, stakeholders are looking at the corporate governance and control systems of businesses to ensure that they are being managed with the interests of the stakeholders in mind. Although the debate has focused primarily on the financial position and reporting of companies, other concerns are being discussed (e.g., honesty in other information, respect for the environment, etc.).

Since the early 1990s, the debate on corporate governance has been flourishing and regulators in Canada have been setting guidelines to address this issue. This has been in response to worldwide incidences that have brought questions about boards of directors' performance and alleged management incompetence. Most notable have been the WorldCom and Enron scandals (where financial statements were proved to be inaccurate), but Canada has not escaped its own examples (e.g., Bre-X and YBM).[3] As well, companies are expected to be socially responsible in their investing. According to Brian A. Scholfield and Blair W. Feltmate in *Sustainable Development Investing,*

> Stakeholders now require that companies be committed to minimizing environmental disruptions and to contribute to the economic and social advancement of the communities in which they operate, known as sustainable development.[4]

In July 2002, the Canadian Institute of Chartered Accountants, the Canadian Securities Administrators, and the Office of the Superintendent of Financial Institutions announced the creation of the Canadian Public Accountability Board (CPAB). Its mission is to "contribute to public confidence in the integrity of financial reporting of public companies by promoting high-quality, independent auditing."[5]

So what has brought about the need to create the CPAB? There have been many successful attempts by associations to regulate their industries. The provincial legal associations, medical associations, faculty associations, accounting associations, and others have developed strict guidelines that control the responsibilities and actions of their members. But this does not guarantee that every member will follow the guidelines. Typically, when there are serious violations, government bodies react and enact regulations (in the form of laws) to protect society, or, in some cases, governments have been proactive in anticipation of violations.

HOT Links

For more news and updated events, search the Office of the Superintendent of Financial Institutions' Web site at **www.osfi-bsif.gc.ca**

The Legal System

Our legal system affects everyone who lives and does business in Canada. The smooth functioning of society depends on the law, which protects the rights of people and businesses. The purpose of law is to keep the system stable while allowing orderly change. The law defines which actions are allowed or banned and regulates some practices. It also helps settle disputes. The legal system both shapes and is shaped by political, economic, and social systems. All three levels of government, federal, provincial, and municipal, regulate various business activities as set out in the laws of Canada and the provinces.

In any society **laws** are the rules of conduct created and enforced by a controlling authority, usually the government. They develop over time in response to the changing needs of people, property, and business. The legal system in Canada is thus the result of a long and continuing process. In each generation new social problems occur, and new laws are created to solve them. For instance, the Combines Investigation Act and

laws
The rules of conduct in a society, created and enforced by a controlling authority, usually the government.

Statute laws at the federal level are the end result of the legislative process in Ottawa.

its successor, the Competition Act, were enacted to protect consumers in areas such as misleading advertising and abusive marketing practices. These acts also provide provisions that can be grouped under three categories: conspiracies, monopolies, and mergers.

Environmental law is an area that both the federal and provincial governments have concurrent jurisdiction. Increased awareness of pollution and a social movement towards the protection of our environment has made this area an important public issue. The appropriate federal and provincial Environmental Protection Acts apply to all the elements of the environment: air, land, and water.

Another area of law that is important to businesses is the Employment Equity Act. Passed in 1986, the act applies to all employers with 100 or more employees. Employment rights go beyond requiring employers to treat potential and existing employees equally, regardless to their personal characteristics. The employers, at a minimum, are encouraged to make their work force reflect various underrepresented peoples (i.e., their organizations should reflect society as much as possible). Because of the increase of businesses geared towards social responsibility, not only do employers with 100 or more employees try to follow the Employment Equity standards, but smaller organizations do so as well.

Today new areas of law are developing to deal with the Internet. The increasing use of the Internet, as discussed in Chapter 4, requires that industry and the governments respond to various applicable issues, such as privacy.

Public and Private Law

public law
The law relating to the relationship between the individual or business and the government (or its agencies).

Public law is the law relating to the relationship between the individual or business and the government (or its agencies). The Criminal Code and the Income Tax Act are two examples at the federal level. Liquor laws are an example of public law at the provincial level.

private law
The law relating to the relationship between individuals, businesses, or individuals and businesses.

Private law is the law relating to the relationship between individuals, businesses, or individuals and businesses. Statutes that protect one person from the harm of another are private laws.

The Main Sources of Law

common law
The body of unwritten law that has evolved out of judicial (court) decisions rather than being enacted by a legislature; also called *case law*.

Common law is the body of unwritten law that has evolved out of judicial (court) decisions rather than being enacted by legislatures. It is also called case law. It developed in England and applies to most of the English-speaking world. Common law is based on community customs that were recognized and enforced by the courts. Therefore, common law is based on previous decisions. The reliance on previous decisions creates certainty and predictability.

civil code
A body of written law that sets out the private rights of the citizens.

Civil code is a body of written law that sets out the private rights of the citizens. In Quebec much of what would be found in the common law of other provinces has been codified, and is known as the Civil Code.

statute law (or statutory law)
Written law enacted by a legislature (municipal, provincial, or federal).

Statute law (or statutory law) is written law enacted by legislatures at all levels, from municipal and provincial governments to the federal government. Statues are the end result of the legislative process. Statutory laws are the elected representatives of the people's wishes. The particular advantage of statue law over common law is the relative ease that the statues can be changed.

administrative law
The rules, regulations, and orders passed by boards, commissions, and agencies of government (municipal, provincial, and federal).

Related to statutory law is **administrative law**, or the rules, regulations, and orders passed by boards, commissions, and agencies of municipal, provincial, and federal governments. The scope and influence of administrative law have expanded as the number of these government bodies has grown. Examples of the activities of regulatory agencies include the sale of securities by public companies, employment standards, and broadcasting.

Business Law

Business law is the body of law that governs commercial dealings. These laws provide a certainty within which businesses can operate. They serve as guidelines for business decisions. Every businessperson should be familiar with the laws governing his or her field. Some laws, such as the Trade-marks Act, apply to all businesses. Other types of business laws may apply to a specific industry, such as the Canadian Radio-television and Telecommunications Commission Act that regulates and supervises all aspects of the Canadian broadcasting system and regulates telecommunications carriers and service providers that fall under federal jurisdiction.

The Court System

Canada has a highly developed court system. There are basically four levels of courts in Canada. The trials of most business disputes are heard in the Provincial/Territorial Superior Courts. These courts also hear appeals from Provincial Court judgments and judgments from the Provincial Administrative Tribunals. Appeals of these decisions are made to the Provincial Court of Appeal and subsequently to the Supreme Court of Canada. The Federal Court, Trial Division, and the Court of Appeals hear appeals of federally regulated Administrative Tribunals. The highest court in Canada is the Supreme Court of Canada and it is the final court of appeal from all other Canadian courts. Also, there are specialized Federal Courts, including the Tax Court of Canada, where individuals and companies have an opportunity to settle matters relating to federal tax and revenue legislation. See Exhibit 7-1 for an outline of Canada's court system.[6]

e x h i b i t 7 - 1	Outline of Canada's Court System

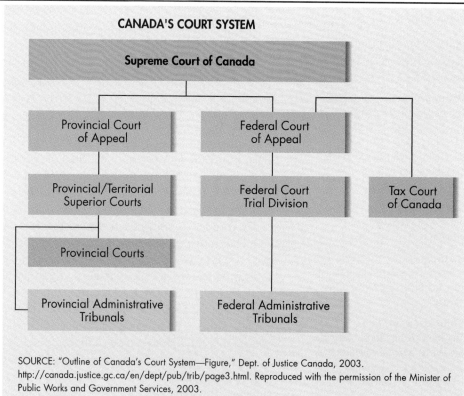

SOURCE: "Outline of Canada's Court System—Figure," Dept. of Justice Canada, 2003.
http://canada.justice.gc.ca/en/dept/pub/trib/page3.html. Reproduced with the permission of the Minister of Public Works and Government Services, 2003.

arbitration
A method of settling disputes in which the parties agree to present their case to an impartial third party and are required to accept the arbitrator's decision.

mediation
The intervention of a third party with a view to persuading the parties to adjust or settle their dispute.

contract
An agreement that sets forth the relationship between parties regarding the performance of a specified action; creates a legal obligation and is enforceable in a court of law.

express contract
A contract in which the terms are specified in either written or spoken words.

implied contract
A contract that depends on the acts and conduct of the parties to show agreement; the terms are not specified in writing or orally.

Nonjudicial Methods of Settling Disputes

Settling disputes by going to court is both expensive and time-consuming. Even if the case is settled prior to the actual trial, a sizable legal expense can be incurred in preparing for trial. Therefore, many companies now use private arbitration and mediation firms as alternatives to litigation. Private firms offer these services, which are a high-growth area within the legal profession.

With **arbitration**, the parties agree to present their case to an impartial third party and are required to accept the arbitrator's decision. **Mediation** is similar, but the mediator intervenes with the view of persuading the parties to adjust or settle their dispute. The mediator may or may not offer a resolution, but if the mediator does offer a solution, neither party is bound by the mediator's decision. The mediator may suggest alternative solutions and primarily tries to help the parties negotiate a settlement. Mediation is more flexible than arbitration and allows for compromise. If the parties cannot reach a settlement, they can then go to court, an option not available in most arbitration cases.

In addition to saving time and money, corporations like the confidentiality of testimony and settlement terms in these proceedings. Arbitration and mediation also allow businesses to avoid the risks associated with going to trial. Generally speaking, once court action is initiated the information is then public.

Contract Law

A **contract** is an agreement that sets forth the relationship between parties regarding the performance of a specified action. The contract creates a legal obligation and is enforceable in a court of law. Contracts are an important part of business law. Contract law is also incorporated into other fields of business law, such as property and agency law, which we'll discuss later. Some of the business transactions that involve contracts are buying materials and property, selling goods, leasing equipment, and hiring consultants.

A contract can be an **express contract**, which specifies the terms of the agreement in either written or spoken words, or an **implied contract**, which depends on the acts and conduct of the parties to show agreement. An example of an express contract is the written contract an employee might sign that outlines the obligations of the employee and the employer. For example, an implied contract exists when you order and receive a sandwich at Jason's Grill. You and the restaurant have an implied contract that you will pay the price shown on the restaurant's menu in exchange for an edible sandwich.

Michelle Sales, a 22-year-old owner of a small cosmetics company, is looking for a supplier to provide her store with inventory. She found a supplier she had confidence in and after some negotiating, she and the supplier agree on a price of $11 000 and the supplier writes up a contract, which they both sign. Has Michelle legally bought the inventory for $11 000? The answer is yes, because the transaction meets all the requirements for a valid contract.

A contract may be verbal or written, express or implied.

Contract Requirements[7]

Businesses deal with contracts all the time, so it's important to know the requirements of a valid contract. For a contract to be legally enforceable, all of the following elements must be present:

- *Mutual agreement.* This is evidenced by the offer of one party being accepted by another party. Each party to the contract must have entered into it freely, without duress. Using physical or economic harm to force the signing of the contract—threatening injury or refusing to place another large order, for instance—invalidates a contract. Likewise, fraud—misrepresenting the facts of a transaction—makes a contract unenforceable. Telling a prospective used-car buyer that the brakes are new when in fact they have not been replaced makes the contract of sale invalid.
- *Capacity of the parties.* Legal ability of a party to enter into contracts. Under the law, minors (those who have not attained the age of majority according to the law of their province or territory), mental incompetents, and drug and alcohol addicts cannot enter into contracts.
- *Legal consideration.* Exchange of something of legal value or benefit between the parties. Consideration can be in the form of money, goods, or a legal right given up. Suppose that an electronics manufacturer agrees to rent an industrial building for a year at a monthly rent of $1500. Its consideration is the rent payment of $1500, and the building owner's consideration is permission to occupy the space. But if you offer to type a term paper for a friend for free and your offer is accepted, there is no contract. Your friend has not given up anything, so you are not legally bound to honour the deal.
- *Lawful object (legal purpose).* Absence of illegality. The purpose of the contract must be legal for it to be valid. A contract cannot require performance of an illegal act. A contract to smuggle a banned substance into Canada for a specified amount of money would not be legally enforceable.
- *Legal form.* Oral or written form, as required. Many contracts can be oral (although a written contract provides an accurate record to the parties of their obligations). For instance, an oral contract exists when Bridge Corp. orders office supplies by phone from Ace Stationery Store and Ace delivers the requested goods. Written contracts include leases, sales contracts, and property deeds. Some types of contracts must be in writing to be legally binding.

As you can see, Michelle's inventory purchase meets all the requirements for a valid contract. Both parties have freely agreed to the terms of the contract. Michelle is not a minor and presumably does not fit any of the other categories of incapacity. Both parties are giving consideration, Michelle by paying the money and the supplier by delivering the inventory. The purchase of the inventory is a legal activity. And the written contract is the correct form because the cost of the inventory is over the legal amount that requires a written contract (this varies by province).

Breach of Contract

breach of contract
The failure by one party to a contract to fulfill the terms of the agreement without a legal excuse.

A **breach of contract** occurs when one party to a contract fails (without legal excuse) to fulfill the terms of the agreement. The other party then has the right to seek a remedy in the courts. There are three legal remedies for breach of contract:
- *Payment of damages.* Money awarded to the party who was harmed by the breach of contract, to cover losses incurred because the contract wasn't fulfilled. Suppose that Ajax Roofing contracts with Fred Wellman to fix the large hole in the roof of his factory within three days. But the roofing crew doesn't show up as promised. When a thunderstorm four days later causes $45 000 in damage to Wellman's machinery, Wellman can sue for damages to cover the costs of the water damage because Ajax breached the contract.
- *Specific performance of the contract.* A court order that requires the breaching party to perform the duties under the terms of the contract. Specific performance is a common method of settling a breach of contract. Wellman might ask the court to direct Ajax to fix the roof at the price and conditions in the contract.
- *Restitution.* Cancelling the contract and returning both parties to the situation that existed before the contract. If one party fails to perform under the contract,

neither party has any further obligation to the other. Because Ajax failed to fix Wellman's roof under the terms of the contract, Wellman does not owe Ajax any money. Ajax must return the 50 percent deposit it received when Wellman signed the contract.

Warranties

Express warranties are specific statements of fact or promises about a product by the seller. This form of warranty is considered part of the sales transaction that influences the buyer. Express warranties appear in the form of statements that can be interpreted as fact. The statement "This machine will process 1000 gallons of paint per hour" is an express warranty, as is the printed warranty that comes with a computer or a telephone answering machine.

Implied warranties are neither written nor oral. These guarantees are imposed on sales transactions by statute or court decision. They promise that the product will perform up to expected standards. For instance, a man bought a used car from a dealer, and the next day the transmission fell out as he was driving on the highway. The dealer fixed the car, but a week later the brakes failed. The man sued the car dealer. The court ruled in favour of the car owner because any car without a working transmission or brakes is not fit for the ordinary purpose of driving. Similarly, if a customer asks to buy a copier to handle 5000 copies per month, she relies on the salesperson to sell her a copier that meets those needs. The salesperson implicitly warrants that the copier purchased is appropriate for that volume.

Patents, Copyrights, and Trademarks

Canadian law protects authors, inventors, and creators of other intellectual property by giving them the rights to their creative works. Patents, copyrights, and registration of trademarks are legal protection for key business assets.

A **patent** gives an inventor the exclusive right to manufacture, use, and sell an invention for 20 years. The Patent Act grants patents for ideas that meet its requirements of being new, unique, and useful. The physical process, machine, or formula is what is patented. Patent rights—pharmaceutical companies' rights to produce drugs they discover, for example—are considered intangible personal property (i.e., they do not have physical form, but are of value).

The government also grants copyrights. A **copyright** is an exclusive right, shown by the symbol © (but does not necessarily need it), given to a writer, artist, composer, or playwright to use, produce, and sell her or his creation. This protection is automatic. Works protected by copyright include printed materials (books, magazine articles, lectures), works of art, photographs, and movies. Under current copyright law, the copyright is issued for the life of the creator plus 50 years after the creator's death. Patents and copyrights, which are considered intellectual property, are the subject of many lawsuits today.

A **trademark** is a design, name, or other distinctive mark that a manufacturer uses to identify its goods in the marketplace. Apple Computer's multicoloured apple logo (symbol) is an example of a trademark.

Trademarks are valuable because they create uniqueness in the minds of customers. At the same time, companies don't want a trademark to become so well known that it is used to describe all similar types of products. For instance, Coke is often used to refer to any cola soft drink, not just those produced by the Coca-Cola Company. Companies spend millions of dollars each year to keep their trademarks from becoming generic words, terms used to identify a product class rather than the specific product. Coca-Cola employs many investigators and files 70 to 80 lawsuits each year to prevent its trademarks from becoming generic words.

➡ lg 4

patent
A form of protection (limited monopoly) established by the government to inventors; gives an inventor the exclusive right to manufacture, use, and sell an invention for 20 years.

copyright
A form of protection established by the government for creators of works of art, music, literature, or other intellectual property; gives the creator the exclusive right to use, produce, and sell the creation during the lifetime of the creator and for 50 years thereafter.

trademark
The legally exclusive design, name, or other distinctive mark that a manufacturer uses to identify its goods in the marketplace.

HOT Links

For more information about patents, copyrights and trademarks go to CanadaOne's Web site and search for information at www.canadaone.com

A patent gives the inventor exclusive rights to the manufacture, use, and sale of the invention for 20 years. There may be no more Elmos for a while but similar products soon flooded the marketplace.

tort
A civil, or private, act that harms other people or their property.

product liability
The responsibility of manufacturers and sellers for defects in the products they make and sell.

Once a trademark becomes generic (which a court decides), it is public property and can be used by any person or company. Names that were once trademarked but are now generic include aspirin, thermos, linoleum, and zipper.

Tort Law

A **tort** is a civil, or private, act that harms other people or their property. The harm may involve physical injury, emotional distress, invasion of privacy, or defamation (injuring a person's character by publication of false statements). The injured party may sue the wrongdoer to recover damages for the harm or loss. A tort is not the result of a breach of contract, which would be settled under contract law. Torts are part of common law. Examples of tort cases are medical malpractice, slander (an untrue oral statement that damages a person's reputation), libel (an untrue written statement that damages a person's reputation), product liability (discussed in the next section), professional negligence, and fraud.

A tort is generally not a crime, although some acts can be both torts and crimes. (Assault and battery, for instance, is a criminal act that would be prosecuted by the government and is also a tort because of the injury to the person.) Torts are private wrongs and are settled in courts. Crimes are violations of public law punishable by the government in the criminal courts. The purpose of criminal law is to punish the person who committed the crime. The purpose of tort law is to provide remedies to the injured party.

For a tort to exist and damages to be recovered, the harm must be done through either negligence or deliberate intent. Negligence occurs when reasonable care is not taken for the safety of others. For instance, a woman attending a baseball game was struck on the head by a foul ball that came through a hole in the screen behind home plate. The court could rule that a sports team charging admission has an obligation to provide structures free from defects and seating that protects spectators from danger. Therefore, the baseball organization could be found negligent. Negligence does not apply when an injury is caused by an unavoidable accident, an event that was not intended and could not have been prevented even if the person used reasonable care. This area of tort law is quite controversial, because the definition of negligence leaves much room for interpretation.

Product-Liability Law

Product liability refers to manufacturers' and sellers' responsibility for defects in the products they make and sell. It has become a specialized area of law combining aspects of contracts, warranties, torts, and statutory law.

An important concept in product-liability law is **strict liability**. A manufacturer or seller is liable for any personal injury or property damage caused by defective products or packaging that does not meet industry standards.

Bankruptcy and Insolvency Act

It may be possible to save a business, even though it is insolvent, by using the provisions under the *Bankruptcy and Insolvency Act*. **Bankruptcy** is the legal act by which individuals or businesses that cannot meet their financial obligations are relieved of

strict liability
A concept in products-liability laws under which a manufacturer or seller is liable for any personal injury or property damage caused by defective products or packaging that does not meet industry standards.

bankruptcy
The legal procedure by which individuals or businesses that cannot meet their financial obligations are relieved of some, it not all, of their debt.

HOT Links

For more information on corporate bankruptcy, see the Web site that helps people and businesses get a fresh financial start at
www.BankruptcyCanada.com

cartel
An agreement between enterprises to lessen competition.

monopoly
A situation where there is no competition and the benefits of a free market are lost.

→ lg 5

consumerism
A movement that seeks to increase the rights and powers of buyers vis-à-vis sellers.

some, if not all, of their debt. Working through a Trustee in Bankruptcy, the company (or individual) files a Proposal ("offer") to the company's creditors asking them to accept less than the actual monies owed so that the company can survive.

Competition Act

As stated earlier in this chapter, the Competition Act was enacted to protect consumers and provide provisions that can be grouped under three categories: conspiracies, monopolies, and mergers. Each of these three categories is briefly discussed below.

Many measures have been taken to try to keep the marketplace free from influences that would restrict competition. The Competition Act sets out the basic prohibition against cartels, (the expression that is often used is *antitrust law)* among other issues. A **cartel** is an agreement between enterprises to lessen competition. If it can be proven that enterprises entered into an agreement or arrangement (a conspiracy) to lessen competition, they can be charged with a criminal offence.

Some of the more common methods of reducing or eliminating competition are:
- *Parallel pricing*—competing firms adopt similar pricing strategies.
- *Setting quotas*—imposing limits of production.
- *Market-sharing*—dividing the market based on a geographical basis.
- *Product specialization*—each firm agrees to specialize their products.

According to the free market economy (as discussed in Chapter 1), the essential characteristic of an efficient market is competition. If customers have a choice of products to purchase (i.e., competition), prices will be generally lower or quality will be better or both. A **monopoly** is a situation when there is no competition and the benefits of a free market are lost.

For various reasons (e.g., small population, large geographical area, etc.) some monopolies are allowed to exist in Canada. Some examples have been utilities and telecommunications services, but these have been governed by regulatory agencies (e.g., utility boards) that protected the consumers' rights. These *natural monopolies* have been disappearing in the past decade as government regulations have promoted more competition in reaction to the stronger move to increased competition.

The third area where the Competition Act protects the consumer is mergers and acquisitions. As discussed in Chapter 6, mergers and acquisitions are often an important means to seek efficiencies in business. The Competition Act allows the government to stop any mergers and acquisitions that may lessen competition.

Employment Standards Acts

One issue that many businesses face is the ability to recruit good employees. Further, each province has an Employment Standards Act (or an equivalent, such as an Employment Standards Code) that outlines the minimum terms of employment in such areas as minimum wages, payment of earnings, hours of work, overtime, general (statutory) holidays, vacations, maternity and parental leaves, termination, layoff and recall, and the employment of children.

Without the knowledge of these minimum standards, employers can potentially be violating the standards and can incur considerable costs if action is taken against them. Particularly at risk are the smaller organizations that do not have a human resource department with professional human resource personnel.

Consumer Protection

Consumerism reflects the struggle for power between buyers and sellers. Specifically, it is a movement seeking to increase the rights and powers of buyers vis-à-vis sellers often resulting in consumer protection laws. Sellers' rights and powers include the following:

- To introduce into the marketplace any product, in any size and style, that is not hazardous to personal health or safety, or if it is hazardous, to introduce it with the proper warnings and controls.
- To price the product at any level they wish, provided they do not discriminate among similar classes of buyers.
- To spend any amount of money they wish to promote the product, so long as the promotion does not constitute unfair competition.
- To formulate any message they wish about the product, provided that it is not misleading or dishonest in content or execution.
- To introduce any buying incentives they wish.

Meanwhile, buyers have the following rights and powers:
- To refuse to buy any product that is offered to them.
- To expect products to be safe.
- To expect a product to be essentially as the seller represents it.
- To receive adequate information about the product.

Deregulation of Industries

deregulation

The removal or rules and regulations governing business competition.

Since the 1980s, the Canadian governments (federal and provincial/territorial) have actively promoted **deregulation**, the removal of rules and regulations governing business competition. Deregulation has drastically changed some once-regulated industries (especially the transportation, telecommunications, and financial services industries) and created many new competitors. The result has been entries into and exits from some industries.

Taxation of Business

Taxes are sometimes seen as the price we pay to live in this country. Taxes are assessed by all levels of government on both business and individuals, and they are used to pay for the services provided by government.

income taxes

Taxes that are based on the income received by businesses and individuals.

Income Taxes

Income taxes are based on the income received by businesses and individuals. Most personal income taxes are progressive, meaning that rates increase as income increases (one exception is the flat tax for individuals in Alberta). The tax rates for the federal government apply to all Canadians (with few exceptions) equally, but the provinces are free to set their own rates. Income taxes for businesses are flat (i.e., same rate regardless of income).

As we discussed in Chapter 5, the net income for sole proprietorships and partnerships are included in the personal income taxes of the owners. For corporations, it is the responsibility of the corporation.

Other Types of Taxes

Besides income taxes, individuals and businesses pay a number of other taxes. The four main types are property taxes, payroll taxes (only as a remittance), sales taxes, and excise taxes.

Property taxes are assessed on real property, based on the assessed value of the property. Most jurisdictions tax land and buildings. Property taxes may be based on fair market value (what a buyer would pay), a percentage of fair market value, or replacement value (what it would cost today to rebuild or buy something like the original). The value on which the taxes are based is the *assessed value.*

Consumerism has played an important part in enhancing the reputation of used car lots by pressuring dealers to provide a product that is essentially as represented.

property taxes
Taxes that are imposed on real and personal property based on the assessed value of the property.

payroll taxes
Income taxes that are collected by the employer and remitted to the federal government, usually in the form of a deduction from the employee's pay.

sales taxes
Taxes that are levied on goods and services when they are sold; calculated as a percentage of the price.

excise taxes
Taxes that are imposed on specific items such as gasoline, alcoholic beverages, and tobacco.

Any individual that is employed is required to pay federal and provincial taxes on the money that he or she earns (after the personal exemption is deducted), called income taxes. These taxes must be paid on wages, salaries, and commissions. The employer deducts the income taxes from the employee's pay and remits them to the federal government where they are called **payroll taxes**.

Sales taxes are levied on goods when they are sold and are a percentage of the sales price. These taxes are imposed by the federal government (the goods and services tax, or GST) and most provincial governments in the form of a provincial sales tax (PST). (One exception is that there is no provincial sales tax in Alberta.) Some provinces now have a harmonized sales tax (HST), which is a combination of the GST and the PST. The PSTs vary in amount and in what is considered taxable. Sales taxes increase the cost of goods to the consumer. Businesses are responsible for collecting sales taxes and remitting them to the government.

Excise taxes are placed on specific items, such as gasoline, alcoholic beverages, and tobacco. They can be assessed by federal and provincial governments. In many cases, these taxes help pay for services related to the item taxed. For instance, gasoline excise taxes are often used to build and repair highways. Other excise taxes—like those on alcoholic beverages and tobacco—are used to control practices that may cause harm.

CAPITALIZING ON TRENDS IN BUSINESS

As stakeholders increasingly see companies as "corporate citizens," businesses will be expected to carry out the obligations that society dictates. An argument can be made that organizations exist only because society allows them to exist, and therefore they must abide by certain rules of conduct or their survival could be jeopardized. As society expects more responsible corporate governance, they will expect that companies ensure that their boards of directors and company officers are ethical.

Stakeholders want to ensure that there is sustainable development and that companies contribute in a positive manner to society. Companies are expected to add to the well-being of society, and as their stakeholders' attitudes change, so must the companies. For some time it has been acknowledged by many in business that the bottom line is important, but it is not the only factor.

Industries, usually through associations, have increased their responsibility to ensure that corporations are adhering to laws and following the rules. Unfortunately, there have been recent events that have caused increased public outcry, causing both industry and government to respond. Even though these incidences have been few, they have shaken the confidence of many stakeholders.

APPLYING THIS CHAPTER'S TOPICS

This chapter has been about businesses governing themselves in a legal manner to respond to their stakeholders. Corporate governance is increasingly becoming important and it is necessary for businesses to be aware of their ethical and legal responsibilities.

Our environment is always changing, and businesses must be proactive to respond to the changes, or governments are forced to act. Associations can encourage strict adherence to the ethical standards that they set out, but these have little power to stop someone from acting unethically, or even illegally, often until it is too late.

Organizations, associations, industry, and government are increasingly working together to protect the stakeholders to ensure that business is governed in a ethical and legal manner.

1. Find Out about Employment Standards Go to your provincial government's Web site and search for employment standards for your province. Why do you think that these employment standards were legislated?

2. Know How the Law Is Changing Consider the changes that you can see in the legal and tax system that will affect business in the next five years. How do changes in our environment (e.g., values, economics, etc.) affect or cause these changes?

>looking ahead

at Business Law and the Tax System

Sandra Malach believes that proper corporate governance and understanding the company's legal and tax responsibilities will minimize the risk of making serious errors that could impact the sustainability of the business. Understanding the legal environment helps to minimize the risk in decision-making and helps the company to respond to customers.

The law does add certainty to business (e.g., contracts) and helps to protect the various stakeholder groups from being harmed by others. The law goes far beyond dictating actions, as many see it. The laws protect employees, consumers, suppliers, and other stakeholders and gives minimum guidelines for behaviours. Many organizations are far exceeding their expected roles and promoting behaviours that ensure good corporate governance.

SUMMARY OF LEARNING GOALS

➡lg 1 **What is corporate governance and why is it important?**
Corporate governance is the way in which an organization is being governed, directed, and administered. Increasingly, organizations must be seen as acting in the interests of its various stakeholders or its survival could be in jeopardy. If a corporation is acting in a perceived unethical manner, it could lose sales, have regulations imposed on it, have difficulty attracting employees, and so on.

➡lg 2 **How does the legal system govern business transactions and settle business disputes?**
Laws are the rules governing a society's conduct that are created and enforced by a controlling authority. The Canadian court system governs the legal system and includes both federal and provincial courts, each organized into three levels. The courts settle disputes by applying and interpreting laws. Most cases start in trial courts. Decisions can be appealed to appellate courts. The Supreme Court of Canada is the nation's highest court and the court of final appeal. To avoid the high costs of going to court, many firms now use private arbitration or mediation as alternatives to litigation.

➡lg 3 **What are the required elements of a valid contract; and what are the key types of business law?**
A contract is an agreement between two or more parties that meets five requirements: mutual agreement, capacity of the parties, legal consideration, lawful object (legal purpose), and legal form. If one party breaches the contract terms, the remedies are damages, specific performance, or restitution.

Tort law settles disputes involving civil acts that harm people or their property. Torts include physical injury, mental anguish, and defamation. Product-liability law governs the responsibility of manufacturers and sellers for product defects. Bankruptcy law gives business or individuals who cannot meet their financial obligations a way to be relieved of their debts. Some laws are designed to keep the marketplace free from influences that would restrict competition such as price fixing and deceptive advertising. Laws protecting consumer rights are another important area of government control.

➡lg 4 **What are patents, copyright, and trademarks? How do these help businesses?**

A patent is a form of protection (limited monopoly) established by the government to inventors. It gives an inventor the exclusive right to manufacture, use, and sell an invention for 20 years. A copyright is established by the government to protect creators of works of art, music, literature, or other intellectual property. It gives the creator the exclusive right to use, produce, and sell the creation during the lifetime of the creator and for 50 years thereafter. A trademark is a design, name, or other distinctive mark that a manufacturer uses to identify its goods in the marketplace.

Patents, copyrights, and trademarks help businesses protect their rights for the exclusive use of their inventions, creations (e.g., music), names, and designs.

➡lg 5 **What are Employment Standards Acts?**

Each province has an Employment Standards Act (or an equivalent act) that outlines the minimum terms of employment in such areas as minimum wages, payment of earnings, hours of work, overtime, statutory holidays, vacations, maternity and parental leaves, termination, layoff and recall, and the employment of children.

➡lg 6 **What are the most common taxes paid by businesses?**

Income taxes are based on the income received by businesses and individuals. Income taxes are paid to both the federal and provincial governments, who are responsible for setting their own rates. In addition to income taxes, individuals and businesses also pay property taxes (assessed on real property), payroll taxes (employers are responsible for collecting the income taxes from their employees and remitting them to the federal government), sales taxes (e.g., GST and HST, which are levied on goods and services), and excise taxes (levied on specific products such as gasoline, alcoholic beverages, and tobacco).

WORKING THE NET

1. As companies are expected to become more responsive and responsible to their stakeholders, the Canadian Public Accountability Board (CPAB) will respond with new regulations and expectations from public companies. Find out what is new in the area of corporate governance at **www.osfi-bsif.gc.ca/eng/issues/cpab_e.asp.**

2. Whether we are purchasing a computer or a vehicle, it is important to fill out a bill of sale. Connect to **www/lawdepot.com/contracts/canada/billofsale** to view what a legal bill of sale should contain to ensure that both the purchaser and the buyer are protected in case of later disagreements.

3. As discussed in Chapter 6, entrepreneurs play a vital role in the Canadian economy. Many of you will start (or have started) your own business at some point, and it's important to understand the government regulations regarding such issues as registering your company, taxes, and so on. Search the Government of Canada's Web site at **www.ccra-adrc.gc.ca/tax/business/menu-e.html** to see how government regulations will affect you and your business.

CREATIVE THINKING CASE

Second Chance Body Armour

Second Chance Body Armour (**www.sruniforms.com/second.html**) makes protective clothing—body armour that is worn underneath a person's street clothes.

The company produces comfortable, concealable, everyday body armour. It is made with lightweight materials that stop the penetration of a bullet or a knife, thereby protecting the wearer against serious or fatal injury. The armour is designed to be comfortable so that people will wear it on a daily basis.

Richard Davis, president of Second Chance Body Armour, invented the concept of concealable body armour in 1971. Though he had a good product, he found that the market was not aware of it. To promote market awareness, Davis developed advertisements in which he shot himself at point-blank range while wearing the body armour. He survived, sustaining only superficial abrasions.

Since those early days, Second Chance Body Armour has expanded its line of personal protection products. Second Chance's business strategy is quite simple: focus on customer needs for comfortable, custom-fit body armour. Carrying out this strategy requires strong customer service, the use of new technology, and the creation and maintenance of brand identity.

Second Chance now produces several different types of concealable body armour. The SUPERfeatherlite Body Armour, advertised as its "good" armour, is made with DuPont Kevlar 129. The SUPERfeatherlite SC229 is billed as the "better" model. It is made with Akzo-Nobel TWARON T-2000 Microfilament fibres and Butterfly Lite fabrication technology. Second Chance's "best" body armour, the Monarch, combines three fourth-generation ballistics technologies "to produce revolutionary improvement in wear-ability and performance." The Monarch model incorporates ARAFLEX IV ballistics fibres; Butterfly Lite stitch patterns to protect against multihits, multiangle hits, and blunt trauma; and Gore-Tex ComfortCOOL ballistic pad covers for moisture protection and breathability. Second Chance also produces the Monarch +P+, which combines antiballistic properties and antipuncture properties into a single body armour model. Promoted as Second Chance's "bonus" model, this product provides protection from both gunshots and penetration by knives and other sharp instruments. No matter which type of body armour a Second Chance customer purchases, it is designed for comfort and custom fit to the customer using five different body measurements.

The Second Chance brand has become so widely accepted in law enforcement circles that it has become a generic name just as Kleenex has for facial tissue. There is only one Second Chance brand, but people commonly refer to any body armour as "providing them with their second chance." By following the business strategy of focusing on customer needs for comfortable, custom-fit body armour, Second Chance has developed into the worldwide leader in body armour.[8]

Critical Thinking Questions

1. What are the legal and employment regulations that Davis should be concerned with that are associated with his employees?
2. What do you think are the legal implications of such a product? How do you think Davis can protect his investment?

Mad Science and Franchising

The Mad Science Group is a successful company operating out of Montreal. The founders, Ariel and Ron Shlien, were interested in science as teenagers, with Ariel purchasing his first laser at the age of 12. By their early teens, Ariel and Ron were doing shows at the local YMCA and at birthday parties for children. From such humble beginnings, a multi-million-dollar enterprise has grown. Today the company has over 150 franchisees in Canada, the U.S., and overseas and boasts sales in excess of $30 million.

On the franchise side of the business, Mad Science provides support, equipment, and training for their franchisees. In return, the franchisees pay 8 percent of their sales to the company. Franchisees are from a variety of backgrounds, such as air force instructors, clerical workers, and those just wanting a change of pace. The success of individual franchisees depends on their ability to grow their own business. They must seek out business in order to become profitable. Birthday parties alone won't do it. The franchise costs approximately $55 000. Performing at two parties every day only nets the franchisee $50 000—not a great return on investment. Successful franchisees are the ones who have the drive to excel in a competitive environment. After a three-week training period in Montreal, they are provided with additional support and the necessary equipment to begin their business. The director of franchise support feels that the required support had been lacking in the past and plans to increase the level of support to help franchisees grow their businesses. When the franchises make more money, so does Mad Science. Meanwhile, the head office staff continues to experiment with new and exciting shows and products.

Today, Mad Science has grown beyond all expectations and is found in theme parks in the U.S., as well as in all major North American markets.

Critical Thinking Questions

1. Franchising has benefits for the franchisee and for the franchisor. What are the benefits for the Mad Science franchisees and for the company?
2. Why might someone decide to open his or her own entertainment business rather than buy a franchise?
3. What are the advantages and disadvantages of this approach?
4. What is the status of this company today?

The Litebook Company

Larry Pederson, an entrepreneur from Medicine Hat, Alberta, has suffered from seasonal adaptive disorder (SAD) all his life. Larry described the lethargy resulting from living through the long winter days with their minimal light as "living in molasses." His Litebook product was designed to mimic the effect of the sun's rays and thus banish the winter blues. For two-and-a-half years, Larry spent his time, energy, and money to develop the product. He obtained initial investment capital from local construction company owners and local dentists, and enlisted the help of defence research experts and engineers to build the prototype.

Larry realized that to have his product perceived as a credible solution to SAD, he would need an expert recommendation. This he received from Dr. Raymond Lam of Vancouver. Dr. Lam advised Larry of the American Psychiatric Association's conference soon to be held in New Orleans. There would be over 1500 psychiatrists from all over the world. If Larry could win the endorsement of the psychiatrists, it would help his sales immensely. Larry attended the conference trade show and was excited about the response to his product. His assistant, Martin, who spoke three languages and was an excellent trade show host, helped make Larry's booth one of the hits of the show. He received many orders despite the fact that he had no Litebooks in stock, and returned home enthusiastic about the future of his business.

Once back in Medicine Hat with his orders, Larry learned about many of the issues that can affect business success despite the efforts of the entrepreneur. Even with interest expressed on many fronts, Larry needed a big-time buyer to get the business off the ground. The events of September 11, 2001, had a major effect on Larry's business, but with the enduring support of his investors, Larry was able to continue on to become the chairman, president, and CEO of a very successful company.

Critical Thinking Questions

1. What characteristics of an entrepreneur did Larry exhibit?
2. What sources of financing did he access? Were there other possible sources?
3. Research Larry's company today and discuss factors that impacted on his success.

Marketing—The Customer Focus

In this chapter we will start to take a look at the internal environment of a business, or more simply, the functional areas of a business. This is what most people think of when they think of a business or a career in business—marketing, operations, finance and accounting, and human resources.

Before we take a look inside each of these areas in detail in separate chapters, one very important message must be communicated clearly at the outset. Even though each of these areas is discussed separately in different chapters in introductory textbooks and later in separate courses in business schools, they cannot act separately if the business is to be successful. They are all part of the integrated business model that has been the central theme of this text. Each of these areas must work together to make the business successful overall. For example, a company cannot design and market a product for which it does not have the human, operational, and financial resources. Just imagine The Bay attempting to produce a new all-terrain vehicle and introduce it to the market. It could perhaps alter its store setup to sell the vehicle, but does it have the facilities and people skills to produce it? Would it even have the financial resources to put towards this type of endeavour, considering the tight budgets most businesses are working with today to keep their core business alive?

You will see in Chapter 14, which deals with management and planning, that all decisions made at the tactical level in the functional areas come from decisions made at a higher *strategic* level that affect the whole company. Top management would first scan the external environment (PEST model) to look for opportunities and threats and match those with the strengths and weaknesses of the company in the different functional areas to decide the direction of the company. It is therefore unlikely that a decision like this one would ever be made by The Bay. Even if there were opportunities in the market for ATVs, it would not match with the strengths of the company. Financial resources would therefore not be released for this type of project to begin with.

Marketers make decisions about what products to bring to market in conjunction with the overall strategic direction of the company, and then work with *operations* to design those products and allocate the resources needed to provide them—whether that be production facilities or alliances with other firms if it is a good that is being produced, or layouts and procedures to be followed if it is a service. And, of course, both marketing and operations need to work with *human resources* to make sure people with the needed skills are in place in all areas, as well as with *finance* to make sure the product is financially worthwhile for the company to pursue and that funds will be available to pursue it. It is an integrated effort. This is evident from the example of Lexus in the chapter. The company "adopted a customer-driven approach with particular emphasis on service" by stressing "product *quality* with a standard of zero defects in manufacturing" and a service goal to "treat each customer as a guest in one's home." Marketing couldn't do this alone. It would have to work with operations to provide this level of product quality as well as human resources to provide this level of customer service. And it would also need an investment of funds to pull it all together.

It is also evident at your own college or university. This same integrative approach was used there. If you are taking this course on campus, how could the college provide it without the operations people making classroom space available and scheduling it at times determined to be in demand by the marketing people, but also fitting with other perhaps conflicting courses chosen by the same students who would be taking this course? How could it provide the course without trained faculty to deliver it? And how could it continue to provide the course without fees being collected, as well as financial resources provided for faculty, facilities, administrative support, and so on, and managed to ensure profitability? Again, all the areas have to work together.

But just think for a minute what would happen if there were no customer demand for ATVs, quality cars, or business courses? Obviously, just as the decisions that are made in the functional areas to bring a product to market are integrated, the decisions about which products to bring to market obviously have to be integrated with the outside environment—they must come ultimately from the customer. The customer is the central focal point of any successful business. Look at the critical success factors. As we've said many times, you can't *achieve financial* success if you aren't earning revenue, and you can't earn revenue if customers aren't buying your products. And they won't buy your products if they don't at least *meet and at best exceed their needs*. That is what this chapter is all about—understanding the customer and creating products that satisfy.

This requires that the company keep an eye on all areas of the external environment that may affect *marketing* decisions, as discussed in the chapter, but particularly on the *social* environment to understand the trends that affect customer needs. As the chapter explains, it is important to do market research to understand the customer, and advances in *technology* have made that easier.

Many concepts in this chapter are important for understanding marketing and its integrative nature. For example, in this chapter you'll discuss the marketing concept—focusing on customer wants and needs, and integrating the organization's activities in the functional areas to satisfy the customer, but doing so with a responsibility toward the *stakeholders*—profitably for the owners, ethically for the customer, and fairly for the employee. The marketing concept is an important integrative concept. It is the thread that ties all the marketing activities together in order to stay focused on the customer. It is also the thread that ties the functional areas together again to satisfy the customer. But it also ties the business as a whole together so that decisions are made responsibly and success is achieved with all the stakeholders in mind and all critical success factors met.

You'll also discuss relationship marketing. This is critical to the long-term success of the company—meeting the critical success factors over time by establishing long-term relationships with customers. This can be done through loyalty programs as one example, but also requires commitment from your employees to be customer oriented. The example in the chapter is of WestJet airlines. Just give them a call and chat with one of their reps, and then call another airline, and you'll see the difference in customer service.

Target marketing is another important concept. Identifying a target market helps a company focus marketing efforts on those customers most likely to buy its products. The unique features of the product that appeal to this target group are the company's competitive advantage. If that competitive advantage is cost—operating at a lower cost than competitors and passing this saving on to the customer (as in Wal-Mart)—we see another integration of marketing with the other functional areas. As the chapter explains, this cost advantage is gained through using less expensive raw materials and/or controlling overhead costs (finance), and making plant operations more efficient and/or designing products that are easier to manufacture (operations), and so on. This

is done by these areas through *people committed* to this goal and often with the help of technology. If this competitive advantage is something unique about the product, it also often requires integration with other functional areas—Maytag's differential advantage of product reliability, for example, requires that the products be produced to exacting standards.

And finally, the target market of consumers whose needs the company is focusing on is determined after segmenting the market. Though it seems like a purely marketing exercise—dividing up the market of consumers into different groups based on some common characteristics—it has some very definite integrative implications. Take Air Canada's attempt, since November 2001, to get back in the black by creating a series of sub-brands to target specialized segments of the market. Some of these names may be familiar to you—Tango, ZIP, and Jazz. Although unsuccessful at staving off bankruptcy protection announced in the spring of 2003, this move nonetheless came as a result of several environmental variables. Some of these include the September 11, 2001, terrorist attacks and the resulting effect they had on both the economic and social environments—changing attitudes of customers toward the safety of airline travel, constant pressure from Ottawa to make the Canadian airline industry more competitive, competitive pressure from rival WestJet, and the bursting of the technology bubble, which slashed business-class revenues from large technology companies.

Whatever the environmental influences were, the end result was changes in each functional area to accommodate this new marketing strategy. Financially, the market segmentation allowed Air Canada to lower its overall operating costs and improve its profit margins. Actually, in the third quarter of 2002, it had its second profitable quarter in a row, at a time when most other major airlines were losing money. From a human resource standpoint, the market segmentation gave Air Canada the ability to pay their employees different lower rates on the new smaller carriers than on the main Air Canada flights. From an operations standpoint, it meant redoing the planes to accommodate the different segments that were being targeted with each different sub-brand.[1] Marketing is without a doubt a very central integrative function within a successful business.

Marketing—The Customer Focus

CHRYSLER

CHAPTER 8

Learning Goals

→ **lg 1** What are the marketing concept and relationship building?

→ **lg 2** How do managers create a marketing strategy?

→ **lg 3** What is the marketing mix?

→ **lg 4** How do consumers and organizations make buying decisions?

→ **lg 5** What are the five basic forms of market segmentation?

→ **lg 6** How is marketing research used in marketing decision-making?

→ **lg 7** What are the trends in understanding the consumer?

Targeting Baby Boomers at DaimlerChrysler

In 1955, Chrysler needed an icon. It had no Corvette, no Thunderbird for crew-cut young men in blue jeans to drool over. That year the company found its muscle car: the C-300. Touted as "America's most powerful car," the C-300 tore up the tracks at NASCAR and Daytona. This positioned Chrysler as a leader in high-performance, upscale North American automobiles. The company launched a new model in its "letter-car" series every year until the 300L in 1965 and then discontinued the line.

Now, more than 45 years later, Chrysler had merged with Germany's Daimler Benz, and the new company, DaimlerChrysler (**www.daimlerchrysler.com**) needed an icon to catch the attention of 40-something baby boomers. "Bringing a car to market is a $1 billion investment," says Steven Bruyn, large-car marketing executive at the Chrysler division of DaimlerChrysler. "As a result, you like to be right." The company didn't have to go far for its concept: it resurrected the 300 letter series from the 1950s and 1960s, and simply picked up where it left off in the alphabet. After three years of development, engineering, tinkering, and intense market research, the carmaker launched the 300M in 1998. Sales have been booming since, and it was named the Motor Trend 1999 Car of the Year.

Steering the 300M from drafting table to dealer has been no easy task. At the start of the project, Bruyn and his team studied the potential of the near-luxury car market by looking at population trends and forecasts for its target customers. North America's baby boomers were aging and well educated, and their personal income was growing, courtesy of a strong economy. They wanted room for their expanding waistlines—and were willing to pay for it.

Factors like these indicated a robust future for near-luxury car sales, but how did the 300M fit into the picture? Through marketing research, DaimlerChrysler honed its profile of the car's typical driver. "To 300M drivers, the car is more than just something to get them from point A to point B," says Bruyn.

Target customers are real car enthusiasts. They read *Motor Trend* and other car magazines. And, says Paul Leinberger, senior vice-president at Roper Starch Worldwide, they're looking for a product that represents who they are. "It's not about status, but their sense of identity," he says.

North America's mood swing toward nostalgia also influenced the design of the 300M, both inside and out. The egg-crate grille harks back to earlier styles in the letter series, and simple analogue dials dot the dashboard. Chrysler restored the series vintage silver-winged badge, which now appears on the hood of all of the brand's cars and trucks. Of course, not everything about the 300M recalls the 1950s—standard features include leather seats, climate control, and a stereo

CRITICAL THINKING QUESTIONS

As you read this chapter, consider the following questions as they relate to DaimlerChrysler:

- Why do companies identify target customers for their products?
- Why is it important to differentiate a product?
- How does a company like DaimlerChrysler find out what customers and potential customers want in a car?

system with nine speakers. Today the 300M is popular with drivers who are middle aged, male, and have interests such as golf, politics, travel, and current affairs. The car sells for US$29 565–$32 995.[2]

BUSINESS IN THE 21ST CENTURY

marketing
The process of discovering the needs and wants of potential buyers and customers and then providing goods and services that meet or exceed their expectations.

Marketing played an important role in DaimlerChrysler's successful launch of its 300M. Marketing is the process of getting the right goods or services to the right people at the right place, time, and price, using the right promotion techniques. This concept is referred to as the *"right" principle*. We can say that **marketing** is finding out the needs and wants of potential buyers and customers and then providing goods and services that meet or exceed their expectations. Marketing is about creating exchanges. An **exchange** takes place when two parties give something of value to each other to satisfy their respective needs. In a typical exchange, a consumer trades money for a good or service.

exchange
The process in which two parties give something of value to each other to satisfy their respective needs.

To encourage exchanges, marketers follow the "right" principle. If your local DaimlerChrysler dealer doesn't have the right car for you when you want it, at the right price, you will not exchange money or credit for a new car. Think about the last exchange (purchase) you made: What if the price had been 30 percent higher? What if the store or other source had been less accessible? Would you have bought anything? The "right" principle tells us that marketers control many factors that determine marketing success. In this chapter, you will learn about the marketing concept and how organizations create a marketing strategy. You will learn how the marketing mix is used to create sales opportunities. Next, we examine how and why consumers and organizations make purchase decisions. Then, we discuss the important concept of market segmentation, which helps marketing managers focus on the most likely purchasers of their wares. We conclude the chapter by examining how marketing research and decision support systems help guide marketing decision making.

➡ **lg 1**

The Marketing Concept

marketing concept
Identifying consumer needs and then producing the goods or services that will satisfy them while making a profit for the organization.

If you study today's best organizations, you'll see that they have adopted the **marketing concept**, which involves identifying consumer needs and then producing the goods or services that will satisfy them while making a profit. The marketing concept is oriented toward pleasing consumers by offering value. Specifically, the marketing concept involves:

- Focusing on customer wants so the organization can distinguish its product(s) from competitors' offerings.
- Integrating all of the organization's activities, including production, to satisfy these wants.
- Achieving long-term goals for the organization by satisfying customer wants and needs legally and responsibly.

Ganong Brothers Ltd. of St. Stephen, New Brunswick, found that the identification of consumer needs led them to move toward a healthier snack food in addition to their long-established Ganong Chocolates. They introduced a line of fruit juice gummy snacks and bought the Canadian licence to market them under the Sunkist brand name. The kid appeal of the snacks, which are shaped like sharks, dinosaurs, and UFOs, was promoted through ads on YTV. Since, in most cases, parents make the purchasing decision, the healthy aspect of the snack was enhanced by the use of the Sunkist name. Chocolates still remain the Ganong flagship product. However, the goal is to double sales on both products as the company believes it must respect the decades-old tradition of Ganong's chocolate while addressing the needs of health-conscious consumers.[3]

production orientation
An approach in which a firm works to lower production costs without a strong desire to satisfy the needs of customers.

Firms have not always followed the marketing concept. Around the time of the Industrial Revolution in North America (1860–1910), firms had a **production orientation**, which meant that they worked to lower production costs without a strong desire to satisfy the needs of their customers. To do this, organizations concentrated on mass production, focusing internally on maximizing the efficiency of operations, increasing output, and ensuring uniform quality. They also asked such questions as: What can we do best? What can our engineers design? What is economical and easy to produce with our equipment?

There is nothing wrong with assessing a firm's capabilities. In fact, such assessments are necessary in planning. But the production orientation does not consider whether what the firm produces most efficiently also meets the needs of the marketplace. By implementing the marketing concept, an organization looks externally to the consumers in the marketplace and commits to customer value, customer satisfaction, and relationship marketing, as explained in this section.

Customer Value

customer value
The ratio of benefits to the sacrifice necessary to obtain those benefits, as determined by the customer; reflects the willingness of customers to actually buy a product.

Customer value is the ratio of benefits to the sacrifice necessary to obtain those benefits. The customer determines the value of both the benefits and the sacrifices. Creating customer value is a core business strategy of many successful firms. Customer value is rooted in the belief that price is not the only thing that matters. A business that focuses on the cost of production and price to the customer will be managed as though it were providing a commodity differentiated only by price. In contrast, businesses that provide customer value believe that many customers will pay a premium for superior customer service.

The automobile industry illustrates the importance of creating customer value. To penetrate the fiercely competitive luxury automobile market, Lexus adopted a customer-driven approach, with particular emphasis on service. Lexus stresses product quality with a standard of zero defects in manufacturing. Driver and passenger comfort is enhanced in some models through steering wheel audio controls, rain-sensing wipers, and rear-seat audio. The service quality goal is to treat each customer as one would treat a guest in one's home, to pursue the perfect person-to-person relationship, and to strive to improve continually. This strategy has enabled Lexus to establish a clear quality image and capture a significant share of the luxury car market.

customer satisfaction
The customer's feeling that a product has met or exceeded expectations.

Customer Satisfaction

Customer satisfaction is the customer's feeling that a product has met or exceeded expectations. David Ho, owner of HMY Airlines, feels that the future success of the company will depend on "the travel experience of each and every passenger." The new airline expects to provide flights from Vancouver, Calgary, and Edmonton to points such as Cancun, Puerto Vallarta, Ixtapa, Mazatlan, the Mayan Riviera, Manchester, and eventually Hawaii. Mr. Ho, heir to the Hong Kong tobacco fortune, decided to establish the airline after an extremely dissatisfying experience with another airline where he and his daughter were stranded in an airport in Maui for 18 hours. He is pleased with the results of his efforts and the enthusiasm of his passengers.[4]

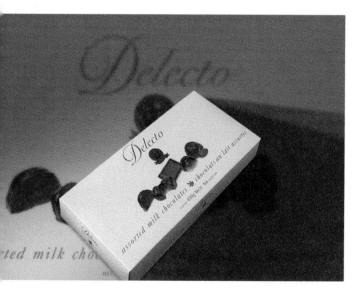

Ganong identified a consumer need and then produced a product to meet that need, but retained its flagship product, Ganong's Chocolates.

At Double Tree Hotels, guests are asked to fill out a CARE card several times during their stay to let staff know how they are doing. Managers check the cards daily to solve guests' problems before they check out. Guests can also use a CARE phone line to call in their complaints at the hotel. A CARE committee continually seeks ways to improve guest services. The goal is to offer a solution to a CARE call in 15 minutes. Embassy Suites goes one step further by offering a full refund to guests who are not satisfied with their stay.

Who delivers the most customer satisfaction? Exhibit 8-1 gives some examples of high levels of customer satisfaction.

Customer satisfaction may indicate how consumers feel about a product, but it may not indicate their willingness to actually purchase that product. General Motors' Cadillac Division, for example, was quite pleased that more than 90 percent of its customers reported that they were either "satisfied" or "highly satisfied" with their recent purchase of a new Cadillac, figures comparable with those reported by purchasers of Japanese automobiles. But Cadillac was quite dismayed to learn that only 30 to 40 percent of these new Cadillac owners would buy another Cadillac, compared with more than 80 percent of Japanese auto purchasers.[5] GM had been asking only about customer satisfaction, not customer value—the willingness of customers to actually buy a new Cadillac.

Building Relationships

relationship marketing
A strategy that focuses on forging long-term partnerships with customers by offering value and providing customer satisfaction.

Relationship marketing is a strategy that focuses on forging long-term partnerships with customers. Companies build relationships with customers by offering value and providing customer satisfaction. Companies benefit from repeat sales and referrals that lead to increases in sales, market share, and profits. Costs fall because it is less expensive to serve existing customers than to attract new ones. Keeping a customer costs about one-fourth of what it costs to attract a new customer, and the probability of retaining a customer is over 60 percent, whereas the probability of landing a new customer is less than 30 percent.[6]

Customers also benefit from stable relationships with suppliers. Business buyers have found that partnerships with their suppliers are essential to producing high-quality products while cutting costs. Customers remain loyal to firms that provide them greater value and satisfaction than they expect from competing firms.

Frequent buyer clubs are an excellent way to build long-term relationships. Most major airlines, including American Airlines and Air Canada, have frequent flyer programs. After you fly a certain number of miles, you become eligible for a free ticket. Now, cruise lines, hotels, car rental agencies, credit card companies, and even real estate companies give away "airline miles" with purchases. Consumers patronize the airline and its partners because they want the free tickets. Thus, the program helps to create a long-term relationship with the customer. For example, CIBC buys reward miles from Air Canada. Each dollar charged to a customer's Aerogold Visa card results in one air

e x h i b i t   8 - 1

Companies That Deliver High Levels of Customer Satisfaction (3rd Quarter of 2002)

Percentage	Company or Division
84%	Sara Lee
88%	H.J. Heinz (food processing)
84%	Colgate-Palmolive (pet foods)
81%	H.J. Heinz (pet foods)
83%	Mars (food processing)
83%	Nestlé
87%	Quaker Oats
81%	Kellogg
87%	Hershey Foods
81%	Kraft Foods
86%	PepsiCo
85%	Coca-Cola
80%	Campbell's Soup
83%	General Mills

SOURCE: "The Economy: Consumer Satisfaction is Rising—Lower Prices Translate into a Sense of More Value from Products Services" by Jon E. Hilsenrath. Copyright 2002 by Dow Jones & Co Inc. Reproduced with permission of Dow Jones & Co Inc. in the format Textbook via Copyright Clearance Center.

HOT Links

See www.marriot.com or www.hiltonhotels.com to see how these companies attempt to build customer loyalty.

HOT Links

See www.westjet.com and check out the WestJet spirit.

mile being added to their Aeroplan account. Hotel chains also attempt to build relationships with guests by offering free accommodation after a certain number of nights stay.

If an organization is to build relationships with customers, its employees' attitudes and actions must be customer oriented. Any person, department, or division that is not customer oriented weakens the positive image of the entire organization. An employee may be the only contact a potential customer has with the firm. In that person's eyes, the employee is the firm. If greeted discourteously, the potential customer may well assume that the employee's attitude represents the whole firm. Calgary-based WestJet is proud of their customer orientation. Travellers are referred to as "guests" and are treated accordingly. The values statement captures WestJet's philosophy with such terms as "positive, passionate, friendly and caring" and concludes with the phrase "We are team WestJet!"

concept check

- What is marketing?
- Explain the marketing concept.
- Explain the difference between customer value and customer satisfaction.
- What is meant by relationship marketing?

→ **lg 2**

Creating a Marketing Strategy

There is no secret formula for creating goods and services that provide customer value and customer satisfaction. An organization that is committed to providing superior customer satisfaction puts customers at the very centre of its marketing strategy. Creating a customer-focused marketing strategy involves four main steps: understanding the external environment, defining the target market, creating a competitive advantage, and developing a marketing mix. This section will examine the first three steps, and the next section will discuss how a company develops a marketing mix.

environmental scanning
The process in which a firm continually collects and evaluates information about its external environment.

Understanding the External Environment

Unless marketing managers understand the external environment, a firm cannot intelligently plan for the future. Thus, many organizations assemble a team of specialists to continually collect and evaluate environmental information, a process called **environmental scanning**. The goal in gathering the environmental data is to identify future market opportunities and threats.

For example, as technology continues to blur the lines between personal computers, television, and compact disc players, a company like Sony may find itself competing against a company like Compaq. Research shows that children would like more games bundled with computer software, while adults desire various types of word-processing and business-related software. Is this information an opportunity or a threat to Compaq marketing managers?

In general, six categories of environmental data shape marketing decisions:

As a "guest" on WestJet, you can expect friendly, casual, yet competent service from everyone you encounter from captain to customer service representative.

- Social forces such as the values of potential customers and the changing roles of families and women working outside the home (see Chapter 3).
- Demographic forces such as the ages, birth and death rates, and locations of various groups of people (see Chapter 3).

- Economic forces such as changing incomes, inflation, and recession (see Chapter 1).
- Technological forces such as advances in communications and data retrieval capabilities (see Chapter 4).
- Political and legal forces such as changes in laws and regulatory agency activities (see Chapter 2).
- Competitive forces from domestic and foreign-based firms.

Defining the Target Market

Managers and employees focus on providing value for a well-defined target market. The **target market** is the specific group of consumers toward which a firm directs its marketing efforts. It is selected from the larger overall market. For instance, Carnival Cruise Lines says its main target market is "blue-collar entrepreneurs," people with an income of $25 000 to $50 000 a year who own auto supply shops, dry cleaners, and the like. Unlike other cruise lines, it does not seek affluent retirees. Quaker Oats targets its grits to blue-collar consumers in the Southern United States. Kodak targets Ektar colour print film, designed for use only in rather sophisticated cameras, to advanced amateur photographers. Holt Renfrew targets affluent fashion- and quality-conscious consumers. Subway targets health- and value-conscious consumers.

Identifying a target market helps a company focus its marketing efforts on those who are most likely to buy its products or services. Concentrating on potential customers lets the firm use its resources efficiently. Check out the advertising in your neighbourhood bus shelter. Who is the target market for the product advertised? Is the advertising aimed at those waiting for the bus? Those driving down the street? The neighbourhood itself?

Creating a Competitive Advantage

A **competitive advantage**, also called a differential advantage, is a set of unique features of a company and its products that are perceived by the target market as significant and superior to those of the competition. As Andrew Grove, CEO of Intel, says, "You have to understand what it is you are better at than anybody else and mercilessly focus your efforts on it." Competitive advantage is the factor or factors that cause customers to patronize a firm and not the competition. There are three types of competitive advantage: cost, product/service differential, and niche.

Cost Competitive Advantage

A firm that has a **cost competitive advantage** can produce a product or service at a lower cost than all its competitors while maintaining satisfactory profit margins. Firms become cost leaders by obtaining inexpensive raw materials, making plant operations more efficient, designing products for ease of manufacture, controlling overhead costs, and avoiding marginal customers. DuPont, for example, has an exceptional cost competitive advantage in the production of titanium dioxide. Technicians created a production process using low-cost feedstock that gives DuPont a 20 percent cost advantage over its competitors. The cheaper feedstock technology is complex and can be accomplished only by investing about $100 million and several years of testing time.

Differential Competitive Advantage

A product/service **differential competitive advantage** exists when a firm provides something unique that is valuable to buyers beyond simply offering a low price. Differential competitive advantages tend to be longer lasting than cost competitive advantages because cost advantages are subject to continual erosion as competitors catch up. Cost advantages fail to last for two reasons. For one thing, technology is

The "milk moustache" ads target different market segments to promote the consumption of milk. This one targets the youth market with an ad featuring actress Neve Campbell.

target market
The specific group of consumers toward which a firm directs its marketing efforts.

competitive advantage
A set of unique features of a company and its products that are perceived by the target market as significant and superior to those of the competition; also called *differential advantage*.

cost competitive advantage
A firm's ability to produce a product or service at a lower cost than all other competitors in an industry while maintaining satisfactory profit margins.

differential competitive advantage
A firm's ability to provide a unique product or service that offers something of value to buyers besides simply a lower price.

transferable. For example, Bell Labs invented fibre-optic cable that reduced the cost of voice and data transmission by dramatically increasing the number of calls that could be transmitted simultaneously through a 5 cm cable. Within five years, however, fibre optic technology had spread throughout the industry. Second, for most production processes or product categories (e.g., running shoes and laptop computers), there are alternative suppliers. Over time, high-cost producers tend to seek out lower-cost suppliers and they can compete more effectively with the industry's low-cost producers.

The durability of a differential competitive advantage tends to make this strategy more attractive to many top managers. Common differential advantages are brand names (Lexus), a strong dealer network (Caterpillar Tractor for construction work), product reliability (Maytag washers), image (Sears in retailing), and service (Federal Express). Brand names such as Coca-Cola, BMW, and Cartier stand for quality the world over. Through continual product and marketing innovations and attention to quality and value, managers at these organizations have created enduring competitive advantages. Arthur Doppelmayer, an Austrian manufacturer of aerial transport systems, believes his main differential advantage, besides innovative equipment design, is his service system, which allows the company to come to the assistance of users anywhere in the world within 24 hours. Doppelmayer uses a worldwide system of warehouses and skilled personnel prepared to move immediately in emergency cases.

Niche Competitive Advantage

niche competitive advantage
A firm's ability to target and effectively serve a single segment of the market within a limited geographic area.

A company with a **niche competitive advantage** targets and effectively serves a single segment of the market within a limited geographic area. For small companies with limited resources that potentially face giant competitors, "niche-ing" may be the only viable option. A market segment that has good growth potential but is not crucial to the success of major competitors is a good candidate for a niche strategy. Once a potential segment has been identified, the firm needs to make certain it can defend against challengers through its superior ability to serve customers in the segment. For example, Thyme Maternity is a small chain of retail stores that sells maternity clothes. Its quality materials, innovative designs, and reasonable prices serve as a barrier against competition. Margaret Nemeth offers home-cooked organic food in her Primal Grounds restaurant. The food is high quality, value-priced and served in pleasant surroundings.

➡ **lg 3**

Developing a Marketing Mix

marketing mix
The blend of product offering, pricing, promotional methods, and distribution system that brings a specific group of consumers superior value.

four Ps
Product, price, promotion, and place (distribution), which together make up the marketing mix.

Once a firm has defined its target market and identified its competitive advantage, it can create the **marketing mix**, that is, the blend of product offering, pricing, promotional methods, and distribution system that brings a specific group of consumers superior value. Distribution is sometimes referred to as place, so the marketing mix is based on the **four Ps**: product, price, promotion, and place. Every target market requires a unique marketing mix to satisfy the needs of the target consumers and meet the firm's goals. A strategy must be constructed for each of the four Ps and blended with the strategies for the other elements. Thus, the marketing mix is only as good as its weakest part. An excellent product with a poor distribution system could be doomed to failure. Product, price, and promotion are discussed in Chapter 9 and distribution in Chapter 10.

A successful marketing mix requires careful tailoring. For instance, at first glance you might think that McDonald's and Wendy's have roughly the same marketing mix. After all, they are both in the fast-food business. But McDonald's targets parents with young children through Ronald McDonald, heavily promoted children's Happy Meals, and playgrounds. Wendy's is targeted to a more adult crowd. Wendy's has no playgrounds but it does have pleasant background audio (a more adult atmosphere), and Wendy's pioneered fast-food specialty salads.

HOT Links

Compare McDonald's and Wendy's marketing efforts by visiting their home pages at www.mcdonalds.com and www.wendys.com

Product Strategy

Marketing strategy typically starts with the product. You can't plan a distribution system or set a price if you don't know what you're going to market. Marketers use the term *product* to refer to both *goods*, such as tires, stereos, and clothing, and *services*, such as hotels, hair salons, and restaurants. Thus, the heart of the marketing mix is the good or service. Creating a **product strategy** involves choosing a brand name, packaging, colours, a warranty, accessories, and a service program.

Marketers view products in a much larger context than you might imagine. They include not only the item itself but also the brand name and the company image. The names Ralph Lauren and Gucci, for instance, create extra value for everything from cosmetics to bath towels. That is, products with those names sell at higher prices than identical products without the names. We buy things not only for what they do, but also for what they mean. (Product strategies are discussed further in Chapter 9.)

Pricing Strategy

Pricing strategy is based on demand for the product and the cost of producing it. Some special considerations can also influence the price. Sometimes, for instance, a special introductory price is used to get people to try a new product. Some firms enter the market with low prices and keep them low, such as Carnival Cruise Lines and Saturn cars. Others enter a market with very high prices and then lower them over time, such as producers of high-definition televisions and personal computers. (You can learn more about pricing strategies in Chapter 9.)

Distribution Strategy

Distribution is the means (the channel) by which a product flows from the producer to the consumer. One aspect of **distribution strategy** is deciding how many stores and which specific wholesalers and retailers will handle the product in a geographic area. Cosmetics, for instance, are distributed in many different ways. Avon has a sales force of several hundred thousand representatives who call directly on consumers. Clinique and Estée Lauder are distributed through selected department stores. Cover Girl and Del Laboratories use mostly chain drugstores and other mass merchandisers. Redken sells through beauticians. Revlon uses several of these distribution channels. (Distribution is examined in detail in Chapter 10.)

Promotion Strategy

Many people feel that promotion is the most exciting part of the marketing mix. **Promotion strategy** covers personal selling, advertising, public relations, and sales promotion. Each element is coordinated with the others to create a promotional blend. An advertisement, for instance, helps a buyer get to know the company and paves the way for a sales call. A good promotion strategy can dramatically increase a firm's sales. (Promotion is discussed in Chapter 9.)

Public relations plays a special role in promotion. It is used to create a good image of the company and its products. Bad publicity costs nothing to send out, but it can cost a firm a great deal in lost business. Good publicity, such as a television or magazine story about a firm's new product, may be the result of much time, money, and effort spent by a public relations department.

Sales promotion directly stimulates sales. It includes trade shows, catalogues, contests, games, premiums, coupons, and special offers. McDonald's contests offering money and food prizes are an example. The company also issues discount coupons from time to time.

product strategy
The part of the marketing mix that involves choosing a brand name, packaging, colours, a warranty, accessories, and a service program for the product.

pricing strategy
The part of the marketing mix that involves establishing a price for the product based on the demand for the product and the cost of producing it.

distribution strategy
The part of the marketing mix that involves deciding how many stores and which specific wholesalers and retailers will handle the product in a geographic area.

promotion strategy
The part of the marketing mix that involves personal selling, advertising, public relations, and sales promotion of the product.

HOT Links

Considering a career in marketing? Visit
www.the-cma.org

Not-for-Profit Marketing

Profit-oriented companies are not the only ones that analyze the marketing environment, find a competitive advantage, and create a marketing mix. The application of marketing principles and techniques is also vital to not-for-profit organizations. Marketing helps not-for-profit groups identify target markets and develop effective marketing mixes. In some cases, marketing has kept symphonies, museums, and other cultural groups from having to close their doors. In other organizations, such as the Canadian Cancer Society and Foster Parents Plan International, marketing ideas and techniques have helped managers do their jobs better.

In the private sector, the profit motive is both an objective for guiding decisions and a criterion for evaluating results. Not-for-profit organizations do not seek to make a profit for redistribution to owners or shareholders. Rather, their focus is often on generating enough funds to cover expenses. For example, the Salvation Army does not gauge its success by the amount of money left in offering plates, and the Ontario Science Centre does not base its performance evaluations on the dollar value of admission charges.

social marketing
The application of marketing techniques to social issues and causes.

Not-for-profit marketing is also concerned with **social marketing**, that is, the application of marketing to social issues and causes. The goals of social marketing are to effect social change (e.g., by creating racial harmony), further social causes (e.g., by helping the homeless), and evaluate the relationship between marketing and society (e.g., by asking whether society should allow advertising on television shows for young children). Individual organizations also engage in social marketing. MADD counsels against drunk driving, and the World Wildlife Federation asks your help in protecting endangered animals and birds.

concept check

- What is meant by the marketing mix?
- What are the components of the marketing mix?
- How can marketing techniques help not-for-profit organizations?
- Define social marketing.

buyer behaviour
The actions people take in buying and using goods and services.

Buyer Behaviour

An organization cannot reach its goals without understanding buyer behaviour. **Buyer behaviour** is the actions people take in buying and using goods and services. Marketers who understand buyer behaviour, such as how a price increase will affect a product's sales, can create a more effective marketing mix.

To understand buyer behaviour, marketers must understand how consumers make buying decisions. The decision-making process has several steps, which are shown in Exhibit 8-2. The entire process is affected by a number of personal and social factors. A buying decision starts (step 1) with a stimulus. A stimulus is anything that affects one or more of our senses (sight, smell, taste, touch, or hearing). A stimulus might be the feel of a sweater, the sleek shape of a new-model car, the design on a package, or a brand name mentioned by a friend. The stimulus leads to problem recognition (step 2): "This sweater feels so soft and looks good on me. Should I buy it?" In other words, the consumer decides that there's a purchase need.

The consumer next gets information about the purchase (step 3). What other styles of sweaters are available? At what price? Can this sweater be bought at a lower price elsewhere? Next, the consumer weighs the options and decides whether to make the purchase (step 4). If the consumer buys the product (step 5), certain outcomes are expected. These outcomes may or may not become reality: the sweater may last for years, or the shoulder seams may pull out the first time it's worn. Finally, the consumer assesses the experience with the product (step 6) and uses this information to update expectations about future purchases (step 7).

Influences on Consumer Decision Making

As Exhibit 8-2 shows, individual and social factors can influence the consumer decision-making process. *Individual factors* are within the consumer and are unique to each person. They include perception, beliefs and attitudes, values, learning, self-concept, and personality. Companies often conduct research to better understand individual factors that cause consumers to buy or not to buy. For instance, Hyatt Hotels found that people who stayed at Hyatt while on business chose other hotels when they travelled on vacation with their children. Hyatt was perceived as a businessperson's hotel. So Hyatt came up with a program called Camp Hyatt, which caters to children with a year-round program that varies by season. It combines attractive rates that appeal to parents with lots of activities for kids.

Social factors that affect the decision-making process include all interactions between a consumer and the external environment: family, opinion leaders, social class, and culture. Families may be the most important of these social factors. Yet fam-

e x h i b i t   8 - 2 | Consumer Decision-Making Process

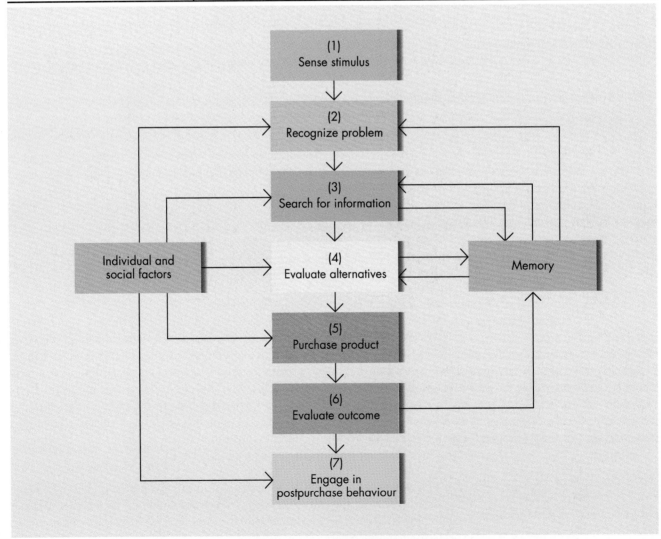

ilies have limited resources, so many buying decisions are compromises. Since a number of decisions include input from several family members, marketing managers sometimes promote products using a family theme, such as Camp Hyatt.

Business-to-Business Purchase Decision Making

Business buyer behaviour and business markets are different from consumer markets. Business markets include institutions such as hospitals and schools, manufacturers, wholesalers and retailers, and various branches of government. The key difference between a consumer product and a business product is the intended use. If you purchase a certain model Dell computer for your home so you can surf the Internet, it is a consumer good. If a purchasing agent for MTV buys exactly the same computer for an MTV scriptwriter, it is a business good. Why? The reason is that MTV is a business, so the computer will be used in a business environment.

Characteristics of the Business-to-Business Market

The main differences between consumer markets and business markets are as follows:

1. *Purchase volume.* Business customers buy in much larger quantities than consumers. Think how many truckloads of sugar Mars must purchase to make one day's output of M&Ms. Imagine the number of batteries Sears buys each day for resale to consumers. Think of the number of pens the federal government must use each day.

2. *Number of customers.* Business marketers usually have far fewer customers than consumer marketers. As a result, it is much easier to identify prospective buyers and monitor current needs. Think about how few customers for airplanes or industrial cranes there are compared to the number of customers for dish detergent in Canada.

3. *Location of buyers.* Business customers tend to be much more geographically concentrated than consumers. The aircraft simulation industry is concentrated in the Montreal area. Automobile manufacturing is found in the Hamilton area. Suppliers to these manufacturers often locate close to the manufacturers to lower distribution costs and facilitate communication.

4. *Direct distribution.* Business sales tend to be made directly to the buyer because such sales frequently involve large quantities or custom-made items like heavy machinery. Consumer goods are more likely to be sold through intermediaries like wholesalers and retailers.

5. *Rational purchase decisions.* Unlike consumers, business buyers usually approach purchasing rather formally. Businesses use professionally trained purchasing agents or buyers who spend their entire career purchasing a limited number of items. They get to know the items and the sellers quite well.

concept check

- Explain the consumer decision-making process.
- How do business markets differ from consumer markets?

➡ lg 5

market segmentation
The process of separating, identifying, and evaluating the layers of a market in order to design a marketing mix.

Market Segmentation

The study of buyer behaviour helps marketing managers better understand why people make purchases. To identify the target markets that may be most profitable for the firm, managers use **market segmentation**, which is the process of separating, identifying, and evaluating the layers of a market to design a marketing mix. For instance, a target market might be segmented into two groups: families with children and families without children. Families with young children are likely to buy hot cereals and presweetened cereals. Families with no children are more likely to buy health-oriented cereals. You can be sure that cereal companies plan their marketing mixes with this difference in mind. A business market may be segmented by large customers and small customers or by geographic area. See the Chapter 9 opening vignette for a discussion of how Steve Smith of ZIP Airlines conducted his marketing segmentation exercise.

The five basic forms of consumer market segmentation are demographic, geographic, psychographic, benefit, and volume. Their characteristics are summarized in Exhibit 8-3 and discussed in the following sections.

Demographic Segmentation

demographic segmentation
The differentiation of markets through the use of categories such as age, education, gender, income, and household size.

Demographic segmentation uses categories such as age, education, gender, income, and household size to differentiate among markets. This form of market segmentation is the most common. Statistics Canada provides a great deal of demographic data. For example, marketing researchers can use census data to find areas within cities that contain high concentrations of high-income consumers, singles, blue-collar workers, and so forth.

HOT Links

Find a vast array of census data at **www.statcan.ca**

You don't have to be an adult to have market clout. One study found that aggregate spending by or on behalf of children ages 4 to 12 roughly doubled every decade in the 1960s, 1970s, and 1980s. It tripled in the 1990s.[7] And whereas children in the 1960s spent almost all their money on candy, today only one-third of the money goes to food and drink, with the balance spent on toys, clothes, movies, and games.

Mature Canadians (those born before 1945), baby boomers (consumers born between the late 1940s and the mid-1960s), and Generation Xers or baby busters (younger consumers born between the mid-1960s and the late 1970s) all have different needs, tastes, and consumption patterns. Baby boomers tend to be nostalgic and prefer the old to the new, whereas Generation Xers tend to be video oriented and would rather see the movie than read the book. However, in a *Maclean's* poll examining value systems, a remarkable consistency was seen across the age groups. The participants were asked to rank eight key values according to their importance. The rankings in order of the most important, with strong consistency across age groups, were as follows:

1. Being a good parent (98%)
2. Having a fulfilling job (96%)
3. Being in a good relationship (95%)
4. Being physically fit (93%)
5. Having a healthy sex life (85%)
6. Living according to a strict moral standard (82%)
7. Developing a spiritual side (75%)
8. Making money (58%)[8]

e x h i b i t   8 - 3 | Forms of Consumer Market Segmentation

Form	General Characteristics
Demographic segmentation	Age, education, gender, income, race, social class, household size
Geographic segmentation	Regional location (e.g. The Maritimes, Central Canada, Quebec); population density (urban, suburban, rural); city or county size; climate
Psychographic segmentation	Lifestyle, personality, interests, values, attitudes
Benefit segmentation	Benefits provided by the good or service
Volume segmentation	Amount of use (light versus heavy)

Certain markets are segmented by gender. These include clothing, cosmetics, personal care items, magazines, jewellery, and footwear. Gillette, for example, is one of the world's best-known marketers of personal care products and has historically targeted men for the most part. Yet women's products have generated a considerable amount of Gillette's growth since 1992. Overall net sales for 2002 were US$8.45 billion, 5 percent above 2001. Sales growth was driven by the success of premium shaving systems, specifically the Mach3 for men and Venus for women. There have been strong shipments of the Venus system in North America and Europe.[9]

Income is another popular way to segment markets. Income level influences consumers' wants and determines their buying power. Housing, clothing, automobiles, and alcoholic beverages are among the many markets segmented by income. Michelina frozen dinners are targeted to lower-income groups, whereas the Le Menu line is aimed at higher-income consumers.

Geographic Segmentation

Geographic segmentation means segmenting markets by region of the country, city or county size, market density, or climate. Market density is the number of people or businesses within a certain area. Many companies segment their markets geographically to meet regional preferences and buying habits. Harvey's, for instance, gives Quebeckers and Maritimers extra cheese in the form of poutine (French fries, gravy, and cheese), not a popular menu item in other parts of Canada. "Duckies," a type of rubberized slip-on footwear, are found on both east and west coasts but are not widely worn in Central Canada or on the Prairies.

Psychographic Segmentation

Race, income, occupation, and other demographic variables help in developing strategies but often do not paint the entire picture of consumer needs. Demographics provide the skeleton, but psychographics add meat to the bones. **Psychographic segmentation** is market segmentation by personality or lifestyle. People with common activities, interests, and opinions are grouped together and given a "lifestyle name."

Benefit Segmentation

Benefit segmentation is based on what a product will do rather than on consumer characteristics. For years Crest toothpaste was targeted toward consumers concerned with preventing cavities. Recently, Crest subdivided its market. It now offers regular Crest, Crest Tartar Control for people who want to prevent cavities and tartar buildup, Crest for kids with sparkles that taste like bubble gum, and another Crest that prevents gum disease. Another toothpaste, Topol, targets people who want whiter teeth—teeth without coffee, tea, or tobacco stains. Sensodyne toothpaste is aimed at people with highly sensitive teeth.

Volume Segmentation

The fifth main type of segmentation is **volume segmentation**, which is based on the amount of the product purchased. Just about every product has heavy, moderate, and light users, as well as nonusers. Heavy users often account for a very large portion of a product's sales. Thus, a firm might want to target its marketing mix to the heavy-user segment. Kraft recently ran a US$30 million advertising campaign directed at heavy users of Miracle Whip. A heavy user consumes 550 servings or about 7.5 kg of Miracle Whip a year.[10]

Retailers are aware that heavy shoppers not only spend more, but also visit each outlet more frequently than other shoppers. Heavy shoppers visit the grocery store 122 times per year, compared with 93 annual visits for the medium shopper. They

HOT Links

A comprehensive list of Canadian advertising, marketing, and media associations is found at
www.ad-freaks.com

geographic segmentation
The differentiation of markets by region of the country, city or county size, market density, or climate.

psychographic segmentation
The differentiation of markets by personality or lifestyle.

benefit segmentation
The differentiation of markets based on what a product will do rather than on customer characteristics.

volume segmentation
The differentiation of markets based on the amount of the product purchased.

In the marketing of Cartier watches, psychographic segmentation would help identify the target market.

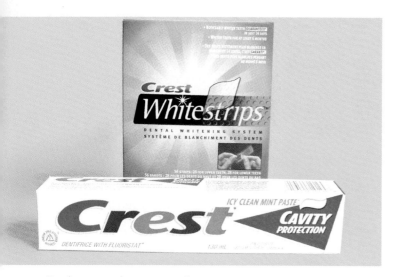

Toothpaste marketers stress the benefits of their various products.

➡ **lg 6**

marketing research
The process of planning, collecting, and analyzing data relevant to a marketing decision.

visit discount stores more than twice as often as medium shoppers, and they visit convenience/gas stores more than five times as often. On each trip, they consistently spend more than their medium-shopping counterparts.[11]

concept check

* Define market segmentation.
* List and discuss the five basic forms of market segmentation.

Using Marketing Research to Serve Existing Customers and Find New Customers

How do successful companies learn what their customers value? Through marketing research, companies can be sure they are listening to the voice of the customer. **Marketing research** is the process of planning, collecting, and analyzing data relevant to a marketing decision. The results of this analysis are then communicated to management. The information collected through marketing research includes the preferences of customers, the perceived benefits of products, and consumer lifestyles. Research helps companies make better use of their marketing budgets. Marketing research has a range of uses from fine-tuning products to discovering whole new marketing concepts.

For example, everything at the Olive Garden restaurant chain from the decor to the wine list is based on marketing research. Each new menu item is put through a series of consumer taste tests before being added to the menu. Hallmark Cards uses marketing research to test messages, cover designs, and even the size of the cards. Hallmark's experts know which kinds of cards will sell best in which places.

➡ **lg 7**

CAPITALIZING ON TRENDS IN BUSINESS

To discover exactly what customers value most, organizations are using innovative techniques for collecting customer information. Some of the more sophisticated marketing research techniques that are growing in popularity are advanced observation research methods, decision support systems (DDSs), and database marketing.

Advanced Observation Research Methods

All forms of observation research are increasingly using more sophisticated technology. The major television networks, for example, are supporting an advanced technology that provides highly accurate market data about television viewers' behaviour.

The networks have been discouraged by the data flowing from A.C. Nielsen media research, which indicate that the networks are losing market share. The networks say that Nielsen's research is faulty and are backing a new measurement system created by Statistical Research Inc. (SRI). The stakes are about US$13 billion in advertising revenue generated annually by the major networks.[12] SRI has developed Systems for Measuring And Reporting Television, or SMART, at a cost of US$160 million. The SMART setup consists of meters with sensors that can pick up signals from the air. The meter looks like a VCR and sits on top of the television. Users log in and out before and after watching television by pressing a device similar to a TV remote control, which was designed for ease of use. The device accurately tracks which program is being watched and by whom.

Technology is also being applied to measure Internet traffic. Web sites measure their own popularity, largely by the number of "hits," or the times a page or parts of a page are called up. Sites then try to convert that measurement into "unique visitors" so that one person calling up several pages is not counted more than once.

Perhaps most astounding of all is the new technology that is allowing us to learn how the brain receives and processes information. Brain science has come so far that researchers are now able to routinely eavesdrop on brains while they think. The new technology offers insights about how we perceive, think, and make decisions. This information will enable researchers to uncover consumers' root motivations—or hot buttons. These come from the subliminal regions of our brains, where values, needs, and motivations originate.[13]

Decision Support Systems

decision support system (DSS)
An interactive, flexible, computerized information system that allows managers to make decisions quickly and accurately; used to conduct sales analyses, forecast sales, evaluate advertising, analyze product lines, and keep tabs on market trends and competitors' actions.

More and more managers are turning to another form of technology called a **decision support system (DSS)**, an interactive, flexible computerized information system that allows managers to make decisions quickly and accurately. Managers use DSS to conduct sales analyses, forecast sales, evaluate advertising, analyze product lines, and keep tabs on market trends and competitors' actions. A DSS not only allows managers to ask "what if" questions, but enables them to slice the data any way they want. A DSS has the following characteristics:

1. *Interactive.* The manager gives simple instructions and sees results generated on the spot. The process is under the manager's direct control; no computer programmer is needed.
2. *Flexible.* It can sort, regroup, total, average, and manipulate the data in a variety of ways. It will shift gears as the user changes topics, matching information to the problem at hand. For example, the chief executive can see highly aggregated figures, while the marketing analyst views detailed breakouts.
3. *Discovery oriented.* It helps managers probe for trends, isolate problems, and ask new questions.
4. *Easy to learn and use.* Managers need not be particularly computer knowledgeable. Novice users can elect a standard, or "default," method of using the system that enables them to bypass optional features and work with the basic system while they gradually learn its possibilities. This minimizes the frustration that frequently accompanies new computer software.

Using Databases for Micromarketing

database marketing
The creation of a large computerized file of the profiles and purchase patterns of customers and potential customers, usually required for successful micro marketing.

Perhaps the fastest growing use of DSS is for **database marketing**, which is the creation of a large computerized file of the profiles and purchase patterns of customers and potential customers. Using the very specific information in the database, a company can, if it wishes, direct a different individualized message to every customer or potential customer.

Beginning in the 1950s, network television enabled advertisers to "get the same message to everyone simultaneously." Database marketing can get a customized, individual message to everyone simultaneously through direct mail. This is why database marketing is sometimes called *micromarketing*. Specifically, database marketing can:

- Identify the most profitable and least profitable customers.
- Identify the most profitable market segments or individuals and target efforts with greater efficiency and effectiveness.
- Aim marketing efforts to those goods, services, and market segments that require the most support.
- Increase revenue through repackaging and re-pricing products for various market segments.
- Evaluate opportunities for offering new products and services.
- Identify products and services that are best-sellers and most profitable.

Database marketing can create a computerized form of the old-fashioned relationship that people used to have with the corner grocer, butcher, or baker. American Express, for example, can pull from its database all cardholders who made purchases at golf pro-shops in the past six months, attended symphony concerts, or travelled to Europe more than once in the last year.

concept check

- How is technology being used in marketing research?
- What is a decision support system (DSS) and what is its purpose?
- Explain what database marketing is and describe some of its uses.

APPLYING THIS CHAPTER'S TOPICS

As a consumer, you participate in shaping consumer products by the choices you make and the products and services you buy. You can become a better consumer by actively participating in marketing surveys and learning more about the products you buy.

Participate in Marketing Research Surveys

All of us get tired of telephone solicitations where people try to sell us everything from new carpet to chimney cleaning. Recognize that marketing research surveys are different. A true marketing research survey will never involve a sales pitch nor will the research firm sell your name to a database marketer. The purpose of marketing research is to build better goods and services for you and me. Help out the researchers and ultimately help yourself.

Conduct Your Own Market Research

A good idea is to read everything you can find about your intended purchase. Go to the Internet and use the search engines to find articles relevant to your purchase. Find Internet chat rooms about your product and join in the discussion. And, before you buy, check out the *Consumer Reports* ratings on your product at **www.consumerreports.org**.

TRY IT NOW!

1. **Stop Junk Mail** If you are upset about junk mail, contact the Canadian Marketing Association (CMA) and have your name removed from mailing lists. Visit the CMA's Web site at www.the-cma.org. You can also join an umbrella organization dedicated to stopping the flood of junk e-mail, intrusive telemarketing

calls, and junk mail. One such organization is Zero Junk Mail. It can be found at www.junkbusters.com.

2. **Know Your Profile** Do you wonder where marketers place you in their psychographic profiles? To find out, go to www.mbgoldfarb.com.

>looking ahead
at DaimlerChrysler

Before a company can create a marketing mix, it must identify the target market for the product. Thus, DaimlerChrysler first had to identify the target market for the 300M. To be successful, the company had to identify one or more competitive advantages unique to the 300M. DaimlerChrysler used marketing research to identify the target market for the 300M and then determined the needs and desires of these potential buyers. With this information, the company could build customer value into the 300M. The automaker must continue to use marketing research to identify the ever-changing desires of the target market. DaimlerChrysler can retain its leadership position with the 300M by continuing to deliver value to target buyers.

SUMMARY OF LEARNING GOALS

➡lg 1 **What are the marketing concept and relationship building?**

Marketing includes those business activities that are designed to satisfy consumer needs and wants through the exchange process. Marketing managers use the "right" principle—getting the right goods or services to the right people at the right place, time, and price, using the right promotional techniques. Today, many firms have adopted the marketing concept. The marketing concept involves identifying consumer needs and wants and then producing goods or services that will satisfy them while making a profit. Relationship marketing entails forging long-term relationships with customers, which can lead to repeat sales, reduced costs, and stable relationships.

➡lg 2 **How do managers create a marketing strategy?**

A firm creates a marketing strategy by understanding the external environment, defining the target market, determining a competitive advantage, and developing a marketing mix. Environmental scanning enables companies to understand the external environment. The target market is the specific group of consumers toward which a firm directs its marketing efforts. A competitive advantage is a set of unique features of a company and its products that are perceived by the target market as significant and superior to those of the competition.

➡lg 3 **What is the marketing mix?**

To carry out the marketing strategy, firms create a marketing mix—a blend of products, distribution systems, prices, and promotion. Marketing managers use this mix to satisfy target consumers. The mix can be applied to non-business as well as business situations.

➡ lg 4   How do consumers and organizations make buying decisions?

Buyer behaviour is what people and businesses do in buying and using goods and services. The consumer decision-making process consists of the following steps: responding to a stimulus, recognizing a problem or opportunity, seeking information, evaluating alternatives, purchasing the product, judging the purchase outcome, and engaging in post-purchase behaviour. A number of factors influence the process. Individual factors are within the individual consumer and are unique to each person. Social factors include all interactions between a consumer and the external environment, such as family, social classes, and culture. The main differences between consumer and business markets are purchase volume, number of customers, location of buyers, direct distribution, and rational purchase decisions.

➡ lg 5   What are the five basic forms of market segmentation?

Success in marketing depends on understanding the target market. One technique used to identify a target market is market segmentation. The five basic forms of segmentation are demographic (population statistics), geographic (location), psychographic (personality or lifestyle), benefit (product features), and volume (amount purchased).

➡ lg 6   How is marketing research used in marketing decision-making?

Much can be learned about consumers through market research, which involves collecting, recording, and analyzing data important in marketing goods and services. The results are then communicated to management. Marketing researchers may use primary data, which are gathered from door-to-door, telephone, Internet, and mail interviews. The Internet is becoming a quick, cheap, and efficient way to gather primary data. Secondary data are available from a variety of sources including government, trade, and commercial associations. Secondary data save time and money, but they may not meet the researchers' needs. Both primary and secondary data give researchers a better idea of how the market will respond to the product. Thus, they reduce the risk of producing something the market does not want.

➡ lg 7   What are the trends in understanding the consumer?

New technology has increased the sophistication of observation research techniques and improved the accuracy of data, such as measurements of the size of television audiences and Web traffic to specific sites. Researchers are also analyzing the brain to better understand how people think. A second trend is the growing use of decision support systems. These enable managers to make decisions quickly and accurately. A third trend is the growing use of databases for micromarketing.

WORKING THE NET

1. You've been hired by a snack food manufacturer that is interested in adding popcorn snacks to its product line. First, however, the company asks you to find some secondary data on the current market for popcorn. Go to the Dogpile Search Engine (**www.dogpile.com**) and do a search for "popcorn consumption." Can you find how much popcorn is sold annually? The geographic locations with the highest popcorn sales? The time of the year when the most popcorn is sold? What are the limitations of doing research like this on the Internet?

2. You and a friend want to start a new magazine for people who work at home. Do a search of Statistics Canada at **www.statcan.ca** to get information about the work-at-home market.

CREATIVE THINKING CASE

The American Automobile Association—Building Long-Term Relationships?

This case is built upon the experience of Don Schultz, a marketing professor at Northwestern University. He tells his story in the first person.

Almost every car owner knows about the American Automobile Association. They're the people who slog through rain and snow to rescue stranded motorists. Whether it's a flat tire on the expressway or a broken axle or keys locked in a car parked in a lot, the AAA professionals come running. And they do a good job. I've been a member of the Chicago Motor Club, a "Triple A" affiliate, for 20 years. They have given good service to me, my wife, my children, and my mother.

In recent months, my car has had a problem. For reasons known only to the car, the battery discharges at random. Sometimes it happens overnight, sometimes weeks go by without a problem. When the battery discharges itself, I call AAA. No matter where I am, they come out and give me a jump. Seemingly my problem is no problem for them. They provide cheerful, friendly service, day and night.

Until recently, that is, when apparently I triggered their brand relationship destroying mechanism. While other service suppliers were sending end-of-the-year calendars and thank-you letters, I got threats from AAA. In a letter, Gerald F. Svarz, manager of member relations, wrote:

> Our records indicate that you have requested Emergency Road Service four times during the past 12 months. As outlined in the Member's Handbook, the Club reserves the right to notify a member when they have used four or more service calls in the previous 12 months. Excessive use of Emergency Road Service can result in the nonrenewal or the cancellation of a membership. The nonrenewal or cancellation of membership is based solely on the number of calls in a membership year.

Wow, talk about *building* brand *relationships!* Here's an organization that's going to kick me out of its club, whose primary claim to fame and only reason for being—at least for most of its members—is emergency road service. Only don't use our service too much, they say, or we'll cancel your membership. We reserve that right.

Just to make sure I wasn't overlooking something, I checked out AAA in the Yellow Pages. "Emergency Road Service," the ad says. Same for the newspaper ads I found. And "Emergency Road Service" is splashed all over the relation-building magazine they send me every few months. Their promotional literature says "Emergency Road Service" in big bold letters.

The problem is, they reserve the right to limit the Emergency Road Service you need. Am I a better AAA customer if I don't ever use their services? It sure sounds like it. What about all those years I paid the membership fee and never used the service? They didn't write to thank me for that, nor did they adjust my membership fee the way auto insurance companies do for safe drivers.[14]

Critical Thinking Questions

1. Is AAA following the marketing concept?
2. Doesn't it make economic sense to "weed out" people who use the service too much?
3. Insurance companies cancel people's auto insurance if they get too many speeding tickets. Isn't AAA's policy the same thing?
4. Does the CAA use the same policy? Check it out at **www.caa.ca**.

Marketing—Product, Price, and Promotion

In this chapter we will continue to look at the functional area of marketing but more specifically at three of the four Ps of the marketing mix—product, price, and promotion. One of the keys to success in marketing is to provide something of unique value to the customer in order to achieve the critical success factor of meeting their needs. The second is to market it in such a way that you convince the customer of its benefit. They must believe that it will satisfy their needs or they won't buy it. This is where the four Ps come in. Not only does marketing have to work with the other functional areas in an integrative fashion as we discussed in Chapter 8, but the marketing functions themselves must work together in an integrative way to convince the customer of the unique benefit of the product. For example, if a company wants to promote a product that is of better quality than the competition and therefore designs it to have the features as well as the look of higher quality, promotes it in high-end publications, distributes it in high-end stores, but prices it below the competition, consumers will be confused about its quality. All four of the elements must give a consistent message—they must form an integrative whole.

This is quite evident when you consider that consumers make purchase decisions after considering many attributes of the product, including price. They consider the total value package—what they get at the price they have to pay. Integration is also evident in looking at product design alone. The chapter discusses how consumers buy packages of benefits; for example, Burger King sells burgers and fries, but along with that—quick food preparation and cleanliness. Therefore, product design must take into consideration human resource and operational issues as well.

Another very integrative product concept is the product life cycle. It sounds like just a product concept but the implications of what stage in the life cycle a product is at go far beyond the product itself, into how it is priced, promoted, and distributed. At the new product stage, there are also obvious connections to the other parts of our business model. New product goals are usually financially stated, and ideas are rejected if they don't meet financial goals. It also must be considered whether the firm has the operational facilities to produce the product, as well as access to the necessary technology, human, and financial resources. New product ideas need to be checked against long-range strategies as well, to ensure that plans at all levels relate back to the overall corporate strategy.

Pricing has obvious connections to finance. The company must set a price that will earn a fair return but also provide value to the consumer. This connection with finance is no more obvious than in the discussion of the breakeven point. If the costs from operations, human resources, and marketing cannot be covered from the revenue generated by the product, then financially it is not feasible and can't be done within the current cost structure, regardless of its marketing appeal.

Promotion is also affected by other areas of the business. For example, one of the elements of a promotional mix is personal selling. This has definite human resource implications. The sales force must be managed to communicate the intended message. And how much is spent on personal selling as opposed to other forms of promotion depends to a great extent on the financial situation of the company. But the factors in the external environment also affect promotion—the government (political environment) sets guidelines on what can and cannot be done in advertising, the competition (economic environment) has to be monitored carefully to be aware of what message they are projecting versus your company's message, social trends will influence your advertising design, and of course technology is always changing and expanding the limits of what can be done. For example, the Internet cannot be ignored as a potential vehicle for building a brand presence (in fact, more quickly than traditional methods), nor can it be ignored as a powerful tool for tailoring the message to meet the needs of specific consumers. Just go visit Amazon.com.

The clearest example of integration in promotion is the need for integrated marketing communications. Just as all of the four Ps must project the same message, so do all elements of the promotional mix. If this is not done, the company risks confusing the consumer, who will simply buy a different product. The area where there is the least control is in personal selling. Your salespeople are your message, and therefore, the message may not be the same every time. This creates obvious human resource issues that must be handled very carefully to ensure consistency.

Marketing— Product, Price, and Promotion

CHAPTER 9

Learning Goals

➡ **lg 1** What is a product, and how is it classified?

➡ **lg 2** How does branding distinguish a product from its competitors?

➡ **lg 3** How do organizations create new products?

➡ **lg 4** What are the stages of the product life cycle?

➡ **lg 5** What is the role of pricing in marketing?

➡ **lg 6** How are product prices determined?

➡ **lg 7** What are the goals of promotional strategy?

➡ **lg 8** What is the promotional mix, and what are its elements?

➡ **lg 9** What are the types of advertising?

➡ **lg 10** What are the advertising media, and how are they selected?

➡ **lg 11** How does public relations fit into the promotional mix?

Product, Price, and Promotion at 4321ZIP

Steve Smith, president and CEO of ZIP Airlines, describes the process ZIP management followed in order to create its product. Initially, the company identified an underserved market in the airline passenger transportation business. Steve suggests finding out whom you are going to go after and what they want. For ZIP's market segmentation, three customer segments were identified: business travellers, VFRs (visiting friends and relatives), and leisure travellers. The product was divided into short-haul and long-haul trips with the various differentiating factors for each segment determined. For example, business travellers tend to be time sensitive and therefore frequency is critical. As we move from the short haul to the long haul, comfort also becomes important. For the VFRs and leisure travellers, price is the deciding factor for short and long hauls. The key to establishing an attractive product is to determine which segment is not being well served and to target that segment. ZIP chose to go after the VFR market segment and, by offering differentiating features, they hope to gain significant market share. The differentiating features of a ZIP flight when competing with a regular low-fare carrier include more legroom, Aeroplan points accumulation, and pre-assigned seating available when booking. The goal is to move passengers away from other low-fare carriers by offering additional value for the price. Steve believes that to be successful the price must drive the cost structure and not the other way around. ZIP has been designed to focus on customer service at a low cost to the consumer. People must be hired correctly in order to ensure that they are moving in the same direction as the company (i.e., providing best value and "spirited" service). In promoting the product, Steve recommends promoting what is important to your target market segment and creating awareness in the marketplace. What is the image? Why would a customer choose ZIP? The image of ZIP is promoted using TV advertisements to create a general warm and fuzzy feeling about the company. The hard-hitting tactical advertising is found in newspaper and radio ads where the goal is to bring in the bookings—as Steve says, "a call to action." Public relations is huge in the creation of the image, and Steve wants the public to know why ZIP is doing what it's doing. This is accomplished through interviews with the media. Here accessibility is critical. Through speeches presented at various venues the message is given—straight, clean, and simple. The distribution system includes the direct booking on the Net and also the travel agents as distributors. ZIP has identified an underserved market segment and created a company outside of Air Canada to service this market. It has successfully differentiated itself from its immediate competition and has promoted itself as a friendly, flexible, low-fare carrier serving many Canadian destinations. Read more about ZIP on its Web site at **www.4321zip.com**.[1]

CRITICAL THINKING QUESTIONS

As you read this chapter, consider the following questions as they relate to ZIP:

- How do companies use pricing as a competitive edge?
- How do companies choose the products and services that they offer?
- How do companies ensure that they are using their resources properly to promote their products and services?

BUSINESS IN THE 21ST CENTURY

The creation of a marketing mix normally begins with the first of the four Ps, product. Only when there is something to sell can marketers create a promotional theme, set a price, and establish a distribution channel. Organizations prepare for long-term success by creating and packaging products that add value and pricing them to meet the organization's financial objectives. In addition, organizations respond to changing customer needs by creating new products. Very few goods and services can survive in the marketplace without good promotion. Marketers, such as those touting Levi's Dockers, promote their products to build consumer demand. **Promotion** is an attempt by marketers to inform, persuade, or remind consumers and industrial users to engage in the exchange process. Once the product has been created, promotion is often used to convince target customers that it has a **differential advantage** over the competition. A differential advantage is a set of unique features that the target market perceives as important and better than the competition's features. Such features may include high quality, fast delivery, low price, good service, and the like. Lexus, for example, is seen as having a quality differential advantage over other luxury cars. Therefore, promotion for Lexus stresses the quality of the vehicle.

This chapter will examine products, brands, and the importance of packaging and promotion. We discuss how new products are created and how they go through periods of sales growth and then decline. Next, you will discover how managers set prices to reach pricing goals. We will look at trends in products and pricing and conclude with a discussion of marketing communications to promote products and services. The fourth P, place, or distribution, will be covered in Chapter 10.

promotion
The attempt by marketers to inform, persuade, or remind consumers and industrial users to engage in the exchange process.

differential advantage
A set of unique features of a product that the target market perceives as important and better than the competition's features.

➡ **lg 1**

product
In marketing, any good or service, along with its perceived attributes and benefits, that creates value for the customer.

What Is a Product?

In marketing, a **product** is any good or service, along with its perceived attributes and benefits, that creates value for the customer. Attributes can be tangible or intangible. Among the tangible attributes are packaging and warranties. Intangible attributes are symbolic, such as brand image. People make decisions about which products to buy after considering both tangible and intangible attributes of a product. For example, when you buy a pair of jeans, you consider price, brand, store image, and style before you buy. These factors are all part of the marketing mix. Exhibit 9-1 illustrates both the tangible and intangible attributes of a product.

Products are often a blend of goods and services as shown in Exhibit 9-2. For example, Honda Accord (a good) would have less value without Honda's maintenance agreement (a service). Although Burger King sells such goods as sandwiches and French fries, customers expect quality service as well, including quick food preparation and cleanliness. When developing a product, an organization must consider how the combination of goods and services will provide value to the customer.

Classifying Consumer Products

Because most things sold are a blend of goods and services, the term *product* can be used to refer to both. After all, consumers are really buying packages of benefits that deliver value. The person who buys a plane ride on Air Canada is looking for a quick way to get from one city to another (the benefit). Providing this benefit requires goods (a plane, food) and services (ticketing, maintenance, piloting).

Marketers must know how consumers view the types of products their companies sell so that they can design the marketing mix to appeal to the selected target market. To help them define target markets, marketers have devised product categories. Products that are bought by the end user are called *consumer products*. They include electric razors, sandwiches, cars, stereos, magazines, and houses. Consumer products

e x h i b i t 9 - 1 | Tangible and Intangible Attributes of a Product Create Value for the Buyer

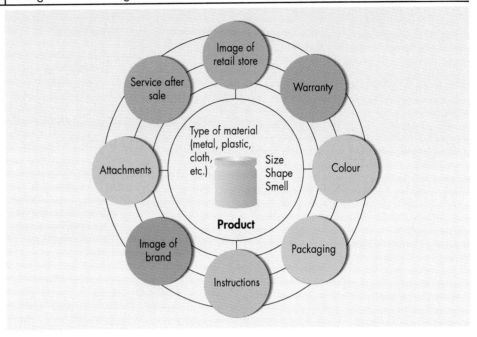

that get used up, such as Dove soap and Lays potato chips, are called *consumer non-durables*. Those that last for a long time, such as Whirlpool washing machines and computers, are *consumer durables*.

Another way to classify consumer products is by the amount of effort consumers are willing to make to acquire them. The four major categories of consumer products are unsought products, convenience products, shopping products, and specialty products, as summarized in Exhibit 9-3.

Unsought products are products unknown to the potential buyer or known products that the buyer does not actively seek. New products fall into this category until advertising and distribution increase consumer awareness of them. Some goods are always marketed as unsought items, especially products we do not like to think about or care to spend money on. Insurance, burial plots, encyclopedias, and similar items require aggressive personal selling and highly persuasive advertising. Salespeople actively seek leads to potential buyers. Because consumers usually do not seek out this type of product, the company must go directly to them through a salesperson, direct mail, telemarketing, or direct-response advertising.

unsought products
Products that either are unknown to the potential buyer or are known but the buyer does not actively seek them.

e x h i b i t 9 - 2 | Products Are Typically a Blend of Goods and Services

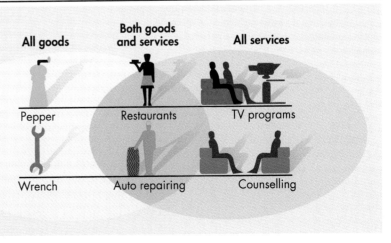

| Classification of Consumer Products by the Effort Expended to Buy Them

Consumer Product	Examples	Expended by Consumer
Unsought products	Life insurance Burial plots New products	No effort
Convenience products	Soft drinks Bread Milk Coffee	Very little or minimum effort
Shopping products	Automobiles Homes Vacations	Considerable effort
Specialty products	Expensive jewellery Gourmet dinners Limited-production automobiles	Maximum effort

convenience products
Relatively inexpensive items that require little shopping effort and are purchased routinely without planning.

shopping products
Items that are bought after considerable planning, including brand-to-brand and store-to-store comparisons of price, suitability, and style.

specialty products
Items for which consumers search long and hard and for which they refuse to accept substitutes.

capital products
Large, expensive items with a long life span that are purchased by businesses for use in making other products or providing a service.

expense items
Items, purchased by businesses, that are smaller and less expensive than capital products and usually have a life span of less than one year.

Convenience products are relatively inexpensive items that require little shopping effort. Soft drinks, candy bars, milk, bread, and small hardware items are examples. We buy them routinely without much planning. This does not mean that such products are unimportant or obscure. Many, in fact, are well known by their brand names—such as Pepsi-Cola, Campbell's Soup, Domino's pizza, Secret deodorant, and UPS shipping.

In contrast to convenience products, **shopping products** are bought only after a brand-to-brand and store-to-store comparison of price, suitability, and style. Examples are furniture, automobiles, a vacation in Europe, and some items of clothing. Convenience products are bought with little planning, but shopping products may be chosen months or even years before their actual purchase.

Specialty products are products for which consumers search long and hard and for which they refuse to accept substitutes. Expensive jewellery, designer clothing, state-of-the-art stereo equipment, limited-production automobiles, and gourmet dinners fall into this category. Because consumers are willing to spend much time and effort to find specialty products, distribution is often limited to one or two sellers in a given region, such as Holt Renfrew, Ralph Lauren, or the Porsche dealer.

Classifying Business Products

Products bought by businesses or institutions for use in making other products or in providing services are called *business* or *industrial products*. They are classified as either capital products or expense items. **Capital products** are usually large, expensive items with a long life span. Examples are buildings, large machines, and airplanes. **Expense items** are typically smaller, less expensive items that usually have a life span of less than a year. Examples are printer cartridges and paper. Industrial products are sometimes further classified in the following categories:

1. *Installations.* These are large, expensive capital items that determine the nature, scope, and efficiency of a company. Capital products like General Motors' Saturn assembly plant in Ontario represent a big commitment against future earnings and profitability. Buying an installation requires longer negotiations, more planning, and the judgments of more people than buying any other type of product.

2. *Accessories.* Accessories do not have the same long-run impact on the firm as installations, and they are less expensive and more standardized. But they are still capital products. Xerox copy machines, IBM personal computers (PCs), and smaller machines such as Black and Decker table drills and saws are typical accessories. Marketers of accessories often rely on well-known brand names and extensive advertising as well as personal selling.

3. *Component parts and materials.* These are expense items that are built into the end product. Some component parts are custom-made, such as a drive shaft for an automobile or a case for a computer; others are standardized for sale to many industrial users. Intel's Pentium chip for PCs and cement for the construction trade are examples of standardized component parts and materials.

4. *Raw materials.* Raw materials are expense items that have undergone little or no processing and are used to create a final product. Examples include lumber, copper, and zinc.

5. *Supplies.* Supplies do not become part of the final product. They are bought routinely and in fairly large quantities. Supply items run the gamut from pencils and paper to paint and machine oil. They have little impact on the firm's long-run profits. Bic pens, Xerox copier paper, and Pennzoil machine oil are typical supply items.

6. *Services.* These are expense items used to plan or support company operations; for example, janitorial cleaning and management consulting.

concept check

- What is a product?
- What are the classes of consumer goods?
- Explain how business products are classified.

---

brand

A company's product identifier that distinguishes the company's products from those of competitors.

trademark

The legally exclusive design, name, or other distinctive mark that a manufacturer uses to identify its goods in the marketplace.

➡ **lg 2**

brand equity

The value of company and brand names.

These brand names for laundry detergents are effective because they are short, distinctive, and easy to pronounce, recognize, and remember.

Building Brand Equity and Master Brands

Most industrial and consumer products have a brand name. If everything came in a plain brown wrapper, life would be less colourful and competition would decrease. Companies would have less incentive to put out better products because consumers would be unable to tell one company's products from those of another.

The product identifier for a company is its **brand**. Brands appear in the form of words, names, symbols, or designs. They are used to distinguish a company's products from those of its competitors. Examples of well-known brands are Kleenex tissues, Jeep automobiles, and IBM computers. A **trademark** is the legally exclusive design, name, or other distinctive mark that a manufacturer uses to identify its goods in the marketplace. No other company can use that same trademark.

Benefits of Branding

Branding has three main purposes: product identification, repeat sales, and new product sales. The most important purpose is product identification. Branding allows marketers to distinguish their products from all others. Exhibit 9-4 identifies the characteristics of an effective brand name. Many brand names are familiar to consumers and indicate quality. The term **brand equity** refers to the value of company and brand names. A brand that has high awareness, perceived quality, and brand loyalty among customers has high brand equity. Brand equity is more than awareness of a brand—it is the personality, soul, and emotion associated with the brand. Think of the feelings you have when you see the brand name Harley-Davidson, Nike, or even Microsoft. A brand with strong brand equity is a valuable asset. Some brands such as Coke, Kodak, Cadbury, and Chevrolet are worth millions of dollars.

- Easy to pronounce (by both domestic and foreign buyers)
- Easy to recognize
- Easy to remember
- Short
- Distinctive, unique
- Describes the product
- Describes the product's use
- Describes the product's benefits
- Has a positive connotation
- Reinforces the desired product image
- Is legally protectable in home and foreign markets of interest

master brand
A brand so dominant that consumers think of it immediately when a product category, use, attribute, or customer benefit is mentioned.

brand loyalty
A consumer's preference for a particular brand.

A brand so dominant in consumers' minds that they think of it immediately when a product category, use, attribute, or customer benefit is mentioned is a **master brand.** Exhibit 9-5 lists some of North America's master brands in several product categories.

Building Repeat Sales with Brand Loyalty

A consumer who tries one or more brands may decide to buy a certain brand regularly. The preference for a particular brand is **brand loyalty.** It lets consumers buy with less time, thought, and risk. Brand loyalty ensures future sales for the firm. It can also help protect a firm's share of the market, discourage new competitors, and thus prolong the brand's life. Brand loyalty even allows companies to raise prices. Quaker Oats Co., maker of Cap'n Crunch, Life, and Quaker oatmeal, recently raised its prices 3.8 percent. Analysts said that Quaker could do this, even though other cereal makers didn't raise prices, because of the strong consumer loyalty to Quaker products.[2]

What makes people loyal to a brand? Though pricing, promotion, and product quality are important, customer interaction with the company may be most critical. A recent study found that 90 percent of consumers who were delighted with their experience say they will continue to buy the product/service, whereas only 37 percent of the customers who were dissatisfied with their experience say they will remain loyal.[3] Brand loyalty to a particular company's products is a marketer's dream come true.

Facilitating New Product Sales

The third main purpose of branding is to facilitate *new product sales*. Let's assume that your class forms a company to market frozen tarts and pies under the name "University Frozen Desserts." Now, assume that Pepperidge Farms develops a new line of identical

HOT Links

See how one consulting firm helps clients pick the right name by pointing your Web browser to
www.namebase.com

Product Category	Master Brand
Adhesive bandages	Band-Aid
Antacids	Alka-Seltzer
Laundry detergent	Tide
Cellophane tape	Scotch Tape
Fast food	McDonald's
Gelatin	Jell-O
Rum	Bacardi
Chocolate	Cadbury
Soft drinks	Coca-Cola
Soup	Campbell's

frozen tarts and pies. Which ones will consumers try? The Pepperidge Farm products, without a doubt. Pepperidge Farm is known for its quality frozen bakery products. Consumers assume that its new tarts and pies will be of high quality and are therefore willing to give them a try. The well-known Pepperidge Farm brand is facilitating new product introduction.

Many consumers don't want to pay the costs of manufacturer or dealer brands. One popular way to save money is to buy **generic products**. These products carry no brand name, come in plain containers, and sell for much less than brand-name products. They are typically sold in yellow and white packages with such simple labels as "liquid bleach" or "spaghetti." Generic products are sold by most supermarkets. Sometimes manufacturers simply stop the production line and substitute a generic package for a brand package, though the product is exactly the same. The most popular generic products are garbage bags, jelly, paper towels, coffee cream substitutes, cigarettes, and paper napkins.

In launching his line of cologne and personal care products, entrepreneur Michael Jordon enjoys high brand equity because people associate the brand with Jordan's status as one of the world's best athletes.

generic products
Products that carry no brand name, come in plain containers, and sell for much less than brand-name products.

HOT Links

Curious about how generic and private label products are manufactured? Visit the Private Label Manufacturers Association at **www.plma.com**

➡ **lg 3**

focus group
A group of 8 to 12 participants led by a moderator in an in-depth discussion on one particular topic or concept.

brainstorming
A method of generating ideas in which group members suggest as many possibilities as they can without criticizing or evaluating any of the suggestions.

concept ✓ check

- Define the terms *brand* and *trademark*.
- Describe the three benefits of branding.
- What is a generic product?

How New Products Are Developed

Developing new products is both costly and risky. To increase their chances for success, most firms use the following product development process, which is also summarized in Exhibit 9-6.

1. *Set new product goals.* New product goals are usually stated as financial objectives. For example, a company may want to recover its investment in three years or less. Or it may want to earn at least a 15 percent return on the investment. Nonfinancial goals may include using existing equipment or facilities.

2. *Develop new product ideas.* Smaller firms usually depend on employees, customers, investors, and distributors for new ideas. Larger companies use these sources and more structured marketing research techniques, such as focus groups and brainstorming. A **focus group** consists of 8 to 12 participants led by a moderator in an in-depth discussion on one particular topic or concept. The goal of focus group research is to learn and understand what people have to say and why. The emphasis is on getting people talking at length and in detail about the subject at hand. The intent is to find out how they feel about a product, concept, idea, or organization, how it fits into their lives, and their emotional involvement with it. Focus groups often generate excellent product ideas. A few examples are the interior design of the Ford Taurus, Stick-Up room deodorizers, Dustbusters, and Wendy's salad bar. In the industrial market, machine tools, keyboard designs, aircraft interiors, and backhoe accessories evolved from focus groups.

   Brainstorming is also used to generate new product ideas. With **brainstorming** the members of a group think of as many ways to vary a product or solve a problem as possible. Criticism is avoided, no matter how ridiculous an idea seems at the time. The emphasis is on sheer numbers of ideas. Evaluation of these ideas is postponed to later steps of development.

3. *Screen ideas and concepts.* As ideas emerge, they are checked against the firm's new product goals and its long-range strategies. Many product concepts are rejected because they don't fit well with existing products, needed technology is not available, the company doesn't have enough resources, or the sales potential is low.

e x h i b i t   9 - 6 | Steps to Develop New Products That Satisfy Customers

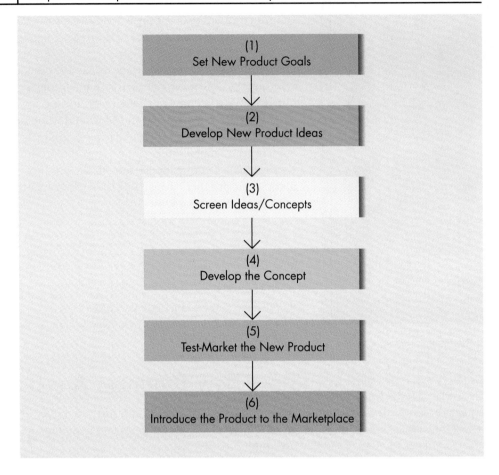

4. *Develop the concept.* Developing the new product concept involves creating a prototype of the product, testing the prototype, and building the marketing strategy. The type and amount of product testing vary, depending on such factors as the company's experience with similar products, how easy it is to make the item, and how easy it will be for consumers to use it. Suppose that Kraft is developing a new salad dressing flavour. The company already has a lot of experience in this area, so the new dressing will go directly into advanced taste tests and perhaps home-use tests. If they were to develop a new line of soft drinks, however, Kraft would most likely do a great deal of testing. Since they would be entering a totally new market, they would study many aspects of the new product before actually making it.

While the product is tested, the marketing strategy is refined. Channels of distribution are selected, pricing policies are developed and tested, the target market is further defined, and demand for the product is estimated. Management also continually updates the profit plan.

As the marketing strategy and prototype tests mature, a communication strategy is developed. A logo and package wording are created. As part of the communication strategy, promotion themes are developed, and the product is introduced to the sales force.

test marketing
The process of testing a new product among potential users.

5. *Test-market the new product.* **Test-marketing** is testing the product among potential users. It allows management to evaluate various strategies and to see how well the parts of the marketing mix fit together. Few new product concepts reach this stage. For those that pass this stage, the firm must decide whether to introduce the product on a regional or national basis.

6. *Introduce the product.* A product that passes test-marketing is ready for market introduction, called *rollout*, which requires a lot of logistical coordination. Various divisions of the company must be encouraged to give the new item the attention it deserves. Packaging and labelling in a different language may be required. Sales training sessions must be scheduled, spare parts inventoried, service personnel trained, advertising and promotion campaigns readied, and wholesalers and retailers informed about the new item. If the new product is to be sold internationally, it may have to be altered to meet the requirements of the target countries. For instance, electrical products may have to run on different electrical currents.

concept check

• What are the steps in the new product development process?

→ lg 4

The Product Life Cycle

product life cycle
The pattern of sales and profits over time for a product or product category; consists of an introductory state, growth stage, maturity, and decline (and death).

Product managers create marketing mixes for their products as they move through the life cycle. The **product life cycle** is a pattern of sales and profits over time for a product (e.g., Ivory dishwashing liquid) or a product category (e.g., liquid detergents). As the product moves through the stages of the life cycle, the firm must keep revising the marketing mix to stay competitive and meet the needs of target customers.

Stages of the Life Cycle

As illustrated in Exhibit 9-7, the product life cycle consists of the following stages:

exhibit 9 - 7 | Sales and Profits during the Product Life Cycle

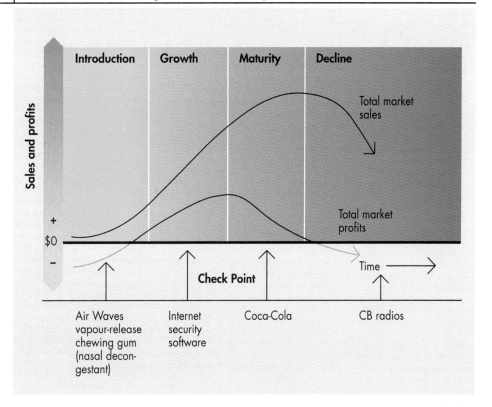

1. *Introduction.* When a product enters the life cycle, it faces many obstacles. Although competition may be light, the introductory stage usually features frequent product modifications, limited distribution, and heavy promotion. The failure rate is high. Production and marketing costs are also high, and sales volume is low. Hence profits are usually small or negative.

2. *Growth stage.* If a product survives the introductory stage, it advances to the growth stage of the life cycle. In this stage, sales grow at an increasing rate, profits are healthy, and many competitors enter the market. Large companies may start to acquire small pioneering firms that have reached this stage. Emphasis switches from primary demand promotion to aggressive brand advertising and communicating the differences between brands. For example, the goal changes from convincing people to buy compact disc players to convincing them to buy Sony versus Panasonic or RCA.

   Distribution becomes a major key to success during the growth stage, as well as in later stages. Manufacturers scramble to acquire dealers and distributors and to build long-term relationships. Without adequate distribution, it is impossible to establish a strong market position.

   Toward the end of the growth phase, prices normally begin falling and profits peak. Price reductions result from increased competition and from cost reductions from producing larger quantities of items (economies of scale). Also, most firms have recovered their development costs by now, and their priority is in increasing or retaining market share and enhancing profits.

3. *Maturity.* After the growth stage, sales continue to mount—but at a decreasing rate. This is the maturity stage. Most products that have been on the market for a long time are in this stage. Thus, most marketing strategies are designed for mature products. One such strategy is to bring out several variations of a basic product (line extension). Kool-Aid, for instance, was originally offered in three flavours. Today there are more than ten, as well as sweetened and unsweetened varieties.

4. *Decline (and death).* When sales and profits fall, the product has reached the *decline stage*. The rate of decline is governed by two factors: the rate of change in consumer tastes and the rate at which new products enter the market. Sony turntables are an example of a product in the decline stage. The demand for turntables has now been surpassed by the demand for compact disc players and cassette players.

The Product Life Cycle as a Management Tool

The product life cycle may be used in planning. Marketers who understand the cycle concept are better able to forecast future sales and plan new marketing strategies. Exhibit 9-8 is a brief summary of strategic needs at various stages of the product life cycle.

e x h i b i t　9 - 8　| Strategies for Success at Each Stage of the Product Life Cycle

	Life Cycle Stage			
Category	**Introduction**	**Growth**	**Maturity**	**Decline**
Marketing objectives	Encourage trial, establish distribution	Get triers to repurchase, attract new users	Seek new users or uses	Reduce marketing expenses, keep loyal users
Product	Establish competitive advantage	Maintain product quality	Modify product	Maintain product
Distribution	Establish distribution network	Solidify distribution relationships	Provide additional incentives to ensure support	Eliminate trade allowances
Promotional	Build brand awareness	Provide information	Reposition product	Eliminate most advertising and sales promotions
Pricing	Set introductory price	Maintain prices	Reduce prices to meet competition	Maintain prices

Marketers must be sure that a product has moved from one stage to the next before changing its marketing strategy. A temporary sales decline should not be interpreted as a sign that the product is dying. Pulling back marketing support can become a self-fulfilling prophecy that brings about the early death of a healthy product.

concept check

- What is the product life cycle?
- Describe each stage of the product life cycle.
- What are the marketing strategies for each stage of the product life cycle?

→ **lg 5**

Pricing Products Right

An important part of the product development process is setting the right price. Price is the perceived value that is exchanged for something else. Value in our society is most commonly expressed in dollars and cents. Thus, price is typically the amount of money exchanged for a good or service. Note that perceived value refers to the time of the transaction. After you've used a product you've bought, you may decide that its actual value was less than its perceived value at the time you bought it. The price you pay for a product is based on the *expected satisfaction* you will receive and not necessarily the *actual satisfaction* you will receive.

Although price is usually a dollar amount, it can be anything with perceived value. When goods and services are exchanged for each other, the trade is called barter. If you exchange this book for a math book at the end of the term, you have engaged in *barter*.

Line extensions of Tostitos salsa products include new flavours such as salsa con queso, which help Tostitos increase its shelf space and brand recognition.

profit maximization
A pricing objective that entails getting the largest possible profit from a product by producing the product as long as the revenue from selling it exceeds the cost of producing it.

Pricing Objectives

Price is important in determining how much a firm earns. The prices charged customers times the number of units sold equals the gross revenue for the firm. Revenue is what pays for every activity of the company (production, finance, sales, distribution, and so forth). What's left over (if anything) is profit. Managers strive to charge a price that will allow the firm to earn a fair return on its investment.

The chosen price must be neither too high nor too low. And the price must equal the perceived value to target consumers. If consumers think the price is too high, sales opportunities will be lost. Lost sales mean lost revenue. If the price is too low, consumers may view the product as a great value, but the company may not meet its profit goals. Three common pricing objectives are maximizing profits, achieving a target return on the investment, and offering good value at a fair price.

Maximizing Profits

Profit maximization means producing a product as long as the revenue from selling it exceeds the cost of producing it. In other words, the goal is to get the largest possible profit from the product. For example, suppose Carl Morgan, a builder of houses, sells each house for $100 000. His revenue and cost projections are shown in Exhibit 9-9. Notice in column 3 that the cost of building each house drops for the second through the fifth house. The lower cost per house results from two things: First, by having several houses under construction at the same time, Morgan can afford to hire a full-time

| Revenue, Cost, and Profit Projections for Morgan's Houses

(1) Unit of Output (House)	(2) Selling Price (Revenue)	(3) Cost of Building House	(4) Profit on House	(5) Total Profit
1st	$100 000	$ 76 000	$ 24 000	$ 24 000
2nd	100 000	75 000	25 000	49 000
3rd	100 000	73 000	27 000	76 000
4th	100 000	70 000	30 000	106 000
5th	100 000	70 000	30 000	136 000
6th	100 000	77 000	23 000	159 000
7th	**100 000**	**90 000**	**10 000**	**169 000**
8th	100 000	115 000	(15 000)	154 000

crew. The crew is more economical than the independent contractors to whom he would otherwise subcontract each task. Second, Morgan can order materials in greater quantities than usual and thus get quantity discounts on his orders.

Morgan decides that he could sell 15 houses a year at the $100 000 price. But he knows he cannot maximize profits at more than seven houses a year. Inefficiencies begin to creep in at the sixth house. (Notice in column 3 that the sixth house costs more to build than any of the first five houses.) Morgan can't supervise more than seven construction jobs at once, and his full-time crew can't handle even those seven. Thus, Morgan has to subcontract some of the work on the sixth and seventh houses. To build more than seven houses, he would need a second full-time crew.

The exhibit also shows why Morgan should construct seven houses a year. Even though the profit per house is falling for the sixth and seventh houses (column 4), the total profit is still rising (column 5). But at the eighth house, Morgan would go beyond profit maximization. That is, the eighth unit would cost more than its selling price. He would lose $15 000 on the house, and total profit would fall to $154 000 from $169 000 after the seventh house.

Achieving a Target Return on Investment

target return on investment
A pricing objective where the price of a product is set so as to give the company the desired probability in terms of return on its money.

Another pricing objective used by many companies is **target return on investment**, where a price is set to give the company the desired profitability in terms of return on its money. Among the companies that use target return on investment as their main pricing objective are 3M, Procter & Gamble, General Electric, and DuPont.

To get an idea of how target return works, imagine that you are a marketing manager for a cereal company. You estimate that developing, launching, and marketing a new hot cereal will cost $2 million. If the net profit for the first year is $200 000, the return on investment will be $200 000 ÷ $2 000 000, or 10 percent. Let's say that top management sets a 15 percent target return on investment. (The average target return on investment for large corporations is now about 14 percent.) Since a net profit of $200 000 will yield only a 10 percent return, one of two things will happen: either the cereal won't be produced, or the price and marketing mix will be changed to yield the 15 percent target return.

Value Pricing

value pricing
A pricing strategy in which the target market is offered a high-quality product at a fair price and with good service.

Value pricing has become a popular pricing strategy. **Value pricing** means offering the target market a high-quality product, at a fair price, with good service. It is the notion of offering the customer a good value. Value pricing doesn't mean high quality that's available only at high prices. Nor does it mean bare-bones service or low-quality products. Value pricing can be used to sell a variety of products, from a $45 000 Jeep Grand Cherokee to a $2.99 package of L'eggs hosiery.

A value marketer does the following:

- *Offers products that perform.* This is the price of entry because consumers have lost patience with shoddy merchandise.
- *Gives consumers more than they expect.* Soon after Toyota launched Lexus, the company had to order a recall. The weekend before the recall, dealers phoned every Lexus owner in the United States and arranged to pick up their cars and provide replacement vehicles.
- *Gives meaningful guarantees.* DaimlerChrysler offers a 70 000-mile (about 113 000 km) power train warranty. Michelin recently introduced a tire warranted to last 80 000 miles (about 130 000 km).
- *Gives the buyer facts.* Today's sophisticated consumer wants informative advertising and knowledgeable salespeople.
- *Builds long-term relationships.* Air Canada's Aeroplan program, Hyatt's Passport Club, and Whirlpool's 800-number hot line all help build good customer relations.

concept check

- Explain the concept of price.
- What is meant by target return on investment, and how does it differ from profit maximization?
- What is value pricing?

➡ lg 6

How Managers Set Prices

After establishing a pricing objective, managers must set a specific price for the product. Two techniques that are often used to set a price are markup pricing and breakeven analysis.

Markup Pricing

markup pricing
A method of pricing in which a certain percentage (the markup) is added to the product's cost to arrive at the price.

One of the most common forms of pricing is **markup pricing**. In this method, a certain percentage is added to a product's cost to arrive at the retail price. (The retail price is thus *cost plus markup.*) The cost is the expense of manufacturing the product or acquiring it for resale. The markup is the amount added to the cost to cover expenses and leave a profit. For example, if Banana Boat suntan cream costs London Drugs $5 and sells for $7, it carries a markup of 29 percent:

Cost	$5	Cost to London Drugs
Markup	+2	London Drugs' markup to cover expenses (utilities, wages, etc.)
Retail price	$7	Banana Boat suntan cream price paid by the consumer

$$\text{London Drugs' markup percentage} = \frac{\text{Markup}}{\text{Retail price}}$$

$$= \frac{\$2}{\$7}$$

$$= 29\%$$

Several elements influence markups. Among them are tradition, the competition, store image, and stock turnover. Traditionally, department stores used a 40 percent markup. But today competition has forced retailers to respond to consumer demand and meet competitors' prices. A department store that tried to sell household appliances at a 40 percent breakeven point markup would lose customers to such discounters as Wal-Mart and Superstore. However, a retailer trying to develop a prestige image will use markups that are much higher than those used by a retailer trying to develop an image as a discounter.

Breakeven Analysis

Manufacturers, wholesalers (companies that buy from manufacturers and sell to retailers and institutions), and retailers (firms that sell to end users) need to know how much of a product must be sold at a certain price to cover all costs. The point at which the costs are covered and additional sales result in profit is the **breakeven point**.

To find the breakeven point, the firm measures the various costs associated with the product:

- **Fixed costs** do not vary with different levels of output. The rent on a manufacturing facility is a fixed cost. It must be paid whether production is one unit or a million units.
- **Variable costs** change with different levels of output. Wages and expenses of raw materials are considered variable costs.
- The **fixed-cost contribution** is the selling price per unit (revenue) minus the variable costs per unit.
- **Total revenue** is the selling price per unit times the number of units sold.
- **Total cost** is the total of the fixed costs and the variable costs.
- **Total profit** is total revenue minus total cost.

Knowing these amounts, the firm can calculate the breakeven point:

$$\text{Breakeven point in units} = \frac{\text{Total fixed cost}}{\text{Fixed-cost contribution}}$$

Let's see how this works: Grey Corp., a manufacturer of aftershave lotion, has variable costs of $3 per bottle and fixed costs of $50 000. Grey's management believes the company can sell up to 100 000 bottles of aftershave at $5 a bottle without having to lower its price. Grey's fixed-cost contribution is $2 ($5 selling price per bottle minus $3 variable costs per bottle). Therefore, $2 per bottle is the amount that can be used to cover the company's fixed costs of $50 000.

To determine its breakeven point, Grey applies the previous equation:

$$\text{Breakeven point in bottles} = \frac{\$50\ 000\ \text{fixed cost}}{\$2\ \text{fixed-cost contribution}}$$

$$= 25\ 000\ \text{bottles}$$

Grey Corp. will therefore break even when it sells 25 000 bottles of after-shave lotion. After that point, at which the fixed costs are met, the $2 per bottle becomes profit. If Grey's forecasts are correct and it can sell 100 000 bottles at $5 a bottle, its total profit will be $150 000 ($2 per bottle for 75 000 bottles).

By using the equation, Grey Corp. can quickly find out how much it needs to sell to break even. It can then calculate how much profit it will earn if it sells more units. A firm that is operating close to the breakeven point may change the profit picture in two ways. Reducing costs will lower the breakeven point and expand profits. Increasing sales will not change the breakeven point, but it will provide more profits.

concept check

- Explain how markups are calculated.
- Describe breakeven analysis.
- What does it mean to "break even"?

breakeven point
The price at which a product's costs are covered, so additional sales result in profit.

fixed costs
Costs that do not vary with different levels of output; for example, rent.

variable costs
Costs that change with different levels of output; for example, wages and cost of raw materials.

fixed-cost contribution
The selling price per unit (revenue) minus the variable costs per unit.

total revenue
The selling price per unit times the number of units sold.

total cost
The sum of the fixed costs and the variable costs.

total profit
Total revenue minus total cost.

Marketers promote their goods and services by creating advertisements that stimulate consumers to purchase them.

➡ lg 7

HOT Links

Star-Kist uses a variety of promotional methods to sell tuna. Get a peek at some of them at the company's consumer Web site at www.starkist.com

Promotional Goals

Most firms use some form of promotion. The meaning of the Latin root word is "to move forward." Hence actions that move a company toward its goals are promotional in nature. Because company goals vary widely, so do promotional strategies. The goal is to stimulate action. In a profit-oriented firm, the desired action is for the consumer to buy the promoted item. McCain's, for instance, wants people to buy more frozen foods. Not-for-profit organizations seek a variety of actions with their promotions. They tell us not to litter, to buckle up, join the army, and attend the ballet.

Promotional goals include creating awareness, getting people to try products, providing information, retaining loyal customers, increasing the use of products, and identifying potential customers. Any promotional campaign may seek to achieve one or more of these goals:

1. *Creating awareness.* All too often, firms go out of business because people don't know they exist or what they do. Small restaurants often have this problem. Simply putting up a sign and opening the door is rarely enough. Promotion through ads on local radio or television, coupons in local papers, fliers, and so forth can create awareness of a new business or product.

2. *Getting consumers to try products.* Promotion is almost always used to get people to try a new product or to get nonusers to try an existing product. Sometimes free samples are given away. Lever, for instance, mailed over 2 million free samples of its Lever 2000 soap to target households. Coupons and trial-size containers of products are also common tactics used to tempt people to try a product. Pepsi spent US$100 million trying to get consumers to try Pepsi One when it was introduced.[4]

3. *Providing information.* Informative promotion is more common in the early stages of the product life cycle. An informative promotion may explain what ingredients (like fibre) will do for your health, tell you why the product is better (high-definition television versus regular television), inform you of a new low price, or explain where the item may be bought.

   People typically will not buy a product or support a not-for-profit organization until they know what it will do and how it may benefit them. Thus, an informative ad may change a need into a want or stimulate interest in a product. Consumer watchdogs and social critics applaud the informative function of promotion because it helps consumers make more intelligent purchase decisions. Star-Kist, for instance, lets customers know that its tuna is caught in dolphin-safe nets.

4. *Keeping loyal customers.* Promotion is also used to keep people from switching brands. Slogans such as Campbell's "Soups are mmmmm good" and Tim Hortons' "Always fresh" remind consumers about the brand. Marketers also remind users that the brand is better than the competition. Dodge Ram trucks claim that they have superior safety features. For years, Pepsi has claimed it has the taste that consumers prefer. The Old Spaghetti Factory claims to be "a great place to wind up." Such advertising reminds customers about the quality of the product.

   Firms can also help keep customers loyal by telling them when a product or service is improved. Blockbuster guarantees that the hit movie you want to rent is in stock or it's free.

5. *Increasing the amount and frequency of use.* Promotion is often used to get people to use more of a product and to use it more often. When smoking was banned on domestic flights, Wrigley's began promoting its chewing gum as a good alternative

to smoking. The most popular promotion to increase the use of a product may be frequent-flyer programs. Air Canada has enrolled over 6 million frequent flyers. Hotel chains such as Marriott and Hyatt now have frequent-user programs.

6. *Identifying target customers.* Promotion helps find customers. One way to do this is to list a Web site. For instance, the *Wall Street Journal* and *Business Week* include Web addresses for more information on computer systems, corporate jets, colour copiers, and other types of business equipment, to help target those who are truly interested. Charles Schwab ads trumpet, "Learn more about investing online; go to **www.schwab.com**." A full-page ad in the *Wall Street Journal* for Compaq notebook computers invites potential customers to visit **www.compaq.com/whoa**, or call 1-800-AT-COMPAQ.

promotional mix
The combination of advertising, personal selling, sales promotion, and public relations used to promote a product.

The Promotional Mix

The combination of advertising, personal selling, sales promotion, and public relations used to promote a product is called the **promotional mix.** Each firm creates a unique mix for each product. But the goal is always to deliver the firm's message efficiently and effectively to the target audience. These are the elements of the promotional mix:

- *Advertising.* Any paid form of nonpersonal promotion by an identified sponsor.
- *Personal selling.* A face-to-face presentation to a prospective buyer.
- *Sales promotion.* Marketing activities (other than personal selling, advertising, and public relations) that stimulate consumer buying, including coupons and samples, displays, shows and exhibitions, demonstrations, and other types of selling efforts.
- *Public relations.* The linking of organizational goals with key aspects of the public interest and the development of programs designed to earn public understanding and acceptance.

The sections that follow examine the elements of the promotional mix in more detail.

concept check

- List and discuss the goals of promotion.
- What is the promotional mix?

advertising
Any paid form of nonpersonal presentation by an identified sponsor.

Advertising Builds Brand Recognition

Most Canadians are bombarded daily with advertisements to buy things. **Advertising** is any paid form of nonpersonal presentation by an identified sponsor. It may appear on television or radio; in newspapers, magazines, books, or direct mail; or on billboards or transit cards. The money that big corporations spend on advertising is mind-boggling. Total advertising expenses in this country are approximately $14.5 billion.[5] Labatt, for example, donated $2.5 million to the Toronto 2008 Olympic bid. This "donation" is a form of advertising used to promote the company's image as a good corporate citizen.[6]

In this section, you will learn about the different types of advertising, the strengths and weaknesses of advertising media, and the functions of an advertising agency.

product advertising
Advertising that features a specific good or service.

Types of Advertising

The form of advertising most people know is **product advertising,** which features a specific good or service. It can take many different forms. One special form is **comparative advertising,** in which the company's product is compared with competing, named products. Coca-Cola and Pepsi often use comparative advertising. Sprint

comparative advertising
Advertising that compares the company's product with competing, named products.

reminder advertising
Advertising that is used to keep a product's name in the public's mind.

institutional advertising
Advertising that creates a positive picture of a company and its ideals, services, and roles in the community.

advocacy advertising
Advertising that takes a stand on a social or economic issue; also called *grassroots lobbying*.

 **lg 10**

advertising media
The channels through which advertising is carried to prospective customers; includes newspapers, magazines, radio, television, outdoor advertising, direct mail, and the Internet.

audience selectivity
An advertising medium's ability to reach a precisely defined market.

HOT Links

How can you find the right magazine in which to advertise? The MediaFinder Web site at www.mediafinder.com has a searchable database of thousands of magazines.

advertising agencies
Companies that help create ads and place them in the proper media.

Canada claims that the only difference in their local telephone service, as compared to the traditional providers, is the price. Another special form is **reminder advertising,** which is used to keep the product name in the public's mind. It is most often used during the maturity stage of the product life cycle. Reminder advertising assumes that the target market has already been persuaded of the product's merits and just needs a memory boost. Tide laundry detergent, V-8 vegetable juice, and the FTD florist association use reminder promotion.

In addition to product advertising, many companies use **institutional advertising**. This type of advertising creates a positive picture of a company and its ideals, services, and roles in the community. Instead of trying to sell specific products, it builds a desired image and goodwill for the company. Some institutional advertising supports product advertising that targets consumers. Other institutional advertising is aimed at shareholders or the public. **Advocacy advertising** takes a stand on a social or economic issue. It is sometimes called *grassroots lobbying.* Energy companies often use this type of advertising to influence public opinion about regulation of their industry.

Choosing Advertising Media

The channels through which advertising is carried to prospective customers are the **advertising media.** Both product and institutional ads appear in all the major advertising media: newspapers, magazines, radio, television, outdoor advertising, direct mail, and the Internet. Exhibit 9-10 summarizes the advantages and disadvantages of these media. Each company must decide which media are best for its products. Two of the main factors in making that choice are the cost of the medium and the audience reached by it.

Media selection is also a matter of matching the advertising medium with the product's target market. If marketers are trying to reach teenage females, they might select *Seventeen* magazine. If they are trying to reach consumers over 50 years old, they may choose *Modern Maturity*. A medium's ability to reach a precisely defined market is its **audience selectivity.** Some media vehicles, like general newspapers and network television, appeal to a wide cross section of the population. Others—such as *Brides, Popular Mechanic, Architectural Digest,* MTV, ESPN, and Christian radio stations—appeal to very specific groups.

Advertising Agencies

Advertising agencies are companies that help create ads and place them in the proper media. Many firms rely on agencies to both create and monitor their ad campaigns.

Full-service advertising agencies offer the five services shown in Exhibit 9-11 on page 235. Members of the creative services group develop promotional themes and messages, write copy, design layouts, take photos, and draw illustrations. The media services group selects the media mix and schedules advertising. Researchers may conduct market research studies for clients or help develop new products or gauge the firm's or product's image. Merchandising advice may include developing contests and brochures for the sales force. Campaign design and planning are often wholly in the hands of the agency, although some firms prefer to do much of the work in-house, relying on the agency only for scheduling media and evaluating the campaign.

The Canadian Marketing Association (CMA) states that marketers acknowledge that high standards of practice are a fundamental responsibility to the public. Accordingly, the CMA has developed a code of ethics designed to set and maintain these standards. Included in these standards is "accuracy in representation." Advertising managers want to avoid having to drop or modify advertisements or

e x h i b i t   9 - 1 0 | Strengths and Weaknesses of Major Media

Medium	Strengths	Weaknesses
Newspapers	Geographic selectivity and flexibility Short-term advertiser commitments News value and immediacy Constant readership High individual market coverage Low cost	Little demographic selectivity Limited colour facilities Short-lived
Magazines	Good reproduction, especially colour Message permanence Demographic selectivity (can reach affluent audience) Regionality Local-market selectivity Special-interest possibilities Relatively long advertising life	Long-term advertiser commitments Slow audience buildup Limited demonstration capacities Lack of urgency Long lead time for ad placement May be expensive for national coverage

Radio	Low and negotiable costs
	High frequency
	Immediacy of message
	Relatively little seasonal change in
	    audience
	Highly portable
	Short scheduling notice
	Short-term advertiser commitments
	Entertainment carryover
		No visuals
		Advertising message short-lived
		Background sound
		Commercial clutter (a large number of ads
		    in a short time)

Television	Widely diversified audience
	Creative visual and audio opportunities
	    for demonstration
	Immediacy of message
	Entertainment carryover
		High cost
		Limited demographic selectivity
		Advertising message short-lived
		Consumer skepticism about advertising
		    claims

Network	Association with programming prestige	Long-term advertiser commitments
Local	Geographic selectivity Associated with programs of local origin and appeal Short lead time	Narrow audience on independent stations High cost for broad geographic coverage
Outdoor advertising	Repetition possibilities Moderate cost Flexibility	Short messages Lack of demographic selectivity Many distractions when observing the message

Direct mail	Very efficient with good mailing list
	Can be personalized by computer
	Can reach very specific demographic
	    market
	Lengthy message with photos and
	    testimony
		Very costly with poor mailing list
		May never be opened

Internet	Inexpensive global coverage Available at any time Interactive personalized message via e-mail	Not everyone has access Difficult to measure ad effectiveness

commercials. Not only does the controversy create ill will for the company, but the ad must be remade, which can be expensive. In addition, if a substitute commercial is unavailable, the timing of the campaign may be destroyed.

exhibit 9 - 11 | Functions of an Advertising Agency

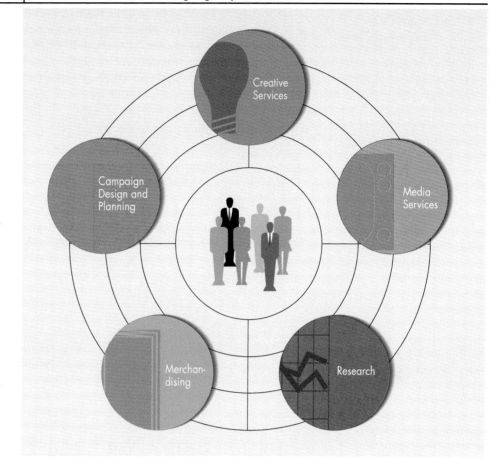

HOT Links

See which companies get the most complaints about their advertising at the Canadian Council of Better Business Bureaus Web site at
www.canadiancouncilbbb.ca

HOT Links

For more information about the Canadian Marketing Association and its governance, see
www.the-cma.org

HOT Links

Check out Advertising Standards Canada for an understanding of the Canadian code of Advertising Standards at
www.adstandards.com

➡ **lg 11**

public relations
Any communication or activity designed to win goodwill or prestige for a company or person.

publicity
Information about a company or product that appears in the news media and is not directly paid for by the company.

concept check

- Define five different types of advertising, and give examples.
- Indicate some of the strengths and weaknesses of the seven main advertising media.
- Describe the services offered by advertising agencies.

Public Relations Helps Build Goodwill

Like sales promotion, public relations can be a vital part of the promotional mix. **Public relations** is any communication or activity designed to win goodwill or prestige for a company or person. Its main form is **publicity,** information about a company or product that appears in the news media and is not directly paid for by the company. Publicity can be good or bad. Children becoming ill from eating tainted hamburgers is an example of negative publicity.

Naturally, firms' public relations departments try to create as much good publicity as possible. They furnish company speakers for business and civic clubs, write speeches for corporate officers, and encourage employees to take active roles in such civic groups as the United Way and the Chamber of Commerce. The main tool of the public relations department is the *press release*, a formal announcement of some newsworthy event connected with the company, such as the start of a new program, the introduction of a new product, or the opening of a new plant.

HOT Links

Learn how to write a press release at www.press-release-writing.com

New Product Publicity

Publicity is instrumental in introducing new products and services. Publicity can help advertisers explain what's different about their new product by prompting free news stories or positive word-of-mouth about it. During the introductory period, an especially innovative new product often needs more exposure than conventional, paid advertising affords. Public relations professionals write press releases or develop videos in an effort to generate news about their new product. They also jockey for exposure of their product or service at major events, on popular television and news shows, or in the hands of influential people.

Event Sponsorship

Public relations managers may sponsor events or community activities that are sufficiently newsworthy to achieve press coverage; at the same time, these events also reinforce brand identification. Sporting, music, and arts activities remain the most popular choices of event sponsors. Many sponsors are also turning to more specialized events that have tie-ins with schools, charities, and other community service organizations.

concept check

- What are the functions of a public relations department?
- Explain the concept of event sponsorship.

Factors That Affect the Promotional Mix

By sponsoring sporting events like the Women's World Cup Soccer championship, McDonald's, Fuji Film, and other marketers increase their brand awareness and enhance their corporate image.

Promotional mixes vary a great deal from product to product and from one industry to the next. Advertising and personal selling are usually a firm's main promotional tools. They are supported by sales promotion. Public relations helps develop a positive image for the organization and its products. The specific promotional mix depends on the nature of the product, market characteristics, and available funds.

The Nature of the Product

Selling toothpaste differs greatly from selling overhead industrial cranes. Personal selling is most important in marketing industrial products and least important in marketing consumer nondurables (consumer products that get used up). Broadcast advertising is used heavily in promoting consumer products, especially food and other nondurables. Print media are used for all types of consumer products. Industrial products may be advertised through special trade magazines. Sales promotion, branding, and packaging are roughly twice as important (in terms of percentage of the promotional budget) for consumer products as for industrial products.

Market Characteristics

When potential customers are widely scattered, buyers are highly informed, and many of the buyers are brand loyal, the promotional mix should include more advertising and sales promotion and less personal selling. But sometimes personal selling is required even when buyers are well informed and geographically dispersed, as is the case with mainframe computers. Industrial installations and component parts may be sold to knowledgeable people with much education and work experience. Yet a salesperson must still explain the product and work out the details of the purchase agreement.

Available Funds

Money, or the lack of it, is one of the biggest influences on the promotional mix. A small manufacturer with a tight budget and a unique product may rely heavily on free publicity. The media often run stories about new products and new businesses. This can help new and smaller businesses with funding their promotions. For example, Christopher Halpin of Manna Catering Services (see Chapter 5) is often featured in his local-market Saturday-morning news show and local newspaper. This form of promotion would be unavailable to him if he were required to pay for the exposure.

concept check

- Explain how the nature of the product, market characteristics, and available funds affect the promotional mix.

CAPITALIZING ON TRENDS IN BUSINESS

As customer expectations increase and competition becomes fiercer, perceptive managers will find innovative strategies to satisfy demanding consumers and establish unique products in the market. For example, strategies that build instant brand recognition and use technology to meet individual consumer needs will help ensure the ultimate success of new products. The explosive growth of Internet advertising and the impact of the digital VCR on television advertising are also discussed in this section.

Building Immediate Brand Recognition

Building brand recognition has traditionally been a long-term process. Popular brand names like Coca-Cola, Chevrolet, Sony, and Whirlpool took decades to become household words. Start-up technology companies, however, don't have decades to build brand recognition. To survive and thrive, they must use powerful, precise strategies for building rapid brand awareness. Consider that many Canadian households are familiar with America Online (AOL) and Yahoo. And PalmPilot, the electronic personal organizer, sold 1 million units in only 18 months, surpassing even the Sony Walkman.

How did these high-tech start-ups accomplish levels of brand recognition that took Procter & Gamble a generation? For one thing, they gave away lots of product. AOL is the leader in giveaways. For several years it has been blanketing the country with diskettes and CD-ROMs offering consumers a one-month free trial. For another, these companies rely heavily on public relations. Sun has built the visibility of Java—

HOT Links

See how Amazon.com uses the Internet to deliver personal customer service at

www.amazon.com

its flagship software platform—within the corporate community almost entirely through public relations techniques such as sending managers out on speaking tours and making high-profile announcements every time a licensing agreement is signed.

A third way to quickly build a brand is to use the Internet effectively. Amazon.com strives to make every customer interaction highly personal, the antithesis of the anonymous strip-mall experience. When customers log on to the site, they are welcomed by name and offered a list of recommended books based on previous purchases. Through a service called BookMatcher, Amazon.com asks customers to rate ten books. The ratings provide more insight into readers' preferences and enable BookMatcher to suggest additional titles the customers might like. All of this adds up to relationship marketing that land-based retailers can only dream about.

The Growth of Internet Auctions

HOT Links

Check out eBay for the most unusual item you can think of. It's probably there!

www.ebay.com

The Internet is also becoming the source of information on competitive prices. Name the product—computers, airline tickets, rare coins—and, chances are, there's a Web site where you can name your price. You can think of Internet auctions as a new distribution outlet where companies with excess inventory can reach eager customers. Web auctions aren't necessarily a great place to save money. The advantage of the auctions is that they give consumers access to products that are hard to find (like a concert poster from an old Rolling Stones tour) or that aren't available in stores (like overstocked computer inventory, refurbished laser printers, or last year's fancy consumer electronics equipment).

concept check

- How can a new company build immediate brand recognition?
- What advantages do Internet auctions offer to companies and to consumers?

The Growth of Web Advertising

The explosive growth of the Internet has led to similar growth in Web advertising. More that half of the Fortune 500 companies launched online advertising campaigns in the last quarter of 2002.[7] For companies whose businesses are based on the Internet, building a recognized brand name is important. With nothing to pick up or touch and hundreds of similar-sounding sites to choose from, online consumers have little to go on except a familiar name. In cyberspace, anyone with enough resources to rent space on a server and build some buzz for its brand is a potentially dangerous competitor.

There's a growing recognition among marketers, however, that the advertising tactics they have tried so far on the Web have been ineffective. The emotion-laden vignettes that work so well on TV simply don't excite viewers in cyberspace. Meanwhile, the established methods of Internet advertising don't do much better. Pop-up ads that just pop up on the screen are annoying interruptions to the online experience. Spending on banner ads is expected to drop as companies conclude that computer users are ignoring them. On the Internet, the consumer is in charge. That means marketers set on building their brands in the online world have to persuade consumers to participate in their marketing efforts. The latest theory on how to do that is called **rational branding.** The idea is to marry the emotional sell of traditional brand marketing—the message that links "Disney" with "family" or "Volvo" with "safety"— with a concrete service that is offered only online. Rational branding strives to both move and help the online consumer at the same time. In essence, the advertiser "pays" the consumer to endure the brand message by performing some kind of service. But the tactic poses a real challenge to makers of consumer products. There are very few

rational branding
A tactic for advertising on the Internet that combines the emotional aspect of traditional brand marketing with a concrete service that is offered only online.

ways to make soap or soda useful in the virtual world. Indeed, most of the top five buyers of TV advertising (General Motors, Procter & Gamble, Johnson & Johnson, Philip Morris, and Ford) are nearly invisible online.

The Impact of Digital VCRs on Television

Though the digital VCR is made of little more than a few integrated circuits, a power supply, and a massive multi-gigabyte hard drive, it will render traditional VCRs obsolete.[8] Here's why. Most people these days use VCRs to play prerecorded tapes. Although you can use a VCR to tape your favourite programs and watch them on your own time, that doesn't happen very often. The gadgets are too hard to use. This won't be the case with digital VCRs. With some simple programming through a remote control, a digital VCR will proactively record the shows you want to see. Tell it you are an Oprah Winfrey fan, and it automatically records all *Oprah* shows so that you can watch them when it's convenient. These devices take note of which programs you watch and recommend shows you didn't know about. They'll even record more than one show at a time.

Why will this technology affect advertising? The reason is that TV advertisers—not to mention viewers—are used to a world of synchronous viewing. For the past 50 years, shows have belonged in time slots, and people have watched whatever is on at that particular time. As a result, ad sales are typically based on Nielsen audience ratings, which measure how many people are watching a show at a given moment.

But the digital VCR makes it very easy to watch shows on your own time—in other words, asynchronously. Watching TV will be more like surfing the Web than viewing a movie. That may reduce the Nielsen influence and make it even more difficult to measure the size of the audience watching any single program. This, in turn, will make it more difficult for the television networks to price their airtime for commercials. It will also make it difficult for advertisers to know if the price is fair.

concept check

- Define rational branding, and explain why it may not be useful for all products.
- How will digital VCRs affect television advertising?

APPLYING THIS CHAPTER'S TOPICS

Two important points from this chapter apply directly to you now. By understanding how advertising is changing to benefit you, you will be a better-informed consumer. By realizing the importance of selling yourself, you will be better able to take advantage of life's opportunities.

Advertising Will Be More Beneficial to You

More and more advertising dollars will be directed to online promotion in the future. For the online advertiser, the challenge is to educate, entertain, or otherwise give you a benefit. Advertisers know that no one can be compelled to pay attention online—they must deliver benefits up front. If Colgate Palmolive wants to advertise toothpaste online, it needs more than photogenic lovers with toothy smiles. Unilever has created a Web site for Mentadent toothpaste that offers potential customers the chance to order a free sample, get oral-care advice, and send questions to a dental hygienist. Amazon.com, for example, will e-mail you to remind you of your spouse's birthday and anyone else you specify. Amazon.com will also e-mail you if a favourite author is conducting an online chat or has published a new work. It's a far cry from impersonal mass advertising. This is strictly for you. You can and should expect to receive benefits from online advertisers.

Using the Internet to Find Product Information

It has been said that people can raise their standard of living by one-third by becoming intelligent consumers. Now the Internet makes intelligent shopping easier than ever. You can go to *Consumer Reports* (**www.consumerreports.org**) on the Net and find out how products are ranked. Go to **www.bizrate.com** and compare products feature-by-feature and dollar-for-dollar. You can shop for an infinite variety of products and then ask your local retailer to meet or beat the price. You can also bid on almost anything in an Internet auction.

Always Sell Yourself

If you stop and think about it, all of us must be salespeople. If you are going to be successful in business, and in life in general, you must be a salesperson. You must be able to effectively explain and sell your plans, ideas, and hopes. A straight "A" student who can't do this will not be successful. Conversely, a "C" student who can will be successful. *Always* be prepared to sell yourself and your ideas. It's the best way to get ahead in business and in life.

TRY IT NOW!

1. **Check Your Prices** Travelocity.ca lets you check out prices for airline tickets, hotel rooms, and so on. You can compare the prices found here with those offered on the airline or hotel Web sites. Also look at Expedia.ca for more information. Become an informed consumer!

2. **Know When to Bid** If you decide to bid at an Internet auction, visit Auction Insider (www.auctioninsider.com) on the Web and learn how to be a smart bidder. This site offers strategies and tactics for the first-time bidder—including tips on how to avoid winning an auction that you're better off losing.

For example, Auction Insider advises against bidding on used items (not to be confused with refurbished items, which can be a good deal). It also provides updated rankings of the top 10 auction sites for computers, electronics, and collectibles, and lists hundreds of other auctions as well.

3. **Sell Yourself** Go to www.amazon.com and under the search engine type "selling yourself." Order one or more of the books available to improve your selling skills. Also, consider a Dale Carnegie training course. For more information, go to www.dale-carnegie.com/.

>looking ahead
at 4321ZIP

ZIP is planning to add new flights to various Canadian destinations over the next few months. These decisions will result from the consideration of many factors such as the state of the economy, the fate of Air Canada, the entrance of any new carriers, and so forth. Steve Smith is excited about ZIP's future. Check out the latest on ZIP at **www.4321zip.com**.

SUMMARY OF LEARNING GOALS

➡ lg 1   What is a product, and how is it classified?

A product is any good or service, along with its perceived attributes and benefits, that creates customer value. Tangible attributes include the good itself, packaging, and warranties. Intangible attributes are symbolic like a brand's image.

Most items are a combination of goods and services. Services and goods are often marketed differently. Products are categorized as either consumer products or industrial products. Consumer products are goods and services that are bought and used by the end users. They can be classified as unsought products, convenience products, shopping products, or specialty products, depending on how much effort consumers are willing to exert to get them.

Industrial products are those bought by organizations for use in making other products or in rendering services. Capital products are usually large, expensive items with a long life span. Expense items are typically smaller, less expensive items that usually have a life span of less than a year.

➡ lg 2   How does branding distinguish a product from its competitors?

Products usually have brand names. Brands identify products by words, names, symbols, designs, or a combination of these things. The two major types of brands are manufacturer (national) brands and dealer (private) brands. Generic products carry no brand name. Branding has three main purposes: product identification, repeat sales, and new product sales.

➡ lg 3   How do organizations create new products?

To succeed, most firms must continue to design new products to satisfy changing customer demands. But new product development can be risky. Many new products fail. To be successful, new product development requires input from production, finance, marketing, and engineering personnel. In large organizations, these people work in a new product development department. The steps in new product development are setting new product goals, exploring ideas, screening ideas, developing the concept (creating a prototype and building the marketing strategy), test-marketing, and introducing the product. When the product enters the marketplace, it is often managed by a product manager.

➡ lg 4   What are the stages of the product life cycle?

After a product reaches the marketplace, it enters the product life cycle. This cycle typically has four stages: introduction, growth, maturity, and decline (and possibly death). Profits usually are small in the introductory phase, reach a peak at the end of the growth phase, and then decline. Marketing strategies for each stage are listed in Exhibit 9-8 on page 226.

➡ lg 5   What is the role of pricing in marketing?

Price indicates value, helps position a product in the marketplace, and is the means for earning a fair return on investment. If a price is too high, the product won't sell well, and the firm will lose money. If the price is too low, the firm may lose money even if the product sells well. Prices are set according to pricing objectives. Among the most common objectives are profit maximization, target return on investment, and value pricing.

➡ lg 6   How are product prices determined?

A cost-based method for determining price is markup pricing. A certain percentage is added to the product's cost to arrive at the retail price. The markup is the amount added to the cost to cover expenses and earn a profit. Breakeven analysis determines the level of sales that must be reached before total cost equals total revenue. Breakeven analysis provides a quick look at how many units the firm must sell before it starts earning a profit. The technique also reveals how much profit can be earned with higher sales volumes.

➡lg 7 **What are the goals of promotional strategy?**

Promotion aims to stimulate demand for a company's goods or services. Promotional strategy is designed to inform, persuade, or remind target audiences about those products. The goals of promotion are to create awareness, get people to try products, provide information, keep loyal customers, increase use of a product, and identify potential customers.

➡lg 8 **What is the promotional mix, and what are its elements?**

The unique combination of advertising, personal selling, sales promotion, and public relations used to promote a product is the promotional mix. Advertising is any paid form of nonpersonal promotion by an identified sponsor. Personal selling consists of a face-to-face presentation in a conversation with a prospective purchaser. Sales promotion consists of marketing activities—other than personal selling, advertising, and public relations—that stimulate consumers to buy. These activities include coupons and samples, displays, shows and exhibitions, demonstrations, and other selling efforts. Public relations is the marketing function that links the policies of the organization with the public interest and develops programs designed to earn public understanding and acceptance.

➡lg 9 **What are the types of advertising?**

Institutional advertising creates a positive picture of a company. Advocacy advertising takes a stand on controversial social or economic issues. Product advertising features a specific good or service. Comparative advertising is product advertising in which the company's product is compared with competing, named products. Reminder advertising is used to keep a brand name in the public's mind.

➡lg 10 **What are the advertising media, and how are they selected?**

The main types of advertising media are newspapers, magazines, radio, television, outdoor advertising, direct mail, and the Internet. Newspaper advertising delivers a local audience but has a short life span. Magazines deliver special-interest markets and offer good detail and colour. Radio is an inexpensive and highly portable medium but has no visual capabilities. Television reaches huge audiences and offers visual and audio opportunities, but it can be very expensive. Outdoor advertising requires short messages but is only moderately expensive. Direct mail can reach targeted audiences, but it is only as good as the mailing list. The Internet is global in scope and can offer a personalized message response by e-mail, but as yet not everyone is on the Net.

➡lg 11 **How does public relations fit into the promotional mix?**

Public relations is mostly concerned with getting good publicity for companies. Publicity is any information about a company or product that appears in the news media and is not directly paid for by the company. Public relations departments furnish company speakers for business and civic clubs, write speeches for corporate officers, and encourage employees to take active roles in civic groups. These activities help build a positive image for an organization, which is a good backdrop for selling its products.

WORKING THE NET

1. Thousands of new products are introduced each year, but many don't stay on store shelves for long. Check out **www.newproducts.com** and give your opinion on the likelihood of success for some new products. Choose one or two products to review. What type of good is it (i.e., convenience, shopping, or specialty)? Evaluate its chances of succeeding. What pricing issues do you think the manufacturer will face?

2. You're working for a company that plans to introduce gourmet treats for pets. Your job is to determine the market for this new product and the marketing issues that may need to be addressed. Start your information search at **www.google.ca**. Search for "Canadian pets" and research pet ownership, pet food, and pet products. Write a short report summarizing the information.

3. Visit an online retailer such as Amazon.com (**www.amazon.com**) or eToys (**www.eToys.com**). Do online retailers have different pricing considerations from real-world retailers? Explain.

4. Do a search on Yahoo (**www.yahoo.com**) for online auctions for a product you are interested in buying. Visit several auctions and get an idea of how the product is priced. How do these prices compare with the price you might find in a local store? What pricing advantages or disadvantages do companies face in selling their products through online auctions? How do online auctions affect the pricing strategies of other companies? Why?

CREATIVE THINKING CASE

Personality Puffs and Cardio Chips

There was a time when potato chips were just potato chips, their greasy crunch leaving the snacker with an aftertaste of delicious guilt. No more. A new kind of chip aims at tackling the psyche rather than tickling the taste bud, promising to turn customers into kinder, happier, and gentler souls.

The secret? Herbs and plant extracts, such as St. John's wort, gingko biloba, and kava kava, are added to the chips along with essences of edible flowers—violet, chamomile, peppermint, and passion flower—to help combat depression, promote long life, and improve memory. "It's just one of those next steps in the evolution of snacks and food," said the chips' manufacturer, Robert Ehrlich. "There are definitely benefits from the product."

But not everyone is swallowing that claim. Some nutritionists have expressed concern that all the feel-good messages about the snacks are just advertising gimmicks to sell chips. "They're just ridiculous," said Norman Rosenthal, clinical professor of psychiatry and author of *St. John's Wort: The Herbal Way to Feeling Good.* "It would be like having a penicillin pie or an antibiotic apple strudel."

Ehrlich began making his mood-enhancing snacks four years ago. A group of herbalists, zen masters, a psychiatrist, and young consumers help put the products together. At 99 cents for a 2-ounce bag, the chips are sold in supermarkets—in the health food section—in the United States and in some parts of Europe, Asia, and South America.

Low-fat Cardio Chips containing a blend of natural herbs to improve cardiovascular health, metabolic conditions, the immune system, and aging are one of Ehrlich's products. His other herbal products include St. John's Wort Tortilla Chips to improve moods, Gingko Biloba Rings to enhance memory, and Kava Corn Chips to promote relaxation. Personality Puffs, which come in the shape of little people, are made up of a blend of flowers, St. John's wort, and gingko biloba.

Unlike other herbal products, Personality Puffs come with a set of printed rules that will "open you to the magic that is ready to happen in your life." Snackers are asked to buy at least two bags and give one away to a stranger within one hour of purchase. That, Ehrlich said, will create goodwill and kindness.[9]

Critical Thinking Questions

1. How would you classify these consumer goods?
2. Using the criteria discussed in the chapter, evaluate Ehrlich's brand names.
3. Describe the pricing strategy for the herbal chips.

CHAPTER 10

Achieving World-Class Operations and Timely Distribution

Nothing in an introductory text could indicate the integrative nature of business more quickly than the title of this chapter. Rather than look at each functional area on its own, this chapter combines two areas—operations and distribution—simply because it makes sense to do so. In this chapter we'll be examining the fourth of the four Ps—place (or distribution), as well as the operations area. Due primarily to the importance placed on managing the supply chain in today's businesses (that is, the route the product takes from provider to consumer), these two areas are inseparable.

The chapter starts with a discussion of Harley-Davidson's operations. For years Harley tried to sell freedom and adventure but with a poor-quality product sold at a high price due to outdated and inefficient facilities. Its *financial performance* was extremely poor because it simply did not *meet customer needs*—poor *quality* at a high price did not provide the customer with anything of value. Once it stopped trying to produce quantity and focused instead on quality, Harley turned it all around. Today the company is a leader in quality management. But it required a view of the business as a whole—meeting the needs of the customer (*marketing*) through *committed employees* (*human resources*) and providing quality (*operations*) at the lowest cost to improve the bottom line (*finance*).

As explained in the chapter, sound operations management is vital to the financial success of the company because this area accounts for as much as three-quarters of the company's costs. Therefore it must work very closely with the other functional areas to achieve maximum financial performance. Most obviously, operations must develop processes to provide for the demand created and forecasted by marketing, but it must also work with marketing to develop and design products so that the operations processes used to provide them are the most efficient and effective. Similarly, operations must work with human resources to have the right numbers of the best qualified people available to produce products and service customers, as well as deciding whether or not to replace this human effort with robots or other computerized techniques. In fact, most of the decisions made in the operations area have wider functional implications. For example, the choice of location can affect transportation costs and thus the final cost of the product as well as the availability and cost of labour, whereas implementing a flexible manufacturing system is expensive but needs little labour to operate and provides consistent quality products that meet individual customer specifications.

Another area where we can see the integration of operations with the other facets of our business model is in the external environment. Many businesses today are faced with environmental challenges in an effort to meet their operational goals. For example, in the *social* environment consumers are expecting customized products of greater quality delivered in a timely manner at a reasonable price. This requires using whatever *technology* is available to allow the company to stay ahead of the competition, and improving relationships with suppliers and vendors (both important *stakeholder* groups) so that there is a smooth flow from provider to consumer. If consumers don't get what they want, they will simply go to the increasing number of competitors in the global *economic* environment who can often produce at a lower cost.

The technology that is available to the operations area of a business has improved tremendously. The chapter outlines many of these new *innovations*. One of the most integrative examples of technology is manufacturing resource planning (MRPII). It uses a complex computerized system to integrate data from the different departments of the company so that they are all working as one to meet customer needs. Enterprise resource planning (ERP) takes this a step further by integrating information about suppliers and customers into the system. These technologies and others help to manage the supply chain so that the entire sequence from securing inputs into the process to delivering goods to the consumer is done in a manner that meets the needs of the customer at the highest possible level.

In this chapter, you'll learn about many trends in operations that allow companies to both enhance innovation in order to meet changing customer needs in a timely manner and adapt to changes in technology, at the same time improving quality, keeping costs down, and gaining employee commitment by involving teams of employees throughout the process. And isn't that what it's all about? Meeting the critical success factors by integrating the functional areas in the context of the dynamic business environment.

Achieving World-Class Operations and Timely Distribution

CHAPTER 10

Learning Goals

➡ **lg 1** Why is operations management important?

➡ **lg 2** What types of processes are used by manufacturers and service firms?

➡ **lg 3** Why are resource planning tasks such as inventory management and supplier relations critical to production?

➡ **lg 4** How do operations managers schedule and control processes?

➡ **lg 5** How can quality management and lean manufacturing techniques help firms?

➡ **lg 6** What are physical distribution (logistics) and logistics management?

➡ **lg 7** What are distribution channels and their functions? What are the three degrees of market coverage? How is physical distribution used to increase efficiency and customer satisfaction?

➡ **lg 8** What key trends are affecting the way companies manage operations?

Harley-Davidson Revs Up Operations

Harley-Davidsons (**www.harley-davidson.com**) aren't just motorcycles. They're a legend, known for their unique style, sound, and power ever since the first one was assembled in a backyard workshop in 1903. "People want more than two wheels and a motor," explains Harley-Davidson CEO Jeffrey Bleustein. "Harleys represent something very basic—a desire for freedom, adventure, and individualism."

Back in the 1980s, Harleys also represented everything that was wrong with manufacturing. The company's main factory was outdated and inefficient, keeping prices high. Quality was so poor that owners sometimes joked they needed two Harleys—one to ride and one for parts. Fed-up consumers started buying motorcycles made by Japanese and German manufacturers. Harley-Davidson's future looked grim.

To turn things around, the company designed new models and borrowed state-of-the-art quality and production techniques from Japanese manufacturers. It cut the number of parts stored in inventory at the company's factories, keeping costs—and prices—under control. As quality improved and prices stabilized, Harley-Davidson's sales began to climb.

By the mid-1990s, however, Harley's existing factories were having trouble keeping up with demand. Customers often had to wait a year or longer to get a new Harley. The choice was clear: either the firm must rev up its production capability, or it would risk losing customers to foreign competitors once again.

The first order of business was a new US$86 million factory in Kansas City. The 330 000-square-foot plant, opened in 1998, puts Harley-Davidson at the forefront of modern manufacturing and management practice.

In a special lightproof room, lasers automatically pierce holes in fenders for taillights and other attachments. Robots then polish the finished fenders, along with gas and oil tanks, while other robots paint the various components needed to build a Harley. The components are loaded onto three dozen specially designed carts that swivel 360 degrees and can be lowered or raised to suit different workers or tasks. The carts move among workstations where employees assemble motorcycle frames. By the end of the line, 70 employees have assembled 650 parts at 20 different workstations.

No motorcycle leaves the plant without a final stop at station 20. A team of test drivers revs up and rides each motorcycle, checking operating quality and listening for the classic Harley sound. Any bikes that don't meet rigid standards are sent back to the factory for adjustments and fine-tuning.

Employees are integral to the success of Harley's new factory. They are grouped in work teams, and every employee is cross-trained to perform a variety of production tasks. Each work team

CRITICAL THINKING QUESTIONS

As you read this chapter, consider the following questions as they relate to Harley-Davidson:

- How has a focus on manufacturing supported Harley-Davidson's growth?
- What factors outside the company have led to this focus?
- What are the implications for a company if it cannot deliver its products or services to its customers in a timely manner?

must constantly look for ways to build a better Harley. The result has been many employee-generated ideas for better equipment, factory layout, and production processes.

Looking back, CEO Bleustein believes production and operations have been vital to Harley-Davidson's continued growth. "In the last 10 years, we were very much internally focused," he says. "We had to fix our manufacturing and bring it to a new level. With that in place, our focus can be more external, bringing new and exciting products to the marketplace."[1]

→ lg 1

BUSINESS IN THE 21ST CENTURY

Finding the most efficient and effective methods of producing the goods or services it sells to customers is an ongoing focus of nearly every type of business organization. Today more than ever, changing consumer expectations, technological advances, and increased competition are all forcing business organizations to rethink where, when, and how they will produce products or services. Also, organizations must consider how to use a distribution system to enhance the value of a product or service. The customer focus is very important and we need to examine the methods available to move products to locations where consumers wish to buy them.

Like Harley-Davidson in the chapter's opening vignette, manufacturers are discovering that it is no longer enough to simply push products through the factory and onto the market. Consumers are demanding higher quality at reasonable prices. They often expect some degree of customization; the product must meet the customer's requirements. They also expect products to be delivered in a timely manner. Firms that can't meet these expectations often face strong competition from businesses that can. To compete, many manufacturers are reinventing how they make their products by developing new production processes (such as factory automation), tightening their relationships with suppliers, and seeking a better understanding of their customers' needs.

Service organizations are also facing challenges. Their customers are demanding better service, shorter waits, and more individualized attention. Just like manufacturers, service organizations are using new methods to deliver what customers need and want. Banks, for example, are using technology such as ATMs and the Internet to make their services more accessible to customers. Many colleges and universities now offer weekend courses or courses delivered over the Internet for students that cannot attend the traditional classes. Tax services are filing tax returns directly via the Internet.

In this chapter, we will examine how manufacturers and service firms manage and control the creation of products and services. Following a brief overview, we'll discuss production planning, including the choices firms must make concerning the type of production process they will use, the location where production will occur, and the management of resources needed in production. Next, we'll explain routing and scheduling, two critical tasks for controlling production and operations efficiency. Many businesses are improving productivity by employing new methods like quality control and automation. We will also look at transportation logistics and how the physical distribution can enhance customer satisfaction.

Operations Management—An Overview

operations
The creation of products and services by transforming inputs, such as natural resources, raw materials, human resources, and capital, into outputs, products, and services.

operations management
The design and management of the transformation process.

Operations, the creation of products and services, is an essential function in every firm. Production turns inputs, such as natural resources, raw materials, human resources, and capital, into outputs, products, and services. This process is shown in Exhibit 10-1. Managing this transformation process is the role of **operations management**.

| Operations Process for Products and Services

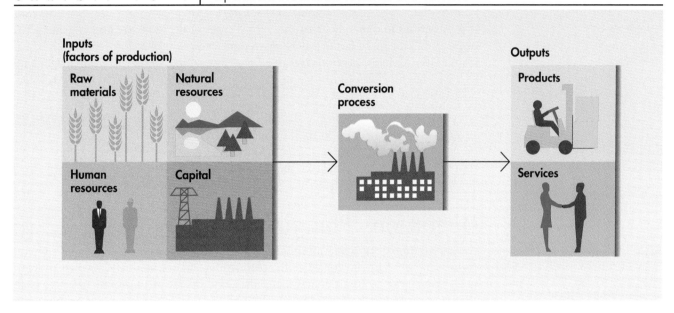

In the 1980s, many North American industries, such as automotive, steel, and electronics, lost customers to foreign competitors because their production systems could not provide the quality customers demanded. As a result, most of these companies, both large and small, now consider a focus on quality to be a central component of effective operations management.

The goal of customer satisfaction, closely linked to quality, is also an important part of effective operations. In the past, the manufacturing function in most companies was focused on efficiencies. Manufacturing had little contact with customers and didn't always understand their needs and desires and how they would use the product. Today, however, stronger links between customers (often through marketing efforts) and manufacturing have encouraged operations managers to be more outwardly focused and to consider decisions in light of their effect on customer satisfaction. Service companies have also found that making operating decisions with customer satisfaction in mind can be a competitive advantage. Also, service companies have been examining their processes to ensure they provide value to the customer and trying to avoid the "bureaucracy."

Operations managers, the personnel charged with managing and supervising the conversion process, play a vital role in today's firm. They control as much as three-fourths of a firm's costs, including inventories, wages, and benefits. They work closely with other major functions of the firm, such as marketing, finance, accounting, and human resources, to help ensure that the firm continually provides customer satisfaction. They face the challenge of combining people and other resources to produce high-quality goods and services, on time and at a reasonable cost. Working with customers, they help to decide which products to make or which services to offer. They become involved with the development and design of goods and services to determine what processes will be most effective.

Operations management involves three main types of decisions that are made at three different stages:

1. *Operations planning.* The first decisions facing operations managers come at the planning stage. At this stage, decisions are made regarding where, when, and how operations will occur. Resources are obtained and site locations determined.
2. *Operations control.* At this stage, the decision-making process focuses on scheduling, controlling quality and costs, and the actual day-to-day operations.

3. *Improving operations.* In the final stage, operations management focuses on developing more efficient methods of producing the firm's goods and services.

It is important to remember that these three types of decisions are ongoing and often occur simultaneously. In the following sections, we will take a closer look at the decisions and considerations firms face in each of these stages of operations management.

concept check

• Define operations and operations management.
• What are the three main types of decisions operations managers must make?

Operations Planning

operations planning
The aspect of operations management in which the firm considers the competitive environment and its own strategic goals in an effort to find the best methods.

An important part of operations management is **operations planning**. During operations planning, the firm considers the competitive environment and its own strategic goals in an effort to find the best methods. Good operations planning balances goals that may conflict such as providing high-quality service while keeping operating costs down, or keeping profits high while maintaining adequate inventories of finished products and service levels.

Operations planning involves three phases. Long-term planning has a time frame of three to five years (strategic issues). It focuses on which goods and services to provide, how much to produce, and where they should be produced. Medium-term planning decisions cover about two years (tactical issues). They concern the layout of factory or service facilities, where and how to obtain the resources needed for production, and labour issues. Short-term planning (operational issues) are usually shorter than a one-year time frame. The short-term planning converts these broader goals into specific production plans and materials management strategies.

Four important decisions must be made in operations planning. They involve the type of process that will be used, site selection, facility layout, and resource planning.

process
The way a good is made or a service provided.

Process

In planning, the first decision to be made is which type of **process**—the way a good is made or a service provided—best fits with the company's goals and customer demands. Another important consideration is the type of good or service being produced, as different goods and services may require different processes. In general, there are three types of processes: mass production, mass customization, and customization.

Mass Production

mass production
The ability to manufacture many identical goods or provide many identical services at once.

Mass production is the ability to manufacture many identical goods or provide many identical services at once. Henry Ford's Model-T automobile is a good example of mass production. Each car turned out by Ford's factory was identical, right down to its colour. If you wanted a car in any colour except black, you were out of luck. Canned goods, over-the-counter drugs, and household appliances are examples of goods that are still mass-produced. For services, an example would be the service that a ski lift provides. The emphasis in mass production is on keeping costs low by producing highly uniform products and services.

A quality-control employee inspects the uniformity of cookies, a product that is mass-produced to keep manufacturing costs low.

mass customization
A manufacturing process in which modules are mass-produced and then assembled to meet the needs or desires of individual customers.

customization
The production of goods or services one at a time according to the specific needs or wants of individual customers.

HOT Links

Check out what Dell has to offer at www.dell.com/ca

Mass Customization and Customization

In **mass customization**, a relatively new concept in manufacturing, modules are produced using mass production techniques. The modules can then be assembled to suit the customer's particular needs or desires. For example, Dell mass produces the modules that a customer can combine to customize his or her own computer.

Customization is the opposite of mass production. In customization, the firm produces goods one at a time according to the specific needs or wants of individual customers. Unlike mass customization, each product or service produced is unique. For example, a print shop may handle a variety of projects, including newsletters, brochures, stationery, and reports. Each print job varies in quantity, type of printing process, binding, colour of ink, and type of paper.

Some types of service businesses also deliver customized services. Doctors, for instance, usually must consider the individual illnesses and circumstances of each patient before developing a customized treatment plan. Real estate agents also develop a customized service plan for each customer based on the type of house the person is selling or wants to buy. The differences between mass production, mass customization, and customization are summarized in Exhibit 10-2.

In addition to production type, operations managers also classify processes in two ways: (1) by how inputs are converted into outputs and (2) by the timing of the process.

Converting Inputs to Outputs

The transformation process involves converting inputs (raw materials, parts, human resources) into outputs (products or services). In a manufacturing company, the inputs, the transformation process, and the final outputs are usually obvious. Harley-Davidson, for instance, converts steel, rubber, paint, and other inputs into motorcycles. The transformation process in a service company involves a less obvious conversion. For example, a hospital converts the knowledge and skills of its medical personnel, along with equipment and supplies from a variety of sources, into health care services for patients. Examples of the inputs and outputs used by other types of businesses are shown in Exhibit 10-3.

e x h i b i t   1 0 - 2 | Classification of Production Types

Mass Production	Mass Customization	Customization
Highly uniform products or services. Many products made sequentially.	Uniform and standardized production to a point, then unique features added to each product.	Each product or service produced according to individual customer requirements.
Examples: Breakfast cereals, soft drinks, and computer keyboards	Examples: Dell computers, tract homes, and Taylor Made Golf clubs.	Examples: Custom homes, legal services, and haircuts.

e x h i b i t   1 0 - 3 | Converting Inputs to Outputs

Type of Organization	Input	Output
Airline	Pilots, crew, flight attendants, reservations system, ticketing agents, customers, airplanes, fuel, maintenance crews, ground facilities	Movement of customers and freight
Grocery store	Merchandise, building, clerks, supervisors, store fixtures, shopping carts, customers	Groceries for customer sales
University	Faculty, curriculum, buildings, classrooms, library, students, staff	Graduates, public service
Manufacturer	Machinery, raw materials, plant, workers, managers	Finished products for consumers and other firms
Restaurant	Food, cooking equipment, serving personnel, chefs, dishwashers, host, patrons, furniture, fixtures	Meals for customers

process manufacturing
A transformation process in which the basic input is broken down into one or more outputs (products).

assembly process
A transformation process in which the basic inputs are either combined to create the output or transformed into the output.

There are two basic processes for converting inputs into outputs. In **process manufacturing**, the basic input (raw materials, parts) is broken down into one or more outputs (products). For instance, raw natural gas (the input) is processed to extract natural gas, sulphur, and other materials (the output). The **assembly process** is just the opposite. The basic inputs, such as parts, raw materials, or human resources, are either combined to create the output or transformed into the output. An airplane, for example, is created by assembling thousands of parts. Iron and other materials are combined and transformed by heat into steel. In services, customers may play a role in the transformation process. For example, a tax preparation service combines the knowledge of the tax preparer with the customer's information in order to complete tax returns.

Site Selection

One strategic decision that must be made early in production and operations planning is where to locate the facility, be it a factory or a service office. Site selection affects operating costs, the price of the product or service, and the company's ability to compete. For instance, the costs of shipping raw materials and finished goods can be as much as 25 percent of a manufacturer's total cost. Locating a factory where these and other costs are as low as possible can make a major contribution to a firm's success. Another consideration is the location of the major customers. Mistakes made at this stage can be expensive. It is hard and costly to move a factory or service facility once production begins. Firms must weigh a number of factors to ensure that the right decision is made.

Availability of Production Inputs

As we discussed earlier, organizations need certain resources in order to produce products and services for sale. Access to these resources, or inputs, is a huge consideration in site selection. For example, the availability and cost of labour are very important to both manufacturing and service businesses. Payroll costs can vary widely from one location to another because of differences in the cost of living, the number of jobs available, and the skills and productivity of the local work force. For services, typically there is a need to near the customers. However for some businesses technology is

HOT Links

Ontario? France? Sri Lanka? Get a clear picture of what these and other business locations offer at
www.corporatelocation.com

changing this. For example, many of the call centres that companies have set up are located in areas where the unemployment rate is high and where they could secure government incentives, and this has no effect the customers.

Executives must also assess the availability of raw materials, parts, and equipment for each production site under consideration. It can be costly to ship these resources long distances so companies that use heavy or bulky raw materials may choose to be located near suppliers. Mining companies want to be near ore deposits, oil refiners near oil fields, paper mills near forests, and food processors near farms.

Marketing Factors

Businesses must also evaluate how the location of their facility will affect their ability to serve their customers. For some firms, it may not be necessary to be located near customers. Instead, the firm will need to assess the difficulty and costs involved with distributing its goods to customers from the location chosen.

Other firms may find that locating near customers can provide marketing advantages. When a factory or service centre is close to customers, the firm can often offer better service at a lower cost. Other firms may gain a competitive advantage by locating their facilities so that customers can easily buy their products or services. The location of competitors may also be a factor. Businesses with more than one facility may also need to consider how far apart their locations should be in order to maximize market coverage and at the same time not compete with themselves. Some businesses, such as franchises, have rules that govern this situation.

Local Incentives

Incentives offered by governments may also influence site selection. Tax breaks are a common incentive. The locality may reduce the amount of taxes the firm will pay. Other government incentives can also convince businesses to choose one location over another. Local governments sometimes offer exemption from certain regulations or financial assistance in order to attract or keep production facilities in their area.

Manufacturing Environment

Another factor to consider is the manufacturing environment in a potential location. Some localities have a strong existing manufacturing base. When a large number of manufacturers, perhaps in a certain industry, are already located in an area, that area is likely to offer greater availability of resources, such as manufacturing workers, better accessibility to suppliers and transportation, and other factors that can increase a plant's operating efficiency.

International Location Considerations

In recent years, manufacturers in many industries have opened new production facilities internationally. There are often sound financial reasons for considering a foreign location. Labour costs are considerably lower in countries such as Singapore, Ireland, and Mexico. Labour costs are important, but companies have other considerations too when it comes to labour. They must also consider the skill level of the population, the literacy rate, productivity rate, and so on.

Hamilton, Ontario, is a world-class manufacturing city where a high percentage of the work force is employed in the steel and automotive industries, despite recent declines in the manufacturing sector.

Foreign countries may have fewer regulations governing how factories operate. Or with a foreign location, production may be closer to new markets. That's exactly why Cabot Corp.'s Microelectronics Materials Division decided to open a plant in Japan. The company, which makes industrial slurries that are used to form computer chips, recognized a growing demand for its product in Asia. Opening a plant in Japan gave the company the ability to take advantage of this market growth.[2]

Facility Layout

After the site location decision has been made, the next focus in planning is the facility's layout. Here, the goal is to determine the most efficient and effective design for the particular production process. For example, an assembly line set up at Big Rock Brewery is set up in order of how the product is put together with inbound materials unloaded at the beginning of the line and the outbound product loaded at the end of the line.

Service organizations must also consider layout, but they are more concerned with how it affects customer behaviour and employee movements. It may be more convenient for a hospital to place its freight elevators in the centre of the building, but doing so may block the flow of patients, visitors, and medical personnel between floors and departments.

There are three main types of facility layouts: product, process, and fixed-position layouts. All three layouts are illustrated in Exhibit 10-4.

Product Layout

The **product** (or **assembly-line**) **layout** is used for a continuous or repetitive production process. When large quantities of a product must be processed on an ongoing basis, the workstations or departments are arranged in a line with products moving along the line. Automobile and appliance manufacturers, as well as food-processing plants, usually use a product layout. Service companies may also use a product layout for routine processing operations. For example, film processors use assembly-line techniques.

Process Layout

The **process layout** arranges workflow around the production process. All workers performing similar tasks are grouped together. Products pass from one workstation to another (but not necessarily to every workstation). For example, all grinding would be done in one area, all assembling in another area, and all inspection in yet another. The process layout is best for firms that produce small batches of a wide variety of products, typically using general-purpose machines that can be changed rapidly to new operations for different product designs. For example, an auto-body repair shop (which would do painting, sanding, electrical, etc.) would use a process layout.

Fixed-Position Layout

Some products cannot be put on an assembly line or moved about in a plant. A **fixed-position layout** lets the product stay in one place while workers and machinery move to it as needed. Products that are impossible to move—ships, airplanes, and road and building construction projects—are typically produced using a fixed-position layout. Limited space at the project site often means that parts of the product must be assembled at other sites, transported to the fixed site, and then assembled. The fixed-position layout is also common for on-site services like housecleaning services, pest control, and landscaping.

product (assembly-line) layout
A facility arrangement in which workstations or departments are arranged in a line with products moving along the line.

process layout
A facility arrangement in which work flows according to the production process. All workers performing similar tasks are grouped together, and products pass from one workstation to another.

fixed-position layout
A facility arrangement in which the product stays in one place and workers and machinery move to it as needed.

e x h i b i t   1 0 - 4 | Facility Layouts

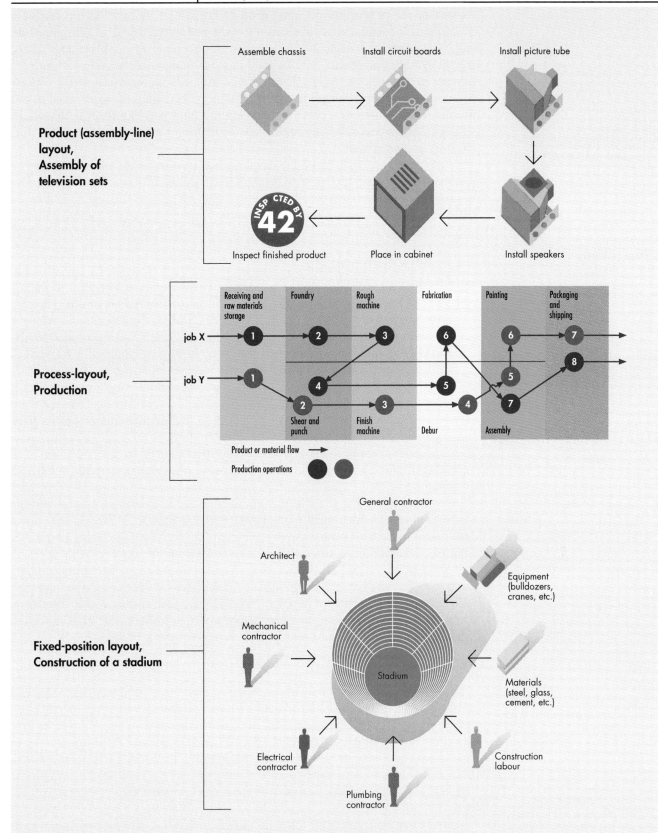

Product (assembly-line) layout, Assembly of television sets

Assemble chassis → Install circuit boards → Install picture tube → Install speakers → Place in cabinet → Inspect finished product (INSPECTED BY 42)

Process-layout, Production

Receiving and raw materials storage | Foundry | Rough machine | Fabrication | Painting | Packaging and shipping

job X → 1 → 2 → 3 → 6 → 6 → 7
job Y → 1 → 2 → 4 → 3 → 4 → 5 → 7 → 5 → 8

Shear and punch | Finish machine | Debur | Assembly

Product or material flow →
Production operations

Fixed-position layout, Construction of a stadium

General contractor
Architect
Mechanical contractor
Equipment (bulldozers, cranes, etc.)
Stadium
Materials (steel, glass, cement, etc.)
Electrical contractor
Plumbing contractor
Construction labour

SOURCE: From *Production and Operations Management* 8th edition by Gaither/Frazier. © 1999. Reprinted with permission of South-Western, a division of Thomson Learning: www.thomsonrights.com. Fax 800-730-2215.

➡ lg 3

Resource Planning

As part of the production planning process, firms must ensure that the resources needed for production, such as human resources, raw materials, parts, and equipment, will be available at strategic moments in the production process. This can be a huge challenge. The components used to build just one Bombardier aircraft, for instance, number in the millions. Cost is also an important factor. In many industries, the cost of materials and supplies used in the production process amounts to as much as half of sales revenues. Resource planning is therefore a large part of any firm's operations strategy. The process of buying operations inputs from various sources is called **purchasing**, or *procurement*.

Resource planning begins by specifying which raw materials, parts, and components will be required, and when, to produce finished goods. To determine the amount of each item needed, the expected quantity of finished goods to be produced must be forecast. A **bill of material** is then drawn up that lists the items and the number of each required to make the product.

purchasing
The process of buying production inputs from various sources; also called *procurement*.

bill of material
A list of the items and the number of each required to make a given product.

Internal or Outsourcing

make-or-buy decision
The determination by a firm of whether to make its own production materials or buy them from outside sources.

Next, the firm must decide whether to make its own materials or buy them from outside sources. This is the **make-or-buy decision**. Companies need to consider what are they in business to do and what their competitive strengths are. The quantity of items needed is another consideration. If a part is used in only one of many products, buying the part may be more cost-effective than making it. Buying standard items, such as screws, bolts, rivets, and nails, is usually cheaper and easier than producing them internally. Sometimes purchasing larger components from another manufacturing firm is cost-effective as well. Purchasing items from an outside source instead of making them internally is called **outsourcing**. Harley-Davidson, for example, purchases its tires, brake systems, and other motorcycle components from other businesses that make them to Harley's specifications. If a product has special design features that need to be kept secret to protect a competitive advantage, however, a firm may decide to produce all parts internally.

outsourcing
The purchase of items from an outside source rather than making them internally.

In deciding whether to make or buy, a firm must also consider whether outside sources can provide high-quality supplies in a reliable manner. Having to shut down production because vital parts weren't delivered on time can be a costly disaster. For example, General Motors relies on hundreds of suppliers for parts. When workers in two of the plants that supplied parts went on strike, GM was forced to shut down virtually all of its North American production.[3] Just as bad are inferior parts or materials, which can damage a firm's reputation for producing high-quality goods. Therefore, firms that buy some or all of their production materials from outside sources need to pay close attention to building strong relationships with quality suppliers.

Inventory Management

inventory
The supply of goods that a firm holds for use in production or for sale to customers.

A firm's **inventory** is the supply of goods it holds for use in production or for sale to customers. Deciding how much inventory to keep on hand is one of the biggest challenges facing operations managers. On the one hand, with large inventories, the firm can meet most production and customer demands. Buying in large quantities can also allow a company to take advantage of quantity discounts. On the other hand, large inventories can tie up the firm's money, are expensive to store, can become obsolete, and may decrease in quality if the inventory becomes old, expires, or goes bad.

inventory management
The determination of how much of each type of inventory a firm will keep on hand and the ordering, receiving, storing, and tracking of inventory.

Inventory management involves deciding how much of each type of inventory to keep on hand and the ordering, receiving, storing, and tracking of it. The goal of inventory management is to keep down the costs of ordering and holding inventories while maintaining enough on hand for production and sales. Good inventory management enhances product quality, makes operations more efficient, and increases profits. Poor inventory management can result in dissatisfied customers, financial difficulties, and even bankruptcy!

To control inventory levels, managers often track the use of certain inventory items. Most companies keep a **perpetual inventory,** a continuously updated list of inventory levels, orders, sales, and receipts, for all major items. Today, due to advances in technology, companies often use point-of-sale terminals to track inventory levels, calculate order quantities, and issue purchase orders at the right times.

Computerized Resource Planning

Many manufacturing companies have adopted computerized systems to control the flow of resources and inventory. **Materials requirement planning (MRP)** is one such system. MRP uses a master schedule to ensure that the materials, labour, and equipment needed for production are at the right places in the right amounts at the right times. The schedule is based on forecasts of demand for the company's products. It says exactly what will be manufactured during the next few weeks or months and when the work will take place. Sophisticated computer programs coordinate all the elements of MRP. The computer comes up with materials requirements by comparing production needs to the materials the company already has on hand. Orders are placed so items will be on hand when they are needed for production. MRP helps ensure a smooth flow of finished products.

Manufacturing resource planning II (MRPII) was developed in the late 1980s to expand on MRP. It uses a complex computerized system to integrate data from many departments, including finance, marketing, accounting, engineering, and manufacturing. MRPII can generate a production plan for the firm, as well as management reports, forecasts, and financial statements. The system lets managers make more accurate forecasts and assess the impact of production plans on profitability. If one department's plans change, the effects of these changes on other departments are transmitted throughout the company.

Whereas MRP and MRPII systems are focused internally, **enterprise resource planning (ERP)** systems go further and incorporate information about the firm's suppliers and customers into the flow of data. ERP provides timely information of a firm's major departments into a single source. For instance, production can call up sales information and know immediately how many units must be produced to meet customer orders. By providing information about the availability of resources, including both human resources and materials needed for production, the system allows for better cost control and eliminates production delays. The system automatically notes any changes, such as the closure of a plant for maintenance and repairs on a certain date or a supplier's inability to meet a delivery date, so that all functions can adjust accordingly. ERP is being used to improve operations not only in large corporations, such as Bombardier and General Motors, but in small businesses as well.

Supply Chain Management

In the past, the relationship between purchasers and suppliers was often competitive and antagonistic. Businesses used many suppliers and switched among them frequently. During contract negotiations, each side would try to get better terms at the expense of the other. Communication between purchasers and suppliers was often limited to purchase orders and billing statements.

Today, however, many firms are moving toward a new concept in supplier relationships. The emphasis is increasingly on developing a strong **supply chain.** The supply chain can be thought of as the entire sequence of securing inputs, producing goods, and delivering goods to customers. If any of the links in this process are weak, the customers—the end point of the supply chain—will end up dissatisfied since they are not receiving the products they want in a timely manner.

perpetual inventory
A continuously updated list of inventory levels, orders, sales, and receipts.

materials requirement planning (MRP)
A computerized system of controlling the flow or resources and inventory. A master schedule is used to ensure that the materials, labour, and equipment needed for production are at the right places in the right amounts at the right times.

manufacturing resource planning II (MRPII)
A complex computerized system that integrates data from many departments to control the flow of resources and inventory.

enterprise resource planning (ERP)
A computerized resource planning system that includes information about the firm's suppliers and customers as well as data generated internally.

supply chain
The entire sequence of securing inputs, producing goods, and delivering goods to customers.

Strategies for Supply Chain Management

Ensuring a strong supply chain requires that firms implement supply chain management strategies. **Supply chain management** focuses on using information along the supply chain, with the ultimate goal of satisfying customers with quality products and services. A critical element of effective supply chain management is to work closely with suppliers. In many cases, this means reducing the number of suppliers used and asking those suppliers to offer more services or better prices in return for long-term contracts, often with guaranteed volumes. Instead of being viewed as "outsiders" in the production process, many suppliers are now playing an important role in supporting the operations of their customers. They are expected to meet higher quality standards, offer suggestions that can help reduce production costs, and even contribute to the design of new products.

Improving Supplier Communications

Underlying supply chain management is the development of strong communications with suppliers. Technology is providing new ways to do this. Some manufacturing firms are using the Internet to keep key suppliers informed about their requirements. Intel, for example, has set up a special Web site for its suppliers and potential suppliers. Would-be suppliers can visit the site to get information about doing business with Intel; once they are approved, they can access a secure area to make bids on Intel's current and future resource needs. The Internet also streamlines purchasing by providing firms with quick access to a huge database of information about the products and services of hundreds of potential suppliers.

Another communications tool is **electronic data interchange (EDI)**, in which two trading partners exchange information electronically, such as order placement. EDI can be conducted via a linked computer system or over the Internet. The advantages of exchanging information with suppliers electronically include speed, accuracy, and lowered communication costs.

supply chain management
The process of using information along the supply chain so that the firm can satisfy its customers with quality products and services; includes working closely with suppliers.

electronic data interchange (EDI)
The electronic exchange of information between two trading partners.

routing
The aspect of production control that involves setting out the workflow—the sequence of machines and operations through which the product or service progresses from start to finish.

c o n c e p t   c h e c k

- Describe the various types of processes and explain for what type of firm each is best suited.
- What factors does a firm consider when making a site selection decision?
- Describe the various types of facility layouts and explain for what type of production each is best suited.
- How is technology being used in resource planning?

➡ lg 4

Operations Control

Every company needs to have systems in place to see that operations are carried out as planned and to correct errors when they are not. The area of operations control that is concerned with the coordination of materials, equipment, and human resources to achieve operating efficiencies is called production control. Two of its key aspects are routing and scheduling.

Routing Production

Routing is the first step in controlling production. It sets out a workflow, that is, the sequence of machines and operations through which a product or service progresses from start to finish. Routing depends on the type of goods being produced and the facility layout. Good routing procedures increase productivity and cut unnecessary costs.

McDonald's has experimented with new food preparation routes in many of its restaurants. The changes are part of McDonald's "Made For You" program, a strategic decision to offer customers more choices in how their orders are prepared. First, the restaurant chain redesigned its kitchens to improve the way orders are prepared and routed through the kitchen. New high-tech food preparation equipment that automates much of the order preparation process was added. Finally, a centralized computer system improved the flow of communications between the customer counter and the kitchen. When a customer orders a Big Mac, the order taker enters it into a specially designed cash register that simultaneously sends the information to a video screen in the kitchen. Before the customer has even finished paying, kitchen workers have almost a third of the order completed. Within a few moments, the order, including customizations such as extra ketchup or tomatoes, is on its way out to the customer.[4]

Scheduling

Closely related to routing is **scheduling.** Scheduling involves specifying and controlling the time required for each step in the production process. The operations manager prepares timetables showing the most efficient sequence of production and then tries to ensure that the necessary materials and labour are in the right place at the right time.

Scheduling is important to both manufacturing and service firms. The production manager in a factory schedules material deliveries, work shifts, and production processes. Trucking companies schedule drivers, clerks, truck maintenance and repair with customer transportation needs. Scheduling at a university or college entails deciding when to offer which courses in which classrooms with which instructors. A museum must schedule its special exhibits, ship the works to be displayed, market its services, and conduct educational programs and tours.

Scheduling can range from simple to complex. Giving numbers to customers waiting in a bakery and making interview appointments with job applicants are examples of simple scheduling. Organizations that must produce large quantities of products or services, or service a diverse customer base, face more complex scheduling problems (e.g., ZIP Airlines).

Three common scheduling tools used for complex situations are Gantt charts, the critical path method, and PERT.

Gantt Charts

Named after their originator, Henry Gantt, **Gantt charts** are bar graphs plotted on a time line that show the relationship between scheduled and actual production. Exhibit 10-5 is an example. On the left, the chart lists the activities required to complete the job or project. Both the scheduled time and the actual time required for each activity are shown, so the manager can easily judge progress.

Gantt charts are most helpful when only a few tasks are involved, when task times are relatively long (days or weeks rather than hours), and when job routes are short and simple. In the past, one of the biggest shortcomings of Gantt charts was that they were static (i.e., not flexible), but now there are various planning software packages that allow for adjustments, so this is less of an issue. Another problem is that they fail to show how tasks are related.

The Critical Path Method and PERT

To control large projects, operations managers need to closely monitor resources, costs, quality, and budgets. They also must be able to see the "big picture"—the interrelationships of the many different tasks necessary to complete the project. Finally, they must be able to revise scheduling and divert resources quickly if any tasks fall behind schedule. The critical path method (CPM) and the program evaluation and review technique (PERT) are related project management tools that were developed in the 1950s to help managers accomplish this.

Redesigned food preparation routes and a computer system that links kitchen workers with order takers are helping McDonald's to serve customized food quickly.

scheduling
The aspect of production control that involves specifying and controlling the time required for each step in the production process.

Gantt charts
Bar graphs plotted on a time line that show the relationship between scheduled and actual production.

exhibit 10-5 | A Typical Gantt Chart

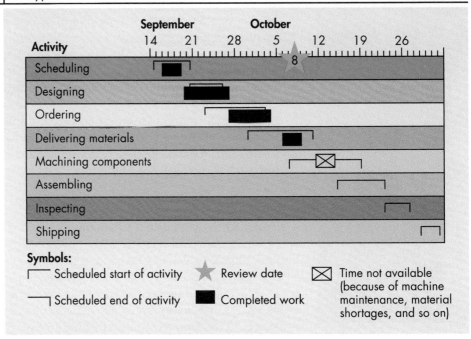

critical path method (CPM)
A scheduling tool that enables a manager to determine the critical path of activities for a project—the activities that will cause the entire project to fall behind schedule if they are not completed on time.

critical path
In a critical path method network, the longest path through the linked activities.

In the **critical path method (CPM)**, the manager identifies all of the activities required to complete the project, the relationships between these activities, and the order in which they need to be completed. Then, the manager develops a diagram that uses arrows to show how the tasks are dependent on each other. The longest path through these linked activities is called the **critical path**. If the tasks on the critical path are not completed on time, the entire project will fall behind schedule.

To better understand how CPM works, look at Exhibit 10-6, which shows a CPM diagram for constructing a house. All of the tasks required to finish the house and an estimated time for each have been identified. The arrows indicate the links between the various steps and their required sequence. As you can see, most of the jobs to be done

exhibit 10-6 | A CPM Network for Building a House

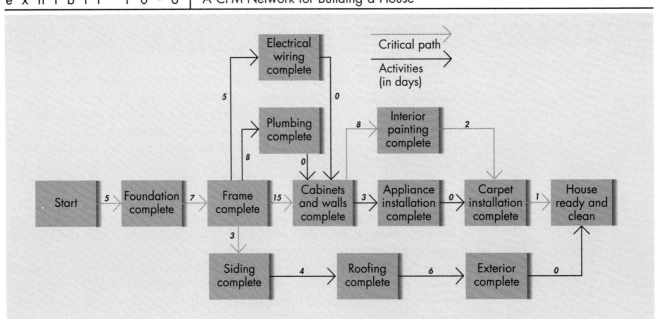

can't be started until the house's foundation and frame are completed. It will take five days to finish the foundation and another seven days to erect the house frame. The activities linked by orange arrows form the critical path for this project. It tells us that the fastest possible time the house can be built is 38 days, the total time needed for all of the critical path tasks. The non-critical path jobs, those connected with black arrows, can be delayed a bit or done early. Short delays in installing appliances or roofing won't delay construction of the house because these activities don't lie on the critical path.

Like CPM, **program evaluation and review technique (PERT)** helps managers identify critical tasks and assess how delays in certain activities will affect operations or production. In both methods, managers use diagrams to see how operations and production will flow. PERT differs from CPM in one important respect, however. CPM assumes that the amount of time needed to finish a task is known with certainty; therefore, the CPM diagram shows only one number for the time needed to complete each activity. In contrast, PERT assigns three time estimates for each activity: an optimistic time for completion, the most probable time, and a pessimistic time. These estimates allow managers to anticipate delays and potential problems and schedule accordingly.

program evaluation and review technique (PERT)
A scheduling tool that is similar to the CPM method but assigns three time estimates for each activity (optimistic, most probable, and pessimistic); allows managers to anticipate delays and potential problems and schedule accordingly.

concept check

- What is production control, and what are its key aspects?
- Identify and describe three commonly used scheduling tools.

➡ **lg 5**

Process Improvement

Competing in today's business world is difficult. The process of producing and delivering goods and services is becoming increasingly complex. Customers are demanding higher levels of quality and satisfaction. The lower production costs enjoyed by many foreign competitors can be difficult to compete against. In light of these challenges, businesses are continually looking for new ways to keep quality high, costs low, and processes flowing smoothly. Among the methods that many companies have successfully implemented are total quality management, lean manufacturing, and automation.

Total Quality Management

Successful businesses recognize that quality and productivity are interrelated. Defective products waste materials and time, thus increasing costs. Worse, poor quality causes customer dissatisfaction; this often can mean the loss of the current sales (i.e., returns) and future sales.

To a consumer, quality is how well a good serves its purpose or a service meets their needs. From the company's point of view, quality is the degree to which a good or service conforms to a set of predetermined standards, such as dimensions or timeliness. **Quality control** involves creating those quality standards and measuring finished products and services against them. At one time quality control was simply a matter of inspecting products before they went out the door. Today, it's a company-wide commitment that involves every facet of operations, with an emphasis on doing it right the first time.

One of the first to say that quality control should be a company-wide goal was an American, Dr. W. Edwards Deming. His ideas were adopted by the Japanese in the 1950s but largely ignored in North America until the 1980s when NBC aired *If Japan Can, Why Can't We*. Deming suggested that merely inspecting products after they are produced is not enough to ensure quality. He believed that quality control must start

quality control
The process of creating standards for quality and then measuring finished products and services against them.

total quality management (TQM)
The use of quality principles in all aspects of a company's production and operations.

with top management, who must foster a culture dedicated to producing quality. Teamwork between managers and workers helps to identify ways to improve the production process, leading to better quality.

Total quality management (TQM) refers to the use of quality principles in all aspects of a company's production and operations. It emphasizes that all employees involved with bringing a product or service to customers—marketing, purchasing, accounting, shipping, manufacturing—contribute to its quality. TQM focuses on improving operations to achieve greater efficiency and, in turn, higher quality. Nearly every decision involved in production and operations management can affect a firm's ability to produce high-quality products and services.

The Move toward Lean Manufacturing

lean manufacturing
Streamlining production by eliminating steps in the production process that do not add benefits that customers are willing to pay for.

Manufacturers are discovering that they can better respond to rapidly changing customer demands, while keeping inventory and production costs down, by adopting lean manufacturing techniques. **Lean manufacturing** can be defined as streamlining production by eliminating steps in the production process that do not add benefits that customers are willing to pay for. In other words, non-value-added production processes are eliminated so that the company can concentrate its production and operations resources on items essential to satisfying customers. Toyota was a pioneer in developing these techniques, but today manufacturers in many industries have also adopted the lean manufacturing philosophy.

just-in-time (JIT)
A system in which materials arrive exactly when they are needed for production, rather than being stored on site.

Another Japanese concept, **just-in-time (JIT)**, is closely related to lean manufacturing. JIT is based on the belief that materials should arrive exactly when they are needed for production, rather than being stored on site. Relying closely on computerized systems such as MRP, MRPII, and ERP, manufacturers determine what parts will be needed and when, and then order them from suppliers so they arrive "just in time." Under the JIT system, inventory and products are "pulled" through the production process in response to customer demand. JIT requires close teamwork between vendors and production and purchasing personnel because any delay in deliveries of supplies could bring JIT production to a halt. If employed properly, however, a JIT system can greatly reduce inventory holding costs and can also smooth production cycles.

Automation Operations Management

Technology is helping many firms improve their operating efficiency and ability to compete. Computer systems, in particular, are enabling businesses to automate production and the provision of services in ways never before possible.

Among the technologies helping to automate manufacturing are computer-aided design (CAD, the use of computers to design and test new products and modify existing ones), computer-aided manufacturing (CAM, the use of computers to develop and control the production process), and robotics (the technology involved in designing, constructing, and operating computer-controlled machines that can perform tasks independently). Another technology is the flexible manufacturing system (FMS). This system combines automated workstations with computer-controlled transportation devices—automatic guided vehicles (AGVs)—that move materials between workstations and into and out of the system. In addition, computer-integrated manufacturing (CIM) combines computerized manufacturing processes (like robots and flexible manufacturing systems) with other computerized systems that control design, inventory, production, and purchasing.

Technology and Automation in Nonmanufacturing Operations

Manufacturers are not the only businesses benefiting from technology. Nonmanufacturing firms are also using automation to improve customer service and productivity. Banks now offer services to customers through automated teller machines (ATMs), via automated telephone systems, and even over the Internet. Retail stores of all kinds use point-of-sale (POS) terminals that track inventories, identify items that need to be reordered, and tell which products are selling well. Wal-Mart, the leader in retailing automation, has its own satellite system connecting POS terminals directly to its distribution centres and headquarters.

Consider how technology and automation have helped the airline industry and consumers. Today airline reservation systems are able to search various routes at different times to secure the best fare for passengers. Customers can also search various Web sites, find the best pricing and the best routes, and book their seats, meals, car rentals, and so on.

With computer-aided design, engineers can design, analyze, modify, and test prototypes before products are manufactured.

concept check

- Define total quality management, lean manufacturing, and just-in-time, and explain how each can help a firm improve its production and operations.
- How are both manufacturing and nonmanufacturing firms using technology and automation to improve operations?

HOT Links

Travel through Travelocity's Web site to find out what is available for your next trip at www.travelocity.ca

physical distribution (logistics)
The movement of products from the producer to industrial users and consumers.

manufacturer
A producer; an organization that converts raw materials to finished products.

logistics management
The management of the physical distribution process.

vendor-managed inventory
A system of managing inventory in which the supplier manages the distributor's inventory, thereby reversing the traditional arrangement.

The Role of Distribution

Physical distribution (logistics) is the movement of products from the producer or **manufacturer,** to industrial users and consumers. It is important to note that timely distribution (i.e., when the customer wants the product) is imperative for customer satisfaction. Physical distribution activities are usually the responsibility of the marketing department and are part of the large series of activities included in the supply chain. As discussed earlier, a supply chain is the system through which an organization acquires raw material, produces products, and delivers the products and services to its customers. Exhibit 10-7 illustrates a supply chain. The physical distribution process is managed through **logistics management,** which involves managing (1) the movement of raw materials, (2) the movement of materials and products within plants and warehouses, and (3) the movement of finished goods to intermediaries and buyers. Supply chain management helps increase the efficiency of logistics service by minimizing inventory and moving goods efficiently from producers to the ultimate users.[5]

A recent innovation in logistics management is **vendor-managed inventory,** pioneered by Wal-Mart when it challenged the traditional roles of suppliers and distributors in building its superb supply chain. Using its vast wealth of sales information and working directly with manufacturers, the company surrendered responsibility for managing its warehouse inventories to its suppliers in exchange for having the right products delivered to the right store exactly when needed. Key manufacturers like Procter & Gamble placed managers at Wal-Mart's headquarters; there they managed

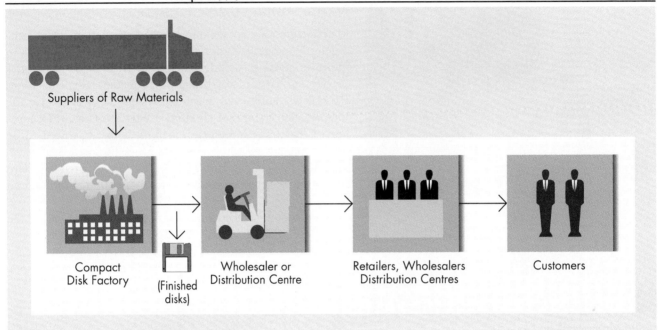

An efficient distribution system allows Home Depot to offer customers a vast assortment of building materials, appliances, and tools.

the restocking of stores, replacing Wal-Mart buyers. The outside managers also pooled sales information and market research with Wal-Mart executives, helping the retailer improve store sales and the manufacturers to focus their marketing efforts. Vendor-managed inventory is now sweeping across a variety of industries from processed foods to health care.

concept check

- Define physical distribution and logistics management
- What are the advantages of vendor-managed inventory?

The Nature and Functions of Distribution Channels

On their way from producers to end users and consumers, goods and services pass through a series of marketing entities known as a **distribution channel.** This section will look first at the entities that make up a distribution channel and then will examine the functions that channels serve.

distribution channel
The series of marketing entities through which goods and services pass on their way from producers to end users.

marketing intermediaries
Organizations that assist in moving goods and services from producers to end users.

agents
Sales representatives of manufacturers and wholesalers.

brokers
Go-betweens that bring buyers and sellers together.

industrial distributors
Independent wholesalers that buy related product lines from many manufacturers and sell them to industrial users.

wholesalers
Firms that sell finished goods to retailers, manufacturers, and institutions.

retailers
Firms that sell goods to consumers and to industrial users for their own consumption.

Marketing Intermediaries in the Distribution Channel

A distribution channel is made up of **marketing intermediaries,** or organizations that assist in moving goods and services from producers to end users and consumers. Marketing intermediaries are so called because they are in the middle of the distribution process between the producer and the end user. The following marketing intermediaries most often appear in the distribution channel:

- *Agents and brokers.* **Agents** are sales representatives of manufacturers and wholesalers, and **brokers** are entities that bring buyers and sellers together. Both agents and brokers are usually hired on commission basis by either a buyer or a seller. Agents and brokers are go-betweens whose job is to make deals. They do not own or take possession of goods.
- *Industrial distributors.* **Industrial distributors** are independent wholesalers that buy related product lines from many manufacturers and sell them to industrial users. They often have a sales force to call on purchasing agents, make deliveries, extend credit, and provide information. Industrial distributors are used in such industries as aircraft manufacturing, mining, and petroleum.
- *Wholesalers.* **Wholesalers** are firms that sell finished goods to retailers, manufacturers, and institutions (such as schools and hospitals). Historically, their function has been to buy from manufacturers and sell to retailers.
- *Retailers.* **Retailers** are firms that sell goods to consumers and to industrial users for their own consumption.

At the end of the distribution channel are final consumers, like you and me, and industrial users. Industrial users are firms that buy products for internal use or for producing other products or services. They include manufacturers, utilities, airlines, railroads, and service institutions, such as hotels, hospitals, and schools.

Exhibit 10-8 shows various ways marketing intermediaries can be linked. For instance, a manufacturer may sell to a wholesaler that sells to a retailer that in turn sells to a customer. In any of these distribution systems, goods and services are physically transferred from one organization to the next. As each takes possession of the products, it may take legal ownership of them. As the exhibit indicates, distribution channels can handle either consumer products or industrial products.

The Functions of Distribution Channels

Why do distribution channels exist? Why can't every firm sell its products directly to the end user or consumer? Why are go-betweens needed? Channels serve a number of functions.

Channels Reduce the Number of Transactions

Channels make distribution simpler by reducing the number of transactions required to get a product from the manufacturer to the consumer. Assume for the moment that only four students are in your class. Also assume that your professor requires five textbooks, each from a different publisher. If there were no bookstore, 20 transactions would be necessary for all students in the class to buy the books, as shown in Exhibit 10-9 on page 267. If the bookstore serves as a go-between, the number of transactions is reduced to nine. Each publisher sells to one bookstore rather than to four students. Each student buys from one bookstore instead of from five publishers.

Dealing with channel intermediaries frees producers from many of the details of distribution activity. Producers are traditionally not as efficient or as enthusiastic about selling products directly to end users as channel members are. First, producers may wish to focus on production. They may feel that they cannot both produce and distribute in a competitive way. Some firms also may not have the resources to invest in distributing their products.

e x h i b i t   1 0 - 8 | Channels of Distribution for Industrial and Consumer Products

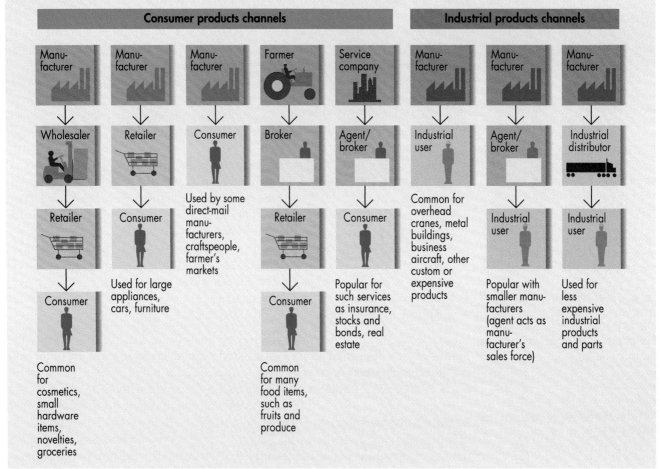

Channels Ease the Flow of Goods

Channels make distribution easier in several ways. The first is by *sorting*, which consists of the following:

- *Sorting out.* Breaking many different items into separate stocks that are similar. Eggs, for instance, are sorted by grade and size.
- *Accumulating.* Bringing similar stocks together into a larger quantity. Twelve large grade-A eggs could be placed in some cartons and 12 medium grade B eggs in other cartons.
- *Allocating.* Breaking similar products into smaller and smaller lots. (Allocating at the wholesale level is called **breaking bulk.**) For instance, a tank-car load of milk could be broken down into four-litre jugs. The process of allocating generally is done when the goods are dispersed by region and as ownership of the goods changes.

breaking bulk
The process of breaking large shipments of similar products into smaller, more usable lots.

Without the sorting, accumulating and allocating processes, modern society would not exist. We would have home-based industries providing custom or semi-custom products to local markets. In short, we would return to a much lower level of consumption.

A second way channels ease the flow of goods is by locating buyers for merchandise. A wholesaler must find the right retailers to sell a profitable volume of merchandise. A sporting goods wholesaler, for instance, must find the retailers who are most likely to reach sporting goods consumers. Retailers have to understand the buying habits of consumers and put stores where consumers want and expect to find the merchandise. Every member of a distribution channel must locate buyers for the products it is trying to sell.

| How Distribution Channels Reduce the Number of Transactions

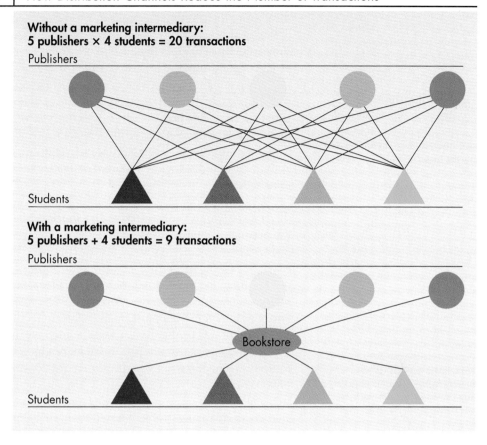

Channel members also store merchandise so that goods are available when consumers want to buy them. The high cost of retail space often means that goods are stored by the wholesaler or the manufacturer.

Channels Perform Needed Functions

The functions performed by channel members help increase the efficiency of the channel. Yet consumers sometimes feel that the go-betweens create higher prices. They doubt that these intermediaries perform useful functions. Actually, however, if channel members did not perform important and necessary functions at a reasonable cost, they would cease to exist. If firms could earn a higher profit without using certain channel members, they would not use them.

A useful rule to remember is that, although channel members can be eliminated, their functions cannot. The manufacturer must either perform the functions of the intermediaries itself or find new ways of getting them carried out. Publishers can bypass bookstores, for instance, but the function performed by the bookstores then has to be performed by the publishers or by someone else.

concept check

- List and define the marketing intermediaries that make up a distribution channel.
- How do channels reduce the number of transactions?
- What is meant by sorting out and accumulating?
- Define breaking bulk.

The Intensity of Market Coverage

All types of distribution systems must be concerned with market coverage. How many dealers will be used to distribute the product in a particular area? As Exhibit 10-10 shows, the three degrees of coverage are exclusive, selective, and intensive. The type of product determines the intensity of the market coverage.

When a manufacturer selects one or two dealers in an area to market its products, it is using **exclusive distribution.** Only items that are in strong demand can be distributed exclusively because consumers must be willing to travel some distance to buy them. If Wrigley's chewing gum were sold in only one drugstore per city, Wrigley's would soon be out of business. However, Bang and Olufsen stereo components, Jaguar automobiles, and Adrienne Vittadini designer clothing are distributed exclusively with great success.

A manufacturer that chooses a limited number of dealers in an area (but more than one or two) is using **selective distribution.** Since the number of retailers handling the product is limited, consumers must be willing to seek it out. Timberline boots, a high-quality line of footwear, are distributed selectively. So are Sony televisions, Maytag washers, Waterford crystal, and Tommy Hilfiger clothing. When choosing dealers, manufacturers look for certain qualities. Sony may seek retailers that can offer high-quality customer service. Tommy Hilfiger may look for retailers with high-traffic locations in regional shopping malls. All manufacturers try to exclude retailers that are a poor credit risk or that have a weak or negative image.

A manufacturer that wants to sell its products everywhere there are potential customers is using **intensive distribution.** Such consumer goods as bread, tape, and light bulbs are often distributed intensively. Usually, these products cost little and are bought frequently, which means that complex distribution channels are necessary. Coca-Cola is sold in just about every type of retail business, from gas stations to supermarkets.

exclusive distribution
A distribution system in which a manufacturer selects only one or two dealers in an area to market its products.

selective distribution
A distribution system in which a manufacturer selects a limited number of dealers in an area (but more than one or two) to market its products.

intensive distribution
A distribution system in which a manufacturer tries to sell its products wherever there are potential customers.

concept check

- Name the three degrees of market coverage.
- How does each differ from the others?
- What are some examples of products, other than those mentioned, that would fit into each of the three degrees?

e x h i b i t   1 0 - 1 0 | Different Products Require Different Degrees of Market Coverage

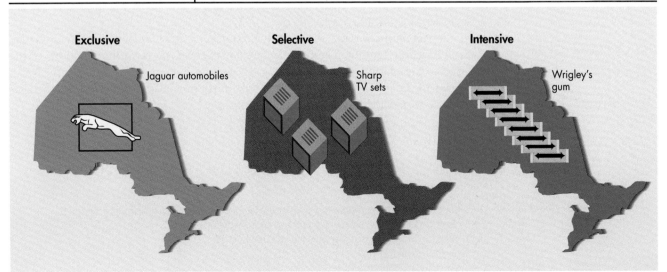

Exclusive — Jaguar automobiles

Selective — Sharp TV sets

Intensive — Wrigley's gum

Business and retail customers pay cash for and carry their purchases from Costco, a limited-service wholesaler that doesn't offer credit or delivery service.

HOT Links

Many publishers use wholesaler Ingram Book Group to distribute their books, audiotapes, and periodicals to bookstores and libraries. For a clear look at the services this wholesaler provides, visit Ingram's Web site at

www.ingrambook.com

Manufacturers' representatives (manufacturers' agents)
Salespeople who represent noncompeting manufacturers.

Wholesaling

Wholesalers are channel members that buy finished products from manufacturers and sell them to retailers. Retailers in turn sell the products to consumers. Manufacturers that use selective or exclusive distribution normally sell directly to retailers. Manufacturers that use intensive distribution often rely on wholesalers.

Wholesalers also sell products to institutions, such as manufacturers, schools, and hospitals, for use in performing their own missions. A manufacturer, for instance, might buy typing paper from Nationwide Papers, a wholesaler. A hospital might buy its cleaning supplies from Lagasse Brothers, one of the wholesalers of janitorial supplies.

Sometimes wholesalers sell products to manufacturers for use in the manufacturing process. A builder of custom boats, for instance, might buy batteries from a battery wholesaler and switches from an electrical wholesaler. Some wholesalers even sell to other wholesalers, creating yet another stage in the distribution channel.

About half of all wholesalers offer financing for their clients. They sell products on credit and expect to be paid within a certain time, usually 60 days. Other wholesalers operate like retail stores. The retailer goes to the wholesaler, selects the merchandise, pays cash for it and transports it to the retail outlet.

Because wholesalers usually serve limited areas, they are often located closer to retailers than the manufacturers are. Retailers can thus get faster delivery at lower cost from wholesalers. A retailer who knows that a wholesaler can restock store shelves within a day can keep a low level of inventory on hand. More money is then available for other things because less cash is tied up in items sitting on the shelves or in storerooms.

Agents and Brokers

As mentioned earlier, agents represent manufacturers and wholesalers. **Manufacturers' representatives** (also called **manufacturers' agents**) represent noncompeting manufacturers. These salespeople function as independent agents rather than as salaried employees of manufacturers. They do not take title to or possession of merchandise. They get commissions if they make sales—and nothing if they don't. They are found in a variety of industries, including electronics, clothing, hardware, furniture, and toys.

Brokers bring buyers and sellers together. Like agents, brokers do not take title to merchandise, they receive commissions on sales, and they have little say over company sales policies. They are found in markets where the information that would join buyers and sellers is scarce. These markets include real estate, agriculture, insurance, and commodities.

concept check

- Define wholesaling and describe what wholesalers do.
- Explain the difference between agents and brokers.

Using Physical Distribution to Increase Efficiency and Customer Satisfaction

Physical distribution is an important part of the marketing mix. Retailers don't sell products they can't deliver and salespeople don't (or shouldn't) promise deliveries they can't make. Late deliveries and broken promises may mean loss of a customer. Accurate order filling and billing, timely delivery, and arrival in good condition are important to the success of the product.

Distribution managers are responsible for making decisions that affect the successful delivery of a product to the end consumer in a timely manner (i.e., when the customer wants it). These decisions, presented in this section, include choosing a warehouse location and type, setting up a materials-handling system, and choosing among the available modes of transportation.

Choosing a Warehouse Location and Type

Deciding where to put a warehouse is mostly a matter of deciding which markets will be served and where production facilities will be located. A *storage warehouse* is used to hold goods for a long time. For instance, Jantzen makes bathing suits at an even rate throughout the year to provide steady employment and hold down costs. It then stores them in a warehouse until the selling season.

distribution centres
Warehouses that specialize in changing shipment sizes, rather than in storing goods.

Distribution centres are a special form of warehouse. They specialize in changing shipment sizes rather than storing goods. Such centres make bulk (put shipments together) or break bulk. They strive for rapid inventory turnover. When shipments arrive, the merchandise is quickly sorted into orders for various retail stores. As soon as the order is complete, it is delivered. Distribution centres are the wave of the future, replacing traditional warehouses. Companies simply can't afford to have a lot of money tied up in idle inventory.

Setting Up a Materials-Handling System

A materials-handling system moves and handles inventory. The goal of such a system is to move items as quickly as possible while handling them as little as possible. When Kodak built a new plant for making photographic coated paper, for example, it designed a way to minimize materials handling. It built a ten-level concrete rack to hold the one-ton rolls of raw paper. A computer handles inventory control and commands machines that can retrieve and carry the rolls without damage and then load the paper onto the assembly line.

Making Transportation Decisions

Transportation typically accounts for between 5 and 10 percent of the price of goods.[6] Physical distribution managers must decide which mode of transportation to use to move products from producer to buyer. This decision is, of course, related to all other physical distribution decisions. The five major modes of transportation are railroads, motor carriers, pipelines, water transportation, and airways. Distribution managers generally choose a mode of transportation on the basis of several criteria:

- *Cost.* The total amount a specific carrier charges to move the product from point of origin to the destination.
- *Transit time.* The total time a carrier has possession of goods, including the time required for pickup and delivery, handling, and movement between the point of origin and the destination.
- *Reliability.* The consistency with which the carrier delivers goods on time and in acceptable condition.

HOT Links

The Freight World Web site offers detailed information on various transportation modes and links to transportation companies. Visit it at www.freightworld.com

- *Capability.* The carrier's ability to provide the appropriate equipment and conditions for moving specific kinds of goods, such as those that must be transported in a controlled environment (for example, under refrigeration).
- *Accessibility.* The carrier's ability to move goods over a specific route or network.
- *Traceability.* The relative ease with which a shipment can be located and transferred.[7]

Using these six criteria, a shipper selects the mode of transportation that will best meet its needs. Exhibit 10-11 shows how the basic modes of transportation rank in terms of these criteria.

concept check

- Discuss the functions of physical distribution.
- What factors are considered when selecting a mode of transportation?

exhibit 10-11 | Criteria for Ranking Modes of Transportation

	Highest				Lowest
Relative cost	Air	Truck	Rail	Pipe	Water
Transit time	Water	Rail	Pipe	Truck	Air
Reliability	Pipe	Truck	Rail	Air	Water
Capability	Water	Rail	Truck	Air	Pipe
Accessibility	Truck	Rail	Air	Water	Pipe
Traceability	Air	Truck	Rail	Water	Pipe

➡ lg 8

CAPITALIZING ON TRENDS IN BUSINESS

The past decade has seen the Canadian economy grow at an unprecedented rate. Stock prices and corporate profits in many industries have soared, and unemployment and inflation have plummeted. Changes in production and operations management have made a huge contribution to this success and are likely to continue to propel productivity and economic growth in the new millennium.

Nonmanufacturing firms also face operating challenges. Like manufacturers, they must keep up with the constant pace of change and carefully manage how they use and deploy resources. As the service sector grows, so do customer expectations about the speed and quality of service. This puts increased pressure on nonmanufacturing firms to be ever vigilant in their search for new ways of streamlining service production and operations. In this section, we will look at some of the trends likely to alter how companies manage and control the production of goods and services in the future.

Modular Production

The executives at Palm Computing knew they had a good idea: a small electronic personal organizer called the Pilot. They also knew that their competitive advantage would depend on getting the Pilot on the market as quickly as possible, a schedule that would be impossible to meet without help. The Pilot's designers wrote detailed specifications for how the product should be produced; then the company invited 3500 other firms to create different parts of the product. Working together, Palm and its suppliers soon had the Pilot on the market. It became one of history's hottest products, selling more than 1 million units in its first 18 months.

Palm Computing's success highlights a growing trend in the business world, *modular production*. Modular production involves breaking a complex product, service, or process into smaller pieces that can be created independently and then combined quickly to make a whole. Modular production not only cuts the cost of developing and designing innovative products, but it also gives businesses a tool for meeting rapidly changing conditions. Modular production also makes it easier to implement mass customization or pure customization strategies. With access to a variety of components that can be assembled in different ways, endless combinations of product features are possible.

Agile Manufacturing

Another concept businesses are using to stay flexible and move fast is *agile manufacturing*. Investing millions of dollars in production processes, resources, and equipment that can be used only to produce one particular product doesn't always make economic sense. When customer demands shift or new technological innovations occur, the firm must be able to adapt. In agile manufacturing, firms strive to develop a production system comprised of flexible tools and processes that can be quickly changed to produce new or different products. Toyota uses agile manufacturing methods at its Kentucky plant. The factory builds both Camry and Avalon cars and the Siena minivans on the same assembly line. All three vehicles basically rely on the same underlying body platform. As the vehicles move through the plant, different components and parts are added depending on whether workers are producing a car or a minivan.[8]

concept check

- Explain modular production.
- How can agile manufacturing help a company obtain a competitive advantage?

Services and Physical Distribution

The fastest-growing part of our economy is the service sector. Although distribution in the service sector is difficult to visualize, the same skills, techniques, and strategies used to manage goods inventory can also be used to manage service inventory, such as hospital beds, bank accounts, or airline seats. The quality of the planning and execution of distribution can have a major impact on costs and customer satisfaction. Because service industries are so customer oriented, customer service is a priority. Service distribution focuses on three main areas:

- *Minimizing wait times.* Minimizing the amount of time customers wait to deposit a cheque, obtain their food at a restaurant, or see a doctor for an appointment is a key factor in maintaining the quality of service. FedEx, for example, revolutionized the delivery market when it introduced guaranteed overnight delivery of packages and documents to commercial and residential customers.
- *Managing service capacity.* For a product manufacturer, inventory acts as a buffer, enabling it to provide the product during periods of peak demand without extraordinary efforts. Service firms don't have this luxury. If they don't have the capacity to meet demand, they must either turn down some prospective customers, let service levels slip, or expand capacity. For instance, at tax time so many customers may desire tax-preparation services that a tax-preparation firm will have to either turn business away or add temporary offices or preparers.

- *Improving delivery through new distribution channels.* Like manufacturers, service firms are now experimenting with different distribution channels for their services. These new channels can increase the time that services are available (like round-the-clock automated teller machines) or add to customer convenience (like pizza delivery or walk-in medical clinics). For example, alternatives to hospitals called medical malls now offer one-stop shopping for all types of medical services. Like traditional malls, these shopping areas are equipped with fountains, food courts, and other amenities. The only difference lies in their product assortment, which ranges from radiology and cardiac treatment to outpatient surgery.[9]

concept check

- How are service firms changing their distribution systems to improve customer service?
- How does physical distribution influence service delivery?

APPLYING THIS CHAPTER'S TOPICS

As we've seen throughout this chapter, every organization produces something or provides a service or a combination of both. Cereal manufacturers turn grains into breakfast foods. Law firms turn the skills and knowledge of lawyers into legal services. Retailers provide a convenient way for consumers to purchase a variety of goods. Universities and colleges convert students into educated individuals. Therefore, no matter what type of organization you end up working for in the future, you will be involved, to one degree or another, with your employer's production and operations processes.

In some jobs, such as plant manager and quality-control manager, you will have a direct role in the operations process. But employees of manufacturing firms are not the only ones involved with production. Software developers, bank tellers, medical personnel, magazine writers, and a host of other jobs are also actively involved in turning inputs into outputs. If you manage people in these types of jobs, you'll need insight into the tools used to plan, schedule, and control production processes. Understanding operations processes, resource management, and techniques for increasing productivity is vital to becoming a more valuable employee, who sees how his or her job fits into "the big picture" of the firm's operating goals.

Other professionals also need to understand production and operations management in order to help the firm reach its goals. Want to be a sales representative? An awareness of how, when, and where goods or services are made will help you better serve customer needs. Or, perhaps you plan to work in new product development. The best idea for a new product will fail if production cannot produce it in a timely, cost-effective manner. Human resource managers need to know the type of work operations personnel do in order to do a good job of recruiting and retaining employees. Financial personnel, such as accountants, also need to understand what goes on in production and operations. That knowledge helps them in budgeting, pricing products, and managing financial resources.

If you plan to start your own business, you'll also face many production and operations decisions. You can use the information from this chapter to help you find suppliers, design an operating facility (no matter how small), and put customer-satisfying processes in place. This information can also help you make decisions about whether to manufacture goods yourself or rely on outside contractors to handle production.

TRY IT NOW!

Track a Project with a Gantt Chart Your instructor has just announced a huge assignment, due in three weeks. Where do you start? How can you best organize your time? A Gantt chart can help you plan and schedule more effectively. First, break the assignment down into smaller tasks. Say, for instance, that you have a ten-page research paper due in three weeks. Your list of tasks would include picking a topic, researching information at the library and on the Internet, organizing your notes, developing an outline, and writing and proofreading the paper. Next, estimate how much time each task will take.

Try to be realistic. There's no sense saying it will only take you a day to write the paper when you know you have spent a week or more writing similar papers in the past. At the top of a piece of paper, list all of the days until the assignment is due. Along the side of the paper, list all of the tasks you've identified in the order they need to be done. Starting with the first task, block out the number of days you estimate each task will take. If you run out of days, you'll know you need to adjust how you've scheduled your time. If you know that you will not be able to work on some days, note them on the chart as well. Hang the chart where you can see it. Your Gantt chart will give you a visual tool for tracking your progress. Instead of worrying about the entire project all at once, you'll be able to see exactly what you should be doing on a particular day. The end result should be a terrific paper turned in on time!

>looking ahead
at Harley-Davidson

Harley-Davidson's Kansas City plant has helped rev up the company's sales and profits. The new plant is so efficient that when daily production was recently increased from 161 bikes a day to 180, the factory only needed to hire 11 new workers. The factory's quality is high, too. The number of parts or sections rejected because of poor quality is only 5 percent at the Kansas City plant, compared with 20 percent at Harley's other finishing plants. Thanks in part to the greater efficiency of the new plant, the company plans to manufacture 202 000 motorcycles in 2000, up from just 150 000 the previous year. "That means we will have accomplished our goal of producing 200 000 units per year by 2003 a full three years ahead of our original schedule," says CEO Bleustein. The company's target for 2001 is to produce 223 000 units.

Harley-Davidson continues to increase production while slashing costs by making an enormous investment in new technology. New computer systems in its factories automate how production and operations information is managed and used throughout the company.

The company has also launched a new computer system that has improved its relationships with suppliers. Since 1995, the company has cut the number of its suppliers from 1000 to just over 400. The new system allows the company to order parts, components, and materials electronically and involves suppliers more closely in the design and development of new products.

Although some analysts criticize Harley-Davidson's slow and deliberate pace of incorporating technology and other changes into production, others are convinced that's the secret to the motorcycle manufacturer's growing profits and success. "This is a company that gets better every quarter," says one analyst. "There's nothing wrong with being an intelligent tortoise as opposed to a hare."[10]

KEY TERMS

SUMMARY OF LEARNING GOALS

➡ lg 1 **Why is operations management important?**

In the 1980s, many Canadian manufacturers lost customers to foreign competitors because their operations management systems did not support the high-quality, reasonably priced products consumers demanded. Service organizations also rely on effective operations management in order to satisfy consumers. Operations managers, the personnel charged with managing and supervising the conversion of inputs into outputs, work closely with other functions in organizations to help ensure quality, customer satisfaction, and financial success.

➡ lg 2 **What types of processes are used by manufacturers and service firms?**

Products are made using one of three types of production processes. In mass production, many identical goods are produced at once, keeping production costs low. Mass production, therefore, relies heavily on standardization, mechanization, and specialization. When mass customization is used, goods are produced using mass production techniques up to a point, after which the product or service is custom tailored to individual customers by adding special features. In general, mass customization is more expensive than mass production, but consumers are often willing to pay more for mass-customized products. When a firm's process is built around customization, the firm makes many products and provide services at a time according to the very specific needs or wants of individual customers.

➡ lg 3 **Why are resource planning tasks such as inventory management and supplier relations critical to production?**

Production converts input resources, such as raw materials and labour, into outputs, finished products and services. Firms must ensure that the resources needed for production will be available at strategic moments in the production process. If they are not, productivity, customer satisfaction, and quality may suffer. Carefully managing inventory can help cut production costs while maintaining enough supply for production and sales. Through good relationships with suppliers, firms can get better prices, reliable resources, and support services that can improve production efficiency.

➡ lg 4 **How do operations managers schedule and control processes?**

Routing is the first step in scheduling and controlling production. Routing analyzes the steps needed in production and sets out a workflow, the sequence of machines and operations through which a product or service progresses from start to finish. Good routing increases productivity and can eliminate unnecessary cost. Scheduling involves specifying and controlling the time and resources required for each step in the production process. It can range from simple to complex. Operations managers use three methods to schedule production: Gantt charts, the critical path method, and PERT.

➡ lg 5 **How can quality management and lean manufacturing techniques help firms?**

Successful businesses recognize that quality and productivity are interrelated. Quality control involves creating those quality standards and measuring finished products and services against them. This can save material wastage and time, and therefore money for the organization. Total quality management, the use of quality principles in all aspects of a company's production and operations, focuses on achieving greater efficiency and higher quality. Lean manufacturing streamlines production by eliminating steps in the production process that do not add value.

➡lg 6   **What are physical distribution (logistics) and logistics management?**
Physical distribution, or logistics, is the movement of products from the producer to industrial users and consumers. Logistics management involves managing (1) the movement of raw materials, (2) the movement of materials and products within plants and warehouses, and (3) the movement of finished goods to intermediaries and buyers. Supply chain management helps increase the efficiency of logistics service by minimizing inventory and moving goods efficiently.

➡lg 7   **What are distribution channels and their functions? What are the three degrees of market coverage? How is physical distribution used to increase efficiency and customer satisfaction?**
Distribution channels are the series of marketing entities through which goods and services pass on their way from producers to end users. Distribution systems focus on the physical transfer of goods and services and on their legal ownership at each stage of the distribution process. Channels (1) reduce the number of transactions, (2) ease the flow of goods, and (3) increase channel efficiency.

The three degrees of market coverage are exclusive distribution (only one or two dealers in an area), selective distribution (a limited number of dealers in an area, but more than two), and intensive distribution (as many dealers as possible in an area).

Physical distribution is an important part of the marketing mix. Late deliveries and broken promises may mean the loss of a customer. Distribution managers are responsible for making decisions that affect the successful delivery of a product to the end consumer in a timely manner (i.e., accurate order filling and billing, timely delivery, and arrival in good condition). This includes choosing a warehouse location and type, setting up a materials-handling system, and making transportation decisions.

➡lg 8   **What key trends are affecting the way companies manage operations?**
Faced with growing global competition, increased product complexity, and more demanding consumers, manufacturers are rethinking how, when, and where they produce the goods they sell. Modular production involves breaking a complex product, service, or process into smaller pieces that can be created independently and then combined quickly to make a whole. Agile manufacturing is a concept that helps manufacturers stay fast and flexible. Firms strive to develop production systems composed of tools and processes that can be quickly changed to produce new or different products. Because of these trends and the increased use of technology in production, firms are recognizing that smarter, better-motivated workers are an asset. Both manufacturing and nonmanufacturing firms are therefore putting new emphasis on empowering employees—giving them greater say in deciding how their jobs should be done and a larger role in company decision making.

WORKING THE NET

1. Go to **purchasing.miningco.com/msub-corp.htm**. Pick two or three of the companies listed and visit their supplier information Web sites. Compare the requirements the companies set for their suppliers. How do the requirements differ? How are they similar?

2. Visit the *Advanced Manufacturing* Web site at **www.advancedmanufacturing.com/** for the latest news about lean manufacturing.

3. Canadian manufactures that choose to place their operations in other countries have to consider specific ethical and social issues. Using the North-South Institute's Web site (at **www.nsi-ins.ca**), search for current research initiatives that are intended to increase cooperation effectiveness, maintain development

sustainability, and improve global governance by Canadian companies that choose to operate outside of Canada. What do you think are these companies' responsibilities to their host country?

4. Using a search engine like Excite (**www.excite.com**) or Info Seek (**www.infoseek.com**), search for information about technologies like robotics, CAD/CAM systems, or ERP. Find at least three suppliers for one of these technologies. Visit their Web sites and discuss how their clients are using their products to automate production.

CREATIVE THINKING CASE

New Patterns for Jody B Fashions

Jody Branson is the owner of Jody B Fashions, a small manufacturer of women's dresses. Jody designs the dresses herself and personally orders fabrics, trims, and other materials needed for production from a number of different suppliers. Jody has a work crew of 40. Production begins when the fabric is cut using Jody's patterns. After cutting, the pieces for each dress style are placed into bundles, which are then moved through the factory from worker to worker. Each worker opens each bundle and does one assembly task, such as sewing on collars, hemming the dresses, or adding decorative items like appliqués and lace. Then the worker puts the bundle back together and passes it on to the next person in the production process. Finished dresses are pressed and packaged for shipment.

Things were running smoothly until recently when Jody sold her first big order to a large retailer. Unlike the small boutique stores Jody usually sells to, the retailer wants to buy hundreds of dresses in different style and fabric combinations all at one time. If the retailer is pleased with this first order, chances are good it will give Jody a steady stream of future business. In the past, some of Jody's suppliers haven't sent their fabrics on time, so she has always ordered extra material to avoid shortages. She tried to do the same to prepare for the retailer's order, but her inventory room has become a disorganized nightmare. Jody had to shut down production twice this week because the workers who do the cutting couldn't find the fabric she had specified.

Jody knows she is beginning to fall behind on the retailer's order. She needs to cut the amount of time her workers take to finish each dress, but she doesn't want to sacrifice quality. Luckily, Jody has set aside some emergency capital that she can use to help solve this problem. She sees only three options:

- Hire additional workers for her production crew and hope to speed up production.
- Automate some of her production systems.
- Call retailer's buyer and ask for an extension on the order delivery deadline.[11]

Critical Thinking Questions

1. Evaluate Jody's production processes. Could she change them in any way to increase production?
2. Discuss the effectiveness of Jody's supply chain. Make recommendations for improvement.
3. Draw a diagram of how work flows through Jody's factory. Could Jody improve production by using a different layout? Draw a diagram of how this might look.
4. What do you think Jody should do? Are there any other options she could consider? Discuss whether each option is a short-term or long-term solution.

MAKING THE CONNECTION MAKING THE CONN

Using Financial Information and Accounting

In the previous three chapters we examined the functional areas of marketing and operations and saw that they must work together in a very integrative way to achieve the goals of the company. It is obvious that these two areas affect the level of product *quality* and *innovativeness* and thus the ability to *meet customer needs*, and that they therefore affect the ability of the company to achieve *financial success*. In this chapter we will begin to look more specifically at the functional area of *finance*, starting with how a firm develops and uses financial information through the function of accounting.

It couldn't be said more clearly than at the beginning of this chapter—"Regardless of your position, you need to understand accounting!" All decisions that are made in an organization eventually have financial consequences and therefore show up in the accounting information. For example, on the income statement you may find advertising expenses and sales revenue from *marketing*, production and operating costs from *operations*, payroll and training costs from *human resources*, and of course the interest costs on debt financing to pay for it all. On the balance sheet you can also see the impact of each area on the numbers. For example, in the accounts payable section there may be payments outstanding for employee wages, for marketing expenses, and for operating expenses, as well as for interest on debt financing or dividends payable to shareholders. In the current assets sections you may find marketable securities (money invested in financial products to earn a return for a short period of time—a financing decision), accounts receivable from customers for invoices they have not yet paid (a marketing decision), and inventories of goods on hand (an operating decision).

All areas of the company, and employees at all levels, must therefore understand the financial implications of the decisions they make. They must see the integration of their decisions with each area and eventually on the "bottom line." Internal accounting reports help functional areas to make these decisions; for example, marketing sales reports assess how well different marketing strategies are working, and production cost reports help control operating costs.

On the other hand, external accounting reports, such as balance sheets and income statements that are contained in annual reports to shareholders, are used by many outside *stakeholder* groups. Potential employees use them to assess the stability of a company and therefore job security and job prospects before taking job offers, and potential investors use them to assess investment opportunities just as current shareholders use them to assess the investments they have already made. These stakeholder relationships cannot be dealt with casually, particularly in light of recent scandals that have called into question the integrity of the accounting profession. The impact that these scandals, such as WorldCom and Enron, have had on the financial markets (*economic* environment) suggest quite clearly the far-reaching integrative impact of financial information, and the importance of operating with the highest ethical standards. In fact, this demand for greater ethical conduct (*social* environment) has resulted in many new regulations (*political* environment) governing what firms can and cannot do in reporting accounting information.

The other aspect of the external environment that affects this functional area is *technology*. The advances in technology today have sped up the pace with which accounting information can be gathered and disseminated throughout an organization, thus giving all areas an opportunity to examine the impact of their decisions in an integrative way and focus more on the analysis of the information to make better decisions. In Chapter 12 we'll continue with the finance area and look at these decisions in more detail.

Using Financial Information and Accounting

CHAPTER 11

Learning Goals

➡ **lg 1** Why are financial reports and accounting information important, and who uses them?

➡ **lg 2** What are the differences between public and private accountants?

➡ **lg 3** What are the six steps in the accounting cycle?

➡ **lg 4** In what terms does the balance sheet describe the financial condition of an organization?

➡ **lg 5** How does the income statement report a firm's profitability?

➡ **lg 6** Why is the statement of cash flows an important source of information?

➡ **lg 7** How can ratio analysis be used to identify a firm's financial strengths and weaknesses?

➡ **lg 8** What major trends are affecting the accounting industry today?

Regardless of Your Position, You Need to Understand Accounting!

Barry Sadrehashemi, a university instructor, consultant, and chartered accountant, started his accounting career when everything was manual except for the simplistic calculator. "I remember taking spreadsheets, filling the complete top of my desk to input the financial transactions," he says. "Technology and the new accounting systems now allow us to focus more on the analysis of the accounting information to make better decisions." He believes that accountants and the accounting professions add great value to the success of a company. "It is important for students to understand accounting basics and financial statements, regardless of whether they want to be an accountant or not." Most students will be responsible, at some point, for budgets (personal and corporate), making financial decisions (e.g., to carry debt or to issue equity), and so forth, and without the basic accounting knowledge, good financial decisions will only come by chance. "By being able to read financial reports and understanding the markets, people can make informed decisions and minimize the risks involved and thereby create more certainty," Barry says.

According to Barry, "for our capital markets to function, there is a need for timely and accurate reporting to all the stakeholders of a company." (*Capital markets* is a general term that encompasses all the various markets for financial investments.) "Accounting information provides the needed information to both management and employees, as well as the other stakeholders, such as shareholders, creditors, and regulatory and tax authorities, in order to make less risky decisions." Barry strongly believes that in the absence of accurate and timely financial information, there is very little chance of having a well-functioning capital market, and without an efficient capital market there is very little chance of proper allocation of resources in the economy.

Accountants work in different capacities. Some work in industry, some work for the various levels of government, and some provide services needed by industry and commerce by way of providing assurance, bookkeeping, valuation, tax, and other services for industry. All these roles are necessary to have an accurate picture of a business's financial position.

"Most stakeholders are interested in all three reports that make up the financial statements—the balance sheet, income statement, and the statement of cash flows. By analyzing the three reports together, the person can get a better picture of what is happening in the business. Sometimes, people will only look at the balance sheet and income statement but do not analyze the statement of cash flows. This can cause more risky decisions to be made. It is similar to making a

CRITICAL THINKING QUESTIONS

As you read this chapter, consider the following questions as they relate to Barry Sadrehashemi's discussion:

- Why is it important to understand accounting and its reports even if you are not planning on working in the profession?
- How can understanding the financial statements help you in your professional life? Your personal life?
- By understanding the basics of accounting, the accounting statements, and ratio analysis, what can you gain?

decision with only part of the available information and ignoring the other parts. For instance, the company may be very profitable (from the income statement), have lots of assets (from the balance sheet), but may be having trouble in collecting its receivables, so it may have problems paying its bills when they become due. The statement of cash flows shows the sources and uses of cash and therefore reconciles the cash position."

Ratio analysis is another concern that Barry has. He cautions students not evaluate financial ratios independently. Analyzing ratios independent of the other ratios often gives the wrong message. The intent of ratio analysis is to divide (pull each of the ratios out from the financial reports), and then conquer (analysis the appropriate ratios together). "Numbers on their own do not tell much about how a business is doing, but when we compare them with other numbers or prior-year numbers they show how those numbers are related to each other and become much more meaningful."

Barry's final thoughts of the accounting profession: "Today accountants and the professions now need to take a look at what has been happening and react accordingly. Like most professions, we try to regulate ourselves but sometimes it is not enough. We have seen scandals recently that have caused our profession to lose some of its credibility. It is time to be more proactive and respond accordingly to bring back the 'professionalism in our profession' and regain the public confidence that we once had."

In business and in the classroom, Barry has seen it all. People making decisions based on wrong information or partial information and suffering the consequences. Understanding the basics of accounting will help each and every one of you to be able to make good investment choices, understand budgets and the budgeting process, and ultimately provide you with the knowledge to make profitable decisions.[1]

BUSINESS IN THE 21ST CENTURY

Financial information is central to every organization. To operate effectively, businesses must have a way to track income, expenses, assets, and liabilities in an organized manner. Financial information is also essential for decision making. Managers prepare financial reports using accounting, a set of procedures and guidelines for companies to follow when preparing financial reports. Unless you understand basic accounting concepts, you will not be able to "speak" the standard financial language of businesses.

This chapter starts by discussing why accounting is important for businesses and for users of financial information and then presents an overview of accounting procedures. Next, the three main financial statements—the balance sheet, the income statement, and the statement of cash flows—are described. The chapter then discusses how to analyze financial statements using ratio analysis. Finally, it explores some of the trends affecting accounting.

→ **lg 1**

accounting
The process of collecting, recording, classifying, summarizing, reporting, and analyzing financial activities.

The Purpose of Accounting

Accounting is the process of collecting, recording, classifying, summarizing, reporting, and analyzing financial activities. It results in reports that describe the financial condition of an organization. All types of organizations—businesses, hospitals, schools, government agencies, civic groups—use accounting procedures. Accounting provides a framework for looking at past performance, current financial health, and possible future performance. It also provides a framework for comparing the financial positions and financial performances of different firms. Understanding how to prepare and interpret financial reports will enable you to evaluate two computer companies and choose the one that is more likely to be a good investment.

As Exhibit 11-1 shows, the accounting system converts the details of financial transactions (sales, payments, and so on) into a form that people can use to evaluate the firm and make decisions. Data become information, which in turn become reports. These reports describe a firm's financial position at one point in time and its financial performance during a specified period. Financial reports include financial statements (such as balance sheets and income statements) and special reports (such as sales and expense breakdowns by product line).

Who Uses Financial Reports?

managerial accounting
Accounting that provides financial information that managers inside the organization can use to evaluate and make decisions about current and future operations.

financial accounting
Accounting that focuses on preparing external financial reports that are used by outsider stakeholders such as creditors, suppliers, investors, and government agents to assess the financial strength of a business.

generally accepted accounting principles (GAAP)
The financial accounting standards followed by accountants in Canada in preparing financial statements.

The accounting system generates two types of financial reports, as shown in Exhibit 11-2: internal and external. Internal reports are used within the organization. As the term implies, **managerial accounting** provides financial information that managers inside the organization can use to evaluate and make decisions about current and future operations. For instance, the sales reports prepared by managerial accountants show how well marketing strategies are working. Production cost reports help departments track and control costs. Managers may prepare very detailed financial reports for their own use and provide summary reports to top management.

Financial accounting focuses on preparing external financial reports that are used by outsiders, that is, people who have an interest in the business but are not part of management. Although these reports also provide useful information for managers, they are primarily used by lenders, suppliers, investors, and government agencies to assess the financial strength of a business.

To ensure accuracy and consistency in the way financial information is reported, accountants in Canada follow **generally accepted accounting principles (GAAP)** when preparing financial statements. The professional association responsible for setting the standards for all Canadian accountants is the Canadian Institute of Chartered Accountants (CICA).

exhibit 11-1	The Accounting System

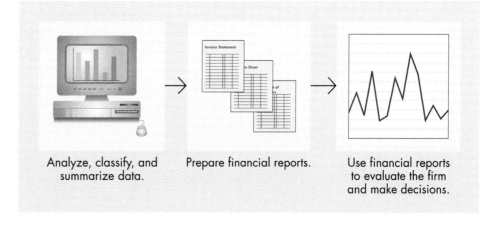

Analyze, classify, and summarize data.   Prepare financial reports.   Use financial reports to evaluate the firm and make decisions.

In managerial accounting, internal reports detailing financial information such as the costs of labour and material in production are shared with other managers to assess the organization's performance.

annual report
A yearly document that describes a firm's financial status and usually discusses the firm's activities during the past year and its prospects for the future.

chartered accountant (CA)
An accountant who has completed an approved bachelor's degree program, completed an educational program, and passed a comprehensive examination. Only a CA can issue an auditor's opinion on a firm's financial statements.

At the present time, there are no international accounting standards, although the International Accounting Standards Committee is trying to develop them. Because accounting practices vary from country to country, a multinational company must make sure that its financial statements conform to both its own country's accounting standards and those of the parent company's country.

Financial statements are the chief element of the **annual report,** a yearly document that describes a firm's financial status. Annual reports usually discuss the firm's activities during the past year and its prospects for the future. Three primary financial statements included in the annual report are discussed and illustrated later in this chapter:

1. The balance sheet (statement of position)
2. The income statement (statement of profit and loss or statement of earnings)
3. The statement of cash flows

The Accounting Profession

In Canada there are three accounting associations that grant professional designations. They are the Canadian Institute of Chartered Accountants (CICA), the Society of Management Accountants of Canada (CMA Canada), and the Certified General Accountants Association of Canada (CGA-Canada). Each of the professional accounting associations provides specialized services and has certain educational and work experience requirements in order for the accountant to be granted the professional designation.

A **chartered accountant (CA)** typically provides tax, audit, and management services. This kind of accountant focuses on the external reporting and certifies that the financial statements accurately reflect the company's financial health. To become a chartered accountant, an accountant must complete an approved bachelor's degree program, complete an educational program, and pass a comprehensive examination. Each province also has requirements for CAs such as several years' on-the-job experience and continuing education. Only CAs can provide the auditor's opinion on a firm's financial statements. Most CAs first work for public accounting firms and later become private accountants or financial managers.

e x h i b i t 1 1 - 2 | Reports Provided by the Accounting System

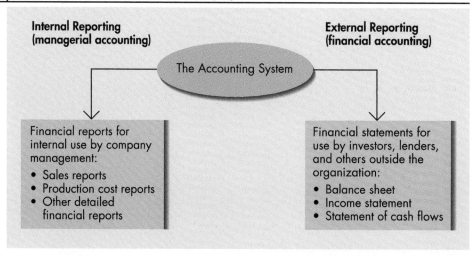

HOT Links

To find out more about the accounting profession, visit the Canadian Institute of Chartered Accountants site at www.cica.ca, the CMA Canada site at www.cma-canada.org, or the Certified General Accountants site at www.cga-canada.org.

certified management accountant (CMA)
An accountant that works primarily in industry and focuses on internal management accounting.

certified general accountant (CGA)
An accountant that focuses primarily on external financial reporting.

 lg 2

public accountants
Independent accountants who serve organizations and individuals on a fee basis.

auditing
The process of reviewing the records used to prepare financial statements and issuing a formal auditor's opinion indicating whether the statements have been prepared in accordance with accepted accounting rules.

private accountants
Accountants who are employed to serve one particular organization.

CAs generally work in four key areas: public practice, industry, government, or education. In public practice they provide accounting and business advice to clients such as small business taxation, auditing, information technology, personal finance planning, business valuation, receivership, insolvency, and forensic investigation. In industry, CAs develop financial and administrative policies, analyze information, and provide strategic leadership. They often add value to organizations as CEO/president, treasurer/V.P. finance, controller, or systems developer. All areas of government require accounting expertise to guide the financial planning and to maintain fiscal control. Additionally, many of Canada's top educators are CAs.

A **certified management accountant (CMA)** works primarily in industry and focuses on internal management accounting. They combine their accounting expertise and business know-how with professional management skills to provide strategic financial management, strategic planning, sales and marketing, information technology, human resources, finance, and operations. According to CMA Canada, "They monitor, interpret, and communicate operating results, evaluate performance, control operations, and make decisions about the strategic direction of the organization. They also bring a strong market focus to strategic management and resource deployment and analyze both financial and non-financial management to develop total business solutions, identify new market opportunities and maximize shareholder value."[2]

Certified general accountant (CGA) roles have far expanded from the primary focus on external financial reporting. They also provide tax and financial advice to individuals and businesses. Many own their own accounting business, while others are employed in industry and government. According to CGA Canada, "A CGA offers the highest standards of expertise in taxation, finance, information technology and strategic business management."[3]

A CA, CMA, or a CGA can be either a public accountant or a private accountant.

Public Accountants

Independent accountants who serve organizations and individuals on a fee basis are called **public accountants.** Public accountants offer a wide range of services, including preparation of financial statements and tax returns, independent auditing of financial records and accounting methods, and management consulting. **Auditing,** the process of reviewing the records used to prepare financial statements, is an important responsibility of public accountants. They provide a formal auditor's opinion indicating whether the statements have been prepared in accordance with accepted accounting rules. This written opinion is an important part of the annual report.

Private Accountants

Accountants employed to serve one particular organization are **private accountants.** Their activities include preparing financial statements, auditing company records to be sure employees follow accounting policies and procedures, developing accounting systems, preparing tax returns, and providing financial information for management decision making.

concept check

- Explain who uses financial information.
- Differentiate between financial accounting and managerial accounting.
- Compare the responsibilities of public and private accountants.

Basic Accounting Procedures

Using generally accepted accounting principles, accountants record and report financial data in similar ways for all firms. They report their findings in financial statements that summarize a company's business transactions over a specified time period. As mentioned earlier, the three major financial statements are the balance sheet, income statement, and statement of cash flows.

People sometimes confuse accounting with bookkeeping. Accounting is a much broader concept. Bookkeeping, the system used to record a firm's financial transactions, is a routine, clerical process. Accountants take bookkeepers' transactions, classify and summarize the financial information, and then prepare and analyze financial reports. Accountants also develop and manage financial systems and help plan the firm's financial strategy.

The Accounting Equation

The accounting procedures used today are based on those developed in the late 15th century by an Italian monk, Brother Luca Pacioli. He defined the three main accounting elements as assets, liabilities, and owners' equity. **Assets** are things of value owned by a firm. They may be *tangible*, such as cash, equipment, and buildings, or *intangible*, such as a patent or trademarked name. **Liabilities**—also called *debts*—are what a firm owes to its creditors. **Owners' equity** is the total amount of investment in the firm minus any liabilities. Another term for owners' equity is *net worth*.

The relationship among these three elements is expressed in the accounting equation:

$$\text{Assets} = \text{Liabilities} + \text{Owners' equity}$$

The accounting equation must always be in balance (that is, the total of the elements on one side of the equals sign must equal the total on the other side).

Suppose you start a bookstore and put $10 000 in cash into the business. At that point, the business has assets of $10 000 and no liabilities. This would be the accounting equation:

$$\text{Assets} = \text{Liabilities} + \text{Owners' equity}$$
$$\$10\ 000 = \$0 \qquad + \$10\ 000$$

The liabilities are zero and owner's equity (the amount of your investment in the business) is $10 000. The equation balances.

To keep the accounting equation in balance, every transaction must be recorded as two entries. As each transaction is recorded, there is an equal and opposite event so that two accounts or records are changed. This method is called **double-entry bookkeeping.**

Suppose that after starting your bookstore with $10 000 cash, you borrow another $10 000 from the bank. The accounting equation will change as follows:

Assets	= Liabilities	+ Owners' equity	
$10 000	= $0	+ $10 000	Initial equation
$10 000	= $10 000	+ $0	Borrowing transaction
$20 000	= $10 000	+ $10 000	Equation after borrowing

Now you have $20 000 in assets—your $10 000 in cash and the $10 000 loan proceeds from the bank. The bank loan is also recorded as a liability of $10 000 because it's a debt you must repay. Making two entries keeps the equation in balance.

assets
Possessions of value owned by a firm.

liabilities
What a firm owes to its creditors; also called *debts*.

owners' equity
The total amount of investment in the firm minus any liabilities; also called *net worth*.

double-entry bookkeeping
A method of accounting in which each transaction is recorded as two entries so that two accounts or records are changed.

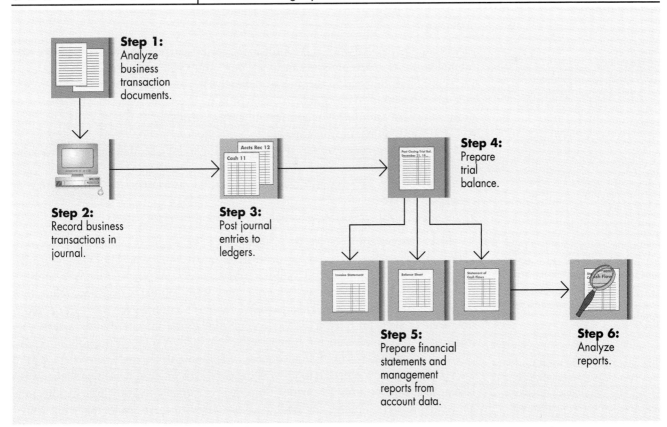

→ **lg 3**

The Accounting Cycle

The *accounting cycle* refers to the process of generating financial statements, beginning with a business transaction and ending with the preparation of the report. Exhibit 11-3 shows the six steps in the accounting cycle. The first step in the cycle is to analyze the data collected from many sources. All transactions that have a financial impact on the firm—sales, payments to employees and suppliers, interest and tax payments, purchases of inventory and the like—must be documented. The accountant must review the documents to make sure they're complete.

Next each transaction is recorded in a journal, a listing of financial transactions in chronological order. Then the journal entries are recorded in ledgers, which show increases and decreases in specific asset, liability, and owners' equity accounts. The ledger totals for each account are summarized in a trial balance, which is used to confirm the accuracy of the figures. These values are used to prepare financial statements and management reports. Finally, individuals analyze these reports and make decisions based on the information in them.

Computers in Accounting

Computers have become part of the accounting activity in almost all firms, performing most of the mechanics of accounting. Because they can quickly and accurately handle large amounts of data, computers streamline the routine aspects of accounting so the accountant can focus on interpreting financial information. With computerized accounting systems, an entry generates the appropriate changes to other related parts.

Computerized accounting programs do many different things. Most accounting packages offer six basic modules that handle general ledger, sales order, accounts receivable, purchase order, accounts payable, and inventory control functions. Tax

e x h i b i t   1 1 - 3 | The Accounting Cycle

Step 1: Analyze business transaction documents.

Step 2: Record business transactions in journal.

Step 3: Post journal entries to ledgers.

Step 4: Prepare trial balance.

Step 5: Prepare financial statements and management reports from account data.

Step 6: Analyze reports.

programs use accounting data to prepare tax returns and tax plans. Computerized point-of-sale terminals used by many retail firms automatically record sales and do some of the bookkeeping.

concept check

• Explain the accounting equation.
• Describe the six-step accounting cycle.
• What role do computers play in accounting?

 **lg 4**

balance sheet
A financial statement that summarizes a firm's financial position at a specific point in time; also known as the *statement of financial position*.

liquidity
The speed with which an asset can be converted to cash.

The Balance Sheet

The **balance sheet** (also known as the statement of financial position), one of three financial statements generated from the accounting system, summarizes a firm's financial position at a specific point in time. It reports the resources of a company (assets), the company's obligations (liabilities), and the difference between what is owned (assets) and what is owed (liabilities), or owners' equity.

The assets are listed in order of their **liquidity,** the speed with which they can be converted to cash. The most liquid assets come first, and the least liquid are last. Because cash is the most liquid asset, it is listed first. Buildings, on the other hand, must be sold to be converted to cash, so they are listed after cash. Liabilities are arranged similarly: liabilities due in the short term are listed before those due in the long term.

The balance sheet at December 31, 200X, for Delicious Desserts, Inc., an imaginary bakery, is illustrated in Exhibit 11-4. The basic accounting equation is reflected in the three totals highlighted on the balance sheet: assets of $148 900 equal the sum of liabilities and owners' equity ($70 150 + $78 750). The three main categories of accounts on the balance sheet are explained below.

Assets

current assets
Assets that can or will be converted to cash within the next 12 months (within the next fiscal year).

Assets can be divided into three broad categories: current assets, fixed assets, and intangible assets. **Current assets** are assets that can or will be converted to cash within the next 12 months (within the next fiscal year). They are important because they provide the funds used to pay the firm's current bills. They also represent the amount of money the firm can quickly raise. Current assets include:
• *Cash.* Funds on hand or in a bank.
• *Marketable securities.* Temporary investments of excess cash that can readily be converted to cash.
• *Accounts receivable.* Amounts owed to the firm by customers who bought goods or services on credit.
• *Inventory.* Stock of goods being held for production or for sale to customers.

fixed assets
Long-term assets used by a firm for more than a year, such as land, buildings, and machinery; also referred to as *capital assets* or *property, plant, and equipment* (PPE).

Fixed assets (also referred to as *capital assets* or *property, plant, and equipment* [PPE]) are long-term assets used by the firm for more than a year. They tend to be used in production and include land, buildings, machinery, equipment, furniture, and fixtures. Except for land, fixed assets wear out and become outdated over time. Thus, they decrease in value every year. This declining value is accounted for through depreciation. **Depreciation** (also referred to as *amortization*) is the allocation of the asset's original cost to the years in which it is expected to produce revenues. A portion of the cost of a depreciable asset—a building or piece of equipment, for instance—is charged to each of the years it is expected to provide benefits. This practice helps match the asset's cost against the revenues it provides. Since it is impossible to know exactly how long an asset will last, estimates are used. They are based on past experience with similar

depreciation
The allocation of an asset's original cost to the years in which it is expected to produce revenues; also referred to as *amortization*.

exhibit 11-4 | Balance Sheet for Delicious Desserts

Delicious Desserts, Inc.
Balance Sheet as of December 31, 200X

Assets

Current assets:

Cash		$15 000	
Marketable securities		4 500	
Accounts receivable	$45 000		
Less: Allowance for doubtful accounts	1 300	43 700	
Notes receivable		5 000	
Inventory		15 000	
Total current assets			$83 200

Fixed assets:

Bakery equipment	$56 000		
Less: Accumulated depreciation	16 000	$40 000	
Furniture and fixtures	$18 450		
Less: Accumulated depreciation	4 250	14 200	
Total fixed assets			54 200

Intangible assets:

Trademark		$4 500	
Goodwill		7 000	
Total intangible assets			11 500
Total assets			**$ 148 900**

Liabilities and Owners' Equity

Current liabilities:

Accounts payable	$30 650		
Notes payable	15 000		
Accrued expenses	4 500		
Income taxes payable	5 000		
Current portion of long-term debt	5 000		
Total current liabilities		$60 150	

Long-term liabilities:

Bank loan for bakery equipment	$10 000		
Total long-term liabilities		$10 000	
Total liabilities			$70 150

Owners' equity

Common shares (10 000 shares outstanding)		$30 000	
Retained earnings		48 750	
Total owners' equity			**$ 78 750**
Total liabilities and owners' equity			**$148,900**

items or Canada Customs and Revenue agency guidelines for assets of that type. Notice that, through 200X, Delicious Desserts has taken a total of $16 000 in depreciation on its bakery equipment.

Note: On the balance sheet, the original cost of the fixed asset is recorded. From that we subtract the accumulated depreciation (the total of all years' depreciation amounts for the fixed asset) to determine the book value of the fixed asset ($40 000 in this case).

Intangible assets are long-term assets with no physical existence. Common examples are patents, copyrights, trademarks, and goodwill. Patents and copyrights shield the firm from direct competition, so their benefits are more protective than productive. For instance, no one can use more than a small amount of copyrighted material

intangible assets
Long-term assets with no physical existence, such as patents, copyrights, trademarks, and goodwill.

On its balance sheet, this paper mill and wood-processing plant would list long-term resources such as land, buildings, machinery, furniture, and fixtures as fixed assets.

current liabilities
Short-term claims that are due within a year of the date of the balance sheet.

long-term liabilities
Claims that come due more than one year after the date of the balance sheet.

retained earnings
The amounts left over from profitable operations since the firm's beginning; equal to total profits minus all dividends paid to shareholders.

without permission from the copyright holder. Trademarks are registered names that can be sold or licensed to others. Delicious Desserts' intangible asset is a trademark valued at $4500. Goodwill occurs when a company pays more for an acquired firm than the value of its tangible assets.

Liabilities

Liabilities are the amounts a firm owes to creditors. Those liabilities coming due sooner—current liabilities—are listed first on the balance sheet, followed by long-term liabilities.

Current liabilities are those due within a year of the date of the balance sheet. These short-term claims may strain the firm's current assets because they must be paid in the near future. Current liabilities include:

- *Accounts payable.* Amounts the firm owes for credit purchases due within a year. This account is the liability counterpart of accounts receivable.
- *Notes payable.* Short-term loans from banks, suppliers, or others that must be repaid within a year. For example, Delicious Desserts has a six-month, $15 000 loan from its bank that is a note payable.
- *Income taxes payable.* Taxes owed for the current operating period but not yet paid. Taxes are often shown separately when they are a large amount.
- *Current portion of long-term debt.* Any repayment on long-term debt due within the year. Delicious Desserts is scheduled to repay $5000 on its equipment loan in the coming year.

Long-term liabilities come due more than one year after the date of the balance sheet. They include bank loans (such as Delicious Desserts' $10 000 loan for bakery equipment), mortgages on buildings, and the company's bonds sold to others.

Owners' Equity

Owners' equity is the owners' total investment in the business after all liabilities have been paid. For sole proprietorships and partnerships, amounts put in by the owners are recorded as capital. In a corporation, the owners provide capital by buying the firm's common shares. For Delicious Desserts, the total investment in common shares is $30 000. **Retained earnings** are the amounts left over from profitable operations since the firm's beginning. They are total profits minus all dividends (distributions of profits) paid to shareholders. Delicious Desserts has $48 750 in retained earnings.

concept check

- What is a balance sheet?
- What are the three main categories of accounts on the balance sheet, and how do they relate to the accounting equation?
- How do retained earnings relate to owners' equity?

➡ lg 5

income statement
A financial statement that summarizes a firm's revenues and expenses and shows its total profit or loss over a period of time; also referred to as a *profit and loss statement* or *statement of earnings*.

revenues
The dollar amount of a firm's sales plus any other income it received from sources such as interest, dividends, and rents.

gross sales
The total dollar amount of a company's sales.

The Income Statement

The balance sheet shows the firm's financial position at a certain point in time. The **income statement** (also referred to as a *profit and loss statement* or *statement of earnings*) summarizes the firm's revenues and expenses and shows its total profit or loss over a period of time. Most companies prepare monthly income statements for management and quarterly and annual statements for use by investors, creditors, and other outsiders. The primary elements of the income statement are revenues, expenses, and net income (or net loss). The income statement for Delicious Desserts for the year ended December 31, 200X, is shown in Exhibit 11-5.

Revenues

Revenues are the dollar amount of sales plus any other income received from sources such as interest, dividends, and rents. The revenues of Delicious Desserts arise from sales of its bakery products. Revenues are determined starting with **gross sales,** the total dollar amount of a company's sales. Delicious Desserts had two deductions from gross sales. Sales discounts are price reductions given to customers that pay their bills

e x h i b i t   1 1 - 5 | Income Statement for Delicious Desserts

Delicious Desserts, Inc.
Income Statement for the Year Ended December 31, 200X

Revenues		
Gross sales	$275 000	
Less: Sales discounts	2 500	
Less: Returns and allowances	2 000	
Net Sales		$270 500
Cost of Goods Sold		
Beginning inventory, January 1	$ 18 000	
Cost of goods manufactured	109 500	
Total cost of goods available for sale	$127 500	
Less: Ending inventory December 31	15 000	
Cost of goods sold		112 500
Gross profit		**$158 000**
Operating Expenses		
Selling expenses		
Sales salaries	$31 000	
Advertising	16 000	
Other selling expense	18 000	
Total selling expenses	$65 000	
General and administrative expenses		
Professional and office salaries	$20 500	
Utilities	5 000	
Office supplies	1 500	
Interest	3 600	
Insurance	2 500	
Rent	17 000	
Total general and administrative expenses	50 100	
Total operating expenses		115 100
Net profit before taxes		**$42 900**
Less: Income taxes		10 725
Net profit		**$ 32 175**

net sales
The amount left after deducting sales discounts and returns and allowances from gross sales.

expenses
The costs of generating revenues.

cost of goods sold
The total expense of buying or producing a firm's goods or services.

early. For example, Delicious Desserts gives sales discounts to restaurants that buy in bulk and pay at delivery. Returns and allowances is the dollar amount of merchandise returned by customers because they didn't like a product or because it was damaged or defective. **Net sales** is the amount left after deducting sales discounts and returns and allowances from gross sales. Delicious Desserts' gross sales were reduced by $4500, leaving net sales of $270 500.

Expenses

Expenses are the costs of generating revenues. Two types are recorded on the income statement: cost of goods sold and operating expenses.

The **cost of goods sold** is the total expense of buying or producing the firm's goods or services. For manufacturers, cost of goods sold includes all costs directly related to production: purchases of raw materials and parts, labour, and factory overhead (utilities, factory maintenance, machinery repair). For wholesalers and retailers, it is the cost of goods bought for resale. For all sellers, cost of goods sold includes all the expenses of preparing the goods for sale, such as shipping and packaging.

Delicious Desserts' cost of goods sold is based on the value of inventory on hand at the beginning of the accounting period, $18 000. During the year, the company spent $109 500 to produce its baked goods. This figure includes the cost of raw materials, labour costs for bakery workers, and the cost of operating the bakery area. Adding the cost of goods manufactured to the value of beginning inventory, we get the total cost of goods available for sale, $127 500. To determine the cost of goods sold for the year, we subtract the cost of inventory at the end of the period:

$$\$127\ 500 - \$15\ 000 = \$112\ 500$$

gross profit
The amount a company earns after paying to produce or buy its products but before deducting operating expenses.

operating expenses
The expenses of running a business that are not directly related to producing or buying its products.

The amount a company earns after paying to produce or buy its products but before deducting operating expenses is the **gross profit**. It is the difference between net sales and cost of goods sold. Since service firms do not produce goods, their gross profit equals net sales. Gross profit is a critical number for a company because it is the source of funds to cover all the firm's other expenses.

The other major expense category is **operating expenses.** These are the expenses of running the business that are not related directly to producing or buying its products. The two main types of operating expenses are selling expenses and general and administrative expenses. Selling expenses are those related to marketing and distributing the company's products. They include salaries and commissions paid to salespeople and the costs of advertising, sales supplies, delivery, and other items that can be linked to sales activity, such as insurance, telephone and other utilities, and postage. General and administrative expenses are the business expenses that cannot be linked to either cost of goods sold or sales. Examples of general and administrative expenses are salaries of top managers and office support staff; office supplies; fees for accounting, consulting, and legal services; insurance; rent; and utilities. Delicious Desserts' operating expenses totalled $115 100.

net profit (net income or net earnings)
The amount obtained by subtracting all of a firm's expenses from its revenues, when the revenues are more than the expenses.

net loss
The amount obtained by subtracting all of a firm's expenses from its revenues, when the expenses are more than the revenues.

Net Profit or Loss

The final figure—or bottom line—on an income statement is the **net profit** (or **net income** or **net earnings**) or **net loss.** It is calculated by subtracting all expenses from revenues. If revenues are more than expenses, the result is a net profit. If expenses exceed revenues, a net loss results.

Several steps are involved in finding net profit or loss. (These are shown in the right-hand column of Exhibit 11-5.) First, cost of goods sold is deducted from net sales to get the gross profit. Then total operating expenses are subtracted from gross profit to get the net profit before taxes. Finally, income taxes are deducted to get the net profit. As shown in Exhibit 11-5, Delicious Desserts earned a net profit of $32 175 in 200X.

It is very important to recognize that profit does not represent cash. The income statement is a summary of the firm's operating results during some time period. It does not present the firm's actual cash flows during the period. Those are summarized in the statement of cash flows, which is discussed briefly in the next section.

concept check

- What is an income statement? How does it differ from the balance sheet?
- Describe the key parts of the income statement. Distinguish between gross sales and net sales.
- How is the cost of goods sold calculated? Define the two types of expenses. How is net profit or loss calculated?

⇒ lg 6

The Statement of Cash Flows

statement of cash flows
A financial statement that provides a summary of the money flowing into and out of a firm.

Net profit or loss is one measure of a company's financial performance. However, creditors and investors are also keenly interested in how much cash a business generates and how it is used. The **statement of cash flows,** a summary of the money flowing into and out of a firm, is the financial statement used to assess the sources and uses of cash during a certain period, typically one year. All publicly traded firms must include a statement of cash flows in their financial reports to shareholders. The statement of cash flows tracks the firm's cash receipts and cash payments. It gives financial managers and analysts a way to identify cash flow problems and assess the firm's financial viability.

Using income statement and balance sheet data, the statement of cash flows divides the firm's cash flows into three groups:
- *Cash flow from operating activities.* Those related to the production of the firm's goods or services.
- *Cash flow from investment activities.* Those related to the purchase and sale of fixed assets.
- *Cash flow from financing activities.* Those related to debt and equity financing.

Delicious Desserts' statement of cash flows for 200X is presented in Exhibit 11-6. It shows that the company's cash and marketable securities have increased over the last year. And during the year the company generated enough cash flow to increase inventory and fixed assets and to reduce accounts payable, accruals, notes payable, and long-term debt.

concept check

- What is the purpose of the statement of cash flows?

⇒ lg 7

Analyzing Financial Statements

ratio analysis
The calculation and interpretation of financial ratios taken from the firm's financial statements in order to assess its condition and performance.

Individually, the balance sheet, income statement, and statement of cash flows provide insight into the firm's operations, profitability, and overall financial condition. By studying the relationships among the financial statements, however, one can gain even more insight into a firm's financial condition and performance.

Ratio analysis involves calculating and interpreting financial ratios taken from the firm's financial statements to assess its condition and performance. A financial ratio states the relationship between amounts as a percentage. For instance, current assets

| Statement of Cash Flows for Delicious Desserts

Delicious Desserts, Inc.
Statement of Cash Flows for 200X

Cash Flow from Operating Activities		
Net profit after taxes	$32 175	
Depreciation	1 500	
Decrease in accounts receivable	3 140	
Increase in inventory	(4 500)	
Decrease in accounts payable	(2 065)	
Decrease in accruals	(1 035)	
Cash provided by operating activities		$29 215
Cash Flow from Investment Activities		
Increase in gross fixed assets	($5 000)	
Cash used in investment activities		($5 000)
Cash Flow from Financing Activities		
Decrease in notes payable	($3 000)	
Decrease in long-term debt	(1 000)	
Cash used by financing activities		($4 000)
Net increase in cash and marketable securities		**$ 20 215**

might be viewed relative to current liabilities or sales relative to assets. The ratios can then be compared over time, typically three to five years. A firm's ratios can also be compared to industry averages or to those of another company in the same industry.

It's important to remember that ratio analysis is based on historical data and may not indicate future financial performance. Ratio analysis merely highlights potential problems; it does not prove that they exist. However, ratios can help managers understand operations better and identify trouble spots.

Ratios can be classified by what they measure: liquidity, profitability, activity, and debt. Using Delicious Desserts' 200X balance sheet and income statement (Exhibits 11-4 and 11-5), we can calculate and interpret the key ratios in each group. Exhibit 11-7 summarizes the calculations of these ratios for Delicious Desserts.

Liquidity Ratios

liquidity ratios
Ratios that measure a firm's ability to pay its short-term debts as they come due.

Liquidity ratios measure the firm's ability to pay its short-term debts as they come due. These ratios are of special interest to the firm's creditors. The three main measures of liquidity are the current ratio, the acid-test (quick) ratio, and net working capital.

current ratio
The ratio of total current assets to total current liabilities; used to measure a firm's liquidity.

The **current ratio** is the ratio of total current assets to total current liabilities. Traditionally, a current ratio of 2 ($2 of current assets for every $1 of current liabilities) has been considered good. Whether it is sufficient depends on the industry in which the firm operates. Utility companies and financial institutions, for example, will have a very steady cash flow and operate quite well with a current ratio below 2. A current ratio of 2 might not be adequate for manufacturers and merchandisers that carry high inventories and have lots of receivables. The current ratio for Delicious Desserts for 200X, as shown in Exhibit 11-7, is 1.4. This means little without a basis for comparison. If the analyst found that the industry average for small bakeries was 2.4, Delicious Desserts would appear to have low liquidity.

acid-test (quick) ratio
The ratio of total current assets excluding inventory to total current liabilities; used to measure a firm's liquidity.

The **acid-test (quick) ratio** is like the current ratio except that it excludes inventory, which is the least liquid current asset. The acid-test ratio is used to measure the firm's ability to pay its current liabilities without selling inventory. The name acid test implies that this ratio is a crucial test of the firm's liquidity. An acid-test ratio of at least 1 is preferred. But again, what is an acceptable value varies by industry. The acid-test ratio is a good measure of liquidity when inventory cannot easily be converted to cash (e.g., if it consists of very specialized goods with a limited market). If inventory is

exhibit 11-7 | Ratio Analysis for Delicious Desserts at Year-End 200X

Ratio	Formula	Calculation	Result
Liquidity Ratios			
Current ratio	$\dfrac{\text{Total current assets}}{\text{Total current liabilities}}$	$\dfrac{\$83\ 200}{\$60\ 150}$	1.4
Acid-test (quick) ratio	$\dfrac{\text{Total current assets} - \text{inventory}}{\text{Total current liabilities}}$	$\dfrac{\$83\ 200 - \$15\ 000}{\$60\ 150}$	1.1
Net working capital	$\begin{array}{c}\text{Total current assets} -\\ \text{Total current liabilities}\end{array}$	$\$83\ 200 - \$60\ 150$	$23 050
Profitability Ratios			
Net profit margin	$\dfrac{\text{Net profit}}{\text{Net sales}}$	$\dfrac{\$32\ 175}{\$270\ 500}$	11.9%
Return on equity	$\dfrac{\text{Net profit}}{\text{Total owners' equity}}$	$\dfrac{\$32\ 175}{\$78\ 750}$	40.9%
Earnings per share	$\dfrac{\text{Net profit}}{\begin{array}{c}\text{Number of common}\\ \text{shares outstanding}\end{array}}$	$\dfrac{\$32\ 175}{10\ 000}$	$3.22
Activity Ratio			
Inventory turnover	$\dfrac{\text{Cost of goods sold}}{\text{Average inventory}}$		
	$\dfrac{\text{Cost of goods sold}}{(\text{Beginning inventory} + \text{Ending inventory})/2}$	$\dfrac{\$112\ 500}{(\$18\ 000 + \$15\ 000)/2}$	
		$\dfrac{\$112\ 500}{\$16\ 500}$	6.8 times
Debt Ratio			
Debt-to-equity ratio	$\dfrac{\text{Total liabilities}}{\text{Owners' equity}}$	$\dfrac{\$70\ 150}{\$78\ 750}$	89.1%

net working capital
The amount obtained by subtracting total current liabilities from total current assets; used to measure a firm's liquidity.

profitability ratios
Ratios that measure how well a firm is using its resources to generate profit and how efficiently it is being managed.

net profit margin
The ratio of net profit to net sales; also called *return on sales*. It measures the percentage of each sales dollar remaining after all expenses, including taxes, have been deducted.

liquid, the current ratio is better. Delicious Desserts' acid-test ratio for 200X is 1.1. Because the bakery's products are perishable, it does not carry large inventories. Thus, the values of its acid-test and current ratios are fairly close. At a manufacturing company, however, inventory typically makes up a large portion of current assets, so the acid-test ratio will be lower than the current ratio.

Net working capital, though not really a ratio, is often used to measure a firm's overall liquidity. It is calculated by subtracting total current liabilities from total current assets. Delicious Desserts' net working capital for 200X is $23 050. Comparisons of net working capital over time often help in assessing a firm's liquidity.

Profitability Ratios

To measure profitability, a firm's profits can be related to its sales, equity, or stock value. **Profitability ratios** measure how well the firm is using its resources to generate profit and how efficiently it is being managed. The main profitability ratios are net profit margin, return on equity, and earnings per share.

The ratio of net profit to net sales is the **net profit margin,** also called return on sales. It measures the percentage of each sales dollar remaining after all expenses, including taxes, have been deducted. Higher net profit margins are better than lower ones. The net profit margin is often used to measure the firm's earning power. "Good" net profit margins differ quite a bit from industry to industry. A grocery store usually has a very low net profit margin, perhaps below 1 percent, while a jewellery store's net profit margin would probably exceed 10 percent. Delicious Desserts' net profit margin for 200X is 11.9 percent. In other words, Delicious Desserts is earning 11.9 cents on each dollar of sales.

return on equity (ROE)
The ratio of net profit to total owners' equity; measures the return that owners receive on their investment in the firm.

The ratio of net profit to total owners' equity is called **return on equity (ROE).** It measures the return that owners receive on their investment in the firm, a major reason for investing in a company's stock. Delicious Desserts has a 40.9 percent ROE for 200X. On the surface, a 40.9 percent ROE seems quite good. But the level of risk in the business and the ROE of other firms in the same industry must also be considered. The higher the risk, the greater the ROE investors look for. A firm's ROE can also be compared to past values to see how the company is performing over time.

earnings per share (EPS)
The ratio of net profit to the number of common shares outstanding; measures the number of dollars earned by each share.

Earnings per share (EPS) is the ratio of net profit to the number of common shares outstanding. It measures the number of dollars earned by each share. EPS values are closely watched by investors and are considered an important sign of success. EPS also indicates a firm's ability to pay dividends. Note that EPS is the dollar amount earned by each share, not the actual amount given to shareholders in the form of dividends. Some earnings may be put back into the firm. Delicious Desserts' EPS for 200X is $3.22.

Activity Ratios

activity ratios
Ratios that measure how well a firm uses its assets.

Activity ratios measure how well a firm uses its assets. They reflect the speed with which resources are converted to cash or sales. A frequently used activity ratio is inventory turnover.

inventory turnover ratio
The ratio of cost of goods sold to average inventory; measures the speed with which inventory moves through a firm and is turned into sales.

The **inventory turnover ratio** measures the speed with which inventory moves through the firm and is turned into sales. It is calculated by dividing cost of goods sold by the average inventory. (Average inventory is estimated by adding the beginning and ending inventories for the year and dividing by 2.) On average, Delicious Desserts' inventory is turned into sales 6.8 times each year, or about once every 54 days (365 days ÷ 6.8). The acceptable turnover ratio depends on the line of business. A grocery store would have a high turnover ratio, maybe 20 times a year, whereas the turnover for a heavy equipment manufacturer might be only three times a year.

Debt Ratios

Debt ratios measure the degree and effect of the firm's use of borrowed funds (debt) to finance its operations. These ratios are especially important to lenders and investors. They want to make sure the firm has a healthy mix of debt and equity. If the firm relies too much on debt, it may have trouble meeting interest payments and repaying loans. The most important debt ratio is the debt-to-equity ratio.

The **debt-to-equity ratio** measures the relationship between the amount of debt financing (borrowing) and the amount of equity financing (owners' funds). It is calculated by dividing total liabilities by owners' equity. In general, the lower the ratio, the better. But it is important to assess the debt-to-equity ratio against both past values and industry averages. Delicious Desserts' ratio for 200X is 89.1 percent. The ratio indicates that the company has 89 cents of debt for every dollar the owners have provided. A ratio above 100 percent means the firm has more debt than equity. In such a case, the lenders are providing more financing than the owners.

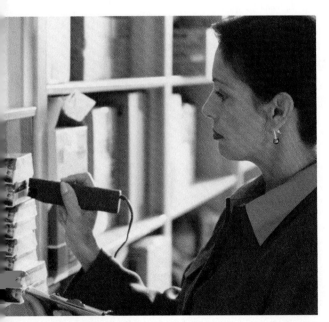

Inventory must move through the firm and be turned into sales as quickly as possible in order to maximize profits.

debt ratios
Ratios that measure the degree and effect of a firm's use of borrowed funds (debt) to finance its operations.

debt-to-equity ratio
The ratio of total liabilities to owners' equity; measures the relationship between the amount of debt financing and the amount of equity financing.

 **lg 8**

concept check

- How can ratio analysis be used to interpret financial statements?
- Name the two main liquidity ratios and explain what they indicate.
- Describe the main profitability ratios and the aspect of profitability measured by each.
- What kinds of information do activity ratios give?
- Why are debt ratios of concern to lenders and investors?

CAPITALIZING ON TRENDS IN BUSINESS

In the past accountants were portrayed primarily as "bean-counters" who overanalyzed financial data and were of little help to the managers and employees who produced the numbers the auditors examined. Still many people make this assumption! Although accountants still perform the important task of assuring that a company's financial reporting conforms to GAAP, they have become a valuable part of the financial team and consult with clients on information technology and other areas as well.

The increasing complexity of today's business environment creates additional challenges for the accounting profession. The information explosion means that the CICA must consider a greater number of new regulations and develop more position statements to keep up with the pace of change. The CICA also has an emerging issues task force that studies ways to make accounting standards more relevant for today's companies.

No longer can a company's assets be measured solely in terms of its bricks and mortar. Knowledge assets—brand names, patents, research and development (R&D) costs, and similar expenses—make up a large portion of the value of many information technology companies. As yet, however, there are few accepted ways to value those assets; indeed, there is disagreement over whether companies should even try. In other areas, GAAP is either unclear or subject to different interpretations.

Accountants Expand Their Role

Moving beyond their traditional task of validating a company's financial information, accountants now take an active role advising their clients on systems and procedures, accounting software, and changes in accounting regulations. They also delve into operating information to discover what's behind the numbers. By examining the risks and weaknesses in a company, they can help managers develop financial controls and procedures to prevent future trouble spots. For example, auditors in a manufacturing company may spend more time on inventory, a likely problem area.

Accounting firms have greatly expanded the consulting services they provide clients. As a result, accountants have become more involved in the operations of their clients. This raises the question of potential conflicts of interest. Can auditors serve both the public and the client? Auditors' main purpose is to certify financial statements. Will they maintain sufficient objectivity to raise questions while auditing a client that provides significant consulting revenues? Can they review systems and methods that they recommended? According to one expert, "If the financial markets don't believe in a firm's audit, the firm has nothing."

Valuing Knowledge Assets

As the world's economy becomes knowledge-based rather than industrial-based, more of a company's value may come from internally generated intangible intellectual assets such as R&D, brands, trademarks, and employee talent than from traditional tangible assets. Consider, for example, Loblaw's President Choice brand image, Dell Computer's direct marketing strategy, and an Internet provider's subscriber base. How should these be valued? Today's accounting system is based on historical costs of physical assets. There is ongoing research and study for estimating and reporting the value of investments in intangibles. The stock market, on the other hand, places a value on them. In fact, the value of knowledge assets now approaches or even exceeds the value of reported book assets. This is what creates the huge discrepancy between book value and market value.[4]

Whether and how to value intangibles is a controversial issue. Some people believe that because intangibles are uncertain and risky, they do not belong on the balance sheet. Costs related to intangibles may bear no relationship to their actual value. On the other hand, placing a value on intangibles allows companies to know whether they are earning adequate returns on R&D, whether patents are worth renewing, and whether they should invest more to build brands. Clearly, there are no quick and easy solutions to this issue, which will continue to be studied in the coming years.

Tightening the GAAP

Although GAAP is supposed to ensure uniformity of Canadian companies' financial reporting, in reality companies have some discretion in how they interpret certain accounting standards. Companies appear to be taking advantage of loopholes in GAAP to manipulate numbers. There have been examples of companies accused of fraudulently inflating income by claiming inflated revenues. Many companies are pushing accounting to the edge—and over it—to keep earnings rising to meet the expectations of investment analysts, who project earnings, and investors, who panic when a company misses the analysts' forecasts. This has raised serious concerns about the quality of earnings and questions about the validity of financial reports.

One of the most common issues involves write-offs of certain large one-time charges. What is a legitimate one-time charge, and what are normal operating costs that are written off as they are incurred? GAAP doesn't provide a clear answer. In this category are charges like restructuring charges (combining several years of expected future expenses and writing them off at once) and costs associated with acquisitions, such as "in-process R&D," the estimated value of R&D at an acquired company. The acquirer can write off the estimated value of products still in development. The benefits of this R&D are unknown and may be worthless in the future, so companies must take the charge against earnings now.

concept check

- What new roles are accountants playing? Do you see any potential problems from these new roles?
- What are knowledge assets, and why have they become so important?
- How can large one-time write-offs distort a company's financial results?
- What problems might the declining quality of financial reporting present for investors, lenders, and the economy in general?

APPLYING THIS CHAPTER'S TOPICS

By now it should be very clear that basic accounting knowledge is a valuable skill to have, whether you start your own company, work for someone else, or are looking for an investment opportunity. Analyzing a company's financial statements before you take a job there can tell you quite a bit about its financial health. Once you are on the job, you need to understand how to read financial statements and how to develop financial information for business operations. It's almost impossible to operate effectively in a business environment otherwise. Especially in a small company, you will wear many hats, and having accounting skills may help you get the job or provide an opportunity for advancement. In addition, accounting will help you manage your personal finances.

If you own your own firm, you can't rely on someone else to take charge of your accounting system. You must decide what financial information you need to manage your company better and to track its progress. If you can't understand the reports your accountant prepares, you will have no idea whether they are accurate.

Managing your personal finances is also a lot easier if you understand accounting. Suppose your Great-Aunt Helen wants to buy you a few shares of stock to encourage your interest in business. Her stockbroker suggests two computer companies, and Aunt Helen asks you to choose one of them. The product lines of the companies are nearly identical. Where can you get more information to help you make your choice? Someone suggests that you should study their financial statements. The companies send you their financial statements upon request. Now that you have a basic understanding of accounting, you have an idea of what all those numbers mean and how you can use them to make your decision.

As you will see in Question 2 in the Try It Now box, accounting can also help you create personal financial statements. And as noted above, financial statements are at the core of investment analysis.

TRY IT NOW!

1. **Learn to Read Financial Statements** To become more familiar with annual reports and key financial statements, head for IBM's Guide to Understanding Financials at www.ibm.com/investor/ FinancialGuide/. The material offers a good overview of financial reporting and shows you what to look for when you read these documents.

2. **Prepare Personal Financial Statements** One of the best ways to learn about financial statements is to prepare them. Put together your personal balance sheet and income statement, using Exhibits 11-4 and 11-5 as samples. You will have to adjust the account categories to fit your needs. Here are some suggestions:

   - Current assets—cash on hand, balances in savings and chequing accounts.
   - Investments—stocks and bonds, retirement funds.
   - Fixed assets—real estate, personal property (cars, furniture, jewellery, etc.).
   - Current liabilities—charge card balances, loan payments due in one year.

   - Long-term liabilities—mortgage on real estate, loan balances that will not come due until after one year.
   - Income—employment income, investment income (interest, dividends).
   - Expenses—housing, utilities, food, transportation, medical, clothing, insurance, loan payments, taxes, personal care, recreation and entertainment, and miscellaneous expenses.

After you complete your personal financial statements, use them to see how well you are managing your finances. Consider the following questions:

   - Should you be concerned about your debt ratio?
   - Would a potential creditor conclude that it is safe or risky to lend you money?
   - If you were a company, would people want to invest in you? Why or why not? What could you do to improve your financial condition?

>looking ahead
at Accounting

As Barry Sadrehashemi says, regardless of your position in an organization you need to understand accounting and how the processes can work in your favour. Sufficient knowledge of accounting and the tax system (see Chapter 7) can change the bottom line for a company. If you are able to read a balance sheet, income statement, and statement of cash flows, you will be able to make less risky decisions about matters such as what company you want to work for and what company you should invest in.

Now that you have some basic knowledge of accounting, you should be asking yourself questions such as these: How can this information help me in the future? Do I have at least some knowledge to make better decisions?

In addition, you can develop realistic forecasts, something that was impossible without basic accounting knowledge. With accounting knowledge not only can you have an accurate picture of where your personal financial life is—but you can also be informed about where the company you choose to work for (or own) is going financially. This knowledge provides a reality check.

SUMMARY OF LEARNING GOALS

➡ lg 1   **Why are financial reports and accounting information important, and who uses them?**

Accounting involves collecting, recording, classifying, summarizing, and reporting a firm's financial activities according to a standard set of procedures. The financial reports resulting from the accounting process give managers, employees, investors, customers, suppliers, creditors, and government agencies a way to analyze a company's past, current, and future performance. Financial accounting is concerned with the preparation of financial reports using generally accepted accounting principles. Managerial accounting provides financial information that management can use to make decisions about the firm's operations.

➡ lg 2   **What are the differences between public and private accountants?**

Public accountants work for independent firms that provide accounting services—such as financial report preparation and auditing, tax return preparation, and management consulting—to other organizations on a fee basis. Private accountants are employed to serve one particular organization and may prepare financial statements, tax returns, and management reports.

➡ lg 3   **What are the six steps in the accounting cycle?**

The accounting cycle refers to the process of generating financial statements. It begins with analyzing business transactions, recording them in journals, and posting them to ledgers. Ledger totals are then summarized in a trial balance that confirms the accuracy of the figures. Next the accountant prepares the financial statements and reports. The final step involves analyzing these reports and making decisions.

➡ lg 4   **In what terms does the balance sheet describe the financial condition of an organization?**

The balance sheet represents the financial condition of a firm at one moment in time, in terms of assets, liabilities, and owners' equity. The key categories of assets are current assets, fixed assets, and intangible assets. Liabilities are divided into current and long-term liabilities. Owners' equity, the amount of the owners' investment in the firm after all liabilities have been paid, is the third major category.

⇒lg 5 **How does the income statement report a firm's profitability?**
The income statement is a summary of the firm's operations over some period. The main parts of the statement are revenues (gross and net sales), cost of goods sold, operating expenses (selling and general and administrative expenses), taxes, and net profit or loss.

⇒lg 6 **Why is the statement of cash flows an important source of information?**
The statement of cash flows summarizes the firm's sources and uses of cash during a financial reporting period. It breaks the firm's cash flows into those from operating, investment, and financing activities. It shows the net change during the period in the firm's cash and marketable securities.

⇒lg 7 **How can ratio analysis be used to identify a firm's financial strengths and weaknesses?**
Ratio analysis is a way to use financial statements to gain insight into a firm's operations, profitability, and overall financial condition. The four main types of ratios are liquidity ratios, profitability ratios, activity ratios, and debt ratios. Comparing a firm's ratios over several years and comparing them to ratios of other firms in the same industry or to industry averages can indicate trends and highlight financial strengths and weaknesses.

⇒lg 8 **What major trends are affecting the accounting industry today?**
The accounting industry is responding to the rise in information technology in several ways. The role of accountants has expanded beyond the traditional audit and tax functions and now includes management consulting in areas such as computer systems, human resources, and electronic commerce. A major issue facing the industry is how to treat key intangible assets—knowledge assets such as patents, brands, research and development—and whether they should be valued and included on a company's balance sheet. In addition, the CICA has raised concerns about the quality of reported earnings. Loose interpretation of GAAP has given companies leeway in how they deal with items like restructuring charges and write-offs resulting from acquisitions.

WORKING THE NET

1. What is the latest news in business? CBC has up-to-the-minute news and information about business and what is happening, not only for Canadian companies but companies that affect Canadian business. See **www.cbc.ca/business** for the most current business news stories. Discuss the current business news stories with classmates.

2. The cornerstone of the Canadian financial system (see Chapter 12) is the TSX Group Inc. To view this public company's annual report see **www.tsx.ca**. What are the different areas within the TSX Group?

3. Can you judge an annual report by its cover? Bornemann Communications has developed "secrets to developing a successful annual report." Check out these secrets at **www.bccreative.com/secrets.html**. How do you think using these secrets can influence the stakeholders of a company?

4. Go to the Web site of a company that is traded on the TSX (**www.tsx.ca**) and look for its annual report. Consider the statement from the chartered accountancy firm that audited the financial statements. What have the auditors said about the company's financial statements according to GAAP? What letters to the shareholders are included? Who signed the letter to the shareholders? Do you think that the secrets mentioned in Question 3 could improve this annual report? Do you think companies should put their financial information online? Why or why not?

CREATIVE THINKING CASE

The Weathervane Terrace Inn and Suites

Charlevoix is a resort community located in a valley between Lake Charlevoix and Lake Michigan. With its majestic maple trees, picket fences, Victorian homes, three-masted schooners and gleaming yachts, blue water, and white sand beaches, Charlevoix is reminiscent of a summer resort town from the 1800s. In the winter, it offers scenic cross-country ski trails and snowmobiling trails. In short, Charlevoix is a year-round tourist destination.

One of Charlevoix's premier lodging facilities is the Weathervane Terrace Inn and Suites (**www.weathervane-chx.com/**). The Weathervane Inn, housed in an "architectural and historic masterpiece," provides "a special and unique lodging experience" for guests. The inn has special guest packages such as the Charlevoix Sampler and several different golf packages. The Weathervane's staff readily accommodates guests' special requests, whether they involve organizing special outings, making reservations with other hotels on a guest's itinerary, arranging a charter fishing expedition, or renting a sailboat.

In addition to offering these services, the Weathervane Inn seeks to provide a luxurious and restful experience for its guests by providing numerous amenities, including a pool, a hot tub spa, a massive stone fireplace in the game room, and spectacular views of Lake Michigan. All rental units are oversized. Each unit is furnished with a refrigerator, a microwave oven, and a videocassette recorder. Some rooms feature two-person Jacuzzi tubs and wet bars. The one-bedroom suites feature a kitchenette and fireplace. Conference and meeting facilities are available as well.

The Weathervane Inn has an interesting, if not unique, ownership structure. The rooms and suites are essentially condominium units that are owned by individual investors. A management team operates the inn for the owners. The managers' duties include promoting the inn, renting units to guests when they are not being used by the owners, cleaning and maintaining the rental units, and regularly reporting operating results to the owners. The managers strive to equitably allocate rentals across all the units. By doing this, they assure that all owners receive reasonable rental income from their condominium properties.

Essentially, the Weathervane's staff are sales and management agents for the condominium owners. As agents, they have a stewardship responsibility with regard to the investors' assets. This agency relationship also imposes important financial reporting requirements on the managers.

To enable them to do an effective and efficient job of financial reporting, the Weathervane Inn's managers use a computerized accounting information system. This system tracks all the accounting and financial data for each condominium unit, including rental activity and income, operating expenses, and maintenance expenses. This information is used to generate monthly accounting reports for each condominium owner. Thus, the owners are able to monitor and evaluate the management of their investment properties.[5]

Critical Thinking Questions

1. Why is it important for the Weathervane Inn to have an effective and efficient accounting information system?
2. What types of accounting reports are likely to be most useful to the condominium owners? Explain your answer.
3. How can the condominium owners make use of financial accounting? How can they make use of managerial accounting?

MAKING THE CONNECTION MAKING THE CONN

Financial Management and the Securities Markets

In this chapter we will continue to look at the finance area. The primary role of the financial manager is to maximize the value of the firm for the owners. This is to achieve the main critical success factor of *financial performance*. This, we know, cannot be done without the other four success factors, reiterating the need for the managers of all departments to work closely with each other and the finance area in particular.

As we saw in Chapter 11, the relationship between finance and the major *stakeholders*, particularly the owners, is a difficult but important one. One important decision that financial managers have to make is how much of the company's profit will be distributed to the shareholders in the form of a dividend. The shareholders expect a return, so if a regular dividend is not paid then they expect the return in the form of an increased share price. This can only happen if the investing community sees potential in the value of the stock. If neither of these happens, the price of the stock will fall as shareholders sell their shares. The company must therefore consider the stakeholder response to the decisions it makes, as they will affect its ability to maximize the value of the firm for the owners.

The dividend decision also provides us with an example of how the securities markets are affected by decisions made in the finance area. The securities markets themselves also affect the finance area. For example, whether it is a bull market or a bear market affects the ability of the company to raise funds in the market, as well as the value of the company's shares.

As we also saw in Chapter 11, all decisions have financial consequences, but financial decisions have consequences in the other areas as well. For example, policies for granting credit affect *marketing's* ability to generate sales. Just imagine if Chrysler did not offer financing packages on its vehicles. Also, money spent on research and development or new production facilities has an impact on what *operations* is capable of doing, just as the company's policies on payroll costs have an impact on attracting and keeping key employees (human resources). To make money the firm must first spend money, but it must also control that money

in order to continue to be profitable and stay viable. It's a fine balance that must be achieved between taking the risks and reaping the rewards—one that the finance manager must consider and that affects all areas of the company.

Cash flow provides an example of this need for integration and balance. In order to aid marketing in selling the firm's products, the supply chain must be set up to make sure that inventory is available for customers, and credit is generally extended. But that means that finance must balance the time that it takes to sell the inventory and then collect the accounts receivable from customers, with the payments on that inventory and other expenses. If it does not do this, the company will not have enough cash coming in to pay its bills and will go bankrupt! Another example is with inventory. The operations area needs raw materials on hand to avoid delays in production and marketing needs enough finished goods on hand to *satisfy customers*, but finance must balance these needs with the cost of carrying inventory, and therefore it tries to keep inventory levels at a minimum. In Chapter 10 we discussed techniques for dealing with inventory, and saw that technology provides many new options.

Technology is just one of the many environmental factors that must be taken into account in making financial decisions. For example, as market demand changes (*social* environment), funds need to be shifted between projects. As interest rates and exchange rates fluctuate (*economic* environment), some projects and methods of financing projects will either need to be abandoned or will become more possible. General economic conditions in domestic and world markets may cause firms to speed up or slow down the rate of investment in different projects, and government policies in the home and foreign countries (*political* environment) may make investment in certain projects more attractive than others; and as *technology* advances and costs drop, some projects become more accessible.

In the internal business environment when budgets are set, the finance area must work with the other functional areas to develop plans for financing the company that help it meet its strategic goals. Each area has a role to play in helping the organization achieve its strategic goals, and the resources they will need must be considered. Finance uses various forecasts to develop financial plans for the business.

Financial Management and the Securities Markets

CHAPTER 12

Learning Goals

➡ **lg 1** What roles do finance and the financial manager play in the firm's overall strategy?

➡ **lg 2** How does a firm develop its financial plans, including forecasts and budgets?

➡ **lg 3** What types of short-term and long-term expenditures does a firm make?

➡ **lg 4** What are the main sources and costs of unsecured and secured short-term financing?

➡ **lg 5** How do the two primary sources of long-term financing compare?

➡ **lg 6** What are the major types, features, and costs of long-term debt?

➡ **lg 7** When and how do firms issue equity, and what are the costs?

➡ **lg 8** Where can investors buy and sell securities?

➡ **lg 9** What trends are affecting the field of financial management?

Financial Acumen at Acumen Capital Financial Partners Ltd.

What does it take to be a successful chief financial officer (CFO) today? CFOs are no longer behind-the-scenes players but key members of the executive team, setting the firm's overall strategy and participating in managerial activities that go well beyond traditional areas. Team building, strategic and operational planning, managing risks, selling and acquiring companies—it's all in a day's work for financial managers like Bruce Ramsay, a founder and chairman of Acumen Capital Financial Partners Limited.

Acumen is defined by *Webster's Dictionary* as "keenness and depth of perception, discernment or discrimination, especially in practical matters." Acumen in financial matters is a key to the success of most businesses today. As Bruce Ramsay says, "a lack of financial acumen can lead to your banker handing your head to you on a platter." Acumen Capital Financial Partners is a fully licensed investment dealer specializing in the technology and manufacturing sectors. The objective of the founders was to have fun while doing something different. Offering corporate financial services and research services to smaller, high-growth companies seems like fun to Bruce and his partner, Kim Wong. In addition to these services, the firm seeks out external growth capital for corporate clients. Client companies need injections of cash to execute their business plans and purchase assets such as inventories, buildings, machinery, and so forth. The planning and the finance go hand in hand. The financial markets serve as an intermediary between the corporate client and the institutional investors, the real source of capital. As there is only a cyclical ability to raise money in the markets, the equity market must be good in order for the capital to be available. The financial officer of the company must know where the firm is in the economic cycle. What is the receptivity of the market? When the economy is down, the investment trend is toward larger companies rather than the smaller high-growth operations.

As Bruce says, "If the cookie train is going by, better take a cookie." See more on Acumen at **www.acumencapital.com**.[1]

CRITICAL THINKING QUESTIONS

As you read this chapter, consider the following questions as they relate to Acumen Capital Financial Partners Limited:

- In addition to raising funds, what other types of financial activities would Bruce Ramsey oversee?

- What types of economic, industry, and other information would be important to Acumen's financial analysts in developing forecasts of revenues and operating expenses?

- How do financiers such as Bruce Ramsay help to achieve the financial manager's primary goal of maximizing the value of the firm to its owners?

BUSINESS IN THE 21ST CENTURY

In today's fast-paced global economy, managing a firm's finances is more complex than ever. For financial managers like Bruce Ramsey, a thorough command of traditional finance activities—financial planning, investing money, and raising funds—is only part of the job. Financial managers are more than number crunchers. As part of the top management team, chief financial officers (CFOs) need a broad understanding of their firm's business and industry, as well as leadership ability and creativity. They must never lose sight of the primary goal of the financial manager: to maximize the value of the firm to its owners.

Financial management—raising and spending a firm's money—is both a science and an art. The science is analyzing numbers and flows of cash through the firm. The art is answering questions such as these: Is the firm using its financial resources in the best way? Aside from costs, why choose a particular form of financing? How risky is each option?

This chapter focuses on the financial management of a firm. We'll start with an overview of the role of finance and of the financial manager in the firm's overall business strategy. Next we consider the basics of financial planning—forecasts and budgets. Discussions of investment decisions and sources of short- and long-term financing follow. We'll also look at key trends affecting financial management in the 21st century and then discuss the securities markets.

The Role of Finance and the Financial Manager

Finance is critical to the success of all companies. It may not be as visible as marketing or production, but management of a firm's finances is just as much a key to its success.

Financial management—the art and science of managing a firm's money so it can meet its goals—is not just the responsibility of the finance department. All business decisions have financial consequences. Managers in all departments must work closely with financial personnel. If you are a sales representative, for example, the company's credit and collection policies will affect your ability to make sales.

Any company, whether it's a two-lawyer partnership or Loblaw Companies Limited, needs money to operate. To make money, it must first spend money—on inventory and supplies, equipment and facilities, and employee wages and salaries.

Revenues from sales of the firm's products should be the chief source of funding. But money from sales doesn't always come in when it's needed to pay the bills. Financial managers must track how money is flowing into and out of the firm (see Exhibit 12-1). They work with the firm's other department managers to determine how available funds will be used and how much money is needed. Then they choose the best sources to obtain the required funding.

For example, a financial manager will track day-to-day operational data such as cash collections and disbursements to ensure that the company has enough cash to meet its obligations. Over a longer time horizon, the manager will thoroughly study whether and when the company should open a new manufacturing facility. The manager will also suggest the most appropriate way to finance the project, raise the funds, and then monitor the project's implementation and operation.

Financial management is closely related to accounting. In most firms both areas are the responsibility of the vice-president of finance or the CFO. Accountants' main function is to collect and present financial data. Financial managers use financial statements and other information prepared by accountants to make financial decisions. Financial managers focus on **cash flows,** the inflow and outflow of cash. They plan and monitor the firm's cash flows to ensure that cash is available when needed. It is not uncommon for those working in the finance area to have an accounting designation.

→ lg 1

financial management
The art and science of managing a firm's money so that it can meet its goals.

HOT Links

When you come across a finance term you don't understand, visit the Fiscal Agents Financial Services Group's financial glossary at www.fiscalagents.com/newsletter/gloss/Glossary/a.shtml

cash flows
The inflow and outflow of cash for a firm.

e x h i b i t   1 2 - 1 | How Cash Flows through a Business

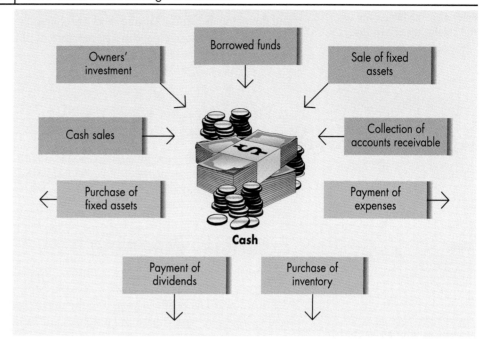

The Financial Manager's Responsibilities and Activities

Financial managers have a complex and challenging job. They analyze financial data prepared by accountants, monitor the firm's financial status, and prepare and implement financial plans. One day they may be developing a better way to automate cash collections; the next they may be analyzing a proposed merger or acquisition. The key activities of the financial manager are:

- *Financial planning.* Preparing the financial plan, which projects revenues, expenditures, and financing needs over a given period.
- *Investment (spending money).* Investing the firm's funds in projects and securities that provide high returns in relation to the risks.
- *Financing (raising money).* Obtaining funding for the firm's operations and investments and seeking the best balance between debt (borrowed funds) and equity (funds raised through the sale of ownership shares in the business).

The Goal of the Financial Manager

How can financial managers make wise planning, investment, and financing decisions? The main goal of the financial manager is *to maximize the value of the firm to its owners.* The value of a publicly owned corporation is measured by the share price of its stock. A private company's value is the price at which it could be sold.

To maximize the firm's value, the financial manager has to consider both short- and long-term consequences of the firm's actions. Maximizing profits is one approach, but it should not be the only one. Such an approach favours making short-term gains over achieving long-term goals. What if a firm in a highly technical and competitive industry did no research and development? In the short run, profits would be high because research and development is very expensive. But in the long run, the firm might lose its ability to compete because of its lack of new products.

Financial managers constantly strive for a balance between the opportunity for profit and the potential for loss. In finance, the opportunity for profit is termed **return;** the potential for loss, or the chance that an investment will not achieve the expected level of return, is **risk.** A basic principle in finance is that the higher the risk, the greater

return
The opportunity for profit.

risk
The potential for loss or the chance that an investment will not achieve the expected level of return.

risk-return trade-off
A basic principle in finance that holds that the higher the risk, the greater the return that is required.

the return that is required. This widely accepted concept is called the **risk-return trade-off.** Financial managers consider many risk and return factors when making investment and financing decisions. Among them are changing patterns of market demand, interest rates, general economic conditions, market conditions, and political and social issues (such as environmental effects and equal employment opportunity policies).

concept check

- What is the role of financial management in a firm?
- How do the three key activities of the financial manager relate?
- What is the main goal of the financial manager? How does the risk-return trade-off relate to the financial manager's main goal?

→ **lg 2**

Financial Planning

Companies use several types of plans to determine how to achieve organizational objectives. A company's *financial plan* is part of the overall company plan and guides the firm toward its business goals and the maximization of its value. The financial plan enables the firm to estimate the amount and timing of its investment and financing needs.

To prepare a financial plan, the financial manager must first consider existing and proposed products, the resources available to produce them, and the financing needed to support production and sales. Forecasts and budgets are essential to the firm's financial planning. They should be part of an integrated planning process that links them to strategic plans and performance measurement.

short-term forecasts
Projections of revenues, costs of goods, and operating expenses over a one-year period.

long-term forecasts
Projections of a firm's activities and the funding for those activities over a period that is longer than one year; from a financial point typically covers two to ten years.

Forecasts

The financial planning process starts with financial forecasts, or projections of future developments within the firm. The estimated demand for the firm's products (the sales forecast) and other financial and operating data are key inputs. For example, many manufacturing companies' economic analysts estimate expected production and sales for each line of cars and trucks. Then financial analysts prepare detailed short- and long-term financial forecasts based on these assumptions.

Short-term forecasts, or *operating plans,* project revenues, costs of goods, and operating expenses over a one-year period. Using short-term forecasts, financial managers estimate the next year's expenses for inventory, labour, advertising, and other operating activities. These estimates form the basis for cash budgets (described below) that forecast cash inflows and outflows over the same period.

Long-term forecasts, or *strategic plans,* from the financial point typically cover two to ten years and take a broader view of the firm's financial activities. With these forecasts, management can assess the financial effects of various business strategies: What would be the financial results of investing in new facilities and equipment? Of developing new products? Of eliminating a line of business? Of acquiring other firms? Long-term forecasts also show where the funding for these activities is expected to come from.

Financial managers at the Ford Motor Company plan and monitor cash flow to ensure that funds are available to finance the labour and material costs of producing vehicles.

Budgets

budgets
Formal written forecasts of revenues and expenses that set spending limits based on operational forecasts; include cash budgets, capital budgets, and operating budgets.

Firms prepare **budgets** to plan and control their future financial activities. These are formal written forecasts of revenues and expenses that set spending limits based on operational forecasts. All budgets begin with forecasts. Budgets are a way to control expenses and compare the actual performance to the forecast.

Firms use several types of budgets. Most cover a one-year period. **Cash budgets** forecast the firm's cash inflows and outflows and help the firm plan for cash surpluses and shortages. Because having enough cash is so critical to their financial health, many firms prepare annual cash budgets subdivided into months or weeks. Then they project the amount of cash needed in each shorter time period. **Capital budgets** forecast outlays for fixed assets (plant and equipment). They usually cover a period of several years and ensure that the firm will have enough funds to buy the equipment and buildings it needs. **Operating budgets** combine sales forecasts with estimates of production costs and operating expenses in order to forecast profits. They are based on individual budgets for sales, production, purchases of materials, factory overhead, and operating expenses. Operating budgets then are used to plan operations: dollars of sales, units of production, amounts of raw materials, cost of wages, and so forth.

cash budgets
Budgets that forecast a firm's cash inflows and outflows and help the firm plan for cash surpluses and shortages.

capital budgets
Budgets that forecast a firm's outlays for fixed assets (plant and equipment), typically for a period of several years.

operating budgets
Budgets that combine sales forecasts with estimates of production costs and operating expenses in order to forecast profits.

Budgets are routinely used to monitor and control the performance of a division, a department, or an individual manager. When actual outcomes differ from budget expectations, management must take action.

concept check

- What is a financial plan? Name two types of financial planning documents.
- Distinguish between short- and long-term forecasts. How are both used by financial managers?
- Briefly describe three types of budgets.

→ lg 3

How Organizations Use Funds

To grow and prosper, a firm must keep investing money in its operations. The financial manager decides how best to use the firm's money. Short-term expenses support the firm's day-to-day activities. For instance, Roots Canada Ltd. regularly spends money to buy such raw materials as fabrics and to pay employee salaries. Long-term expenses are typically for fixed assets. For Nike, these would include outlays to build a new factory, buy automated manufacturing equipment, or acquire a small manufacturer of sports apparel.

Short-Term Expenses

Short-term expenses, often called *operating expenses*, are outlays used to support current production and selling activities. They typically result in current assets, which include cash and any other assets (accounts receivable and inventory) that can be converted to cash within a year. The financial manager's goal is to manage current assets so the firm has enough cash to pay its bills and to support its accounts receivable and inventory.

Cash Management: Assuring Liquidity

cash management
The process of making sure that a firm has enough cash on hand to pay bills as they come due and to meet unexpected expenses.

Cash is the lifeblood of business. Without it, a firm could not operate. An important duty of the financial manager is **cash management,** or making sure that enough cash is on hand to pay bills as they come due and to meet unexpected expenses.

Businesses use budgets to estimate the cash requirements for a specific period. Many companies keep a minimum cash balance to cover unexpected expenses or changes in projected cash flows. The financial manager arranges loans to cover any shortfalls. If the size and timing of cash inflows closely match the size and timing of cash outflows, the company needs to keep only a small amount of cash on hand. A company whose sales and receipts are fairly predictable and regular throughout the year needs less cash than a company with a seasonal pattern of sales and receipts. A toy company, for instance, whose sales are concentrated in the fall, spends a great deal of cash during the spring and summer to build inventory. It has excess cash during the winter and early spring, when it collects on sales from its peak selling season.

Because cash held in chequing accounts earns little, if any, interest, the financial manager tries to keep cash balances low and to invest the surplus cash. Surpluses are invested temporarily in **marketable securities,** short-term investments that are easily converted into cash. The financial manager looks for low-risk investments that offer high returns. Three of the most popular marketable securities are Treasury bills, certificates of deposit, and commercial paper. **Commercial paper** is unsecured short-term debt (an IOU) issued by a financially strong corporation.

In addition to seeking the right balance between cash and marketable securities, the financial manager tries to shorten the time between the purchase of inventory or services (cash outflows) and the collection of cash from sales (cash inflows). The three key strategies are to collect money owed to the firm (accounts receivable) as quickly as possible, to pay money owed to others (accounts payable) as late as possible without damaging the firm's credit reputation, and to minimize the funds tied up in inventory.

Managing Accounts Receivable

Accounts receivable represent sales for which the firm has not yet been paid. Because the product has been sold but cash has not yet been received, an account receivable amounts to a use of funds. For example, the average manufacturing firm's accounts receivable represent about 15 to 20 percent of total assets.

The financial manager's goal is to collect money owed to the firm as quickly as possible—while offering customers credit terms attractive enough to increase sales. Accounts receivable management involves setting *credit policies,* guidelines on offering credit, and *credit terms,* specific repayment conditions, including how long customers have to pay their bills and whether a cash discount is given for quicker payment. Another aspect of accounts receivable management is deciding on *collection policies,* the procedures for collecting overdue accounts.

Setting up credit and collection policies is a balancing act for financial managers. On the one hand, easier credit policies or generous credit terms (a longer repayment period or larger cash discount) result in increased sales. On the other hand, the firm has to finance more accounts receivable. The risk of uncollectible accounts receivable also rises. Businesses consider the impact on sales, timing of cash flow, experience with bad debt, customer profiles, and industry standards when developing their credit and collection policies.

Companies that want to speed up collections can use several strategies. They can actively manage their accounts receivable, rather than passively letting customers pay when they want to. Michael Churchman, owner of Rocky Mountain Radar, an electronics company, waited three months for his first payment from one of his corporate customers. Not content to settle for the customer's typically slow payment process, he took steps to be paid in 15 days: good follow-up with both the buyer and the person who handles his accounts payable and offering a 5 percent cash discount for payment within 15 days. The benefits of faster collections offset the small discount.[2]

Technology can also help firms speed up collections. To cope with the dramatic rise in sales and, hence, accounts receivable, Dell Computer implemented an automated receivables collection system. Customized software improved order processing

marketable securities
Short-term investments that are easily converted into cash.
commercial paper
Unsecured short-term debt (an IOU) issued by a financially strong corporation.

HOT Links

Find an introduction to the types of personal and business services offered by Scotiabank at www.scotiabank.com

accounts receivable
Sales for which a firm has not yet been paid.

and collection methods. The new system also took over labour-intensive tasks such as sending letters to overdue accounts at specified times and creating activity reports with current account status. Dell's days receivables outstanding dropped from 50 to 37 days, freeing up a significant amount of cash.[3]

Inventory

Another use of funds is to buy inventory needed by the firm. In a typical manufacturing firm, inventory is nearly 20 percent of total assets. The cost of inventory includes not only its purchase price, but also ordering, handling, storage, interest, and insurance costs.

Production, marketing, and finance managers usually have differing views about inventory. Production managers want lots of raw materials on hand to avoid production delays. Marketing managers want lots of finished goods on hand so customer orders can be filled quickly. But financial managers want the least inventory possible without harming production efficiency or sales. Financial managers must work closely with production and marketing to balance these conflicting goals. Techniques for reducing the investment in inventory—efficient order quantities, the just-in-time system, and materials requirement planning—are discussed in Chapter 10.

Long-Term Expenditures

capital expenditures
Investments in long-lived assets, such as land, buildings, machinery, and equipment, that are expected to provide benefits over a period longer than one year.

A firm also uses funds for its investments in long-lived assets, such items as land, buildings, machinery, and equipment. These are called **capital expenditures.** Unlike operating expenses, which produce benefits within a year, the benefits from capital expenditures extend beyond one year. For instance, a printer's purchase of a new printing press with a usable life of seven years is a capital expenditure. It appears as a fixed asset on the firm's balance sheet. Paper, ink, and other supplies, however, are expenses. Mergers and acquisitions are also considered capital expenditures.

Firms make capital expenditures for many reasons. The most common are to expand and to replace or renew fixed assets. Another reason is to develop new products. Most manufacturing firms have a big investment in long-term assets. For example, Bombardier Aerospace, the third largest civil airframe manufacture in the world, invests millions of dollars a year into its manufacturing facilities.

capital budgeting
The process of analyzing long-term projects and selecting those that offer the best returns while maximizing the firm's value.

Because capital expenditures tend to be costly and have a major effect on the firm's future, the financial manager must analyze long-term projects and select those that offer the best returns while maximizing the firm's value. This process is called **capital budgeting.** Decisions involving new products or the acquisition of another business are especially important. Another challenge managers face is assessing the value of proposed information technology expenditures.

concept check

- Distinguish between short- and long-term expenses.
- What is the financial manager's goal in cash management? List the three key cash management strategies.
- Describe the firm's main motives in making capital expenditures.

➡ **lg 4**

Obtaining Short-Term Financing

How do firms raise the funding they need? They borrow money (debt), sell ownership shares (equity), and retain earnings (profits). The financial manager must assess all these sources and choose the one most likely to help maximize the firm's value.

Like expenses, borrowed funds can be divided into short- and long-term loans. A short-term loan comes due within one year; a long-term loan has a maturity greater than a year. Short-term financing is shown as a current liability on the balance sheet. It is used to finance current assets and support operations. Short-term loans can be unsecured or secured.

Unsecured Short-Term Loans

unsecured loans
Short-term loans for which the borrower does not have to pledge specific assets as security.

Unsecured loans are made on the basis of the firm's creditworthiness and the lender's previous experience with the firm. An unsecured borrower does not have to pledge specific assets as security. The three main types of unsecured short-term loans are trade credit, bank loans, and commercial paper.

Trade Credit: Accounts Payable

trade credit
The extension of credit by the seller to the buyer between the time the buyer receives the goods or services and when it pays for them.

When Cott Corporation, the world's largest supplier of premium retailer brand beverages, sells its products to Loblaw Companies Limited, Loblaw does not have to pay cash on delivery. Instead, Cott regularly bills Loblaw for its purchases, and Loblaw pays at a later date. This is an example of **trade credit**—the seller extends credit to the buyer between the time the buyer receives the goods or services and when it pays for them. Trade credit is a major source of short-term business financing. The buyer enters the credit on its books as an **account payable.** In effect, the credit is a short-term loan from the seller to the buyer of the goods and services. Until Loblaw pays Cott, Cott has an account receivable from Loblaw—and Loblaw has an account payable to Cott.

accounts payable
Purchase for which a buyer has not yet paid the seller.

Bank Loans

Unsecured bank loans are another source of short-term business financing. Companies often use these loans to finance seasonal (cyclical) businesses. For instance, a swimwear manufacturer has strong sales in the spring and summer and lower sales during the fall and winter. It needs short-term bank financing to increase inventories before its strongest selling season and to finance accounts receivable during late winter and early spring, as shown in Exhibit 12-2. The company repays these bank loans when it sells the inventory and collects the receivables.

e x h i b i t   1 2 - 2 | Swimwear Manufacturer's Seasonal Cash Flows

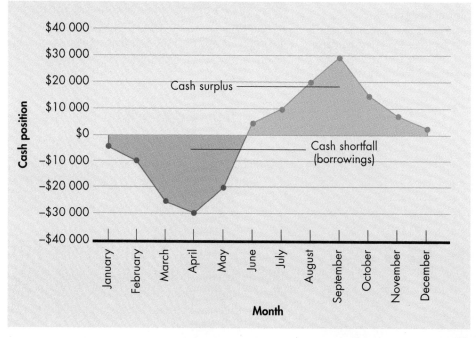

line of credit
An agreement between a bank and a business that specifies the maximum amount of unsecured short-term borrowing the bank will allow the firm over a given period, typically one year.

revolving credit agreement
A guaranteed line of credit whereby a bank agrees that a certain amount of funds will be available for a business to borrow over a given period.

Unsecured bank loans include lines of credit and revolving credit agreements. A **line of credit** is an agreement between a bank and a business. It specifies the maximum amount of unsecured short-term borrowing the bank will allow the firm over a given period, typically one year. A line of credit is not a guaranteed loan; the bank agrees to lend funds only if it has money available. Usually, the firm must repay any borrowing within a year. It must also either pay a fee or keep a certain percentage of the loan amount (10 to 20 percent) in an account at the bank.

Another bank loan, the **revolving credit agreement,** is basically a guaranteed line of credit. Because the bank guarantees that a certain amount of funds will be available, it charges an extra fee in addition to interest. Revolving credit agreements are often arranged for a two- to five-year period.

Firms often obtain annual lines of credit based on their expected seasonal needs. Then they can quickly borrow without having to reapply to the bank each time funds are needed. Suppose the swimwear manufacturer projected a cash shortfall of $80 000 for the period from February to June. The financial manager might get a $100 000 line of credit from the bank. (The extra $20 000 would be there to cover any unexpected expenses.) The firm could borrow funds as needed—$10 000 in February, $25 000 in March, $30 000 in April. Then it could gradually repay the loan as it collects cash during the summer months.

Commercial Paper

As noted earlier, *commercial paper* is an unsecured short-term debt (an IOU) issued by a financially strong corporation. Thus, it is a short-term investment for firms with temporary cash surpluses, and it is a financing option for major corporations. Corporations issue commercial paper in multiples of $100 000 for periods ranging from 30 to 270 days. Many big companies use commercial paper instead of short-term bank loans because the interest rate on commercial paper is usually 1 to 3 percent below bank rates.

BetzDearborn, a manufacturer of water treatment chemicals, saved US$800 000 a year by replacing a portion of its short-term financing with a US$500 million commercial paper program. Not only was the interest rate lower, but commercial paper was more flexible, allowing BetzDearborn to issue it as needed. By fine-tuning the timing of its borrowing, the company reduced expenses even further.[4]

Secured Short-Term Loans

secured loans
Loans for which the borrower is required to pledge specific assets as collateral, or security.

Secured loans require the borrower to pledge specific assets as *collateral*, or security. The secured lender can legally take the collateral if the borrower doesn't repay the loan. Commercial banks and commercial finance companies are the main sources of secured short-term loans to business. Borrowers whose credit is not strong enough to qualify for unsecured loans use these loans.

Typically, the collateral for secured short-term loans is accounts receivable or inventory. Because accounts receivable are normally quite liquid (easily converted to cash), they are an attractive form of collateral. The appeal of inventory—raw materials or finished goods—as collateral depends on how easily it can be sold at a fair price.

factoring
A form of short-term financing in which a firm sells its accounts receivable outright at a discount to a *factor*.

Another form of short-term financing using accounts receivable is **factoring.** A firm sells its accounts receivable outright to a *factor*, a financial institution (usually a commercial bank or commercial finance company) that buys accounts receivable at a discount. Factoring is widely used in the clothing, furniture, and appliance industries. Factoring allows a firm to turn its accounts receivable into cash without worrying about collections. Because the factor assumes all the risks and expenses of collecting the accounts, firms that factor all of their accounts can reduce the costs of their credit and collection operations. Factoring is more expensive than a bank loan, however,

HOT Links

When working capital is a problem, one option is factoring. Learn more about factoring by searching Export Development Canada's Web site at www.edc.ca

because the factor buys the receivables at a discount from their actual value. But often a company has no choice because it has neither the track record to get unsecured financing nor other collateral to pledge as security for a loan.

concept check

• Distinguish between unsecured and secured short-term loans.
• Briefly describe the three main types of unsecured short-term loans.
• Discuss the two ways that accounts receivable can be used to obtain short-term financing.

➡ **lg 5**

financial risk
The chance that a firm will be unable to make scheduled interest and principal payments on its debt.

Raising Long-Term Financing

A basic principle of finance is to match the term of the financing to the period over which the benefits are expected to be received from the associated outlay. Short-term expenses should be financed with short-term funds, and long-term expenses should be financed with long-term funds. Long-term financing sources include both debt (borrowing) and equity (ownership). Equity financing comes either from selling new ownership interests or from retaining earnings.

Debt versus Equity Financing

Say that Bombardier Aerospace plans to spend $2 billion over the next four years to build and equip new factories to make jet aircraft. Bombardier's top management will assess the pros and cons of both debt and equity and then consider several possible sources of the desired form of long-term financing.

The major advantage of debt financing is the deductibility of interest expense for income tax purposes, which lowers its overall cost. In addition, there is no loss of ownership. The major drawback is **financial risk**—the chance that the firm will be unable to make scheduled interest and principal payments. The lender can force a borrower that fails to make scheduled debt payments into bankruptcy. Most loan agreements have restrictions to ensure that the borrower operates efficiently.

Equity, on the other hand, is a form of permanent financing that places few restrictions on the firm. The firm is not required to pay dividends or repay the investment. However, equity financing gives common shareholders voting rights that provide them with a voice in management. Equity is more costly than debt. Unlike the interest on debt, dividends to owners are not tax-deductible expenses. Exhibit 12-3 summarizes the major differences between debt and equity financing.

Financial managers try to select the mix of long-term debt and equity that results in the best balance between cost and risk. Company policies about the mix of debt and equity vary. Some companies have high debt compared to equity. Others keep debt to a minimum.

Yahoo co-founder Jerry Yang held a press conference to announce that his Internet search engine firm was going public to finance the expansion of Yahoo's online services.

exhibit 1 2 - 3 | Major Differences between Debt and Equity Financing

	Debt Financing	Equity Financing
Voice in management	Creditors typically have none, unless borrower defaults on payments. Creditors may be able to place restraints on management in event of default.	Common shareholders have voting rights.
Claim on income and assets	Debt holders rank ahead of equity holders. Payment of interest and principal is a contractual obligation of the firm.	Equity owners have a residual claim on income (dividends are paid only after interest and any scheduled principal payments are paid) and assets. The firm has no obligation to pay dividends.
Maturity	Debt has a stated maturity and requires repayment of principal by a specified maturity date.	The company is not required to repay equity, which has no maturity date.
Tax treatment	Interest is a tax-deductible expense.	Dividends are not tax-deductible and are paid from after-tax income.

HOT Links

In Chapter 11 we discussed the debt to equity ratio. Search for the annual reports of some of the public companies that you are interested in (found on their Web sites) and calculate the company's relationship of debt to equity. For example, check out the Hudson Bay Company at www.hbc.com

 lg 6

term loan
A business loan with a maturity of more than one year; can be unsecured or secured.

bonds
Securities that represent long-term debt obligations (liabilities) issued by corporations and governments.

interest
A fixed amount of money paid by the issuer of a bond to the bondholder on a regular schedule, typically every six months; stated as the *coupon rate*.

principal
The amount borrowed by the issuer of a bond; also called *par value*.

Debt Financing

Long-term debt is used to finance long-term (capital) expenditures. The maturities of long-term debt typically range between 5 and 20 years. Three important forms of long-term debt are term loans, bonds, and mortgage loans.

Term Loans

A **term loan** is a business loan with a maturity of more than one year. Term loans generally have 5- to 12-year maturities and can be unsecured or secured. They are available from commercial banks, insurance companies, pension funds, commercial finance companies, and manufacturers' financing subsidiaries. A contract between the borrower and the lender spells out the amount and maturity of the loan, the interest rate, payment dates, the purpose of the loan, and other provisions such as operating and financial restrictions on the borrower to control the risk of default. Term loans may be repaid on a quarterly, semi-annual, or annual schedule. The payments include both interest and principal, so the loan balance declines over time. Borrowers try to arrange a repayment schedule that matches the forecast cash flow from the project being financed.

Bonds

Bonds are securities that represent long-term debt obligations (liabilities) of corporations and governments. A bond certificate is issued as proof of the obligation. The issuer of a bond must pay the buyer a fixed amount of money—called **interest,** stated as the *coupon rate*—on a regular schedule, typically every six months. The issuer must also pay the bondholder the amount borrowed—called the **principal,** or *par value*—at the bond's maturity date (due date). Bonds are usually issued in units of $1000—for instance, $1000, $5000, or $10 000. The two sources of return on bond investments are interest income and gains from sale of the bonds.

Bonds do not have to be held to maturity. They can be bought and sold in the securities markets (discussed below). Unlike common and preferred shareholders, who are owners, bondholders are creditors (lenders) of the issuer. In the event of liquidation, the bondholders' claim on the assets of the issuer comes before that of any shareholders.

CORPORATE BONDS   Corporate bonds, as the name implies, are issued by corporations. They usually have a par value of $1000. They may be secured or unsecured, include special provisions for early retirement, or be convertible to common shares.

High-yield, or **junk**, **bonds** are high-risk, high-return bonds that became popular during the 1980s, when they were widely used to finance mergers and takeovers. Today, they are used by companies whose credit characteristics would not otherwise allow them access to the debt markets. Because of their high risk, these bonds generally earn 3 percent or more above the returns on high-quality corporate bonds.

Corporate bonds can be either secured or unsecured. **Secured bonds** have specific assets pledged as collateral, which the bondholder has a right to take if the bond issuer defaults. **Mortgage bonds** are secured by property, such as land, equipment, or buildings. **Debentures** are unsecured bonds. They are backed only by the reputation of the issuer and its promise to pay the principal and interest when due. In general, debentures have a lower risk of default than secured bonds and therefore have lower interest rates. Of course, a debenture issued by a financially shaky firm probably has a greater default risk than a mortgage bond issued by a sound one.

Corporate bonds may be issued with an option for the bondholder to convert them into common shares. **Convertible bonds** generally allow the bondholder to exchange each bond for a specified number of common shares. For instance, a $1000 par value convertible bond may be convertible into 40 common shares—no matter what happens to the market price of the common shares. Because convertible bonds could be converted to stock when the price is very high, these bonds usually have a lower interest rate than nonconvertible bonds.

Mortgage Loans

A **mortgage loan** is a long-term loan made against real estate as collateral. The lender takes a mortgage on the property, which lets the lender seize the property, sell it, and use the proceeds to pay off the loan if the borrower fails to make the scheduled payments. Long-term mortgage loans are often used to finance office buildings, factories, and warehouses. Life insurance companies are an important source of these loans. They issue billions of dollars worth of mortgage loans to businesses each year.

high-yield (junk) bonds
High-risk, high-return bonds.

secured bonds
Corporate bonds for which specific assets have been pledged as collateral.

mortgage bonds
Corporate bonds that are secured by property, such as land, equipment, or buildings.

debentures
Unsecured bonds that are backed only by the reputation of the issuer and its promise to pay the principal and interest when due.

convertible bonds
Corporate bonds that are issued with an option that allows the bondholder to convert them into common shares.

mortgage loan
A long-term loan made against real estate as collateral.

concept check

- Describe the common features of all bonds. What are the advantages and disadvantages of bonds for investors?
- What are corporate bonds? Discuss secured and unsecured types.
- What is a mortgage loan?

→ lg 7

Equity Financing

Equity is the owners' investment in the business. In corporations, the common and preferred shareholders are the owners. A firm obtains equity financing by selling new ownership shares (external financing) or by retaining earnings (internal financing).

Common Shares

common shares
Securities that represent one form of ownership interest in a corporation.

Common shares are securities that represent one form of ownership interest in a corporation. A share is issued for each unit of ownership. The shareholder (owner) gets a stock certificate to prove ownership, and ownership gives the shareholder certain rights.

As a shareholder, you have a right to the profits of the corporation. You would receive them as dividends on your common shares. *Dividends* are the part of the profits of a corporation that the firm distributes to shareholders. Dividends are paid only after all the other obligations of the firm—payments to suppliers, employees, bondholders, and other creditors, plus taxes and preferred share dividends—have been met. Dividends can be paid in cash or stock (called *stock dividends*). Some firms, especially rapidly growing companies and those in high-technology industries, pay no dividends. Instead, they reinvest their profits (retained earnings) in more buildings, equipment, and new products to earn greater future profits. (Dividends, stock dividends, and retained earnings are discussed in more detail below.)

Common shareholders also have *voting rights*. They usually get one vote for each share they own. They can vote on such issues as election of the board of directors, mergers/acquisitions, and the selection of an independent auditor.

POTENTIAL RETURNS TO INVESTORS   Common shares offer two types of potential returns: dividends and share-price increases. Dividends are declared annually or quarterly (four times a year) by the board of directors (discussed below).

An investor can also benefit by selling a stock when its price increases, or *appreciates,* above the original purchase price. Suppose you bought shares of a company in January 200X at $52 and sold them for $76 in October 200X. The per-share profit of $24 ($76 sales price − $52 original price) represents a 46 percent *rate of return* ($24 profit ÷ $52 original price). Common shareholders have no guarantee that they will get any return on their investment and sometimes will lose money on their investment.

ADVANTAGES AND DISADVANTAGES OF COMMON SHARES   The returns from common-share dividends and price appreciation can be quite attractive. Over the long term, common-share investments have been better than most other types of investments. The historical average annual return on common shares since World War II has been about 12 percent. Another advantage is liquidity: many stocks are actively traded in securities markets and can be quickly bought and sold.

The major disadvantage is the risky nature of common-share investments. Shareholders may not get any return at all. Stocks are subject to many risks related to the economy, the industry, and the company. These risks can hold down a stock's dividends and its price, making it hard to predict the stock's return.

Preferred Shares

preferred shares
Equities for which the dividend amount is set at the time the stock is issued.

Another form of equity is **preferred shares.** Unlike common shares, preferred shares usually have a dividend amount that is set at the time the stock is issued. These dividends must be paid before the company can pay any dividends to common shareholders. Also, if the firm goes bankrupt and sells its assets, preferred shareholders get their money back before common shareholders do.

Like debt, preferred shares increase the firm's financial risk because they obligate the firm to make a fixed payment. But preferred shares are more flexible. The firm can miss a dividend payment without suffering the serious results of failing to pay back a debt.

FEATURES OF PREFERRED SHARES   Preferred shares have features of both common shares and bonds. Like common shares, preferred shares are a form of ownership. Dividends may not be paid on either type of shares if the company encounters financial hardships. But most preferred shares are *cumulative preferred shares.* Owners must receive all unpaid dividends before any dividends can be paid to the holders of common shares. Suppose that a company with a $5-per-year preferred dividend missed its annual dividend payment in 200X. It must pay the preferred shareholders $10 ($5 in unpaid preferred dividends from 200X plus the $5 preferred dividend for the current year) before it can pay any dividends to common shareholders. Like bonds, preferred shares provide fixed income to investors, and their claim on income and assets comes before that of common shareholders (but after bondholders).

ADVANTAGES AND DISADVANTAGES OF PREFERRED SHARES   Investors like preferred shares because of the steady dividend income. Although companies are not legally obligated to pay preferred dividends, most have an excellent record of doing so. But the fixed dividend is also a disadvantage because it limits the cash paid to investors. Thus, preferred shares have less potential for price appreciation than common shares.

concept check

- Define common shares, and describe their features.
- What are the advantages and disadvantages of common shares for investors and corporations?
- What are preferred shares, and how are they different from common shares?

Dividends and Retained Earnings

dividends
Payments to shareholders from a corporation's profits.

stock dividends
Payments to shareholders in the form of more shares; may replace or supplement cash dividends.

Dividends are payments to shareholders from a corporation's profits. A company does not have to pay dividends to shareholders. But if investors buy the shares expecting to get dividends and the firm does not pay them, the investors may sell their shares. If too many sell, the value of the shares decreases. Dividends can be paid in cash or in stock. **Stock dividends** are payments in the form of more shares. Stock dividends may replace or supplement cash dividends. After a stock dividend has been paid, more shares have a claim on the same company, so the value of each share often declines.

At their meetings, the company's board of directors (with the advice of its financial managers) decides how much of the profits to distribute as dividends and how much to reinvest. A firm's basic approach to paying dividends can greatly affect its share price. A stable history of dividend payments indicates good financial health. If a firm that has been making regular dividend payments cuts or skips a dividend, investors start thinking it has serious financial problems. The increased uncertainty often results in lower share prices. Thus, most firms set dividends at a level they can keep paying.

retained earnings
Profits that have been reinvested in a firm.

Retained earnings, profits that have been reinvested in the firm (i.e., not distributed as dividends), have a large advantage over other sources of equity capital: they do not incur underwriting costs. Financial managers strive to balance dividends and retained earnings to maximize the value of the firm. Often the balance reflects the nature of the firm and its industry. Well-established firms and those that expect only modest growth, like public utilities, typically pay out much of their earnings in dividends.

concept check

- Compare the advantages and disadvantages of debt and equity to the issuer.
- Discuss the advantages and disadvantages of owning common shares.
- Briefly describe retained earnings and preferred shares.

➡ lg 8

securities
Investment certificates issued by corporations or governments that represent either equity or debt.

institutional investors
Investment professionals who are paid to manage other people's money.

primary market
The securities market where *new* securities are sold to the public.

HOT Links

What are some of the IPOs available today? Check out the premium investor resource centre at ipo.investcom.com

secondary market
The securities market where (already issued) old securities are traded among investors; includes the organized stock exchanges, the over-the-counter market, and the commodities exchanges.

initial public offer (IPO)
A company's first issuance of shares to the public.

Securities Markets

Shares, bonds, and other securities are traded in securities markets. These markets streamline the purchase and sales activities of investors by allowing transactions to be made quickly and at a fair price. They make the transfer of funds from lenders to borrowers much easier. **Securities**—investment certificates issued by corporations or governments—represent either equity (ownership in the issuer) or debt (a loan to the issuer).

Institutional investors are investment professionals who are paid to manage other people's money. Most of these professional money managers work for financial institutions, such as banks, mutual funds, insurance companies, and pension funds. Institutional investors control very large sums of money, often buying stock in 10 000-share blocks. They aim to meet the investment goals of their clients. Institutional investors are a major force in the securities markets, accounting for about half of the dollar volume of equities traded.

Businesses and governments also take part in the securities markets. Corporations issue bonds and shares to raise funds to finance their operations. They are also among the institutional investors that purchase corporate and government securities.

Types of Markets

Securities markets can be divided into primary and secondary markets. The **primary market** is where *new* securities are sold to the public, usually with the help of investment bankers. In the primary market, the issuer of the security gets the proceeds from the transaction. A security is sold in the primary market just once—when it is first issued.

Later transactions take place in the **secondary market,** where *old* (already issued) securities are bought and sold, or traded, among investors. The issuers generally are not involved in these transactions. The vast majority of securities transactions take place in secondary markets, which include the organized stock exchanges (in Canada these include the Toronto Stock Exchange and the TSX Venture Exchange), the over-the-counter securities market, and the commodities exchanges.

Selling New Stocks in a Primary Market

When a company first issues shares to the public, it is an example of a company *going public*—its first sale of stock to the public. Usually, a high-growth company has an **initial public offering (IPO)** because it needs to raise more funds to finance continuing growth. (Companies that are already public can issue and sell additional common shares to raise equity funds.) An IPO often enables existing shareholders, usually employees, family, and friends who bought the shares privately, to earn big profits on their investment. But going public has some drawbacks. For one thing, there is no guarantee an IPO will sell. It is also expensive. Large fees must be paid to investment bankers, brokers, lawyers, accountants, and printers. Once the company is public, it is closely watched by regulators, shareholders, and securities analysts. The firm must reveal such information as operating and financial data, product details, financing plans, and operating strategies. Providing this information is often costly.

Contributing to the growing number of individual investors are discount brokerages, online trading firms, home computers, and the Internet.

The Role of Investment Bankers and Stockbrokers

Two types of investment specialists play key roles in the functioning of the securities markets. **Investment bankers** help companies raise long-term financing. These firms act as intermediaries, buying securities from corporations and governments and reselling them to the public. This process, called **underwriting,** is the main activity of the investment banker, which acquires the security for an agreed-upon price and hopes to be able to resell it at a higher price to make a profit. Investment bankers advise clients on the pricing and structure of new securities offerings, as well as on mergers, acquisitions, and other types of financing. Most of the Canadian banks now offer investment-banking services.

A **stockbroker** is a person who is licensed to buy and sell securities on behalf of clients. Also called *account executives,* these investment professionals work for brokerage firms and execute the orders customers place for shares, bonds, mutual funds, and other securities.

The Primary Canadian Stock Exchanges

The cornerstone of the Canadian financial system is the TSX Group. The TSX Group owns and operates the two national stock exchanges, the Toronto Stock Exchange and the TSX Venture Exchange. The Toronto Stock Exchange serves the senior equity market (a broad range of established businesses from across Canada, the United States, and other countries), and the public venture equity market is served by the TSX Venture Exchange (which provides emerging companies with access to capital).

Other Exchanges Important to Canadian Businesses

Of all the foreign exchanges, the New York Stock Exchange (NYSE) is the most important to Canadian business. Canadian companies that are listed on the NYSE have access to a greater pool of potential investors due to the sheer number of people who live in and invest in the United States. Only companies that meet certain minimum requirements are eligible for being listed on the NYSE.

The Over-the-Counter Market

Unlike the organized stock exchanges, the **over-the-counter (OTC) market** is not a specific institution with a trading floor. It is a sophisticated telecommunications network that links dealers and enables them to trade securities. The **National Association of Securities Dealers Automated Quotation (NASDAQ) system,** the first electronic-based stock market, is the fastest-growing part of the stock market. It provides up-to-date bid and ask prices on about 6400 of the most active OTC securities. Its sophisticated electronic communication system is the main reason for the popularity and growth of the OTC market.

The securities of many well-known companies, some of which could be listed on the organized exchanges, trade on the OTC market. Examples include Apple Computer, Coors, Dell Computer, Intel, Microsoft, Nordstrom Department Stores, Qualcomm, and Starbucks. The stocks of most commercial banks and insurance companies also trade in this market, as do most government and corporate bonds. About 440 foreign companies also trade on the OTC market.

What makes the NASDAQ different from an organized exchange? On the NYSE, for example, one specialist handles all transactions in a particular stock, but on the NASDAQ system, a number of dealers handle ("make a market in") a security. For instance, about 40 dealers make a market in Apple Computer stock. Thus, dealers compete, improving investors' ability to get a good price.

Many of the world's previously organized stock markets are opting for an OTC market based on the NASDAQ system due to technology changes, user sophistication, and lower operating costs.

---

investment bankers
Firms that act as underwriters, buying securities from corporations and governments and reselling them to the public.

underwriting
The process of buying securities from corporations and governments and reselling them to the public; the main activity of investment bankers.

stockbroker
A person who is licensed to buy and sell securities on behalf of clients.

HOT Links

To learn more about the Toronto Stock Exchange, the TSX Venture Exchange, how companies get listed on the exchanges, and the most current stock price quotes, visit **www.tsx.ca**

HOT Links

The Montreal Exchange trades primarily in the options, futures, and derivative markets. To find out more about these, visit **www.me.org**

over-the-counter (OTC) market
A sophisticated telecommunications network that links dealers and enables them to trade securities.

National Association of Securities Dealers Automated Quotation (NASDAQ) system
The first electronic-based stock market and the fastest-growing part of the stock market.

HOT Links

For more information about the NYSE go to **www.nyse.com**

Many Canadian firms and other firms outside of Japan list their stock on the Tokyo Stock Exchange, one of the world's largest foreign exchanges.

bull markets
Markets in which securities prices are rising.

bear markets
Markets in which securities prices are falling.

Market Conditions: Bull Market or Bear Market?

Two terms that often appear in the financial press are "bull market" and "bear market." Securities prices rise in **bull markets.** These markets are normally associated with investor optimism, economic recovery, and government action to encourage economic growth. In contrast, prices go down in **bear markets.** Investor pessimism, economic slowdown, and government restraint are all possible causes. As a rule, investors earn better returns in bull markets; they earn low, and sometimes negative, returns in bear markets.

Bull and bear market conditions are hard to predict. Usually, they can't be identified until after they begin. Over the past 50 years, the stock market has generally been bullish, reflecting general economic growth and prosperity. Bull markets tend to last longer than bear markets. The bull market that started in 1982 lasted a full five years, and the bear market that preceded it lasted just over a year and a half. The longest bull market on record began in October 1990 and was still going strong into 2001. Since then, the markets have been relatively flat (i.e., neither a bull nor a bear market) with short pockets of a bear market.

concept check

- How do securities markets help businesses and investors?
- Distinguish between primary and secondary securities markets.
- How does an investment banker work with companies to issue securities?

HOT Links

To find out what happens when you place an order, follow the "anatomy of a trade" on the NYSE at
www.nyse.com/floor/1022221392895.html

➡ **lg 9**

CAPITALIZING ON TRENDS IN BUSINESS

Many of the key trends shaping financial management as we proceed through the first decade of the 21st century echo those in other disciplines. For example, technology is improving the efficiency with which financial managers run their operations. As in other areas, the increasing interdependence of the world's economies requires an international approach to finance. One different note, however, is the expanding role of the financial manager in risk management.

Finance Goes Global

Just as venturing overseas affects marketing, production, and general management practices, globalization brings additional complexity to financial management. Today's financial managers can make investments and raise financing in Canada and around the world. They may have to compare the costs, risks, and benefits of relocating manufacturing facilities to another country versus expanding at home. And they must pay attention not only to the Canadian economy, but to economic developments in the United States, Mexico, South America, Europe, and other areas.

Take Karl Strauss Breweries, for example. The microbrewery tried for over a year to break into foreign markets. It was already exporting to Taiwan when the financial turmoil in Asia erupted. Not only did those shipments stop, but attempts to enter other

Asian markets failed. Next Karl Strauss focused on several Russian cities—only to have the ruble collapse due to political and economic conditions in Russia just as the company was finalizing the deal. The ruble's devaluation pushed the price of Karl Strauss's product to more than double that of Russian beer. Rather than abandon plans to enter international markets, the brewery has continued to focus on a long-term strategy but now looks closer to home.[5]

Managing foreign currency exposure and developing strategies to protect against increased foreign currency risk are now major activities for many financial managers. Fluctuating exchange rates affect the revenues, costs, and profits of businesses that operate in global markets. And because once-stable currencies can become extremely volatile, as happened in Asia in the fall of 1998, companies must track currency rates closely and change their strategies as necessary.

On January 1, 2002, euro cash was introduced as the legal tender in 12 countries in Europe. The introduction of the euro should make global financial markets more efficient and improve access to European capital markets. It can also bring advantages to early adopters. Rapidly growing technology companies, for example, can bring their products to a unified European market more quickly and at a lower cost. Other advantages include elimination of currency transaction costs, streamlined financial and accounting systems, simplified currency risk management, and reduced hedging costs.

Risk Management

The 1998 turmoil in Asian and Russian financial markets proved that going global increases a company's risk, whether or not the company has operations in those regions. As a result, financial managers are spending more time on **risk management,** the process of identifying and evaluating risks and selecting and managing techniques to adapt to risk exposures. Companies face a wide range of risks, including:

- *Credit risk.* Exposure to loss as a result of default on a financial transaction or a reduction in a security's market value due to decline in the credit quality of the debt issuer.
- *Market risk.* Risk resulting from adverse movements in the level or volatility of market prices of securities, commodities, and currencies.
- *Operational risk.* The risk of unexpected losses arising from deficiencies in a firm's management information, support, and control systems and procedures.

A failure in a company's risk control procedures can lead to substantial financial losses. Major financial institutions like Daiwa and Sumitomo Corp. lost huge amounts of money because their control systems collapsed. A breakdown in risk control eventually costs the shareholders money. They may have to invest more capital to bail out the troubled firm. Otherwise their equity investment will decline in value when the company's problems become known to the public.[6]

Recently, some insurance companies have entered the risk management arena. They offer new types of policies to protect companies against disappointing financial results. Reliance Group, an insurer, introduced Enterprise Earnings Protection Insurance. This policy reimburses a company for any operating earnings shortfall that is due to forces beyond management's control, such as drought, floods, or the Asian economic crisis. Reliance is hoping that CFOs will buy its policies to prevent earnings surprises. Guaranteeing results is likely to be an expensive proposition, however. And predicting the volatility of a client's earnings is a new area for insurers.[7]

HOT Links

For everything you need to know about the euro, start at the U.K.'s official Web site for the euro at
www.euro.gov.uk

risk management
The process of identifying and evaluating risks and selecting and managing techniques to adapt to risk exposures.

HOT Links

Learn more about risk management services on the Web site of Wilfrid Laurier University's School of Business and Economics Clarica Financial Services Research Centre at
www.wlu.ca/~wwwsbe/
sbe2000/html/clarica.html

Anyone investing in the securities market is wise to keep up to date on the latest business trends and, as Bruce Ramsay says, "Research, research, research!"

APPLYING THIS CHAPTER'S TOPICS

Whether you are a marketing manager, purchasing agent, or systems analyst, knowledge of finance will help you to do your job better. You'll be able to understand your company's financial statements, its financial condition, and management's investment and financing decisions. Financial information also provides feedback on how well you are doing and identifies problems. On a more practical note, you may be asked to prepare a budget for your department or unit. Employees who understand the financial decision-making process will be able to prepare proposals that address financial concerns. As a result, they will be more likely to get the resources they require to accomplish the firm's goals.

If you own a business, you must pay close attention to financial management. Without financial plans you may find yourself running out of cash. It's easy to get so caught up in growing sales that you neglect your billing and collection methods. In fact, managing accounts receivable is often one of the more challenging aspects of running a young company. But you can't rely on revenue increases to solve your cash flow problems. Good receivables practices start with credit policies. Be choosy when it comes to offering trade credit and check customers' credit references and payment history thoroughly. Set the initial credit limit fairly low until the customer establishes a prompt payment history. Here are some other ways to improve collections:

- Bill frequently, not just at the end of the month, so that money flows in throughout the month.
- Clearly state payment terms.
- Establish regular and frequent follow-up procedures. Some companies call to notify the customer that the bill has been sent and to make sure the customer is satisfied. Weekly calls are in order for late payments.
- Monitor results of outstanding receivables collection.
- Don't fill new orders from customers who are continually delinquent.[8]

You can also apply financial management techniques to your personal life. See the budget exercise in the Try It Now! box.

TRY IT NOW!

Prepare a Personal Budget A personal budget is one of the most valuable tools for personal financial planning. It will help you evaluate your current financial situation, spending patterns, and goals.

- Using credit card receipts, cheque records, and other documents, record your income and expenses for the past 30 days. Based on this information, develop a personal budget for the next month. Follow the worksheet in Exhibit 12-4. Include scholarships or grants as other income sources.

- Track your actual income and expenses for one month. Write down everything you spend on a daily basis, or you will forget little things (like snacks) that add up over the course of a month.

- At the end of the budget period, compare your budget to your actual results. How close were you to your budget estimates? In what categories did you overspend? Where did you underspend? Did creating the budget have any impact on how you allocated your money to different categories and how you spent your money?

- *Optional*: Use the results of your first month's budget to project next month's income and expenses. And repeat the monitoring process.

e x h i b i t   1 2 - 4 | Monthly Budget Worksheet

Name:_____
Month of _____

	Planned	Actual	Variance

Income
  Wages (take-home pay)
  Support from relatives
  Loans
  Withdrawals from savings
  Other _____
  Other _____
  (1) Total Available Income

Expenses
  Fixed Expenses
  Housing
  Automobile payment
  Insurance
  Loan repayment
  Savings for goals
  Tuition and fees
  Other _____
      Subtotal, Fixed Expenses

  Flexible Expenses
  Food
  Clothing
  Personal care
  Entertainment and recreation
  Transportation
  Telephone
  Utilities (electricity, gas, water)
  Cable TV
  Medical and dental
  Books, magazines, educational
      supplies
  Gifts
  Other _____
  Other _____
      Subtotal, Flexible Expenses

  (2) Total Expenses

Cash Surplus (Deficit) [(1)–(2)]

>looking ahead
at Acumen Capital Financial Partners

What trends should you monitor to maintain your financial acumen? It seems a tightening of government regulations is imminent, and a review of corporate governance is likely. With the internationalization of the business world, the market is wide open. The day-trader trend seems to have stabilized with investors, solidifying the relationship between themselves and a financial advisor. A final word for the novice investor from Bruce Ramsay, chairman of Acumen Capital Financial Partners: "Before parting with your money, do your homework … research, research, research."

SUMMARY OF LEARNING GOALS

➡️lg 1 **What roles do finance and the financial manager play in the firm's overall strategy?**

Finance involves managing the firm's money. The financial manager must decide how much money is needed and when, how best to use the available funds, and how to get the required financing. The financial manager's responsibilities include financial planning, investing (spending money), and financing (raising money). Maximizing the value of the firm is the main goal of the financial manager, whose decisions often have long-term effects.

➡️lg 2 **How does a firm develop its financial plans, including forecasts and budgets?**

Financial planning enables the firm to estimate the amount and timing of the financial resources it needs to meet its business goals. The planning process begins with forecasts based on the demand for the firm's products. Short-term forecasts project expected revenues and expenses for one year. They are the basis for cash budgets, which show the flow of cash into and out of the firm and are used to plan day-to-day operations. Long-term forecasts project revenues and expenses for two to ten years. These strategic plans allow top management to analyze the impact of different options on the firm's profits.

➡️lg 3 **What types of short-term and long-term expenditures does a firm make?**

A firm invests in short-term expenses—supplies, inventory, and wages—to support current production, marketing, and sales activities. The financial manager manages the firm's investment in current assets so that the company has enough cash to pay its bills and support accounts receivable and inventory. Long-term expenditures (capital expenditures) are made for fixed assets such as land, buildings, and equipment. Because of the large outlays required for capital expenditures, financial managers carefully analyze proposed projects to determine which offer the best returns.

➡️lg 4 **What are the main sources and costs of unsecured and secured short-term financing?**

Short-term financing comes due within one year. The main sources of unsecured short-term financing are trade credit, bank loans, and commercial paper. Secured loans require a pledge of certain assets, such as accounts receivable or inventory, as security for the loan. Factoring, or selling accounts receivable outright at a discount, is another form of short-term financing.

➡️lg 5 **How do the two primary sources of long-term financing compare?**

Financial managers must choose the best mix of debt and equity for their firm. The main advantage of debt financing is the tax-deductibility of interest. But debt involves financial risk because it requires the payment of interest and principal on specified dates. Equity—common and preferred shares—is considered a permanent form of financing on which the firm may or may not pay dividends. Dividends are not tax-deductible.

➡️lg 6 **What are the major types, features, and costs of long-term debt?**

The main types of long-term debt are term loans, bonds, and mortgage loans. Term loans can be secured or unsecured and generally have 5- to 12-year maturities. Bonds usually have maturities of 10 to 30 years. Mortgage loans are secured by real estate. Long-term debt usually costs more than short-term financing because of the greater uncertainty that the borrower will be able to make the scheduled loan payments.

➡️lg 7 **When and how do firms issue equity, and what are the costs?**

The chief sources of equity financing are common shares, retained earnings, and preferred shares. The cost of selling shares includes issuing costs and potential dividend payments. Retained earnings are profits reinvested in the firm. For the issuing firm, preferred shares are more expensive than debt because their dividends are not tax-deductible and their claims are secondary to those of debtholders, but less expensive than common shares.

➡lg 8   Where can investors buy and sell securities?
Securities are resold on organized stock exchanges, like the Toronto Stock Exchange and the TSX Venture Exchange, and in the over-the-counter market, a telecommunications network linking dealers throughout the world. The most actively traded securities are listed on the NASDAQ system, so dealers and brokers can perform trades quickly and efficiently.

➡lg 9   What trends are affecting the field of financial management?
Globalization brings additional complexity to financial management. Financial managers must be prepared to invest and raise funds overseas and make transactions in multiple currencies. Financial managers are spending more time on risk management, identifying and evaluating risks, and selecting techniques to control and reduce risk. Companies face a wide range of risks, including credit risk, market risk, and operational risk.

WORKING THE NET

1. GetSmart (**www.getsmart.com**) is an information service that offers advice on business as well as personal loans. Click on Business Finance Center and move through the various types of loans. Try the questionnaires in each area, using different answers, to see what is necessary to qualify for that financing option.
2. If factoring accounts receivable is still a mystery to you, visit "#1 Factoring Company" by J & D at **www.1-factoring-company.com/index.asp**. List the benefits of receivables financing and briefly describe the factoring process.
3. The International Finance and Commodities Institute (IFCI) Risk Watch site, **risk.ifci.ch/index.htm**, offers an excellent introduction to risk management concepts. Explore the site, especially the Key Concepts page, develop a list of sources and types of financial risks, and give an example of each. Discuss briefly the consequences of not controlling these risks. How can companies implement sound risk management procedures?

CREATIVE THINKING CASE

Pets.com Ends Up in the Doghouse

Pets.com was the cat's meow of online pet stores. Founded in February 1999, it caught the fancy of investors who were looking to grab some dot-com riches for themselves. Money flowed in from major venture capital firms and partners like Amazon.com. By December 1999, Pets.com raised US$110 million in four financing rounds and seemed destined for Internet stardom. It scheduled its initial public offering (IPO) for its first birthday in February 2000.

With a lavish US$27 million advertising campaign featuring their Sock Puppet mascot, Pets.com courted pet lovers who spared no expense on their pets, dressing them in diamond-studded collars, special coats, and other pricey accessories. However, the business model for pet e-tailers was not sustainable. "Pet products simply do not lend themselves very well to online purchases," says Andrew Bartels of Giga Information Group. "You can certainly order a 50-pound bag of dry dog food online, but think about the overnight shipping costs." To counter high shipping costs, Pets.com offered discounts to attract customers. As a result, it sold most products below cost, losing as much as $5 for every $1 of merchandise sold in the first quarter of 2000 alone.

"It was astounding to see how few pure dot-com e-tailers had a grasp of their gross margins," says Jim Breyer, managing partner at Accel Partners, a venture capital firm. They assumed that building sales to a high enough level would bring profits. Instead they discovered that expenses like marketing and personnel rose along with sales. At Pets.com, overall sales volume was slow to build; customers never returned to buy the higher-margin pet toys. The company quickly ran through their cash on hand.

By the time Pets.com went public, investors shunned Internet companies with small revenues, heavy losses, and no profits in sight. The stock never sold above the US$11 offering price as the once-hot market for dot-coms fizzled. From there it was all downhill. Pets.com launched a private-label food line, started selling sock-puppet merchandise, and built a second distribution centre to improve profitability and develop brand awareness. However, these strategies failed to interest new investors in providing the additional US$20 million necessary for Pets.com to continue operations. On November 7, 2000, Pets.com closed its doors.[9]

Critical Thinking Questions

1. In an interview just after the company's demise, Pets.com chairman and chief executive Julie Wainwright said, "In the end, we thought [closing the company] was the best thing for our shareholders, who are our primary concern, since we're a public company." Do you agree with Wainwright? Why? How does being a public company change the picture for Pets.com? What additional responsibilities and risks does it involve?

2. How could better financial planning have helped Pets.com in the early stages of its life?

3. Assume you were Pets.com's chief financial officer in early 2000. What steps could you have taken to possibly avoid the company's downfall?

MAKING THE CONNECTION MAKING THE CONN

Managing Human Resources

In this chapter we'll take a look at our last functional area, and last critical success factor. The old adage "last but not least" certainly applies here. As we discussed earlier, *gaining the commitment of employees* is the most critical factor because all of the other four critical success factors are achieved through the people in the company. Without a strong human resource area, and strong commitment of the employees toward organizational goals, the company simply cannot be successful in any functional area or overall.

The business environment today provides many challenges for the human resource manager. In the *political* environment regulations govern many different aspects of the human resource function, such as how workers can be selected (e.g., drug testing, human rights legislations governing the application and interview process, etc.). The mix of people hired is also regulated for some companies through employment equity legislation. Issues relating to diversity are critically important because without a diverse work force companies will have a difficult time understanding the diverse global marketplace and designing products and marketing plans to appeal to our diverse society. In the *economic* environment organizations are competing not only for customers but also for a shrinking pool of qualified job applicants, and they must also pay attention to the salaries of the competition in order to remain competitive. In the *social* environment workers are seeking to better balance their home and work lives, making it more critical and more difficult to gain commitment in the traditional ways, and the aging work force is also creating difficulties. The *technological* environment is reshaping how work is done, offering options to human labour and changing the nature of many jobs and the skills required to do them. Technology also affects how the human resource department does its job. You'll find many examples both in the chapter and in trying to find a job yourself, such as using the Internet to recruit workers and using specially designed software to pick out key phrases from résumés in order to sort through them more quickly.

As with the other functional areas, the main basis for all decisions is the company's goals and *strategy*. The role of the human resource area is to provide the right numbers of the right kinds of people in the right places at the right times to assist the other functional areas to help the organization achieve its objectives. To do this the human resource area must work very closely with *marketing*, *operations*, and *finance* to understand their objectives and thus their human resource requirements. It must also understand the jobs that need to be done to determine the skills that it must recruit and train for.

One area in which human resources must work especially closely with finance is in the area of employee compensation and benefits. Because of the relative size of this expense, it has a tremendous impact on the bottom line on the one hand, but on the other it also affects the level of commitment from employees, and therefore an integrative approach must be taken in determining compensation. This matter is becoming more important as workers are changing jobs more often.

Compensation is just one decision area in which the human resource manager must develop and implement policies to create a more committed work force. For example, one common approach in recruitment and selection is to first promote from within. This practice shows employees that the organization is committed to them, which is an essential ingredient in gaining commitment from employees. A particular integrative example is telecommuting. The technological environment has made telecommuting possible, thus improving the productivity of workers, saving companies money, and helping firms retain key people who would otherwise have to leave. In training and development as well, the organization can show its commitment to the employees by helping them to achieve their potential. Again, employees will be more committed to an organization that shows commitment to them in its human resource policies. And this loyalty translates into being more *innovative*, providing greater *quality*, and working harder to meet and exceed *customer needs*, thereby allowing the organization to *achieve financial performance*.

Managing Human Resources

CHAPTER 13

Learning Goals

→ **lg 1** What is the human resource management process?

→ **lg 2** How are human resource needs determined?

→ **lg 3** How do human resource managers find good people to fill the jobs?

→ **lg 4** What is the employee selection process?

→ **lg 5** What types of training and development do organizations offer their employees?

→ **lg 6** What is a performance appraisal?

→ **lg 7** How are employees compensated?

→ **lg 8** What is organizational career management?

→ **lg 9** What is the key legislation affecting human resource management?

→ **lg 10** What trends are affecting human resource management?

The Changing Role of HR at Right Axsmith

Right Axsmith (**www.right.com/ca**) is a leading organizational consulting and career transition firm with over 30 locations across Canada. The firm provides such services as coaching, leadership development, talent management, succession planning, mergers and acquisitions, employee opinion surveys, organizational culture analyses, career transitioning, and organizational assessment. Approximately 50 percent of their business is organizational consulting, and 50 percent is career transitioning.

According to Dianne Bond, a vice-president of the company, the role of the HR professional has changed dramatically over the years. In the 1970s the primary functions of the HR staff revolved around recruitment and selection. Their role was primarily administrative in nature and did not involve decision making. In the 1980s it became more important to involve HR in some decision making as many changes were occurring in organizations. The "job for life" era was over, a pay increase just for showing up was less common, and employees were expected to be more productive. As these changes occurred, the role of HR changed accordingly. The HR professional became more of a change agent and mediator, but still in an advisory role rather than a decision-making role.

According to Dianne, the goal of HR is now to be part of the strategic planning process. Many challenges face organizations today, including lack of employee loyalty, inability to attract and retain the top people, inadequate employee development, and ineffective (or nonexistent) succession planning. In addition, HR call centres are being established, new technology is being used more frequently, benefits plans are becoming self-administered, and a great deal of administrative work is being contracted out. All of these challenges affect the HR role. As usual, this scenario offers good news and bad news for the HR professional. The good news is that roles should become more strategic, HR may be included in the planning process, and organizational cultures may become more people focused as a result. As for the bad news, there are not as many HR jobs at the higher levels, HR departments are getting smaller, HR professionals must have an understanding of the entire business including the financial side, and there's more lateral movement into HR.

The bottom line, to quote Dianne Bond, "This is not a touchy-feely business anymore." If you're planning a career in HR, you must have a broad understanding of all business functional areas if you plan on sitting down at the strategic planning table.[1]

CRITICAL THINKING QUESTIONS

As you read this chapter, consider the following questions as they relate to Right Axsmith:

- What advice would you give a first-year student who is planning to go into HR because "I like to work with people"?
- What factors in the political, social, economic, and technological environments have contributed to the changed role of the HR professional?

BUSINESS IN THE 21ST CENTURY

Human resource management in contemporary organizations is instrumental in driving an organization toward its objectives. Today, human resource professionals face numerous challenges in recruiting, selecting, and retaining employees:

- Organizations are competing with each other for a shrinking pool of applicants.
- Workers seek to balance work and home/life activities.
- Technology is reshaping the way business is done.
- Laws govern many aspects of the employee–employer relationship.

Each day, human resource experts and front-line supervisors deal with these challenges while sharing responsibility for attracting and retaining skilled, motivated employees. Whether faced with a large or small human resource problem, managers need to understand the process for finding and retaining excellent employees.

In this chapter, you will learn about the role of human resource management in building and maintaining an exceptional work force. We will explore human resource planning, recruiting and selection, training, and motivating employees toward reaching organizational objectives. The chapter will also cover employee job changes within an organization and the laws guiding human resource decisions. Finally, we will look at important trends influencing human resource management.

Human resource managers at FedEx train employees to use computer technology that improves communication among employees and increases worker efficiency and productivity.

 lg 1

human resource management (HRM)
The process of hiring, developing, motivating, and evaluating employees to achieve organizational goals.

Developing People to Help Reach Organizational Goals

Human resource management (HRM) is the process of hiring, developing, motivating, and evaluating employees to achieve organizational goals. Organizational strategies and objectives form the basis for making all human resource management decisions. All companies strive to hire and develop well-trained, motivated employees. The human resources management process includes these steps, as illustrated in Exhibit 13-1:

- Job analysis and design
- Human resource planning and forecasting
- Employee recruitment
- Employee selection
- Training and development
- Performance planning and evaluation
- Compensation and benefits
- Organizational career management: employee job changes and disengagement.

In the following sections, you will learn more about each of these important functions.

concept check

- Define human resource management.
- Describe the human resource management process.

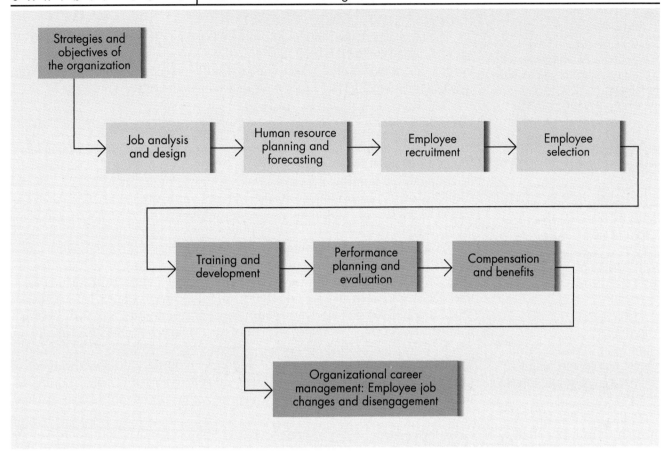

→ lg 2

Human Resource Planning

Firms need to have the right number of people, with the right training, in the right jobs, to do the organization's work when it needs to be done. Human resource specialists are the ones who must determine future human resource needs. Then they assess the skills of the firm's existing employees to see if new people must be hired or existing ones retrained.

human resource (HR) planning
Creating a strategy for meeting future human resource needs.

Creating a strategy for meeting future human resource needs is called **human resource (HR) planning.** Two important aspects of HR planning are job analysis and forecasting the firm's people needs. The HR planning process begins with a review of corporate strategy and policy. By understanding the mission of the organization, planners can understand its human resource needs. When Compaq Computer bought Digital Equipment Corp. (DEC), the acquisition resulted in several thousand DEC employees losing their jobs, while hundreds of Compaq employees were transferred to DEC's former headquarters in Boston. Many transferred employees assumed managerial positions.

Job Analysis and Design

job analysis
A study of the tasks required to do a particular job well.

Human resource planners must know what skills different jobs require. Information about a specific job is typically assembled through a **job analysis**, a study of the tasks required to do a job well. This information is used to specify the essential skills, knowledge, and abilities. For instance, when General Dynamics was awarded the contract for a new military plane, several new jobs were created for industrial engineers. Job

job description
The tasks and responsibilities of a job.

job specification
A list of the skills, knowledge, and abilities a person must have to fill a job.

analysts from the company's human resource department gathered information from other department heads and supervisors to help recruiters hire the right people for the new jobs.

The tasks and responsibilities of a job are listed in a **job description**. The skills, knowledge, and abilities a person must have to fill a job are spelled out in a **job specification**. These two documents help human resource planners find the right people for specific jobs. A sample job description is shown in Exhibit 13-2.

Human Resource Planning and Forecasting

Forecasting an organization's human resource needs, known as an HR *demand forecast*, is an essential aspect of HR planning. This process involves two forecasts: (1) determining the number of people needed by some future time (in one year, for example), and (2) estimating the number of people currently employed by the organization who will be available to fill various jobs at some future time. This is an *internal* supply forecast.

By comparing human resource demand and supply forecasts, a future personnel surplus or shortage can be determined and appropriate action taken. For example, United Airlines hired approximately 2000 additional flight attendants when it developed the Star Alliance, an air transport network consisting of United, Lufthansa, SAS, Thai, Varig, and Air Canada. On the other hand, major oil and gas companies terminate hundreds of employees when oil prices drop. Exhibit 13-3 summarizes the process of forecasting an organization's needs.

Today, many firms with employee shortages are hiring **contingent workers**, or persons who prefer temporary employment, either part-time or full-time. College students and retired persons comprise a big portion of the contingent work force. Other

HOT Links

Does Ceridian Canada, a leading payroll management company, live up to its motto "The freedom to succeed"? Find out how a company like this can help businesses of all sizes at www.ceridian.ca

contingent workers
Persons who prefer temporary employment, either part-time or full-time.

---

e x h i b i t 1 3 - 2 | Job Description

Position: College Recruiter   **Location:** Corporate Offices
Reports to: Vice-President of Human Resources   **Classification:** Salaried/Exempt

Job Summary: Member of HR corporate team. Interacts with managers and department heads to determine hiring needs for college graduates. Visits 20 to 30 college and university campuses each year to conduct preliminary interviews of graduating students in all academic disciplines. Following initial interviews, works with corporate staffing specialists to determine persons who will be interviewed a second time. Makes recommendations to hiring managers concerning best-qualified applicants.

Job Duties and Responsibilities: Estimated time spent and importance
15% Working with managers and department heads, determines college recruiting needs.
10% Determines colleges and universities with degree programs appropriate to hiring needs to be visited.
15% Performs college relations activities with numerous colleges and universities.
25% Visits campuses to conduct interviews of graduating seniors.
15% Develops applicant files and performs initial applicant evaluations.
10% Assists staffing specialists and line managers in determining who to schedule for second interviews.
5% Prepares annual college recruiting report containing information and data about campuses, number interviewed, number hired, and related information.
5% Participates in tracking college graduates who are hired to aid in determining campuses that provide the most outstanding employees.

Job Specification (Qualifications):   Bachelor's degree in human resource management or a related field. Minimum of two years of work experience with the firm in HR or department that annually hires college graduates. Ability to perform in a team environment, especially with line managers and department heads. Very effective oral and written communication skills. Reasonably proficient in Excel, Word, and Windows computer environment and familiar with People Soft.

exhibit 13-3 | Human Resource Planning Process

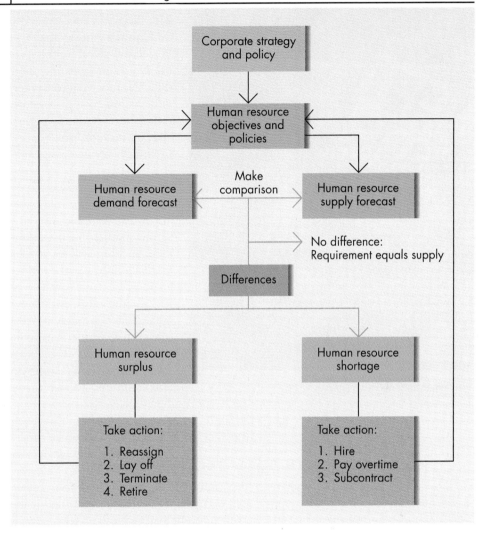

people who want to work but don't want to be permanent employees join a professional employer organization (PEO). A PEO performs staffing, training, and compensation functions by contracting with a business to provide employees for a specified period of time. A firm with a shortage of accountants can rent or lease an accountant from the PEO for the expected duration of the shortage.

concept check

- Describe the job analysis and design process.
- What is the process for human resource forecasting?

➡ lg 3   Employee Recruitment

When a firm creates a new position or an existing one becomes vacant, it starts looking for people with qualifications that meet the requirements of the job. Two sources of job applicants are the internal and external labour markets. The internal labour market consists of employees currently employed by the firm; the external labour market is the pool of potential applicants outside the firm.

Many organizations find qualified job applicants for professional positions through recruitment programs at university and college campuses.

recruitment
The attempt to find and attract qualified applicants in the external labour market.

job fair
An event, typically one day, held at a convention centre to bring together thousands of job seekers and hundreds of firms searching for employees.

Most companies, including UPS, WestJet, and Wal-Mart, follow a policy of promotion from within and try to fill positions with their existing employees. The internal search for job applicants usually means that a person must change his or her job. People are typically either promoted or transferred. A firm's *skills inventory* can help find the right person for a job opening. A skills inventory is a computerized employee database containing information on each employee's previous work experience, educational background, performance records, career objectives, and job location preferences. General Electric has used a skills inventory for many years as a means of determining promotions and transfers.

If qualified job candidates cannot be found inside the firm, the external labour market must be tapped. **Recruitment** is the attempt to find and attract qualified applicants in the external labour market. The type of position determines which recruitment method will be used and which segment of the labour market will be searched. Boeing will not recruit an experienced engineer the same way it would recruit a secretary or clerk typist.

Nontechnical, unskilled, and other nonsupervisory workers are recruited through newspaper, radio, and sometimes even television help wanted ads in local media. Starbucks placed ads in the *Beijing Youth Daily* to attract workers for its Beijing coffee shops.[2] Entry-level accountants, engineers, and systems analysts are commonly hired through college campus recruitment efforts. Each year companies send recruiters to dozens of colleges and universities across the country.

A firm that needs executives and other experienced professional, technical, and managerial employees may employ the services of an executive search firm such as International Executive Search. The hiring firm pays the search firm a fee equivalent to one to four months of the employee's first-year salary. Many search firms specialize in a particular occupation, industry, or geographic location.

Many firms participate in local job fairs. A **job fair** is typically a one-day event held at a convention centre to bring together thousands of job seekers and hundreds of firms searching for employees.

Some firms now use the Internet exclusively to attract new employees. A firm can post job announcements at its Web site, and applicants send their résumés via the Internet. Beacon Application Services Corp., a systems integration company, recruits only over the Internet. According to Dan Maude, president of the firm, "A year's worth of Web recruiting for us costs less than one agency fee ... it's also faster."[3]

Other firms such as Coca-Cola utilize artificial intelligence software to scan and track résumés.[4] Restrac and Resumix scan résumés for key words to identify qualified job candidates. Each system can scan and search thousands of résumés in minutes. With such systems, the words you use to describe your education, background, and work experience become very important.

concept check

- What is a skills inventory, and what are the two labour markets?
- Describe different ways that employees are recruited.
- How is technology helping firms find the right recruits?

→ **lg 4**

selection
The process of determining which persons in the applicant pool possess the qualifications necessary to be successful on the job.

Employee Selection

After a firm has attracted enough job applicants, employment specialists begin the selection process. **Selection** is the process of determining which persons in the applicant pool possesses the qualifications necessary to be successful on the job. The steps in the employee selection process are shown in Exhibit 13-4 and described below:

1. *Initial screening.* During the initial screening, an applicant usually completes an application form and has a brief interview of 30 minutes or less. The application form includes questions about education, work experience, and previous job duties. A personal résumé may be substituted for the application form. The interview is normally structured and consists of a short list of specific questions. For example: Are you familiar with any accounting software packages? Did you supervise anyone in your last job? Did you use a company car when making sales calls?

2. *Employment testing.* Following the initial screening, an applicant may be asked to take one or more employment tests, such as the Minnesota Clerical Test or the Wonderlic Personnel Test, a mental ability test. Some tests are designed to measure special job skills, others measure aptitudes, and some are intended to capture characteristics of one's personality. The Myers-Briggs Type Indicator is a personality and motivational test widely used on college campuses as an aid in providing job and career counselling.

3. *Selection interview.* The tool most widely used in making hiring decisions by Intel, Merck, and other firms is the **selection interview**, an in-depth discussion of an applicant's work experience, skills and abilities, education, and career interests. For managerial and professional positions, an applicant may be interviewed by several persons, including the line manager for the position to be filled. This interview is designed to determine an applicant's communication ability and motivation. It is also a means for gathering additional factual information from the applicant such as college major, years of part-time work experience, computer equipment used, and reason for leaving the last job. The applicant may be asked to explain how to solve a particular management problem or how she or he provided leadership to a group in a previous work situation when an important problem had to be solved quickly.

selection interview
An in-depth discussion of an applicant's work experiences, skills and abilities, education, and career interests.

e x h i b i t   1 3 - 4 | Steps of the Employee Selection Process

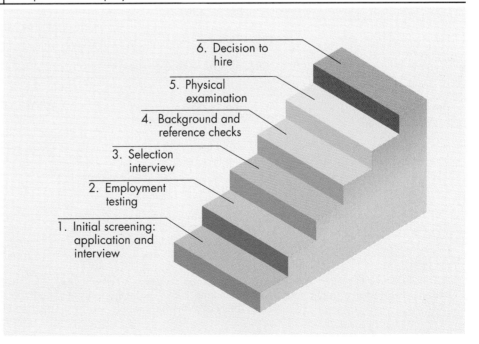

6. Decision to hire

5. Physical examination

4. Background and reference checks

3. Selection interview

2. Employment testing

1. Initial screening: application and interview

HOT Links

Get advice for brushing up
your interview skills at
www.job-interview.net

Carolyn Murray, a recruiter for W.C. Gore and Associates, makers of Gore-Tex, says she pays little attention to a candidate's carefully scripted responses to her admittedly easy questions. Instead, she listens for a casual remark that reveals the reality behind an otherwise thought-out reply. Using a baseball analogy, Carolyn gives examples of how three job candidates struck out in Exhibit 13-5.[5]

4. *Background and reference check.* If applicants pass the selection interview, most firms examine their background and check their references. In recent years an increasing number of employers such as Disney and Microsoft are carefully researching applicants' backgrounds, particularly their legal history, reasons for leaving previous jobs, and even creditworthiness. Retail firms where employees have extensive contact with customers, tend to be very careful about checking applicant backgrounds. Some checking can be easily done using the Internet. In fact, many retired law enforcement officers have started their own firms that specialize in these investigations.

5. *Physical exams.* Companies frequently require job candidates to have a medical checkup to ensure they are physically able to perform a job. Although drug testing is becoming a routine part of physical exams in the United States, particularly in the transportation industry, the Canadian government has decided not to enact legislation on this issue. The private sector is left to decide whether or not to test employees for drugs and alcohol. However, these same employees (in the transportation industry) may be subjected to U.S. drug testing upon crossing the border with their loads. This issue is one of considerable controversy in Canada and while our laws do not prohibit drug testing, there are many related issues of concern such as human rights, wrongful dismissal, and privacy.[6]

6. *Decision to hire.* If an applicant progresses satisfactorily through all the selection steps, a decision to hire the individual is made. The decision to hire is nearly always made by the manager of the new employee.

concept check

- What are the steps in the employee selection process?
- Describe some ways that applicants are tested.

e x h i b i t   1 3 - 5 | Striking Out with Gore-Tex

The Pitch (Question to Applicant)	The Swing (Applicant's Response)	The Miss (Interviewer's Reaction to Response)
"Give me an example of a time when you had a conflict with a team member."	"Our leader asked me to handle all of the Fed Exing for our team. I did it, but I thought that Fed Exing was a waste of my time."	"At Gore, we work from a team concept. Her answer shows that she won't exactly jump when one of her teammates needs help."
"Tell me how you solved a problem that was impeding your project."	"One of the engineers on my team wasn't pulling his weight, and we were closing in on a deadline. So I took on some of his work."	"The candidate may have resolved the issue for this particular deadline, but he did nothing to prevent the problem from happening again."
"What's the one thing that you would change about your current position?"	"My job as a salesman has become mundane. Now I want the responsibility of managing people."	"He's not maximizing his current position. Selling is never mundane if you go about it in the right way."

→ **lg 5**

training and development
Activities that provide learning situations in which an employee acquires additional knowledge or skills to increase job performance.

employee orientation
Training that prepares a new employee to perform on the job; includes information about job assignments, work rules, equipment, and performance expectations, as well as about company policies, salary and benefits, and parking.

on-the-job training
Training in which the employee learns the job by doing it with guidance from a supervisor or experienced co-worker.

Employee Training and Development

To ensure that both new and experienced employees have the knowledge and skills to perform their jobs successfully, organizations invest in training and development. **Training and development** involves learning situations in which the employee acquires additional knowledge or skills to increase job performance. Training objectives specify performance improvements, reductions in errors, job knowledge to be gained, and/or other positive organizational results. The design of training programs at General Electric, for example, includes determining instructional methods, number of trainees per class, printed materials (cases, notebooks, manuals, and the like) to be used, location of training, use of audiovisual equipment and software, and many other matters. The process of creating and implementing training and development activities is shown in Exhibit 13-6.

Training for new employees is instrumental in getting them up to speed and familiar with their job responsibilities. One study found that in the first three months a new hire can accomplish only 60 percent as much as an experienced worker. And even a 5 percent drop in overall employee efficiency can cut annual revenues by "several hundred million dollars."[7] The first type of training that new employees experience is **employee orientation**, which entails getting the new employee ready to perform on the job. Formal orientation (a half-day classroom program) provides information about company policies, salary and benefits, and parking. Although this information is very helpful, the more important orientation is about job assignments, work rules, equipment, and performance expectations provided by the new employee's supervisor and co-workers. This second briefing tends to be more informal and may last for several days or even weeks.

On-the-Job Training

Continuous training for both new and experienced employees is important to keep job skills fresh. Job-specific training, designed to enhance a new employee's ability to perform a job, includes **on-the-job training**, during which the employee learns the job by doing it with guidance from a supervisor or experienced co-worker.

On-the-job training takes place at the job site or workstation and tends to be directly related to the job. This training involves specific job instructions, coaching (guidance given to new employees by experienced ones), special project assignments,

e x h i b i t   1 3 - 6 | Employee Training and Development Process

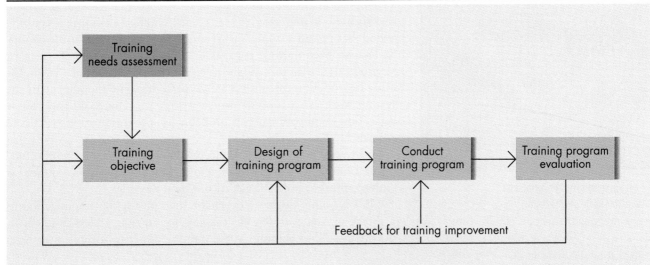

job rotation
Reassignment of workers to several different jobs over time so that they can learn the basics of each job.

apprenticeship
A form of on-the-job training that combines specific job instruction with classroom instruction.

mentoring
A form of on-the-job training in which a senior manager or other experienced employee provides job- and career-related information to a protégé.

or job rotation. **Job rotation** is the reassignment of workers to several different jobs over time. At Sears, management trainees work sequentially in two or three merchandise departments, customer service, credit, and human resources during their first year on the job.

An **apprenticeship** usually combines specific on-the-job instruction with classroom training. It may last as long as four years and can be found in the skilled trades of carpentry, plumbing, and electrical work.

With **mentoring,** another form of on-the-job training, a senior manager or other experienced employee provides job- and career-related information to a protégé. Mentoring is becoming increasingly popular with many firms, including Federal Express, Texaco, and Merrill Lynch. At Coca-Cola Roberto Goizueta mentored Douglas Ivester to become CEO of the company. When Goizueta died suddenly in 1997, Ivester's transition to CEO went very smoothly. The company clearly benefited from this mentoring relationship.

The primary benefits of on-the-job training are that it provides instant feedback about performance and is inexpensive. Trainees produce while learning, and no expensive classroom or learning tools are needed.

Off-the-Job Training

Even with the advantages of on-the-job training, many firms recognize that it is often necessary to train employees away from the workplace. With off-the-job training, employees learn the job away from the job. There are numerous popular methods of off-the-job training. Frequently, it takes place in a classroom where cases, role-play exercises, films, videos, lectures, and computer demonstrations are utilized to develop workplace skills.

vestibule training
A form of off-the-job training in which trainees learn in a scaled-down version or simulated work environment.

programmed instruction
A form of computer-assisted off-the-job training.

Another form of off-the-job training takes place in a facility called a vestibule or a training simulator. In **vestibule training,** used by Honda and Kroger, trainees learn about products, manufacturing processes, and selling in a scaled-down version of an assembly line or retail outlet. When mistakes are made, no customers are lost or products damaged. A training simulator, such as WestJet's flight simulators for pilot training, is much like a vestibule facility. Pilots can practise hazardous flight manoeuvres or learn the controls of a new aircraft in a safe, controlled environment with no passengers.

In a very rapidly developing trend that will undoubtedly accelerate in this century, many companies including Compaq and Microsoft are using computer-assisted, electronically delivered training and development courses and programs. Many of these courses have their origins in **programmed instruction,** a self-paced, highly structured training method that presents trainees with concepts and problems using a modular format. Each module consists of a set of concepts, math rules, or task procedures with test questions at the end of the module. When the trainee or student masters all material presented in a module, he or she advances to the next module, which is somewhat more difficult. Some courses taught on your campus probably use programmed instructional materials.

Finally, trade associations, colleges and universities, and professional organizations offer professional and executive education courses at training centres or professional organization meetings.

By using simulator training, airlines can teach pilots flight manoeuvres and the controls of new aircraft in a safe and controlled off-the-job training environment.

Usually, off-the-job training is more expensive than on-the-job training, and its impact is less direct or the transfer of learning to the job is less immediate. Nevertheless, despite these shortcomings, some training can only be done away from the job.

concept check

• Describe several types of on-the-job training.
• Explain vestibule training and programmed instruction.

➡ lg 6

Performance Planning and Evaluation

Along with employee orientation and training, new employees learn about performance expectations through performance planning and evaluation. Managers provide employees with expectations about the job. These are communicated as job objectives, schedules, deadlines, and product and/or service quality requirements. As an employee performs job tasks, the supervisor periodically evaluates the employee's efforts. A **performance appraisal** is a comparison of actual performance with expected performance to assess an employee's contributions to the organization and to make decisions about training, compensation, promotion, and other job changes. The performance planning and appraisal process is shown in Exhibit 13-7 and described below.

1. The manager establishes performance standards.
2. The employee works to meet the standards and expectations.
3. The employee's supervisor evaluates the employee's work in terms of quality and quantity of output and various characteristics such as job knowledge, initiative, relationships with others, and attendance and punctuality.
4. Following the performance evaluation, reward (pay raise) and job change (promotion) decisions can be made.
5. Rewards are positive feedback and provide reinforcement, or encouragement, for the employee to work harder in the future.

Performance appraisals serve a number of purposes, but they are most often used to make decisions about pay raises, training needs, and advancement opportunities.

performance appraisal
A comparison of actual performance with expected performance to assess an employee's contributions to the organization.

concept check

• What are the steps in the performance planning and appraisal process?
• What purposes do performance appraisals serve?

e x h i b i t   1 3 - 7 | Performance Planning and Evaluation

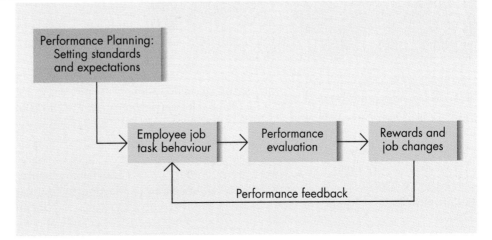

➡ **lg 7**

Employee Compensation and Benefits

Compensation, which includes both pay and benefits, is becoming more closely connected to performance. In a recent study of 191 Canadian companies, it was determined that companies are becoming more targeted in the awarding of salary increases and are aligning employee performance with awards.[8] Factors that affect an employee's pay fall under the following categories:

1. *Pay structure and internal influences.* Wages, salaries, and benefits usually reflect the importance of the job. The jobs that management considers more important are compensated at a higher rate; president, chief engineer, and chief financial officer are high-paying jobs. Likewise, different jobs of equal importance to the firm are compensated at the same rate. For instance, if a drill-press operator and a lathe operator are considered of equal importance, they may both be paid $21 per hour.

2. *Pay level and external influences.* In deciding how much to pay workers, the firm must also be concerned with the salaries paid by competitors. If competitors are paying much higher wages, a firm may lose its best employees. Larger firms conduct salary surveys to see what other firms are paying. An employer can decide to pay at, above, or below the going rate. Most firms try to offer competitive wages and salaries within a geographic area or an industry. If a company pays below-market wages, it may not be able to hire skilled people. The level, or competitiveness, of a firm's compensation is determined by internal factors, such as the firm's financial condition (or profitability) and the employee productivity, as well as external factors, such as the going rates paid by competitors.

Types of Compensation or Pay

External influences affect employee pay and benefits. With a high demand for skilled workers and high turnover rates, firms in the information technology industry offer high wages and many benefits to attract and retain workers like this Netscape employee.

There are two basic types of compensation: direct and indirect. Direct pay is the wage or salary received by the employee; indirect pay consists of various employee benefits and services. Employees are usually paid directly on the basis of the amount of time they work, the amount they produce, or some combination of time and output. The following are the most common types of compensation:

- *Hourly wages.* McDonald's counter staff, drive-through staff, cooks, crew trainers, and shift managers are paid various rates ranging from minimum wage on up.
- *Salaries.* Managerial and professional employees are paid an annual salary either on a biweekly or a monthly basis.
- *Piecework and commission.* Some employees are paid according to how much they produce or sell. A car salesperson might be paid $500 for each car sold or a 3 percent commission on the car's sale price. Thus, a salesperson who sold four cars in one week at $500 per car would earn $2000 in pay for that week. Alternatively, a 3 percent commission on four cars sold with total sales revenue of $70 000 would yield $2100 in pay.

Increasingly, business firms are paying employees using a base wage or salary and an incentive. The incentive feature is designed to increase individual employee, work group, and/or organizational performance. Incentive pay plans are commonly referred to as variable or contingent pay arrangements.

- *Accelerated commission schedule.* A salesperson could be paid a commission rate of 3 percent on the first $50 000 of sales per month, 4 percent on the next $30 000, and 5 percent on any sales beyond $80 000. For a salesperson who made $90 000 of sales in one month, the monthly pay would be as follows:

$$3\% \times \$50\ 000 = \$1500$$
$$4\% \times \$30\ 000 = \$1200$$
$$5\% \times \underline{\$10\ 000} = \underline{\$\ \ 500}$$
$$\$90\ 000 \qquad \$3200$$

- *Bonus.* A bonus is a payment for reaching a specific goal; it may be paid on a monthly, quarterly, or annual basis. A bank with several offices or branches might set monthly goals for opening new accounts, making loans, and customer service. Each employee of a branch that meets all goals would be paid a monthly bonus of $100. Although the bonuses are paid to the employees individually, the employees must function as an effective, high-performing group to reach the monthly goals.
- *Profit sharing.* A firm that offers profit sharing pays employees a portion of the profits over a preset level. For example, profits beyond 10 percent of gross sales might be shared at a 50 percent rate with employees. The company retains the remaining profits. All employees may receive the same profit shares, or the shares may vary according to base pay.
- *Fringe benefits.* **Fringe benefits** are indirect compensation and include pensions, health insurance, vacations, and many others. Some fringe benefits are required by law, including *employment insurance (EI)*, *worker's compensation*, and the *Canada Pension Plan (CPP)*, which are all paid in part by employers. Employment insurance compensation provides former employees with money for a certain period while they are unemployed. To be eligible, the employee must have worked a minimum number of weeks, be without a job, and be willing to accept a suitable position offered by the Employment Insurance office. Worker's compensation pays employees for lost work time caused by work-related injuries and may also cover rehabilitation after a serious injury. CPP is a government pension plan, but it also provides disability and survivor benefits. Medicare is also part of most benefit packages and the cost is usually shared by the employee.

    Many employers also offer fringe benefits not required by law. Among these are paid time off (vacations, holidays, sick days, even pay for jury duty), insurance (health and hospitalization, disability, life, dental, vision, and accidental death and dismemberment), pensions and retirement savings accounts, and stock purchase options.

    Some firms with numerous fringe benefits allow employees to mix and match benefit items or select items based on individual needs. This is a flexible or cafeteria-style benefit plan. A younger employee with a family may desire to purchase medical, disability, and life insurance, whereas an older employee may want to put more benefit dollars into a retirement savings plan. All employees are allocated the same number of benefit dollars but can spend these dollars on different items and in different amounts.

fringe benefits
Indirect compensation such as pensions, health insurance, and vacations.

concept check

- How does a firm establish a pay scale for its employees?
- What is the difference between direct and indirect pay?

➡ **lg 8**

Organizational Career Management

An important aspect of the human resource management process is organizational career management, or facilitating employee job changes, including promotions, transfers, demotions, layoffs, terminations, and retirements.

Job Changes within the Organization

A **promotion** is an upward move in an organization to a position with more authority, responsibility, and pay. Promotion decisions are usually based on merit (ability and performance) and seniority (length of service). Union employees usually prefer a strict seniority system for employee advancement. Managers and technical employees strongly prefer promotions based on merit.

A **transfer** is a horizontal move in an organization to a position with about the same salary and at about the same organizational level. An employee may seek a transfer for personal growth, for a more interesting job, for convenience (better work hours, work location, or training opportunity), or for a job that offers more potential for advancement. Employers may transfer workers from positions where they are no longer needed to ones where they are needed. Or the goal may be to find a better fit for the employee within the firm. Sometimes transfers are made to give employees a different perspective or to re-energize them.

When a person is downgraded or reassigned to a position with less responsibility, it is called a **demotion**. This usually occurs when an employee isn't performing satisfactorily. In most companies, a person is given several warnings before a demotion takes place.

Separations

A **separation** occurs when an employee leaves the company. Layoffs, terminations, resignations, and retirements are all types of separations. Sometimes separations occur because companies are trying to remain competitive in the global marketplace. When oil prices drop significantly many energy firms historically lay off or terminate workers. Often this activity is combined with the offering of early retirement packages to eligible employees.

A **layoff** is a temporary separation arranged by the employer, usually because business is slow. Layoffs can be planned, such as seasonal reductions of employees, or unplanned, as when sales unexpectedly decline. Generally, employees with the least seniority are laid off first.

There are several alternatives to a layoff. With a voluntary reduction in pay, all employees agree to take less pay so that everyone can keep working. Other firms arrange to have all or most of their employees take vacation time during slow periods. Major league baseball teams usually encourage their full-time year-round employees to take vacations during the off-season from November through April. Other employees agree to take *voluntary time off*, or work fewer hours, which again has the effect of reducing the employer's payroll and avoiding the need for a layoff.

A **termination** is a permanent separation arranged by the employer. Reasons for terminations include failure to perform as expected, violation of work rules, dishonesty, theft, sexual harassment, excessive absenteeism, or insubordination (disobedience).

Most companies follow a series of steps before terminating an employee. First, the employee is given an oral warning. The second step is a written statement that the employee's actions are not acceptable. If the employee fails to improve, he or she is suspended from work for a time. If the employee persists in wrongdoing after suspension, his or her employment is terminated.

promotion
An upward move in an organization to a position with more authority, responsibility, and pay.

transfer
A horizontal move in an organization to a position with about the same salary and at about the same organizational level.

demotion
The downgrading or reassignment of an employee to a position with less responsibility.

separation
The departure of an employee from the organization; can be a layoff, termination, resignation, or retirement.

layoff
A temporary separation of an employer from the organization; arranged by the employer, usually because business is slow.

termination
A permanent separation of an employee from the organization, arranged by the employer.

resignation
A permanent separation of an employee from the organization, done voluntarily by the employee.

retirement
The separation of an employee from the organization at the end of his or her career.

Resignation is a permanent form of separation that is undertaken voluntarily by the employee, whereas layoff and termination are involuntary. An employee may resign for almost any reason: to seek a new career, move to a different part of the country, accept an employment offer with a significant pay raise, or join a fast-growing firm with numerous advancement opportunities. For companies in high-growth industries, keeping employees from resigning and moving to "greener pastures" is a number-one priority. This is particularly true in smaller entrepreneurial firms where losing a key employee can be disastrous.

Retirement usually ends one's career. The aging work force in Canada may be the cause of problems in several industry sectors according to a recent study. The resource industries, utilities, education, and health care will be among the first sectors to experience the costs of the exodus of the baby boomers. However, this opens opportunities for younger workers who have the skills and education to move up in the organization.[9]

Workers in companies with too many employees may be offered early-retirement incentives. This option offers retirement benefits to younger employees or adds extra retirement benefits or both. Employees can thus retire more comfortably without working longer. As mentioned earlier, this is a common work force reduction technique in the oil and gas industry.

concept check

- What is organizational career management?
- Define promotion, transfer, termination, and retirement.

➡ **lg 9**

Laws Affecting Human Resource Management

Human resource managers must ensure that their firms accommodate the needs of disabled employees like wheelchair-bound workers who need ramps to facilitate their mobility.

Federal laws help ensure that job applicants and employees are treated fairly and not discriminated against. Hiring, training, and job placement must be unbiased. Promotion and compensation decisions must be based on performance. These laws help all Canadians who have talent, training, and the desire to get ahead.

New legislation and the continual interpretation and reinterpretation of existing laws will continue to make the jobs of human resource managers challenging and complicated. The key laws that currently affect human resource management are shown in Exhibit 13-8.

Employers may not discriminate against disabled persons. They must make "reasonable accommodations" so that qualified disabled employees can perform the job, unless doing so would cause "undue hardship" for the business. Altering work schedules, modifying equipment so a wheelchair-bound person can use it, and making buildings accessible by ramps and elevators are considered reasonable. Two companies often praised for their efforts to hire the disabled are McDonald's and IBM Canada.

Canada's overall employment equity record of the past decade has been mixed. The employment of women in professional occupations continues to grow, but minority representation among professionals has not significantly increased, even though professional jobs have been among the fastest-growing areas. Technical jobs

exhibit 1 3 - 8 | Laws Impacting Human Resource Management

Law	Purpose	Applicability
Charter of Rights and Freedoms (contained in the Constitution Act of 1982)	Provides the right to live and seek employment anywhere in Canada.	Takes precedence over all other laws.
Human rights legislation	Provides equal opportunity for members of protected groups in areas such as accommodation, contracts, provision of goods and services, and employment.	Comprised of federal, provincial, and territorial laws with a common objective.
Canadian Human Rights Act (1977)	Prohibits discrimination on a number of grounds.	Applies to federal government agencies, Crown corporations, and businesses under federal jurisdiction.
Employment Equity Act (amended in 1995)	Attempts to remove employment barriers and promote equality for the members of four designated groups: women, visible minorities, Aboriginal people, and persons with disabilities.	Employers under federal jurisdiction having more than 100 employees or firms with 100 employees wishing to bid on federal contracts of more than $200 000.
Occupational Health and Safety Act	Designed to protect the health and safety of workers by minimizing work-related accidents and illness.	All provinces, territories, and the federal jurisdiction have occupational health and safety legislation.
WHMIS (Workplace Hazardous Materials Information System)	Designed to protect workers by providing information about hazardous materials in the workplace.	Canada-wide legally mandated system.

HOT Links

Check out the Canadian Human Rights Commission Web site at www.chrc-ccdp.ca

HOT Links

Look through a variety of interesting information on the HRDC Web site at www.hrdc-drhc.gc.ca

have the most equitable utilization rates of minorities. Almost 400 federal and federally regulated organizations under the Employment Equity Act submit annual reports to Human Resources Development Canada (HRDC). The organizations are then graded on an alphabetical scale.

concept check

- What are the key laws affecting employment?
- What is employment equity?

➡ lg 10

CAPITALIZING ON TRENDS IN BUSINESS

Social change, evolving demographics, advancing technology, and global competition are driving the trends in human resource management in the 21st century.

Social Change

The most dramatic social change that is occurring is the increasing number of women joining the labour force—a trend that began in the 20th century and continues today. Today, women comprise about 45 percent of the Canadian labour force. The entry of women into the work force has created some new human resource management issues including dual-career couples, child and elder care, and workplace sexual harassment.

Another social change is the new attitude toward changing jobs. Only a few years ago, recent college graduates could expect to change jobs and employers three to five times during their 25 to 40 years of professional experience. Now, a 22- to 25-year-old college graduate can expect six to ten of these changes and one or two significant occupational changes, such as from engineer to accountant. This increased frequency of job changes may mean that employees and employers are less loyal to one another.

Demographics

Changes in demographics have resulted in a more diverse work force. **Diversity** refers to employee differences in age, race and ethnicity, gender, educational background, and work experience. Managing a diverse work group is more difficult than managing a homogeneous group, such as all white males, for example, because each group brings its own ideas, habits, culture, and communication skills to the work environment. Progressive human resource practices of diversity management focus on mentoring women and minority persons and removing the glass ceiling, or the invisible barrier in many firms that prevents women, minorities, and others from advancing to high-level management and executive positions.

Advantages of Employment Equity in the Workplace

In order to sell employment equity to some employers it can be useful to stress the positive effects on the bottom line. It is estimated that there are over 4 million persons with disabilities and more than 3 million racial minority members in Canada. This represents a huge consumer group. In order to access this market, employment equity has to be linked with marketing, customer relations, product design, and service delivery. What better way is there to do this than to have members of these groups employed in the business? By having women, Aboriginals, persons with disabilities, and visible minorities working in various departments, a company is better able to understand and take advantage of such market factors as differing lifestyles, nontraditional consumption patterns, culturally based purchasing preferences, various reading and TV-watching patterns, and so forth. These diverse groups can contribute knowledge, skills, and experience, which can then become part of the marketing focus in order to access those segments of the consumer population. As stated in Chapter 3, the Aboriginal segment of the Canadian population is growing at a faster rate than any other segment, a fact that cannot be overlooked by human resource professionals or marketers.

Including women in all areas of the workplace is also beneficial to modern companies. The following represents some interesting facts concerning women and spending:

- Women control 80 percent of the consumer dollar spent in North America.

HOT Links

For the latest news in the human resources field, visit the Web site of the Society for Human Resource Management at **www.shrm.org**

diversity
Employee differences in age, race and ethnicity, gender, educational background, and work experience.

- Women purchase 53 percent of all stocks sold in North America.
- Four out of five businesses started by young Canadians are started by women.
- Women make 89 percent of choices of bank accounts.
- Women buy 50 percent of the cars sold in Canada and influence 85 percent of the purchasing decisions.[10]

With data such as that above, the human resource specialist can more easily convince a manager or employer of the importance of recognizing a diverse work force as an integral part of the organization.

Advancing Technology

outsourcing
The assignment of various functions, such as human resources, accounting, or legal work, to outside organizations.

Advances in information technology have greatly improved the efficiency of handling many transaction-based aspects (payroll and expense reimbursement) of employee services. Technology enables instant communication of human resource data from far-flung branches to the home office. Ease of communication has also led many companies to outsource some or all of their human resource functions. **Outsourcing** is the assignment of various functions, like human resources, accounting, or legal work, to outside organizations. The National Geographic Society outsourced all of its employee benefits programs to Workforce Solutions. Administaff is a large company that handles compensation and benefits processing, training, and even performance appraisal for many large corporate clients. Without computer databases and networks, such outsourcing would be impossible.

telecommuting
An arrangement in which employees work at home and are linked to the office by phone, fax, and computer.

Technology has also made telecommuting a reality for many workers. **Telecommuting** involves employees working at home and being linked to the office by phone, fax, and computer. At Cisco Systems, a computer-networking giant based in San José, California, telecommuters have improved their productivity by up to 25 percent, while the company has saved about US$1 million on overhead and retained key employees who might otherwise have left.[11] What's more, those who have traded suits for sweats say they love setting their own schedules, skipping rush hour, spending more time with their kids, and working at least part-time in comfortable surroundings. "It's surprising the number of engineers who will respond to a question at 11:00 on a Saturday night," says John Hotchkiss, Cisco's human resource manager. "We can solve a problem that would not have been solved until Monday morning."[12]

Global Competition

As more firms "go global," they are sending an increasing number of employees overseas. Procter & Gamble, IBM, Caterpillar, Microsoft, Federal Express, and many others have tens of thousands of employees abroad. Such companies face somewhat different human resource management issues than do firms that operate only within North America. For example, criteria for selecting employees include not only technical skills and knowledge of the business, but also the ability to adapt to a local culture and to learn a foreign language.

Once an individual is selected for an overseas assignment, language training and cultural orientation become important. Salary and benefits, relocation expenses, and special allowances (housing, transportation, and education) can increase human resource costs by as much as three times normal annual costs. After an overseas assignment of one year or more, the firm must repatriate the employee, or bring the individual back home. Job placement and career progression frequently become issues during repatriation because the firm has changed and the employee's old job may no longer exist. After spending a year in Brussels, Belgium, Mike Rocca, a financial executive with Honeywell, experienced "re-entry shock" when he returned to his corporate office and saw how new software had changed accounting.

concept check

- How is the entry of more women into the work force affecting human resource management?
- What is diversity, and how does it affect human resource management?
- What benefits does telecommuting offer?
- What issues does "going global" present for human resource management?

APPLYING THIS CHAPTER'S TOPICS

It's never too early to start thinking about your career in business. No, you don't have to decide today, but it's important to decide fairly soon how you will spend your life's work. A very practical reason for doing so is that it will save you a lot of time and money. We have seen too many third- and fourth-year students, and even graduate students, who aren't really sure what they want to do upon graduation. The longer you wait to choose a profession, the more credit hours you may have to take in your new field and the longer it will be before you start earning real money.

A second reason to choose a career field early is that you can get a part-time or summer job and "test-drive" the profession. If it's not for you, you will find out very quickly.

A good source of career information is the Internet. Go to any search engine, such as Excite or Lycos, and enter "careers in business," or narrow your search to a specific area such as management or marketing.

HOT Links

Interested in a career in human resources? At www.hrmguide.net/hrm/Links/can.htm you'll find valuable tips to point you in the right direction.

TRY IT NOW!

Make Telecommuting Work for You Maybe a part-time job might require too much driving time. Perhaps there are simply no jobs in the immediate area that suit you. Try telecommuting right now. Is telecommuting for you? It's not for every person or every job, and you'll need plenty of self-discipline to make it work for you. Ask yourself if you can perform your duties without close supervision. Also, think about whether you would miss your co-workers.

If you decide to give telecommuting a try, consider these suggestions to maintain your productivity:

- *Set ground rules with your family.* Spouses and small children have to understand that even though you're in the house, you are busy earning a living. It's fine to throw in a few loads of laundry or answer the door when the plumber comes. It's another thing to take the

kids to the mall or let them play games on your office PC.

- *Clearly demarcate your workspace by using a separate room with a door you can shut.* Let your family know that, emergencies excepted, the space is off-limits during working hours.

- *If you have small children, you may want to arrange for child-care during your working hours.*

- *Stay in touch with your co-workers and professional colleagues.* Go into the office from time to time for meetings to stay connected.

Above all, you can make telecommuting work for you by being productive. Doing your job well whether on-site or telecommuting will help assure you of a bright future.

>looking ahead
at Right Axsmith

Dianne Bond, of Right Axsmith, sees the role of the HR professional moving toward greater decision-making responsibilities. Therefore, anyone planning on entering the HR field must be prepared to acquire a solid understanding of accounting, finance, marketing, the business environment, general management, and labour relations. Basically, a more in-depth knowledge of the material introduced in this book and related topics. As the role of the HR professional expands, opportunities arise for companies like Right Axsmith to provide training and development in the strategic aspect of human resources. Given this expanded role, more students may decide to look toward a career in HR in order to become part of the strategic management team of a major corporation.

KEY TERMS

apprenticeship 340
contingent workers 334
demotion 344
diversity 347
employee orientation 339
fringe benefits 343
human resource management (HRM) 332
human resource (HR) planning 333
job analysis 333
job description 334
job fair 336
job rotation 340
job specification 334
layoff 344
mentoring 340
on-the-job training 339
outsourcing 348
performance appraisal 341
programmed instruction 340
promotion 344
recruitment 336
resignation 345
retirement 345
selection 337
selection interview 337
separation 344
telecommuting 348
termination 344
training and development 339
transfer 344
vestibule training 340

SUMMARY OF LEARNING GOALS

➡lg 1   **What is the human resource management process?**
The human resource management process consists of a sequence of activities that begins with job analysis and HR planning; progresses to employee recruitment and selection; then focuses on employee training, performance appraisal, and compensation; and ends when the employee leaves the organization. Human resource decisions and activities along this series of events increase the value and contributions the employee makes to the firm. Over several years for a given employee, training, performance appraisal, and changes in compensation form a repeated set of activities that facilitate career development and increase a person's contributions to the firm.

➡lg 2   **How are human resource needs determined?**
Creating a strategy for meeting human resource needs is called human resource planning, which begins with job analysis. Job analysis is a process for studying a job to determine its tasks and duties for setting pay, determining employee job performance, specifying hiring requirements, and designing training programs. Information from the job analysis is used to prepare a job description, which lists the tasks and responsibilities of the job. A job specification describes the skills, knowledge, and abilities a person needs to fill the job described in the job description. By examining the human resource demand forecast and the internal supply forecast, human resource professionals can determine if the company faces a personnel surplus or shortage.

➡lg 3   **How do human resource managers find good people to fill the jobs?**
When a job vacancy occurs, most firms begin by trying to fill the job from within. If a suitable internal candidate is not available, the firm begins an external search. Firms use local media to recruit nontechnical, unskilled, and nonsupervisory workers. To locate highly trained recruits, employers use college recruiters, executive search firms, job fairs, and company Web sites to promote job openings.

➡lg 4   **What is the employee selection process?**
Typically, an applicant submits an application, or résumé, and then receives a short, structured interview. If an applicant makes it past the initial screening, he or she may be asked to take an aptitude, personality, or skills test. The next step is the selection interview, which is an in-depth discussion of the applicant's work experience, skills and abilities, education, and career interests. An

applicant seeking a professional or managerial position will typically be interviewed by several people. After the selection interview, successful applicants may be asked to undergo a physical exam before being offered a job.

➡lg 5 **What types of training and development do organizations offer their employees?**

Training and development programs are designed to increase employees' knowledge, skills, and abilities in order to foster job performance improvements. Formal training (usually classroom in nature and off-the-job) takes place shortly after being hired. Development programs prepare employees to assume positions of increasing authority and responsibility. Job rotation, executive education programs, mentoring, and special project assignments are examples of employee development programs.

➡lg 6 **What is a performance appraisal?**

A performance appraisal compares an employee's actual performance with the expected performance. Performance appraisals serve several purposes but are typically used to determine an employee's compensation, training needs, and advancement opportunities.

➡lg 7 **How are employees compensated?**

Direct pay is the hourly wage or monthly salary paid to an employee. In addition to the base wage or salary, direct pay may include bonuses and profit sharing. Indirect pay consists of various benefits and services. Some benefits are required by law: employment insurance, worker's compensation, and the Canada Pension Plan. Others are voluntarily made available by employers to employees. These include paid vacations and holidays, pensions, health and other insurance products, employee wellness programs, and college tuition reimbursement.

➡lg 8 **What is organizational career management?**

Organizational career management is the facilitation of employee job changes, including promotions, transfers, layoffs, and retirements. A promotion is an upward move with more authority, responsibility, and pay. A transfer is a horizontal move in the organization. When a person is downgraded to a position with less responsibility, it is a demotion. A layoff is a temporary separation arranged by the employer, usually when business is slow. A termination is a permanent separation arranged by the employer. A resignation is a voluntary separation by the employee. Retirement is a permanent separation that ends one's career.

➡lg 9 **What is the key legislation affecting human resource management?**

A number of federal, and provincial, territorial laws affect human resource management. These include the Charter of Rights and Freedoms (contained in the Constitution Act of 1982), the Canadian Human Rights Act (1977), the Employment Equity Act (amended in 1995), the Occupational Health and Safety Act, and the Workplace Hazardous Materials Information System.

➡lg 10 **What trends are affecting human resource management?**

Women now comprise 45 percent of the work force in Canada. As a result, we are seeing growing numbers of dual-career couples. In turn, companies are now facing issues like sexual harassment and nonwork lifestyle issues such as child-care and elder care. Workers also now change jobs three to five times during their career. This lessens the loyalty between employer and employee. As the Canadian work force becomes increasingly more diverse, companies are offering diversity training and mentoring of minorities.

Technology continues to improve the efficiency of human resource management. It also enables firms to outsource many functions done internally in the past. Telecommuting is becoming increasingly popular among employers and employees.

As more firms enter the international market, they are sending an increasing number of employees overseas. In addition to normal job requirements, selected workers must have the ability to adapt to a local culture and perhaps to learn a foreign language.

WORKING THE NET

1. Go to the Monster Board at **content.monster.com/resume/** to learn how to prepare an electronic résumé that will get results. Develop a list of rules for creating effective electronic résumés, and revise your own résumé into electronic format.
2. Working as a contingent employee can help you explore your career options. Visit the site at **www.canadajobsearch.com** to link to a variety of job sites. Search for several types of jobs that interest you. What are the advantages of being a temporary worker?
3. As a corporate recruiter, you must know how to screen prospective employees. The Integrity Center Web site at **www.integctr.com** offers a brief tutorial on pre-employment screening, a glossary of key words and phrases, and related information. Prepare a short report that tells your assistant how to go about this process.

CREATIVE THINKING CASE

"Do-It-Yourself" Human Resource Management at Spectrum Signal Processing

Some companies are now managing all or part of their human resource functions with employee teams. Martin McConnell decided that this was the way to go at Spectrum Signal Processing, Inc. McConnell is vice-president of finance for Spectrum, a hardware and software designer with 180 employees in Burnaby, British Columbia. He says his company has no human resource department at all. Instead, it uses rotating human resource committees.

In a 1996 employee-satisfaction survey, Spectrum's managers discovered that its employees were not all that satisfied with the way the company was dealing with human resource issues. So Spectrum created a cross-functional employee team to focus on those issues. McConnell initially thought the committee would be only short term; it would deal with the immediate problems and then disband. "But it gained so much interest and momentum, it became part of our culture," he says.

Now the committee regularly discusses and addresses most of the company's typical human resource functions: performance appraisals and the employee handbook, as well as company training, recognition, mentoring, and orientation programs. (Payroll and benefits administration are handled by the accounting department.)

The committee consists of 12 elected members from various job functions. Member-involvement dates are staggered, so the committee is constantly getting new members and perspectives. McConnell and CEO Barry Jinks also serve on the team, albeit in an advisory role. According to group chair Carol Schulz, the bosses' presence doesn't present a hindrance. "They have the same say as anybody else," says Schulz. "Plus it gives employees the feeling that they really do care."

McConnell admits that at first he worried that the committee might establish some overly expensive policies. "But it's not us versus them," he says. "Whatever decision they made would be modified for what works for the environment. Or maybe we'd implement it in stages."[13]

Critical Thinking Questions

1. What are the advantages and possible disadvantages of a do-it-yourself human resource department?
2. Would this concept work at a large company like Ford Motor Co., or is it best suited for smaller organizations?

3. One problem that has surfaced at Spectrum is that serving on the committee takes a lot of time and distracts committee members from their jobs. McConnell is thinking about using a co-op student from a local university to do detail and leg work. Do you think that this is a good idea? Why or why not?

China Toys

Need to find the perfect gift for someone who has everything? Try checking out Luc and Don of Prelam Enterprises (**www.prelam.com**).

Every year a huge gadget and gizmo trade show is held in Hong Kong, where new products are displayed. One of the trade shows had over 4000 displays and hundreds of thousands of attendees. Don and Luc of Moncton, New Brunswick, search the show for the perfect product, which they call a "WOW." The two businessmen want to find the new products before anyone else brings them to Canada and, hence, get a jump on the competition. With a bank of existing customers, they want to find new products for these customers. The name of the game seems to be hustle, hustle, hustle. The goal is to discover something "never seen before." In order to attract customers that enjoy these types of products, advertising is needed to stimulate demand.

One of the "WOW" products brought to Canada by Luc and Don is an "Anysizer" battery converter. The package contains converters that will change any AAA battery into an AA-, C-, or D-size battery. When the product was first ordered, Luc felt that the packaging was inappropriate for the Canadian market and therefore had it repackaged using more suitable colours. The Anysizer has a 98.8 percent positive feedback rate on eBay.

Luc had made four trips to China in one year in an attempt to find his "WOW" products. Some of the new products included spring-loaded magnetic hammers, runners that converted to roller blades, snowboards with wheels, fruit- and vegetable-shaped candles, and a new type of car air freshener.

In order to distribute their unusual products, Luc and Don set up in a Moncton mall. They also launched a catalogue of products and were able to land a deal with Wal-Mart. Luc feels that you must always be quicker on your feet than the competition so that you can get the product to market first. As some of these products have a very short life, one must always be looking for the next "WOW" in order to stay ahead.

Critical Thinking Questions

1. What is the importance of packaging in a self-service economy?
2. What channels of distribution did Don and Luc use?
3. What do you think would be the best way to distribute "WOW" products and why would you choose this particular channel?

Cobra Cars

Len and Allan Skok are unlikely business partners. The father and son team have very different backgrounds, with Allan being a young professional just out of school and Len being a 30-year veteran of the automotive industry. Allan's strength is in marketing while Len is a long-time mechanic and the principal of the Macro Automotive Group. The duo have one major thing in common—they love fast, high-performance luxury cars. In order to market a product such as classic car replicas, an appropriate strategy must be devised. The company is trying to tap into a very small market niche, the luxury "replicar" market. The cars sell for a lot of money, which immediately limits their potential customer base. For example, the Cobra replicar sells for around $85 000. The Cobra replicas sold by Len and Allan are manufactured in South Africa and assembled in Ontario.

Many problems need to be addressed. In order to remain viable, the company must increase its sales, but with a price tag of $85 000, the size of the market is relatively small. They would like to open a Vancouver office but simply don't have the volume to justify it. Len helps finance the current venture through his used-car business. Bank financing seems to be out of the question for the moment, and import problems plague the business. The customers tend to be very demanding—understandable given the price they are paying for the car. Assembly doesn't always go as planned, with the expected assembly time being one week. The guys ended up with a defective demo car, which didn't help things either.

In order to be successful, Len and Allan believe that expansion is needed but are not sure they can afford to expand. Read more about the Cobra replicar at **www.superformance.ca** or **www.cobracar.ca**

Critical Thinking Questions

1. Using the PEST model, discuss the various environmental factors impacting on Len and Allan as they attempt to grow their business.
2. How would Len and Allan use market segmentation to help identify the target markets that might be most profitable for the company?
3. What promotional methods might be most effective?
4. What marketing strategy would you suggest for Len and Allan?

Management and Planning in Today's Organization

In this chapter you will be introduced to management and the first function of a manager in the act of managing a business—*planning*. Management is what managers do to ensure that the organization achieves the critical success factors. As the chapter states, "management is the process of guiding the development, maintenance, and allocation of resources to attain organizational goals." That is why the process of management encircles our model of a successful business. It is the process that implements all the activities of a business toward achieving the factors critical to its success. It ties everything together and, when done properly, ensures that activities are integrated.

All of the activities within the process of management—planning, organizing, leading/motivating, and controlling—are highly integrated. As you'll read in this chapter, they form a tightly integrated cycle of thoughts and actions. They are highly interdependent, and are performed in such a way that it is difficult, if not impossible, to separate them. Just watch a manager at work. Let's suppose that she has just made a decision to promote a particular individual and leave that person's previous position permanently vacant. You might say that this was a decision made to reward an individual for a job well done and therefore to *motivate* him to continue to work hard by recognizing his efforts. However, *planning* would have gone into that decision as well, because managers can't just move people around without looking ahead to the implications of those moves on other employees. One of those implications is that a change would have occurred to the structure of the *organization*, as a position was left vacant, perhaps causing that individual's subordinates to change managers and the number of managers to be reduced at that level. It also would require that the performance of that individual had been monitored in order to determine that he was worthy of this promotion. This is called *control*—results are measured and compared against objectives, and changes are made to keep everything on track, or under control.

But remember that managers don't perform this highly integrative process in a vacuum. They make plans contingent upon the opportunities and threats they see in the external environment in relation to the strengths and weaknesses the business has internally. What is done to implement the plan, with respect to organizational structure, motivational tactics, and control mechanisms, also depends on the internal and external environments. For example, a company might choose an open, flexible structure with less bureaucracy to encourage employees to be more creative and seek and pursue opportunities that exist in a rapidly changing and highly competitive *economic* environment. This would in turn be dependent on the types of employees the company has, whether or not they would grow and develop in that type of environment, and whether they would need more direction to be motivated to perform. In other words, the strengths and weaknesses of the employees would need to be considered.

The planning process itself is also highly integrative. As mentioned in the chapter, there are different levels of planning—strategic, tactical, and operational. But they must all work together. *Strategic* planning is broad-based and determines the goals and plans for the entire organization. Then, at the tactical level each functional area determines its own goals and plans that enable that area to fulfill its role in achieving the overall strategic plan. Finally, at the operational level each unit within each functional area determines its goals and plans to implement those at the next higher level. For example, if a company decided strategically to develop a new product line to compete with another company that is threatening to reduce its market share, then at a tactical level *marketing* would need to determine how to promote this new product line and *operations* would need to determine the most efficient and cost-effective way to produce it. At the operational level, sales quotas, territories, and strategies for salespeople would then be established, and production schedules would be established in the plant. The important factor is that all these plans are related to each other. They are connected as if by a string to the next higher level; each one helps to achieve the objectives of the next level, so ultimately, the company achieves its overall goals and the critical factors of success.

Management and Planning in Today's Organization

CHAPTER 14

Learning Goals

→ **lg 1**   What is the role of management?

→ **lg 2**   What roles do managers take on in different organizational settings?

→ **lg 3**   What set of managerial skills is necessary for managerial success?

→ **lg 4**   What are the four types of planning?

→ **lg 5**   What is a mission statement?

→ **lg 6**   What are contingency plans and why are they important?

→ **lg 7**   What trends will affect management in the future?

Carewest: Planning to Survive

Blair Phillips of Carewest describes the company as a care organization for adults with long-term needs or disabilities, located in Calgary, Alberta. Carewest has been in operation for over 40 years and operates ten facilities as well as many day programs and clinics. The goal of Carewest is "to provide the very best care and services so those we serve can be as comfortable and independent as possible." Carewest's structure consists of a board of directors and a management team, which includes the CEO of the board, the HR service leader, the finance service leader, the site leaders, and the service development leader. Under the direction of this team are areas of business enabling (HR and finance), operations (which includes site leaders of the ten facilities), and organizational capabilities (which includes planning and analyzing responsibilities). This structure seems to serve Carewest very well. However, troubled times have led to the structure of today.

In the 1994–95 period, Carewest was facing a major crisis. Costs were very high, regionalization in the health-care sector was imminent, and funding cuts were made by the Alberta government. Carewest had to plan for survival. The management decided that they must fundamentally change the way they do business and become customer focused.

The first step in this very long process involved recreating the organizational memory. The board of directors at that time reviewed the minutes of all board meetings from 1963 to 1994 in order to track the focus, movement, and history over the years. They needed to answer several important questions such as "What are our values, mission, and vision?" and "Who are our customers?" The goal was to create a new service delivery model for Carewest. In order to do this, management needed to identify core processes. They did this by looking at the desired outcomes and working backwards to determine how to achieve these outcomes. Needless to say, this was a very long process and buy-in from all staff was critical. Carewest management involved the frontline caregivers and created teams with leaders drawn from all sectors of the organization. They had to determine a new way to operate, define their customer, and create a new identification for Carewest while working within the constraints of their new fiscal reality. By looking at the organizational memory, a new frame of reference was determined, including a mission statement, a vision statement, a statement of values, and a list of key results (see Exhibit 14-8 on page 367). The resulting strategy for Carewest was one of diversification, where the organization offers not only long-term and disability care but also rehabilitation, recovery, respite, community-based options, and comprehensive community care. See the Carewest Web site at **www.carewest.org** for more information on their services. The ultimate goal of Carewest is to provide services that allow people to stay in their own homes longer, a true win–win scenario.[1]

CRITICAL THINKING QUESTIONS

As you read this chapter, consider the following questions as they relate to Carewest:

- What factors in the political, economic, social, and technological environments are critical for this organization to consider in its planning process?
- What was management's greatest challenge in changing this organization from a publicly funded nonprofit focus to a customer-driven business focus?

BUSINESS IN THE 21ST CENTURY

Today's companies rely on managers to guide the daily process using human, technological, financial, and other resources to create competitive advantage. For many beginning business students, being in "management" is an attractive, but somewhat vague, future goal. This vagueness is due in part to an incomplete understanding of what managers do and how they contribute to organizational success or failure. This chapter introduces the basic functions of management and the skills required by managers to drive an organization toward its goals. We will also discuss the importance of planning in achieving organizational goals and highlight the trends that are shaping the future role of managers.

The Role of Management

Management is the process of guiding the development, maintenance, and allocation of resources to attain organizational goals. Managers are the people in the organization responsible for developing and carrying out this management process. Management is dynamic by nature and evolves to meet needs and constraints in the organization's internal and external environments. In a global marketplace where the rate of change is rapidly increasing, flexibility and adaptability are crucial to the managerial process. This process is based in four key functional areas of the organization: planning, organization, leadership, and control. Although these activities are discussed separately in the following chapters, they actually form a tightly integrated cycle of thoughts and actions. From this perspective, the managerial process can be described as (1) anticipating potential problems or opportunities and designing plans to deal with them, (2) coordinating and allocating the resources needed to implement plans, (3) guiding personnel through the implementation process, and (4) reviewing results and making any necessary changes. This last stage provides information to be used in ongoing planning efforts, and thus the cycle starts over again.

As shown in Exhibit 14-1, managerial work can be divided into four activities: planning, organizing, leading, and controlling. The four functions are highly interdependent, with managers often performing more than one of them at a time and each

HOT Links

Check out the wide range of courses and seminars offered through the Canadian Management Centre at **www.cmcamai.org**

➡ **lg 1**

management
The process of guiding the development, maintenance, and allocation of resources to attain organizational goals.

e x h i b i t   1 4 - 1 | What Managers Do and Why

Good management consists of proper		And leads to achievement of	Which results in
Planning • Set objectives and state mission • Examine alternatives • Determine needed resources • Create strategies to reach objectives **Organizing** • Design jobs and specify tasks • Create organization structure • Staff positions • Coordinate work activities • Set policies and procedures • Allocate resources	**Leading** • Lead and motivate employees to accomplish organizational goals • Communicate with workers • Resolve conflicts • Manage change **Controlling** • Measure performance • Compare performance to standards • Take necessary action to improve performance	Organizational mission and objectives	Organizational efficiency and effectiveness

of them many times over the course of a normal workday. As you will learn in the following chapters, all of the functions require sound decision making and communication skills.

concept check

- Define the term *management.*
- What are the four key functions of managers?

→ **lg 2**

informational roles
A manager's activities as an information gatherer, an information disseminator, or a spokesperson for the company.

interpersonal roles
A manager's activities as a figurehead, company leader, or liaison.

decisional roles
A manager's activities as an entrepreneur, resource allocator, conflict resolver, or negotiator.

Managerial Roles

In carrying out the responsibilities of planning, organizing, leading, and controlling, managers take on many different roles. A role is a set of behavioural expectations, or a set of activities that a person is expected to perform. Managers' roles fall into three basic categories: **informational roles, interpersonal roles**, and **decisional roles**. These roles are summarized in Exhibit 14-2. In an informational role, the manager may act as an information gatherer, an information distributor, or a spokesperson for the company. A manager's interpersonal roles are based on various interactions with other people. Depending on the situation, a manager may need to act as a figurehead, a company leader, or a liaison. When acting in a decisional role, a manager may have to think like an entrepreneur, make decisions about resource allocation, help resolve conflicts, or negotiate compromises.

e x h i b i t   1 4 - 2 | The Many Roles That Managers Play in an Organization

Role	Description	Example
Informational Roles		
Monitor	Seeks out and gathers information relevant to the organization.	Finding out about legal restrictions or product technology.
Disseminator	Provides information where it is needed in the organization.	Providing current figures to workers on the assembly line.
Spokesperson	Transmits information to people outside the organization.	Representing the company at a shareholders' meeting.
Interpersonal Roles		
Figurehead	Represents the company in a symbolic way.	Cutting the ribbon at ceremony for the opening of a new building.
Leader	Guides and motivates employees to achieve organizational goals.	Helping subordinates to set monthly performance goals.
Liaison	Acts as a go-between among individuals inside and outside the organization.	Representing the retail sales division for the company at a regional sales meeting.
Decisional Roles		
Entrepreneur	Searches out new opportunities and initiates change.	Implementing a new production procedure using new technology.
Disturbance handler	Handles unexpected events and crises.	Handling a crisis situation such as a fire.
Resource allocator	Designates the use of financial, human, and other organizational resources.	Approving the funds necessary to purchase computer equipment and hire personnel.
Negotiator	Represents the company at negotiating processes.	Participating in salary negotiations with union representatives.

Decision making is an ongoing activity at all levels in all organizations.

nonprogrammed decisions
Responses to infrequent, unforeseen, or very unusual problems and opportunities where the manager does not have a precedent to follow in decision making.

Planning for the G-8 Summit in Kananaskis required many nonprogrammed decisions in response to very unusual problems and circumstances.

Managerial Decision Making

In every function performed, role taken on, and set of skills applied, a manager is a decision maker. Decision making means choosing among alternatives. Decision making occurs in response to the identification of a problem or an opportunity. The decisions managers make fall into two basic categories: programmed and nonprogrammed. Programmed decisions are made in response to routine situations that occur frequently in a variety of settings throughout an organization. For example, the need to hire new personnel is a common situation for most organizations. Therefore, standard procedures for recruitment and selection are developed and followed in most companies.

Infrequent, unforeseen, or very unusual problems and opportunities require **nonprogrammed decisions** by managers. Because these situations are unique and complex, the manager rarely has a precedent to follow.

A very unique and complex situation requiring months of planning was the protection of the G-8 Summit held in the remote Kananaskis Valley of Alberta in June 2002. Over $200 million was spent to provide surface-to-air missiles, CF-18 jets, and thousands of troops to patrol the 12-kilometre-wide secure zone. Many nonprogrammed decisions comprised the security plan known as Operation Grizzly by the RCMP.[2]

Addressing these sorts of problems requires a systematic approach to decision making, as illustrated in Exhibit 14-3. Managers typically follow five steps in the decision-making process:

1. Recognize or identify a problem or opportunity. Although it is more common to focus on problems because of their obvious negative effects, managers who do not take advantage of new opportunities may lose competitive advantage to other firms.
2. Gather information so as to identify alternative solutions or actions.
3. Analyze the alternatives, including their advantages and disadvantages.
4. Select one or more alternatives after evaluating the strengths and weaknesses of each possibility.
5. Put the chosen alternative into action.
6. Gather information to obtain feedback on the effectiveness of the chosen plan. Some very practical questions to ask during the decision-making process are shown in Exhibit 14-4.

concept check

- What are the three types of managerial roles?
- Give examples of things managers might do when acting in each of the different types of roles.
- List the six steps in the decision-making process.

exhibit   1 4 - 3 | The Decision-Making Process

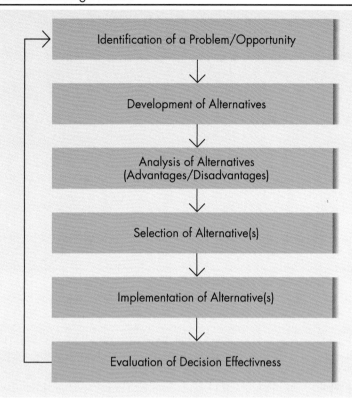

→ lg 3   Managerial Skills

In order to be successful in planning, organizing, leading, and controlling, managers must use a wide variety of skills. A *skill* is the ability to do something proficiently. Managerial skills fall into three basic categories: conceptual, human relations, and technical skills. The degree to which each type of skill is used depends upon the level of the manager's position as seen in Exhibit 14-5. Additionally, in an increasingly global marketplace, it pays for managers to develop a special set of skills to deal with global management issues.

exhibit   1 4 - 4 | Questions to Ask Yourself to Help Make Better Decisions

1. *What's my decision problem?* What, broadly, do I have to decide? What specific decisions do I have to make as a part of the broad decision?
2. *What are my fundamental objectives?* Have I asked "Why?" enough times to get to my bedrock wants and needs?
3. *What are my alternatives?* Can I think of more good ones?
4. *What are the consequences of each alternative in terms of the achievement of each of my objectives?* Can any alternatives be safely eliminated?
5. *What are the trade-offs among my more important objectives?* Where do conflicting objectives concern me the most?
6. *Do any uncertainties pose serious problems?* If so, which ones? How do they impact consequences?
7. *How much risk am I willing to take?* How good and how bad are the possible consequences? What are ways of reducing my risk?
8. *Have I thought ahead, planning out into the future?* Can I reduce my uncertainties by gathering information? What are the potential gains and costs in time, money, and effort?
9. *Is the decision obvious or pretty clear at this point?* What reservations do I have about deciding now? In what ways could the decision be improved by a modest amount of added time and effort?
10. *What should I be working on?* If the decision isn't obvious, what do the critical issues appear to be? What facts and opinions would make my job easier?

SOURCE: Reprinted by permission of Harvard Business School Press. From *Smart Choices: A Practical Guide to Making Better Decisions*, by John S. Mannond, Ralph L. Keeney, and Howard Raiffa. Boston, MA 1998. Copyright © 1998 by John S. Hammond, Ralph L. Keeney, and Howard Raiffa; all rights reserved.

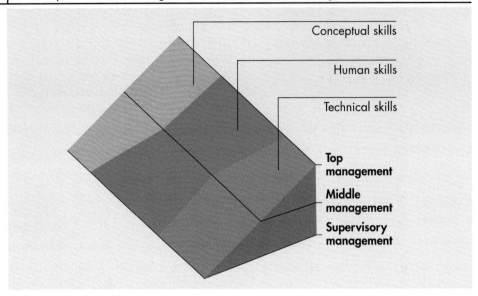

Technical Skills

Specialized areas of knowledge and expertise and the ability to apply that knowledge make up a manager's **technical skills**. Preparing a financial statement, programming a computer, designing an office building, and analyzing market research are all examples of technical skills. These types of skills are especially important for supervisory managers because they work closely with employees who are producing the goods and/or services of the firm. Supervisory managers need to be knowledgeable about the specific production and operation tools, techniques, and methods relevant to their specific area of the organization.

Human Relations Skills

Human relations skills are the interpersonal skills managers use to accomplish goals through the use of human resources. This set of skills includes the ability to understand human behaviour, to communicate effectively with others, and to motivate individuals to accomplish their objectives. Giving positive feedback to employees, being sensitive to their individual needs, and showing a willingness to empower subordinates are all examples of good human relations skills.

Consistently, human relations skills are cited as essential for business leaders. In a July 2002 article in *Human Resource Magazine*, Dave Opton, founder and CEO of ExecuNet, a recruitment firm, states "Clearly, it's not enough merely to be able to manage staff. Instead, employers are looking for executives who can effect change and who have all of the soft skills."[3]

Edna Morris, president of Red Lobster, credits much of her success to her people skills and her realization that people make a company successful. Ms. Morris oversees more than 60 000 employees at 670 units with total sales of over US$2 billion a year. She is described as passionate and approachable (people skills), as well as having industry insight (conceptual and technical skills).[4]

Conceptual Skills

Conceptual skills include the ability to view the organization as a whole, understand how the various parts are interdependent, and assess how the organization relates to its external environment. These skills allow managers to evaluate situations and develop alternative courses of action. Good conceptual skills are especially necessary for managers at the top of the management pyramid where strategic planning takes place.

---

technical skills
A manager's specialized areas of knowledge and expertise, as well as the ability to apply that knowledge.

human relations skills
A manager's interpersonal skills that are used to accomplish goals through the use of human resources.

HOT Links

Most successful managers work hard at continually updating their managerial skills. One organization that offers many ongoing training and education programs is the Chartered Accountants of Canada. Visit their site at www.cica.ca

conceptual skills
A manager's ability to view the organization as a whole, understand how the various parts are interdependent, and assess how the organization relates to its external environment.

Global Management Skills

The increasing globalization of the world market, as discussed in Chapters 2 and 3, has created a need for managers who have **global management skills**, that is, the ability to operate in diverse cultural environments. With more and more companies choosing to do business in multiple locations around the world, employees are often required to learn the geography, language, and social customs of other cultures. It is expensive to train employees for foreign assignments and pay their relocation costs; therefore, choosing the right person for the job is especially important. Individuals who are open-minded, flexible, willing to try new things, and comfortable in a multicultural setting are good candidates for international management positions.

global management skills
A manager's ability to operate in diverse cultural environments.

c o n c e p t   c h e c k

- Define the basic managerial skills.
- How important is each of these skill sets at the different levels of the management pyramid?
- What new challenges do managers face due to increasing globalization?

Planning

Planning begins by anticipating potential problems or opportunities the organization may encounter. Managers then design strategies to solve current problems, prevent future problems, or take advantage of opportunities. These strategies serve as the foundation for goals, objectives, policies, and procedures. Put simply, planning is deciding what needs to be done to achieve organizational objectives, identifying when and how it will be done, and determining by whom it should be done. Effective planning requires extensive information about the external business environment in which the firm competes, as well as its internal environment.

There are four basic types of planning: strategic, tactical, operational, and contingency. Most of us use these different types of planning in our own lives. Some plans are very broad and long term (more strategic in nature), such as planning to attend graduate school after earning a bachelor's degree. Some plans are much more specific and short term (more operational in nature), such as planning to spend a few hours in the library this weekend. Your short-term plans support your long-term plans. If you study now, you have a better chance of achieving some future goal, such as getting a job interview or attending graduate school. Like you, organizations tailor their plans to meet the requirements of future situations or events. A summary of the four types of planning appears in Exhibit 14-6.

Strategic planning involves creating long-range (one to five years), broad goals for the organization and determining what resources will be needed to accomplish those goals. An evaluation of external environmental factors such as economic, technological, and social issues is critical to successful strategic planning (see Exhibit 14-7). Once the analyses are completed, the vision, mission, strategy, and policy statements are formulated. An organization's mission is formalized in its **mission statement,** a document that states the purpose of the organization and its reason for existing.

For example, Carewest's mission statement, as part of its frame of reference document, clearly explains why the organization exists. The document also includes the vision and values statement and identifies the key result areas (see Exhibit 14-8 on page 367).

planning
The process of deciding what needs to be done to achieve organizational objectives; identifying when and how it will be done; and determining by whom it should be done.

 **lg 4**

strategic planning
The process of creating long-range (one to five years), broad goals for the organization and determining what resources will be needed to accomplish those goals.

mission statement
The formalized statement of an organization's purpose and reason for existing.

Operational planning is conducted by supervisory-level management to implement and activate specific objectives.

e x h i b i t   1 4 - 6 | Types of Planning

Type of Planning	Time Frame	Level of Management	Extent of Coverage	Purpose and Goal	Breadth of Content	Accuracy/ Predictability
Strategic	1–5 Years	Top management (CEO, vice-presidents, directors, division heads)	External environment and entire organization	Establish mission and long-term goals	Broad and general	High degree of certainty
Tactical	Less than 1 year	Middle management	Strategic business units	Establish mid-range goals for implementation	More specific	Moderate degree of certainty
Operational	Current	Supervisory management	Geographic and functional divisions	Implement and activate specific objectives	Specific and concrete	Reasonable degree of certainty
Contingency	When an event occurs or a situation demands	Top and middle management	External environment and entire organization	Meet unforeseen challenges and opportunities	Both broad and detailed	Reasonable degree of certainty once event of situation occurs

➡ **lg 5**

In all organizations, plans and goals at the tactical and operational levels should clearly support the organization's mission statement. Carewest's strategic planning process can be examined using Exhibit 14-7. The current mission, objectives, and strategies were identified as described in the vignette at the beginning of this chapter. The organization then identified its internal strengths and weaknesses. In analyzing the

e x h i b i t   1 4 - 7 | The Strategic Planning Process

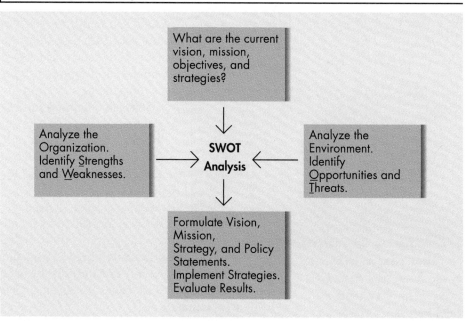

HOT Links

How does Carewest's mission statement translate into company action? Visit Carewest's home page at www.carewest.org to learn more.

external environment of Carewest, the management team looked at the political (Chapter 2), economic (Chapter 1), social (Chapter 3), and technological (Chapter 4) trends on the horizon. Recall the PEST model discussed in the Introduction on page 1. Political and economic trends would drive the fiscal considerations, while the social trends would impact such aspects as accessibility and capacity for Carewest. Comparing the internal strengths and weaknesses (SW) to the external opportunities and threats (OT) comprises a SWOT analysis. Carewest was then able to formulate a vision, mission, and strategy for the future, as shown in Exhibit 14-8.

e x h i b i t   1 4 - 8 | Carewest's "Frame of Reference" Document

Our Frame of Reference
Why We Exist

Our Mission....
Our Mission is to provide specialized care and support in an appropriate environment to:
> Adults who require transitional services to enable them to return to the community
> Adults who require residential or short-term services for complex health needs
> Seniors who require assessment and treatment services

What We Want To Be

Our Vision....
Carewest, leading the way in specialized continuing care.

How We Want To Work

Statement of Values
We Value:
commitment to the needs of the whole person
clients being involved and offered choices to enhance their quality of life
a learning environment which encourages innovation, research, and evaluation to foster best practice.
optimizing quality while managing costs
community involvement, partnerships, and the contribution of volunteers to respond to customer needs
a collaborative approach with other service providers to further an integrated health system
shared responsibility in creating a healthy, productive working environment, open communication and consultation

What We Need To Do

Key Result Areas
KRA (Key Result Area) #1 – Satisfied Clients
To provide services that earn high client satisfaction and promote quality of life

KRA #2 – Targeted Service Development
To respond to changing client needs and support the health region through appropriate implementation of services

KRA #3 – Progressive Work Environment
To provide an open, honest, responsive, healthy environment that supports continuous learning, quality improvement, and customer service

KRA #4 – Cost-Effective Organization
To manage finances and seek alternative funding to support and improve service delivery, facilities and support new options

SOURCE: Reprinted by permission of Carewest, a wholly owned subsidiary of the Calgary Health Region.

➡ **lg 6**

tactical planning
The process of beginning to implement a strategic plan by addressing issues of coordination and allocating resources to different parts of the organization; has a shorter time frame (less than one year) and more specific objectives than strategic planning.

operational planning
The process of creating specific standards, methods, policies, and procedures that are used in specific functional areas of the organization; helps guide and control the implementation of tactical plans.

contingency plans
Plans that identify alternative courses of action for very unusual or crisis situations; typically stipulate the chain of command, standard operating procedures, and communication channels the organization will use during an emergency.

HOT Links

To learn more about how firms develop contingency plans for all sorts of crises, visit *Contingency Planning* magazine's Web site at www.contingencyplanning.com

➡ **lg 7**

Tactical planning begins the implementation of strategic plans. Tactical plans have a shorter (less than one year) time frame than strategic plans and more specific objectives designed to support the broader strategic goals. Tactical plans begin to address issues of coordinating and allocating resources to different parts of the organization.

Operational planning creates specific standards, methods, policies, and procedures that are used in specific functional areas of the organization. Operational objectives are current, narrow, and resource focused. They are designed to help guide and control the implementation of tactical plans.

The key to effective planning is anticipating future situations and events. Yet even the best-prepared organization must sometimes cope with unforeseen circumstances such as a natural disaster, an act of terrorism, or a radical new technology. Therefore, many companies have developed **contingency plans** that identify alternative courses of action for very unusual or crisis situations. The contingency plan typically stipulates the chain of command, standard operating procedures, and communication channels the organization will use during an emergency. Failure to have adequate contingency plans for emergencies can have serious consequences for an organization.

Mike Howell, a former employee of Fred Alger Management Inc. who perished on September 11, 2001, had taken contingency planning to a new level. Mike, a chief technology officer, had built an emergency back-up office seven kilometres west of Manhattan in Morristown, New Jersey, which contained every portfolio for every client. All financial models, research notes, information services, and databases were operational. As Dan Chung, chief investment officer at Fred Alger says, "The firm would have had nowhere to operate from but for the planning … of Mike Howell and his team."[5]

concept check

• What is the purpose of planning, and what is needed to do it effectively?
• Identify the unique characteristics of each type of planning.

CAPITALIZING ON TRENDS IN BUSINESS

Three important trends in management today are the increasing empowerment of employees, the growing use of information technology, and the increasing need for global management skills. Each will be examined in turn.

Managers Empowering Employees

Most of the firms discussed in this chapter, including Carewest, Red Lobster, and Fred Alger Management Inc., are including more employees in the decision-making process than ever before. This increased level of employee involvement comes from the realization that people at all levels in the organization possess unique knowledge, skills, and abilities that can be of great value to the company. With empowerment, managers share information and responsibility with employees at all levels in the organization. Along with the authority to make decisions, empowerment also gives employees the control over resources needed to implement those decisions. Empowering employees enhances their commitment to the organization by giving them a feeling of ownership in the firm and an increased sense of competency.

In order for empowerment to work, managers have to facilitate employee decision making by providing access to necessary information, clear expectations for results, behavioural boundaries, and the resources employees need to carry out their decisions.

The employee empowerment trend allows employers to tap the knowledge and talent of all employees and gives workers a greater sense of ownership in their work and commitment to their employers.

HOT Links

Check out the PeopleSoft Web site at www.peoplesoft.com

HOT Links

Many organizations offer services to help companies who deal and work with various cultures. For an example of what is available, check out www.managingcultures.com

This concept is illustrated by Steve Miller, group managing director of the Royal Dutch/Shell Group of Companies. Royal Dutch/Shell, one of the largest companies in the world, has a strong sense of tradition and a very structured way of doing things. When Miller set out to change the way things were done at his company, he knew he would have to involve the people on the front lines, the "grassroots" positions of the company. He calls his form of empowerment *grassroots leadership*. Grassroots leadership means finding a way to empower the frontline people, "to challenge them, to provide them with the resources they need, and then to hold them accountable."[6]

Managers and Information Technology

The second trend having a major impact on managers is the proliferation of information technology. An increasing number of organizations are selling technology, and an increasing number are looking for cutting-edge technology to make and market the products and services they sell. A brief look at PeopleSoft, a rapidly growing provider of automated human resource functions, provides some insight into the crucial role information technology can play in today's organizations.[7] Plenty of new technology is being used at PeopleSoft, but it is "people-oriented" technology, and it starts with a backpack. Every new employee is issued a backpack filled with a laptop, pager, cell phone, and digital assistant. Steve Zarate, chief information officer at PeopleSoft, calls it "information-to-go." Every employee has access to PeopleSoft's "massive information infrastructure that spans continents and time zones." PeopleSoft uses information systems to create an "infomacracy," an organization where members have access to the information they need to make and implement decisions. By using the latest technology to empower people and keep members of the organization connected, PeopleSoft has grown to be a US$10 billion company.

Managing in a Global Marketplace

Geographic boundaries no longer constrain businesses the way they once did. To fully realize their potential, many companies must look to international markets to expand the sales of their products and services. This presents significant new challenges to managers. Global management can mean flying thousands of kilometres a week to keep up with business units spread across the world. Although new information technology makes communication easier than ever before, sometimes it cannot substitute for face-to-face contact. Ensuring that employees in far-flung locations still feel part of a cohesive organizational team can be difficult. Global managers often have to adapt to a new culture, learn a new language, manage a diverse work force, and operate in a foreign economic system. For many managers, accepting an international position also means helping their spouses and children adapt to the new environment. And in some companies, managers must try to translate an entire company philosophy into another language and culture.

concept check

- What steps must managers take if employee empowerment is to work?
- How can information technology aid in decision-making?
- What special problems do global managers face?

APPLYING THIS CHAPTER'S TOPICS

Many of the skills managers use to accomplish organizational goals can be applied outside the organizational setting. You could be using these skills in your life right now to accomplish your personal goals. This section provides some examples.

Effective Time Management

Successful managers use their time wisely. Adopting the following time management techniques will help you become a more successful student now and will help prepare you for the demands of your future workplace:

- *Plan ahead.* This is first and most obvious. Set both long-term and short-term goals. Review your list often and revise it when your situation changes.
- *Establish priorities.* Decide what is most important and what is most urgent. Sometimes they are not the same thing. Keep in mind the 80–20 rule: 20 percent of one's effort delivers 80 percent of the results.
- *Delegate.* Ask yourself if the task can be accomplished as effectively by someone else. Empower other people, and you may be surprised by the quality of the outcome.
- *Learn to say no.* Be stingy with your time. Be realistic about how long tasks will take. Don't feel guilty when you don't have the time, ability, or inclination to take on an additional task.
- *Batch.* Group activities together so they take up less of your day. For example, set aside a certain time to return phone calls, answer e-mail, and do any necessary written correspondence.
- *Stay on task.* Learn how to handle diversions. For example, let your answering machine take messages until you finish a particular task. Create a routine that helps you stay focused.
- *Set deadlines.* Don't let projects drag on. Reward yourself each time you cross a certain number of items off your "to do" list.

TRY IT NOW!

1. **Try a SWOT Analysis** Every university and college has distinctive strengths and weaknesses. Identify the various strengths and weaknesses of your school. What opportunities and threats do you feel are in your school's environment? Is your school positioned to take advantage of any of these opportunities? Is it prepared to deal with the threats you have identified?

2. **Use a Decision Model** List the various options open to you upon graduation from your program. What are the advantages and disadvantages of each option? Use the decision-making process to help choose the next step in your career planning.

>looking ahead
at Carewest

The Carewest management team sees several key issues to consider: access, capacity, fiscal constraints, and the arrival of P3s (public/private partnerships). A diversification strategy is evolving to address the access problems of the future. Offerings could include rehabilitation and recovery, community-based options such as a "health campus," a virtual care centre, and comprehensive community care (known as "C3"). Nursing rounds could include the neighbourhood, with the ultimate goal of keeping people in their own homes longer. This could be a win–win–win solution as the seniors are more satisfied, the government saves money, and the employees have an opportunity for a much more diverse workload.

KEY TERMS

conceptual skills 364
contingency plans 368
decisional roles 361
global management skills 365
human relations skills 364
informational roles 361
interpersonal roles 361
management 360
mission statement 365
nonprogrammed decisions 362
operational planning 368
planning 365
strategic planning 365
tactical planning 368
technical skills 364

SUMMARY OF LEARNING GOALS

➡lg 1   **What is the role of management?**
Management is the process of guiding the development, maintenance, and allocation of resources to attain organizational goals. Managers are the people in the organization responsible for developing and carrying out this management process. The four primary functions of managers are planning, organizing, leading, and controlling.

➡lg 2   **What roles do managers take on in different organizational settings?**
In an informational role, the manager may act as an information gatherer, an information distributor, or a spokesperson for the company. A manager's interpersonal roles are based on various interactions with other people. Depending on the situation, a manager may need to act as a figurehead, a company leader, or a liaison. When acting in a decisional role, a manager may have to think like an entrepreneur, make decisions about resource allocation, help resolve conflicts, or negotiate compromises.

➡lg 3   **What set of managerial skills is necessary for managerial success?**
Managerial skills fall into three basic categories: technical, human relations, and conceptual skills. Specialized areas of knowledge and expertise and the ability to apply that knowledge make up a manager's technical skills. Human relations skills include the ability to understand human behaviour, to communicate effectively with others, and to motivate individuals to accomplish their objectives. Conceptual skills include the ability to view the organization as a whole, understand how the various parts are interdependent, and assess how the organization relates to its external environment.

➡lg 4   **What are the four types of planning?**
Planning is deciding what needs to be done, identifying when and how it will be done, and determining by whom it should be done. Managers use four different types of planning: strategic, tactical, operational, and contingency planning. Strategic planning involves creating long-range (one to five years), broad goals and determining the necessary resources to accomplish those goals. Tactical planning has a shorter time frame (less than one year) and more specific objectives that support the broader strategic goals. Operational planning creates specific standards, methods, policies, and procedures that are used in specific functional areas of the organization. Contingency plans identify alternative courses of action for very unusual or crisis situations.

➡lg 5   **What is a mission statement?**
A mission statement is a formal document that states an organization's purpose and reason for existing and describes its basic philosophy.

➡lg 6   **What are contingency plans and why are they important?**
Contingency plans identify alternative courses of action for very unusual or crisis situations. They typically stipulate the chain of command, standard operating procedures, and emergency communication channels. They are important in that they allow companies to cope effectively with emergency situations by providing guidance and direction.

➡lg 7   **What trends will affect management in the future?**
Three important trends in management today are increasing employee empowerment, the increasing use of information technology, and the growing need for global management skills. Empowerment means giving employees increased autonomy and discretion to make their own decisions, as well as control of the resources needed to implement those decisions. When decision-making power is shared at all levels in the organization, employees feel a greater sense of ownership in, and responsibility for, organizational outcomes. Using the latest information technology, managers can make quicker, better-informed decisions. It also keeps organization members connected. As more companies "go global," the need for global management skills is growing. Global managers often have to adapt to a new culture, learn a new language, manage a diverse work force, and operate in a foreign economic system.

WORKING THE NET

1. Find information about how to develop a business plan by doing a search on the Dogpile mega-search engine (**www.dogpile.com**). Make a list of the resources available and suggest which ones would be most useful for (a) top executives of a large corporation, (b) a small business owner, and (c) a middle manager in a large corporation preparing an operational plan for her or his department. See if you can also find a site that has examples of completed business plans.

2. What is your image of successful management and leaders? Why? Try to find real-world examples that support your argument by searching the archives of business magazines such as *Forbes* (**www.forbes.com**), *Fortune* (**www.fortune.com**), or *Business Week* (**www.businessweek.com**).

CREATIVE THINKING CASE

Anatomy of Dragonflies and Empowerment

Once a week, Duncan Highsmith closets himself for two hours in a small room adjacent to his office and tries to wrap his brain around the world. Seated at a large wooden table, the president and CEO of Highsmith, Inc., sifts through stacks of articles on subjects ranging from juvenile crime to semiotics to the anatomy of dragonflies. In this eclectic mix he is searching for nascent trends, provocative contradictions, and, most important, connections that could eventually reshape his business.

Highsmith's pursuit—called Life, the Universe, and Everything—springs from his conviction that you can't take a narrow approach to the future. "We tend to behave as though the future will be like the present, only bigger and faster," says Highsmith, whose US$55 million business is the United States' leading mail-order supplier of equipment such as book displays, audio-video tools, and educational software for schools and libraries.

Life, the Universe, and Everything is significant for the information it gathers, but Highsmith also intends it as a teaching tool that will ultimately prod everyone in the company to see and understand the kinds of big-picture connections CEOs generally make in isolation. Toward that end, he's beginning to broaden participation in the project, asking other staff members to pass along scraps of intriguing information and using his research as the basis for presentations at executive meetings.

Highsmith's overarching goal is for all employees in the company to shed their tactical blinders and begin thinking strategically—about customers, about the industry, and about forces for which the words big picture seem inadequate. "Life, the Universe, and Everything is in many ways in its infancy," says Highsmith. "The concrete benefits still have more to do with my role than with the rest of the organization. But thinking about what's next is becoming part of the routine work of the organization."[8]

Critical Thinking Questions
1. How would you describe Duncan Highsmith's leadership style?
2. Is Life, the Universe, and Everything a tool for employee empowerment? Why or why not?
3. Is Life, the Universe, and Everything more beneficial for strategic planning or tactical planning, or is it equally beneficial for both?

MAKING THE CONNECTION MAKING THE CONNECTIO

Designing Organizational Structures

We saw in the previous chapter how all the functions of a manager are highly integrated. They are done almost as if simultaneously, and they affect and are affected by each other. They are the glue that binds the organization together, because it is the process of management that guides the internal organization to achieve its critical success factors, within the external environment that it is faced with, and to the satisfaction of its stakeholders. Sounds complicated, doesn't it? Well management isn't easy. The rewards of a successful business don't come easy, but they are definitely worth it. To make it easier we will examine each of the functions of a manager in a separate chapter. Just remember that they are connected.

In this chapter we will examine the design of organizational structures suitable to achieve the goals of the company. Take the example in the chapter of Procter & Gamble (P&G). Its goal was faster product *innovation*. This goal came in response to today's rapidly changing business environment, which demands that businesses respond more quickly to meet both competitive threats and changing customer needs. Innovation, we know, is a critical success factor; P&G needs to be a step ahead of the competition. In order to achieve this goal, it shifted from a geographically based structure to a structure based on products. It also introduced a new compensation system to encourage innovation. This is a very integrative example. We can see that the strategic plan fits with the environment, that the organizational structure fits with the strategic plan, and that the tactical plan for compensation was changed to fit with the strategic plan as well.

In fact, you'll see that when organizations change their structures, they are attempting to increase their ability to *satisfy the customer*—whether through centralizing some operations to reduce costs (and ultimately price), decentralizing to be more responsive to customer needs, or using information technology to get closer to the customer.

A formal organizational structure is the result of this design process. The chapter describes this formal organization as "human, material, financial, and information resources deliberately connected to form the business organization." In other words, the resources of each functional area are structured in such a way that even though they are in separate areas—human resources, operations, finance, and marketing—they are linked together so that the organization can achieve its goals. If the organization is not structured in this way, with all the parts working together in an integrative way, success is not possible. We know from our discussion in the Introduction to the model, that all the critical success factors are connected. They are also connected to each of the functional areas. The most obvious connections are:

- Achieving financial performance (*finance*)
- Meeting and exceeding customer needs (*marketing*)
- Providing value—quality products at a reasonable price (*operations* and marketing)
- Encouraging creativity and innovation (all areas)
- Gaining employee commitment (*human resources*)

However they can't work independently and achieve these success factors. It all starts, as we've said, with the customer. As you'll see in the chapter, every organization is structured with the customer as the central thread. With this in mind, operations and marketing must work together. Marketing determines the needs of the customer and works with operations to design a product to meet those needs. Operations provides it in a quality manner, and marketing prices it to reflect the level of quality and provide something of value to the customer. They can't do this without people committed to making it work, and they can't keep doing it without fresh ideas that keep the organization providing something that distinguishes it from the competition. All of these areas provide the income for the business, but that money must flow back to each of the areas as needed to fuel the plans. It is therefore necessary that whatever structure is designed take into consideration the inseparable connections between the different areas of the business.

Certain structures specifically integrate the different functional areas intentionally so that they are working together on specific projects. A matrix structure is one such example. All areas are represented so that conflicting objectives can be balanced and overall, rather than individual, goals become the priority. It also allows for other factors that contribute to success—different minds working together increases creativity and innovation, for example.

Another type of structure takes the topic of integration beyond the borders of the business, as in the case with most successful businesses today. The virtual corporation is a "network of independent companies linked by information technology" that allows them to take advantages of opportunities they couldn't alone, and share each other's key competen-cies to become a truly integrative organization. Cisco is one such company that is at the forefront of this new type of structure. As discussed in the chapter, Cisco CEO John Chambers's beliefs reflect the essence of this integrative structure—organizations should be built on change, organized as networks, and based on interdependencies.

Designing Organizational Structures

CHAPTER 15

Learning Goals

→ **lg 1** What are the five structural building blocks that managers use to design organizations?

→ **lg 2** What are the five types of departmentalization?

→ **lg 3** How can the degree of centralization/decentralization be altered to make an organization more successful?

→ **lg 4** How do mechanistic and organic organizations differ?

→ **lg 5** What is the difference between line positions and staff positions?

→ **lg 6** What is the goal of re-engineering?

→ **lg 7** How does the informal organization affect the performance of the company?

→ **lg 8** What trends are influencing the way businesses organize?

Procter & Gamble Reorganizes to Sell US$70 Billion in 2005

The people who bring you Crest toothpaste, Pringles potato chips, and Hugo Boss cologne are really shaking things up. In an attempt to increase sales worldwide and bring new products to market more quickly, Procter & Gamble (**www.pg.com**) is reorganizing its corporate structure. The consensus of consumers, chain-store customers, and industry insiders is that P&G needs to be simpler and to move faster.

To achieve these goals, the company has undertaken "Organization 2005!" To achieve its 2005 sales goal of US$70 billion and reinvigorate its corporate culture, P&G is revamping its entire corporate management structure. The old P&G bureaucracy was based on geography, with four executive vice-presidents overseeing the North American, Asian, Latin American, European, Middle Eastern, and African operations. Under this system, senior regional managers had wide latitude in setting prices and handling products. The old structure is being replaced by seven product-based global business units organized by category, such as baby care, food and beverage, and laundry and cleaning. These global business units will develop and sell products on a worldwide basis. P&G hopes that this shift from geographic departmentalization to a product-based structure will lead to faster product innovation and increase flexibility and response time.

As part of the restructuring process, P&G is streamlining its corporate staff and creating a global business services organization. Services that are currently spread throughout the organization, such as finance, accounting, and information technology, are being consolidated. According to top management, this will provide P&G with greater economies of scale and will improve both the quality and speed of those service areas. Additionally, P&G plans to introduce a new compensation system that will encourage employee innovation, flexibility, and customer service.

In 1998, P&G named Durk Jager to implement the new structure. Jager earned the nickname "Crazy Man Durk" for his earlier aggressive turnaround of P&G's failing Japanese operation. His aggressiveness, however, proved his undoing at rigidly structured P&G. He simply tried to do too much too fast. Alan Lafley, a man known for his people skills, was made CEO in the summer of 2000. Some observers say that the change was a mistake. Despite Jager's aggressive style, he may have been the best hope for changing P&G's entrenched bureaucracy.[1]

CRITICAL THINKING QUESTIONS

As you read this chapter, consider the following questions as they relate to Procter & Gamble:

- What are the structural building blocks that Procter & Gamble can use in its reorganization?
- How does decentralization enter into the reorganization?
- How can the informal organization affect the reorganization?

BUSINESS IN THE 21ST CENTURY

In today's dynamic business environment, organizational structures need to be designed so that the organization can quickly respond to new competitive threats and changing customer needs. In the future, companies such as Procter & Gamble will achieve long-term success only if they have the ability to manage change and organize their resources effectively. In this chapter, we'll present the five structural building blocks of organizations and look at how each can be used to build unique organizational structures. We'll explore how communication, authority, and job specialization are combined to create both formal and informal organizational structures. Finally, we'll consider how re-engineering and new business trends are changing the way businesses organize.

➡ lg 1

Structural Building Blocks

As you learned in Chapter 14, the key functions that managers perform include planning, organizing, leading, and controlling. This chapter focuses specifically on the organizing function. Organizing involves coordinating and allocating a firm's resources so that the firm can carry out its plans and achieve its goals. This organizing, or structuring, process is accomplished by

- determining work activities and dividing up tasks (*division of labour*),
- grouping jobs and employees (*departmentalization*), and
- assigning authority and responsibilities (*delegation*).

formal organization
The order and design of relationships within a firm; consists of two or more people working together with a common objective and clarity of purpose.

The result of the organizing process is a formal organizational structure. A **formal organization** is the order and design of relationships within the firm. It consists of two or more people working together with a common objective and clarity of purpose. Formal organizations also have well-defined lines of authority, channels for information flow, and means of control. Human, material, financial, and information resources are deliberately connected to form the business organization. Some connections are long lasting, such as the links among people in the finance or marketing department. Others can be changed at almost any time, as when a committee is formed to study a problem.

Five structural building blocks are used in designing an efficient and effective organizational structure. They are division of labour, departmentalization, managerial hierarchy, span of control, and centralization of decision making.

Division of Labour

division of labour
The process of dividing work into separate jobs and assigning tasks to workers.

The process of dividing work into separate jobs and assigning tasks to workers is called **division of labour**. In a fast-food restaurant, for example, some employees take or fill orders, others prepare food, a few clean and maintain equipment, and at least one supervises all the others. In an auto assembly plant, some workers install rear-view mirrors, while others mount bumpers on bumper brackets. The degree to which the tasks are subdivided into smaller jobs is called **specialization**. Employees who work at highly specialized jobs, such as assembly-line workers, perform a limited number and variety of tasks. Employees who become specialists at one task, or a small number of tasks, develop greater skill in doing that particular job. This can lead to greater efficiency and consistency in production and other work activities. However, a high degree of specialization can also result in employees who are disinterested or bored due to the lack of variety and challenge.

specialization
The degree to which tasks are subdivided into smaller jobs.

Currently, most managers recognize that there is a trade-off between the economic benefits and the human costs associated with specialization. At Harley-Davidson's Kansas City assembly plant, managers and workers together have created an environment that maximizes the benefits and minimizes the drawbacks of highly specialized motorcycle assembly jobs.[2] To streamline the production process and at the same time keep employees involved and motivated, line workers are required to share their opinions and to make decisions about how to build better bikes. There is no denying the benefits of specialization in designing an efficient production system. But Harley has discovered that those benefits are best realized in an atmosphere that allows employees to experience challenge, empowerment, and ownership.

Departmentalization

The second building block used to create a strong organizational structure is called **departmentalization**. After the work is divided into jobs, jobs are then grouped together so that similar or associated tasks and activities can be coordinated. This grouping of people, tasks, and resources into organizational units facilitates the planning, leading, and control processes.

An **organization chart** is a visual representation of the structured relationships among tasks and the people given the authority to do those tasks. In the organization chart in Exhibit 15-1, each figure represents a job, and each job includes several tasks. The sales manager, for instance, must hire salespeople, establish sales territories, motivate and train the salespeople, and control sales operations. The chart also indicates the general type of work done in each position.

As Exhibit 15-2 shows, five basic types of departmentalization are commonly used in organizations:

- **Functional departmentalization**, which is based on the primary functions performed within an organizational unit (marketing, finance, production, sales, and so on).
- **Product departmentalization**, which is based on the goods or services produced or sold by the organizational unit (such as outpatient/emergency services, pediatrics, cardiology, and orthopedics).

➡ lg 2

departmentalization
The process of grouping jobs together so that similar or associated tasks and activities can be coordinated.

organization chart
A visual representation of the structured relationships among tasks and the people given the authority to do those tasks.

functional departmentalization
Departmentalization that is based on the primary functions performed within an organizational unit.

product departmentalization
Departmentalization that is based on the goods or services produced or sold by the organizational unit.

---

e x h i b i t   1 5 - 1 | Organizational Chart for a Typical Appliance Manufacturer

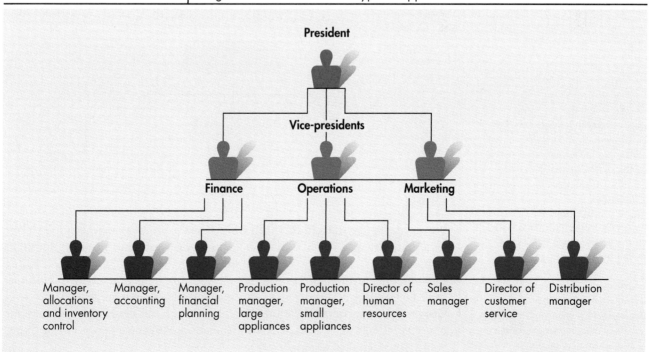

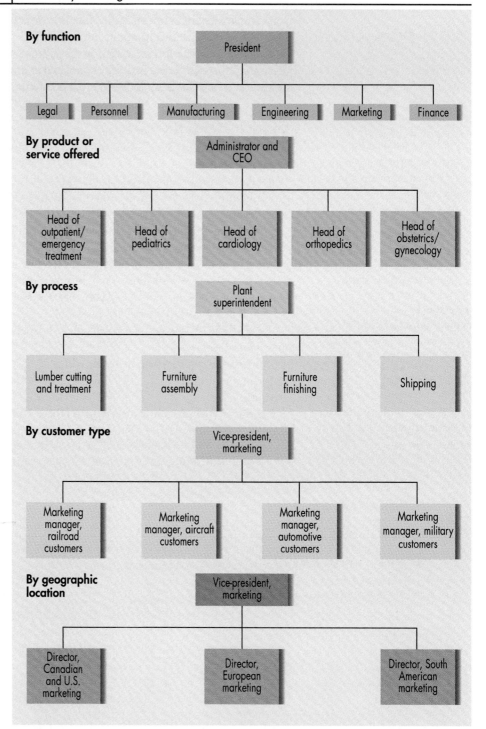

process departmentalization
Departmentalization that is based on the production process used by the organizational unit.

customer departmentalization
Departmentalization that is based on the primary type of customer served by the organizational unit.

geographic departmentalization
Departmentalization that is based on the geographic segmentation of the organizational units.

- **Process departmentalization,** which is based on the production process used by the organizational unit (such as lumber cutting and treatment, furniture finishing, shipping).
- **Customer departmentalization,** which is based on the primary type of customer served by the organizational unit (such as wholesale or retail purchasers).
- **Geographic departmentalization,** which is based on the geographic segmentation of organizational units (such as U.S. and Canadian marketing, European marketing, South American marketing).

People are assigned to a particular organizational unit because they perform similar or related tasks, or because they are jointly responsible for a product, client, or market. Decisions about how to departmentalize affect the way management assigns authority, distributes resources, rewards performance, and sets up lines of communication. Many large organizations use several types of departmentalization. For example, a global company may be departmentalized first geographically (North American, European, and Asian units), then by product line (foods/beverages and health care), and finally by functional area (marketing, operations, finance, and so on). As Procter & Gamble illustrates, the type(s) of departmentalization an organization uses can directly affect organizational performance.

Managerial Hierarchy

managerial hierarchy
The levels of management within an organization; typically includes top, middle, and supervisory management.

The third building block used to create effective organizational structure is the **managerial hierarchy** (also called the *management pyramid*), or the levels of management within the organization. Generally, the management structure has three levels: top, middle, and supervisory management (see Exhibit 15-3).

In a managerial hierarchy, each organizational unit is controlled and supervised by a manager in a higher unit. The person with the most formal authority is at the top of the hierarchy. The higher a manager, the more power he or she has. Thus, the amount of power decreases as you move down the management pyramid. At the same time, the number of employees increases as you move down the hierarchy.

Although the trend in organizations today is to eliminate layers of middle management in order to create a leaner, "flatter" organization, sometimes companies find that adding another layer to the hierarchy can actually simplify the reporting relationships in the company. Home Depot, the world's biggest home improvement retailer, recently discovered this.[3] The company's phenomenal growth rate was straining the capabilities of the six division heads who reported directly to the CEO. So the company hired four new group presidents, adding a layer of management between the CEO and the division heads. As often happens when a structure is changed, there was some

e x h i b i t   1 5 - 3 | The Managerial Pyramid

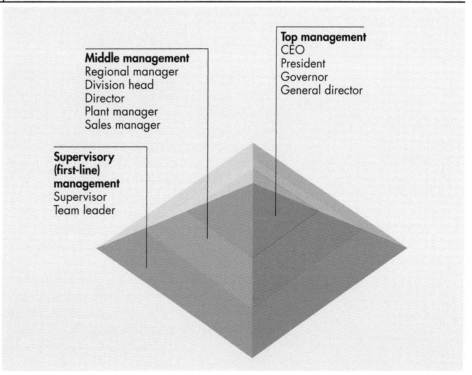

Top management
CEO
President
Governor
General director

Middle management
Regional manager
Division head
Director
Plant manager
Sales manager

Supervisory
(first-line)
management
Supervisor
Team leader

initial negative reaction to the decision. Eventually, most of the resistance was overcome as managers realized the new positions were needed to deal with business areas outside the company's traditional core competencies (for example, a direct marketing expert and a retail sales expert). Adding the new positions actually freed the division heads to concentrate on the duties central to their particular area of the business.

An organization with a well-defined hierarchy has a clear **chain of command**, which is the line of authority that extends from one level of the organization to the next, from top to bottom, and makes clear who reports to whom. The chain of command is shown in the organization chart and can be traced from the CEO all the way down to the employees producing goods and services. Under the *unity of command* principle, everyone reports to and gets instructions from only one boss. Unity of command guarantees that everyone will have a direct supervisor and will not be taking orders from a number of different supervisors. Unity of command and chain of command give everyone in the organization clear directions and help coordinate people doing different jobs.

Individuals who are part of the chain of command have authority over other persons in the organization. **Authority** is legitimate power, granted by the organization and acknowledged by employees, that allows an individual to request action and expect compliance. Exercising authority means making decisions and seeing that they are carried out. Most managers delegate, or assign, some degree of authority and responsibility to others below them in the chain of command. The **delegation of authority** makes the employees accountable to their supervisor. Accountability means responsibility for outcomes. Typically, authority and responsibility move downward through the organization as managers assign activities to, and share decision making with, their subordinates. Accountability moves upward in the organization as managers in each successively higher level are held accountable for the actions of their subordinates.

Span of Control

The fourth structural building block is the managerial span of control. Each firm must decide how many managers are needed at each level of the management hierarchy to effectively supervise the work performed within organizational units. A manager's **span of control** (sometimes called *span of management*) is the number of employees the manager directly supervises. It can be as narrow as two or three employees or as wide as 50 or more. In general, the larger the span of control, the more efficient the organization. As Exhibit 15-4 shows, however, both narrow and wide spans of control have benefits and drawbacks.

If hundreds of employees perform the same job, one supervisor may be able to manage a very large number of employees. Such might be the case at a clothing plant, where hundreds of sewing machine operators work from identical patterns. But if employees perform complex and dissimilar tasks, a manager can effectively supervise only a much smaller number. For instance, a supervisor in the research and development area of a pharmaceutical company might oversee just a few research chemists due to the highly complex nature of their jobs.

The optimal span of control is determined by the following five factors:

- *Nature of the task.* The more complex the task, the narrower the span of control.
- *Location of the workers.* The more locations, the narrower the span of control.
- *Ability of the manager* to delegate responsibility. The greater the ability to delegate, the wider the span of control.
- *Amount of interaction* and feedback between the workers and the manager. The more feedback and interaction required, the narrower the span of control.
- *Level of skill and motivation of the workers.* The higher the skill level and motivation, the wider the span of control.

chain of command
The line of authority that extends from one level of an organization's hierarchy to the next, from top to bottom, and makes clear who reports to whom.

HOT Links

To understand the chain of command in the United Nations, check out the organizational chart at
www.un.org

authority
Legitimate power, granted by the organization and acknowledged by employees, that allows an individual to request action and expect compliance.

delegation of authority
The assignment of some degree of authority and responsibility to persons lower in the chain of command.

span of control
The number of employees a manager directly supervises; also called *span of management*.

e x h i b i t   1 5 - 4 | Narrow and Wide Spans of Control

	Advantages	Disadvantages
Narrow span of control	• High degree of control • Fewer subordinates may mean manager is more familiar with each individual • Close supervision can provide immediate feedback.	• More levels of management, therefore more expensive. • Slower decision making due to vertical layers. • Isolation of top management • Discourages employee autonomy
Wide span of control	• Fewer levels of management means increased efficiency and reduced costs. • Increased subordinate autonomy leads to quicker decision making. • Greater organizational flexibility. • Higher levels of job satisfaction due to employee empowerment.	• Less control. • Possible lack of familiarity due to large number of subordinates. • Managers spread so thin that they can't provide necessary leadership or support. • Lack of coordination or synchronization.

 lg 3

centralization
The degree to which formal authority is concentrated in one area or level of an organization.

decentralization
The process of pushing decision-making authority down the organizational hierarchy.

Centralization of Decision Making

The final component in building an effective organizational structure is deciding at what level in the organization decisions should be made. **Centralization** is the degree to which formal authority is concentrated in one area or level of the organization. In a highly centralized structure, top management makes most of the key decisions in the organization, with very little input from lower-level employees. Centralization lets top managers develop a broad view of operations and exercise tight financial controls. It can also help to reduce costs by eliminating redundancy in the organization. But centralization may also mean that lower-level personnel don't get a chance to develop their decision-making and leadership skills and that the organization is less able to respond quickly to customer demands.

Decentralization is the process of pushing decision-making authority down the organizational hierarchy, giving lower-level personnel more responsibility and power to make and implement decisions. Benefits of decentralization can include quicker decision making, increased levels of innovation and creativity, greater organizational flexibility, faster development of lower-level managers, and increased levels of job satisfaction and employee commitment. But decentralization can also be risky. If lower-level personnel don't have the necessary skills and training to perform effectively, they may make costly mistakes. Additionally, decentralization may increase the likelihood of inefficient lines of communication, incongruent or competing objectives, and duplication of effort.

Several factors must be considered when deciding how much decision-making authority to delegate throughout the organization. These factors include the size of the organization, the speed of change in its environment, managers' willingness to give up authority, employees' willingness to accept more authority, and the organization's geographic dispersion. Decentralization is usually desirable when the following conditions are met:

- The organization is very large, like Exxon, Ford, or General Electric.
- The firm is in a dynamic environment where quick, local decisions must be made, as in many high-tech industries.
- Managers are willing to share power with their subordinates.
- Employees are willing and able to take more responsibility.
- The company is spread out geographically, such as Sears, Shell, or Procter & Gamble.

As organizations grow and change, they continually re-evaluate the organizational structure to determine whether it is helping the company to achieve its goals. Firms can alter the degree of centralization/decentralization in the organizational structure as the needs of the company change.

concept check

- What are the five building blocks of organizational structure?
- List the five types of departmentalization.
- What factors determine the optimal span of control?
- What are the primary characteristics of a decentralized organization?

➡ lg 4

mechanistic organization
An organizational structure that is characterized by a relatively high degree of job specialization, rigid departmentalization, many layers of management, narrow spans of control, centralized decision making, and a long chain of command.

organic organization
An organizational structure that is characterized by a relatively low degree of job specialization, loose departmentalization, few levels of management, wide spans of control, decentralized decision making, and a short chain of command.

Mechanistic versus Organic Structures

Using different combinations of the building blocks described above, organizations can build a wide variety of organizational structures. Nevertheless, structural design generally follows one of the two basic models described in Exhibit 15-5: mechanistic or organic. A **mechanistic organization** is characterized by a relatively high degree of job specialization, rigid departmentalization, many layers of management (particularly middle management), narrow spans of control, centralized decision making, and a long chain of command. This combination of elements results in what is called a *tall organizational structure*. Military organizations typically have tall structures. In contrast, an **organic organization** is characterized by a relatively low degree of job specialization, loose departmentalization, few levels of management, wide spans of control, decentralized decision making, and a short chain of command. This combination of elements results in what is called a *flat organizational structure*. Colleges and universities tend to have flat organizational structures, with only two or three levels of administration between the faculty and the president. Exhibit 15-6 shows examples of flat and tall organizational structures.

Although few organizations are purely mechanistic or purely organic, most organizations tend more toward one type or the other. The decision to create a more mechanistic or a more organic structural design is based on factors such as the firm's overall strategy, the size of the organization, the types of technologies used in the organization, and the stability of its external environment.

concept check

- Compare and contrast mechanistic and organic organizations.
- What factors determine whether an organization should be mechanistic or organic?

Apple Computers uses an organic structure to develop new products like the iMac computer. Organic structures allow firms like Apple to succeed in rapidly changing environments.

exhibit 1 5 - 5 | Mechanistic versus Organic Structure

Structural Characteristic	Mechanistic	Organic
Job specialization	High	Low
Departmentalization	Rigid	Loose
Management hierarchy (levels of management)	Tall (many levels)	Flat (few levels)
Span of control	Narrow	Wide
Decision-making authority	Centralized	Decentralized
Chain of command	Long	Short

Common Organizational Structures

There is no single best way to design an organization. Within the basic mechanistic and organic models and the hybrids that contain elements of both, an almost infinite variety of organizational structures can be developed. Many organizations use a combination of elements from different structural types to meet their unique organizational needs. Some of the most common structural designs are discussed in this section.

exhibit 1 5 - 6 | Tall versus Flat Organizational Structures

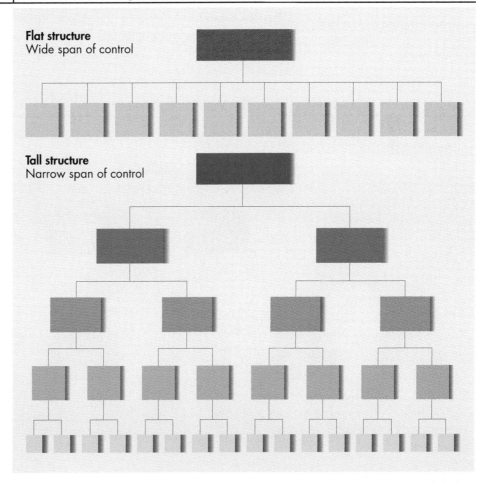

Flat structure
Wide span of control

Tall structure
Narrow span of control

⇒ **lg 5**

line organization
An organizational structure with direct, clear lines of authority and communication flowing from the top managers downward.

line-and-staff organization
An organizational structure that includes both line and staff positions.

line positions
All positions in the organization directly concerned with producing goods and services and which are directly connected from top to bottom.

staff positions
Positions in an organization held by individuals who provide the administrative and support services that line employees need to achieve the firm's goals.

committee structure
An organizational structure in which authority and responsibility are held by a group rather than an individual.

Line Organization

The **line organization** is designed with direct, clear lines of authority and communication flowing from the top managers downward. Managers have direct control over all activities, including administrative duties. An organization chart for this type of structure would show that all positions in the firm are directly connected via an imaginary line extending from the highest position in the organization to the lowest (where production of goods and services takes place). This structure with its simple design, clear chain of command, and broad managerial control is often well suited to small, entrepreneurial firms.

Line-and-Staff Organization

As an organization grows and becomes more complex, the line organization can be enhanced by adding staff positions to the design. Staff positions provide specialized advisory and support services to line managers in the **line-and-staff organization**, shown in Exhibit 15-7. In daily operations, those individuals in **line positions** are directly involved in the processes used to create goods and services. Those individuals in **staff positions** provide the administrative and support services that line employees need to achieve the firm's goals. Line positions in organizations are typically in areas such as production, marketing, and finance. Staff positions are found in areas such as legal counselling, managerial consulting, public relations, and human resource management.

Committee Structure

In **committee structure**, authority and responsibility are held by a group rather than an individual. Committees are typically part of a larger line-and-staff organization. Often the committee's role is only advisory, but in some situations the committee has the power to make and implement decisions. Committees can make the coordination of tasks in the organization much easier. At Toyota, for example, product and

e x h i b i t   1 5 - 7 | Line and Staff Organization

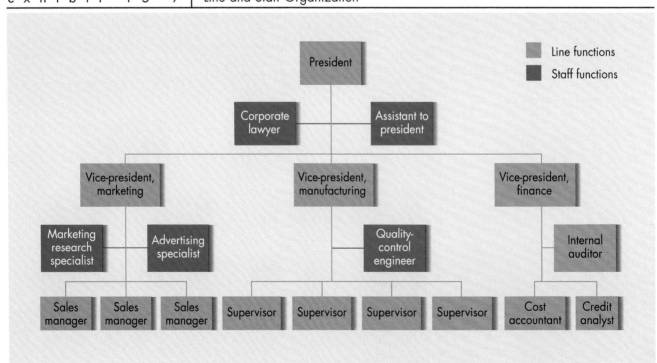

manufacturing engineers work together in committees. Using this process, factory machinery is developed concurrently with new car prototypes so it is able to accommodate them. Committees bring diverse viewpoints to a problem and expand the range of possible solutions, but there are some drawbacks. Committees can be slow to reach a decision and are sometimes dominated by a single individual. It is also more difficult to hold any one individual accountable for a decision made by a group.

Committee meetings can sometimes go on for long periods of time with little seemingly being accomplished. This is why many workers quickly develop an aversion to serving on committees. Blair Phillips of Carewest (profiled in Chapter 14) describes the effectiveness of the committees formed at that organization: "All the teams (committees) have charters and involve the frontline caregivers. We had to create time for meetings within the business strategy in order for them to happen. Our values, mission, and vision have been internalized by our employees and the result is a highly committed work force who believe in what they do because they helped to create our business model."

Matrix Structure

The **matrix structure** (also called the **project management** approach) is sometimes used in conjunction with the traditional line-and-staff structure in an organization. Essentially, this structure combines two different forms of departmentalization, functional and product, that have complementary strengths and weaknesses. The matrix structure brings together people from different functional areas of the organization (such as manufacturing, finance, and marketing) to work on a special project. Each employee has two direct supervisors: the line manager from her or his specific functional area and the project manager. Exhibit 15-8 shows a matrix organization with four special project groups (A, B, C, D), each with its own project manager. Because of the dual chain of command, the matrix structure presents some unique challenges for both managers and subordinates.

matrix structure (project management)
An organizational structure that combines functional and product departmentalization by bringing together people from different functional areas of the organization to work on a special project.

HOT Links

To learn more about matrix management, go to www.strategicfutures.com and select the "matrix management" icon.

e x h i b i t 1 5 - 8 | Matrix Organization

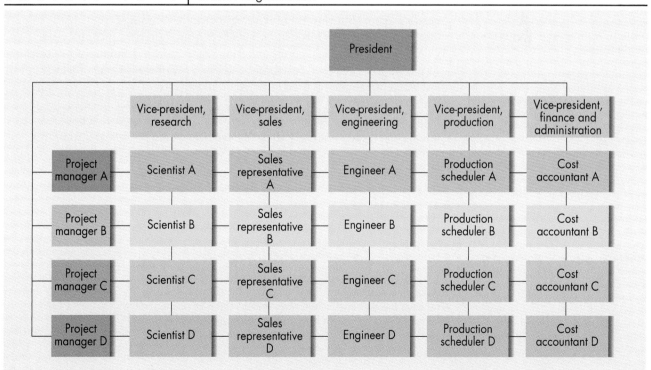

Advantages of the matrix structure include:

- *Teamwork.* By pooling the skills and abilities of various specialists, the company can increase creativity and innovation and tackle more complex tasks.
- *Efficient use of resources.* Project managers use only the specialized staff they need to get the job done, instead of building large groups of underused personnel.
- *Flexibility.* The project structure is flexible and can adapt quickly to changes in the environment; the group can be disbanded quickly when it is no longer needed.
- *Ability to balance conflicting objectives.* The customer wants a quality product and predictable costs. The organization wants high profits and the development of technical capability for the future. These competing goals serve as a focal point for directing activities and overcoming conflict. The marketing representative can represent the customer, the finance representative can advocate high profits, and the engineers can push for technical capabilities.
- *Higher performance.* Employees working on special project teams may experience increased feelings of ownership, commitment, and motivation.
- *Opportunities for personal and professional development.* The project structure gives individuals the opportunity to develop and strengthen technical and interpersonal skills.

Disadvantages of the matrix structure include:

- *Power struggles.* Functional and product managers may have differing goals and management styles.
- *Confusion among team members.* Reporting relationships and job responsibilities may be unclear.
- *Lack of cohesiveness.* Team members from different functional areas may have difficulty communicating effectively and working together as a team.

How do you keep project teams on track in a matrix structure? Chris Higgins, BankAmerica's "Mr. Project," has some basic rules for getting things done.[4] Higgins joined the bank several years ago as a vice-president in charge of project management in the payment services division. His span of control has increased from a team of 8 to 140 project managers, with a current combined budget of US$100 million. Higgins gives this advice for keeping projects on track in a matrix organization:

1. Spend less time doing and more time planning. Higgins believes teams are often quick at acting, but slow to think things through. Planning is particularly important when the team is made up of members from different functional areas.
2. Don't rely on electronic communication. Face-to-face communication can prevent confusion, clarify expectations, and build relationships—all of which can be lost when only e-mail is used to transmit information. Take time to communicate with team members.
3. Look for the commonality among projects. Although project teams often have unique challenges, not every challenge requires a unique plan of operation.
4. Project work isn't just about problem solving and timetables—it also requires encouraging employees to maintain momentum and keep up morale. Celebrate the achievement of interim goals, and make the project challenging as well as fun!

concept check

- How do line and staff positions differ?
- Why does the matrix structure have a dual chain of command?
- What are the advantages of a matrix structure? Disadvantages?

→ **lg 6**

re-engineering
The complete redesign of business structures and processes in order to improve operations.

HOT Links

An excellent source of links and information about the ins and outs of the re-engineering process is the Reengineering Resource Center at

www.reengineering.com

Re-engineering Organizational Structure

Periodically, all businesses must re-evaluate the way they do business. This includes assessing the effectiveness of the organizational structure. To meet the formidable challenges of the future, companies are increasingly turning to **re-engineering**—the complete redesign of business structures and processes in order to improve operations. An even simpler definition of re-engineering is "starting over." In effect, top management asks, "If we were a new company, how would we run this place?" The purpose of re-engineering is to identify and abandon the outdated rules and fundamental assumptions that guide current business operations. Every company has many formal and informal rules based on assumptions about technology, people, and organizational goals that no longer hold. Thus, the goal of re-engineering is to redesign business processes to achieve improvements in cost control, product quality, customer service, and speed. The re-engineering process should result in a more efficient and effective organizational structure that is better suited to the current (and future) competitive climate of the industry.

concept check

- What is meant by re-engineering?
- What is the purpose of re-engineering?

→ **lg 7**

informal organization
The network of connections and channels of communication based on the informal relationships of individuals inside an organization.

The Informal Organization

Thus far in the chapter we have focused on the elements of formal organizational structures, many of which can be seen in the boxes and lines of the organization chart. Yet many important relationships within an organization do not show up on an organization chart. Nevertheless, these relationships can affect the decisions and performance of employees at all levels of the organization. The network of connections and channels of communication based on the informal relationships of individuals inside the organization is known as the **informal organization**. Informal relationships can be between people at the same hierarchical level or between people at different levels and in different departments. Some connections are work related, such as those formed among people who carpool or ride the same train to work. Others are based on non-work commonalties such as belonging to the same church or health club or having children who attend the same school. The informal channels of communication of the informal organization are often referred to as the grapevine, the rumour mill, or the intelligence network.

Informal relationships between co-workers promote friendships among employees and keep employees informed about what's happening at their firm.

Functions of the Informal Organization

The informal organization has several functions. First, it provides a source of friendships and social contact for organization members. Second, the interpersonal relationships and informal groups help employees feel better informed and connected with what is going on in their firm, thus giving them some sense of control over their work environment. Third, the informal organization can provide status and recognition that the formal organization cannot or will not provide employees. Fourth, the network of relationships can aid the socialization of new employees by informally passing along rules, responsibilities, basic objectives, and job expectations. Finally, the organizational grapevine helps employees to be more aware of what is happening in their workplace by transmitting information quickly and conveying it to places that the formal system does not reach.

Although the informal organization can help the formal organization to achieve its goals, it can also create problems if not managed well. Group norms (commonly accepted standards of behaviour) may conflict with the company's standards and cause problems. For instance, during a merger or acquisition, informal groups may strongly resist change (especially structural change), spread incorrect information through the grapevine, and foster fear and low morale among employees. With this in mind, managers need to learn to use the existing informal organization as a tool that can potentially benefit the formal organization. An excellent way of putting the informal organization to work for the good of the company is to bring informal leaders into the decision-making process.

concept check

- What is the informal organization?
- How can informal channels of communication be used to improve operational efficiency?

➡ **lg 8**

CAPITALIZING ON TRENDS IN BUSINESS

To achieve long-term objectives, organizations constantly evaluate and alter their organizational structures. The increased use of information technology and globalization are creating new options for organizing a business.

The Virtual Corporation

One of the biggest challenges for companies today is adapting to the technological changes that are affecting all industries. Organizations are struggling to find new organizational structures that will help them transform information technology into a competitive advantage. One alternative that is becoming increasingly prevalent is the **virtual corporation**, which is a network of independent companies (suppliers, customers, even competitors) linked by information technology to share skills, costs, and access to one another's markets. This network structure allows companies to come together quickly to exploit rapidly changing opportunities. The key attributes of a virtual corporation are:

- *Technology*. Information technology helps geographically distant companies form alliances and work together.
- *Opportunism*. Alliances are less permanent, less formal, and more opportunistic than in traditional partnerships.
- *Excellence*. Each partner brings its core competencies to the alliance, so it is possible to create an organization with higher quality in every functional area and increase competitive advantage.
- *Trust*. The network structure makes companies more reliant on each other and forces them to strengthen relationships with partners.
- *No borders*. This structure expands the traditional boundaries of an organization.

In the concept's purest form, each company that links up with others to create a virtual corporation is stripped to its essence. Ideally, the virtual corporation has neither central office nor organization chart, no hierarchy, and no vertical integration. It

virtual corporation
A network of independent companies linked by information technology to share skills, costs, and access to one another's markets; allows the companies to come together quickly to exploit rapidly changing opportunities.

HOT Links

Read about virtual organizations at
www.virtual-organization.net

HOT Links

For an inside look at a virtual corporation, point your browser to the Linux home page at www.linux.org

HOT Links

How does Cisco handle continual change without chaos? Read about the company's strategies at www.cisco.com

contributes to an alliance only its core competencies, or key capabilities. It mixes and matches what it does best with the core competencies of other companies and entrepreneurs. For example, a manufacturer would only manufacture, while relying on a product design firm to decide what to make and a marketing company to sell the end result.

Although firms that are purely virtual organizations are still relatively scarce, many companies are embracing several of the characteristics of the virtual structure. One of the best examples is Cisco Systems, Inc., the global leader of networking for the Internet. Cisco produces the tools needed to build the powerful networks that link businesses to their customers and suppliers—access products, Web scaling products, security products, and many more. Perhaps because of the nature of its products, Cisco has been at the forefront of developing a new approach to organizational structure and management, incorporating information technology in every conceivable way. Along with an innovative organizational design, Cisco has built a unique corporate culture, relentlessly pursued alliances to acquire and retain intellectual capital, focused obsessively on customer needs, and developed some of the most progressive human resource policies in the industry. Cisco CEO John Chambers believes strongly that organizations should be built on change, not stability; organized as networks, not hierarchies; based on interdependencies, not self-sufficiency; and, above all, based on technological advantage. According to Chambers, Cisco has found "the sweet spot" where technology and the future meet to transform not just business, but all of life.[5]

Structuring for Global Mergers

Recent mergers creating mega-firms raise some important questions regarding corporate structure. How can managers hope to organize the global pieces of these huge, complex new firms into a cohesive, successful whole? Should decision making be centralized or decentralized? Should the firm be organized around geographic markets or product lines? And how can managers consolidate distinctly different corporate cultures? These issues and many more must be resolved if mergers of global companies are to succeed.

APPLYING THIS CHAPTER'S TOPICS

How is organizational structure relevant to you? A common thread linking all of the companies profiled in this chapter is you, the consumer. Companies structure their organizations to facilitate achieving their overall organizational goals. In order to be profitable, companies must have a competitive advantage, and competition is based on meeting customer expectations. The company that best satisfies customer wants and demands is the company that will lead the competition.

When companies make changes to their organizational structures, they are attempting to increase, in some way, their ability to satisfy the customer. They may try to become more efficient and reduce costs, which should translate into better customer service and/or more reasonable prices. They may decentralize operations, giving departments or divisions more autonomy to respond to customer demands. Many companies are embracing new information technologies that bring them closer to their customers faster than was previously possible. Internet commerce is benefiting consumers in a number of ways. When you buy books at **www.amazon.com** or use **www.ebay.com**, you are sending a message that the virtual company is a structure you will patronize and support. Increasing globalization and use of information technology will continue to alter the competitive landscape and the big winner should be the consumer, in terms of increased choice, increased access, and reduced price.

Build a Web Site How computer literate are you? Have you ever built your own Web page? Could you build one for someone else? Find out what it takes to be a freelance Web builder! Visit bailiwick.lib.uiowa.edu/webbuilder/ to get information about building Web sites for fun and profit. You can set your own hours, name your own price, and choose your own projects. This site gives you a wide variety of information about Web-based businesses. Not sure whether you have the right skills, or uncertain what skills you should develop to work in this field? Don't know the difference between a content creator and a technical developer? Answers to those questions and many more can be found at this site. Companies are adapting their organizations to compete in cyberspace. Learn the skills you need to be a part of these new organizations.

>looking ahead
at Procter & Gamble

The structural building blocks for any organization are division of labour, departmentalization, and delegation. Durk Jager was not known as a great delegator. However, under Lafley P&G has managed to stay focused on its mission and returned to consistent, reliable earnings and cash growth. Decentralization can push decision making down into an organization. It can make an organization more responsive to local cultures and change. As Lafley says, "We've sharpened our focus on operational excellence. Execution determines success in a very competitive marketplace. And, every P&Ger knows what he or she can do every day to execute with excellence."[6]

SUMMARY OF LEARNING GOALS

➡lg 1   **What are the five structural building blocks that managers use to design organizations?**
The five structural building blocks that are used in designing an efficient and effective organizational structure are (1) division of labour, which is the process of dividing work into separate jobs and assigning tasks to workers; (2) departmentalization; (3) the managerial hierarchy (or the *management pyramid*), which is the levels of management within the organization (generally consists of top, middle, and supervisory management); (4) the managerial span of control (sometimes called *span of management*), which is the number of employees the manager directly supervises; and (5) the amount of centralization or decentralization in the organization, which entails deciding at what level in the organization decisions should be made. Centralization is the degree to which formal authority is concentrated in one area or level of the organization.

➡lg 2   **What are the five types of departmentalization?**
Five basic types of departmentalization (see Exhibit 15-2 on page 380) are commonly used in organizations:
- *Functional.* Based on the primary functions performed within an organizational unit.
- *Product.* Based on the goods or services produced or sold by the organizational unit.
- *Process.* Based on the production process used by the organizational unit.

- *Customer.* Based on the primary type of customer served by the organizational unit.
- *Geographic.* Based on the geographic segmentation of organizational units.

➡️lg 3 **How can the degree of centralization/decentralization be altered to make an organization more successful?**

In a highly centralized structure, top management makes most of the key decisions in the organization with very little input from lower-level employees. Centralization lets top managers develop a broad view of operations and exercise tight financial controls. In a highly decentralized organization, decision-making authority is pushed down the organizational hierarchy, giving lower-level personnel more responsibility and power to make and implement decisions. Decentralization can result in faster decision-making and increased innovation and responsiveness to customer preferences.

➡️lg 4 **How do mechanistic and organic organizations differ?**

A mechanistic organization is characterized by a relatively high degree of work specialization, rigid departmentalization, many layers of management (particularly middle management), narrow spans of control, centralized decision making, and a long chain of command. This combination of elements results in a tall organizational structure. In contrast, an organic organization is characterized by a relatively low degree of work specialization, loose departmentalization, few levels of management, wide spans of control, decentralized decision making, and a short chain of command. This combination of elements results in a flat organizational structure.

➡️lg 5 **What is the difference between line positions and staff positions?**

In daily operations, those individuals in line positions are directly involved in the processes used to create goods and services. Those individuals in staff positions provide the administrative and support services that line employees need to achieve the firm's goals. Line positions in organizations are typically in areas such as production, marketing, and finance. Staff positions are found in areas such as legal counselling, managerial consulting, public relations, and human resource management.

➡️lg 6 **What is the goal of re-engineering?**

Re-engineering is a complete redesign of business structures and processes in order to improve operations. The goal of re-engineering is to redesign business processes to achieve improvements in cost control, product quality, customer service, and speed.

➡️lg 7 **How does the informal organization affect the performance of a company?**

The informal organization is the network of connections and channels of communication based on the informal relationships of individuals inside the organization. Informal relationships can be between people at the same hierarchical level or between people at different levels and in different departments; the relationships can be based on connections made inside or outside the workplace. Informal organizations give employees more control over their work environment by delivering a continuous stream of company information throughout the organization, thereby helping employees stay informed.

➡️lg 8 **What trends are influencing the way businesses organize?**

The virtual corporation is a network of independent companies (suppliers, customers, even competitors) linked by information technology to share skills, costs, and access to one another's markets. This network structure allows companies to come together quickly to exploit rapidly changing opportunities. The key attributes of a virtual corporation are technology, opportunism, excellence, trust, and no borders.

KEY TERMS

authority 382
centralization 383
chain of command 382
committee structure 386
customer departmentalization 380
decentralization 383
delegation of authority 382
departmentalization 379
division of labour 378
formal organization 378
functional departmentalization 379
geographic departmentalization 380
informal organization 389
line-and-staff organization 386
line organization 386
line positions 386
managerial hierarchy 381
matrix structure (project management) 387
mechanistic organization 384
organic organization 384
organization chart 379
process departmentalization 380
product departmentalization 379
re-engineering 389
span of control 382
specialization 378
staff positions 386
virtual corporation 390

Large global mergers raise important issues in organizational structure. The ultimate question is how does management take two huge global organizations and create a single, successful, cohesive organization? Should it be centralized or decentralized? Should it be organized along product or geographic lines? These are some of the questions management must answer.

WORKING THE NET

1. Find at least three examples of organization charts on the Internet by searching on Alta Vista (**www.altavista.digital.com**) for the term "company organizational charts." Analyze each company's organizational structure. Are the companies organized by function, product/service, process, customer type, or geographic location?

2. At either the *Fortune* magazine (**www.fortune.com**) or the *Forbes* (**www.forbes.com**) Web site, search the archives for stories about companies that have re-engineered. Find an example of a re-engineering effort that succeeded and one that failed and discuss why.

3. Visit the *Inc.* magazine Web site (**www.inc.com**) and use the search engine to find articles about virtual corporations. Using a search engine, find the Web site of at least one virtual corporation and look for information about how the company uses span of control, informal organization, and other concepts from this chapter.

CREATIVE THINKING CASE

Organizing the Monster

Tyrannosaurus rex, pterodactyl, and brontosaurus—dinosaurs all. But what's a trumpasaurus? In fact, he's no dinosaur at all, but a friendly monster—a 10-foot-high, bright green-and-purple mascot, affectionately dubbed "Trump"—who greets you as you step off the fifth-floor elevator at the new 75 000-square-foot headquarters of the Monster Board, a job search Web site. Founded in April 1994 by Jeffrey Taylor, the Monster Board became part of the interactive division of TMP Worldwide in 1995. Today the company, based in Maynard, Massachusetts, boasts that it is the most successful career centre on the Internet. Serving both job seekers and recruiters, the site receives more than 2.5 million visits per month, contains more than 50 000 job postings from 40 000 companies, and posts nearly 500 000 résumés.

The Monster Board Web site makes it easy for job hunters and recruiters to find each other. That business model is reflected in the design principle behind the company's new headquarters—and especially in the 22 team areas built into the space. The goal: to make sure that people can connect with one another whenever and wherever they need to—without having to wait for an empty room.

Teams are encouraged to name their rooms—the Creative Group meets in "Brain Forest"; the Alliance Team convenes in "Raise the Roof"—and each group has a small budget for decorating its rooms. "There's something that happens when you get together in your own comfortable space," says Danielle McCabe, the creative director of the Monster Board. "Ideas start to happen."

The largest, most-often-used meeting spot is the Monster Den—a cavernous area that features a kitchen, pool and ping-pong tables, oversize armchairs, and a mural decorated with monsters. Every Monday morning, all 180 Monster Board employees gather in the Den for a meeting whose purpose is to ensure that everyone in the company is on the same (Web) page.[7]

Critical Thinking Questions

1. How would you describe the organizational structure at the Monster Board?
2. Do you think that the informal organization might be very important at the Monster Board?
3. Would you be happy working in this type of organizational structure? Why or why not?

CHAPTER 16

Leadership and Motivation

In this chapter we'll look at the third step in the process of management—*leading* and *motivating* employees toward the accomplishment of organizational goals. As we saw in Chapter 15, organizational structures are designed to support the accomplishment of the overall plans of the company. But these plans cannot be accomplished, appropriate structure or not, if the individuals responsible for their implementation are not committed to the outcome. As we've said numerous times, without the final critical success factor—*gaining employee commitment*— none of the critical success factors can be accomplished. This is therefore perhaps our most important management function, but unfortunately also one of the most difficult. We're dealing with human beings not push-button machines, and therefore it is extremely important that managers understand what makes people tick.

For example, have you ever gone into a restaurant, up to a service counter in a store, or called a company's customer service department on the phone and been served by an employee that didn't appear to be overjoyed to answer your questions? Most of us have. The important question here is, did you just assume that the employee was having a bad day and not let it affect your perception of the company, or did it enter your mental database and register as a less than pleasurable experience with that company as a whole. Probably the latter. We all see our contact with employees in different companies as a contact with the company, and one employee's attitude as the company's attitude—consciously or not. As customers we see it in a very integrative way—we see it as the whole company. As managers in that company, we need to recognize that and focus on understanding our employees' needs in order to gain their commitment.

This chapter discusses three motivation theories to help you understand what motivates individuals to work harder to please the customer. But everyone is different. This is therefore a truly integrative role that a manager plays here. A manager must see each employee as an individual but also in the context of how that person fits in the larger organization. Managers must integrate the different theories to find a style that works both for them and their employees. Also, many different personalities are needed to make a successful business work—so people with different skills and motivations must work together as one.

The chapter begins by looking at leadership—the process of guiding and motivating others toward the achievement of organizational goals. Just as teams need coaches, organizations need leaders to keep everyone moving in the same direction. There are many different leadership styles, but as you'll see in the chapter the most effective are those that result in individuals working together as a team. These styles result in the greatest commitment, which is of course our primary objective—that employees take ownership in the results of the company as if it were their own—as mentioned by Tim Morgan of WestJet in the opening vignette. Ideally we want employees to work toward the big picture, to see how their jobs help achieve the overall goals, rather than focusing on the immediate task with no context and watching the clock until the end of the workday. As Tim says, "You can't *drag* people down the road." The chapter discusses how important a leader is in developing a vision for the company and inspiring employees to be committed to that vision.

You'll see how different techniques are used to integrate employees in the organization—to get them working together toward goals. Cross-functional teams are one example, made up of employees from different functional areas working together on a common task. This is critically important as we have seen in our discussion of the functional areas. Without this integration and commitment of the employees toward integration, the areas can't work together to achieve the overall goals of the company. We've also seen this through our discussion of *planning*. Different departments or areas within the organization have a different role to play in the overall plan, but they must work together in an integrative fashion to achieve these overall goals.

You'll also learn that when a company shows commitment to its employees it gets commitment in return. A commitment to education and training, for example, goes a long way to showing employees that they are valued and that the organization is a place where they can grow to their full potential.

Remember as you learn the different theories of motivation to keep in mind that the manager's job here is to gain employee commitment in order to achieve the other factors critical to a successful business. Each of the success factors is achieved through people, and thus the people at all levels in the organization must be motivated to achieve these success factors. They must be committed to the organization's success for it to happen.

One factor not discussed so far but integral to achieving this success is the external environment. The external environment can and does have concrete implications on the work environment, as well as affecting the mindset that people bring to work every day, thereby affecting their levels of motivation. Managers must therefore take into consideration the elements in the external environment that may affect employee motivation—for example, the *political* environment and its affect on legislation pertaining to employment standards, the *economy* and its effect on job security and levels of pay, the *social* environment and the resulting expectations that people have regarding the work environment, and the *technological* environment and how it changes the demands of different jobs.

Leadership and Motivation

CHAPTER 16

Learning Goals

➡ **lg 1** What are the five bases of power?

➡ **lg 2** What leadership styles are determined by the amount of authority held by the leader?

➡ **lg 3** What three contemporary theories on employee motivation offer insights into improving employee performance?

➡ **lg 4** How can managers redesign existing jobs to increase employee motivation and performance?

➡ **lg 5** What different types of teams are being used in organizations today?

➡ **lg 6** What initiatives are organizations using today to motivate and retain employees?

Leadership at WestJet Airlines

Leadership means different things to different people. You may think of a political leader such as George W. Bush or Jean Chrétien or even our former prime minister and darling of the media, Pierre Elliott Trudeau. These men are very dissimilar in their styles and presentation of self. Trudeau was an irreverent, independent, loner who enjoyed a playboy lifestyle and wore sandals on Parliament Hill. George W. Bush wears the best-cut suits, and Chrétien is somewhere in between. Or you may think of leaders in the fight for human rights, such as Dr. Sima Samar, a physician and educator as well as a role model for thousands of women and girls, not only in Afghanistan but around the world. Or you may think of Paul Tellier, former CEO of CN Rail and now president and CEO of Bombardier. Any and all of these people are leaders, but what does that mean?

Tim Morgan, senior vice-president and co-chief operating officer of WestJet Airlines, believes leadership can be relatively easy if you can encourage people to follow your vision, whether in a business situation or not. At WestJet, Tim wants to create a corporate culture where everyone has the same goals, where the team feels it is a great place to work, and where they see WestJet as *their* company. A corporate culture evolves over time and stems from the influence of the founders of the company. At WestJet, everyone owns a piece of the airplane and therefore everyone grooms the planes—from Clive Beddoe, the president, on down. Tim feels it is important to hire the right people and to allow them to make their own decisions: "I like to hire people smarter than me, and if they are the right people, they will make me look good as well." If a management decision is required, it is important to explain *why* and to be honest with your employees. To avoid damaging a strong positive culture, keep your promises and avoid micro-management. Tim believes that the leader doesn't have to be the smartest one in the company, but that person must be able to inspire others and earn their trust. "You must have everyone pointed in the same direction, you can't drag people down the road!"[1]

CRITICAL THINKING QUESTIONS

As you read this chapter, consider the following questions as they relate to WestJet:
- Do you see any similarities in leading a company like WestJet and leading a country?
- Can a leader affect the corporate culture in a positive way as well as a negative way?

BUSINESS IN THE 21ˢᵀ CENTURY

Several Canadian CEOs have shared their views on leadership in a recent article published in *Canadian HR Reporter*. Here are some sample comments:

- Bill Black, president and CEO, Maritime Life: "People who are super-achievers can't lead a team. They're actually very dangerous in leadership positions because they tend to do too much themselves and not delegate to others. They don't build a strong team around them."
- John David, president EDS Canada, Information Solutions: "Leadership has to be committed, it has to be thoughtful, it has to be determined, it has to be passionate and at times it has to be charismatic."
- Philip Hughes, president and CEO, Newfoundland Power: "Senior managers really have to earn [employees'] respect each and every day and if they don't then no one is going to follow them and you'll be ignored and you'll be in the corporate obituaries."[2]

Do you agree or disagree with these opinions? Which of these CEOs would you like to have as your boss?

Leadership

Leadership, one of the key management functions, is the process of guiding and motivating others toward the achievement of organizational goals. Managers are responsible for directing employees on a daily basis as the employees carry out the plans and work within the structure created by management. Organizations need strong effective leadership at all levels in order to meet goals and remain competitive.

To be effective leaders, managers must be able to influence others' behaviour. This ability to influence others to behave in a particular way is called **power**. Researchers have identified five primary sources, or bases, of power:

- **Legitimate power**, which is derived from an individual's position in an organization.
- **Reward power**, which is derived from an individual's control over rewards.
- **Coercive power**, which is derived from an individual's ability to threaten negative outcomes.
- **Expert power**, which is derived from an individual's extensive knowledge in one or more areas.
- **Referent power**, which is derived from an individual's personal charisma and the respect and/or admiration the individual inspires.

Many leaders use a combination of all of these sources of power to influence individuals toward goal achievement. Bill Gates, for example, gets his legitimate power from his position as CEO of Microsoft. He is able to offer incentives such as stock options to reward high-performing employees and to threaten low performers with undesirable consequences. His technical expertise in computer software, technological innovation, and financial management allows him to greatly influence the decisions made at Microsoft, and many people find his strong focus and ability to convey his vision compelling enough to warrant great respect and admiration.

Leadership Styles

Individuals in leadership positions tend to be relatively consistent in the way they attempt to influence the behaviour of others, meaning that each individual has a tendency to react to people and situations in a particular way. This pattern of behaviour is referred to as **leadership style**. As Exhibit 16-1 shows, leadership styles can be placed on a continuum that encompasses three distinct styles: autocratic, participative, and free rein.

→ lg 1

leadership
The process of guiding and motivating others toward the achievement of organizational goals.

power
The ability to influence others to behave in a particular way.

legitimate power
Power that is derived from an individual's position in an organization.

reward power
Power that is derived from an individual's control over rewards.

coercive power
Power that is derived from an individual's ability to threaten negative outcomes.

expert power
Power that is derived from an individual's extensive knowledge in one or more areas.

referent power
Power that is derived from an individual's personal charisma and the respect and/or admiration the individual inspires.

→ lg 2

leadership style
The relatively consistent way that individuals in leadership positions attempt to influence the behaviour of others.

e x h i b i t 1 6 - 1 | Leadership Styles of Managers

Amount of authority held by the leader

Autocratic Style	Participative Style (Democratic, Consensual, Consultative)	Free-Rein (Laissez-Faire) Style
• Manager makes most decisions and acts in authoritative manner. • Manager is usually unconcerned about subordinates' attitudes toward decisions. • Emphasis is on getting task accomplished. • Approach is used mostly by military officers and some production line supervisors. • Manager encourages discussion of issues and alternatives.	• Manager shares decision making with group members and encourages teamwork. • Manager is concerned about subordinates' ideas and attitudes • Manager coaches subordinates and helps coordinate efforts. • Approach is found in many successful organizations.	• Manager turns over virtual authority and control to group. • Members of group are presented with task and given freedom to accomplish it. • Approach works well with highly motivated, experienced, educated personnel. • Approach is found in high-tech firms, labs, and colleges.

Amount of authority held by group members

autocratic leaders
Directive leaders who prefer to make decisions and solve problems on their own with little input from subordinates.

Autocratic leaders are directive leaders, allowing for very little input from subordinates. These leaders prefer to make decisions and solve problems on their own and expect subordinates to implement solutions according to very specific and detailed instructions. In this leadership style, information typically flows in one direction, from manager to subordinate. The military, by necessity, is generally autocratic. When autocratic leaders treat employees with fairness and respect, they may be considered knowledgeable and decisive. But often autocrats are perceived as narrow-minded and heavy-handed in their unwillingness to share power, information, and decision making in the organization. The trend in organizations today is away from the directive, controlling style of the autocratic leader.

There are three types of **participative leadership**: democratic, consensual, and consultative. **Democratic leaders** solicit input from all members of the group and then allow the group members to make the final decision through a voting process. This approach works well with highly trained professionals. The president of a physicians' clinic might use the democratic approach. **Consensual leaders** encourage discussion about issues and then require that all parties involved agree to the final decision. This is the general style used by labour mediators. **Consultative leaders** confer with subordinates before making a decision, but retain the final decision-making authority. This technique has been used to dramatically increase the productivity of assembly-line workers.

The third leadership style, at the opposite end of the continuum from the autocratic style, is **free-rein** or **laissez-faire** (French for "leave it alone") **leadership**. Managers who use this style turn over all authority and control to subordinates. Employees are assigned a task and then given free rein to figure out the best way to accomplish it. The manager doesn't get involved unless asked. Under this approach, subordinates have unlimited freedom as long as they do not violate existing company policies. This approach is also sometimes used with highly trained professionals as in a research laboratory. Although one might at first assume that

Microsoft CEO Bill Gates uses all five bases of power—legitimate, reward, coercive, expert, and referent—in leading his employees to achieve organizational goals.

participative leadership
A leadership style in which the leader shares decision making with group members and encourages discussion of issues and alternatives; includes democratic, consensual, and consultative styles.

democratic leaders
Leaders who solicit input from all members of the group and then allow the members to make the final decision through a vote.

consensual leaders
Leaders who encourage discussion about issues and then require that all parties involved agree to the final decision.

consultative leaders
Leaders who confer with subordinates before making a decision, but who retain the final decision-making authority.

free-rein (laissez-faire) leadership
A leadership style in which the leader turns over all authority and control to subordinates.

empowerment
The process of giving employees increased autonomy and discretion to make decisions, as well as control over the resources needed to implement those decisions.

corporate culture
The set of attitudes, values, and standards of behaviours that distinguishes one organization from another.

subordinates would prefer the free-rein style, this approach can have several drawbacks. If free-rein leadership is accompanied by unclear expectations and lack of feedback from the manager, the experience can be frustrating for an employee. Employees may perceive the manager as being uninvolved and indifferent to what is happening or as unwilling or unable to provide the necessary structure, information, and expertise.

Employee Empowerment

Participative and free-rein leaders use empowerment, as discussed in Chapter 14, to share decision-making authority with subordinates. As you may recall, **empowerment** means giving employees increased autonomy and discretion to make their own decisions, as well as control over the resources needed to implement those decisions. When decision-making power is shared at all levels of the organization, employees feel a greater sense of ownership in, and responsibility for, organizational outcomes. Jack Welch, former CEO of General Electric Corp. and a consummate manager, says that "Giving people self-confidence is by far the most important thing that I can do. Because then they will act."[3]

Leadership Theories

Many leadership theories have been proposed over the years, beginning with the *trait theory of leadership*, which suggests that there are certain traits that will predict leadership success. While this approach may seem intuitively reasonable, it has not been substantiated in the leadership research. Rather, there seem to be characteristics, traits, and behaviours consistently exhibited by successful leaders, but these do not necessarily predict leadership.

In recent research, Bennis and Thomas found that there are four qualities that, when combined in the proper proportion, produce great leaders. These include:

- Adaptive capacity—the ability to transcend adversity.
- Ability to engage others in a shared meaning.
- A distinctive and compelling voice.
- A sense of integrity including a strong set of values.

While the authors of this study admit these four qualities are nothing new in the leadership research field, the interrelated nature of these qualities is groundbreaking. To quote Bennis and Thomas, "This is the most thrilling discovery we made as we studied our geeks and geezers: they are the same factors that make a person a healthy, fully integrated human being."[4] Which of the qualities identified in the Bennis and Thomas research do you feel were exhibited by Prime Minister Trudeau?

Many Canadian CEOs are concerned about the shortage of good leaders in their organizations. A 2001 study found 70 percent of Canadian CEOs feel that building leadership capability is their number one issue. The Conference Board of Canada has concluded that there is a leadership gap in Canada that can affect the competitiveness of companies. Why has this gap occurred? There appear to be flaws in the leadership development practice itself, with a focus on a more generic approach rather than an organization-specific approach. Leadership development is a growing business for consultants, and courses on all aspects of leadership are being offered.

A *Canadian HR Reporter* article suggests the following leadership development strategies:

- Engage senior leaders. Make it part of the CEO's agenda, not just the HR agenda.
- Define the leadership story. Make it specific to the organization.
- Integrate leadership development strategies to bring a sense of cohesion and coordination to the process.
- Focus on the leadership life cycle.
- Help leaders learn from experience.[5]

Consultative leaders confer with their work group before making a decision but retain the final decision-making authority.

HOT Links

What management leadership traits are necessary to succeed in today's competitive business world? Read the article in *Trendwaves Magazine*, Issue 75, at **www.trendwaves.com**

Pierre Elliott Trudeau, former Canadian prime minister, may or may not have exhibited Bennis and Thomas's leadership qualities, depending on your point of view.

Corporate Culture

The leadership style of managers in an organization is usually indicative of the underlying philosophy or values of the organization. The set of *attitudes*, *values*, and *standards of behaviour* that distinguishes one organization from another is called **corporate culture**. A corporate culture evolves over time and is based on the accumulated history of the organization, including the vision of the founders. It is also influenced by the dominant leadership style within the organization. Evidence of a company's culture is seen in its heroes (e.g., Clive Beddoe, president of WestJet), myths (again, Clive Beddoe grooming the cabin on a WestJet flight), symbols (e.g., the Nike swoosh), and ceremonies.

Although culture is intangible and its rules are often unspoken, it can have a strong impact on the company's success. Therefore, managers must try to influence the corporate culture so that it will contribute to the success of the company.

concept check

- How do leaders influence other people's behaviour?
- How can managers empower employees?
- What is corporate culture?

Motivation

Successful managers help employees to achieve organizational goals and guide workers through the motivation process using the leadership skills discussed earlier in the chapter. To succeed, managers must understand human relations, how employees interact with one another, and how managers interact with employees to improve effectiveness. Human relations skills include the ability to motivate, lead, communicate, build morale, and teach others. The rest of this chapter presents the three theories on human motivation and the modern application of these theories. We also explore the use of teams in creating and maintaining a motivated work force.

Contemporary Views on Motivation

The early management scholars laid a foundation that enabled managers to better understand their workers and how best to motivate them. Since then, new theories have given us an even better understanding of worker motivation. We will look at three of these theories: the expectancy theory, the equity theory, and the goal-setting theory.

Expectancy Theory

One of the best-supported and most widely accepted theories of motivation is expectancy theory, which focuses on the link between motivation and behaviour. According to **expectancy theory**, the probability of an individual acting in a particular way depends on the strength of that individual's belief that the act will have a particular outcome and on whether the individual values that outcome. The degree to which an employee is motivated depends on three important relationships, shown in Exhibit 16-2:

1. The link between *effort and performance*, or the strength of the individual's expectation that a certain amount of effort will lead to a certain level of performance.
2. The link between *performance and outcome*, or the strength of the expectation that a certain level of performance will lead to a particular outcome.

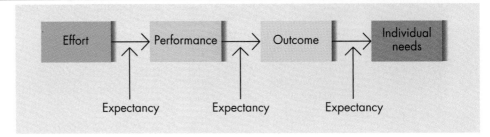

→ **lg 3**

HOT Links

Check out your own leadership skills at

www.myskillsprofile.com

HOT Links

Find out more about three companies that made the *Report on Business*'s "50 Best Companies to Work for in Canada" by visiting

www.hbc.com,

ww.intuit.com, and

www.flightcentre.com

expectancy theory
A theory of motivation that holds that the probability of an individual acting in a particular way depends on the strength of that individual's belief that the act will have a particular outcome and on whether the individual values that outcome.

equity theory
A theory of motivation that holds that worker satisfaction is influenced by employees' perceptions about how fairly they are treated compared with their co-workers.

goal-setting theory
A theory of motivation based on the premise that an individual's intention to work toward a goal is a primary source of motivation.

3. The link between *outcomes and individual needs*, or the degree to which the individual expects the anticipated outcome to satisfy personal needs. Some outcomes have more valence, or value, to individuals than others do.

Based on the expectancy theory, managers should do the following to motivate employees:[6]

- Determine the rewards valued by each employee.
- Determine the desired performance level and then communicate it clearly to employees.
- Make the performance level attainable.
- Link rewards to performance.
- Determine what factors might counteract the effectiveness of a reward.
- Make sure the reward is adequate for the level of performance.

Equity Theory

Another contemporary explanation of motivation, **equity theory** is based on individuals' perceptions about how fairly they are treated compared with their co-workers. Equity means justice or fairness, and in the workplace it refers to employees' perceived fairness of the way they are treated and the rewards they earn. Employees evaluate their own outcomes (e.g., salary, benefits) in relation to their inputs (e.g., number of hours worked, education, and training) and then compare the outcomes-to-inputs ratio to one of the following: (1) the employee's own past experience in a different position in the current organization, (2) the employee's own past experience in a different organization, (3) another employee's experience inside the current organization, or (4) another employee's experience outside the organization.

According to equity theory, if employees perceive that an inequity exists, they will make one of the following choices:

- *Change their work habits* (exert less effort on the job).
- *Change their job benefits and income* (ask for a raise, steal from the employer).
- *Distort their perception of themselves* ("I always thought I was smart, but now I realize I'm a lot smarter than my co-workers").
- *Distort their perceptions of others* ("Joe's position is really much less flexible than mine").
- *Look at the situation from a different perspective* ("I don't make as much as the other department heads, but I make a lot more than most graphic artists").
- *Leave the situation* (quit the job).

Managers can use equity theory to improve worker satisfaction. Knowing that every employee seeks equitable and fair treatment, managers can make an effort to understand an employee's perceptions of fairness and take steps to reduce concerns about inequity.

Goal-Setting Theory

Goal-setting theory is based on the premise that an individual's intention to work toward a goal is a primary source of motivation. Once set, the goal clarifies for the employee what needs to be accomplished and how much effort will be required for completion. The theory has three main components: (1) specific goals lead to a higher level of performance than do more generalized goals ("do your best"); (2) more difficult goals lead to better performance than do easy goals (provided the individual accepts the goal); and (3) feedback on progress toward the goal enhances performance. Feedback is particularly important because it helps the individual identify the gap between the real (the actual performance) and the ideal (the desired outcome defined by the goal).

Given the trend toward employee empowerment in the workplace, more and more employees are participating in the goal-setting process. Are employees who set their own work goals more motivated to achieve them? Research on the benefits of shared goal setting versus assigned goals has produced mixed results. Still, it is clear that when employees are encouraged to participate in the goal-setting process, they are more likely to accept a goal as desirable, especially if the goal is difficult.

concept check

- Discuss the three relationships central to expectancy theory.
- Explain the comparison process that is a part of equity theory.
- How does goal-setting theory contribute to our understanding of motivation?

From Motivation Theory to Application

The material presented thus far in the section on motivation demonstrates the wide variety of theories and research studies that have contributed to our current understanding of employee motivation. Now we turn our attention to more practical matters, to ways that these concepts can be applied in the workplace to meet organizational goals and improve individual performance.

Motivational Job Design

How might managers redesign or modify existing jobs to increase employee motivation and performance? The following three options have been used extensively in the workplace.

The horizontal expansion of a job, increasing the number and variety of tasks that a person performs, is called **job enlargement**. Increasing task diversity can enhance job satisfaction, particularly when the job is mundane and repetitive in nature. A potential drawback to job enlargement is that employees may perceive that they are being asked to work harder and do more with no change in their level of responsibility or compensation. This can cause resentment and lead to dissatisfaction.

Job enrichment is the vertical expansion of an employee's job. Whereas job enlargement addresses the breadth or scope of a job, enrichment attempts to increase job depth by providing the employee with more autonomy, responsibility, and decision-making authority. In an enriched job, the employee can use a variety of talents and skills and has more control over the planning, execution, and evaluation of the required tasks. In general, job enrichment has been found to increase job satisfaction and reduce absenteeism and turnover.

Also called *cross-training*, **job rotation** is the shifting of workers from one job to another. This may be done to broaden an employee's skill base or because an employee has ceased to be interested in or challenged by a particular job. The organization may benefit from job rotation because it increases flexibility in scheduling and production, since employees can be shifted to cover for absent workers or changes in production or operations. It is also a valuable tool for training lower-level managers in a variety of functional areas. Drawbacks of job rotation include an increase in training costs and decreased productivity while employees are getting "up to speed" in new task areas.

job enlargement
The horizontal expansion of a job by increasing the number and variety of tasks that a person performs.

job enrichment
The vertical expansion of a job by increasing the employee's autonomy, responsibility, and decision-making authority.

job rotation
The shifting of workers from one job to another; also called *cross-training*.

Work-Scheduling Options

As companies try to meet the needs of a diverse work force and retain quality employees while remaining competitive and financially prosperous, managers are challenged to find new ways to keep workers motivated and satisfied. Increasingly popular are alternatives to the traditional work schedule, such as the compressed workweek, flextime, job sharing, and telecommuting.

One option for employees who want to maximize their leisure hours, indulge in three-day weekends, and avoid commuting during morning and evening rush hours is the compressed workweek. Employees work the traditional 40 hours, but fit those hours into a shorter workweek. Most common is the 4-40 schedule, where employees work four 10-hour days a week. Organizations that offer this option claim benefits ranging from increased motivation and productivity to reduced absenteeism and turnover.

Another scheduling option, called flextime, allows employees to decide what their work hours will be. Employees are generally expected to work a certain number of hours per week, but have some discretion as to when they arrive at work and when they leave for the day. The flexible work hours schedule offers many of the benefits of the compressed workweek, including increased morale and productivity and reduced absenteeism. Additionally, flextime may reduce employee tardiness and increase satisfaction due to the increased feelings of autonomy. A significant drawback is that flextime cannot be adapted to every job, particularly service jobs where customers expect personnel to be present at specific times.

job sharing
A scheduling option that allows two individuals to split the tasks, responsibilities, and work hours of one 40-hour-per-week job.

Job sharing is a scheduling option that allows two individuals to split the tasks, responsibilities, and work hours of one 40-hour-per-week job. Though used less frequently than flextime and the compressed workweek, this option can also provide employees with job flexibility. The primary benefit to the company is that it gets "two for the price of one"—the company can draw on two sets of skills and abilities to accomplish one set of job objectives.

Telecommuting is a work-scheduling option that allows employees to work from home via a computer that is linked with their office, headquarters, or colleagues. It is the fastest growing of the four scheduling options. Working at home allows employees a high degree of flexibility and autonomy—they can wear what they want, set their own hours, work at their own pace, and control their own work environment. Telecommuting also gives employees the option of living geographically distant from their employer without the headaches of traditional long-distance commuting. Potential drawbacks to telecommuting include lost productivity due to distractions at home, feelings of isolation, and lack of inclusion in the corporate culture and informal communication network.

Recognition, Empowerment, and Economic Incentives

All employees have unique needs that they seek to fulfill through their jobs. Organizations must devise a wide array of incentives to ensure that a broad spectrum of employee needs can be addressed in the work environment, thus increasing the likelihood of motivated employees. A sampling of these motivational tools is discussed here.

Formal recognition of superior effort by individuals or groups in the workplace is one way to enhance employee motivation. Recognition serves as positive feedback and reinforcement, letting employees know what they have done well and that their contribution is valued by the organization. Recognition can take many forms, both formal and informal. Some companies use formal awards ceremonies to acknowledge and celebrate their employees' accomplishments. Others take advantage of informal interaction to congratulate employees on a job well done and offer encouragement for the future. Recognition can take the form of an employee of the month plaque, a monetary reward, a day off, a congratulatory e-mail, or a verbal "pat on the back."

variable pay
A system of paying employees in which a portion of an employee's pay is directly linked to an individual or organizational performance measure.

Employee empowerment, sometimes called employee involvement or participative management, involves delegating decision-making authority to employees at all levels of the organization. Employees are given greater responsibility for planning, implementing, and evaluating the results of decisions. Empowerment is based on the premise that human resources, especially at lower levels in the firm, are an underutilized asset. Employees are capable of contributing much more of their skills and abilities to organizational success if they are allowed to participate in the decision-making process and are given access to the resources needed to implement their decisions.

Any discussion of motivation has to include the use of monetary incentives to enhance performance. Currently, companies are using a variety of variable-pay programs such as piece-rate plans, profit sharing, gain sharing, and bonuses to encourage employees to be more productive. Unlike the standard salary or hourly wage, **variable pay** means that a portion of an employee's pay is directly linked to an individual or organizational performance measure. In piece-rate pay plans, for example, employees are paid a given amount for each unit they produce, directly linking the amount they earn to their productivity. *Profit-sharing plans* are based on overall company profitability. Using an established formula, management distributes some portion of company profits to all employees. Gain-sharing plans are incentive programs based on group productivity. Employees share in the financial gains attributed to the increased productivity of their group. This encourages employees to increase productivity within their specific work area regardless of the overall profit picture for the organization as a whole. A *bonus* is simply a one-time lump-sum monetary reward.

Although all of these monetary incentives can be used very successfully to enhance employee motivation and performance, the incentive that is fast becoming most popular with new members of the work force is the stock option.[7] Two of the most successful companies to use employee stock options (ESOPs) as a recruiting and performance tool are Microsoft and WestJet. Early on, Bill Gates and Clive Beddoe recognized the advantages of offering employees the opportunity to accumulate wealth through stock ownership. Employees are often willing to forgo larger salaries and other benefits in favour of stock that may be worth a great deal in the future. And, if managers want talented employees who will work for the company with the enthusiasm that comes with ownership, then they must be willing to trade equity for talent.

c o n c e p t   c h e c k

• Explain the difference between job enlargement and job enrichment.
• What are the four work-scheduling options that can enhance employee performance?
• Are all employees motivated by the same economic incentives? Explain.

Using Teams to Enhance Motivation and Performance

One of the most apparent trends in business today is the use of teams to accomplish organizational goals. Using a team-based structure can increase individual and group motivation and performance. This section gives a brief overview of group behaviour, defines work teams as specific types of groups, and provides suggestions for creating high-performing teams.

Understanding Group Behaviour

Teams are a specific type of organizational group. Every organization contains groups, social units of two or more people who share the same goals and cooperate to achieve those goals. Understanding some fundamental concepts related to group behaviour and group processes provides a good foundation for understanding concepts about work teams. Groups can be formal or informal in nature. Formal groups are designated and sanctioned by the organization; their behaviour is directed toward accomplishing organizational goals. Informal groups are based on social relationships and are not determined or sanctioned by the organization.

Formal organizational groups must operate within the larger organizational system. To some degree, elements of the larger system, such as organizational strategy, policies and procedures, available resources, and corporate culture, determine the behaviour of smaller groups within the organization. Other factors that affect the behaviour of organizational groups are individual member characteristics (e.g., ability, training, personality), the roles and norms of group members, and the size and cohesiveness of the group. Norms are the implicit behavioural guidelines of the group, or the standards for acceptable and unacceptable behaviour. These standards are conveyed through socialization, a process by which new group members learn:

- The basic goals of the group.
- The preferred means for reaching those goals.
- The behaviour patterns expected for effective performance within the group.
- The basic rules and attitudes that help maintain the group's identity and integrity.

Work socialization occurs both formally in training programs and informally by watching and talking with other group members. Group performance is related to how rapidly new members are socialized.

Group cohesiveness refers to the degree to which group members want to stay in the group and tend to resist outside influences (such as a change in company policies). When group performance norms are high, group cohesiveness will have a positive impact on productivity. Cohesiveness tends to increase when the size of the group is small, individual and group goals are congruent, the group has high status in the organization, rewards are group-based rather than individual based, and the group competes with other groups within the organization. Work group cohesiveness can benefit the organization in several ways, including increased productivity, enhanced worker self-image because of group success, increased company loyalty, reduced employee turnover, and reduced absenteeism. On the other hand, cohesiveness can also lead to restricted output, resistance to change, and conflict with other work groups in the organization.

The opportunity to turn the decision-making process over to a group with diverse skills and abilities is one of the arguments for using work groups (and teams) in organizational settings. For group decision making to be most effective, however, both managers and group members must acknowledge its strengths and weaknesses (see Exhibit 16-3).

Work Groups versus Work Teams

We have already noted that teams are a special type of organizational group, but we also need to differentiate between work groups and work teams. **Work groups** share resources and coordinate efforts to help members better perform their individual duties and responsibilities. The performance of the group can be evaluated by adding up the contributions of the individual group members. **Work teams** require not only coordination but also collaboration, the pooling of knowledge, skills, abilities, and resources in a collective effort to attain a common goal. A work team creates synergy, causing the performance of the team as a whole to be greater than the sum of team members' individual contributions. Simply assigning employees to groups and labelling them a team does not guarantee a positive outcome. Managers and team members must be committed to creating, developing, and maintaining high-performance work teams. Factors that contribute to their success are discussed later in this section.

Types of Teams

The evolution of the team concept in organizations can be seen in three basic types of work teams: problem solving, self-managed, and cross-functional. Japanese companies used problem-solving teams, known as quality circles, as early as the 1950s to improve

---

group cohesiveness
The degree to which group members want to stay in the group and tend to resist outside influences.

work groups
Groups of employees who share resources and coordinate efforts so as to help members better perform their individual duties and responsibilities. The performance of the group can be evaluated by adding up the contributions of the individual group members.

work teams
Groups of employees who not only coordinate their efforts, but also collaborate by pooling their knowledge, skills, abilities, and resources in a collective effort to attain a common goal, causing the performance of the team to be greater than the sum of the members' individual efforts.

exhibit 16-3 | Strengths and Weaknesses of Group Decision Making

Strengths	Weaknesses
• Groups bring more information and knowledge to the decision process.	• Groups typically take a longer time to reach a solution than an individual takes.
• Groups offer a diversity of perspectives and, therefore, generate a greater number of alternatives.	• Group members may pressure others to conform, reducing the likelihood of disagreement.
• Group decision making results in a higher-quality decision than individual decision making.	• The process may be dominated by one or a small number of participants.
• Participation of group members increases the likelihood that a decision will be accepted.	• Groups lack accountability, because it is difficult to assign responsibility for outcomes to any one individual.

➡ **lg 5**

problem-solving teams
Teams of employees from the same department or area of expertise and from the same level of the organizational hierarchy who meet regularly to share information and discuss ways to improve processes and procedures in specific functional areas.

self-managed work teams
Highly autonomous teams of employees who manage themselves without any formal supervision and take responsibility for setting goals, planning and scheduling work activities, selecting team members, and evaluating team performance.

HOT Links

Visit Harley-Davidson's recent annual report at www.harley-davidson.com to learn how the circle organizational design promotes interdependent work teams.

cross-functional teams
Teams of employees who are from about the same level in the organizational hierarchy but from different functional areas; for example, task forces, organizational committees, and project teams.

virtual teams
Teams of employees in different geographic or organizational locations who come together as a team via a combination of telecommunications and information technologies.

quality and efficiency in manufacturing processes. **Problem-solving teams** are typically made up of employees from the same department or area of expertise and from the same level of the organizational hierarchy. They meet on a regular basis to share information and discuss ways to improve processes and procedures in specific functional areas. Problem-solving teams generate ideas and alternatives and may recommend a specific course of action, but they typically do not make final decisions, allocate resources, or implement change.

Many organizations that experienced success using problem-solving teams were willing to expand the team concept to allow team members greater responsibility in making decisions, implementing solutions, and monitoring outcomes. These highly autonomous groups are called **self-managed work teams**. They manage themselves without any formal supervision, taking responsibility for setting goals, planning and scheduling work activities, selecting team members, and evaluating team performance. PepsiCo, Hewlett-Packard, Digital Equipment Corp., and Xerox are just a few of the well-known, highly successful companies using self-managed work teams.

The most recent adaptation of the team concept is called a **cross-functional team**. These teams are made up of employees from about the same hierarchical level, but different functional areas of the organization. Many task forces, organizational committees, and project teams are cross-functional. Often the team members work together only until they solve a given problem or complete a specific project. Cross-functional teams allow people with various levels and areas of expertise to pool their resources, develop new ideas, solve problems, and coordinate complex projects. Both problem-solving teams and self-managed teams may also be cross-functional teams.

Increasing globalization and advances in information technology are changing the competitive landscape and forcing organizations to re-evaluate organizational structures and work processes. Downsizing is common, and many organizations have become increasingly decentralized and geographically dispersed. The problem? Given these trends, it has become more and more challenging for organizations to retain the advantages of team-based organizational structures. The answer? Virtual teams.

Virtual teams are made up of employees in different geographic or organizational locations who come together as a team via a combination of telecommunications and information technologies. Virtual teams work together to accomplish a common goal, but rarely (if ever) meet in a face-to-face setting. Membership is often dynamic, changing to accommodate project or task requirements. The emergence of virtual teams can be attributed to five factors:

1. The increase in flat (horizontal) organizational structures.
2. Increased interorganizational cooperation (e.g., strategic alliances).
3. Changing employee expectations regarding the use of technology (i.e., increased technological sophistication).
4. The ongoing shift from production to service/knowledge work environments.
5. The increasing globalization of business activities.

Work teams pool their knowledge, skills, abilities, and resources.

Virtual teams can exist because of relatively recent advances in computer and telecommunications technology. The infrastructure of virtual teamwork is made up of three basic types of technology: desktop video conferencing systems (DVCS), collaborative software systems, and Internet/Intranet systems. These technologies allow virtual team members to interact and facilitate the accomplishment of complex work assignments.

Virtual teams provide an exciting opportunity to change the way in which work gets done, but they also present unique management challenges:

- The lack of traditional social interaction that facilitates trust and commitment.
- Increased team diversity (e.g., geographic location, language, culture, functional area, company outsiders).
- The need for team members to be technologically savvy.
- Increased difficulty coordinating resources and tasks (the teams are virtual, but the work is real).
- Increased difficulty monitoring individual and team performance.

In the workplace today, the use of virtual teams is an innovative way for companies to create competitive advantage. In the future such teams may become a necessity, perhaps even a dominant organizational form.

Building High-Performance Teams

What are the factors that contribute to highly motivated and productive teams? Based on a study of teams in organizations, researchers have identified some basic building blocks of high-performance teams: (1) the skills of team members, (2) the accountability of the team, and (3) the commitment of the team members.[8] WestJet, for example, has a very strong team orientation. The team members exhibit excellent interpersonal skills, as well as problem-solving and technical/functional skills. In order to maintain a high level of customer satisfaction, your travel experience should be positive and the WestJet team is focused on providing that positive experience. Exhibit 16-4 identifies some specific aspects of those building blocks that contribute to a high-performance team.

The following are some guidelines for enhancing team performance:[9]

- Team work assignments should focus on specific, concrete issues.
- Work should be broken down and delegated to individuals or subgroups (teams are not the same as group meetings).
- Team membership should be based on skills and abilities rather than formal authority or organizational position.
- Team members should do roughly the same amount of work to maintain equity within the group.
- Traditional hierarchical patterns of communication and interaction must be broken down.
- Teams must work to create an atmosphere of openness, commitment, and trust.

e x h i b i t   1 6 - 4 | Building Blocks of High-Performance Teams

Skills	Accountability	Commitment
• Problem solving	• Small number of members	• Specific goals
• Technical/functional	• Mutual accountability	• Common approach
• Interpersonal	• Individual accountability	• Meaningful purpose

concept check

- What is the difference between a work team and a work group?
- Identify and describe three types of work teams.
- What are some ways to build a high-performance team?

⇒ lg 6

CAPITALIZING ON TRENDS IN BUSINESS

Education and Training

Companies that provide educational and training opportunities for their employees reap the benefits of a more motivated, as well as a more skilled, work force. Employees who are properly trained in new technologies are more productive and less resistant to job change. Education and training provide additional benefits by increasing employees' feelings of competence and self-worth. When companies spend money to upgrade employee knowledge and skills, they convey the message "we value you and are committed to your growth and development as an employee."

Employee Ownership

Companies are always looking for new ways to increase employee commitment and thus decrease absenteeism and turnover. Jim Porter, vice-president at Honeywell, Inc., claims that competitive advantage boils down to employees who are committed to making the company successful, and that commitment is driven by a sense of ownership in the organization.[10] In Porter's words, "owners behave very differently from hired hands." Like an increasing number of companies today, Honeywell creates a sense of economic ownership by giving employees stock options in the company. Employee stock ownership increases employees' feelings of responsibility for the performance of the organization.

Work–Life Benefits

In another growing trend in the workplace, companies are helping their employees to manage the numerous and sometimes competing demands in their lives. Organizations are taking a more active role in helping employees achieve a balance between their work responsibilities and their personal obligations. The desired result is employees who are less stressed, better able to focus on their jobs, and, therefore, more productive. Ford Motor Co. is a leader in providing work–life benefits for employees. The company offers telecommuting, part-time positions, job sharing, subsidized child-care, elder-care referral, and on-site fitness centres.

concept check

- What benefits can an organization derive from offering training and educational opportunities for its employees?
- How can employee stock ownership programs benefit both the employees and the organization?
- How can work–life benefits help both an organization and its employees?

APPLYING THIS CHAPTER'S TOPICS

Organizations offer a wide variety of incentives to attract and retain high-quality employees. A knowledgeable, creative, committed, and highly skilled work force provides a company with a source of sustainable competitive advantage in an increasingly competitive business environment. What does that mean to you? It means that companies are working harder than ever to meet employee needs. It means that when you graduate from college or university you may choose a prospective employer on the basis of its daycare facilities and fitness programs as well as its salaries. It means that you need to think about what motivates you. Would you forgo a big salary to work for a smaller company that gives you lots of freedom to be creative and make your own decisions? Would you trade extensive health coverage for a share of ownership in the company? Most organizations try to offer a broad spectrum of incentives to meet a variety of needs, but each company makes trade-offs, and so will you in choosing an employer.

>looking ahead
at WestJet Airlines

WestJet continues to grow and expand. The airline is buying new planes regularly and hiring five or six new employees each week. Can the family orientation be maintained at WestJet as the company continues to grow? Is it possible to continue to hire people who support the leaders' vision of the company? Is it sometimes necessary to fire people who may be wrong for the company?

TRY IT NOW!

The accompanying table lists 17 personal characteristics and 13 institutional values you might encounter at a company. Select and rank the ten personal characteristics that best describe you; do the same for the ten institutional values that would be most evident in your ideal workplace. Test your fit at a firm by seeing whether the characteristics of the company's environment match your top ten personal characteristics.

The Choice Menu

Rank Order (1–17)	You Are	Rank Order (1–13)	Your Ideal Company Offers
_____	1. Flexible	_____	1. Stability
_____	2. Innovative	_____	2. High expectations of performance
_____	3. Willing to experiment	_____	3. Opportunities for professional growth
_____	4. Risk taking	_____	4. High pay for good performance
_____	5. Careful	_____	5. Job security
_____	6. Autonomy seeking	_____	6. A clear guiding philosophy
_____	7. Comfortable with rules	_____	7. A low level of conflict
_____	8. Analytical	_____	8. Respect for the individual's rights
_____	9. Team oriented	_____	9. Informality
_____	10. Easygoing	_____	10. Fairness
_____	11. Supportive	_____	11. Long hours
_____	12. Aggressive	_____	12. Relative freedom from rules
_____	13. Decisive	_____	13. The opportunity to be distinctive, or different from others
_____	14. Achievement oriented		
_____	15. Comfortable with individual responsibility		
_____	16. Competitive		
_____	17. Interested in making friends at work		

SUMMARY OF LEARNING GOALS

➡lg 1 What are the five bases of power?

The five basis of power are:

- *Legitimate power*, which is derived from an individual's position in an organization.
- *Reward power*, which is derived from an individual's control over rewards.
- *Coercive power*, which is derived from an individual's ability to threaten negative outcomes.
- *Expert power*, which is derived from an individual's extensive knowledge in one or more areas.
- *Referent power*, which is derived from an individual's personal charisma and the respect and/or admiration the individual inspires.

➡lg 2 What leadership styles are determined by the amount of authority held by the leader?

The leadership styles determined by the amount of authority held by the leader are autocratic, participative, and free reign. The manager makes most of the decisions and the emphasis is on getting the task accomplished in the autocratic style. In the participative style of leadership, the manager encourages discussion of the issues and the alternatives and shares the decision making. The free-rein-style leader turns over virtual authority and control to the group and the members are presented with the task and given the freedom to accomplish it.

➡lg 3 What three contemporary theories on employee motivation offer insights into improving employee performance?

According to expectancy theory, the probability of an individual acting in a particular way depends on the strength of that individual's belief that the act will have a particular outcome and on whether the individual values that outcome. The degree to which an employee is motivated depends on three important relationships: the link between effort and performance, the link between performance and outcome, and the link between outcomes and personal needs.

Equity theory is based on individuals' perceptions about how fairly they are treated compared with their co-workers. Equity means justice or fairness, and in the workplace it refers to employees' perceived fairness of the way they are treated and the rewards they earn. Employees evaluate their own outcomes (e.g., salary, benefits) in relation to inputs (e.g., number of hours worked, education, and training) and then compare the outcomes-to-inputs ratio to their own past experiences or the experiences of another person whose situation is similar.

Goal-setting theory states that employees are highly motivated to perform when specific goals are established and feedback on progress is offered.

➡lg 4 How can managers redesign existing jobs to increase employee motivation and performance?

The horizontal expansion of a job by increasing the number and variety of tasks that a person performs is called job enlargement. Increasing task diversity can enhance job satisfaction, particularly when the job is mundane and repetitive in nature. Job enrichment is the vertical expansion of an employee's job to provide the employee with more autonomy, responsibility, and decision-making authority. In general, job enrichment has been found to increase employee job satisfaction and reduce absenteeism and turnover. Job rotation, also called cross-training, is the shifting of workers from one job to another. This may be done to broaden an employee's skill base or when an employee ceases to be interested in or challenged by the job.

As companies try to meet the needs of a diverse work force and retain quality employees while remaining competitive and financially prosperous, managers are challenged to find new ways to keep workers motivated and satisfied, thereby increasing individual and organizational performance and decreasing absenteeism and turnover. Popular motivational tools include work-scheduling options, employee recognition programs, empowerment, and variable-pay programs.

➡lg 5   **What different types of teams are being used in organizations today?**
Work groups share resources and coordinate efforts to help members better perform their individual duties and responsibilities. The performance of the group can be evaluated by adding up the contributions of the individual group members. Work teams require not only coordination but also collaboration, the pooling of knowledge, skills, abilities, and resources in a collective effort to attain a common goal. The work team creates synergy, causing the performance of the team as a whole to be greater than the sum of team members' individual contributions.

Four types of work teams are used: problem solving, self-managed, cross-functional, and virtual teams. *Problem-solving teams* are typically made up of employees from the same department or area of expertise and from the same level of the organizational hierarchy; they meet on a regular basis to share information and discuss ways to improve processes and procedures in specific functional areas. *Self-managed work teams* are highly autonomous groups that manage themselves without any formal supervision. They take responsibility for setting goals, planning and scheduling work activities, selecting team members, and evaluating team performance. *Cross-functional teams* are made up of employees from about the same hierarchical level, but different functional areas of the organization. These teams allow people with various areas of expertise to pool their resources, develop new ideas, solve problems, and coordinate complex projects. In a *virtual team*, employees in different geographic or organizational locations come together as a team via a combination of telecommunications and information technologies. Virtual teams work together to accomplish a common goal, but rarely (if ever) meet face-to-face. Membership is often dynamic, changing to accommodate project or task requirements.

➡lg 6   **What initiatives are organizations using today to motivate and retain employees?**
Today, firms are using three key tactics to motivate and retain workers. First, companies are investing more in employee education and training, which make workers more productive and less resistant to job change. Second, managers are offering employees a chance for ownership in the company. This can strongly increase employee commitment. Finally, enlightened employers are providing work–life benefits to help employees achieve a better balance between work and personal responsibilities. Examples include telecommuting, job sharing, subsidized child-care, and on-site fitness centres.

WORKING THE NET

1. Looking for ways to motivate or reward your employees? Mark Holmes can help. Visit his people keeper site at **www.peoplekeeper.com/** to get some ideas you can put to use to help you do a better job, either as a manager or as an employee. View articles such as "How to Reduce Turnover and Rev Up Company Performance" or try the free job satisfaction survey.

2. More companies are offering their employees stock ownership plans. To learn more about stock options, see **www.stock-options.com** or visit the National Center for Employee Ownership (NCEO) at **www.nceo.org** and the Foundation for Enterprise Development (FED) at **www.fed.org**.

3. Open-book management is one of the better-known ways to create a participatory work environment. Over 2000 companies have adopted this practice, which involves sharing financial information with nonmanagement employees and

training them to understand financial information. Does it really motivate employees and improve productivity? Check some of the many Web sites on the subject such as **www.greatgame.com** or **www.behindthechair.com**.

4. You've been asked to develop a staff recognition program for your company but don't have a clue where to start! Many companies are proud to display their staff recognition programs on the Web. Check out two or three examples and discuss the program that would appeal to you the most. How would you prefer to be recognized by your employer? Try **www.recognition.org/faqs.asp**.

5. How do you keep your employees satisfied? The Business Research Lab has a series of articles on this topic at **busreslab.com/tips/tipses.htm**. Compile a list of the best ideas—the ones that would motivate you.

6. Knowing how to build and manage effective teams is a necessary skill in today's workplace. Team Building Inc., at **www.teambuildinginc.com**, is a newsletter featuring ways top corporations use innovative team building to improve team performance.

CREATIVE THINKING CASE

A Clash of Cultures as Ford Meets Volvo

In Gothenburg, Sweden, Volvo car workers are nervous about what life will be like under their new owner, Ford Motor Co. After all, they might lose their badminton courts. At Volvo's flagship factory here, employees have the use of a company gym, Olympic-size swimming pool, badminton and tennis courts, an outdoor track, and tanning beds. There's also a hot-water pool, where workers go for physical therapy sessions after a hard day on the assembly line.

Some 1800 Volvo workers, or roughly 9 percent of the total work force at the company's headquarters, use the facilities. Unions and workers worry that Ford, which bought Volvo, may consider it all a bit too lavish. Although workers have to pay US$1.50 a day to get in, Volvo pays as much as 5 million kronor (US$605 500) a year to support the centre. "Everybody at Volvo is wondering what Ford's takeover really means to our future," says Claes Andersson, vice-president of the plant workers union. "Will our Volvo traditions continue?"

For Ford, the Volvo purchase raises a big question of benefit equality. Ford workers in North America are considerably less pampered than Swedish workers. Ford plants usually have free-of-charge fitness centres for employees, as well as weight-reduction programs, but North American workers have to do without the tanning beds and other goodies normally found only at the most exclusive health clubs.

Ford has been vague about its plans. "I respect the Swedish heritage," said Jacques Nasser, Ford's CEO. But he added that "nothing is safe in this world; there are no guarantees."

It's not just the health club that workers worry about, but a host of issues ranging from job security to quality of life. For example, Nasser said he wanted to make Volvo a "volume car" in North America, which could mean a three-shift, round-the-clock production schedule, just like in North America. Volvo employees currently work two shifts.

Nasser's comments disturbed 40-year-old Jari Saarelainen, a Volvo night-shift worker. He now works fewer than 30 hours a week, but gets paid about the same as day-shift workers, who work as many as 40 hours a week, because of a government-mandated allocation for late-shift employees. The setup allows him to spend lots of time with his wife and four children. "It's a human way of work," he says.

Saarelainen realizes he has it good, but argues that his relatively undemanding workload also helps the company because productivity and morale are higher than they would be under a more conventional employer. "We hope that Ford can grasp that this system is better for the company and the workers," he says. Indeed, the absentee rate at Volvo is roughly 4 percent a day, down from well over 10 percent in the late 1980s. "We like to think that the gym contributed to that," says Mats Edenborg, spokesman for Volvo Group.[11]

Critical Thinking Questions

1. Do you think that Volvo has carried employee benefits and perks too far?

2. Swedish income taxes are far higher than those in the United States and Canada. High salaries are taxed away, so many companies try to do a few things extra for their employees. Is this a sufficient reason for Ford to maintain Volvo's benefits for its workers?

3. A Ford worker in the United States or Canada can earn over US$100 000 a year with overtime. A typical Volvo worker earns about US$30 275 per year. Should Ford cut the perks and raise wages at Volvo? The government would take slightly over 50 percent.

4. Should Nasser simply leave benefits and perks at both places as they are? What if Ford workers start to complain or Volvo workers start demanding higher salaries?

MAKING THE CONNECTION MAKING THE CONNECTIO

Information Systems and Effective Control

In this chapter we'll look at the last step in the process of management—*controlling*, or monitoring progress toward the accomplishment of organizational goals. The chapter also covers information systems, because without information we have no control.

Control is an essential integrative element in a successful business. We monitor the environment for its effect on the business, compare the threats and opportunities that the external environment of the business offers with the strengths and weaknesses of the business itself, combine this information with an understanding of the needs of the different *stakeholders*, and then decide what direction the business should take and how to compete on this chosen path. Once the *vision* and *mission* are outlined, managers at all levels decide on the goals and objectives for the business, *plan* for their execution, *organize* resources to implement the plan, and lead people to commit to accomplishing the goals. If anything along the way changes, which it inevitably does in

today's dynamic business environment, or any of our decisions proves to be unsuccessful, which is also inevitable when you are dealing with human beings, it is essential to the success if not very survival of the business that we are aware of these factors and make the appropriate changes to the plans and their execution. This is what control is all about, and that is why it is the step that completes the outer ring of the model. It is the management function that helps to ensure that the business is on track for success, and so without it, our model of a successful business would not be complete.

The only way that a business can be aware of these changes in environmental conditions and deviations from the goals set, is with information. Fortunately, we live in a knowledge-based economy. Rapid and dramatic changes in the technological environment have greatly increased the importance of information in every facet of business success, but they have also increased access to this information. This information is critical to making decisions in the business, as well as to assessing whether those decisions are successful or need to be changed. Information is critical for effective control.

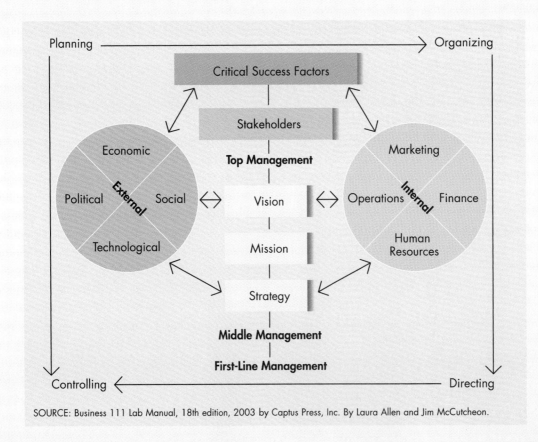

SOURCE: Business 111 Lab Manual, 18th edition, 2003 by Captus Press, Inc. By Laura Allen and Jim McCutcheon.

The most efficient and effective information systems, as you'll see in the chapter, are those that use current *technology* to integrate all the different areas of the business as well as its business partners and customers together into one system. In that way, information is shared and every facet of the business can work in unison, which is essential to success.

Given that business success is defined by the critical success factors, it is important that the information system provide information on how well the business is meeting (or exceeding) the five critical factors. Managers must first decide what the standards are that the company is measuring itself against—the objectives with respect to financial performance, quality, and so on—as set in the planning function. And then they must determine whether these objectives have been achieved. This is the control function. These two functions are intricately connected because without clear objectives, there can be no control. That is, if you aren't sure where

you're headed, you'll never know if you've got there. This is simpler with some of the factors—for example, financial performance, where measuring systems have long been in place. However, determining whether or not employees are committed and the organization is innovative are tougher to do. The organization must decide what indicates success in these areas and measure progress through these indicators—such as the number of customer complaints (*meeting customer needs*), the frequency of product repair (*product quality*), the number of new products each year, and absenteeism and turnover rates (*gaining employee committment*).

What is important is that information is provided to measure progress within each of the five critical success factors to ensure that overall success is monitored and the organization is kept on track to achieve its goals in all areas. Timely and useful information fed into an effective control system is thus essential to a successful business.

Information Systems and Effective Control

Livelink®   Great Minds Working Together™

CHAPTER 17

Learning Goals

➡ **lg 1** How does information play a role in decision making?

➡ **lg 2** Why are computer networks an important part of today's business information systems?

➡ **lg 3** What is the structure of a typical information system?

➡ **lg 4** How can companies manage information technology to their advantage?

➡ **lg 5** How do organizations control activities?

➡ **lg 6** What are the leading trends in information technology?

Open Text Corporation: Reacting Immediately to Critical Situations

In 1991 Open Text Corporation was formed as a result of a spin-off company from the University of Waterloo. With over 6 million people in 31 countries using its products and services, the company is the worldwide leader in delivery collaboration and knowledge management software. Thousands of leading organizations are using Open Text's products and services to leverage their most valuable assets—people and knowledge.

Open Text Corporation has succeeded in harnessing the power of the Internet and delivered the first Web-based document management product—Livelink®. By effectively managing people, processes, and information, Livelink® makes companies more efficient and innovative. Livelink® delivers truly dynamic information and knowledge sharing between individuals, teams, and organizations.

In 2001, Open Text introduced Livelink Wireless, the industry's first wireless technology for collaboration and knowledge management application. Also in that year, Open Text launched Livelink MeetingZone™ (a real-time collaboration tool) and Livelink Records Management™ (the first comprehensive, Web-based document and record management solutions for business) to its tightly integrated services.

Livelink Wireless allows managers and employees to stay in constant contact with the important events in the organization. Livelink Wireless helps organizations become more responsive so that they can react in record time to take advantage of business opportunities and make better decisions—faster. Some of the real-time access that is provided by Livelink includes document management, document viewing, content searching, appointment management, and discussions.

As speed and efficiency are becoming more important for organizations to be effective, people must collaborate in real time. Livelink MeetingZone™ is a real-time virtual meeting tool that helps organizations carry out more effective meetings while reducing expenses and inconvenience. It is fully integrated with Livelink® and facilitates the seamless exchange of ideas and knowledge. Any of the information that is generated during a meeting can be stored and retrieved for future use—thereby providing lasting benefits to the organization. Not only can this be used internally, but it can also be used in collaboration with customers, suppliers, and other stakeholders.

Livelink Records Management™ provides organizations with "life-cycle management" of all its records, whether electronic or in hard-copy form. This module helps businesses meet the stringent regulatory standards by tracking documents, merging paper and electronic records, and creating audit trails that are becoming more complex.

CRITICAL THINKING QUESTIONS

As you read this chapter, consider the following questions as they relate to Open Text Corporation and its products:

- How does managing information give companies a competitive advantage?
- What problems might companies have while implementing a database?
- What steps can companies take to encourage acceptance of the new databases and ensure that employees use it?

Open Text provides companies with efficient and economical information and knowledge management systems to give them greater access to critical information in order to make better decisions. The products ensure integrity of the information and knowledge and ease in the integration of workflow.[1]

BUSINESS IN THE 21ST CENTURY

As most executives and employees know, harnessing the power of information technology gives a company a significant competitive advantage. Data and information can help to cut costs, increase profits, spot market trends faster, and communicate more effectively with customers.

Information helps decision makers reduce risks and make decisions with more confidence. Information systems, such as the ones used by Mark's Work Wearhouse (see Chapter 4) and the computers that comprise them, are so much a part of our lives that we almost take them for granted. In less than 60 years, we have shifted from an industrial society to a knowledge-based economy driven by information. Businesses depend on information technology for everything from running daily operations to making strategic decisions.

Computers are the tools of this information age, performing extremely complex operations as well as everyday jobs such as word processing and creating spreadsheets. Through networks of linked computers, one manager can share information with hundreds of thousands of people around the world almost as easily as with a colleague on another floor of the same office building. Many companies now have a **chief information officer (CIO)**, an executive with responsibility for managing all information resources.

Because most jobs today depend on managing information—obtaining, using, creating, and sharing it—this chapter begins with the role of information in decision-making and the relationship between computers and information systems. The following sections discuss business information systems and the management of information technology. We will also look at the latest trends in information technology. Finally, we will look at how information and managing information help to control the activities of the organization. Throughout the chapter, examples show how managers and their companies are using computers to make better decisions in a highly competitive world.

chief information officer (CIO)
An executive with responsibility for managing all information resources in an organization.

➡ lg 1

information technology (IT)
The equipment and techniques used to manage and process information.

Using Information for Decision-Making

As stated in Chapter 4, **information technology (IT)**, the equipment and techniques used to manage and process information, has changed the way people make business decisions today. Only 30 years ago, well within the careers of many of today's top executives, few companies used computers. Today, IT is one of the fastest-growing industries and includes not only computers but also telecommunications and Internet-related products and services. Computers now reside on almost every employee desktop and provide vast stores of information for decision making. Some of it is useful and some is not. To be useful, information must be:

- *Relevant.* Some kinds of information are more useful than others in making a given decision. For instance, when deciding whether to order raw materials, a manager is more likely to need information about inventories and future production plans than about overtime pay.
- *Accurate.* Obviously, inaccurate information can reduce a manager's ability to make good decisions.

- *Complete.* Partial information may cause a manager to focus on only one aspect of a decision or to make false assumptions. Other important aspects may be overlooked.
- *Timely.* Information that arrives too late is often no more helpful than no information at all in some situations (e.g., stock quotes for traders).

information system (IS)
The hardware, software, people, data, and so on, that provide information about all aspects of a firm's operations.

Managers use **information systems (ISs)**—the hardware, software, people, data, and so on, that provide information about all aspects of a firm's operations—to get the information they need to make decisions.

One function of an information system is to gather **data,** the many facts that together can describe the company's status and/or its environment. For instance, the fact that a worker finished a unit of production on job 23-M-8735 at 2:17 p.m. on March 7 is a data item. When a manager must make a decision, a long list of data is generally not useful. For the production supervisor, a list of the times during the past hour when each unit was completed is far too detailed. Data must be turned into **information,** a meaningful and useful representation or interpretation of data. For example the total number of units produced in the hour would be useful information when examining such things as productivity and efficiencies. The next logical step is **knowledge,** the understanding or awareness of information about a subject. Once the decision-maker has the knowledge, it can now be used to make less risky decisions about future events.

data
The many facts that together describe a company's status and/or its environment.

information
A meaningful and useful representation or interpretation of data.

knowledge
The understanding or awareness of information about a subject.

Businesses collect a great deal of data. Only through well-designed IT systems and the power of computers can managers use such data to make better decisions. Companies are discovering that they cannot operate as effectively or efficiently with a series of separate information systems geared to solving specific departmental problems. They need to integrate the systems throughout the firm. Company-wide systems that bring together the functional units (e.g., human resources, operations) and technology are becoming an integral part of business strategy.

Technology experts are learning more about the way the business operates, and business managers are learning to use technology effectively to create new opportunities. The IS professional has a solid understanding of both of these roles. Once companies know where they want to go, information systems can help them reach those goals. An example could be how a new purchasing system can accomplish the company's goals of automating the purchasing process but also improve inventory management and customer service.

concept check

- What are information systems? Why are they important?
- What makes information useful?
- Distinguish amongst data, information, and knowledge. How are they related?

Computer Software

Computers have greatly increased worker productivity and efficiency at both large and small companies. For example, DaimlerChrysler uses powerful computers to conduct crash simulations, structural analyses, and other tests to improve auto safety and design. Compared to traditional crash testing, each virtual crash saves the company about US$275 000.[2]

software
The general term for various programs used to operate computers; a set of instructions that directs a computer's activities.

Companies now use computers for thousands of activities. The set of instructions that directs the computer's activities is called **software** (i.e., the various programs used to operate computers). Some software is very complex and handles major information processing tasks for finance, accounting, production, sales, and marketing functions. Often companies customize their software to meet the needs of their particular industry. Software falls into two main categories: system software and application software.

system software
Software that controls the computer and provides instructions that enable applications programs to run on a particular computer.

application software
Software that is *applied* to a real-world task; used to perform a specific task or to solve a particular problem.

HOT Links

Confused about how spreadsheets work? Learn some spreadsheet basics at www.quia.com/pages/spreadsheets.html

System software controls the computer and provides instructions that enable applications programs to run on a particular computer. These routines are part of an operating system, a collection of programs that manage the computer system's activities and run application software. Commonly used operating systems include MS-DOS (Microsoft Disk Operating System), Windows (which makes MS-DOS easier to use by adding a *graphical user interface*), IBM's OS/2, Apple's Macintosh system, UNIX, and LINUX.

Application software is *applied* to a real-world task. It is used to perform a specific task or to solve a particular problem. If clerks need to record customer orders, they use an order-entry application program. If service representatives need to type letters in response to customer inquiries, they use a word processing application program. Application software covers a wide range of programs, from the complex software that handles the large-scale processing needs of businesses to PC productivity software used by both businesses and individuals to games and other types of entertainment software.

Sabrina Tam, a sales representative for Homestyle Corp., a large furniture maker, provides a good example of how applications software is used. To help her better serve her customers, Homestyle has given Sabrina a powerful laptop computer with colour display screen, communications modem, and CD-ROM drive that she can carry into a store owner's office and use during her presentations. Her laptop has word processing, spreadsheet, database management, graphics, and communications software (see Exhibit 17-1 for a summary of each of these types of application software). Sabrina can also use the modem to connect to Homestyle's central computers to find current product prices, check merchandise availability, and enter customers' orders while in their offices.

For an example of how graphics software is used, Exhibit 17-2 shows a bar graph of current versus projected sales. Companies often use graphs to visually display concepts, projections, and so on.

concept check

- What is the difference between systems software and applications software?
- What are the main software applications?
- How do word processing software, desktop publishing software, and spreadsheet software differ? How can you use them together to create documents?

e x h i b i t   1 7 - 1 | Summary of Major Application Software

Software	Application
Word processing software	Used to write, edit, and format letters and other text documents.
Spreadsheet software	Used to prepare and analyze numerical data, such that as for financial statements, sales forecasts, and budgets.
Database software	Records, organizes, updates, and processes data.
Graphics software	Used to create tables and graphs.
Desktop publishing software	Combines word processing, graphics, and page layout software; is used to create documents such as sales brochures, catalogues, advertisements, and newscasts.
Communications software	Used in various forms of communication, such as intra-company and inter-company e-mail.
Integrated software (e.g., software suite)	Combines several popular types of programs.

e x h i b i t   1 7 - 2 | Graph Prepared with Spreadsheet Program

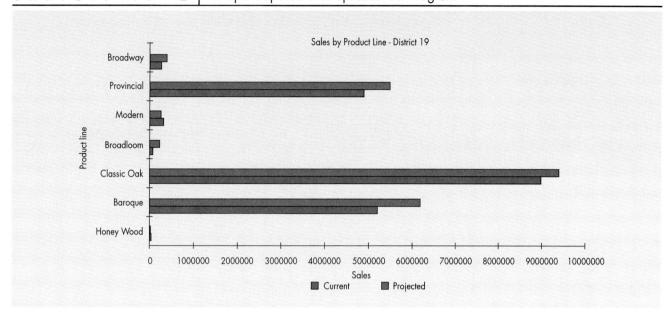

Computer Networks

computer network
A group of two or more computer systems linked together by communications channels to share data and information.

Today most businesses use networks to deliver information to employees, suppliers, and customers. A **computer network** is a group of two or more computer systems linked together by communications channels to share data and information. Networks have been widely used for about 20 years, but microcomputers have made networking much more affordable and popular. Whereas early networks could connect about 20 users and share only data, today's networks link thousands of users and can transmit audio and video as well as data.

By making it easy and fast to share information, networks have created new ways to work and increase productivity. They provide more efficient use of resources, permitting communication and collaboration across distance and time. With file sharing, all employees, regardless of location, have access to the same information. Shared databases also eliminate duplication of effort. Employees at different sites can "screen share" computer files, working on data as if they were in the same room. Their computers are connected by phone lines, they all see the same thing on their display, and anyone can make changes that are seen by the other participants. The employees can also use the networks for videoconferencing.

Networks make it possible for companies to run enterprise software, large programs with integrated modules that manage all of the corporation's internal operations. Enterprise resource planning (ERP) systems run on networks. Typical subsystems include finance, human resources, engineering, sales and order distribution, and order management and procurement. These modules work independently and then automatically exchange information, creating a company-wide system that includes current delivery dates, inventory status, quality control, and other critical information. ERP applications can also be integrated with Web-based resources. Let's now look at the two basic types of networks companies use to transmit data: local area networks and wide area networks.

Local Area Networks

local area network (LAN)
A network that connects computers at one site, enabling the computer users to exchange data and share the use of hardware and software from a variety of computer manufacturers.

A **local area network (LAN)** permits people at one site to exchange data and share the use of hardware and software from a variety of computer manufacturers. LANs offer companies a more cost-effective way to link computers than linking terminals to a mainframe computer. The most common uses of LANs at small businesses, for example, are office automation, accounting, and information management.[3] LANs can help companies reduce staff, streamline operations, and cut processing costs.

Wide Area Networks

wide area network (WAN)
A network that connects computers at different sites via telecommunications media such as phone lines, satellites, and microwaves.

A **wide area network (WAN)** connects computers at different sites via telecommunications media such as phone lines, fibre optics, satellites, and microwaves. A modem connects the computer or a terminal to the telephone line and transmits data. The Internet is essentially a worldwide WAN. Long-distance telephone companies, such as AT&T and Sprint, operate very large WANs. Companies also connect LANs at various locations into WANs. WANs make it possible for companies to work on critical projects around the clock by using teams in different time zones.

Two forms of WANs—intranets and extranets—use Internet technology. We'll look at intranets, internal corporate networks, in this chapter; extranets were discussed in Chapter 4.

Intranets

intranet
An internal corporate-wide area network that uses Internet technology to link employees in many locations and with different types of computers.

Like LANs, **intranets** are private corporate networks. Many companies use both types of internal networks. However, because they use Internet technology to connect computers, intranets are WANs that link employees in many locations and with different types of computers. Essentially mini-Internets that serve only the company's employees, intranets operate behind a *firewall* that prevents unauthorized access. Employees navigate using a standard Web browser, which makes the intranet easy to use. They are also considerably less expensive to install and maintain than other options (e.g., client/server systems) and can take advantage of Internet interactive features such as chat rooms and team workspaces.

Until recently, intranets were too complicated and expensive for small businesses, but the cost has dropped as companies develop off-the-shelf programs. Children's Orchard, a franchiser whose stores sell new, second-hand, and manufacturer's overstock toys and children's clothing, uses an intranet to communicate with franchisees. It is the primary source of company news, corporate services, and peer support. Franchisees have a password to access the intranet through the company's regular Web site. There they can read newsletters, order supplies, and call up statistics on other stores to see how they compare. They can also chat with other franchisees to share ideas and solve problems. CEO Walter Hamilton estimates that the intranet saves the company at least US$40 000 a year.[4]

concept check

- What is a computer network? How do a LAN and a WAN differ?
- What benefits do companies gain by using networks?
- You are an employee in the marketing department of a consumer products company. Make a list of the information you would expect to find on the company's intranet.

➡ **lg 3**

Business Information Systems

While individuals use business productivity software to accomplish a variety of tasks, the job of managing a company's information needs falls to information systems: users, data procedures, hardware, and software that support decision making. Information systems collect and store the company's key data and produce the information needed by managers for analysis, control, and decision making.

Manufacturing businesses often use computer-based information systems to automate production processes and order and monitor inventory. Most companies use them to process customer orders and handle billing and vendor payments. Financial services companies use a variety of information systems to process transactions such as deposits, ATM withdrawals, and loan payments. Most consumer transactions also involve information systems. When you check out at the supermarket, book a hotel room using a toll-free hotel reservations number, or buy CDs over the Internet, information systems record and track the transaction and transmit the data to the necessary places.

Companies typically have several types of information systems:

- *Transaction processing systems* handle the daily business operations of the firm—for example, customer orders, pricing, employee payrolls, and inventory. These operational systems capture and organize raw data and convert these data into information.
- *Management support, or analytic, systems* are dynamic systems that help managers make decisions. These systems allow users to analyze data, including the transaction systems' operational data, to identify business trends, make forecasts, and model business strategies.
- *Office automation systems* use information technology tools such as e-mail, fax machines, and word processing to improve the flow of information throughout an organization. These systems support employees at all levels.

Each type of information system serves a particular level of decision-making: operational, tactical, and strategic. Exhibit 17-3 shows the relationship between transaction processing and management support systems as well as the management levels they serve. Let's now take a more detailed look at how companies and managers use transaction processing and management support systems to manage information.

e x h i b i t   1 7 - 3 | A Company's Integrated Information System

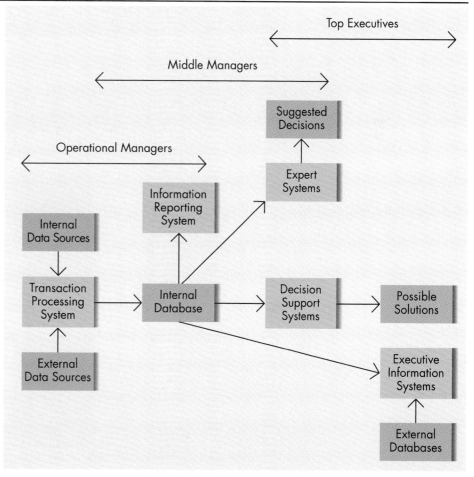

Transaction Processing Systems

transaction processing system (TPS)
An information system that handles the daily business operations of a firm. The system receives and organizes raw data from internal and external sources for storage in a database.

batch processing
A method of updating a database in which data are collected over some time period and then processed together.

online (real-time) processing
A method of updating a database in which data are processed as they become available.

The firm's integrated information system starts with its **transaction processing system (TPS)**. The TPS receives raw data from internal and external sources and prepares these data for storage in a database similar to a microcomputer database but vastly larger. In fact, all the company's key data are stored in a single huge database that becomes the company's central information resource. A *database management system* tracks the data and allows users to query the database for the information they need.

The database can be updated in two ways. With **batch processing**, data are collected over some time period and then processed together. Batch processing uses computer resources very efficiently and is well suited to applications such as payroll processing that require periodic rather than continuous processing. **Online processing,** or **real-time processing** processes data as they become available. When you make an airline reservation, the agent enters your reservation directly into the airline's computer and quickly receives confirmation. Online processing keeps the company's data current. Because absolutely current data are needed for many types of management decisions, many large companies use online processing systems.

The transaction processing systems of large companies are custom-designed to keep and organize the records they need. But some applications in the areas of accounting and finance, human resource management, sales and marketing, and manufacturing are nearly universal. For example, the accounting information system diagrammed in Exhibit 17-4 is a typical TPS. It has subsystems for order entry, accounts receivable (for billing customers), accounts payable (for paying bills), payroll, inventory, and general ledger (for determining the financial status and profitability of the business). The accounting information system provides input to and receives input from the firm's other information systems, such as manufacturing (production planning data, for example) and human resources (data on hours worked and salary increases to generate paycheques).

e x h i b i t   1 7 - 4 | Accounting Information System

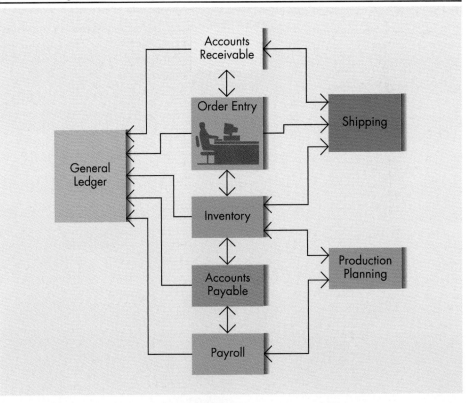

Management Support Systems

Transaction processing systems were the first stage of information technology. By automating routine and tedious back-office processes such as accounting, order processing, and financial reporting, they reduced clerical expenses and provided basic operational information more quickly. As technology improved, businesses realized that computers could do more than merely process data. Managers now have several types of **management support systems** (MSSs) that use the internal database to help them make better decisions.

A **data warehouse** combines many databases across the whole company into one central database that supports management decision making. Data warehouses include software to extract data from operational databases, maintain the data in the warehouse, and provide data to users.

management support system (MSS)
A dynamic information system that helps managers make decisions by allowing them to analyze data, identify business trends, make forecasts, and model business strategies.

data warehouse
An information technology that combines many databases across a whole company into one central database that supports management decision making.

Information Reporting Systems

At the first level of a MSS is an *information reporting system,* which uses summary data collected by the TPS to produce reports with statistics that managers can use to make decisions. Some reports are scheduled and present information on a regular basis. For instance, Homestyle's payroll personnel get a weekly payroll report showing how each employee's paycheque was determined. The next level of report summarizes information. A payroll summary report might show higher-level managers total labour cost by department, overtime as a percentage of total payroll cost by department, and a comparison of current labour costs with those in the prior year. Exception reports help identify problems by telling about cases that fail to meet some standard. An accounts receivable exception report that lists all customers with overdue accounts would help collection personnel focus their work. Demand reports are special reports generated only when a manager requests them. The marketing manager for the Honey Wood furniture line might call for reports on sales by region and type of store to identify reasons for the sales decline.

Decision Support Systems

A **decision support system** (DSS) helps managers make decisions using computer models that describe real-world processes. The DSS also uses data from the internal database but looks for specific data that relate to the problems at hand. It is a tool for answering "what if" questions about what would happen if the manager made certain changes. In simple cases, a manager can create a spreadsheet and try changing some of the numbers. For instance, a manager could create a spreadsheet to show the amount of overtime required if the number of workers increases or decreases. With models, the manager enters into the computer the values that describe a particular situation, and the program computes the results. Homestyle's marketing executives could run DSS models that use sales data and demographic assumptions to develop forecasts of the types of furniture that would appeal to the fastest-growing population groups.

decision support system (DSS)
A management support system that helps managers make decisions using computer models that describe real-world processes.

Executive Information Systems

Although similar to a DSS, an **executive information system** (EIS) is customized for an individual executive. These systems provide specific information for strategic decisions. For example, Homestyle's CEO has an EIS with special spreadsheets that present financial data comparing Homestyle to its principal competitors and graphs showing current economic and industry trends. Belk, Inc., a large privately held department store company, developed an EIS for its buyers, assistant buyers, and executives. Its easy-to-understand interface allows users to quickly get answers to high-level questions such as, "How did last week's markdowns affect the sale of intimate apparel compared to the same time last year?" "Will our current inventory for Kenneth Cole shoes at our Charlotte store be sufficient, given the pending promotion?"[5]

executive information system (EIS)
A management support system that is customized for an individual executive; provides specific information for strategic decisions.

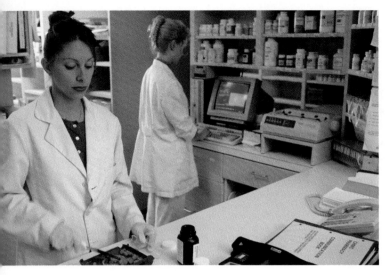

Medical professionals use expert systems to analyze patients' medications, ensuring that they do not cause allergic reactions and potentially dangerous interactions with patients' other prescriptions.

expert system
A management support system that gives managers advice similar to what they would get from a consultant; it uses artificial intelligence to enable computers to reason and learn to solve problems in much the same way humans do.

office automation system
An information system that uses information technology tools such as word processing systems, e-mail systems, cellular phones, pagers, and fax machines, to improve communications throughout an organization.

Expert Systems

An **expert system** gives managers advice similar to what they would get from a human consultant. Artificial intelligence enables computers to reason and learn to solve problems in much the same way humans do. The use of expert systems is growing as more applications are found. To date, expert systems have been used to help explore for oil, schedule employee work shifts, and diagnose illnesses. Some expert systems take the place of human experts, while others assist them.

At Toronto's Hospital for Sick Children, an expert system checks medication orders against patients' known allergies and potentially serious drug interactions. It pages doctors to alert them to problems within seconds. Doctors just can't keep track of 1000 facts on each patient. According to Dr. Jonathan Teich of Boston's Brigham and Women's Hospital, "The computer does it much better." It also suggests alternative medications. The system analyzes about 13 000 orders per day. Its fast response time—no longer does a lab technician have to call the pharmacist, who then finds the doctor—prevents about 400 serious medication errors daily.[6]

Office Automation Systems

Today's **office automation systems** make good use of the computer networks in many companies to improve communications. Office automation systems assist all levels of employees and enable managers to handle most of their own communication. The key elements include:
- *Word processing systems* for producing written messages.
- *E-mail systems* for communicating directly with other employees and customers and transferring computer files.
- *Departmental scheduling systems* for planning meetings and other activities.
- *Cellular phones* for providing telephone service away from the office, as in cars.
- *Pagers* that notify employees of phone calls. Some pagers have the ability to display more extensive written messages sent from a computer network.
- *Voice mail systems* for recording, storing, and forwarding phone messages.
- *Facsimile (fax) systems* for delivering messages on paper within minutes.
- *Electronic bulletin boards* and *computer conferencing systems* for discussing issues with others who are not present.

Office automation systems also make telecommuting and home-based businesses possible. By using microcomputers and other high-tech equipment to keep in touch with the office, employees are spending less time travelling to and from the office, are saving the company money (e.g., overhead), and are able to have a more flexible work schedule.

concept check

- What are the main components of an information system, and what does each do?
- Differentiate between the types of management support systems, and give examples of how each is used.
- How can office automation systems help employees work more efficiently?

→ lg 4

Managing Information Technology

With the help of computers, people have produced more data in the last 30 years than in the previous 5000 years combined. Companies today make sizable investments in information technology to help them manage this overwhelming amount of data, convert the data into information, and deliver it to the people who need it so that knowledge can be gained. In many cases, however, the companies do not reap the desired benefits from these expenditures. Among the typical complaints from senior executives are that the payoff from IT investments is inadequate, IT investments do not relate to business strategy, the firm seems to be buying the latest technology for technology's sake, and communications between IT specialists and IT users are poor.[7]

Managing a company's information resources requires a coordinated effort among a firm's top executives, IT managers, and business unit managers. The goal is to develop an integrated, company-wide technology plan that achieves a balance between business judgment and technology expertise. Protecting company information and privacy concerns are other important aspects of knowledge management.

Technology Planning

Like any other business activity that involves the entire company, IT requires coordinated strategies and planning that take into account the company's strategic objectives. Then managers can select the right technology to help them reach those goals.

The goal of technology planning is to provide employees with the tools they need to perform their jobs at the highest levels of efficiency and effectiveness. The first step is a general needs assessment, followed by ranking of projects and the specific choices of hardware and software. Some basic questions departmental managers and IT specialists should ask when planning technology purchases include:

- What are the company's overall objectives?
- What problems does the company want to solve?
- How can technology help meet those goals and solve the problems?
- What are the company's priorities, both short- and long-term?
- Which technologies meet the company's requirements?
- Are additional hardware and software required? If so, will they integrate with the company's existing systems?
- What are the maintenance (hardware and software) considerations and expandability issues?

Once managers identify the projects that make business sense, they can choose the best products for the company's needs. The final step is to evaluate the potential benefits of the technology, in terms of efficiency and effectiveness. This requires developing specific criteria—not only quantitative measures like cost savings and profit improvement, but also qualitative factors such as employee satisfaction. For example, how will the new technology increase revenues? Will it get products to market faster by shortening the product development cycle or streamlining the production process? Will it save employees time and cut labour costs? What other benchmarks does the company want to achieve? How can prevention strategies guard against information loss?

Many colleges and universities restrict students access to the Internet while labs are being conducted to eliminate the unauthorized use of the Net.

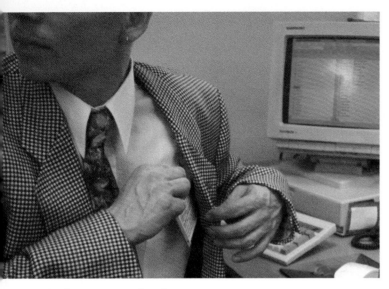

Employers can guard against employee theft of confidential information by installing special authorization systems that prevent unwanted access from inside their organization.

Plans will change over time in response to company needs. "Basically, business and technology plans should become living documents that drive the company forward," says Cheryl Currid, a technology analyst.[8] The planning process can even be a catalyst for growth.

Protecting Computers and Information

Protecting the information stored in computers is no easy task. With the ever-increasing dependence on computers, companies must develop plans to cover power outages, equipment failure, human error, computer viruses and disasters such as major fires, earthquakes, or floods. Many companies install fault-tolerant computer systems designed to withstand such disasters. Preventing costly problems can be as simple as regularly backing up applications and data. Companies should have systems in place that automatically back up the company's data every day or more frequently if appropriate. In addition, employees should back up their own work regularly.

Disasters are not the only threat to data. A great deal of data, much of it confidential, can easily be tampered with or destroyed by anyone knowledgeable about computers.

Data Security Issues

Firms are taking steps to prevent computer crimes, which cost large companies hundreds of thousands of dollars every year. There are several major categories of computer crimes:

- *Unauthorized access and use.* This can create havoc with a company's systems. For example, if an employee uses a company's server to maintain another organization's Web site, it could possibly cause system crashes and network slowdowns. These crashes and slowdowns could potentially cost the company several million dollars from lost employee productivity and missed deadlines—not to mention the risk of unauthorized access to the company's files and research.
- *Security breaches and unauthorized access.* Employees can copy confidential new product information and provide it to competitors. Networking links make it easier for someone outside the organization to gain access to a company's computers. Computer crooks are getting more sophisticated all the time and find new ways to get into "ultrasecure" sites. For example, a British hacker was able to break into the network of the highly secret Rome Laboratory in New York by using computers in Latvia, Colombia, and Chile. Then he attacked defence and government systems.[9]

  To protect data, companies can encode confidential information so only the recipient can decipher it. Special authorization systems can help stop unwanted access from inside or outside. These can be as simple as a password or as sophisticated as fingerprint or voice identification. Companies can also install intrusion-detection systems to monitor networks for activities that signal the possibility of unauthorized access and document suspicious events.
- *Software piracy.* The copying of copyrighted software programs by people who haven't paid for them is another form of unauthorized use. Piracy takes revenue away from the company that developed the program—usually at great cost. Thus, software firms take piracy seriously and go after the offenders. Many also make special arrangements so that large companies can get multiple copies of programs at a lower cost rather than use illegal copies.

- *Deliberate damage to information.* For example, an unhappy employee in the purchasing department could get into the computer system and delete information on past orders and future inventory needs. The sabotage could severely disrupt production and the accounts payable system. Wilful acts to destroy or change the data in computers are hard to prevent. To lessen the damage, companies should back up critical information.

computer virus
A computer program that copies itself into other software and can spread to other computer systems.

- *Computer viruses.* A computer program that copies itself into other software and can spread to other computer systems, a **computer virus** can destroy the contents of a computer's hard drive or damage files. Another form is called a "worm" because it spreads itself automatically from computer to computer. Viruses can hide for weeks or months before starting to damage information. A virus that "infects" one computer or network can be spread to another computer by sharing disks or by downloading infected files over the Internet. To protect data from virus damage, software developers have created virus protection programs. This software automatically monitors computers to detect and remove viruses. Program developers make regular updates available to guard against newly created viruses. In addition, experts are becoming more proficient at tracking down virus authors, who are subject to criminal charges.

Preventing Problems

Firms that take a proactive approach can prevent security and technical problems before they start. Here are some ways to avoid an IT meltdown:

- Set up an IT management service that works closely with other employees to troubleshoot problems in advance rather than just react to them. Act on them *before* they affect the operation.
- Train IT managers to treat employees in other areas as customers.
- Establish a multimedia in-house help centre to respond quickly and professionally to employee concerns. Use e-mail and the Web to minimize phone use for answers to nonurgent questions.
- Know your IT environment. Maintain a complete database of all IT hardware, software, and user details to give help-desk agents the information to assist employees. This speeds up diagnosis of problems and improves management of software licences and updates.
- Give IT support staff remote access to servers and PCs so they can use "remote diagnostics" to provide automatic updates of applications and services and to allow monitoring and fixing of problems.
- Help users help themselves. Establish a database of useful information and FAQs (frequently asked questions) for employees so they can solve problems themselves.
- Develop a healthy communications atmosphere.
- Secure data by making firewalls a priority.
- Invest in skills. Hold frequent staff training sessions to maintain skills and learn about new technology. Investing in adequate training now will save considerable time and money later.[10]

Privacy Concerns

The very existence of huge electronic file cabinets full of personal information presents a threat to our personal privacy. Until recently, our financial, medical, tax, and other records were stored in separate computer systems. Computer networks make it easy to pool these data into data warehouses. Companies also sell the information they collect about you from sources like warranty registration cards, credit card records, registration at Web sites, and grocery store discount club cards. Telemarketers can combine data from different sources to create fairly detailed profiles of consumers.

Increasingly, consumers are fighting to regain control of personal data and how that information is used. Public outcry over a flaw in Microsoft's Windows 98 that allowed it to gather computer identification without the user's knowledge and electronic serial numbers in Intel's Pentium III chips resulted in changes to both products.

According to the Government of Canada, its Bill C-6 will establish the right of all individuals to privacy in a way that is consistent with the reasonable needs of organizations to collect, use, and disclose personal information. The intention of the bill is to protect individual rights and the privacy protection in Bill C-6 has put Canada at the forefront.[11]

The challenge to companies is to find a balance between collecting the information they need while at the same time protecting individual consumer rights. Most registration and warranty forms that ask questions about income and interests have a box for consumers to check to prevent the company from selling their names. Many companies now state their privacy policies to ensure consumers that they will not abuse the information they collect. Although supermarket chain Safeway records purchase data, it will not sell customer information to third parties like telemarketers and direct mail firms or manufacturers who want to send customers coupons. "What we're trying to assess is general shopping patterns," says Debra Lambert, Safeway's corporate director of public affairs.[12]

concept check

- Why is technology planning an essential element of information management? What are its benefits?
- Describe the different threats to data security and the ways companies can protect information from destruction and from unauthorized use.

 lg 5

controlling
The process of assessing the organization's progress toward accomplishing its goals; includes monitoring the implementation of a plan and correcting deviations from the plan.

Controlling

As discussed in Chapters 14, 15, and 16, the managerial process consists of (1) planning, (2) organizing, and (3) leading and motivating; the fourth key function that managers perform is controlling. **Controlling** is the process of assessing the organization's progress toward accomplishing its goals. It includes monitoring the implementation of a plan and correcting deviations from that plan. As Exhibit 17-5 shows, controlling can be visualized as a cyclical process made up of five stages:

1. Setting performance standards (goals).
2. Measuring performance.
3. Comparing actual performance to established performance standards.
4. Taking corrective action (if necessary).
5. Using information gained from the process to set future performance standards.

Performance standards are the levels of performance the company wants to attain. These goals are based on its strategic, tactical, and operational plans. The most effective performance standards state a measurable behavioural objective that can be achieved in a specified time frame. For example, the performance objective for the sales division of a company could be stated as "$100 000 in gross sales for the month of January." Each individual employee in that division would also have a specified performance goal. Actual firm, division, or individual performance can be measured against desired performance standards to see if a gap exists between the desired level of performance and the actual level of performance. If a performance gap does exist, the reason for it must be determined and corrective action taken.

Feedback is essential to the process of control. Most companies have a reporting system that identifies areas where performance standards are not being met. A feedback system helps managers detect problems before they get out of hand. If a problem exists, the managers take corrective action. Toyota uses a simple but effective control system on its automobile assembly lines. Each worker serves as the customer for the process just before his or hers. Each worker is empowered to act as a quality control

e x h i b i t   1 7 - 5 | How Organizations Control Activities

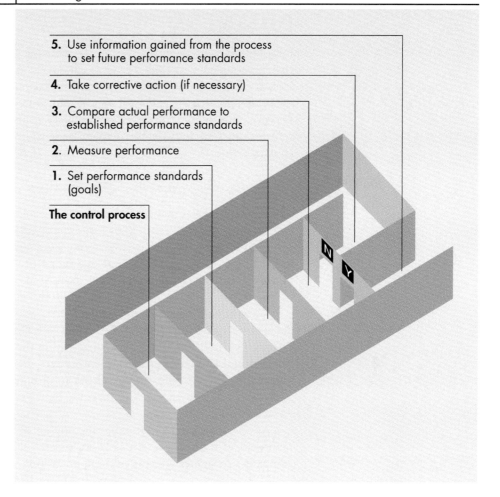

5. Use information gained from the process to set future performance standards

4. Take corrective action (if necessary)

3. Compare actual performance to established performance standards

2. Measure performance

1. Set performance standards (goals)

The control process

inspector. If a part is defective or not installed properly, the next worker won't accept it. Any worker can alert the supervisor to a problem by tugging on a rope that turns on a warning light (i.e., feedback). If the problem isn't corrected, the worker can stop the entire assembly line.

Why is controlling such an important part of a manager's job? First, it helps managers to determine the success of the other three functions: planning, organizing, and leading. Second, control systems direct employee behaviour toward achieving organizational goals. Third, control systems provide a means of coordinating employee activities and integrating resources throughout the organization.

concept check

- Describe the control process.
- Why is the control process important to the success of the organization?

➡ **lg 6**

CAPITALIZING ON TRENDS IN BUSINESS

Information technology is a continually evolving field. The fast pace and amount of change, coupled with IT's broad reach, make it especially challenging to isolate industry trends. From the time we write this chapter to the time you read it—as little as six months—new trends will appear and those that seemed important may fade. However, two trends that are reshaping the IT landscape in the first decade of the 21st century include knowledge management and the emergence of information appliances.

Managing Knowledge Resources

Although companies may have procedures to manage information, they are now tackling the more difficult task of knowledge management (KM). *Information management* involves collecting, processing, and condensing information. *Knowledge management*, however, focuses on gathering and sharing an organization's collective knowledge to improve productivity and foster innovation. Some companies are even creating a new position, chief knowledge officer, to head up this effort.

We've already seen how companies use software tools to comb through company databases seeking information. But better software is not the only answer to KM. Effective KM calls for a cultural change within the company. It's a whole new way of working and communicating that encourages departments and employees to share knowledge. This attitude can be difficult to promote among employees who are used to protecting their own turf. KM's benefits can be significant in terms of both time and money

As KM has become an important company objective, the CIO has joined the top management team. No longer is IT an isolated department focused on keeping the company's computer systems running, managing IT costs, and dealing with IT suppliers. Today the CIO and his or her team are partners in the strategic planning process. IT managers provide input on how to leverage technology to improve business processes, change the business model, and better serve customers.

End of the Personal Computer Era?

"Information appliances," easy-to-use, inexpensive, consumer-oriented products that perform only one or two tasks, may soon replace the PC as our most popular information tool. In addition to simplicity and convenience, many of these appliances use wireless technology to make computing more portable.

These devices run counter to the recent trend to make PCs increasingly complex and powerful. Though businesses may need these PCs, most personal users don't. "The PC is so general purpose that very few of us use more than 5 percent of its capability," says former Hewlett-Packard CEO Lewis Platt. And for users who only want to do one thing—access the Internet, for example—a PC is more than they need. PCs won't disappear, however. They will coexist with other alternatives, but will no longer dominate to the degree that they do now.

Like the palmtop personal digital assistant, information devices are becoming smaller, portable, and easier to use, and are emerging as convenient alternatives to personal computers.

Fuelled by such technological advances as tiny storage devices, efficient microprocessors, and wireless networks, information appliances could revolutionize the way we view computers. A wide variety of these devices are already available: palmtop personal digital assistants, handheld scanners, cell phones that send and receive e-mail, portable music players for music downloaded from the Internet, set-top TV boxes that automatically save favourite programs, and Web phones with touch-screen access. Tiny microprocessors with Internet and digital capabilities make existing products "smarter." For example, fax machines that use the Internet rather than phone lines will save transmission costs.[13]

concept check

- Differentiate between information management and knowledge management. What steps can companies take to manage knowledge?
- What benefits do information appliances offer? Do you think they will diminish the importance of PCs?

APPLYING THIS CHAPTER'S TOPICS

Computer literacy is no longer a luxury. To succeed in business today, and, it appears in our society, almost everyone must develop technological competence. Whether you have a part-time job in a fast-food restaurant that uses computerized ordering systems or perform financial analyses that guide the future of your own company, you will depend on computers. The more you increase your knowledge of technology, the more valuable you will be as an employee in today's information-driven businesses. In addition, the shortage of qualified IT personnel opens up new career avenues to those that enjoy working with technology. You can also take steps to understand and protect your privacy.

Preparation Pays Off

Whether you are an employee or a business owner, you need to be aware of how technology affects the way your firm operates. New applications can change fundamental company operations and employees' roles. For example, many companies now expect individual employees to make more strategic, far-reaching decisions than before. This requires a dramatic shift in employee's roles and the way they should view their jobs. For example, an accountant's responsibilities might now include analyzing budgets, not just auditing expenses. A salesperson's role might expand to include more strategic decision making about customer issues. Your company will see the business benefits sooner if you prepare for these changing roles. A manager should begin teaching employees operational procedures before implementing the new system and help them acquire the necessary analytical skills. As an employee, you can take the initiative to learn as much as possible about the new technology and how it operates.

Keeping Secrets

By understanding how companies collect and use information, you can protect your personal data from being mined. The first step is simply saying no. You can usually get a store's discounts and products even if you withhold some personal information. For example, you may not have to give your name when you get a supermarket card. Some stores allow you to register as an anonymous shopper. Also, have your name removed from direct market lists to curb unwanted mail and data exchange.

Next, check your credit report for unfamiliar accounts and monthly charge card statements for fraudulent charges that signal that someone may have stolen your personal information. Then contact the creditors and let them know the information is not accurate. Major credit reporting agencies must correct the information. Finally, contact the major credit reporting agencies and forbid pre-screening credit rating checks. This puts a stop to unsolicited credit card offers, which can fall into the wrong hands.[14]

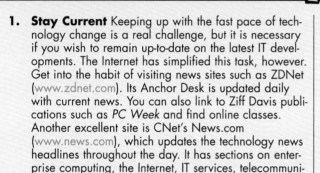

TRY IT NOW!

1. Stay Current Keeping up with the fast pace of technology change is a real challenge, but it is necessary if you wish to remain up-to-date on the latest IT developments. The Internet has simplified this task, however. Get into the habit of visiting news sites such as ZDNet (www.zdnet.com). Its Anchor Desk is updated daily with current news. You can also link to Ziff Davis publications such as *PC Week* and find online classes. Another excellent site is CNet's News.com (www.news.com), which updates the technology news headlines throughout the day. It has sections on enterprise computing, the Internet, IT services, telecommunications, and personal technology.

2. Know Who's Hiring You can benefit from the severe shortage of technology personnel—even if you don't think you want a job in IT. Read the classified employment ads in your local newspaper and the national newspapers. Go online to browse the employment ads from almost any major newspaper and surf through the Web sites with job listings. Many technology company Web sites also post job openings. Make a list of jobs that interest you. In addition, read the general job listings to see how many require computer skills.

>looking ahead

at Open Text Corporation

Open Text Corporation continues to be a world leader in the information technology industry. It is expanding its product lines and customer bases around the world in response to customers' demands and advances in technology. The company presents seminars to demonstrate its products and how they can eliminate waste, save resources, and effectively access the information that companies need to make decisions.

SUMMARY OF LEARNING GOALS

➡lg 1   **How does information play a role in decision making?**
When making decisions, managers compare information about the company's current status to its goals and standards. Some of the information is provided by information systems, which collect and process data.

➡lg 2   **Why are computer networks an important part of today's business information systems?**
Local area networks (LANs) and wide area networks (WANs) are used to link computers so they can share data and expensive hardware. Today companies use networks extensively to improve operating efficiency. Networking techniques like e-mail allow employees to communicate with each other quickly, regardless of their location.

➡lg 3   **What is the structure of a typical information system?**
An information system consists of a transaction processing system, management support systems, and an office automation system. The transaction processing system collects and organizes operational data on the firm's activities.

KEY TERMS

application software 424
batch processing 428
chief information officer (CIO) 422
computer network 425
computer virus 433
controlling 434
data 423
data warehouse 429
decision support system (DSS) 429
executive information system (EIS) 429
expert system 430
information 423
information system (IS) 423
information technology (IT) 422
intranet 426
knowledge 423
local area network (LAN) 425
management support system (MSS) 429
office automation system 430
online (real-time) processing 428
software 423
system software 424
transaction processing system (TPS) 428
wide area network (WAN) 426

Management support systems help managers make better decisions. They include an information reporting system that provides information based on the data to the managers who need it; decision support systems that use models to assist in answering "what if" types of questions; and expert systems that give managers advice similar to what they would get from a human consultant. Executive information systems are customized to the needs of top management. All employees benefit from office automation systems that facilitate communication by using word processing, e-mail, fax machines, and similar technologies.

➡ lg 4 **How can companies manage information technology to their advantage?**
To get the most value from information technology (IT), companies must go beyond simply collecting data and summarizing information. Technology planning involves evaluating the company's goals and objectives and using the right technology to reach them. Because companies are now more dependent on computers than ever before, they need to protect data and equipment from natural disasters and computer crime such as unauthorized access and use and malicious damage. They must also take steps to protect customers' personal privacy rights.

➡ lg 5 **How do organizations control activities?**
Controlling is the process of assessing the organization's progress toward accomplishing its goals. The control process is as follows: (1) set performance standards (goals), (2) measure performance, (3) compare actual performance to established performance standards, (4) take corrective action (if necessary), and (5) use information gained from the process to set future performance standards.

➡ lg 6 **What are the leading trends in information technology?**
Knowledge management focuses on sharing an organization's collective knowledge to improve productivity and foster innovation. The CIO plays a pivotal role in knowledge management. The emergence of simpler information appliances may make the PC a less important information tool. Consumers may prefer these easy-to-use devices to multifunction PCs.

WORKING THE NET

1. The size and cost of computer systems have fallen dramatically in the past few years. Visit the Web site of any of the leading manufacturers of affordable PCs. What type of PC system can you buy for $500? For $700?

2. You are in the market for a new computer system for your five-employee consulting business. Using such resources as **www.directpc.ca** or any other sites you find, conduct research on the latest hardware and software. Put together a list of your recommended purchases. Give reasons for your choices based on product reviews.

3. One of the fastest growing areas of business software is enterprise resource planning (ERP) applications. Visit the site of one of the following companies: SAP (**www.sap.com**); PeopleSoft (**www.peoplesoft.com**); Oracle (**www.oracle.com**); or Baan (**www.baan.com**). Prepare a short presentation for the class about the company's ERP product offerings and capabilities. Include examples of how companies use the ERP software.

4. The Internet has the answer to most computer equipment or software questions—from how to get your computer to stop crashing to which brand of scanner or printer is best for your system. Pick a hardware manufacturer (such as Apple, Compaq, Dell, Epson, Hewlett-Packard, or Iomega) and a software vendor (such as Microsoft, Corel, Adobe, or any other whose products you use) and check out the technical support areas of their Web sites. Start at PC Help Online

(www.pchelponline.com). This site makes it easy to link to a specific company or to find information. Summarize your findings and prepare a brief report to share with the class.

CREATIVE THINKING CASE

Information Management Challenges and Solutions at Archway Cookies

Archway Cookies (www.archwaycookies.com), a family owned business has two company-owned and four licensed bakeries in the United States and Canada, producing more than one billion cookies annually.

Founding the company in 1936, Harold and Ruth Swanson set the standard for what would become a "one-of-a-kind cookie." The Swansons baked cookies that used only the finest quality ingredients and then delivered them fresh to the stores where they were sold. "This commitment to traditional quality and guaranteed freshness is the foundation of Archway Cookies."

Archway Cookies is a bake-to-order company. With over 60 different varieties of home-style, gourmet, fat-free, sugar-free, bag, and holiday cookies, Archway is a "bake today, ship tomorrow" manufacturing operation. Cookies are ordered by distributors, baked by the company, and shipped to distributors within 48 hours.

To "bake today" and "ship tomorrow," Archway must have accurate and timely information. Prior to 1991, the company managed its information using paper-based sales and tracking systems that were introduced in the 1930s. These systems did not provide for the fastest, most effective, and most efficient flow and use of data.

Archway's management recognized the need to automate data collection, improve data flow, and create a single database. Without these information management changes, achieving the company's sales growth goals would be difficult. So in 1991 Archway Cookies began using a system of hardware and software from Intermec Technologies Corporation. Key components of the system were Intermec's Norand Base Bakery database software and Norand 4410 handheld computers.

Before 1991, distributors wrote everything down in route books, and Archway employed people to perform manual data entry. As a result, managers had difficulty understanding, comprehending, and analyzing data on a timely basis. This changed drastically when Archway supplied its distributors with the handheld computers and began using the route accounting software designed specifically for the baking industry. With the new management information system, Archway was able to track, analyze, and adjust sales to customers at the distributor level. In turn, this allowed Archway to "influence production at its two company-owned bakeries in Ashland, Ohio, and Boone, Iowa, as well as its four contract bakeries in Pennsylvania, New Jersey, Oregon, and Canada." Orders are placed by downloading information to the bakeries on a daily basis.

According to Gene H. McKay III, Archway's chief of finance and operations, the use of information technology has produced considerable benefits. He says that "implementing this technology has saved the distributors an enormous amount of time on their routes, so the distributors have additional time for call-backs and for soliciting new sales." In turn, this has contributed to a 3–4 percent sales increase for Archway every year since the system was installed. The system has also provided better information access and information sharing throughout the company.[15]

Critical Thinking Questions

1. Why is timely and accurate information essential for Archway's manufacturing operations?
2. How does Archway Cookies manage information technology to its advantage?
3. Do you think Archway Cookies would be able to achieve its sales growth goals without the use of computerized information technology?

Workplace

Canadians are finding it increasingly difficult to achieve a suitable work–life balance and the toll on physical and mental health is staggering. A lack of balance in work and life can have many negative consequences—such as increased absenteeism, increased stress, increased disability claims (stress leaves, etc.), increased benefits costs in the form of prescription drug claims (antidepressants, sleeping pills), less commitment and loyalty to the organization, and decreased job satisfaction. Without a sense of commitment and loyalty to the organization, employees are unlikely to stay if a more suitable position is found. With the anticipated shortage of skilled labour as a result of retiring baby boomers, companies need to take this problem more seriously.

In the 1980s companies started making accommodations for employees with children in an attempt to retain good workers. Company daycares were a special benefit to help address the needs of these employees. Then the downsizing of the mid-80s led to increased workloads. As job security was fast becoming uncertain, people began working longer hours in an attempt to solidify their position in the organization. With the longer hours came more pressure and stress, and one-quarter of Canadians report working more than 50 hours per week.

Are corporations aware of the problem? Apparently, many are. The Co-operators Group offers an expanded company gym and healthier food in the cafeteria, but according to Linda Duxbury, an expert on work–life balance, the core issue is the amount of work. If the human resources are the company's most valuable assets, then why are people continually expected to do more with less? Is there a way to allow a greater work–life balance but still meet the goals of the company and its need for "intellectual horsepower"?

Critical Thinking Questions

1. How might organizations allow employees to gain a greater work–life balance and yet still meet the goals and objectives of their employer?
2. Would the use of flexible work schedules help?
3. What would be the effect on the motivation of the work force? Use a motivation theory to support your answer.

Nova Scotian Crystal

Nova Scotian Crystal produces mouth-blown, hand-cut glassware available through e-mail (**www.novascotiancrystal.com**), phone order, or regular mail order. Each piece is unique and is crafted using traditional tools and techniques—very unusual in this day of machine manufacturing. The owners are a bit unusual too. Denis Ryan and Rod McCulloch are described as another version of the "odd couple." Denis, the chairman of the board, is the impulsive Irish musician, and Rod, the president, is a forensic accountant. Their leadership and decision-making styles are very different, but are they complementary? Denis had an impulse to make hand-blown crystal in Nova Scotia and jumped in with both feet, forgetting that they also had to sell the product not just make it. With his focus on the manufacturing aspect, and acting on pure impulse, he convinced experienced craftsmen to move to Nova Scotia from Ireland and, as he says, "blew $300 000 in the first year." He then hired his neighbour, Rod, to help sort things out.

Rod put his analytical skills to work in an attempt to increase sales and iron out production problems. With the owners both investing heavily in the business, they felt it was time to access some outside capital. But, who should approach the potential investors? Given their different styles, there was some debate as to who would be most successful relieving people of their investment dollars. Would it be the facts-in-hand analytical accountant or the fast-talking enthusiastic Irishman? In the end, they decided that they would both seek the required funds. With Rod mulling over cash flows and Denis suggesting they open a shop in Toronto, the "spend versus analyze" philosophies continued to confront each other.

The biggest problem seemed to be the inability to increase sales to a level that would generate a reasonable profit. Through Rod's careful number-crunching and Denis's never-ending flood of "wacko" ideas, they have managed to make a reasonable profit and continue to promote the passion of crystal making.

Critical Thinking Questions
1. What managerial skills are exhibited by Denis and Rod?
2. How important is planning in a small business such as Nova Scotian Crystal?
3. Using the PEST model, explain what environmental factors could have an impact on the business?
4. What would be a possible mission statement for Nova Scotian Crystal?

CONCLUSION

BRINGING IT ALL TOGETHER WITH BOB CHANNING, STORE MANAGER, THE BAY

Throughout this textbook, the authors have attempted to integrate the material for the student to illustrate how all the functional areas of business (Chapters 8, 9, 10, 11, 12, and 13), the management processes (Chapters 14, 15, 16, and 17), and Canadian peculiarities (Chapters 5, 6, and 7) all fit together within the PEST model (Chapters 1, 2, 3, and 4) to make a fully functioning whole. Our final goal is to bring all this to life through an interview with a lifelong Bay employee who is now a store manager in Banff, Alberta. Bob Channing has been with the Bay for 34 years. He started as a stock boy in a warehouse in Winnipeg and has worked in stores in Manitoba, Saskatchewan, and Alberta in various capacities. The following interview is the real life integration of the material presented in this book.

Shirley Rose: Can you explain for the students how a knowledge of the business environment, i.e., political, economic, social, and technological (the PEST model), can contribute to business success?

Bob Channing: First of all, it isn't the knowledge of these things, but an *understanding* of them that is necessary. Students often come out of business programs with a vast amount of book knowledge but very little *understanding* of the principles they have learned. To truly understand your PEST model, the students must accept that everything is interconnected and that what happens in one part of the world affects events and people in other parts of the world. For example, look at the mad cow thing [in May of 2003]. One sick cow in Saskatchewan, over 1000 miles from here, has impacted our business in Banff hugely. The Americans shut off the beef trade due to pressure from the Japanese. If the U.S. continues to import our beef, the Japanese will refuse *all* U.S. beef exports and cripple the U.S. beef industry as well. The Japanese perception is that all Canadian beef is dangerous and that all our beef is unfit for human consumption. Add to that the SARS problem in Toronto and West Nile virus and your average Japanese tourist isn't going to come to Canada no matter what incentives we offer. The war in the Middle East has led to fewer Europeans travelling. The Bay store in Banff caters mainly to the tourist trade; hence, our sales are way down. Was there anything we could have done about this? No, of course not, but now we have to deal with it.

From an economic perspective, a change in the interest rates set by the Bank of Canada can have a huge impact on the ability of a business to borrow money. Every business needs to borrow money at some point in order to maintain their level of customer service. The technology today allows us to have instant access to information. This impacts our ability to make informed decisions. In retail, you have to look at the demographics of your area to know what products to offer. In our store the souvenir department is the largest and this is a

function of our location. However, we can't neglect the year-round residents. We must understand what socioeconomic area we are operating in and provide products accordingly. I could go on and on …

Shirley: OK, so given the students have an understanding of the business environment, how do the functional areas tie in to it all?

Bob: Well, of course, an understanding of accounting is critical. You have to know if you're making money or not. But back to your integration of material, for a business to be successful you must have an understanding of the complexity and interdependency of all facets of the business. A change in direction in the marketing area impacts all the other functional areas: accounting, finance, HR. It's all about partnerships, whether it's partnerships with suppliers, partnerships with your employees, partnerships with lenders, etc. If we look at marketing for a minute, my personal favourite given that I am in retail, you have 10–15 seconds to get the customer's attention. Presentation of merchandise is critical. It tells the customer how much you care about the product, about the store, and about them. And advertising creates the perception of who you are. Promotions and products have to be geared to certain socioeconomic areas. For example, in all provinces except Alberta, offering a "Save the GST/PST or HST" promo is a huge success. In Alberta, since there is no sales tax, we offer a "Save double the GST" promo. People love it. The perception is that they are beating the government. Offering a 20-percent-off sale is nowhere near as effective, even though you are offering the same savings. When selecting your product line, you need to know who's out there. You need to be part of the community and listen to your customers.

Shirley: In managing a store such as the Bay, what is important to remember?

Bob: I feel the most important thing is to recognize that your people are an investment. You must treat them as someone who is valued and respected. You need to hire the right people. You need people who are passionate about what they do, who are motivated, and who buy in to your vision. As a leader you must be able to communicate this vision to them and gain their commitment to it. The right people are also those who can change, adjust, and adapt to their environment. There can be some hard decisions involved here because not all *good* people are the *right* people. The days of the manager walking around the store cracking the whip are over. The days of operating a successful business by demanding things from people are long gone. Your people are the ones who deal directly with the customer and they are the most important. The guy up in the office can be replaced tomorrow. Management must accept responsibility if something goes wrong but give credit when things go well. The goal is to hire the right people, give them the tools to do their job, challenge them, and reward them.

Shirley: Any final words of wisdom?

Bob: *Everyone* in your organization is important. The guy who mops the floor and cleans the washrooms is very important. Customers form a perception of your business from things such as a shoddy cleaning job. That says to the customer that you don't care … about the floor, about the store, about the products, about them. Nothing stands alone, everything is interrelated, from the cleaning guy, to mad cow disease, to war in the Middle East, to a drop in the interest rate, to child labour in Indonesia. It's all about learning what we need to do to make things work and respecting everything and everybody along the way.

APPENDIX A

BUSINESS RESEARCH, REPORTS, EXECUTIVE SUMMARIES, AND PRESENTATIONS

For many students, their first job after graduation involves performing research and eventually preparing and presenting business reports. The following is a short-cut guide to help in the preparation of a formal business report and some pointers on presentations.

This is not a comprehensive guide, but it does give the reader some simple rules to follow. Typically, organizations have their own preferred format for reports, so this is only intended as a guide.

Business Research

The two generally accepted forms of business research are qualitative and quantitative. *Qualitative research* involves descriptive reporting of information. Common methods of collecting this information are by observing, interviewing, and focus groups. *Quantitative research*, on the other hand, involves the collection of numerical data for analysis. This is often accomplished with surveys, experiments, or content analysis.

Care must be taken when using qualitative research because the quality of the information is only as good as the researcher's ability to "read the situation" and is subjective as to the interpretations of reality. At the same time, the validity of the quantitative research can be heavily biased without anyone knowing it.

The two principal methods of collecting information for business reports are primary research and secondary research. *Primary research* involves conducting original research. This is usually only undertaken when secondary research is not available. *Secondary research* is information that has been compiled by someone else, and others use this information to analyze the situation.

We must be concerned with gathering relevant and accurate data from both internal and external sources. Internal sources include company records, reports, managers, and so on. Stakeholders (e.g., customers, suppliers, etc.) are examples of external sources.

We must consider what method of collecting information to use and the type of research to analyze. This will depend on many factors, including time, money, concern for validity, and so on. The general rule is that we should use proven methods until they prove to be unreliable or outdated.

Business Reports

Components of typical business report are:
1. Title page
2. Table of contents
3. Executive summary
4. Report
5. Appendices
6. Works cited/bibliography/references

Title Page

The title page is intended to communicate the following information to the reader:

1. Name of the report (this should represent the nature and purpose).
2. Who the report is presented to (including name, title, and organization).
3. The name of the person who is submitting the report.
4. Date of submission.

Formatting of the title page will depend on the expectations of the organization that requests the report. Generally, at a minimum the above information must be included. Exhibit A-1 is an example of a typical title page.

E x h i b i t   A - 1 | Example of a Business Report Title Page

Example of a Business Report Title Page

ANALYSIS OF THE RECRUITING PROGRAM

Presented to

Michelle Sales
Director of Admissions
Bissett School of Business
Mount Royal College

Prepared by

Shabira Warmington
Business Senator
Office of Associated Students

September 15th, 2004

Arrange title in all caps with longer line above shorter line (inverted pyramid styles); use larger font size and bold if desired

Highlights name and title of report recipient

Identifies name and title of report writer

Omits page number

The title page is arranged so that the amount of space above the title is equal to the space below the date. If a report is to be bound on the left, move the left margin and centre point 1/4 inch to the right. Notice that no page number appears on the title page, although it is counted as page one.

If you use scalable fonts, word processing capability, or a laser printer to enhance your report and title page, be careful to avoid anything unprofessional (such as too many type fonts, oversized print, and inappropriate graphics).

Table of Contents

The purpose of the table of contents is to provide the reader with an overview of the report topics and to help the reader to locate the topic. The listings in the table of contents are usually the headings that are used in the report and their initial page numbers (i.e., their starting page number). It is important that the table of contents is prepared after the report is prepared; otherwise, mistakes are probable.

Executive Summary

An executive summary highlights the report's findings, conclusions, and recommendations. It is a condensed version of the report. It is important that the executive summary is labelled as such (i.e., Executive Summary) so that the reader can identify it.

The executive summary is a stand-alone document (i.e., the reader may never read the actual report); therefore, you must include what you did, how you went about doing it, what you found out (with enough support), and your conclusions and recommendations.

The components of the executive summary include the objectives/purposes of the report, a review of the points to follow, methodology (how the research and analysis was completed), the main points of the report with support, and conclusions/recommendations.

Generally, the length is anywhere from one paragraph to two pages in length. A helpful hint when writing the executive summary is to use your table of contents as a guide to ensure that you have covered the major points of the report. The executive summary process is as follows:

- Scan the report.
- Highlight the objectives/purposes.
- Look for key ideas.
- Group similar ideas.
- Eliminate secondary points.

Report

Business reports typically have an introduction to the report, the body of the report, conclusions, and recommendations.

Introduction

The introduction of the report sets the scene for the report to follow. It should include:

- *Background*—events leading up to the problem or need.
- *Problem or purpose*—explains what the report topic is.
- *Significance*—explains why the topic important.
- *Scope*—tells what is included and what is excluded in the report.
- *Organization*—previews the structure of the report.
- *Methodology*—describes secondary sources and details how primary data were collected.

Body of the Report

The body of the report is the principal section of the report. The purpose is to discuss, analyze, interpret, and evaluate the research findings or solutions. It is best to use clear headings for each major section—to help the reader to navigate through the report.

It is important to use your words economically; do not repeat yourself except for emphasis, and do not pad the report with words that do not contribute to your message (e.g., instead of "in order to be able to provide…" use "to provide…"). Other hints for the body of the report are to be consistent with the name or acronym you choose to refer to the target of your investigation, use it throughout the report (i.e., do not use variations), and keep the person and tense consistent (e.g., if the subject is "the company" then the subsequent pronoun should be "it" not "they").

Conclusions

The conclusions tell what the findings mean. This must be tied to the discussion within the body of the report (i.e., do not make conclusions that are not discussed in the report). The conclusions are often combined with the recommendations.

Recommendations

When requested, the recommendations give precise suggestions of different courses of action and their justifications. The writers of the report must use appropriate language (e.g., "The following recommendations are supported by the findings and conclusion of this report.").

Appendices

Appendices are used for incidental or supporting materials that are relevant to the findings of the report and important to some readers but not necessarily to all. Using appendices helps send the message that you have done a thorough job.

Use appendices to expand, highlight, and detail, but do not repeat what you have said in the report. Label the appendices Appendix A, Appendix B, and so on. The order of the appendices should coincide with the order they are mentioned in the report.

References

The purpose of the references is to help the reader to locate the sources of ideas of the report and to give acknowledgement to the originator of the materials or ideas. If you are using information that is not widely known, cite it. Use "*Ibid.*" to repeat a citation on the same page.

Generally, in the social sciences and business, the APA (American Psychological Association) format is used for citing the sources of ideas mentioned in the report. The other two main formats are the Modern Language Association (MLA), used in language papers, and the Science format, used in the sciences and medicine. Regardless of the citing style used, you must include the author, title, publication, date of publication, page number(s), and other significant data for all ideas and quotes that are not your original thought or common understanding.

Whenever you are unsure of the format, check the Web site of Dartmouth College for examples at **www.dartmouth.edu/~sources/about/when.html**.

Below are some examples of proper citation.

Guide to Bibliographies and Reference Notes

Referencing is an integral part of your work term report. Any material that you use that is not your original thought or common knowledge must be referenced. Remember to reference interviews, company publications, Web sites, and CD-ROMS.

The following examples of referencing are taken from the *Publication Manual of the American Psychological Association.*[1] This manual contains over 70 examples of how to reference material from journal articles, CD-ROMS, proceedings of meetings, television broadcasts, and other sources.

Remember that reference style is not as important as actually referencing. Regardless of the citation method used, you must be consistent.

Bibliography

All of the material that you used in your report, whether cited in the text or not, must be listed in the bibliography. Following are examples of bibliographic citation for various media.

BOOKS

Mitchell, T.R. & Larson, J.R. (1987). People in organizations: an introduction to organization behavior. New York: McGraw-Hill.

JOURNAL ARTICLES

Brown, S. (1990). The wheel of retailing: past and future. *Journal of Retailing, 45* (2), 143–147.

MAGAZINE ARTICLES

Serwer, A.E. (1994, October 17). McDonald's conquers the world. *Fortune*, 103–106.

NEWSPAPER OR NEWSLETTER ARTICLES (AUTHOR UNKNOWN)

Partnerships for the commercialization of technology. (1997, Summer). *Network*, p. 1.

NEWSPAPER OR NEWSLETTER ARTICLES (AUTHOR KNOWN)

Howes, C. (1997, January 25). Jobs: but nobody to fill them? *The Calgary Herald*, p. H1.

WEB SITES AND OTHER ELECTRONIC DATA SOURCES

List the author, full title of the document, title of the complete work, date of publication, full http address (URL), and date of visit:

> Burka, L.P. 1993. "A Hypertext History of Multi-User Dimensions." *MUD History*. <http://www.ccs.neu.edu/home/lpb/mud-history.html> (5 Dec. 1994).

Remember that anybody can create a Web page on anything. Web site information has generally *not* undergone any scrutiny whatsoever to ensure its accuracy.

Reference Notes

Any direct quote, reference to a specific fact (event, date, etc.), or paraphrasing of an argument made by the author of a published work should be referenced. This can be done by means of traditional footnotes or endnotes, but an easier and more contemporary method is to put the author, date, and page number(s) in brackets, as in the following example:

> Scotiabank is said to have opened branches in many countries because "the depth and experience of the international staff enabled the branch to make money in countries where its competitors could not" (Cleveland and Huertas, 2004: 263).

Any direct quote must also be enclosed in quotation marks—if you fail to do this, it is plagiarism even if you provide a reference!

Newspaper references can be cited as follows:

> (*Globe and Mail*, July 9, 1990: B5)

Web sites can be cited by providing the author and the URL of the exact page where you found the information (not just the home page). For example:

> http://www.haskayne.ucalgary.ca/coop/coop_handbook.html

Be sure to include all referenced works in your bibliography. You must have both reference notes and a bibliography. Most students don't reference everything they should. If in doubt, reference it.

Plagiarism and How to Avoid It

Below is an extract from *Struggle for South Africa: A Guide to Movements, Organisations and Institutions* by R. Davies, D. O'Meara, and S. Dlamini.[2] It is followed by an *unacceptable* rendering found in a recent student paper, and then by two versions that make it acceptable through (1) use of quotation marks and (2) paraphrasing.

The original source material is as follows:

"Whites, or more especially the Afrikaans-speaking section of the white population, popularly known as the Boers, are presumed to suffer from intense racial prejudice, and this system of racial discrimination is the result. It is certainly true that most whites are highly racially prejudiced, but this explains little. [...]

In other words, the various complex and intersecting class struggles through which capitalist forms of production and relations of production were developed and consolidated under colonialism in South Africa, themselves generated racist ideologies and a racially structured hierarchy of economic and political power. The national oppression of black people in South Africa is a product of, and was indeed the necessary historical condition for, the development of capitalism in that country.

[...] Fundamentally it, like the segregationist policies which preceded it, is a system of economic and political relations designed to produce cheap and controlled black labour, and so generate high rates of profit" (Davies, O'Meara, and Dlamini, 1984, p. 2).

The following is an unacceptable rendering in student paper (plagiarism). Note that the student did not use quotation marks.

It is certainly true that whites, or more especially the Afrikaans-speaking section of the white population, popularly known as the Boers, are highly racially prejudiced. However, the various complex and intersecting class struggles developed and consolidated under colonialism in South Africa, themselves generated racist ideologies and a racially structured hierarchy of economic and political power. The national oppression of blacks in South Africa is a product of, and was a necessary historical condition for, the development of capitalism in that country.

Fundamentally, apartheid is a segregationist policy—a system of economic and political relations designed to produce cheap and controlled black labour, and generate high rates of profit.

[Another paragraph followed that ended with a bracketed reference to the source.]

Here is an acceptable rendering using quotation marks:

As Davies, O'Meara and Dlamini (1984) observe, "whites, or more especially the Afrikaans-speaking section of the white population, popularly known as the Boers... are highly racially prejudiced." However, they maintain that "the various complex and intersecting class struggles developed and consolidated under colonialism in South Africa, themselves generated racist ideologies and a racially structured hierarchy of economic and political power. The national oppression of black people in South Africa is a product of, and was a necessary historical condition for, the development of capitalism in that country." They therefore conclude that fundamentally, apartheid, like earlier similar policies, is "a system of economic and political relations designed to produce cheap and controlled black labour, and so generate high rates of profit" (p. 2).

Here is another acceptable rendering of the same material. This time, the student has used paraphrasing.

> Many South African whites, particularly Afrikaners, are very racially prejudiced. Marxist observers such as Davies, O'Meara, and Dlamini (1984, p. 2) explain this racism as being rooted in a struggle between social classes in which blacks were subjugated to a white power structure to provide a ready supply of cheap labour. Apartheid was thus a means of earning large profits and thereby strengthening the development of capitalism in the country, and not simply an outgrowth of racial prejudice.

It is *not acceptable* simply to take sections (even sentence fragments) from an original text and splice them together to write your paper. If you are using phrases from an original work, they must be put in quotation marks and footnoted. Note that of the two alternatives given above, the paraphrased version would generally be considered preferable because it is shorter, omits jargon (which many readers may not understand), and shows that the writer has understood the gist of the original source, and is not simply parroting the material.

Presentations[3]

Below are some helpful hints to ensure successful presentations:

1. Have an *introduction to the presentation* that tells the audience what will be discussed and in what order.
2. Process for the presentation: tell your audience what you are going to tell them, tell them, then tell them what you told them (i.e., provide an introduction, presentation, and summary).
3. Use an appropriate colour scheme (e.g., do not use a yellow background).
4. Use bullets consistently.
5. Check spelling and grammar.
6. Prepare backups. Things happen (e.g., incompatible technology, etc.)!
7. Dress conservatively. The focus should be on the presentation, not how you are dressed.
8. Remove jewellery that could make noise or could get caught. Also, there is a tendency for presenters to play with their jewellery; this is distracting.
9. Empty your pockets.
10. Secure long hair
11. Go to the washroom prior to the presentation—it is an opportunity to check your appearance.
12. Use presentation notes for reference only. Please do not read them—you must address your audience.
13. Use index cards for notes, not bigger sheets of paper (they are noisy and will shake if you're nervous).
14. Don't hide your notes, if you are using them—they are, what they are!
15. Look at an audience member who appears friendly and supportive if you are nervous during the presentation.
16. Scan your audience to include everyone. Do not focus on one part of the room—look around.
17. Do not read from the slides on the computer or the screen. You must address your audience to show them respect and to retain their interest.
18. Keep your hands out of your pockets and do not fold your arms. Other mannerisms to avoid include jingling your keys/coins, swaying back and forth, rubbing your nose, and so forth—these can be very distracting.

19. Do not chew gum or anything else during your presentation. It interferes with your ability to deliver the presentation in a clear voice.
20. Be sure to keep to the time limit.
21. Make sure that you and (if applicable) your group have rehearsed the presentation—rehearsing helps in meeting the time limit.
22. Have a backup plan prepared for your presentation, both in regard to the visuals (e.g., in case the technology fails you) and the actual presenters (e.g., if a presenter does not show).
23. Do not walk in front of a presenter.
24. Make sure that your audience can read the slides. The font size must be large enough for everyone in the audience to read comfortably.
25. Check the design template for your slides. Make sure that the slides enhance the presentation and are not the presentation, or do not interfere with the message that you are trying to project.
26. Be sure to project your voice—everyone in the audience needs to be informed.
27. Use an open hand to gesture—do not point.
28. Be yourself!

GLOSSARY

A

absolute advantage The situation when a country can produce and sell a product at a lower cost than any other country or when it is the only country that can provide the product.

accounting The process of collecting, recording, classifying, summarizing, reporting, and analyzing financial activities.

accounts payable Purchase for which a buyer has not yet paid the seller.

accounts receivable Sales for which a firm has not yet been paid.

acid-test (quick) ratio The ratio of total current assets excluding inventory to total current liabilities; used to measure a firm's liquidity.

acquisition The purchase of a corporation by another corporation or by an investor group; the identity of the acquired company may be lost.

activity ratios Ratios that measure how well a firm uses its assets.

administrative law The rules, regulations, and orders passed by boards, commissions, and agencies of government (municipal, provincial, and federal).

advertising Any paid form of nonpersonal presentation by an identified sponsor.

advertising agencies Companies that help create ads and place them in the proper media.

advertising media The channels through which advertising is carried to prospective customers; includes newspapers, magazines, radio, television, outdoor advertising, direct mail, and the Internet.

advocacy advertising Advertising that takes a stand on a social or economic issue; also called *grassroots lobbying*.

agents Sales representatives of manufacturers and wholesalers.

angel investors Individual investors or groups of experienced investors who provide funding for start-up businesses.

annual report A yearly document that describes a firm's financial status and usually discusses the firm's activities during the past year and its prospects for the future.

application software Software that is *applied* to a real-world task; used to perform a specific task or to solve a particular problem.

apprenticeship A form of on-the-job training that combines specific job instruction with classroom instruction.

arbitration A method of settling disputes in which the parties agree to present their case to an impartial third party and are required to accept the arbitrator's decision.

assembly process A transformation process in which the basic inputs are either combined to create the output or transformed into the output.

assets Possessions of value owned by a firm.

audience selectivity An advertising medium's ability to reach a precisely defined market.

auditing The process of reviewing the records used to prepare financial statements and issuing a formal auditor's opinion indicating whether the statements have been prepared in accordance with accepted accounting rules.

authority Legitimate power, granted by the organization and acknowledged by employees, that allows an individual to request action and expect compliance.

autocratic leaders Directive leaders who prefer to make decisions and solve problems on their own with little input from subordinates.

B

baby boomers People born between the late 1940s (after World War II) and the mid-1960s.

balance of payments A summary of a country's international financial transactions showing the difference between the country's total payments to and its total receipts from other countries.

balance of trade The differences between the value of a country's exports and the value of its imports during a certain time.

balance sheet A financial statement that summarizes a firm's financial position at a specific point in time; also known as the *statement of financial position*.

Bank of Canada Canada's central bank whose objective is to "promote the economic and financial well-being of Canada."

bankruptcy The legal procedure by which individuals or businesses that cannot meet their financial obligations are relieved of some, if not all, of their debt.

barriers to entry Factors, such as technological or legal conditions, that prevent new firms from competing equally with a monopoly.

batch processing A method of updating a database in which data are collected over some time period and then processed together.

bear markets Markets in which securities prices are falling.

benefit segmentation The differentiation of markets based on what a product will do rather than on customer characteristics.

bill of material A list of the items and the number of each required to make a given product.

board of directors A group of people elected by the shareholders to handle the overall management of a corporation, such as setting corporate goals and policies, hiring corporate officers, and overseeing the firm's operations and finances.

bonds Securities that represent long-term debt obligations (liabilities) issued by corporations and governments.

brainstorming A method of generating ideas in which group members suggest as many possibilities as they can without criticizing or evaluating any of the suggestions.

brand equity The value of company and brand names.

brand loyalty A consumer's preference for a particular brand.

brand A company's product identifier that distinguishes the company's products from those of competitors.

breach of contract The failure by one party to a contract to fulfill the terms of the agreement without a legal excuse.

breakeven point The price at which a product's costs are covered, so additional sales result in profit.

breaking bulk The process of breaking large shipments of similar products into smaller, more usable lots.

brokers Go-betweens that bring buyers and sellers together.

browser Software that allows users to access the Web with a graphical point-and-click interface.

budgets Formal written forecasts of revenues and expenses that set spending limits based on operational forecasts; include cash budgets, capital budgets, and operating budgets.

bull markets Markets in which securities prices are rising.

business cycles Upward and downward changes in the level of economic activity.

Business Development Bank of Canada (BDC) Bank that provides small and medium-sized businesses with flexible financing, affordable consulting services, and venture capital.

business law The body of law that governs commercial dealings.

business plan A formal written statement that describes in detail the idea for a new business and how it will be carried out; includes a general description of the company, the qualifications of the owner(s), a description of the product or service, an analysis of the market, and a financial plan.

business-to-business (B2B) e-commerce Electronic commerce that involves transactions between companies.

business-to-consumer (B2C) e-commerce Electronic commerce that involves transactions between businesses and the end user of the goods or services; also called *e-tailing*.

business-to-enterprise (B2E) Electronic collecting, storing, updating, and using of information within the business.

buyer behaviour The actions people take in buying and using goods and services.

C

Canadian Charter of Rights and Freedoms Legislation that guarantees the rights and freedoms of Canadians.

capital budgeting The process of analyzing long-term projects and selecting those that offer the best returns while maximizing the firm's value.

capital budgets Budgets that forecast a firm's outlays for fixed assets (plant and equipment), typically for a period of several years.

capital expenditures Investments in long-lived assets, such as land, buildings, machinery, and equipment, that are expected to provide benefits over a period longer than one year.

capital products Large, expensive items with a long life span that are purchased by businesses for use in making other products or providing a service.

cartel An agreement between enterprises to lessen competition.

cash budgets Budgets that forecast a firm's cash inflows and outflows and help the firm plan for cash surpluses and shortages.

cash flows The inflow and outflow of cash for a firm.

cash management The process of making sure that a firm has enough cash on hand to pay bills as they come due and to meet unexpected expenses.

centralization The degree to which formal authority is concentrated in one area or level of an organization.

certified general accountant (CGA) An accountant that focuses primarily on external financial reporting.

certified management accountant (CMA) An accountant that works primarily in industry and focuses on internal management accounting.

chain of command The line of authority that extends from one level of an organization's hierarchy to the next, from top to bottom, and makes clear who reports to whom.

chartered accountant (CA) An accountant who has completed an approved bachelor's degree program, completed an educational program, and passed a comprehensive examination. Only a CA can issue an auditor's opinion on a firm's financial statements.

chief information officer (CIO) An executive with responsibility for managing all information resources in an organization.

circular flow The movement of inputs and outputs among households, businesses, and governments; a way of showing how the sectors of the economy interact.

civil code A body of written law that sets out the private rights of the citizens.

code of ethics A set of guidelines prepared by a firm to provide its employees with the knowledge of what the firm expects in terms of their responsibilities and behaviour toward fellow employees, customers, and suppliers.

coercive power Power that is derived from an individual's ability to threaten negative outcomes.

command economy An economic system characterized by government ownership of virtually all resources and economic decision making by central government planning; also known as a *planned economy*.

commercial paper Unsecured short-term debt (an IOU) issued by a financially strong corporation.

committee structure An organizational structure in which authority and responsibility are held by a group rather than an individual.

common law The body of unwritten law that has evolved out of judicial (court) decisions rather than being enacted by a legislature; also called *case law*.

common shares Securities that represent one form of ownership interest in a corporation.

comparative advertising Advertising that compares the company's product with competing, named products.

competitive advantage A set of unique features of a company and its products that are perceived by the target market as significant and superior to those of the competition; also called *differential advantage*.

component lifestyle A lifestyle made up of a complex set of interests and choices.

computer network A group of two or more computer systems linked together by communications channels to share data and information.

computer virus A computer program that copies itself into other software and can spread to other computer systems.

conceptual skills A manager's ability to view the organization as a whole, understand how the various parts are interdependent, and assess how the organization relates to its external environment.

conglomerate merger A merger of companies in unrelated businesses; done to reduce risk.

consensual leaders Leaders who encourage discussion about issues and then require that all parties involved agree to the final decision.

consultative leaders Leaders who confer with subordinates before making a decision, but who retain the final decision-making authority.

consumer fraud The practice of deceiving customers by such means as failing to honour warranties or other promises or selling goods or services that do not meet advertised claims.

consumer price index (CPI) A measure of retail price movements that compares a representative "shopping basket" of goods and services.

consumerism A movement that seeks to increase the rights and powers of buyers vis-à-vis sellers.

consumer-to-business (C2B) e-commerce Electronic commerce that involves transactions between consumers and businesses initiated by the consumer.

consumer-to-consumer (C2C) e-commerce Electronic commerce that involves transactions between consumers.

contingency plans Plans that identify alternative courses of action for very unusual or crisis situations; typically stipulate the chain of command, standard operating procedures, and communication channels the organization will use during an emergency.

contingent workers Persons who prefer temporary employment, either part-time or full-time.

contract manufacturing The practice in which a foreign firm manufacturers private-label goods under a domestic firm's brand name.

contract An agreement that sets for the relationship between parties regarding the performance of a specified action; creates a legal obligation and is enforceable in a court of law.

contractionary policy The use of monetary policy by the Bank of Canada to tighten the money supply by selling government securities or raising interest rates.

controlling The process of assessing the organization's progress toward accomplishing its goals; includes monitoring the implementation of a plan and correcting deviations from the plan.

convenience products Relatively inexpensive items that require little shopping effort and are purchased routinely without planning.

conventional ethics The second stage in the ethical development of individuals in which people move from an egocentric viewpoint to consider the expectations of an organization of society; also known as social ethics.

convertible bonds Corporate bonds that are issued with an option that allows the bondholder to convert them into common shares.

cooperatives Legal entities typically formed by people with similar interests, such as customers or suppliers, to reduce costs and gain economic power. A cooperative has limited liability, an unlimited life span, an elected board of directors, and an administrative staff; all profits are distributed to the member-owners in proportion to their contributions.

copyright A form of protection established by the government for creators of works of art, music, literature, or other intellectual property; gives the creator the exclusive right to use, produce, and sell the creation during the lifetime of the creator and for 50 years thereafter.

corporate culture The set of attitudes, values, and standards of behaviour that distinguishes one organization from another.

corporate governance The way in which an organization is being governed, directed, and administered.

corporate philanthropy The practice of charitable giving by corporations; includes contributing cash, donating equipment and products, and supporting the volunteer efforts of company employees.

corporation A legal entity with an existence and life separate from its owners, who therefore are not personally liable for the entity's debts. A corporation has many of the same legal rights and responsibilities as that of a person: it can own property, enter into contracts, sue and be sued, and engage in business operations.

cost competitive advantage A firm's ability to produce a product or service at a lower cost than all other competitors in an industry while maintaining satisfactory profit margins.

cost of goods sold The total expense of buying or producing a firm's goods or services.

cost-push inflation Inflation that occurs when increases in production costs push up the prices of final goods and services.

critical path method (CPM) A scheduling tool that enables a manager to determine the critical path of activities for a project—the activities that will cause the entire project to fall behind schedule if they are not completed on time.

critical path In a critical path method network, the longest path through the linked activities.

cross-functional teams Teams of employees who are from about the same level in the organizational hierarchy but from different functional areas; for example, task forces, organizational committees, and project teams.

Crown corporations Companies that only the provincial and federal government can set up.

current assets Assets that can or will be converted to cash within the next 12 months (within the next fiscal year).

current liabilities Short-term claims that are due within a year of the date of the balance sheet.

current ratio The ratio of total current assets to total current liabilities; used to measure a firm's liquidity.

custom regulations Regulations on products that are different from generally accepted international standards.

customer departmentalization Departmentalization that is based on the primary type of customer served by the organizational unit.

customer satisfaction The customer's feeling that a product has met or exceeded expectations.

customer value (in economics) The customer's perception of the ratio of benefits (functionality, performance, durability, design, ease of use, and serviceability) to the sacrifice (of money, time, and effort) necessary to obtain those benefits.

customer value (in marketing) The ratio of benefits to the sacrifice necessary to obtain those benefits, as determined by the customer; reflects the willingness of customers to actually buy a product.

customization The production of goods or services one at a time according to the specific needs or wants of individual customers.

cyclical unemployment Unemployment that occurs when a downturn in the business cycle reduces the demand for labour throughout the economy.

D

data The many facts that together describe a company's status and/or its environment.

database marketing The creation of a large computerized file of the profiles and purchase patterns of customers and potential customers, usually required for successful micromarketing.

data warehouse An information technology that combines many databases across a whole company into one central database that supports management decision making.

debentures Unsecured bonds that are backed only by the reputation of the issuer and its promise to pay the principal and interest when due.

debt ratios Ratios that measure the degree and effect of a firm's use of borrowed funds (debt) to finance its operations.

debt A form of business financing consisting of borrowed funds that must be repaid with interest over a stated time period.

debt-to-equity ratio The ratio of total liabilities to owners' equity; measures the relationship between the amount of debt financing and the amount of equity financing.

decentralization The process of pushing decision-making authority down the organizational hierarchy.

decision support system (DSS) An interactive, flexible, computerized information system that allows managers to make decisions quickly and accurately; used to conduct sales analyses, forecast sales, evaluate advertising, analyze product lines, and keep tabs on market trends and competitors' actions.

decisional roles A manager's activities as an entrepreneur, resource allocator, conflict resolver, or negotiator.

delegation of authority The assignment of some degree of authority and responsibility to persons lower in the chain of command.

demand The quantity of a good or service that people are willing to buy at various prices.

demand curve A graph showing the quantity of a good or service that people are willing to buy at various prices.

demand-pull inflation Inflation that occurs when the demand for goods and services is greater than the supply.

democratic leaders Leaders who solicit input from all members of the group and then allow the members to make the final decision through a vote.

demographic segmentation The differentiation of markets through the use of categories such as age, education, gender, income, and household size.

demography The study of people's vital statistics, such as their age, race and ethnicity, and location.

demotion The downgrading or reassignment of an employee to a position with less responsibility.

departmentalization The process of grouping jobs together so that similar or associated tasks and activities can be coordinated.

depreciation The allocation of an asset's original cost to the years in which it is expected to produce revenues; also referred to as *amortization*.

deregulation The removal or rules and regulations governing business competition.

differential advantage A set of unique features of a product that the target market perceives as important and better than the competition's features.

differential competitive advantage A firm's ability to provide a unique product or service that offers something of value to buyers besides simply a lower price.

direct foreign investment Active ownership of a foreign company or of manufacturing or marketing facilities in a foreign country.

distribution centres Warehouses that specialize in changing shipment sizes, rather than in storing goods.

distribution channel The series of marketing entities through which goods and services pass on their way from producers to end users.

distribution strategy The part of the marketing mix that involves deciding how many stores and which specific wholesalers and retailers will handle the product in a geographic area.

diversity Employee differences in age, race and ethnicity, gender, educational background, and work experience.

dividends Payments to shareholders from a corporation's profits.

division of labour The process of dividing work into separate jobs and assigning tasks to workers.

double-entry bookkeeping A method of accounting in which each transaction is recorded as two entries so that two accounts or records are changed.

dumping The practice of charging a lower price for a product in foreign markets than in the firm's home market.

E

earnings per share (EPS) The ratio of net profit to the number of common shares outstanding; measures the number of dollars earned by each share.

economic growth An increase in a nation's output of goods and services.

economic system The combination of policies, laws, and choices made by a nation's government to establish the systems that determine what goods and services are produced and how they are allocated.

economics The study of how a society uses scarce resources to produce and distribute goods and services.

electronic business (e-business) The entire process that involves the full value chain (the entire value-adding process, from the raw materials to the eventual end user, including the disposing of the packaging after use) and how all units of a business operate.

electronic commerce (e-commerce) The actual transaction of selling a product or service via the Internet.

electronic data interchange (EDI) The electronic exchange of information between two trading partners.

embargo A total ban on imports or exports of a product.

employee orientation Training that prepares a new employee to perform on the job; includes information about job assignments, work rules, equipment, and performance expectations, as well as about company policies, salary and benefits, and parking.

empowerment The process of giving employees increased autonomy and discretion to make decisions, as well as control over the resources needed to implement those decisions.

enterprise resource planning (ERP) A computerized resource planning system that includes information about the firm's suppliers and customers as well as data generated internally.

entrepreneurs People with vision, drive, and creativity who are willing to take the risk of starting and managing a new business to make a profit or of greatly changing the scope and direction of an existing firm.

environmental scanning The process in which a firm continually collects and evaluates information about its external environment.

equilibrium The point at which quantity demanded equals quantity supplied.

equity theory A theory of motivation that holds that worker satisfaction is influenced by employees' perceptions about how fairly they are treated compared with their co-workers.

equity A form of business financing consisting of funds raised through the sale of stock in a business.

ethics A set of moral standards for judging whether something is right or wrong.

European Union (EU) An organization of 15 European nations (as of early 2004) that works to foster political and economic integration in Europe; formerly called the European Community.

exchange controls Laws that require a company earning foreign exchange (foreign currency) from its exports to sell the foreign exchange to a control agency, such as a central bank.

exchange The process in which two parties give something of value to each other to satisfy their respective needs.

excise taxes Taxes that are imposed on specific items such as gasoline, alcoholic beverages, and tobacco.

exclusive distribution A distribution system in which a manufacturer selects only one or two dealers in an area to market its products.

executive information system (EIS) A management support system that is customized for an individual executive; provides specific information for strategic decisions.

expansionary policy The use of monetary policy by the Bank of Canada to increase the growth of the money supply.

expectancy theory A theory of motivation that holds that the probability of an individual acting in a particular way depends on the strength of that individual's belief that the act will have a particular outcome and on whether the individual values that outcome.

expense items Items, purchased by businesses, that are smaller and less expensive than capital products and usually have a life span of less than one year.

expenses The costs of generating revenues.

expert power Power that is derived from an individual's extensive knowledge in one or more areas.

expert system A management support system that gives managers advice similar to what they would get from a consultant; it uses artificial intelligence to enable computers to reason and learn to solve problems in much the same way humans do.

exporting The practice of selling domestically produced goods to buyers in another country.

exports Goods and services produced in one country and sold in other countries.

express contract A contract in which the terms are specified in either written or spoken words.

extranet A private computer network that uses Internet technology and a browser interface but is accessible only to authorized outsiders with a valid user name and password.

F

factoring A form of short-term financing in which a firm sells its accounts receivable outright at a discount to a *factor*.

factors of production The resources that are necessary to produce goods and services: labour, capital, entrepreneurs, physical resources, and information.

federal budget deficit The condition that occurs when the federal government spends more for programs than it collects in taxes.

financial accounting Accounting that focuses on preparing external financial reports that are used by outsider stakeholders such as creditors, suppliers, investors, and government agents to assess the financial strength of a business.

financial management The art and science of managing a firm's money so that it can meet its goals.

financial risk The chance that a firm will be unable to make scheduled interest and principal payments on its debt.

fiscal policy The government's use of taxation and spending to affect the economy.

fixed assets Long-term assets used by a firm for more than a year, such as land, buildings, and machinery; also referred to as *capital assets* or *property, plant, and equipment (PPE)*.

fixed costs Costs that do not vary with different levels of output; for example, rent.

fixed-cost contribution The selling price per unit (revenue) minus the variable costs per unit.

fixed-position layout A facility arrangement in which the product stays in one place and workers and machinery move to it as needed.

floating exchange rates A system in which prices of currencies move up and down based upon the demand for and supply of the various currencies.

focus group A group of 8 to 12 participants led by a moderator in an in-depth discussion on one particular topic or concept.

formal organization The order and design of relationships within a firm; consists of two or more people working together with a common objective and clarity of purpose.

four Ps Product, price, promotion, and place (distribution), which together make up the marketing mix.

franchise agreement A contract setting out the terms of a franchising arrangement, including the rules for running the franchise, the services provided by the franchisor, and the financial terms. Under the contract, the franchisee is allowed to use the franchisor's business name, trademark, and logo.

franchisee In a franchising arrangement, the individual or company that sells the goods or services of the franchisor in a certain geographic area.

franchising A form of business organization based on a business arrangement between a franchisor, which supplies the product concept, and the franchisee, who sells the goods or services of the franchisor in a certain geographic area.

franchisor In a franchising arrangement, the company that supplies the product concept to the franchisee.

Free Trade Area of the Americas (FTAA) A proposed free-trading area encompassing 34 democratic nations of the Americas.

free trade The policy of permitting the people of a country to buy and sell where they please without restrictions.

free-rein (laissez-faire) leadership A leadership style in which the leader turns over all authority and control to subordinates.

free-trade zone An area where the nations allow free, or almost free, trade among each other while imposing tariffs on goods of nations outside the zone.

frictional unemployment Short-term unemployment that is not related to the business cycle.

fringe benefits Indirect compensation such as pensions, health insurance, and vacations.

full employment Situation when the economy is producing to its maximum sustainable capacity, using labour, technology, land, capital, and other factors of production to their fullest potential.

functional departmentalization Departmentalization that is based on the primary functions performed within an organizational unit.

G

Gantt charts Bar graphs plotted on a time line that show the relationship between scheduled and actual production.

general partners Partners who have unlimited liability for all of the firm's business obligations and who control its operations.

general partnership A partnership in which all partners share in the management and profits. Each partner can act on behalf of the firm and has unlimited liability for all its business obligations.

generally accepted accounting principles (GAAP) The financial accounting standards followed by accountants in Canada in preparing financial statements.

Generation X Those born between the mid-1960s and the late 1970s.

Generation Y People born from the early 1980s to the mid 1990s.

generic products Products that carry no brand name, come in plain containers, and sell for much less than brand-name products.

geographic departmentalization Departmentalization that is based on the geographic segmentation of the organizational units.

geographic segmentation The differentiation of markets by region of the country, city or county size, market density, or climate.

global management skills A manager's ability to operate in diverse cultural environments.

global vision The ability to recognize and react to international business opportunities, be aware of threats from foreign competition, and effectively use international distribution networks to obtain materials and move finished products to customers.

goal-setting theory A theory of motivation based on the premise that an individual's intention to work toward a goal is a primary source of motivation.

gross domestic product (GDP) The total market value of all final goods and services produced within a nation's borders each year.

gross national product (GNP) The total market value of all final goods and services produced by a country regardless of where the factors of production are located.

gross profit The amount a company earns after paying to produce or buy its products but before deducting operating expenses.

gross sales The total dollar amount of a company's sales.

group cohesiveness The degree to which group members want to stay in the group and tend to resist outside influences.

H

high-yield (junk) bonds High-risk, high-return bonds.

horizontal merger A merger of companies at the same stage in the same industry; done to reduce costs, expand product offerings, or reduce competition.

host computer The central computer for a Web site that stores services and data used by other computers on the network.

human relations skills A manager's interpersonal skills that are used to accomplish goals through the use of human resources.

human resource (HR) planning Creating a strategy for meeting future human resource needs.

human resource management (HRM) The process of hiring, developing, motivating, and evaluating employees to achieve organizational goals.

hypertext A file or series of files within a Web page that links users to documents at the same or other Web sites.

I

implied contract A contract that depends on the acts and conduct of the parties to show agreement; the terms are not specified in writing or orally.

import quota A limit on the quantity of a certain good that can be imported; also known as a *quantitative restraint*.

imports Goods and services that are bought from other countries.

income statement A financial statement that summarizes a firm's revenues and expenses and shows its total profit or loss over a period of time; also referred to as a *profit and loss statement* or *statement of earnings*.

income taxes Taxes that are based on the income received by businesses and individuals.

industrial distributors Independent wholesalers that buy related product lines from many manufacturers and sell them to industrial users.

inflation The situation in which the average of all prices of goods and services is rising.

informal organization The network of connections and channels of communication based on the informal relationships of individuals inside an organization.

information system (IS) The hardware, software, people, data, and so on, that provide information about all aspects of a firm's operations.

information technology (IT) The equipment and techniques used to manage and process information.

information A meaningful and useful representation or interpretation of data.

informational roles A manager's activities as an information gatherer, an information disseminator, or a spokesperson for the company.

infrastructure The basic institutions and public facilities upon which an economy's development depends.

initial public offer (IPO) A company's first issuance of shares to the public.

institutional advertising Advertising that creates a positive picture of a company and its ideals, services, and roles in the community.

institutional investors Investment professionals who are paid to manage other people's money.

intangible assets Long-term assets with no physical existence, such as patents, copyrights, trademarks, and goodwill.

intensive distribution A distribution system in which a manufacturer tries to sell its products wherever there are potential customers.

interest A fixed amount of money paid by the issuer of a bond to the bondholder on a regular schedule, typically every six months; stated as the *coupon rate.*

International Monetary Fund (IMF) An international organization, founded in 1945, that promotes trade, makes short-term loans to member nations, and acts as a lender of last resort for troubled nations.

Internet A worldwide computer network that includes both commercial and public networks and offers various capabilities, including e-mail, file transfer, online chat sessions, and newsgroups.

Internet service provider (ISP) A commercial service that connects companies and individuals to the Internet.

interpersonal roles A manager's activities as a figurehead, company leader, or liaison.

intranet An internal corporate-wide area network that uses Internet technology to link employees in many locations and with different types of computers.

intrapreneurs Entrepreneurs who apply their creativity, vision, and risk taking within a large corporation, rather than starting a company of their own.

inventory management The determination of how much of each type of inventory a firm will keep on hand and the ordering, receiving, storing, and tracking of inventory.

inventory turnover ratio The ratio of cost of goods sold to average inventory; measures the speed with which inventory moves through a firm and is turned into sales.

inventory The supply of goods that a firm holds for use in production or for sale to customers.

investment bankers Firms that act as underwriters, buying securities from corporations and governments and reselling them to the public.

J

job analysis A study of the tasks required to do a particular job well.

job description The tasks and responsibilities of a job.

job enlargement The horizontal expansion of a job by increasing the number and variety of tasks that a person performs.

job enrichment The vertical expansion of a job by increasing the employee's autonomy, responsibility, and decision-making authority.

job fair An event, typically one day, held at a convention centre to bring together thousands of job seekers and hundreds of firms searching for employees.

job rotation Reassignment of workers to several different jobs over time so that they can learn the basics of each job; also called *cross-training.*

job sharing A scheduling option that allows two individuals to split the tasks, responsibilities, and work hours of one 40-hour-per-week job.

job specification A list of the skills, knowledge, and abilities a person must have to fill a job.

joint venture An agreement in which a domestic firm buys part of a foreign firm to create a new entity.

justice What is considered fair according to the prevailing standards of society; in the 21st century, an equitable distribution of the burdens and rewards that society has to offer.

just-in-time (JIT) A system in which materials arrive exactly when they are needed for production, rather than being stored on site.

K

knowledge The understanding or awareness of information about a subject.

L

laws The rules of conduct in a society, created and enforced by a controlling authority, usually the government.

layoff A temporary separation of an employer from the organization; arranged by the employer, usually because business is slow.

leadership The process of guiding and motivating others toward the achievement of organizational goals.

leadership style The relatively consistent way that individuals in leadership positions attempt to influence the behaviour of others.

lean manufacturing Streamlining production by eliminating steps in the production process that do not add benefits that customers are willing to pay for.

legitimate power Power that is derived from an individual's position in an organization.

leveraged buyout (LBO) A corporate takeover financed by large amounts of borrowed money; can be done by outside investors or by a company's own management.

liabilities What a firm owes to its creditors; also called *debts*.

licensing The legal process whereby a firm agrees to allow another firm to use a manufacturing process, trademark, patent, trade secret, or other proprietary knowledge in exchange for the payment of a royalty.

limited partners Partners whose liability for the firm's business obligations is limited to the amount of their investment. They help to finance the business and/or promote the business, but do not participate in the firm's day-to-day operations.

limited partnership A partnership with one or more general partners, who have unlimited liability, and one or more limited partners, whose liability is limited to the amount of their investment.

line of credit An agreement between a bank and a business that specifies the maximum amount of unsecured short-term borrowing the bank will allow the firm over a given period, typically one year.

line organization An organizational structure with direct, clear lines of authority and communication flowing from the top managers downward.

line positions All positions in the organization directly concerned with producing goods and services and which are directly connected from top to bottom.

line-and-staff organization An organizational structure that includes both line and staff positions.

liquidity ratios Ratios that measure a firm's ability to pay its short-term debts as they come due.

liquidity The speed with which an asset can be converted to cash.

local area network (LAN) A network that connects computers at one site, enabling the computer users to exchange data and share the use of hardware and software from a variety of computer manufacturers.

logistics management The management of the physical distribution process.

long-term forecasts Projections of a firm's activities and the funding for those activities over a period that is longer than one year; from a financial point typically covers two to ten years.

long-term liabilities Claims that come due more than one year after the date of the balance sheet.

M

Maastricht Treaty A 1993 treaty concluded by the members of the European Community (now the European Union) that outlines plans for tightening bonds among the members and creating a single market; officially called the Treaty on European Union.

macroeconomics The subarea of economics that focuses on the economy as a whole by looking at aggregate data for large groups of people, companies, or products.

make-or-buy decision The determination by a firm of whether to make its own production materials or buy them from outside sources.

management support system (MSS) A dynamic information system that helps managers make decisions by allowing them to analyze data, identify business trends, make forecasts, and model business strategies.

management The process of guiding the development, maintenance, and allocation of resources to attain organizational goals.

managerial accounting Accounting that provides financial information that managers inside the organization can use to evaluate and make decisions about current and future operations.

managerial hierarchy The levels of management within an organization; typically includes top, middle, and supervisory management.

manufacturer A producer; an organization that converts raw materials to finished products.

Manufacturers' representatives Salespeople who represent non-competing manufacturers; also called *manufacturers' agents*.

manufacturing resource planning II (MRPII) A complex computerized system that integrates data from many departments to control the flow of resources and inventory.

market economy An economic system based on competition in the marketplace and private ownership of the factors of production (resources); also known as the *private enterprise system* or *capitalism*.

market segmentation The process of separating, identifying, and evaluating the layers of a market in order to design a marketing mix.

market structure The number of suppliers in a market.

marketable securities Short-term investments that are easily converted into cash.

marketing The process of discovering the needs and wants of potential buyers and customers and then providing goods and services that meet or exceed their expectations.

marketing concept Identifying consumer needs and then producing the goods or services that will satisfy them while making a profit for the organization.

marketing intermediaries Organizations that assist in moving goods and services from producers to end users.

marketing mix The blend of product offering, pricing, promotional methods, and distribution system that brings a specific group of consumers superior value.

marketing research The process of planning, collecting, and analyzing data relevant to a marketing decision.

markup pricing A method of pricing in which a certain percentage (the markup) is added to the product's cost to arrive at the price.

mass customization A manufacturing process in which modules are mass-produced and then assembled to meet the needs or desires of individual customers.

mass production The ability to manufacture many identical goods or provide many identical services at once.

master brand A brand so dominant that consumers think of it immediately when a product category, use, attribute, or customer benefit is mentioned.

materials requirement planning (MRP) A computerized system of controlling the flow or resources and inventory. A master schedule is used to ensure that the materials, labour, and equipment needed for production are at the right places in the right amounts at the right times.

matrix structure (project management) An organizational structure that combines functional and product departmentalization by bringing together people from different functional areas of the organization to work on a special project.

mechanistic organization An organizational structure that is characterized by a relatively high degree of job specialization, rigid departmentalization, many layers of management, narrow spans of control, centralized decision making, and a long chain of command.

mediation The intervention of a third party with a view to persuading the parties to adjust or settle their dispute.

mentoring A form of on-the-job training in which a senior manager or other experienced employee provides job- and career-related information to a protégé.

Mercosur A trade agreement among Argentina, Brazil, Paraguay, and Uruguay that eliminates most tariffs among the member nations.

merger The combination of two or more firms to form a new company, which often takes on a new corporate identity.

microeconomics The subarea of economics that focuses on individual parts of the economy such as households or firms.

mission statement The formalized statement of an organization's purpose and reason for existing.

mixed economies Economies that combine several economic systems; for example, an economy where the government owns certain industries but others are owned by the private sector.

monetary policy The measures taken by the Bank of Canada to regulate the amount of money in circulation to influence the economy.

monopolistic competition A market structure in which many firms offer products that are close substitutes and in which entry is relatively easy.

monopoly A situation where there is no competition and the benefits of a free market are lost.

mortgage bonds Corporate bonds that are secured by property, such as land, equipment, or buildings.

mortgage loan A long-term loan made against real estate as collateral.

multiculturalism The condition when all major ethnic groups in an area, such as a city, county, or province, are about equally represented.

N

National Association of Securities Dealers Automated Quotation (NASDAQ) system The first electronic-based stock market and the fastest-growing part of the stock market.

national debt The accumulated total of all of the federal government's annual budget deficits.

nationalism A sense of national consciousness that boosts the culture and interests of one country over those of all other countries.

net loss The amount obtained by subtracting all of a firm's expenses from its revenues, when the expenses are more than the revenues.

net profit (net income or net earnings) The amount obtained by subtracting all of a firm's expenses from its revenues, when the revenues are more than the expenses.

net profit margin The ratio of net profit to net sales; also called *return on sales*. It measures the percentage of each sales dollar remaining after all expenses, including taxes, have been deducted.

net sales The amount left after deducting sales discounts and returns and allowances from gross sales.

net working capital The amount obtained by subtracting total current liabilities from total current assets; used to measure a firm's liquidity.

niche competitive advantage A firm's ability to target and effectively serve a single segment of the market within a limited geographic area.

nonprogrammed decisions Responses to infrequent, unforeseen, or very unusual problems and opportunities where the manager does not have a precedent to follow in decision making.

North American Free Trade Agreement (NAFTA) An agreement, launched in 1994, creating a free-trade zone including Canada, the United States, and Mexico.

O

office automation system An information system that uses information technology tools such as word processing systems, e-mail systems, cellular phones, pagers, and fax machines to improve communications throughout an organization.

oligopoly A market structure in which a few firms produce most or all of the output and in which large capital requirements or other factors limit the number of firms.

online (real-time) processing A method of updating a database in which data are processed as they become available.

on-the-job training Training in which the employee learns the job by doing it with guidance from a supervisor or experienced co-worker.

operating budgets Budgets that combine sales forecasts with estimates of production costs and operating expenses in order to forecast profits.

operating expenses The expenses of running a business that are not directly related to producing or buying its products.

operational planning The process of creating specific standards, methods, policies, and procedures that are used in specific functional areas of the organization; helps guide and control the implementation of tactical plans.

operations management The design and management of the transformation process.

operations planning The aspect of operations management in which the firm considers the competitive environment and its own strategic goals in an effort to find the best methods.

operations The creation of products and services by transforming inputs, such as natural resources, raw materials, human resources, and capital, into outputs, products, and services.

organic organization An organizational structure that is characterized by a relatively low degree of job specialization, loose departmentalization, few levels of management, wide spans of control, decentralized decision making, and a short chain of command.

organization chart A visual representation of the structured relationships among tasks and the people given the authority to do those tasks.

outsourcing The assignment of various functions, such as human resources, accounting, or legal work, to outside organizations. Also refers to the purchase of items from an outside source rather than making them internally

over-the-counter (OTC) market A sophisticated telecommunications network that links dealers and enables them to trade securities.

owners' equity The total amount of investment in the firm minus any liabilities; also called *net worth*.

P

participative leadership A leadership style in which the leader shares decision making with group members and encourages discussion of issues and alternatives; includes democratic, consensual, and consultative styles.

partnership An association of two or more persons who agree to operate a business together for profit.

patent A form of protection (limited monopoly) established by the government to inventors; gives an inventor the exclusive right to manufacture, use, and sell an invention for 20 years.

payroll taxes Income taxes that are collected by the employer and remitted to the federal government, usually in the form of a deduction from the employee's pay.

perfect (pure) competition A market structure in which a large number of small firms sell similar products, buyers and sellers have good information, and businesses can be easily opened or closed.

performance appraisal A comparison of actual performance with expected performance to assess an employee's contributions to the organization.

perpetual inventory A continuously updated list of inventory levels, orders, sales, and receipts.

physical distribution (logistics) The movement of products from the producer to industrial users and consumers.

planning The process of deciding what needs to be done to achieve organizational objectives; identifying when and how it will be done; and determining by whom it should be done.

postconventional ethics The third stage in the ethical development of individuals in which people adhere to the ethical standards of a mature adult and are less concerned about how others view their behaviour than about how they will judge themselves in the long run; also known as *principled ethics*.

power The ability to influence others to behave in a particular way.

preconventional ethics A stage in the ethical development of individuals in which people behave in a childlike manner and make ethical decisions in a calculating, self-centred, selfish way, based on the possibility of immediate punishment or reward; also known as *self-centred ethics*.

preferential tariff A tariff that is lower for some nations than for others.

preferred shares Equities for which the dividend amount is set at the time the stock is issued.

pricing strategy The part of the marketing mix that involves establishing a price for the product based on the demand for the product and the cost of producing it.

primary market The securities market where *new* securities are sold to the public.

principal The amount borrowed by the issuer of a bond; also called *par value.*

principle of comparative advantage The concept that each country should specialize in the products that it can produce most readily and cheaply and trade those products for those that other countries can produce more readily and cheaply.

private accountants Accountants who are employed to serve one particular organization.

private corporation Corporation that does not trade publicly and, therefore, is not listed on a stock exchange.

private law The law relating to the relationship between individuals, businesses, or individuals and businesses.

problem-solving teams Teams of employees from the same department or area of expertise and from the same level of the organizational hierarchy who meet regularly to share information and discuss ways to improve processes and procedures in specific functional areas.

process departmentalization Departmentalization that is based on the production process used by the organizational unit.

process layout A facility arrangement in which work flows according to the production process. All workers performing similar tasks are grouped together, and products pass from one workstation to another.

process The way a good is made or a service provided.

process manufacturing A transformation process in which the basic input is broken down into one or more outputs (products).

product advertising Advertising that features a specific good or service.

product (assembly-line) layout A facility arrangement in which workstations or departments are arranged in a line with products moving along the line.

product departmentalization Departmentalization that is based on the goods or services produced or sold by the organizational unit.

product liability The responsibility of manufacturers and sellers for defects in the products they make and sell.

product life cycle The pattern of sales and profits over time for a product or product category; consists of an introductory state, growth stage, maturity, and decline (and death).

product strategy The part of the marketing mix that involves choosing a brand name, packaging, colours, a warranty, accessories, and a service program for the product.

product In marketing, any good or service, along with its perceived attributes and benefits, that creates value for the customer.

production orientation An approach in which a firm works to lower production costs without a strong desire to satisfy the needs of customers.

profit maximization A pricing objective that entails getting the largest possible profit from a product by producing the product as long as the revenue from selling it exceeds the cost of producing it.

profitability ratios Ratios that measure how well a firm is using its resources to generate profit and how efficiently it is being managed.

program evaluation and review technique (PERT) A scheduling tool that is similar to the CPM method but assigns three time estimates for each activity (optimistic, most probable, and pessimistic); allows managers to anticipate delays and potential problems and schedule accordingly.

programmed instruction A form of computer-assisted off-the-job training.

promotion (in employment) An upward move in an organization to a position with more authority, responsibility, and pay.

promotion (in marketing) The attempt by marketers to inform, persuade, or remind consumers and industrial users to engage in the exchange process.

promotion strategy The part of the marketing mix that involves personal selling, advertising, public relations, and sales promotion of the product.

promotional mix The combination of advertising, personal selling, sales promotion, and public relations used to promote a product.

property taxes Taxes that are imposed on real and personal property based on the assessed value of the property.

protectionism The policy of protecting home industries from outside competition by establishing artificial barriers such as tariffs and quotas.

protective tariffs Tariffs that are imposed in order to make imports less attractive to buyers than domestic products are.

psychographic segmentation The differentiation of markets by personality or lifestyle.

public accountants Independent accountants who serve organizations and individuals on a fee basis.

public corporation Corporation that has the right to issue shares to the public.

public law The law relating to the relationship between the individual or business and the government (or its agencies).

public relations Any communication or activity designed to win goodwill or prestige for a company or person.

publicity Information about a company or product that appears in the news media and is not directly paid for by the company.

purchasing The process of buying production inputs from various sources; also called *procurement.*

purchasing power The value of what money can buy.

pure monopoly A market structure in which a single firm accounts for all industry sales and in which there are barriers to entry.

Q

quality control The process of creating standards for quality and then measuring finished products and services against them.

R

ratio analysis The calculation and interpretation of financial ratios taken from the firm's financial statements in order to assess its condition and performance.

rational branding A tactic for advertising on the Internet that combines the emotional aspect of traditional brand marketing with a concrete service that is offered only online.

recession A decline in GDP that lasts for at least two consecutive quarters.

recruitment The attempt to find and attract qualified applicants in the external labour market.

re-engineering The complete redesign of business structures and processes in order to improve operations.

referent power Power that is derived from an individual's personal charisma and the respect and/or admiration the individual inspires.

relationship management The practice of building, maintaining, and enhancing interactions with customers and other parties in order to develop long-term satisfaction through mutually beneficial partnerships.

relationship marketing A strategy that focuses on forging long-term partnerships with customers by offering value and providing customer satisfaction.

reminder advertising Advertising that is used to keep a product's name in the public's mind.

resignation A permanent separation of an employee from the organization, done voluntarily by the employee.

retailers Firms that sell goods to consumers and to industrial users for their own consumption.

retained earnings (in accounting) Profits that have been reinvested in a firm.

retained earnings (in financial management) The amounts left over from profitable operations since the firm's beginning; equal to total profits minus all dividends paid to shareholders.

retirement The separation of an employee from the organization at the end of his or her career.

return The opportunity for profit.

return on equity (ROE) The ratio of net profit to total owners' equity; measures the return that owners receive on their investment in the firm.

revenues The dollar amount of a firm's sales plus any other income it received from sources such as interest, dividends, and rents.

revolving credit agreement A guaranteed line of credit whereby a bank agrees that a certain amount of funds will be available for a business to borrow over a given period.

reward power Power that is derived from an individual's control over rewards.

risk The potential for loss or the chance that an investment will not achieve the expected level of return.

risk management The process of identifying and evaluating risks and selecting and managing techniques to adapt to risk exposures.

risk-return trade-off A basic principle in finance that holds that the higher the risk, the greater the return that is required.

routing The aspect of production control that involves setting out the workflow—the sequence of machines and operations through which the product or service progresses from start to finish.

S

sales taxes Taxes that are levied on goods and services when they are sold; calculated as a percentage of the price.

scheduling The aspect of production control that involves specifying and controlling the time required for each step in the production process.

seasonal unemployment Unemployment that occurs during specific seasons in certain industries.

secondary market The securities market where (already issued) old securities are traded among investors; includes the organized stock exchanges, the over-the-counter market, and the commodities exchanges.

secured bonds Corporate bonds for which specific assets have been pledged as collateral.

secured loans Loans for which the borrower is required to pledge specific assets as collateral, or security.

securities Investment certificates issued by corporations or governments that represent either equity or debt.

selection interview An in-depth discussion of an applicant's work experiences, skills and abilities, education, and career interests.

selection The process of determining which persons in the applicant pool possess the qualifications necessary to be successful on the job.

selective distribution A distribution system in which a manufacturer selects a limited number of dealers in an area (but more than one or two) to market its products.

self-managed work teams Highly autonomous teams of employees who manage themselves without any formal supervision and take responsibility for setting goals, planning and scheduling work activities, selecting team members, and evaluating team performance.

separation The departure of an employee from the organization; can be a layoff, termination, resignation, or retirement.

servers Computers that store data and "serve" information to other computers called clients, upon request.

shareholders The owners of a corporation, who hold shares of stock that provide certain rights; also known as *stockholders*.

shopping products Items that are bought after considerable planning, including brand-to-brand and store-to-store comparisons of price, suitability, and style.

short-term forecasts Projections of revenues, costs of goods, and operating expenses over a one-year period.

small business A business that is independently owned, is owned by an individual or a small group of investors, is based locally, and is not a dominant company in its industry.

social investing The practice of limiting investments to securities of companies that behave in accordance with the investor's beliefs about ethical and social responsibility.

social marketing The application of marketing techniques to social issues and causes.

social responsibility The concern of businesses for the welfare of society as a whole; consists of obligations beyond those required by law or contracts.

socialism An economic system in which the basic industries are owned either by the government itself or by the private sector under strong government control.

software The general term for various programs used to operate computers; a set of instructions that directs a computer's activities.

sole proprietorship A business that is established, owned, operated, and often financed by one person.

span of control The number of employees a manager directly supervises; also called *span of management.*

specialization The degree to which tasks are subdivided into smaller jobs.

specialty products Items for which consumers search long and hard and for which they refuse to accept substitutes.

staff positions Positions in an organization held by individuals who provide the administrative and support services that line employees need to achieve the firm's goals.

stakeholders Individuals or groups (including organizations) to whom the business has a responsibility; including the investors or shareholders (those with a financial interest), employees, customers, suppliers (business partners), governments, local communities, the environment, and society as a whole.

statement of cash flows A financial statement that provides a summary of the money flowing into and out of a firm.

statute law (or statutory law) Written law enacted by a legislature (municipal, provincial, or federal).

stock dividends Payments to shareholders in the form of more shares; may replace or supplement cash dividends.

stockbroker A person who is licensed to buy and sell securities on behalf of clients.

strategic alliance A cooperative agreement between business firms; sometimes called a *strategic partnership.*

strategic giving The practice of tying philanthropy closely to the corporate mission or goals and targeting donations to regions where a company operates.

strategic planning The process of creating long-range (one to five years), broad goals for the organization and determining what resources will be needed to accomplish those goals.

strict liability A concept in products-liability laws under which a manufacturer or seller is liable for any personal injury or property damage caused by defective products or packaging that do not meet industry standards.

structural unemployment Unemployment that is caused by a mismatch between available jobs and the skills of available workers in an industry or region; not related to the business cycle.

supply chain management The process of using information along the supply chain so that the firm can satisfy its customers with quality products and services; includes working closely with suppliers.

supply chain The entire sequence of securing inputs, producing goods, and delivering goods to customers.

supply The quantity of a good or service that businesses will make available at various prices.

supply curve A graph showing the quantity of a good or service that a business will make available at various prices.

system software Software that controls the computer and provides instructions that enable applications programs to run on a particular computer.

T

tactical planning The process of beginning to implement a strategic plan by addressing issues of coordination and allocating resources to different parts of the organization; has a shorter time frame (less than one year) and more specific objectives than strategic planning.

target market The specific group of consumers toward which a firm directs its marketing efforts.

target return on investment A pricing objective where the price of a product is set so as to give the company the desired probability in terms of return on its money.

tariff A tax imposed on imported goods.

technical skills A manager's specialized areas of knowledge and expertise, as well as the ability to apply that knowledge.

telecommuting An arrangement in which employees work at home and are linked to the office by phone, fax, and computer.

term loan A business loan with a maturity of more than one year; can be unsecured or secured.

termination A permanent separation of an employee from the organization, arranged by the employer.

test marketing The process of testing a new product among potential users.

tort A civil, or private, act that harms other people or their property.

total cost The sum of the fixed costs and the variable costs.

total profit Total revenue minus total cost.

total quality management (TQM) The use of quality principles in all aspects of a company's production and operations.

total revenue The selling price per unit times the number of units sold.

trade credit The extension of credit by the seller to the buyer between the time the buyer receives the goods or services and when it pays for them.

trade deficit An unfavourable balance of trade that occurs when a country imports more than it exports.

trade surplus A favourable balance of trade that occurs when a country exports more than it imports.

trademark The legally exclusive design, name, or other distinctive mark that a manufacturer uses to identify its goods in the marketplace.

training and development Activities that provide learning situations in which an employee acquires additional knowledge or skills to increase job performance.

transaction processing system (TPS) An information system that handles the daily business operations of a firm. The system receives and organizes raw data from internal and external sources for storage in a database.

transfer A horizontal move in an organization to a position with about the same salary and at about the same organizational level.

transmission control protocol/Internet protocol (TCP/IP) A communications technology that allows different computer platforms to communicate with each other to transfer data.

U

underwriting The process of buying securities from corporations and governments and reselling them to the public; the main activity of investment bankers.

unemployment rate The percentage of the total labour force that is not working but is actively looking for work.

unsecured loans Short-term loans for which the borrower does not have to pledge specific assets as security.

unsought products Products that either are unknown to the potential buyer or are known but the buyer does not actively seek them.

Uruguay Round A 1994 agreement by 117 nations to lower trade barriers worldwide.

utilitarianism A philosophy that focuses on the consequences of an action to determine whether it is right or wrong; holds that an action that affects the majority adversely is morally wrong.

V

value pricing A pricing strategy in which the target market is offered a high-quality product at a fair price and with good service.

variable costs Costs that change with different levels of output; for example, wages and cost of raw materials.

variable pay A system of paying employees in which a portion of an employee's pay is directly linked to an individual or organizational performance measure.

vendor-managed inventory A system of managing inventory in which the supplier manages the distributor's inventory, thereby reversing the traditional arrangement.

venture capital Financing obtained from investment firms that specialize in financing small, high-growth companies and receive an ownership interest and a voice in management in return for their money.

vertical merger A merger of companies at different states in the same industry; done to gain control over supplies of resources or to gain access to different markets.

vestibule training A form of off-the-job training in which trainees learn in a scaled-down version or simulated work environment.

virtual corporation A network of independent companies linked by information technology to share skills, costs, and access to one another's markets; allows the companies to come together quickly to exploit rapidly changing opportunities.

virtual teams Teams of employees in different geographic or organizational locations who come together as a team via a combination of telecommunications and information technologies.

volume segmentation The differentiation of markets based on the amount of the product purchased.

W

Web sites Locations on the World Wide Web consisting of a *home page* and, possibly, other pages with documents and files.

wholesalers Firms that sell finished goods to retailers, manufacturers, and institutions.

wide area network (WAN) A network that connects computers at different sites via telecommunications media such as phone lines, satellites, and microwaves.

work groups Groups of employees who share resources and coordinate efforts so as to help members better perform their individual duties and responsibilities. The performance of the group can be evaluated by adding up the contributions of the individual group members.

work teams Groups of employees who not only coordinate their efforts, but also collaborate by pooling their knowledge, skills, abilities, and resources in a collective effort to attain a common goal, causing the performance of the team to be greater than the sum of the members' individual efforts.

World Bank An international bank that offers low-interest loans, as well as advice and information, to developing nations.

World Trade Organization (WTO) An organization established by the Uruguay Round in 1994 to oversee international trade, reduce trade barriers, and resolve disputes among member nations.

World Wide Web (WWW) A subsystem of the Internet that consists of an information retrieval system composed of *Web sites.*

ENDNOTES

INTRODUCTION

1. These factors are adapted from Fry, Stoner, and Hattwick, *Business: An Integrative Framework* (New York: McGraw-Hill, 1998).

CHAPTER 1

1. Brandon Mitchener, "Can Daimler's Tiny Swatchmobile Sweep Europe?" *Wall Street Journal* (October 2, 1998), pp. B1, B4.
2. Brandon Mitchener, "Can Daimler's Tiny Swatchmobile Sweep Europe?" *Wall Street Journal* (October 2, 1998); and Philip Siekman, "The Smart Car Is Looking More So," *Fortune* (April 15, 2002).
3. Government of Canada, "Economic Concepts, Full Employment," **www.canadianeconomy.gc.ca/English/ economy/fullemployment.html**, accessed August 5, 2002.
4. Louis Tong, "Consumerism Sweeps the Mainland," *Marketing Management* (Winter 1998), pp. 32–36.
5. "The Amazing Mr. Kuok," *Forbes* (July 28, 1998), pp. 90–98.
6. Ibid.
7. "Revolution in Reverse," *Sydney Morning Herald* (September 27, 1997), p. 6.
8. "Russia's 'Peoples Capitalism' Benefiting Only the Elite; Big Tycoons Squeeze Out Small Business," *Washington Post* (December 28, 1997), p. AO1.
9. Adapted from material contained on the following Internet sites: "Awards & Sponsorships," **www.mercedescenter.com/ black/information-awards.html**; "Meet Our Departments," **www.mercedescenter.com/black/information-departments. html**; and "Our History," **www.mercedescenter.com/black/ information-history.html**; and from material in the video: *A Case Study in Customer Value and Satisfaction: Mercedes-Benz.*

CHAPTER 2

1. McCain Foods Limited, "McCainWorldWide," **www.mccain.com/McCainworldWide/**, accessed May 5, 2003.
2. Statistics Canada, "Canadian Statistics—Imports and Exports of Goods on a Balance-of-Payments Basis," **www.statcan.ca/English/Pgdb/Economy/International/ gblec02a.htm**, accessed May 28, 2002.
3. Government of Canada, Department of Foreign Affairs and International Trade, "Trade Negotiations and Agreements—Why Trade Matters," **www.dfait.maeci.gc.ca/tna-nac/text-e.asp**, accessed June 4, 2002.
4. Ibid.
5. Government of Canada, "Team Canada—What Is Team Canada," **www.tcm-mec.gc.ca/what-e.asp**, accessed June 4, 2002
6. Ibid.
7. Ibid.
8. Government of Canada, Department of Foreign Affairs and International Trade, "Trade Negotiations and Agreements—Why Trade Matters," **www.dfait.maeci.gc.ca/tna-nac/text-e.asp**, accessed June 4, 2002.
9. "Russian Devaluation a High Stakes Gamble," *The Financial Post* (August 18, 1998), p. 9.
10. United States of America, CIA, "CIA-The World Factbook—Ecuador," **www.odci.gov/cia/publications/ factbook/geos/ec.html**, accessed June 6, 2002.
11. Government of Canada, Department of Foreign Affairs and International Trade, "About EPD, Export and Import Controls Bureau," **www.dfait-maeci.gc.ca/~eicb/eicbintro-e.htm**, accessed June 4, 2002.
12. "United States: You've Stumped Us; A Quarrel with Canada," *The Economist* (May 30, 2002).
13. Joel Baglole, "Canada Weighs Imposing Tariffs on Steel—Reaction to U.S. Policy Has Exporters Fearing a Global Trade War," *Wall Street Journal* (March 28, 2002).
14. Government of Canada, Department of Foreign Affairs and International Trade, "Third Phase of the Quota Elimination under WTO Agreement on Textiles and Clothing (ATC)," **www.dfait-maeci.gc.ca/~eicb/textile/WTO%20ATC-e.htm**, accessed June 10, 2002.
15. Government of Canada, Department of Foreign Affairs and International Trade, "About EPD, Export and Import Controls Bureau," **www.dfait-maeci.gc.ca/~eicb/eicbintro-e.htm**, accessed June 4, 2002.
16. World Trade Organization, "The WTO … In Brief," **www.wto.org/English/thewto_e/whatis_e/inbrief_e/ inbr00_e.html**, accessed June 10, 2002.
17. Government of Canada, Department of Foreign Affairs and International Trade, "Trade Negotiations and Agreements—Why Trade Matters, " **www.dfait.maeci.gc.ca/tna-nac/text-e.asp**, accessed June 4, 2002.
18. Government of Canada, Department of Foreign Affairs and International Trade, "The North American Free Trade Agreement (NAFTA), Overview," **www.dfait-maeci.gc.ca/nafta-alena/ over-e.asp**, accessed June 4, 2002.
19. Summit of the Americas Information Network, "Trade and Investment, Trade, Investment and Financial Stability," **www.summit-americas.org/Quebec-Trade/Trade/ trade-trade-eng.html**, accessed June 20, 2002.
20. Government of Canada, "Achieving an FTAA," **www.parl.gc.ca/InfoComDoc/37/1/FAIT/Studies/Reports/ FAITRP22/11-ch3-e.htm**, accessed June 18, 2002.
21. Masuaki Kotabe and Maria de Arruda, "South America's Free Trade Gambit," *Marketing Management* (Spring 1998), pp. 38–46.
22. "Kodak Quickly Develops Deal to Purchase State-Owned Firms," *Journal of Commerce* (October 1, 1998), pp. 1C–3C.
23. "France Rejects Coca-Cola's Purchase of Orangina," *Wall Street Journal* (September 18, 1998), p. A3.
24. Hal Lancaster, "Global Managers Need Boundless Sensitivity, Rugged Constitutions, *Wall Street Journal* (October 13, 1998). p. B1.
25. Gautam Naik, "Inventor's Adjustable Glasses Could Spark Global Correction," *Wall Street Journal* (October 14, 1998), pp. B1, B4.

CHAPTER 3

1. Interview with Randy Gossen, August 13, 2002.
2. "2 Dockers Away," *The Globe and Mail* (April 23, 1998), p. C9.
3. "Retooling for Buying Power of '90s Women," *The Plain Dealer* (August 18, 1998), p. 3C.
4. J. Walker Smith, "Beyond Rocking the Ages," *American Demographics* (May 1998), pp. 45–50.
5. The concept of "Justice" is from John Jackson, Roger Leroy Miller, and Shawn Miller, *Business and Society Today* (Cincinnati: International Thomson Publishing Company, 1997), pp. 89–90.
6. Milton Borden, "The Three R's of Ethics," *Management Review* (June 1998), pp. 59–61.

7. Marianne Moody Jennings, *Case Studies in Business Ethics,* 2nd. ed. (St. Paul: West Publishing Company, 1996), pp. xx–xxiii.
8. Ibid.
9. Jennings, *Case Studies,* p. 11.
10. "3 Out of 4 Say They Have Not Faced Ethical Dilemma at Work," New York Times (October 26, 1998), p. 10D.
11. Canadian Business for Social Responsibility, "CBSR—About Us," **www.cbsr.bc/about_us/index.cfm**, accessed May 23, 2002.
12. Canadian Business for Social Responsibility, "CBSR—Resources—Good Company Guidelines," **www.cbsr.ca/resources/good_guidelines.cfm**, accessed May 23, 2002.
13. Canadian Business for Social Responsibility, "CBSR—What Is CSR," **www.cbsr.bc.ca/what_is_csr/index.cfm**, accessed May 23, 2002.
14. Canadian Business for Social Responsibility, "CBSR—About Us," **www.cbsr.bc/about_us/index.cfm**, accessed May 23, 2002.
15. Ibid.
16. Canadian Business for Social Responsibility, "CBSR—What Is CSR," **www.cbsr.bc.ca/what_is_csr/index.cfm**, accessed May 23, 2002.
17. Ibid.
18. Ibid.
19. Ibid.
20. Ibid
21. "Pollution Fine Hits Cruise Line," *Orlando Sentinel* (September 17, 1998), p. B1.
22. "IOMEGA Agrees to Improve Customer Support," *Business* (March 4, 1998), pp. 1–2.
23. Canadian Tire Corporation, "Canadian Tire & The Community," **www2.canadiantire.ca/CTenglish/enreop_wrd.html**, accessed May 23, 2002.
24. "Bittersweet Charity," *Industry Week* (September 7, 1998), pp. 16–20.
25. Ibid, p. 19.
26. IBM, "IBM—About IBM—Canada—Celebrating 85 Years of Commitment to Canada," **ibm.com/ibm/ca/**, accessed August 12, 2002.
27. Government of Canada, "Canada' National Contact Point for the OECD Guidelines for Multinational Enterprises," **www.ncp-pcn.gc.ca/about_guidelines-en.asp**, accessed November 14, 2002.
28. Eddy Goldberg, "Investing in Tomorrow: Dot-Com Multimillionaires are Changing the Nature of Giving," *Success,* July/August 2000, **www.successmagazine.com**; S.E. Slack, "Spreading the Geek Gospel," *Office.com*, August 23, 2000, **www.office.com**; "Volunteerism: Good Will Geeks," *The Standard*, July 24, 2000, **www.thestandard.com**; "Computer Advocate Works to Develop Geekcorps," *Chicago Tribune*, February 21, 2000, **chicagotribune.com**.

CHAPTER 4

1. Robin Lynas, B. Comm., June 2002.
2. Carolyn C. Kwan, "Restructuring in the Canadian Economy: A Survey of Firms," *Bank of Canada*, April 2002.
3. *The Emerging Digital Economy* (U.S. Department of Commerce, 1998), pp. 2–4, downloaded from **www.ecommerce.gov.**
4. RDS, "Global top 10 countries ranked by percentage of population online, with Internet service provider market size by number of online users for the period 1999 to 2000," **rdsweb1.rdsinc.com/texis/rds/suit/...MewhXtq5Gm5inx"Welhkw5oDqelzHmM/full.html**, accessed June 13, 2002.
5. P. Dickinson and J. Ellison, "Plugging In: The Increase of Household Internet Use Continues," *Canadian Economic Observer*, January 2001, Statistics Canada, Catalogue no. 11-010-XPB.
6. Ibid.
7. RDS, "Global top 10 countries ranked by percentage of population online, with Internet service provider market size by number of online users for the period 1999 to 2000," **rdsweb1.rdsinc.com/texis/rds/suit/...MewhXtq5Gm5inx"Welhkw5oDqelzHmM/full.html**, accessed June 13, 2002.
8. P. Dickinson and J. Ellison, "Plugging In: The Increase of Household Internet Use Continues," *Canadian Economic Observer*, January 2001, Statistics Canada, Catalogue no. 11-010-XPB.
9. "Booz Allen & Hamilton: 89 Percent of Corporates Have a Website," *NUA Internet Surveys* (June 8, 1999), downloaded from **www.nua.ie/surveys.**
10. J. William Gurley, "How the Net Is Changing Competition," *Fortune* (March 15, 1999), p. 168.
11. Canada Tourism, "Canadian tourism Facts and Figures, 2001," **www.candatourism.com/ctxUploads/fr_publications/Tourism2002.pdf**, accessed July 3, 2003.
12. Edward M. Kerchner, Thomas M. Doerflinger, and Michael Geraghty, "The Information Revolution Wars," *PaineWebber Portfolio Managers' Spotlight* (May 18, 1999), pp. 3–40.
13. "The Great Terrain Robbery," *Technology Trends: 1999 Software and Services Annual Report,* Deloitte & Touche LLP, pp. 14–15.
14. David Bank, "Buying Power," *The Wall Street Journal Interactive Edition* (December 7, 1998), downloaded from **interactive.wsj.com.**
15. Penton Media Inc., "Value-Chain Management FAQ," IndustryWeek.com Web site, **www.iwvaluechain.com/FAQ/**, accessed July 19, 2002.
16. Statistics Canada, *The Daily*, "E-commerce: Household shopping on the Internet," **www.statcan.ca/Daily/English/011023/d011023b.htm**, accessed June 17, 2002.
17. *The Technology Primer,* vol. 5, Morgan Stanley Dean Witter (May 1999), p. 351.
18. John R. L. Rizza, "The Internet Gets Down to Business," *Entrepreneurial Edge Magazine* (Summer 1998), downloaded from **www.edgeonline.com.**
19. "Few E-Ventures Will Show Short-Term Profits," Giga Information Group survey, reported by *NUA Internet Surveys,* (January 11, 1999), downloaded from **www.nua.ie/surveys.**
20. Mary Beth Grover, "Lost in Cyberspace," *Forbes* (March 8, 1999), pp. 124–128.
21. Maryann Jones Thompson, "Spotlight: The Economic Impact of E-commerce," *The Industry Standard* (April 26, 1999), downloaded from **www.thestandard.com/metrics/.**
22. Robert D. Hof, "The Click-Here Economy," *Business Week* (June 22, 1998), pp. 122–128.
23. Sandy Reed, "Can't Get No Satisfaction," *Infoworld* (May 24, 1999), p. 83.
24. Jesse Berst, "E-commerce Breakthrough: Finally, an Easy Way to Pay Online," *ZDNet Anchor Desk* (June 14, 1999), downloaded from **www.zdnet.com/anchordesk.**
25. Jan Norman, "E-commerce Is Fast Becoming the Internet's 800-pound Gorilla," *San Diego Union-Tribune* (May 10, 1999), p. C2.
26. Jane Asteroff and Maureen Fleming, "Four Ways to Increase a Web Site's Strategic Value," *Executive Edge* (September 1998), pp. 6–7.
27. "Association of National Advertisers: Report Looks at Corporate Web Spending Effectiveness," *NUA Internet Surveys* (May 17, 1999), downloaded from **www.nua.ie/surveys.**

28. Statistics Canada, *The Daily*, "E-commerce: Household shopping on the Internet," **www.statcan.ca/Daily/English/011023/d011023b.htm**, accessed June 17, 2002.

29. Steven Levy, "The New Digital Galaxy," *Newsweek* (May 31, 1999), pp. 57–62.

30. Robert D. Hof, "Now It's Your Web," *Business Week* (October 5, 1998), pp. 164–176.

31. Ibid.

32. Statistics Canada, **e-com.ic.gc.ca/english/research/b2b/sales/sld001.htm**, accessed July 20, 2002.

33. "Amazon Buys Stake in Homegrocer," *Reuters News Service* (May 18, 1999), downloaded from ZD News Net, **www.zdnet.com/zdnn.**

34. Eleena de Lisser, "For Many Firms, Web Is Still What You Catch Flies In," *Wall Street Journal* (August 17, 1999), p. B2.

35. Bruce Haring, "Untangling the Sticky Habits of Web Users," *USA Today* (April 14, 1999), p. 5D; and "What's the Secret of E-Commerce? Web Designers Offer a Few Hints," *Wall Street Journal Interactive Edition* (December 7, 1998), downloaded from **interactive.wsj.com.**

36. Daniel Roth, "Ticketmaster.com," in "The E-volution of Big Business/Online Report Card: 10 Companies That Get It," *Fortune* (November 8, 1999), downloaded from Electric Library, Business Edition, **business.elibrary.com;** Ticketmaster.com Web site, **www.ticketmaster.com;** "Ticketmaster Group, Inc.," Hoover's Company Capsule, *Hoover's Online*, downloaded from **www.hoovers.com;** Arlene Weintraub, "A Ticket to Dot-Com Heaven?" *Business Week* (April 10, 2000), pp. 87–88.

CHAPTER 5

1. Christopher Halpin, April 10, 2003.

2. Statistics Canada, "Emerging businesses in Canada: Some preliminary results," **www.statcan.ca/english/freepub/61-532-XIE/09-johan.html**, accessed March 11, 2003.

3. Carreen Maloney-Monro, "For Starters, Small Firms Don't Need Big Problems," *San Diego Union-Tribune* (April 19, 1998), Electric Library, Business Edition, downloaded from **business.elibrary.com;** and personal interview with Gail Cecil, January 1, 1999.

4. Jerry Useem, "Partners on the Edge," *Inc.* (August 1998), pp. 52–64.

5. Ken Estey, "The Scope of Canadian Co-ops," downloaded March 10, 2003, from **www.geonewletter.org/Co.html.**

6. Syncrude Canada Ltd., "Who We Are, Joint Venture Ownership," **www.syncrude.com/who_we_are/index.htm**, March 10, 2003.

7. *Profile of Franchising:* vol. 1–*Fact Sheet*, press release from the IFA Educational Foundation (November 9, 1998).

8. "Worldwide Refinishing Announces Expansion into Korea," Franchise Handbook Online NewsBytes, downloaded January 7, 1999, from **www.franchise1.com/articles/newsbyte.html.**

9. Christopher Rhoads, "Low Key GE Capital Expands in Europe," *Wall Street Journal*, (September 17, 1998), p. A18; Bill shepherd, "GE Capital's M&A Strategy, "*Global Finance*, (November 1, 1998), Electric Library, Business Edition, downloaded from **www.business.elibrary.com.**

10. *Canadian Business Franchise Magazine*, "Your Dollar Store With More," **www.cgb.ca/coverstory.html**, accessed March 11, 2003.

11. Gregory Colvin, "The Year of the Mega-Merger," *Fortune* (January 11, 1999), pp. 62–64; and "So How Big Was It?" *Fortune* (January 11, 1999).

12. Richard Behar, "Franchises: Why Subway Is "The Biggest Problem in Franchising," *Fortune* (March 16, 1998) p. 126; "Subway Sandwich Shops Inc.," *Hoover's Company Capsules* (December 1,

1998), downloaded from Electric Library, Business Edition, **business.elibrary.com;** Subway corporate Internet site, **www.Subway.com;** Dan Uhlinger, "Let the Sandwich Wars Begin: Rival Shops to Fight for Fast-Food Business," *Hartford Courant* (June 29, 1998), downloaded from Electric Library, Business Edition, **business.elibrary.com.**

CHAPTER 6

1. Personal interview with Gino Panucci, August 8, 2002.

2. Industry Canada, "Small Business Research and Policy," **www.ic.gc.ca**, accessed July 12, 2003.

3. Canadian Federation of Independent Business, "Building on Canada's Strength: Small Business Outlook & Budget Priorities for 2003," **www.cfib.ca**, accessed January 12, 2003.

4. Ibid.

5. Amazon.com, "Amazon Investor Relations: Press Release," **www.amazon.com**, accessed July 13, 2003.

6. Ibid.

7. Steve Hamm, "Jim Clark Is Off and Running Again," *Business Week* (October 12, 1998), pp. 64–69.

8. Marshall Goldsmith, "Retain Your Top Performers," *Executive Excellence* (November 1, 1997), downloaded from Electric Library Business Edition, **business.elibrary.com;** Jan Norman, "Intrapreneurs Keep Creativity In-House," *Austin-American Statesman* (November 17, 1997), downloaded from Electric Library, Business Edition, **business.elibrary.com;** and Robert G. Stein and Gifford Pinchot, "Are You Innovative?" *Association Management* (February 1, 1998), downloaded from Electric Library, Business Edition, **business.elibrary.com.**

9. Steve Ginsberg, "Xerox Makes New Attempt to Duplicate Research Triumphs," *San Francisco Business Times* (March 28, 1997), downloaded from Electric Library, Business Edition, **business.elibrary.com;** and "Stimulating Creativity and Innovation," *Research-Technology Management* (March 1, 1997), downloaded from Electric Library, Business Edition, **business.elibrary.com.**

10. Daile Tucker, "Are You an Entrepreneur?" *Home Business* (April 1998), downloaded from **www.homebusinessmag.com;** and "Do You Act Like an Entrepreneur?" *Entrepreneur Magazine's Small Business Square* (September 30, 1998), downloaded from **www.entrepreneurmag.com.**

11. Tom Richman, "The Eight Books to Read before You Start Your Business," *Inc. State of Small Business* (May 19, 1998), p. 114.

12. Gary Andrew Poole, "Help Wanted: Desperately: Horizon Communications," *Business Week Enterprise* (May 25, 1998), p. ENT 8.

13. Downloaded from **www.homebusinessreport.com**.

14. John Grossman, "Meeting's at 9. I'll Be the One in Slippers," *Inc. State of Small Business* (May 19, 1998), pp. 47–48.

15. John J. O'Callaghan, "Ten Tips for Would-Be Entrepreneurs," downloaded from Home Business Magazine Web site, **www.homebusinessmag.com**, February 12, 1999; and Bob Weinstein, "What's the Big Idea?" *Entrepreneur* (February 1999), pp. 184A–184C.

CHAPTER 7

1. Personal interview with Sandra Malach, April 13, 2003.

2. Mohammed B Hemraj, "Preventing Corporate Failure: The Cadbury Committee's Governance Report," *Journal of Financial Crime*, London, U.K., October 2002.

3. Colin P. MacDonald, "Where Were the Directors?" *Business Credit*, New York, January 2003.

4. Adapted in part from Brian A. Schofield and Blair W. Feltmate, "Sustainable Development Investing," *Employee Benefits Journal*, Brookfield, March 2003.

5. Government of Canada, "Canadian Public Accountability Board (CPAB), Office of the Superintendent of Financial Institutions Web site, **www.osfi-bsif.gc.ca/eng/issues/cpab_e.asp**, accessed July 10, 2003.

6. Canada, Department of Justice, "Canada's Court System," **canada.justice.gc.ca/en/dept/pub/trib/page3.html.**

7. Adapted from the notes of Robert Malach, LLB, LLM.

8. Adapted from **www.sruniforms.com/fsecond.html**; and from the video *Second Chance Body Armor: A Study of Entrepreneurship*.

CHAPTER 8

1. "Taking a Flyer," *National Post Business Magazine* (December 2002), pp. 68–74.

2. Jennifer Lach, "Boomers on the Drawing Board," *American Demographics* (November 1998), pp. 48–49.

3. Mark Higgins, "A Sweet Twist on a Tasty Tradition: Fruit-Based Gummies and a Partnership with the Mint Are Strengthening Ganong's Longtime Candy Business," *Marketing Magazine* (April 10, 2000) p. 17

4. John Greenwood, "HMY Airways Jets Set to Fly November Skies: Tycoon David Ho Aims to Fill the Void Left by Canada 3000," *Financial Post* (September 17, 2002) p. FP7.

5. Leonard Goodstein and Howard Butz, "Customer Value: The Linchpin of Organizational Change," *ASAP* (June 22, 1998), p. 24.

6. Kevin Clancy and Robert Shulman, "Marketing—Toss Fatal Flaws," *The Retailing Issues Letter* (November 1998), p. 4.

7. "As Children Become More Sophisticated, Marketers Think Older," *Wall Street Journal* (October 13, 1998), pp. A1, A6.

8. Joe Chidley, "Defining Qualities: The Classic Values Are Common to Generations, Genders and Regions," *Maclean's* (December 29, 1997), p. 28.

9. Gillette Home Page, Management's Discussion and Analysis of Financial Condition and Results of Operations, **www.gillette.com/investors/annualreports.asp** (accessed July 14, 2003).

10. "Kraft's Miracle Whip Targets Core Consumers," *Advertising Age* (February 3, 1998), p. 12.

11. "Hard Core Shoppers," *American Demographics* (September 1998), p. 49.

12. "Rating Wars," *American Demographics* (October 1998), p. 31–33.

13. David Wolfe, "What Your Customers Can't Say," *American Demographics* (February 1998), pp. 24–29.

14. Don Schultz, "AAA Gets an 'F' in Building Relationships with Customers," Marketing News (March 30, 1998), pp. 5–6.

CHAPTER 9

1. Personal interview with Steve Smith, March 14, 2003.

2. "Quaker Oats Raises Cereal Prices; Brand Loyalty May Give a Lift to Profit," *Washington Post* (May 23, 1998), p. D1.

3. "New Report Finds How Companies Treat Customers Is a Major Driver of Brand Loyalty and Impacts Future Sales," *PR Newswire* (November 10, 1998), pp. 1–4.

4. "For Pepsi, a Battle to Capture Coke's Fountain Sales," *Wall Street Journal* (May 11, 1998), p. B1.

5. "Net Leads the Way in Spending," *Marketing On-Line* (September 25, 2000).

6. Labatt, **www.labatt.com/enhanced/index_2.html**, downloaded on September 19, 2003.

7. CNET News.com, "Online Ads Pull in Fortune 500 Fans," **news.com.com/2100-1023_3-983146.html**, accessed September 22, 2003.

8. J. William Gurley, "How the Web Will Warp Advertising," *Fortune* (November 9, 1998), pp. 119–120.

9. "Makers of Herb-Dusted Chips Tout Mood-Altering Effects, But Some Are Skeptical," *Dallas Morning News* (September 27, 1998), p. 9A.

CHAPTER 10

1. Cindy Eberting, "The Harley Mystique Comes to Kansas City," *Kansas City Star* (January 6, 1998); Randolph Heaster and Cindy Eberting, "Harley Celebrates Start of Production," *Kansas City Star* (January 7, 1998); Geeta Shjarma Jensen and Dylan Machan, "Is Hog Going Soft?" *Forbes* (March 10, 1997), p. 114; Rick Romell, "With $517.2 Million in Revenue, Harley Sets Another Record," *Milwaukee Journal Sentinel* (July 14, 1998); Stephen Roth, "New Harley Plant Spotlights Training and Empowerment," *Kansas City Business Journal* (January 9, 1998), all articles except Jensen/Machan were downloaded from Electric Library, Business Edition, **business.elibrary.com.**

2. "Cabot's Microelectronics Materials Division Opens New Slurry Manufacturing Facility in Geino, Japan, to Meet Increasing Customer Demand," company press release (January 10, 1999).

3. Emily R. Sendler and Gregory L. White, "Auto Makers Battle Y2K Bug in Vast Supplier Network," *Wall Street Journal* (November 30, 1998), p. B4.

4. Kimberly Koster, "What's Cooking? *Quick Service Restaurant* (September/October 1998), p. 47.

5. Eric Johnson, "Giving 'em What They Want; Effective Supply Chain Management," *Management Review* (November 1998), pp. 62–70.

6. Charles Lamb, Joe Hair, and Carl McDaniel, *Essentials of Marketing* (Cincinnati: SouthWestern Publishing Co. 1999), pp. 291–292.

7. Ibid.

8. Bill Vlasic, "Imitation Is Sincere Form of Productivity: Lean Manufacturing System Focuses on Team Production, *Detroit News* (December 21, 1998), p. F9.

9. Lamb, Hair, and McDaniel *Essentials of Marketing*, p. 293.

10. Bruce Caldwell, "Harley Shifts into High Gear," *Information Week* (November 30, 1998), downloaded from **www.informationweek.com.**

11. Marla Dickerson, "Tailored for Efficiency: Apparel Makers Respond to Need to Automate," *Los Angeles Times* (April 8, 1998), downloaded from Electric Library, Business Edition, **business.elibrary.com**; Clay Parnell, "Supply Chain Management in the Soft Goods Industry," *Apparel Industry Magazine* (June 1, 1998), downloaded from Apparel Industry Magazine Online, **www.aimmagazine.com.**

CHAPTER 11

1. Personal interview with Barry Sadrehashemi, May 13, 2003.

2. CMA Canada, "What Is a CMA" and "About CMA," CMA Canada Web site, **www.cma-canada.org**, accessed July 8, 2003.

3. CGA Canada, "Become a CGA," CGA Canada Web site, **www.cga-canada.org**, accessed July 8, 2003.

4. Bernard Condon, "Gaps in GAAP," *Forbes* (January 25, 1999), pp. 76–80; S.L. Mintz, "Seeing Is Believing," *CFO* (February 1999), downloaded from **www.cfonet.com.**

5. Adapted from **www.charlevoix.org/cvb/**; and **www.weathervane-chx.com/main.htm**; the promotional brochure, *Weathervane Terrace Hotel*; and the video *Accounting Information Systems: A Study of the Weathervane Terrace Inn and Suites*.

CHAPTER 12

1. Personal interview with Bruce Ramsay, May 3, 2003.
2. Mike Hofman, "CEO's Notebook: Speeding Up Government Collections," *Inc.* (December 1998), pp. 122–123.
3. Richard Gamble, "No More Dunning Days," *Treasury & Risk Management* (September 1998), downloaded from **www.cfonet.com.**
4. John F. Greer, Jr., "Commercial Paper Redux," *Treasury & Risk Management* (October 1998), downloaded from **www.cfonet.com.**
5. Diane Lindquist, "Trouble Brewing," *San Diego Union-Tribune* (September 10, 1998), pp. C-1, C-3.
6. Information downloaded July 1, 1999, from the International Finance and Commodities Institute (IFCI) Risk Watch site, **risk.ifci.ch/index.htm.**
7. Diane Brady, "Is Your Bottom Line Covered?" *Business Week* (February 8, 1999), pp. 85–86.
8. Jill Andresky Fraser, "Riding the Economic Roller Coaster," *Inc.* (December 1998), pp. 126–129.
9. Timothy Hanrahan, Danielle Sessa, et al., "Dot-Com Dominoes," *The Wall Street Journal Interactive Edition* (November 7, 2000), downloaded from **www.wsj.com**; Suzanne Koudsi, "Dot-Com Deathwatch: Why Is This Sock Puppet Still Smiling?" *Fortune* (June 26, 2000), p. 54; Pui-Wing Tam and Mylene Mangalindan, "Pets.com Will Shut Down, Citing Insufficient Funding," *The Wall Street Journal Interactive Edition*, November 8, 2000, downloaded from **www.wsj.com**; Fred Vogelstein, Janet Rae-Dupree, Paul Sloan, and William J. Holstein; "Easy Dot Com, Easy Dot Go," *U.S. News & World Report*, May 1, 2000, p. 42; Jerry Useem, "Dot-coms: What have We Learned?" *Fortune* (October 30, 2000), pp. 82–104.

CHAPTER 13

1. Personal interview with Dianne Bond, Right Axsmith, June 13, 2003
2. Joanne Lee-Young, "Starbucks' Expansion in China Is Slated," *Wall Street Journal* (October 5, 1998), p. A27c.
3. Ross Lavers, " Recruiting on the Web: In a Highly Competitive Labour Market, Employers Are Turning to the Net to Find New People," *Maclean's* (May 29, 2000), p. 24.
4. Eileen P. Gunn, "How Mirage Resorts Sifted 75,000 Applicants to Hire 9,600 in 24 Weeks," *Fortune* (October 12, 1998), p. 195.
5. "Gore-Text," *Fast Company* (January 1999), p. 160.
6. Barbara Butler, "Employee Drug Testing in Canada: Motor Carrier Industry," Schaffer Library of Drug Policy, **www.druglibrary.org/schaffer/**, accessed March 3, 2003.
7. "Companies Are Finding It Really Pays to Be Nice to Employees," *Wall Street Journal* (July 22, 1998), p. B1.
8. David Brown, "In a Tough Year, Many Took the Long View," *Canadian HR Reporter* (October 21, 2002), p. 2
9. Michael Kane, "Baby Boomer Retirement Crunch Coming," *The Vancouver Sun* (February 28, 2003), p. D5.
10. Bobby Sui, "Beyond Quotas: The Business Case for Employment Equity," *Canadian HR Reporter* (June 4, 2001), p. 20.
11. Michael J. Flynn, "Crystal Vision," *Telecommute* (January 1999), pp. 14–19.

12. "Making Stay-at-Homes" Feel Welcome, *Business Week* (October 12, 1998), pp. 155–156.
13. Christopher Cuggiano, "Worker, Rule Thyself," *Inc.* (February 1999), pp. 89–90.

CHAPTER 14

1. Personal interview with Blair Phillips, June 16, 2003.
2. Martha Brant, "G-8 Bear It," *Newsweek* (July 8, 2002), p. 8.
3. Steve Bates, " Firms Cite People Skills as Essential for Leaders," *HR Magazine* (July 2002), p. 10.
4. Dina Berta, "Edna Morris: People Skills Propel Red Lobster President to the Top," *Nation's Restaurant News* (August 12, 2002), p. 82.
5. Bob Evans, "Be like Mike," *InformationWeek* (July 22, 2002), p. 60.
6. Richard Pascale, "Grassroots Leadership—Royal Dutch Shell," *Fast Company*, (April 1998), p. 110.
7. "Humane Technology—PeopleSoft," Paul Roberts, *Fast Company* (April 1998), p. 122.
8. Leigh Buchanan, "The Smartest Little Company in America," *Inc.* (January 1999), pp. 43–54.

CHAPTER 15

1. Tara Parker-Pope, "P&G, in Effort to Give Sales a Boost, Plans to Revamp Corporate Structure," *Wall Street Journal* (September 2, 1998), pp. B1, B6; "Warm and Fuzzy Won't Save Procter and Gamble," *Business Week* (June 26, 2000), p. 46.
2. Dana Fields, "Teamwork Powers Harley Bike Factory," *Fort Worth Star-Telegram* (June 16, 1998), Section C, p. 3.
3. Roy S. Johnson, "Home Depot Renovates", *Fortune* (November 23, 1998), pp. 201–219.
4. Gina Imperato, "He's Become BankAmerica's 'Mr. Project,'" *Fast Company* (June 1998; first appeared in *Fast Company* issue 15, p. 42).
5. John A. Byrne, "The Corporation of the Future," *Business Week* (August 31, 1998), pp. 102–106.
6. Procter & Gamble, "Executive Speeches: Chairman's address—2002 Annual Meeting of P&G Shareholders," **www.pg.com/news/executive_speeches** accessed July 13, 2003.
7. Lisa Chadderdon, "Monster World," *Fast Company* (January 1999), pp. 112–117.

CHAPTER 16

1. Personal interview with Tim Morgan, July 9, 2003.
2. "CEO's Talk about Leadership," *Canadian HR Reporter* (December 2, 2002) p. 9
3. John Huey and Jeffrey Colvin, "The Jack and Herb Show," *Fortune* (January 1, 1999), p. 163/
4. Warren G. Bennis and Robert J. Thomas, "The Alchemy of Leadership: Four Qualities That When Mixed Together in Proper Proportion, Produce Great Leaders," *CIO* (December 1, 2002), p. 1.
5. Vince Molinaro, "Filling the Leadership Gap," *Canadian HR Reporter* (December 2, 2002), p. 9.
6. David A. Nadler and Edward E. Lawler III, "Motivation—A Diagnostic Approach," in William Hackman, Edward E. Lawler III, and Michael Porter (Eds.), *Perspectives on Behavior in Organizations* (New York: McGraw-Hill, 1977).
7. Robert B. Reich, "The Company of the Future," *Fast Company* (November 1998), p. 124.

8. John R. Katzenbach and Douglas K. Smith, *The Wisdom of Teams: Creating the High-Performance Organization,* (Boston: Harvard Business School Press, 1993).
9. Ibid.
10. Robert Levering and Milton Moskowitz, "The 100 Best Companies to Work for in America," *Fortune* (January 10, 2000).
11. Almar Latour, "Detroit Meets a Worker Paradise," *Wall Street Journal* (March 3, 1999), pp. B1, B4.

CHAPTER 17

1. Open Text Corporation Web site, **www.opentext.com**.
2. Scott LaJoie, "Size Matters Again," and Carol Pickering, "Blue Mountain," *Forbes ASAP* (February 22, 1999), pp. 51–54.
3. "LANs of Opportunity," *Inc. Technology 1998*, No. 2 (June 16, 1998), p. 20.
4. Emily Esterson, "Inner Beauties," *Inc. Technology 1998,* No. 4 (December 15, 1998), pp. 79–90.
5. "Largest Privately Held Department Store Chain Implements Micro-strategy Decision Support Tech," *M2 PressWIRE* (November 16, 1998), downloaded from Electric Library, Business Edition, **business.elibrary.com.**
6. Michael Menduno, "Software That Plays Hardball," *Hospitals & Health Networks* (May 20, 1998), downloaded from Electric Library, Business Edition, **business.elibrary.com.**
7. M. Bensaou and Michael Earl, "The Right Mind Set for Managing Information Technology," *Harvard Business Review* (September 1, 1998), downloaded from Electric Library, Business Edition, **business.elibrary.com.**
8. Bronwyn Fryer, "No False Moves," *Inc. Technology 1998*, No. 4 (November 17, 1998), pp. 48–58.
9. John Omicinski, "Internet Explosion Has Given Hackers Thousands of New Entry Points," *Gannett News Service* (February 27, 1998), downloaded from Electric Library, Business Edition, **business.elibrary.com.**

10. Marcia Stepanek, "Y2K Is Worse than Anyone Thought," *Business Week* (December 14, 1998), pp. 38–40; Scott Thurm, "A Blitz of Fixes Helps Factories Prepare for 2000," *Wall Street Journal* (January 5, 1999), pp. B1, B6.
11. Government of Canada, "Third Reading Speaking Notes, Bill C-6, Personal Information Protection and Electronic Documents Act," Industry Canada Web site, **www.ic.gc.ca/**, accessed February 24, 2002.
12. Teena Massingill, "Privacy Lost," *The San Diego Union-Tribune* (April 4, 1999), pp. I3, I6.
13. Peter Burrows, "Beyond the PC," *Business Week* (March 8, 1999), pp. 79–88; "High-tech Rejuvenation," *PC Week Online* (March 1, 1999), downloaded from **www.zdnet.com/pcweek/stories;** Stephen Wildstrom, "The Year of the Home Network?" *Business Week* (January 18, 1999), p. 22.
14. Teena Massingill, "Privacy Lost."
15. Adapted from "Archway® News," **www.archwaycookies.com;** "Archway Cookies: Solutions & Success Stories," **www.intermec.com/solutions/archway.htm;** and the video *Management Information Systems: A Study of Archway Cookies.*

APPENDIX A

1. *Publication Manual of the American Psychological Association*, 4th ed. (Washington DC: American Psychological Association, 1994), pp. 194–222.
2. R. Davies, D. O'Meara, and S. Dlamini, *Struggle for South Africa: A Guide to Movements, Organisations and Institutions,* 2 volumes (London, Zed Books, 1984), p. 2.
3. Wilson, K., (2002). Presentation 291 Tips (University of Calgary: Haskayne School of Business), December 4, 2002.

COMPANY INDEX

SUBJECT INDEX

PHOTO CREDITS

This page constitutes an extension of the copyright page. We have made every effort to trace the ownership of all copyrighted material and to secure permission from copyright holders. In the event of any question arising as to the use of any material, we will be pleased to make the necessary corrections in future printings. Thanks are due to the following authors, publishers, and agents for permission to use the material indicated.

Chapter 1
p. 8: © Reuters/ Michael Dalder/ Archive Photos; p. 14: Kim Steele/ PhotoDisc/Getty Images; p. 15: Photo courtesy of Paramount Canada's Wonderland; p. 17: Photolink/ PhotoDisc/Getty Images; p. 23: Photo by Linda Craig; p. 26: Table Mesa Prod/Index Stock Imagery.

Chapter 2
p. 34: Courtesy of McCain's Foods p. 37: Fred Chartrand/CP Picture Archive; p. 38: Linda Craig; p. 43: PhotoDisc Collection/PhotoDisc/Getty Images; p. 49: © European Commission; p. 50: © Mark Richards/PhotoEdit.

Chapter 3
p. 64: Photo by Linda Craig; p. 68: ©Spencer Grant /Photo Edit; p. 75: © Richard T. Nowitz/Corbis/Magma; p. 82: Bernard Weil/Canadian Press TRSTR; p. 83: D. Falconer/PhotoLink/Getty Images; p. 85: Geostock/PhotoDisc/Getty Images; p. 86: Richard Drew/CP Picture Archive.

Chapter 4
p. 92: Photo by Linda Craig; p. 98: © Chip Simons/Getty Images/Taxi; p. 100: © Inge Yspreet/CORBIS/Magma; p. 101: Ryan Remiorz/CP Picture Archive; p.106: Skip Nall/PhotoDisc/Getty Images; p. 107: © Bob Daemmrich/Stock Boston/PNI.

Chapter 5
p. 124: Photo by Linda Craig; p. 128: Photo by Linda Craig; p. 131: Courtesy JobDirect.com. Photo by Bo Parker, Wilton, CT; p. 137: Phil Hossack/CP Picture Archive; p. 139: Courtesy of Indu Ghuman; p. 140: © Reuters/Michael Urban/Archive Photos; p. 142: Courtesy of Elke Price.

Chapter 6
p. 152: Photo courtesy of Doug McMinniman; p. 155: Photo by Linda Craig; p. 158: Photo by Linda Craig; p. 163: © Superstock; p. 167: Photo courtesy of Doug Dokis.

Chapter 7
p. 174: Photo by Linda Craig; p. 177: PhotoDisc Collection/Getty Images; p. 179: Alistair Berg/Photodisc/Getty Images; p. 182: Mark Costantini/CP Picture Archive; p. 184: © Mark Peterson/CORBIS SABA/Magmaphoto.com.

Chapter 8
p. 194: © AP/World Wide Photos; p. 197: Photo courtesy of Ganong Chocolates; p. 199: Photo courtesy of WestJet; p. 200: Courtesy of The National Fluid Milk Processor Promotion Board; p. 207: Richard Drew/CP Picture Archive; p. 208: Nelson Archives.

Chapter 9
p. 216: Photo by Linda Craig; p. 221: ©Bonnie Kamin/Photo Edit; p. 223: © AP/World Wide Photos; p. 227: Nelson Archives; p. 231: © SWCP/Joe Higgins; p. 236: © Jamie Squire/Getty Images/Allsport.

Chapter 10
p. 246: © photolibrary.com pty. ltd./Index Stock Imagery; p. 251: Photo courtesy of Ganong Chocolates; p. 253: Simon Wilson/CP Picture Archive; p. 259: © Bill Aron/PhotoEdit; p. 263: © Bill Aron/PhotoEdit; p. 264: © Michael Newman/Photo Edit; p. 269: © Mark Richards/Photo Edit.

Chapter 11
p. 280: Photo by Linda Craig; p. 284: © Spencer Grant/Photo Edit; p. 290: © Jeff Greenberg/Photo Edit; p. 296: ©Kwame Zikomo/SuperStock.

Chapter 12
p. 304: Photo by Linda Craig; p. 308: © Paul A. Souders/CORBIS/ Magmaphoto.com; p. 314: © AFP/CORBIS/Magmaphoto.com; p. 319: © Amy Etra/Photo Edit; p. 321: PhotoLink/PhotoDisc/Getty Images; p. 323: Photo by Linda Craig.

Chapter 13
p. 330: Photo by Linda Craig; p. 332: © Mark Richards/Photo Edit; p. 336: © Wally McNamee/CORBIS/Magmaphoto.com; p. 340: © Roger Ressmeyer/CORBIS/ Magmaphoto.com; p. 342: © Mark Richards/Photo Edit; p. 345: © Michael Newman/Photo Edit.

Chapter 14
p. 358: Photo by Linda Craig; p. 362 (top left): Keith Brofsky/PhotoDisc/Getty Images; p. 362 (bottom left): Adrian Wyld/CP Picture Archive; p. 365: Walter Hodges/ PhotoDisc/Getty Images; p. 369: Jeff Maloney/PhotoDisc/Getty Images.

Chapter 15
p. 376: © Amy Etra/Photo Edit Inc; p. 384: © AFP/CORBIS/ Magmaphoto.com; p. 389: © Amy Etra/Photo Edit.

Chapter 16
p. 398: Photo by Linda Craig; p. 401: Cheryl Hatch/CP Picture Archive; p. 403 (top left): Ryan McVay/PhotoDisc/Getty Images; p. 403 (bottom left): Jonathan Hayward/CP Picture Archive; p. 410: © Jose Luis Pelaez, Inc./CORBIS/ Magmaphoto.com.